MEDIEVAL DUBLIN XX

This volume is dedicated
by the Friends of Medieval Dublin
to the memory of

Peter Harbison

MA (NUI), PhD (*h.c.* NUI), DPhil (Marburg),
HRHA, FSA, MRIA, Hon. FTCD

Sapientissimus omnium doctorum Europae

Medieval Dublin XX

Seán Duffy

EDITOR

FOUR COURTS PRESS

Typeset in 10.5 pt on 12.5 pt Ehrhardt by
Carrigboy Typesetting Services for
FOUR COURTS PRESS LTD
7 Malpas Street, Dublin 8, Ireland
www.fourcourtspress.ie
and in North America for
FOUR COURTS PRESS
c/o IPG, 814 N Franklin St, Chicago, IL 60610.

A catalogue record for this title is available
from the British Library.

ISBN 978–1–80151–125–4 hbk
ISBN 978–1–80151–126–1 pbk

This book is published with the active support of
Dublin City Council/Comhairle Chathair Átha Cliath.

Printed in England
by CPI Antony Rowe, Chippenham, Wilts.

Contents

Abbreviations

AClon — *The annals of Clonmacnoise, being the annals of Ireland from the earliest period to AD 1408 translated into English AD 1627 by Conell Mageoghagan*, ed. D. Murphy (Dublin, 1896)

AFM — *Annala rioghachta Eireann: annals of the kingdom of Ireland by the Four Masters, from the earliest period to the year 1616*, ed. J. O'Donovan, 7 vols (Dublin, 1851)

AH — *Analecta Hibernica, including the report of the Irish Manuscripts Commission* (IMC, Dublin, 1930–)

AI — *The annals of Inisfallen (MS Rawlinson B. 503)*, ed. S. Mac Airt (DIAS, Dublin, 1951)

ALC — *The annals of Loch Cé: a chronicle of Irish affairs from AD 1014 to AD 1590*, ed. W.M. Hennessy, 2 vols (RS, London, 1871; repr. IMC, Dublin, 1939)

ATig — 'Annals of Tigernach', ed. W. Stokes in *Revue Celtique*, 16 (1895) 374–419; 17 (1896) 6–33, 119–263, 337–420; 18 (1897) 9–59, 150–97, 267–303; reprinted in two vols (Felinfach, 1993).

AU — *Annala Uladh ('Annals of Ulster'), otherwise Annala Senait ('Annals of Senat'): a chronicle of Irish affairs AD 431 to AD 1540*, ed. W.M. Hennessy and B. MacCarthy, 4 vols (Dublin, 1887–1901); *The annals of Ulster (to AD 1131)*, ed. S. Mac Airt and G. Mac Niocaill (Dublin, 1983)

BL — British Library, London

Bradley et al. (eds), *Dublin in the medieval world* — John Bradley, Alan J. Fletcher and Anngret Simms (eds), *Dublin in the medieval world: studies in honour of Howard B. Clarke* (Dublin, 2009)

Cal. S.P. Ire. — *Calendar of state papers relating to Ireland, 1509–73 [etc.]*, 24 vols (London, 1860–1912)

CARD — J.T. Gilbert (ed.), *Calendar of ancient records of Dublin*, 19 vols (Dublin, 1889–1944)

CCD — *Calendar of Christ Church deeds*, ed. M.J. McEnery and Raymond Refaussé (Dublin, 2001)

CCR — *Calendar of the close rolls* [...], *1272–*[*1509*], 47 vols (PRO, London, 1892–1963)

CDI — *Calendar of documents relating to Ireland, 1171–1307*, ed. H.S. Sweetman and G.F. Handcock, 5 vols (PRO, London, 1875–86)

CGG — *Cogadh Gaedhil re Gallaibh*, ed. and trans. James Henthorn Todd (London, 1867)

CIRCLE Peter Crooks (ed.), *A calendar of Irish chancery letters, c.1244–1509* (available at https://virtualtreasury.ie/gold-seams/circle)

Civil Survey *The Civil Survey, AD 1654–56*, ed. R.C. Simington, 10 vols (Dublin, 1931–61)

CJRI *Calendar of the justiciary rolls of Ireland*, ed. James Mills et al., 3 vols (Dublin, 1905–56)

Clarke et al. (eds), *Ireland and Scandinavia*
H.B. Clarke, Máire Ní Mhaonaigh and Raghnall Ó Floinn (eds), *Ireland and Scandinavia in the early Viking Age* (Dublin, 1998)

Clarke, *Dublin, Pt 1* (IHTA)
H.B. Clarke (ed.), *Dublin Part I, to 1610*, IHTA, no. 11 (RIA, Dublin, 2002)

CPL *Calendar of entries in the papal registers relating to Great Britain and Ireland: papal letters* (London, 1893–)

CPR *Calendar of the patent rolls* [...], *1232–*[*1509*], 53 vols (PRO, London, 1911)

CPR Ire., Hen. VIII–Eliz.
Calendar of the patent and close rolls of chancery in Ireland, Henry VIII to 18th Elizabeth, ed. J. Morrin (Dublin, 1862)

CS *Chronicum Scotorum,* ed. W.M. Hennessy (London, 1866).

CStM *Chartularies of Saint Mary's abbey, Dublin*, ed. J.T. Gilbert, 2 vols (RS, London, 1884–6)

DCFR Colm Lennon and James Murray (eds), *The Dublin city franchise roll, 1468–1512* (Dublin, 1998)

DGMR Philomena Connolly and Geoffrey Martin (eds), *Dublin guild merchant roll* (Dublin, 1992)

DHR *Dublin Historical Record*

DIB *Dictionary of Irish biography*, ed. J. McGuire and J. Quinn, 9 vols (Cambridge, 2009)

Duffy (ed.), *MD*
Seán Duffy (ed.), *Medieval Dublin I [etc.]* (Dublin, 2000, etc.)

Gilbert (ed.), *Hist. & mun. docs*
J.T. Gilbert (ed.), *Historic and municipal documents of Ireland, AD 1172–1320, from the archives of the city of Dublin* (RS, London, 1870)

IHS *Irish Historical Studies*

IHTA Irish Historic Towns Atlas, RIA (Dublin, 1986–)

IMC *Coimisiún Láimhscríbhinní na hÉireann* (The Irish Manuscripts Commission)

JRSAI *Journal of the Royal Society of Antiquaries of Ireland*

NAI National Archives of Ireland

NLI National Library of Ireland, Dublin

OED — *Oxford English dictionary*, Oxford University Press, Oxford: oed.com

PRIA — *Proceedings of the Royal Irish Academy*

Reg. St Thomas — *Register of the abbey of St Thomas, Dublin*, ed. J.T. Gilbert (London, 1889)

RIA — Royal Irish Academy

TNA — The National Archives of the United Kingdom [including former PRO], Kew

Williams (ed.), *Pembridge* — Bernadette Williams (ed.), *The Dublin annals of Prior John de Pembridge: an account of Irish affairs, 1162–1370* (Dublin, 2024)

Contributors

SHEA BRENNAN is a graduate of the University of Southern California; she was a visiting student at Trinity College Dublin in 2022–3.

BRUCE M.S. CAMPBELL is emeritus professor of medieval economic history at Queen's University, Belfast.

DENIS CASEY is an independent scholar who holds a PhD in medieval Irish history from the University of Cambridge.

PAUL DUFFY is a licensed archaeologist, working with Irish Archaeological Consultancy Ltd, and has excavated extensively in Dublin and elsewhere.

CAITLIN ELLIS is associate professor of Nordic medieval history at the University of Oslo.

SARAH HENDRIKS is research fellow in early modern history and archival discovery and library network lead at the Virtual Record Treasury of Ireland.

RANDOLPH JONES is an independent scholar, based in England, who has an interest in medieval Ireland.

CAITRÍONA MOORE is a wetland archaeologist and managing director of Archaeology and Built Heritage Ltd.

MUIREANN NÍ CHEALLACHÁIN is associate director and archaeological site director at IAC Archaeology.

JOHN NICHOLL is an independent researcher, leather finds specialist and experimental archaeologist.

EDMOND O'DONOVAN is an archaeologist and archaeological project manager with Edmond O'Donovan & Associates.

VALENTIN ROTHAUPT is a graduate of the University of Stuttgart and was a visiting student at Trinity College Dublin in 2022–3.

PATRICK WADDEN is professor of history at Belmont Abbey College, North Carolina.

Editor's preface

This volume brings to twenty the total in the series so far. It does not seem so long ago – but is in fact a quarter of a century – since I met the late Michael Adams, founder of Four Courts Press, in his then premises in Fumbally Lane to discuss whether it would be possible to publish the proceedings of a one-day symposium on the archaeology and history of medieval Dublin. Michael did not think there was a market for such a book but I talked to him about the seemingly endless archaeological excavations ongoing in Celtic Tiger Dublin and a whole new post-Wood Quay generation of young archaeologists directing them, discovering vast amounts about the city's past, but with no systematic way of sharing this knowledge other than over a Friday evening pint after a hard week's digging. This is why, I said, the Friends of Medieval Dublin had organized a symposium on the subject but that that would have no more lasting impact than the pub debriefings unless we published it for posterity.

Michael was a lovely man but he had no head for business and so he agreed to publish our proceedings. 'What is it to be called?', he asked. I replied, '*Medieval Dublin*', which he thought a great idea, nice and simple. '*Medieval Dublin 1*', I added, at which point he erupted: '*Absolutely* not! Because there'll never be a *Medieval Dublin 2* and if, in the unlikely event there's a *Medieval Dublin 2*, there'll never be a *Medieval Dublin 3*. There'll be nothing left to say.' But I replenished his glass of rioja and we talked quite a bit longer and, in the end, shook on a deal that would see Four Courts allow numbered volumes of *Medieval Dublin*, on condition that the Friends of Medieval Dublin delivered five of them: after that, we could call it quits. And the rest, as they say, is … archaeology (with a little bit of history thrown in).

Of course, none of that could happen had not the then City Manager, John Fitzgerald, supported what the Friends of Medieval Dublin and Four Courts Press were trying to achieve. Nothing we produced would have been affordable to the average Dubliner if he had not seen the importance of providing a modest subvention towards the cost from the Dublin City Council budget, and no one should underestimate how enlightened such an approach was – one continued by his successors, even in times of austerity. Similarly, the day-long Medieval Dublin Symposium from which these volumes emerge has been taking place in Trinity College Dublin for the last twenty-five years, its costs being borne by the College's Department of History, with precious little direct return beyond a commitment to knowledge-creation and engagement with the people of Dublin who attend this free event year after year in their droves. So, we express our gratitude to all concerned and to the authors of the 200 or so papers published in the series to date, while welcoming more in volumes to come, *Deo volente*.

It is a pleasure to acknowledge the support of the City Heritage Officer, Charles Duggan, and the ceaseless encouragement of the City Archaeologist, Dr Ruth Johnson; we express our great gratitude to the outgoing Chief Executive, Mr Owen Keegan – a true Friend of Medieval Dublin – and wish him well on his retirement, while welcoming his successor, Mr Richard Shakespeare, and assuring him of our commitment to promoting awareness of and pride in his city's medieval heritage.

The series continues to be published by Four Courts Press for whose collaboration the Friends of Medieval Dublin remain most grateful: Michael Adams has found worthy successors in the two Martins, Fanning and Healy, whose meticulous attention to detail has left its mark on the pages below, their colleague Anthony Tierney scrupulously spreading word of its publication. Irish academic publishing is fortunate to have such a triumvirate.

As the number of volumes in the series grows, so it becomes a veritable *Who's Who* of Irish medieval scholarship, and it seems that with every volume we lose one of our cherished past contributors. The late Dr Peter Harbison (1939–2023) was involved in the heady days of the Wood Quay controversy and published an important paper on St Doulagh's church in *Medieval Dublin IX*. He was a Friend of Medieval Dublin and a friend to all. Quintessentially professorial, Peter was a brilliant lecturer (though, inexplicably, never formally so in a university, to their great loss), master of the slide projector in the days before PowerPoint killed the art; and, that one regularly accosted Peter in the unlikeliest of locations with a slide carousel tucked under his elbow, only testifies to his generosity in rarely declining a request to 'give a talk', always with the most beaming of smiles and an age-defying energy.

Many of us have wondered what it would be like to travel back in time to meet one of those heroic nineteenth-century polymaths sometimes described as 'antiquarian gentlemen'. I feel sure that if I did, and if he lived up to expectations, he'd look (and sound) a lot like Peter Harbison. A scholar of quite the most extraordinary breadth – whether that be on Irish and European prehistory, on the art of Early Christian Ireland (one thinks especially of the iconography of the Irish High Cross), or the antiquarian artwork of Beranger and his successors – Peter's breadth of knowledge was surpassed only by its depth. Apart from his countless published articles – there must surely be hundreds – who could list all the books Peter wrote? And how many people get to write the bible, the book that is indispensable to an entire generation the way Harbison's *Guide to the national and historic monuments of Ireland* has been? In my household, when we're about to head off on a family outing, if the final question is 'Have you turned off the immersion?', the penultimate one is surely 'Did you remember *Harbison*?' We remember Harbison; we will not see his likes again.

SEÁN DUFFY
Chairman
Friends of Medieval Dublin

The late Dr Peter Harbison MRIA Hon. FTCD

Excavations at St Mary's abbey, Dublin: the archaeology of Ireland's premier Cistercian house

EDMOND O'DONOVAN

INTRODUCTION

St Mary's abbey in Dublin was the subject of two large-scale archaeological excavations conducted between 2021–2 and 2022–4 (fig. 1.1).[1] Traditionally known to have been founded in AD 1139 the abbey was the first site in Ireland where a Continental order, the Benedictine order of Savigny, established a new monastery. It grew to become the wealthiest and one of the most influential monastic foundations in the country until 1539 when it was dissolved by Henry VIII. Having been originally founded as a Savigniac house, it became Cistercian after the Savigniacs were united with the order of Cîteaux. The monastic community at St Mary's adopted the Cistercian rule in 1147. Early historians suggested that the monastery was founded on a pre-existing church site, though Aubrey Gwynn's paper on the origins of St Mary's abbey dismisses a tradition associating its foundation with Olaf (Amlaíb) Cuarán in AD 948,[2] and subsequent scholars have largely accepted 1139 as the primary date of foundation.[3] However, the archaeological excavations at the site have unquestionably found tenth-/eleventh-century burials that predate the arrival of Savigniac monks by 100 years, reigniting the debate around and context of the site's primary foundation.

MEDIEVAL HISTORY[4]

St Mary's abbey followed the Savigniac Benedictine rule from 1139 to 1147. It appears to have become subject as a daughter house to Combermere in

1 The archaeological excavations were undertaken and project managed by Courtney Deery Heritage Consultancy. Edmond O'Donovan directed the excavations on site. Linzi Simpson was the archaeological consultant to both projects, which were project managed by Siobhán Deery. This is foremost a Courtney Deery Heritage Consultancy project. The excavations were carried out under licence to the National Monuments Service and National Museum of Ireland; Arran Street East ref: 21E0604 and Capel Street ref:21E0802. The post-excavation work on the archaeological digs is ongoing and has been managed by and out of the Courtney Deery Heritage Consultancy head office in Dundrum, Co. Dublin. This paper is a preliminary statement which will be significantly developed and expanded with the integration of the analysis of human skeletal remains and other archaeological specialist reports on the excavations. Linzi Simpson and Siobhán Deery have kindly permitted me to publish four C14 dates obtained during the pre-development test excavation stage of the project (Licence ref: 17E0196 Capel Street and 19E0064 for Arran Street East). 2 Aubrey Gwynn, 'The origins of St Mary's abbey, Dublin', *JRSAI*, 79 (1949), 110–25. 3 Colmcille Ó Conbhuí, 'The lands of St Mary's abbey, Dublin', *PRIA*, 62C (1961), 21–86. 4 The

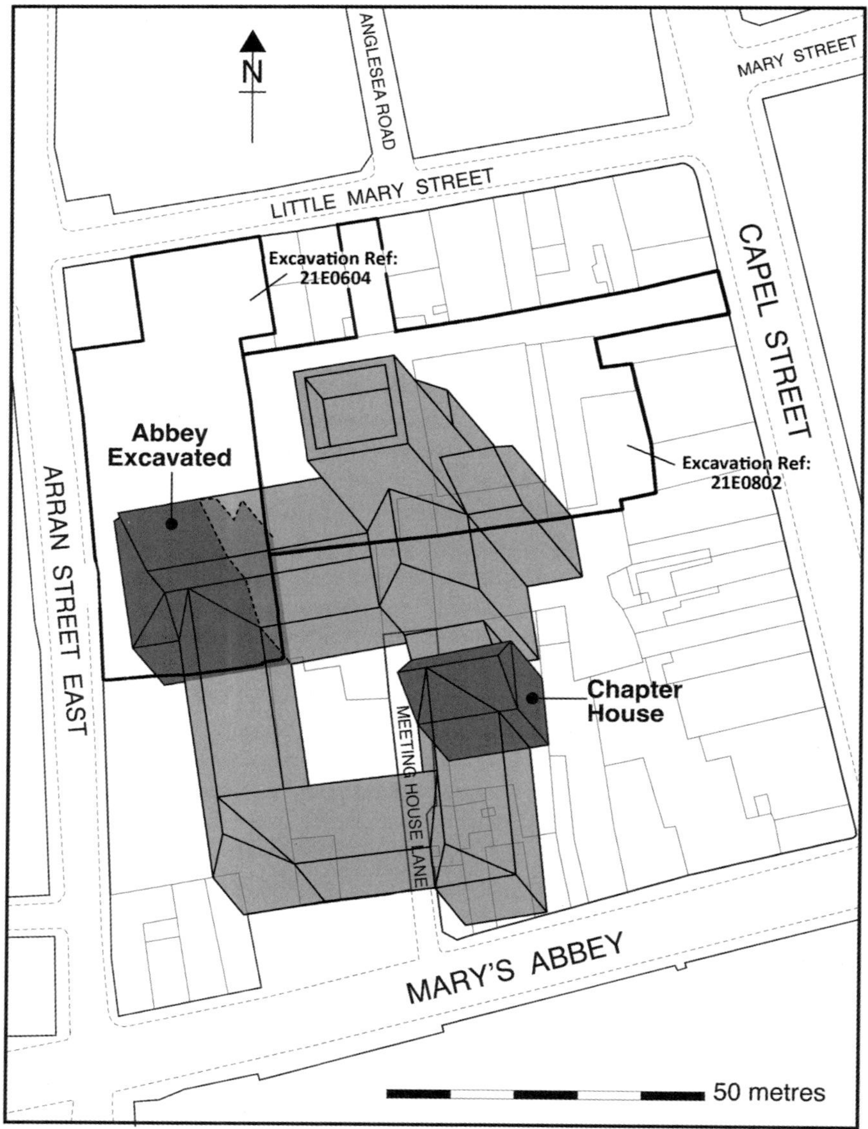

1.1 Site location showing the excavation locations and the postulated layout of monastic building at the core of St Mary's abbey

Cheshire when the monastery was adopted into the Cistercian order. In 1156–7 its affiliation was transferred to Buildwas in Shropshire. St Mary's sent out two colonies to establish daughter houses of its own at Dunbrody in 1182 and Abbeylara in 1214. In 1301 an unsuccessful attempt was made to break with its affiliation with Buildwas. The monks were compelled to undertake extensive reconstruction of the abbey following a great fire in 1304. This not only destroyed the abbey, church and tower but also several streets as far as St Saviour's Dominican priory, located under the Four Courts on Church Street which was also burnt.[5]

Mellifont abbey was established as the primary Cistercian house in Ireland in 1142 when St Mary's was still a Savigniac foundation. However, the fact that St Mary's abbey had been established three years before Mellifont led to conflict and rivalry between them over Cistercian seniority in Ireland. The general chapter of the Cistercians recognized the claims of St Mary's in 1313. The abbey was frequently involved in the affairs of city and state and meetings of the chief governor of Ireland and his council were sometimes held in the abbey's chapter house.[6]

At the time of the Dissolution the total income of the abbey was valued at £537, which made St Mary's by far the richest monastery of the Cistercian order in Ireland. Only two English Cistercian houses, Furness and Fountains, exceeded this income. The abbey was dissolved in 1539 when the last abbot, William Laundie, surrendered his title. Following the dissolution of the house, the goods and chattels were sold off by the royal commissioners: the sale yielded the huge sum of £192. By 1541 the abbey had been taken over by John Travers, master of the king's ordnance, and the church was transformed into an arsenal for the royal army. The abbot's lodging and garden was occupied by Leonard Grey, the lord deputy, as a convenient dwelling close to the city of Dublin. However, he was not in possession for long, for Grey was executed for treason in 1541. In 1543 a substantial part of the abbey was leased to James, earl of Desmond; the grant included the abbot's lodgings, the abbot's chambers and the infirmary.

The site has almost completely disappeared from the city's streetscape. King Henry VIII's courtiers and later property speculators such as Humprey Jervis, were ruthless in picking the monastic buildings apart as a source of building materials and development land for the burgeoning post-medieval city. Placenames, such as Mary Street and Abbey Street, are the principal reminder of the once great monastery. Jervis set out new streets and quays, such as Capel Street and Ormond Quay, leasing newly built houses above and around the old monastery. Recent medieval archaeological research has focused on the wider environs of the medieval abbey and its setting as a liberty and walled medieval precinct north the River Liffey.[7]

following is based on Aubrey Gwynn and R.N. Hadcock (eds), *Medieval religious houses Ireland*, 2nd edn (Dublin, 1988), pp 130–1 and also borrows from historical accounts forming part of unpublished archaeological test-excavation reports by Linzi Simpson on both the Capel Street and Arran Street East sites. **5** Williams (ed.), *Pembridge*, pp 106–7; J.A. Culliton, 'The Four Courts, Dublin', *DHR*, 21, no. 4 (1967), 116–31, at 116. **6** A.J. Otway-Ruthven, 'The chief governors of mediaeval Ireland', *JRSAI*, 95 (1965), 227–236. **7** Geraldine Stout, 'The topography of St Mary's abbey and precinct, Dublin' in Duffy

ANTIQUARIAN INVESTIGATIONS

The archaeological excavations are the first study of a large area of the inner monastic precinct of the monastery since the 1880s. Antiquarian investigations were undertaken during the construction above the remains of the monastery of Boland's Bakery completed in 1882.[8] The work uncovered a significant collection of floor-tiles and led to an interpretive illustration of the floor plan of the monastery by Thomas Drew. Very limited descriptions of what was uncovered in 1880 other than Drew's plan were published and it has been difficult to understand the basis for the plan as proposed given that much of the area depicted lies outside of the former Boland's Bakery complex.

ARCHAEOLOGICAL EXCAVATIONS 2021–4

The recent phase of archaeological work is the first to be undertaken on the core of the monastery. The two archaeological excavations are on separate landholdings but were located on immediately adjoining commercial development sites (fig. 1.1). The Arran Street East excavation (Licence ref: 21E0604) was located at 26–32 Arran Street East and 14–20 Little Mary Street, Dublin 7 (fig. 1.2). The archaeological excavations revealed the footprint of the western end of the abbey church that originally fronted onto Arran Street East. Given that the abbey was one of the most powerful and influential monastic foundations in Ireland, its buildings would have dominated the north bank of the Liffey in the Middle Ages. Elements of the abbey church, portions of the abbey graveyard to the north of the church, and the north western inner precinct and boundary were discovered. The dig also uncovered a series of lime and tile-kilns used in the construction, extension and renovation of the abbey from the twelfth to the sixteenth century. The site was demolished after the Dissolution from 1540 when the abbey buildings were finally dismantled, quarried and parcelled into post-medieval property plots and later subsumed into the expanding modern city in the seventeenth and eighteenth century around Capel Street and the Fruit Market.

The archaeological dig also identified an early monastic church (presumably Savigniac) with a later church built above it (presumably Cistercian). Some 250 human burials were excavated within the church and to the north of the church within the abbey graveyard. The skeletal remains included burials of men, women and children and the osteological analysis of the human bone is not complete at the time of writing. High-status stone-lined burials were

(ed.), *MD XII*, pp 138–60; and Paul Duffy, this volume. 8 J.W. Donnelly, *Remains of St Mary's abbey, Dublin* (Dublin, 1886), which includes a map of the 'Problematical Plan of the Buildings which formed Old St Mary's abbey Dublin' by Thomas Drew, R.H.A.

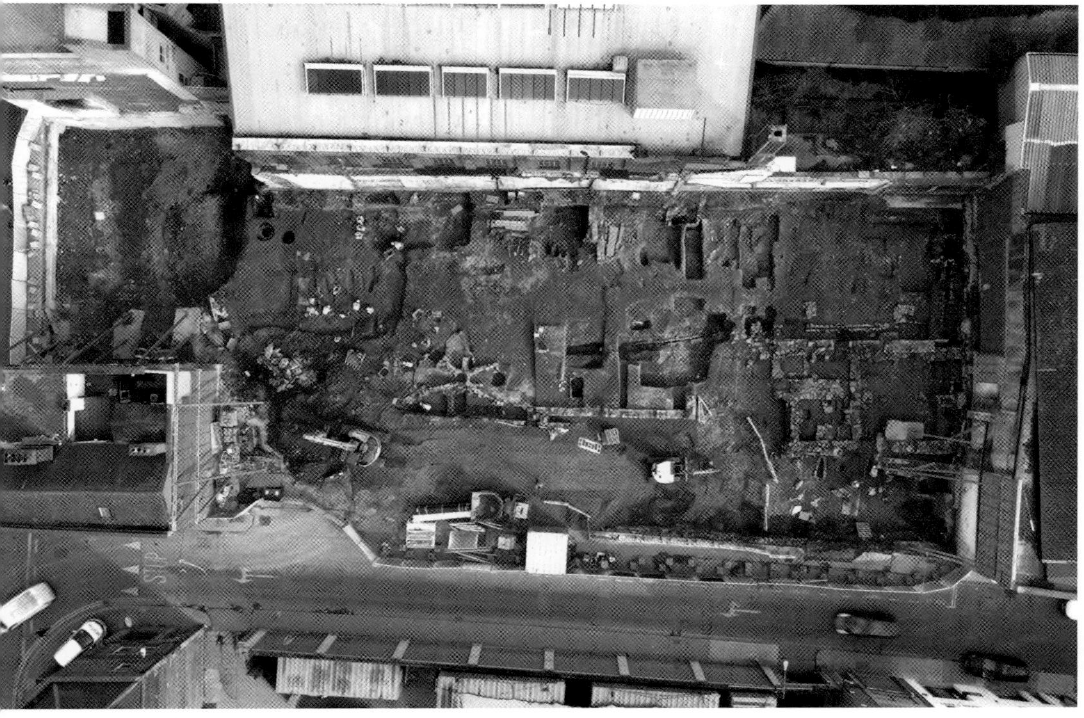

1.2 Aerial view of the archaeological excavations at Arran Street East (21E0604)

identified within a stone portico or narthex porch structure built adjoining the western end of the church. These burials included infants, adolescents and adult inhumation burials, some within elaborate stone-lined graves (fig. 1.3).

In addition to the surviving foundation courses of the abbey's walls, robbed-out foundation-trenches and pillar foundations in the church were also identified that indicated the alignment and size of the monastic buildings in tandem with the surviving masonry. The medieval foundation-trenches were filled with mortar, broken medieval roof-slates and small-stones deposits. The larger building stones of the church were completely removed as a source of stone for the later rebuilding of the evolving post-medieval city. Medieval earth-cut field-boundaries and walled enclosures were discovered that formed the western graveyard boundary north of the church.

The archaeological remains were all identified below the original floor or floor levels of the church. *In situ* tiled floors did not survive. However, significant quantities of broken decorated floor-tiles dating from the twelfth to the sixteenth century were recovered from the archaeological soils. Limited *in situ* dressed Dundry moulded fragments were recorded in the surviving walls. Nonetheless, a large and significant collection of decorated Dundry and other

1.3 Burial XX (20) Arran St East, located in the narthex structure; the bones in the grave have been disturbed by later activity, the stone-lined grave was intact

moulded architectural stone was recovered from later contexts. The decorated masonry remains coupled with the floor-tiles assist in the understanding of styles associated with the decoration of the monastery as it grew and expanded up to its destruction in 1540. The dissolution was so effective that one of Ireland's greatest monasteries disappeared beneath the city. The excavations also uncovered the foundations of later seventeenth- to nineteenth-century dwellings built after and above the buried medieval remains.

The second archaeological excavation (Licence ref: 21E0802) was conducted at 133 Capel Street, Dublin 1. This excavation was under and around a former Presbyterian meeting-house situated at the northern end of Meeting House Lane on the boundary of Dublin 1 and Dublin 7. The excavation was located within the core of an urban block defined by Capel Street on its east side, Mary's abbey to the south, Arran Street East to the west and Little Mary Street to the north, set back from the streets on all sides. The archaeological work has established that early burial at the monastery dates from the tenth/eleventh century AD. This is an intriguing finding as it suggests the existence of a pre-Savigniac ecclesiastical foundation at the site prior to the arrival of the Continental orders.

The site was located to the immediate north of the abbey church and uncovered surviving elements of the medieval abbeys graveyard on the northern side of the church, with *c*.300 human burials recovered. A seventeenth-century Presbyterian meeting-house along and seventeenth- and eighteenth-century houses were built over the old monastery. The site was again remodelled in the mid- to late nineteenth century when a patchwork of buildings set back from the street-fronts was acquired by the Boland family and transformed into the Boland's Bakery premises. The medieval deposits on the site were severely truncated by later seventeenth-century quarrying for gravel, seventeenth-/eighteenth-century cellars and the later nineteenth-century industrial bakery. Both archaeological excavations uncovered extensive evidence for the attrition of the monastery after 1539.

THE MONASTERY IN THE SIXTEENTH AND SEVENTEENTH CENTURY

The transformation of the site from a medieval walled liberty adjacent to but outside of Dublin into a post-medieval suburban quarter is stark, and precious little of the area's medieval character survives above ground-level today. The dismantling of the physical abbey occurred over the centuries after the dissolution of the monastery in a series of events linked to specific and sometimes identifiable construction projects, such as the construction of Essex Bridge by Humprey Jervis in 1676,[9] with the architect Sir William Robinson as designer and builder, stone from the abbey being used in the construction.[10]

The monastic character of the area, its setting and buildings, survived in the late sixteenth/early seventeenth century. The surviving church was used by the king's master of ordnance, William Travers, for the storage of artillery and munitions.[11] In tandem with this, the chapter house continued, after the Dissolution, to be used as a meeting place for the privy council in Ireland up to the establishment of new parliament buildings at College Green. Speed's map of 1610 clearly shows the surviving walls and outer medieval gates around the abbey precinct; also depicted is a cluster of buildings on the site of the abbey church and associated buildings such as the chapter house (the only upstanding building from the abbey which survives to the present day (fig. 1.4). The wider agricultural land holdings west of the monastery are also illustrated.

Redevelopment of the open ground around the abbey began in earnest early in the late seventeenth century. The contrast between early seventeenth-century maps of the abbey precinct, such as Speed's map of 1610 (fig. 1.5) and mid-eighteenth-century depictions of the city, such as Rocque's map of Dublin in 1756 (fig. 1.6), illustrates the dramatic changes witnessed as the

9 Stout, 'Topography of St Mary's abbey', p. 160. 10 See John Gibney, 'Sir William Robinson', *DIB*, https://www.dib.ie/biography/robinson-sir-william-a7736 [accessed 28/01/2025]. 11 Gwynn and Hadcock (eds), *Medieval religious houses*, p. 131.

1.4 A view east of the internal east wall of the chapter house with its triple lancet window and rib vaulted roof

expanding Williamite and early Georgian post-medieval city swallowed the earlier medieval quarter. Arran Street East (formerly Boot Lane), Green Street and Little Green Street made up the principal north–south road in medieval times that was routed through the walls of the precinct and also on the immediate west of abbey church. In 1617 eight corporations representing the

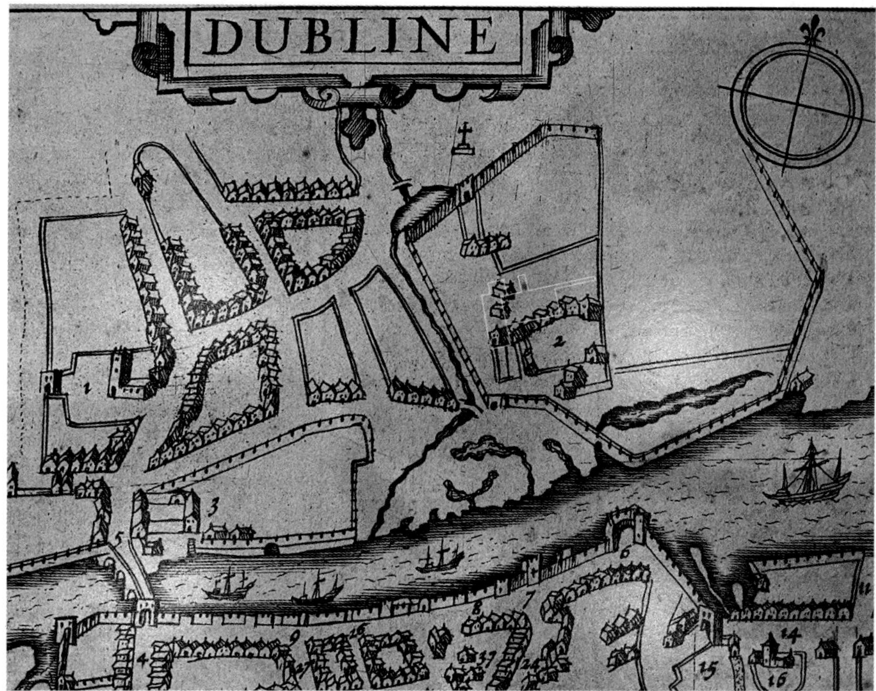

1.5 Speed's map of Dublin, 1610, St Mary's abbey is located on the north side of the Liffey; the abbey precinct is surrounded by a high-gated walled enclosure

seventeen craft guilds and the guild of the Holy Trinity were granted by the city authorities a lease of the lands called the Pill, an area of creeks, inlets and channels around the confluence of the River Bradogue with the Liffey.[12] In 1662 the lease for the Pill and the riverbank as far east as roughly the present Abbey Theatre passed to James Barry, Lord Santry. A heavy straight line along the north bank of the Liffey (similar to Wood Quay, Blind Quay and Merchants Quay) depicted on Bernard de Gomme's map of Dublin in 1673 suggests that Barry had undertaken some straightening of the riverbank on Ormond Quay by this time. To the rear of the riverbank was a large tract of apparently undeveloped land called 'Abbey Parkes' clearly originally belonging to St Mary's abbey. This equates to the tract of enclosed land shown by Speed, east of which was a single building outside the former abbey precinct. The building has been identified (as a result of archaeological excavations by Ian Russell) as a medieval watermill. The Strand Street area of the north inner city has now been the subject of three archaeological excavations by Claire Walsh in 2003,[13] Ian Russell

12 J.W. de Courcy, *The Liffey in Dublin* (Dublin, 1996), p. 281. 13 Claire Walsh, 'Archaeological excavations of the Anglo-Norman waterfront at Strand Street Great, Dublin' in Duffy (ed.), *MD VI*, pp 160–87.

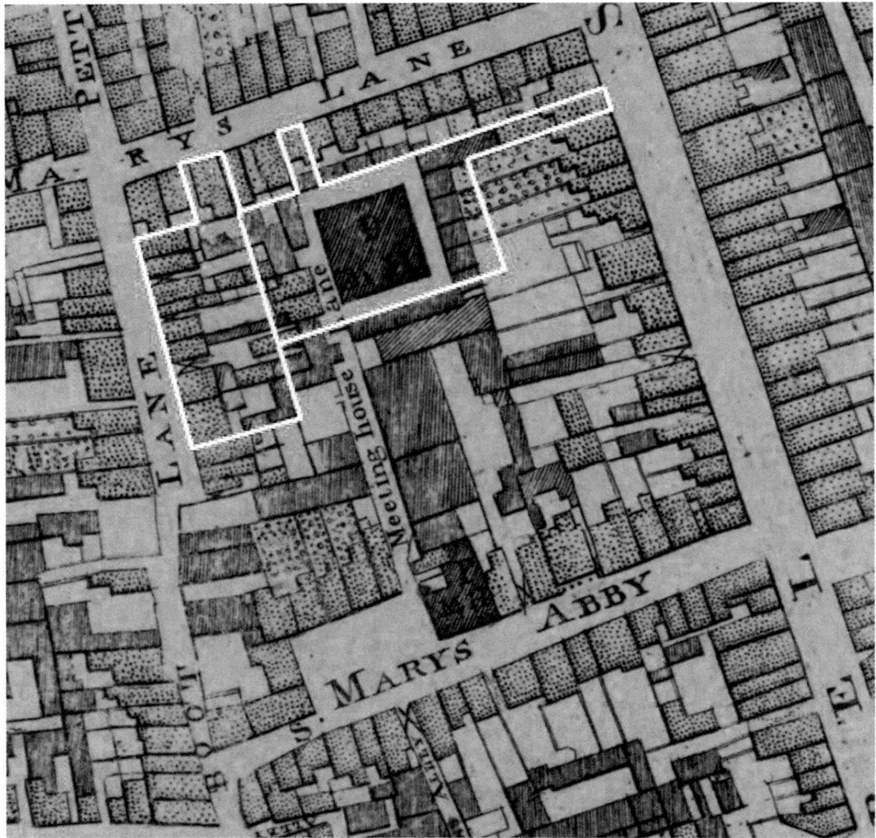

1.6 John Rocque, 'An exact survey of the city and suburbs of Dublin', 1756

in 2019,[14] and Caitríona Moore in 2019.[15] These excavations have located and identified the medieval waterfront, quay wall and the water-powered mill belonging to St Mary's abbey. The lagoon within the precinct wall at this location appears to have formed the head-race for a the tidal mill uncovered by Russell as depicted by Speed.

Humprey Jervis was significantly involved in the development of Capel Street and Ormond Quay in the late seventeenth century. He acquired 20 acres of the lands of St Mary's abbey in 1674 for £3,000.[16] He set out the new streets on the north shore of the Liffey and linked the old city via Parliament Street as

14 Ian Russell directed an excavation at 35–6 Abbey Street Upper, Dublin where a medieval vertical undershot watermill was discovered: https://excavations.ie/report/2019/Dublin/0030955/. 15 Caitríona Moore directed an excavation which linked the Ian Russell excavations and those by Claire Walsh; see Moore, this volume, and https://excavations.ie/report/2019/Dublin/0029061/. 16 Maurice Craig, *Dublin, 1660–1860* (Dublin, 1980), p. 25.

gateway over Essex Bridge to Capel Street. In tandem with Jervis, Jonathon Amory received a lease in 1675, for 299 years, along the Liffey's northeastern bank. Amory's lease extended downstream from a point between modern Arran Street and Capel Street on Ormond Quay Upper to a point near the Abbey Theatre. The southern boundary of the lease was the low-water mark; the northern boundary was roughly on the line of Strand Street Little and Great Strand Street. The name of Strand Street indicates the position of the high-tide shoreline before the strand 'was taken in from the sea' as the Liffey was narrowed and reclaimed.[17] Capel Street was laid out by Jervis in 1680 and was designed to be a new and prestigious residential street and a wide thoroughfare. It was named after Arthur Capel, earl of Essex whom Jervis petitioned for help with the new suburb. The construction by Jervis of Essex Bridge, with masonry taken down from the abbey, opened the new fashionable avenue leading from Dublin Castle and City Hall to the new city suburb that Jervis laid out along Capel Street. Boot Lane became a backstreet as the focus of the city shifted away from the crumbling abbey to the new residential thoroughfare and further east onto Mary Street and Jervis Street, also developed by Jervis.[18]

Jervis set up his building 'yard' adjacent to or on the site of the abbey church above the medieval abbey graveyard. This likely involved a location where stone and other reuseable building materials taken from the abbey ruins could be stored. The exact location of Jervis's Yard is confirmed in a letter to the lord lieutenant of Ireland, Southwell, who in 1703 received a complaint to the privy council of Ireland about a Presbyterian meeting-house being too close to the council chamber in Dublin which was held within the old chapter house of the abbey. The letter records that:

> the opposition which your Grace found in Parliament was discoursed of and threatened by an Assembly of Presbyterian teachers before its convention at the house of the Scotchman, Mr Kennedys, in Capel Street, which Kennedy is the first of twelve elders chosen for the new erected conventicle in St Mary's Abbey in Sir Humfry Jervis' yard in Capell Street aforesaid.[19]

Mr Kennedy's House of the Scotchman, a Presbyterian meeting-house, was founded by William Jacque between 1668 and 1672. William Jacque was a formidable Nonconformist who split from the earliest of Dublin's Presbyterian Conventicles on Bull Alley. Jacque established and built the new meeting-house.[20] He acquired a lease, presumably with help from Jervis, who was a fellow

17 de Courcey, *Liffey*, p. 284. 18 Craig, *Dublin 1660–1860*, pp 25–7. 19 Steven C. Smyrl, *Dictionary of Dublin dissent: Dublin's Protestant dissenting meeting houses 1660–1920* (Dublin, 2009), p. 29. 20 Smyrl, *Dictionary of Dublin dissent*, p. 28.

Dissenter, and constructed the new meeting-house for his newly established congregation known as the Capel Street or the Abbey Congregation on top of the earlier medieval abbey graveyard. This seventeenth-century meeting-house was revealed in the fabric of Boland's Bakery as an upstanding building as part of the wider archaeological work on the second more easterly archaeological excavation. The walls of the meeting-house were later, and cut through the earlier medieval burials interred in the former abbey graveyard. The physical and symbolic act of removing the abbey and constructing the meeting-house on the site of the former Cistercian abbey is not lost on this writer. The new building's foundations physically cut through earlier burials and this fact cannot have been lost on the Nonconformists/Dissenters, while curiously also acquiring the abbey's name at the same time.

Ormond Quay was also developed by Jervis, again with help from the then viceroy, the duke of Ormonde, hence the quay name. Ormonde insisted that the houses were built with a throughfare between the new houses and the quayside as a public carriageway and also for pedestrians. This requirement influenced the later development of the quays in Dublin where, previously, many privately-held inaccessible plots led down to the river with private landing areas. A map by Thomas Phillips (who had worked with Bernard de Gomme), dated 1685, suggests that Ormond Quay Upper and Lower had been substantially formed in the late seventeenth century. The quays were unprotected and were being used by traders.[21] A century later, as depicted on various late eighteenth-century prints, stone parapets to protect citizens from falling into the river had been added on the quays, including along Ormond Quay.[22]

THE RESULTS OF THE ARCHAEOLOGICAL EXCAVATIONS

Prior to the archaeological excavation in 2021 (figs 1.7, 1.8), the location, character, and physical size of the core of the abbey were not clearly defined and we relied almost exclusively on historical sources and antiquarian discoveries to imagine how the abbey looked. The main archaeological evidence stemmed from the location of the chapter house on Meeting House Lane. One of the principal findings of the archaeological excavations was to confirm the location of the abbey church plan and its evolution on the northern side of the cloister. It also established that there were at least two separate phases of church building, an early church building which was replaced with a later church building above it. The second church was substantially larger and built

21 de Courcey, *Liffey*, p. 284. **22** For example, see the mid-eighteenth-century print by Joseph Tudor (fl.1739–d.1759), 'Prospect of the Custom House and Essex Bridge, Dublin, Veue de la Douane, et Dupont d'Essex, a Dublin'.

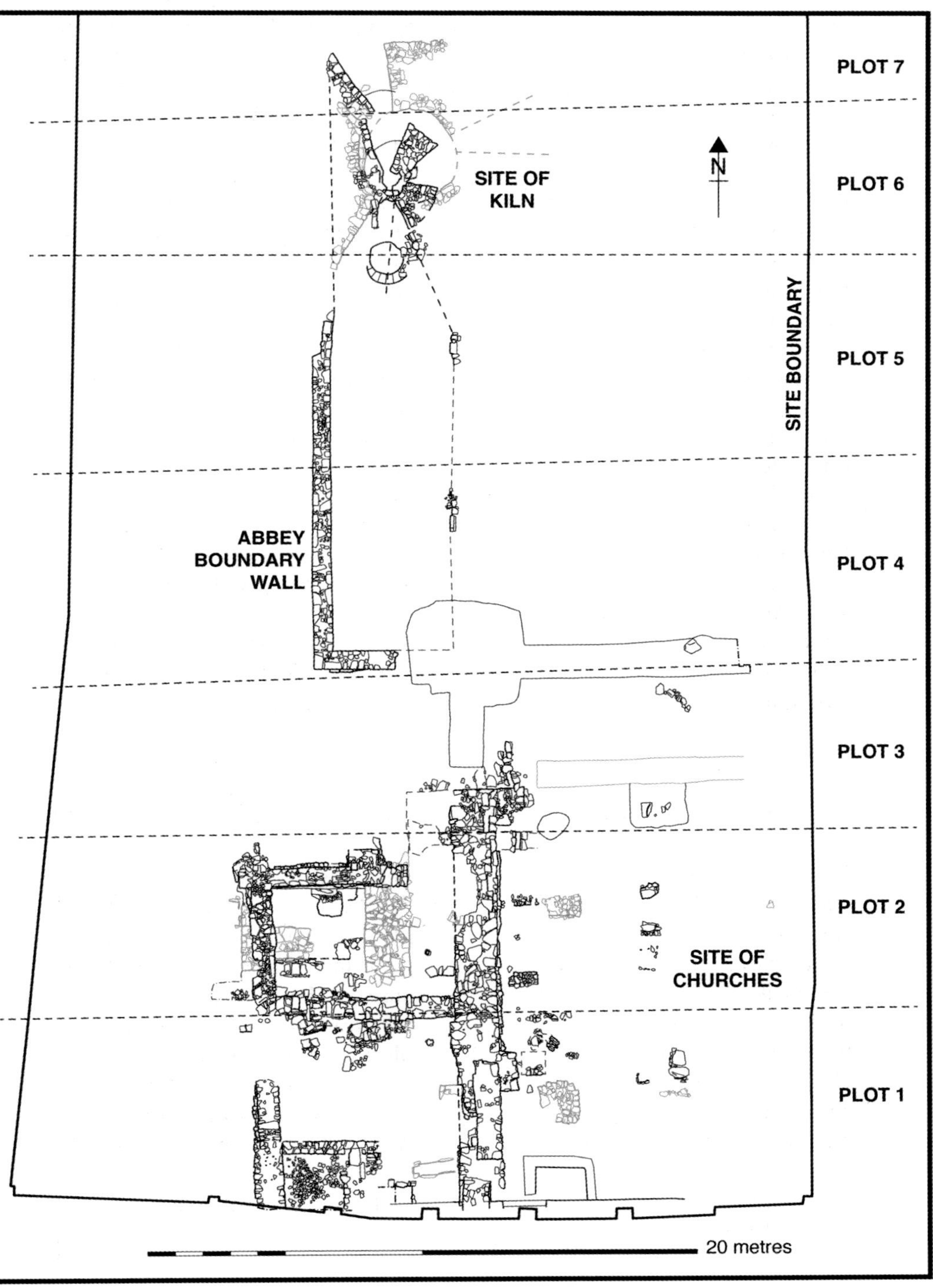

1.7 Location of medieval structures on Arran Street East

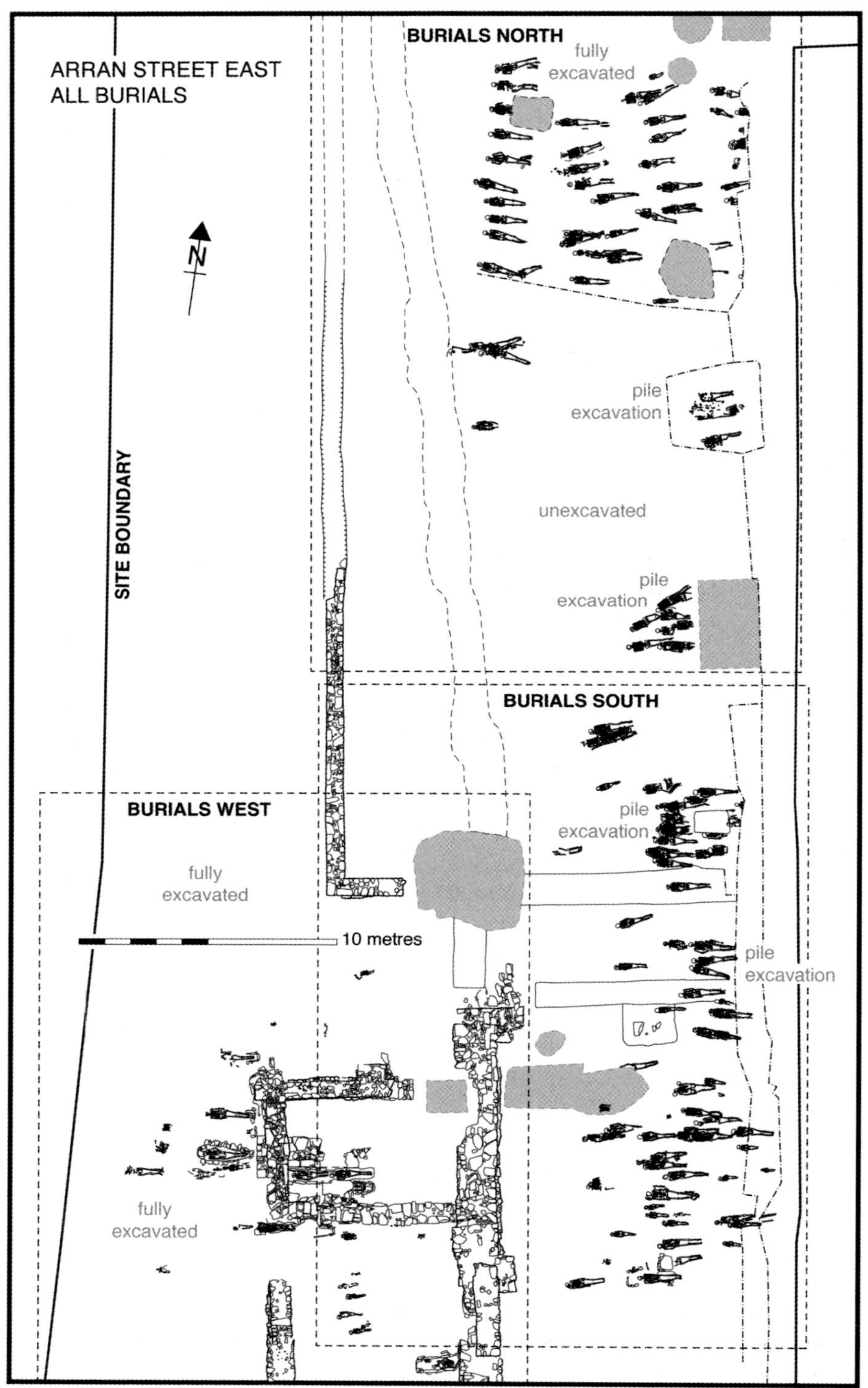

1.8 Location of medieval burials on Arran Street East

slightly to the north of the first church. The location of the cloister remained static, based on the fact that both buildings shared the same southern wall which also formed the southern boundary of excavation. The abbey church was located immediately to the north of the lay brothers' dormitory which presumably was located on the western side of the cloister, possibly built over a store house. The chapter house survives on Meeting House Lane which places its location on the eastern side of the cloister. This suggested layout is common in Cistercian monasteries in Ireland.[23] The distance between the abbey church and chapter house indicated that there was a short southern transept or vestry/sacristy between the chapter house and the chancel of the church. The southern range of buildings on the south side of the cloister would have been domestic areas, such as the refectory and kitchen. These secular medieval ranges on the south side of the cloister appear to have influenced the location of the current buildings that survive at that location today, namely the former Jewish synagogue converted into a banana ripening warehouse that now houses The Complex, a theatre, artist studio and gallery space. The ground plan of The Complex building is set curiously: it is aligned with the excavated medieval foundations plan at Arran Street East rather than being aligned with the later post-medieval street front (Mary's abbey).

The medieval abbey church (mid-twelfth century)

The earliest phase of medieval church building was discovered on the Arran Street East site, where the truncated and robbed-out remains of a rectangular aisled pre-Anglo-Norman monastic church dating from the mid-twelfth century were uncovered. It was located at the very southeastern end of the dig. No original floor levels survived and the excavated remains were fragmentary and truncated. The erosion of the archaeology occurred as a result of a number of factors including, firstly, later medieval church building, secondly, active dismantling of abbey buildings as a source for stone in the post-medieval period, thirdly, late seventeenth-century gravel quarrying and, fourthly, eighteenth- to twentieth-century urban rebuilding above the medieval wall-foundations. In spite of this, a coherent ground plan of the church is proposed (fig. 1.9). The building was orientated east–west and measured 18m wide (north–south) externally. Internally, both side-aisles were 3.4m wide (north–south) and the nave was 6m wide (north–south). The north and south side-aisles were distinguished from the central nave by arcade pillar foundations that would have supported piers and columns forming two parallel arcades running east–west on either side of the nave. The arcade pillars were 2.9m apart (east–west) which presumably reflects the width of the arches supported on the pillars that were located on either side of the nave. The archaeological

23 Roger Stalley, *The Cistercian monasteries of Ireland: an account of the history, art and architecture of the white monks in Ireland from 1142–1540* (London and New Haven, 1987).

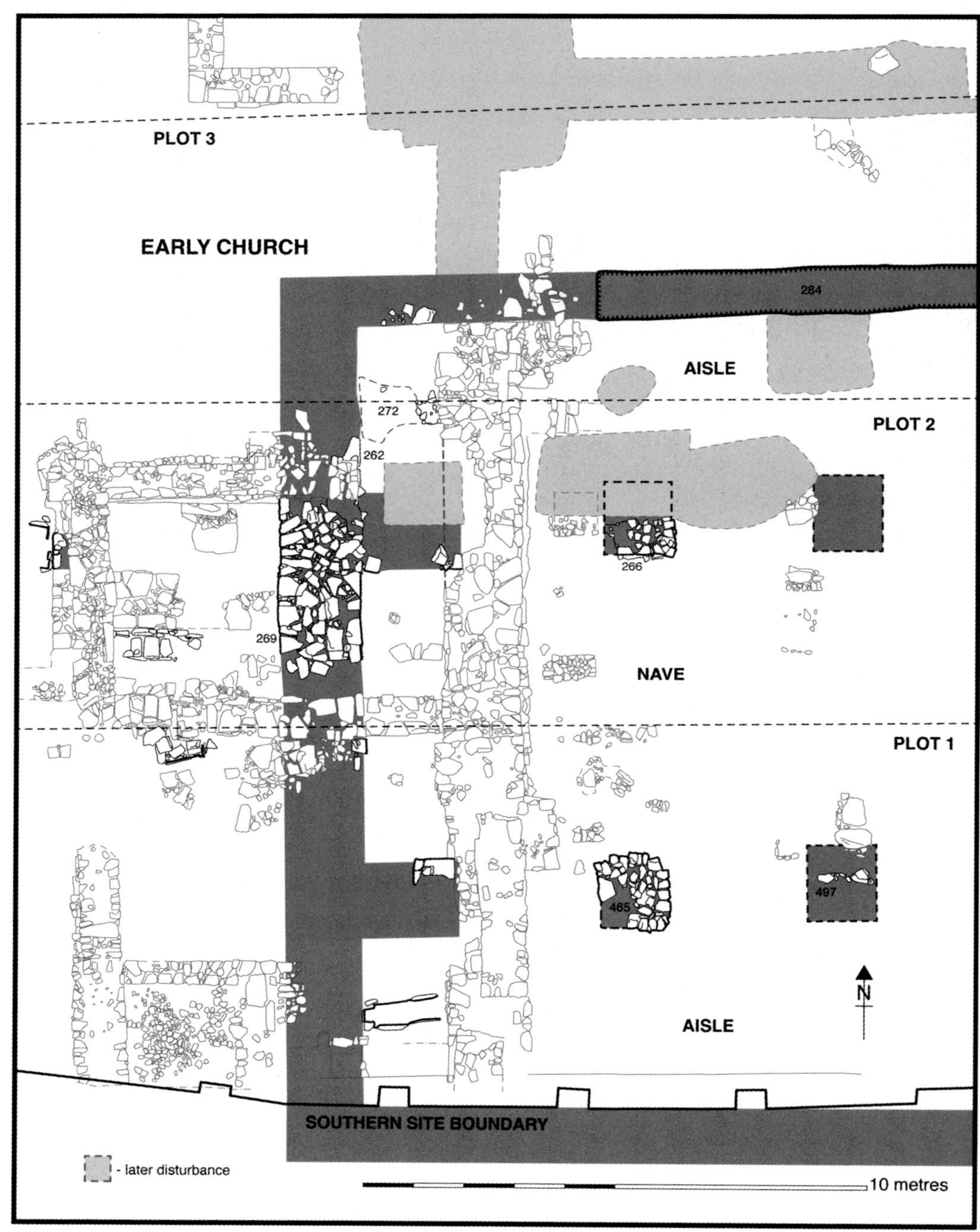

1.9 Pre-Anglo-Norman monastic church plan dating from the mid-12th century

1.10 The Dundry stone-lined door in the south wall of the abbey church reused as a foundation under a later post-medieval wall; the door appears to be the lay brothers' door from the cloister into the church

excavation unearthed a 17.5m-long section (east–west) of the early abbey church. The eastern end of the church is located beyond the sites eastern boundary in the neighbouring derelict property accessed via Meeting House Lane.

This interpretation is based on the discovery of a robbed-out wall-foundation vertically sided trench (F284) marking the north wall of the church. The trench (F284) was 7.5m long and 0.9m wide and filled with medieval mortar, slates and occasional small stone fragments, all that was left after the good building stone had been robbed out. Fragmentary masonry remains survived of the northwest corner of the church but were extensively truncated by a later post-medieval cesspit. Four pillar foundation bases (F266, F498, F465 and F497) were identified in the nave that indicated the alignment and location of the nave and aisles. The pillar bases measured 1.5m square and survived as distinct areas where large foundation stones were bedded in natural gravel (F497 and F498); two of the remaining pillar bases (F495 and F266) survived as truncated lime-bonded masonry foundations. The discovery of the west wall of the church as a partially surviving wall-foundation (F269) also showed evidence for internal wall buttresses that supported the first set of arcade pillars that were built into the west wall of the church. The pillars flanked either side of the west door internally. The south wall of the church was identified under the southern site boundary. The internal north face of the wall was partially exposed. The wall would have also formed the north wall of the cloister as well as the south wall of the church. The cloister is presumably located under the neighbouring property to the south, under The Complex Arts Centre. A blocked Dundry-lined doorway leading through the south wall of the church into the cloister garth was uncovered in the south wall (fig. 1.10).

An ash roundwood charcoal fragment was retrieved from the lime mortar that bounded the stone pillar base (F266). A C14 date was obtained from the feature (F266) which confirmed a date for the structure of AD 1036–1199 (95.4% – 2 sigma). This confirms the likely mid-twelfth-century date of the early church remains.

Reconstruction of the abbey church in the early thirteenth and fourteenth century

The abbey church was substantially rebuilt after AD 1200 as the wealth and influence of the religious house grew as a Cistercian monastery. The church was enlarged to reflect the growing power and status of the foundation and also in response to catastrophic events like the great fire of 1304. The period reflects a phase of expansion, growth and repair and reflects more than one episode of change. A later ground plan of the church is proposed (fig. 1.11). Evidence for this later abbey church survived to a greater extent compared to the more disturbed earlier church building that it partially cut through. The church had the same aisled ground plan reflecting a comparable form to the earlier church plan (figs 1.9, 1.11). However, the later church was constructed with thicker walls enclosing wider spaces that presumably supported a taller, broader and grander Gothic building which would have contrasted with the smaller squatter Romanesque precursor. The church was enlarged to the north and west.

The later church was orientated east–west and followed the alignment of the earlier church incorporating the pre-existing south wall into the new build. It measured 22.5m wide (north–south) externally. Internally, both side-aisles were 4m wide (north–south) and the nave was 8m wide (north–south). The north and south side-aisles were distinguished from the central nave by two large arcade pillar foundations that would have supported piers and columns forming two parallel arcades running east–west on either side of the nave. The arcade pillars were 3.7m apart (east–west) which reflects the taller wider arches supported on the pillars that were located on either side of the new wider nave.

This interpretation is based on the discovery of a robbed-out wall-foundation vertically sided trench (F241) marking the north wall of the church. The trench (F241) was 10.7m long and 1.25m wide and was filled with medieval mortar, slates and occasional small stone fragments, the remnants of walls after building stone had been robbed out. The northwest corner of the church was removed by a later post-medieval cellar. Two substantial pillar foundation bases were identified in the nave that indicated the alignment and

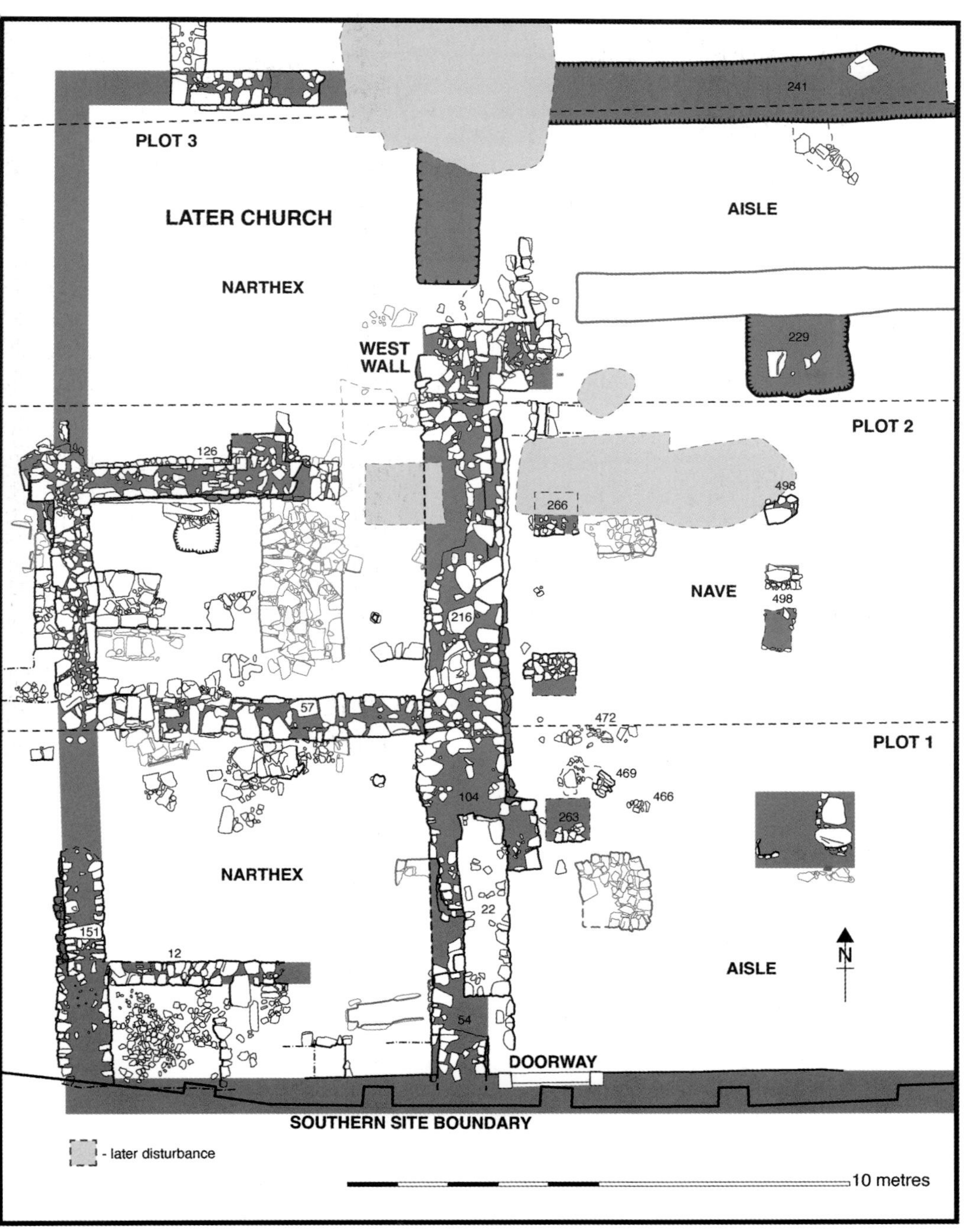

1.11 Later Cistercian monastic church plan dating from the 13th to early 14th century

location of the nave and aisles. These pillar bases measured 2m east–west and 1.6m north–south. The southern pillar base was substantially disturbed by later quarrying but still survived as a distinct area where large foundation stones were bedded into the natural gravel. The northern pillar base (F229) was a robbed-out vertically-sided foundation-trench. The larger west wall of the church (F54 and F216) survived, the wall-foundation was sizeable up to 1.8m wide reflecting the height of the west gable of the church. This contrasted with the narrower side walls (F241) that were constructed in a 1.25m-wide vertically-sided foundation-trench (F241). The west wall of the church (F54 and F216) also showed evidence for internal wall buttresses that supported the first arcade pillar adjoining the internal face of the west wall. The pillars flanked either side of the west door, presumed to be located in the west wall. The south wall of the church was identified under the southern site boundary. It appears that it may not have been necessary to rebuild the south wall of the church given that it also formed the north wall of the cloister. It was difficult to assess fully the south wall as it was partially located under the southern site boundary wall. The Dundry-lined doorway leading through the south wall of the church into the cloister garth continued in use. The archaeological excavation unearthed a 10.7m-long section of the west end of the later abbey church. The eastern end of the church is located beyond the site's eastern boundary in the neighbouring derelict property accessed via Meeting House Lane.

A new west façade (portico or narthex church) was constructed on the western end of the later church that contained high-status adult and child burial (*c.* fourteenth/fifteenth century?). This separate structure was built from lighter less substantial 0.7m-wide walls (F57, F126 and F151) suggesting that the structure was a single storey high. The structure is unusual and may have functioned as a narthex church that adjoined the western end of the abbey church which consisted of a entrance or porch, located at the west end of the nave, opposite the church's main altar. The narthex was a part of the church building, but was not considered part of the church proper.

The purpose of the narthex was to allow those not eligible for admittance into the monastic congregation to hear and partake in the service. The narthex would often include a baptismal font so that infants or adults could be baptized before entering the nave and to remind other believers of their baptism. Significant high-status individuals were interred in stone-lined graves within the structure suggesting that it acted as a quasi-mausoleum for high patrons of the monastery who were granted the familial privilege of burial at the high-status monastery in return for benefaction. The southern end of the narthex also contained a disproportionally high number of child and infant burials. The narthex church or porch may be contemporary with the larger later abbey church or may be later. Church building in the Middle Ages would have taken generations and was constructed piecemeal. At Boyle abbey in

Roscommon the nave of the abbey church, which appears as a single phase, is lined with arcade pillars that change from round arches to pointed arches, perhaps reflecting the slow pace of building rather than the product of rebuilding.

The medieval charcoal, lime and tile-kilns

Four different kilns dating from the Middle Ages were uncovered in the centre of the Arran Street site. The location and continuity of kiln activity north of the abbey church in a repeating location is suggestive of a defined medieval workspace: it was immediately outside but close to the principal abbey buildings, 15m north of the abbey church and immediately adjacent to, and forming the western boundary of, the abbey graveyard.

This craft production area had a lean-to structure that abutted the (eastern) inside edge of a north–south precinct/graveyard wall that enclosed the medieval graveyard on its western side (fig. 1.12). It was a location where materials, tools and finished unused products (including lime) were presumably stored dry and could be retrieved. The kiln was located in the open and abutted the eastern side of the graveyard wall. The lean-to structure was presumably roofed and also abutted the graveyard/precinct wall. The lean-to enclosed an area measuring 15m north–south and 4m east–west located immediately south of the kilns. Very rudimentary wall or post footings were identified parallel and on the eastern side of the wall, indicative of a foundation pad to support the eastern side of the structure. The lime from the kiln was clearly later than the precinct wall as it survived as compact white lime deposits extending from the kiln flues sloping up to and abutting the precinct wall on its eastern face (figs 1.13, 1.14). This area was first devoted to the production of charcoal, then lime mortar production for building and finally for the production of medieval floor-tiles laid in the abbey church.

The location was in use prior to the construction of the Savigniac abbey. A pit with evidence of basal heat-scorching contained significant quantities of oak charcoal dating to between the late ninth and eleventh century (AD 896–1024; UBA-54819). The charcoal pit was from a distinct phase pre-dating the two substantial lime-production kilns. This 'secular' activity pre-dates the abbey. The later episodes of use of the area mark an unbroken sequence of activity starting with the production of lime dating from the early fourteenth century (AD 1325–1428; UBA-54818). This large lime-kiln was reused and rebuilt and a second lime-kiln was constructed above it. The second lime-kiln was also later reused as a kiln to manufacture floor-tiles in the late fifteenth to mid-sixteenth century. The lime-kilns were easily recognizable by the profuse spread of lime mortar surfaces both within and leading from the kiln's central firing chambers, by way of their flues. A significant quantity of burnt lime waste covered the contemporary ground surface and could be identified as distinct phases of lime-production. Archaeologically, at least three phases of

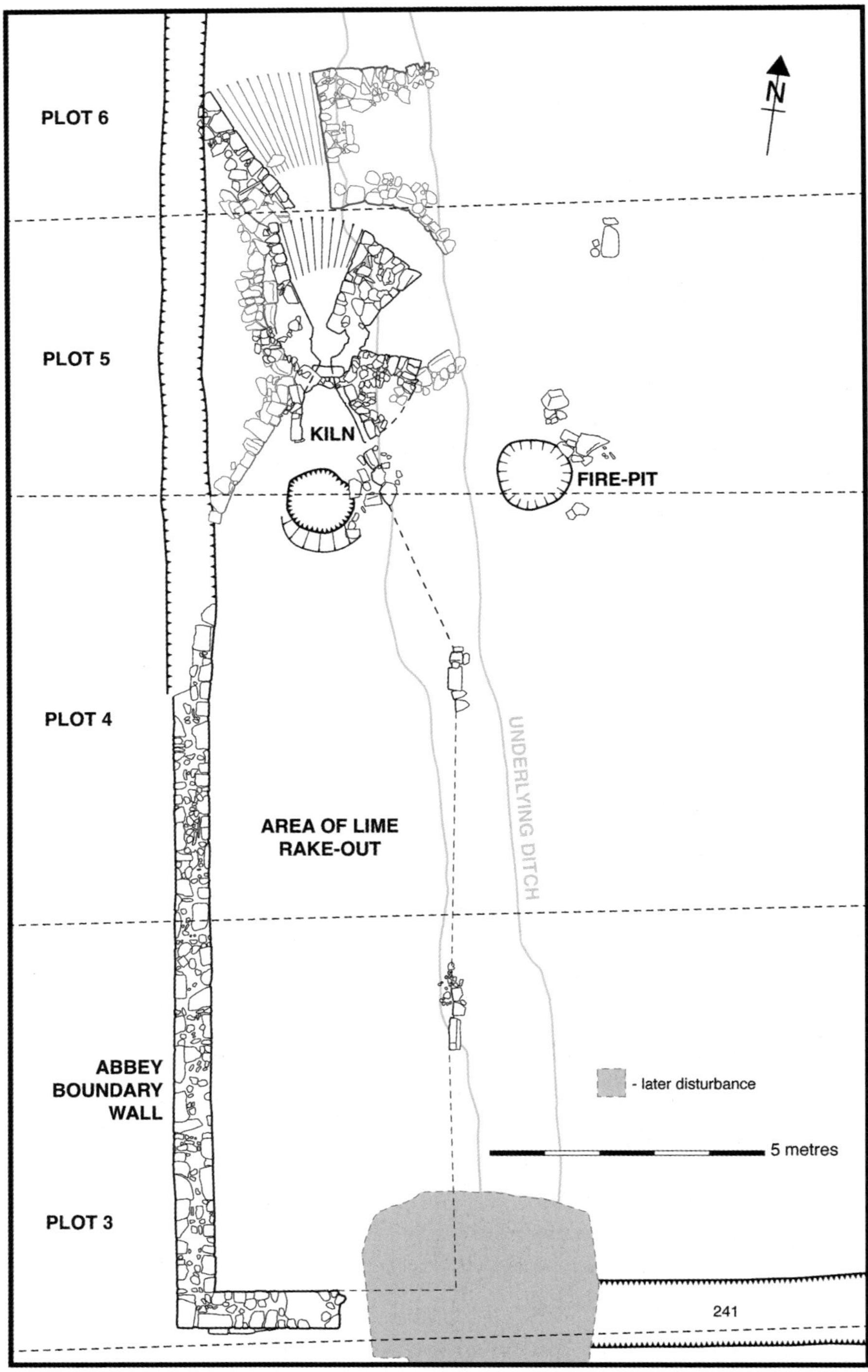

1.12 The location of lime-kiln and craft production area

1.13 The early lime-kiln and flues looking west

1.14 The later lime-kiln with mortar deposits at the flues looking west: note the earlier lime-kiln under the later structure

extensive remodelling or construction work in these kilns was identified coinciding with modifications to the primary monastic complex (church, tower, nave, cloister or its floors, etc.). The lime-kilns were used over a period of 250 years, were long-lived, cleaned out and reused as required.

The supply of lime to produce mortar is essential for bonding stone walls and laying tile floors. Both of these kilns occupied the exact same location, the latter being constructed directly on top of its predecessor. The final phase of activity saw the repurposing of the last lime-kiln chamber into a tile-kiln in the late fifteenth/early sixteenth century. Despite having a common function of burning broken limestone into a lime powder and combining with water to make a bonding mortar, the two structures had significantly different morphology, perhaps suggesting a change of personnel or a different cultural group being active in the abbey over subsequent generations. Similar chronological and typological developments in lime-producing kilns was observed during the archaeological excavations at Trim Castle, Co. Meath.[24] In Trim the assumption was that the large circular kiln excavated by Hayden located in the ditch of the ringwork under the keep was late twelfth or thirteenth century. The primary lime-kiln at St Mary's abbey is morphologically similar, but dates from at least a century later. Kilns of this type therefore appear to have a history of use spanning a wide time period *c.*1200–1400. Three lime-kilns were also excavated at Trim by Sweetman. At the time of the excavation these were thought to be post-medieval in date;[25] however their morphological comparison with the excavated and dated lime-kilns at St Mary's abbey, particularly the later lime-kiln, strongly suggests a medieval date.

The charcoal kiln

A small bowl-shaped circular pit (F1046, 85cm diameter and 17cm depth) was excavated and recorded stratigraphically under a deposit of lime from the later lime-kilns. The feature contained a substantial quantity of oak charcoal lining the base of the feature. The base and sides of the pit were scorched orange indicating that the burning of the oak occurred *in situ* where the natural clay base and sides were oxidized. The eastern side of the kiln or pit (F1046) was cut by a later field-boundary or ditch (F695). Initially the feature was thought to be the remains of a truncated corn-drying kiln; however, no plant cereals were recovered from the sieved soil samples. The environmental analysis of macrofossil plant remains from the pit was undertaken by Dr Ellen O'Carroll; it identified oak charcoal only from the samples.[26] O'Carroll in her analysis of

24 Alan Hayden, *Trim Castle, Co. Meath: Excavations 1995–8*, Archaeological Monograph Series, 6, Stationary Office (Dublin, 2000), pp 137–43. **25** P.D. Sweetman, G.F. Mitchell, R.J. Mansfield and Michael Dolley, 'Archaeological Excavations at Trim Castle, Co. Meath, 1971–74', *PRIA*, 78C (1978), 127–98, at 152–5. **26** Dr Ellen O'Carroll undertook specialist

the feature suggests it was a charcoal production pit. A C14 date (UBA-54819) from the oak charcoal in the feature dates from the tenth or early eleventh century. The date was determined from oak charcoal and therefore the 'old wood effect' has to be considered when dating the feature. This is further discussed in the dating section of the paper below. The feature is stratigraphically earlier than the later earth-cut field-boundary which dates from the twelfth/thirteenth century.

Earth-cut boundary ditch

An earth-cut field-boundary ditch oriented north–south was revealed extending from the northwestern corner of the abbey church. It ran 30m through the centre of the Arran Street site, where it continued beyond the limit of excavation and beneath the modern Hacienda Bar (fig. 1.12). Running parallel to Arran Street East, it was set back 12m east from the modern street front. The ditch dates from the twelfth or thirteenth century and was contemporary with the earlier phase of the Savignac or Cistercian building. The ditch drained water from within and under the wall-foundations of the northwest corner of the abbey church and had a stone culvert along its base taking water away from the abbey building north. The ditch (F695) was narrow at its base (0.44m) and was cut 0.78m deep and was almost vertically-sided with a flat base. It was not entirely straight and was filled with a loose, mid-brown, silty clay with frequent stone inclusions and occasional patches of mortar. The patches of mortar within its fill (F696) are likely to be evidence of the feature silting up during periods of construction. The feature had the archaeological character of a field-boundary or property division. The ditch was backfilled and replaced by a stone wall which replaced the earlier field-boundary. No burials were found on the western side of the ditch. Disarticulated disturbed human remains were found in the ditch fills.

The inner medieval precinct wall

A finely built medieval wall (F366) was constructed replacing the earlier earth-cut ditch (F695). It was located parallel and *c.*2m west of the earthen boundary (figs 1.12, 1.15). It continued to serve as a boundary separating the monastic graveyard from the medieval street which is aligned under the modern Arran Street East. This inner north–south-oriented precinct wall was discovered on the excavation and it appears to be illustrated on Speed's map of Dublin as a linear north–south boundary marking the eastern side of the medieval street. This street later became known as Boot Lane in the eighteenth and nineteenth century and subsequently Arran Street East in the later nineteenth century. The road led from the River Bradoge estuary, known as the Pill. The southern

micro analysis of macrofossil plant remains from soil samples throughout the excavation and on a series of samples from the kilns.

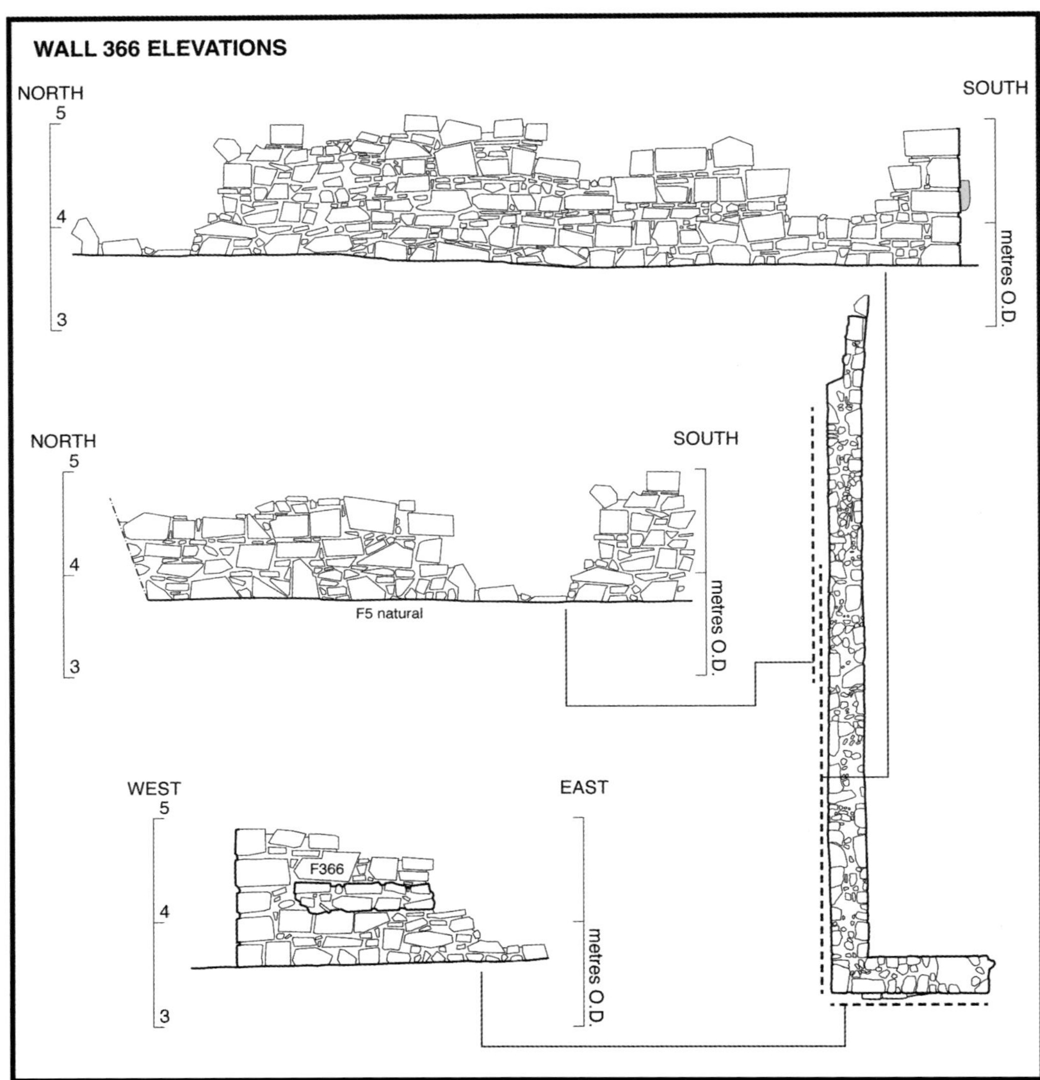

1.15 Plan and elevation of medieval precinct wall

end of the road was marked by a medieval gate (also illustrated on Speed's map). This medieval road followed the line of Arran Street East and Little Green Street inside the monastic precinct. Paul Duffy (see this volume) has excavated and discovered an inner precinct gate (which he calls the cemetery Gate) on Little Green Street which led north to an outer Market Gate on the northern side of the abbey precinct. Speed illustrates all three gates/

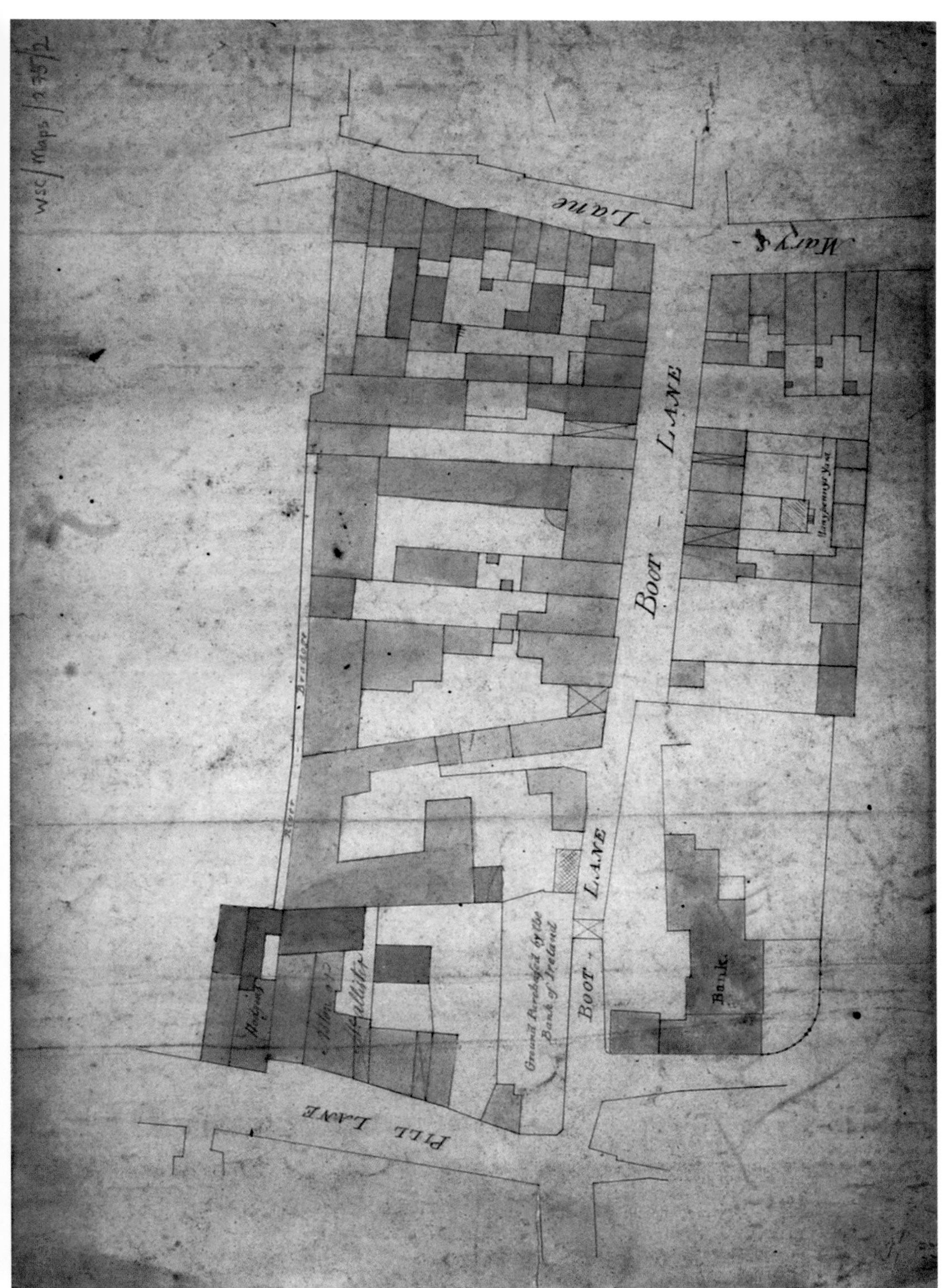

1.16 Wide Street Commission map of Boot Lane and surroundings, 1785

structures: the Water Gate at the Pill, the cemetery Gate on Little Green Street, and the northern Market Gate at the north end of Little Green Street which led to the market green outside of the abbey lands with its market cross (fig. 1.5). Wide Streets Commission maps of Boot Lane illustrate these streets and the junction with Pill Lane.[27] An arched 'gate' is depicted on Boot Lane on the Wide Streets Commission map of 1785 and this appears precisely to locate the medieval gate illustrated by Speed 176 years earlier (fig. 1.16).

The medieval wall (F366) defined the western extent of the abbey graveyard. It was fashioned from finely built limestone calp blocks and survived up to six courses or 1.15m high. It is presumed that it was originally 2–3m high. The wall was contemporary with the earliest phase of a lime-kiln that was constructed at the same time. Spreads of medieval lime forming a working floor at the mouth of the flue of the earliest kiln lapped up onto the edge of the wall. A 5m length of the wall survived and is preserved *in situ* beneath the hotel development. The northern sections of the wall were robbed out and replaced by later post-medieval walls, but the medieval wall cut was still observable. The late seventeenth-century Dutch Billy houses built fronting onto Boot Lane backed up against this earlier medieval wall and demonstrate the continuity of property boundaries into the subsequent post-medieval period.

The earliest lime-kiln

The earliest lime-kiln (F896) was circular, measuring 3.75m in diameter, with part of its structure standing 0.85m high (figs 1.13, 1.17). It had three fan-shaped stone-lined flues or openings for air intake and extracting burnt lime which radiated outwards like a windmill to the east, south and north. It abutted and was contemporary with the medieval graveyard located on its western side (F366). The base of the kiln was circular and was dug into both the back fill of the earth-cut ditch (F696) and the surrounding sandy clayey natural deposits (F629). The blockwork of the kiln was built backing directly against the inner medieval precinct wall. The kiln structure was constructed entirely from large lozenge-shaped water-rolled granite boulders (*c.*0.2m x 0.1m). These rocks were specifically sourced for the core of the kiln as limestone would not withstand the heat generated. Limestone blocks were utilized in the radiating flues. The structure was bonded with a soft, friable off-white lime mortar with sandy grit; only five courses of blockwork remained on the northern side. The structure would have originally been higher throughout its circumference, creating a wide, vertically-sided flat-bottomed

27 See the Dublin City Council Wide Street Commission Conserved Maps Index https://www.dublincity.ie/sites/default/files/media/file-uploads/2018-06/Index_WSC_Maps.pdf [accessed 25/02/2025] for Boot Lane, Map refs: WSC/Maps/057, WSC/Maps/ 220, WSC/Maps/275 and WSC/Maps/295.

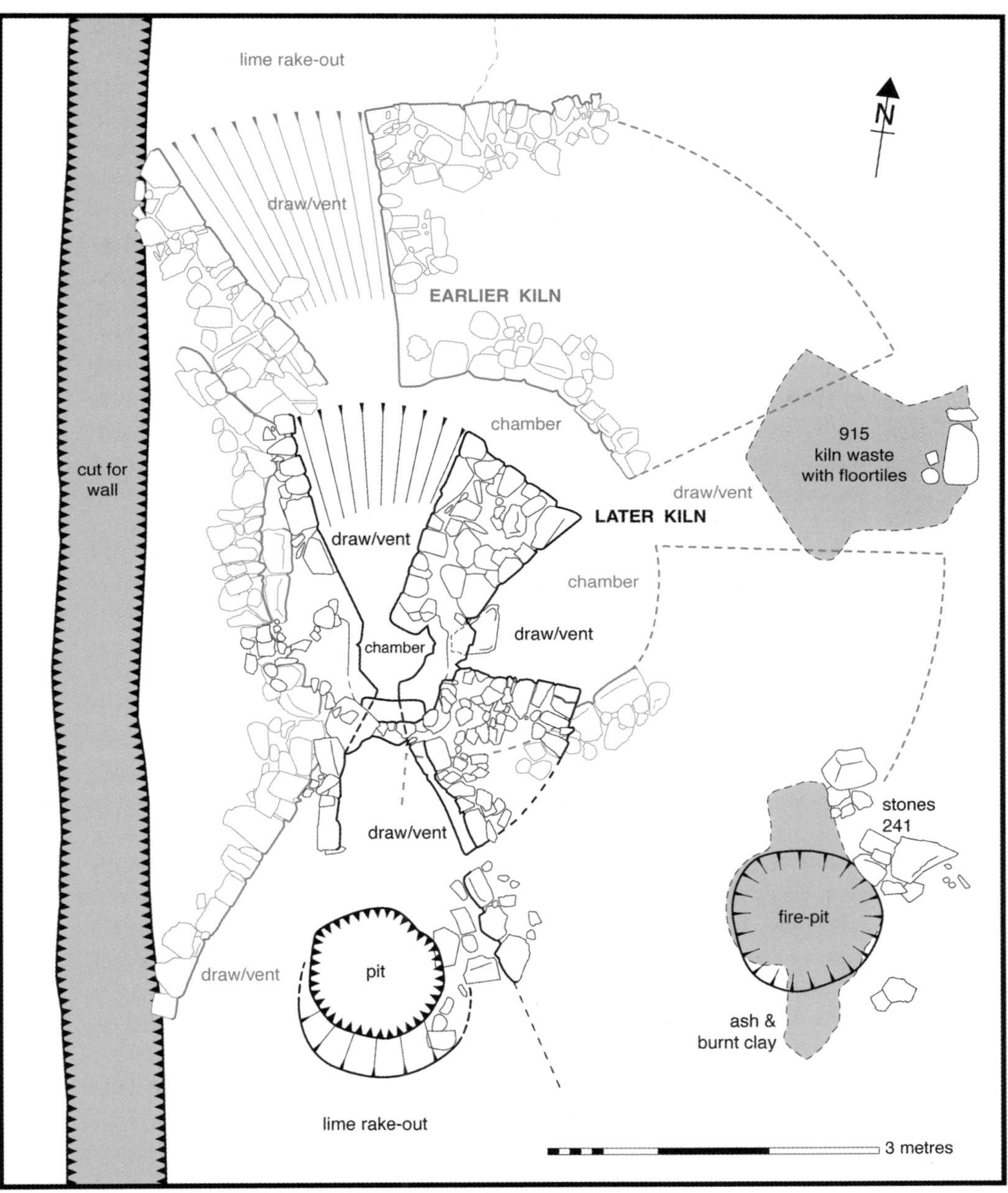

1.17 The medieval early and later lime-kilns

barrel-shaped chamber, suited for retaining burning material. The superstructure of the kiln did not survive and is assumed to have extended upwards with a wider circumference where limestone and a layer of fuel would have filled the structure. Much of the structure of kiln (F896) had been robbed out with the construction of a second later lime-kiln (F627) constructed directly on top of first structure.

The base of the early kiln was filled with a surviving deposit of dark silty clay 0.18m deep, flecked with charcoal and frequent small stones (F882). The deposit appeared to mark a period when the kiln fell out of use and the chamber and flues were no longer maintained. Several fragments of ecclesiastical architectural stone were recovered from this deposit. Many of these pieces were fashioned from Dundry, presumably taken from the abbey during a period of later remodelling of the church. A significant carved column capital with a fanned fluted motif known as a scalloped capital was recovered from this deposit. This piece of stonework is fashioned from a fine-grained sandstone and is likely to have been from one of the earliest Savigniac and/or Cistercian churches built on the site; English parallels date from *c.*1170.[28]

The later lime-kiln

A later lime-kiln (F627) was constructed both above and within the earlier kiln (F896, fig. 1.17). The structure was built with a circular central chamber of granite with three radiating flues composed of limestone blocks, opening to the east, south and north (fig. 1.14). The later kiln (F627) had a similar form but was a considerably smaller structure to the earlier one (F896). The chamber (F943) was formed from repurposed large lozenge-shaped granite boulders likely to have been robbed from the earlier structure. The chamber and the original lintelled flue openings survived on all three sides, with only the top of the structure missing. The flues of the kiln were covered with thick and dense deposits of lime, suggesting a long period of use and reuse for the production of lime mortar and also potentially for slaking out the mortar. The lipping of the slaked out mortar deposits was preserved on site where it was deposited in a wave-like accumulation up against the contemporary medieval precinct wall. The stones from the wall were robbed out (F366), but the precise line of the wall was preserved by the hard lipped lime mortar crust that formerly lay against the wall (fig. 1.14). The second lime-kiln was finally reused to produce medieval floor-tiles, and thousands of fragmentary broken waste floor-tiles were removed from the kiln chamber. The motifs and form of the relief tiles were identified and dated to the late fifteenth/early to mid-sixteenth century.[29] The early kiln was significantly larger and may have been associated with the construction of larger monastic building projects rather than the smaller later kiln which was used for both lime-production and tile-manufacturing. Broken roof-slates taken from medieval buildings were used in the tile-kiln as spacers to separate and stack tiles when they were fired in the kiln. Many of the roof-

28 Paul Duffy, pers. comm. **29** Joanna Wren, pers. comm.

1.18 Roof slate reused as a spacer in the tile kiln with glaze and terracotta residue after firing (21E0604:360:216)

slates were covered with glaze that dripped off the tiles as they were placed in the kiln immediately prior to firing (fig. 1.18). The roof-slates recovered from the kiln and more widely from within grave fills are a variety of colours. No terracotta roof-tiles were found on either excavation, with the exception of a small number of highly decorated ridge roof-tiles. This suggests that the important medieval buildings were covered by roof-slates with the apex of the building set with glazed ridge tiles. Lesser buildings or outbuildings are likely to have been thatched.

Decorative medieval masonry[30]

The abbey buildings were decorated with fine hand-cut masonry typical of the medieval period. A large collection of cut and decorative stone was recovered

30 Paul Duffy has examined the decorated stone from the excavations; the analysis of the stone for the final report is ongoing at the time of writing: his comments and observations

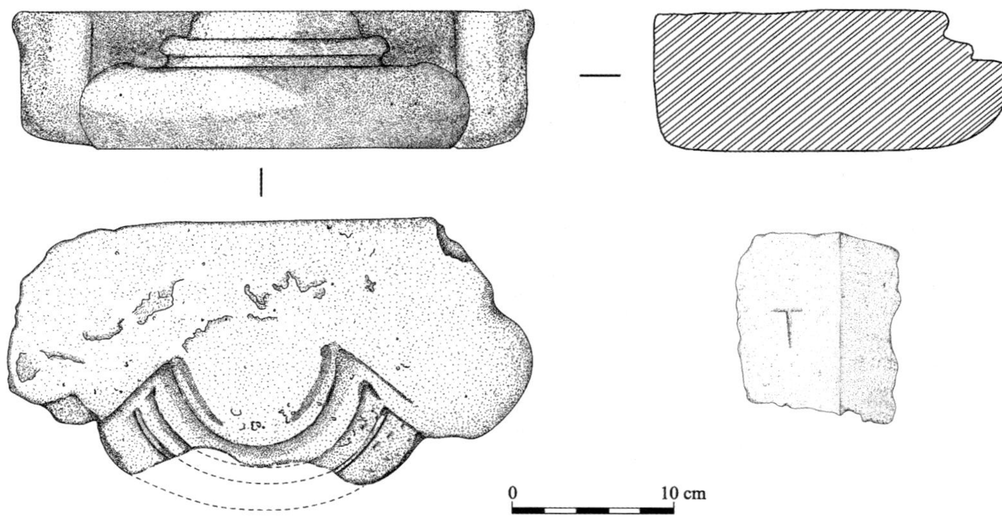

1.19 Carved Dundry moulded column base and medieval mason's mark

during the excavations, almost exclusively at the south end of the Arran Street East excavation. The decorative masonry was not found *in situ*; rather it was recovered in later disturbed contexts, specifically above and around the abbey church wall-foundations. A total of 112 masonry blocks and smaller fragments were accessioned into the National Museum of Ireland. Much of the stone was imported from Britain and was derived from a yellow oolitic limestone known as Dundry stone, from outside Bristol. The vast majority of the larger blocks of Dundry stone were recovered from under the concrete floor of an early twentieth-century warehouse that stood on the site. Additional smaller fragments of broken Dundry with very limited evidence for dressed or cut surfaces were found around the site, indicating the fragmentation of masonry for reuse in later post-medieval buildings. A discrete location within the medieval church porch appeared to have been used as a working surface for the *in situ* dressing of masonry. Small loose Dundry fragments were also retrieved from backfilled grave fills in the abbey cemetery.

Dundry was imported extensively into medieval Ireland *c.*1190–1350, the soft stone being valued for its suitability for hand carving.[31] These carved blocks were used in the most important architectural features of abbeys, cathedrals and castles. Door and window surrounds, including curved pillars and columns, tracery in windows, interlocking arches and cloistral arcading

are greatly appreciated. 31 Paul Duffy and Sara Pavia, 'Quarrying the past: petrographic analysis of Dublin's medieval building stone', unpublished Royal Irish Academy Research Report, 2021.

1.20 Dundry moulded column base with a mason's mark

1.21 Dundry moulded door, column or window block

have all been fashioned from Dundry (figs 1.19–1.21). Many of the pieces are emblematic of the abbey including a carved monk in prayer in a hooded cowl that formed part of a moulded door or cloistral pillar (figs 1.22, 1.23). This hooded monk has been heat-scorched, suggesting it formed part of the church

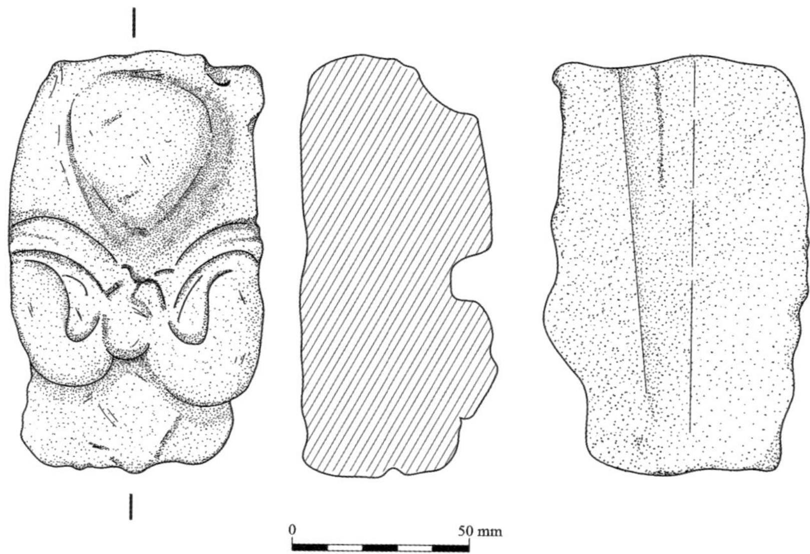

1.22 (*above*) Dundry moulded pillar fragment with the figure of a monk in prayer

1.23 Carved figure in Dundry, pillar fragment of monk in prayer

1.24 Late 12th century trumpet scalloped column capital fragment

burnt in the great fire of 1304. Distinct heat-scorching is present on a number of the Dundry stones found on site.

Later medieval window fragments were fashioned from Irish sandstone, including cusped window tracery carved from a yellow-grey sandstone veined with rust-coloured oxidization. This is thought to be from Carrickleck, Co. Meath,[32] and is possibly the remains of a west window later inserted in the abbey church. Four definite Dundry voussoirs and a probable fifth stone belong to a moulded, trefoil-headed arcade or wall niche. Similar trefoil arches date from the second quarter to the middle of the thirteenth century. Specifically dating these features by comparison is problematic, but a solid thirteenth-century date is proposed. The northern cloister passageway from Fountains abbey in Yorkshire built by Abbot John of Kent (AD 1220–47) offers an obvious stylistic and chronological comparison.[33] In his analysis of the

32 The stone was inspected by Prof. Patrick Wyse Jackson who has made preliminary geological identifications, this helps to distinguish architectural features fashioned from particular stone types, such as the window tracery which is thought to be made from Carrickleck stone. 33 D.M. Robinson and S.A. Harrison, 'The medieval cloister in England and Wales', *Journal of the British Archaeological Association*, 159 (2006), 183–5.

stone, Paul Duffy has also identified two late twelfth-century trumpet-scalloped column capital fragments made from a fine-grained micaceous sandstone (fig. 1.24). Most recently, a scalloped capital fashioned from Dundry dating from the early to mid-twelfth century has been identified from the collection of stone fragments from Christchurch cathedral in Dublin.[34] This architectural fragment may be from the earliest church on the site built in 1139 or shortly thereafter.

THE DECORATIVE FLOOR-TILES FROM THE ABBEY[35]

One of the largest collections of medieval floor-tiles found in Ireland, nearly 3,000 loose floor-tiles, were found during the archaeological excavations. These were the remnants of floors within the abbey, most likely from the church. None of the tiles were found *in situ* and no undisturbed floor levels were uncovered. The tiles were found in the disturbed deposits associated with the demolition of the monastery, in backfilled graves and around and within a late-medieval tile-kiln found in the graveyard north of the church.

At least four phases of decorative flooring were identified in the collection, spanning the period between 1139 and 1539. The tiles were manufactured on site by artisan craftsmen, some of whom may have been monks, producing delicate floral and geometric motifs, combined in panels to form intricate glazed mosaic floors. One such mosaic pattern (21E0604:628:10) has been reproduced on the exterior wall of the Ruby Hotel fronting onto Little Mary Street close to where it was found (figs 1.25, 1.26).

The earliest floors were undecorated mosaic floors, dated to *c.*1200. A collection of two-coloured tiles were the remains of a thirteenth-century floor, probably located within the abbey church. This two-colour tiled floor included tiles depicting a lion and also a fantastical beast, a kind of dragon called a wyvern (fig. 1.27). Images of wyverns are common in medieval art but this is one of the few examples known from a floor-tile and the first of its kind found in Ireland. The floor combined panels of decorated tile and panels of intricate mosaic with a prayer picked out in letter tiles, possibly dedicated to the Virgin Mary, as was the abbey (fig. 1.28). The letter tiles date from *c.*1200–1300. The cross denotes a prayer and the saltire or diagonal cross is used as a full stop. There are letters there which could spell *Ave Maria* or *Beate Marie Virgine* (Table 1). A later floor at the abbey dates to the fourteenth or early fifteenth century and includes panels of decoration with floral and geometric motifs impressed onto the face of the tiles with wooden stamps, these are known as line impressed tiles.

34 Paul Duffy and Rachel Moss, pers. comm. 35 The floor-tiles have been studied by Joanna Wren and the text in this section is largely based on her work.

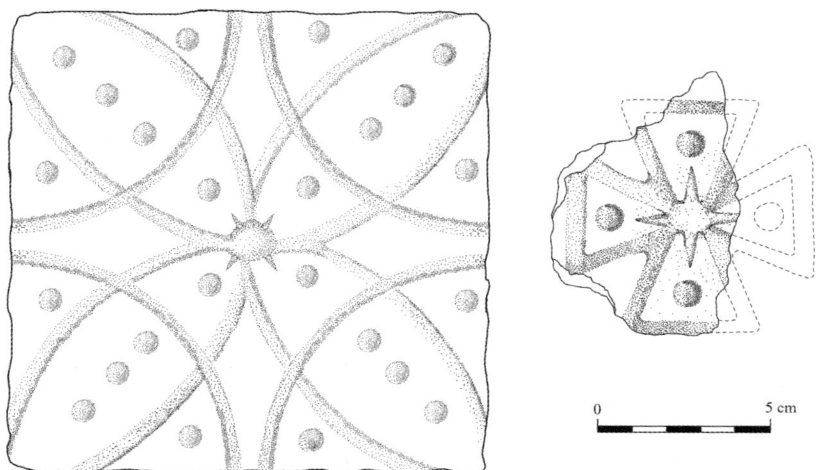

1.25 Relief floor tiles 21E0604:628:10 (L) and 21E0604:915:10 (R)

1.26 Glazed 15th–16th-century relief tile with circular geometric decoration

1.27 Late 12th–early 13th-century two-colour tile of wyvern or dragon

1.28 Late 12th–early 13th-century two-colour tiles: the cross denotes a prayer, the letter tiles 'B', 'M' and 'V' and spell out *Beate Marie Virgine*; the saltire or diagonal cross is used as a full stop

Table 1. The letter tile types

A	a	B	D	d	E	F
L	M	M	N	n	O	R
T	V	X	X	╬		

1.29 Glazed 15th–16th-century relief tile with an image of a lion

A total of 1,134 fragments of wasted tile material and structural fragments from the kiln were by far the largest and most important group in the assemblage, and stylistically dated to the late fifteenth or sixteenth century. Once again this kiln would have been making tiles for use on one of the abbey floors, most likely within the church. The tiles were decorated with a different kind of stamp to produce designs in relief. Among this material there was a

1.30 Glazed 15th–16th-century relief tile with foliage decoration

1.31 Glazed 15th–16th-century relief tile with deer and foliage decoration

wide variety of different forms of decoration, many discovered for the first time. They were mostly floral with some geometric designs and a few notable exceptions. One of these, the face of a lion (fig. 1.29), was taken from heraldry as were many of the images used on medieval tiles. Other tiles depicted a hunting scene of a deer grazing from trees or foliage patterns (figs 1.30, 1.31). Scenes of hunters' dogs and prey were common on floor-tiles. The imagery draws from medieval hunting manuals, which may have been produced or housed in the abbey scriptorium.

Most of the relief tiles were made to work with other tiles with the same image. Some showed parts of a design which became whole when placed on a floor with the other tiles. Others, like the tile depicted on the new hotel built at the Arran Street site show parts of interlocking circles, which again became whole when used in a group. All of these tiles would have formed part of rectangular panels surrounded by border tiles like the one showing the deer.

The abbey graveyard[36]

In excess of 500 burials were excavated on the two archaeological digs (figs 1.32, 1.33), but this forms a small fraction of the wider monastic graveyard. The abbey graveyard was located on the northern side of the church. Burials were also excavated from within the nave of the abbey church and in the church porch or narthex building that was located at the west end of the church outside the west door. The graveyard largely went out of use after 1539 with the dissolution of the monastery, although it is possible that some later burials were still being interred in the graveyard up to the late seventeenth century. The graveyard was completely built over and in places truncated by the construction of the Presbyterian meeting-house in *c.*1670 and also with the development of domestic houses with basements in the seventeenth and eighteenth century on Meeting House Lane, Arran Street East, Little Mary Street and Capel Street.

The burial morphology identified during the archaeological excavations was not entirely consistent. Differing rites of burial were observed during the dig, reflecting changing cultural practices of burial and the status of the individual (figs 1.34–1.36). The predominant burial rite was a simple burial where the individual was placed in an earth-cut grave. The grave was oriented east–west mirroring the alignment of the church or churches. The body was placed in the grave in the supine position (on its back with the hands and legs extended in the grave). Corpses appear to have been interred in shrouds and so the body was placed with the legs extended and the arms either along the side of the body or tightly crossed over the torso wrapped in the shroud. The head was placed at the western end of the grave and was often tilted upwards facing over

36 Dr Denise Keating has provided preliminary findings of the analysis of human skeletal remains found on site. This work is ongoing and may not be complete until 2026.

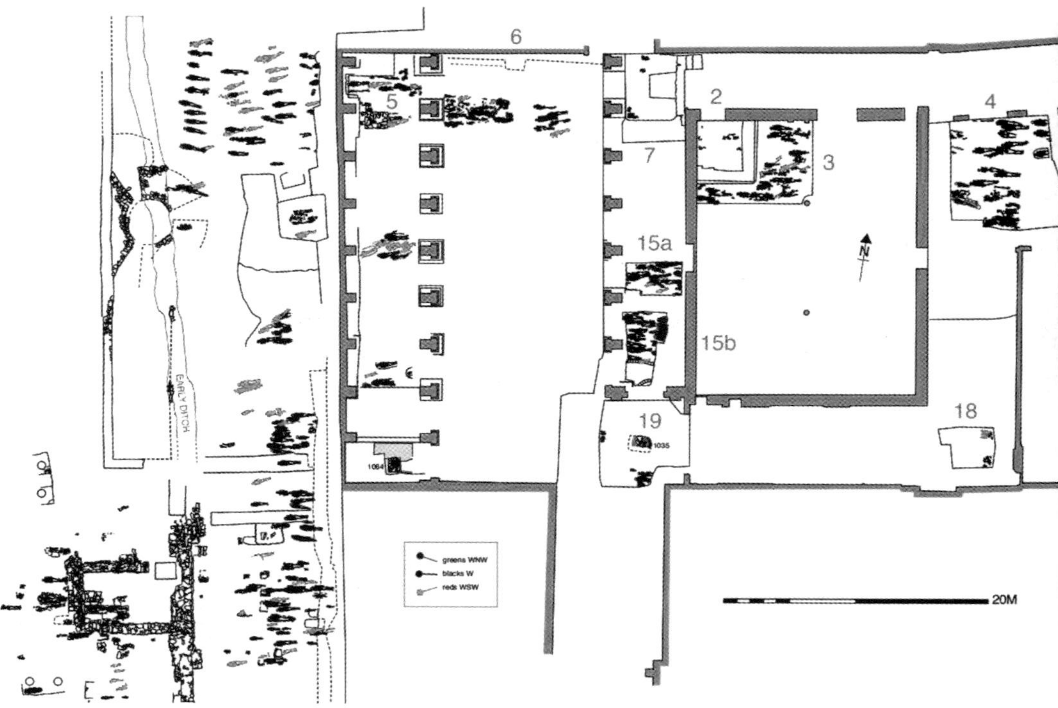

1.32 The location of burials on Capel Street and Arran Street East

the body with the chin lying on the upper torso facing east. This burial rite is complicated by the use of stones or timber to line graves to presumably make them more elaborate, reflecting the social status of the deceased individual or family.

Three distinct early graves were found on the Capel Street excavation (Burial CCLXXIV (274); CCLXXXI (281) and CCXC (290)). These date from at least the early tenth century and are no later than the early eleventh century. The identified burial rites on two of the graves (Burials CCLXXIV (274) and CCXC (290)) were both chronologically early and physically distinct where distinctive ear-muff stones were placed on either side of the skull (figs 1.37–1.39). The third early burial (CCLXXXI (281)) was interred in a rectangular grave-cut where clinker nails or clench bolts were recovered from the cardinal points in the grave, suggesting that the body was placed in a wooden lined grave, potentially derived from fragments of a boat in which the body was placed as part of the burial rite (fig. 1.40). There were a large number of graves from which iron nails were retrieved (fig. 1.41).

A high-status stone-lined grave, Burial CXLVI (146), was uncovered on the Arran Street East excavations, in which Dundry stone was placed around the

1.33 The excavation of burials within the abbey church, Arran Street East

head of the adult male within a mortared limestone cist, creating a pseudo-sarcophagus (fig. 1.36).[37] The burial was contemporary with other more simply interred burials. A copper alloy disc was also recovered between the knees of

37 The stone-lined grave has been preserved and is displayed under a glass floor in a commercial food retail unit on Arran Street East along with other medieval walls and burials that have been entirely preserved *in situ* under the foundations of the new developments. During the course of the archaeological excavation the office of the City Archaeologist within Dublin City Council worked with the writer, the developer and Courtney Deery Heritage Consultancy to tailor the archaeological excavations to preserve medieval walls *in situ* under the new buildings and to identify locations where archaeological deposits should be preserved unexcavated.

1.34 A group of four individuals interred in one grave, located north of the church, Burial XLIX, L, LI and LV (49, 50,51 and 55, Arran Street East), taken looking north

the burial with the fragmentary remains of woollen woven fabric (a cloak or cassock?) attached to the back of the disc (fig. 1.42). The elaborate stone lining, the placement of Dundry around the head, and the decorative mount on the cloak, all indicate the elevated status of the individual. The combined foundation date for the abbey in 1139 and a C14 determination of the grave suggests burial between 1139 and 1157 (see below). A number of high-status stone-lined burials were found (fig. 1.43).

As with many monastic graveyards, the graves were found to include male and female adults of all ages and also children, not just reflecting the burial of monks or novices, but of the wider lay community living around the liberty of St Mary. It would therefore appear that the abbey church, or at least the abbey graveyard, performed some of the functions of a parish church as a burial place for northeastern Dubliners, as distinct from the medieval parish of St Michan serving the community around Church Street. Burials have been found which were interred within the abbey church and these are thought to be most likely monks and/or high-status patrons. The practice of placing burials in discrete separate locations based on individual status is long attested in the Christian and Cistercian tradition. Abbots are known to have been buried

1.35 A group of three individuals interred in the narthex, Burial LXXXV, LXXXVI and LXXXVII (85, 86 and 87, Arran Street East), taken looking west

1.36 Male high-status burial in stone-lined grave, with Dundry stones at the head, Burial CXLVI (146), Arran Street East taken looking west

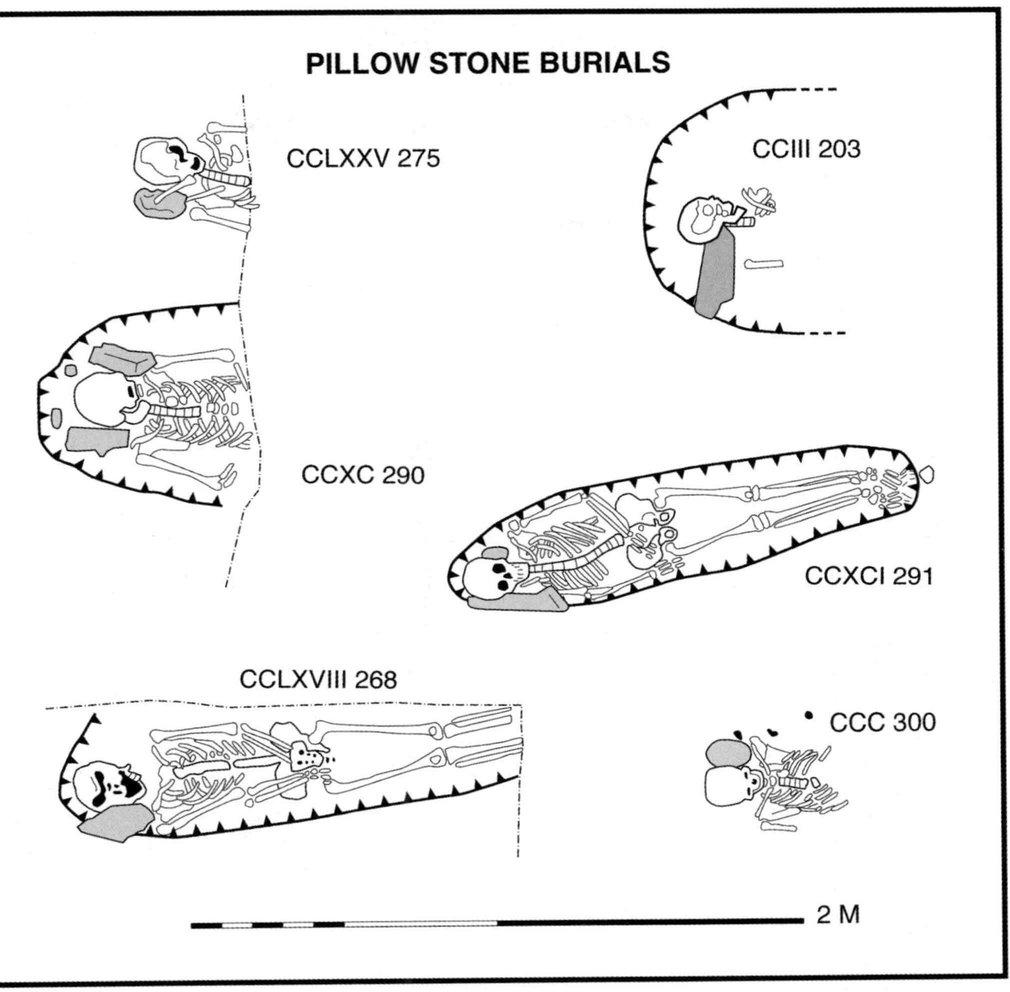

1.37 Burials with ear-muff stones from the Capel Street excavations

under the floor of the chapter house within Cistercian monastic communities, such as Fountains abbey in Yorkshire.[38]

'High status' stone-lined burials were identified within a stone porch or 'narthex' built adjoining the western end of the church. Burial within the Cistercian precinct was at first only permitted to members of the community, although an exception was made if guests died while staying at the abbey. From the mid-twelfth century the general chapter of the order relaxed its stance and

38 https://www.dhi.ac.uk/cistercians/fountains/buildings/chapterhouse/ [accessed 04/02/2025].

1.38 Burial CCLXXIV (274), lying under Burial CCLXXV (275), Capel Street

made various concessions, permitting at first the burial of sovereigns and prelates, thereafter of founders and other outsiders.[39] Hence, we know that patrons of the abbey and their relatives were permitted to be buried within the precinct, such as Thomas de Feipo, who became a monk and his brother

39 In 1152 burial was permitted to sovereigns and prelates; in 1157 this was extended to founders and in 1217 to all who wished if they had the permission of their parish priest:

1.39 Burial CCLXXIV (274), lying under Burial CCLXXV (275), Capel Street

Adam, who left his body to be buried where his brother Thomas had taken the religious habit.[40] Such burial within the monastic precinct became highly prized by the laity, for it was believed that those who were physically present forever within these sacred walls would secure a speedier passage to salvation. The burials within the narthex included infants, adolescents and adult inhumations, some within elaborate stone-lined graves. The completion of the analysis of the excavated remains will test the assumption that individual status is linked to the physical location and furnishing of the burial as permitted by the Cistercian rule.

Preliminary osteological analysis of the skeletal remains has revealed the majority of adults died young, between 25 to 35 years of age with few surviving beyond 45 years of age. The skeletons also reveal how harsh medieval life was, with evidence of people suffering from dental disease, trauma, infections, and conditions such as tuberculosis, syphilis and gouty arthritis. Periods of disease

Statuta capitulorum generalium ordinis Cisterciensis ab anno 1116 ad annum 1786, ed. J. Canivez (8 vols; Louvain, 1933–41), i, 1152: 10 (p. 47); 1157: 63 (p. 68); 1217: 3 (p. 465). **40** Ó Conbhuí, 'Lands of St Mary's abbey', 76.

1.40 Burial CXLVI (146), buried with clinker nails or clench bolts at cardinal point around the body, Capel Street

and malnutrition were not uncommon in childhood, leading to illnesses like scurvy and anaemia, which could affect growth and this may be reflected on this site as the average height of the adults was found to be slightly below normal for the time (men 169.5cm or 5ft 5½ inches tall and women 158.5cm or 5ft 2 inches tall). This reflects the slowing or cessation of growth in childhood during a period of physiological stress (caused by disease, malnutrition, or trauma). There was also evidence of medical care, where fractures had been set and head traumas healed, most likely in the abbey's infirmary. But the evidence of severe disabling conditions, such as advanced spinal arthritis, speaks perhaps of hardworking lay brothers within the abbey community where care and attention were given to the sick and dying. The tradition that elderly or infirm members of the Cistercian community, the lay brethren, were entitled to live out their lives in the monastery infirmary after a life spent working and living in the monastic granges (farms) in the possession of the abbey is well

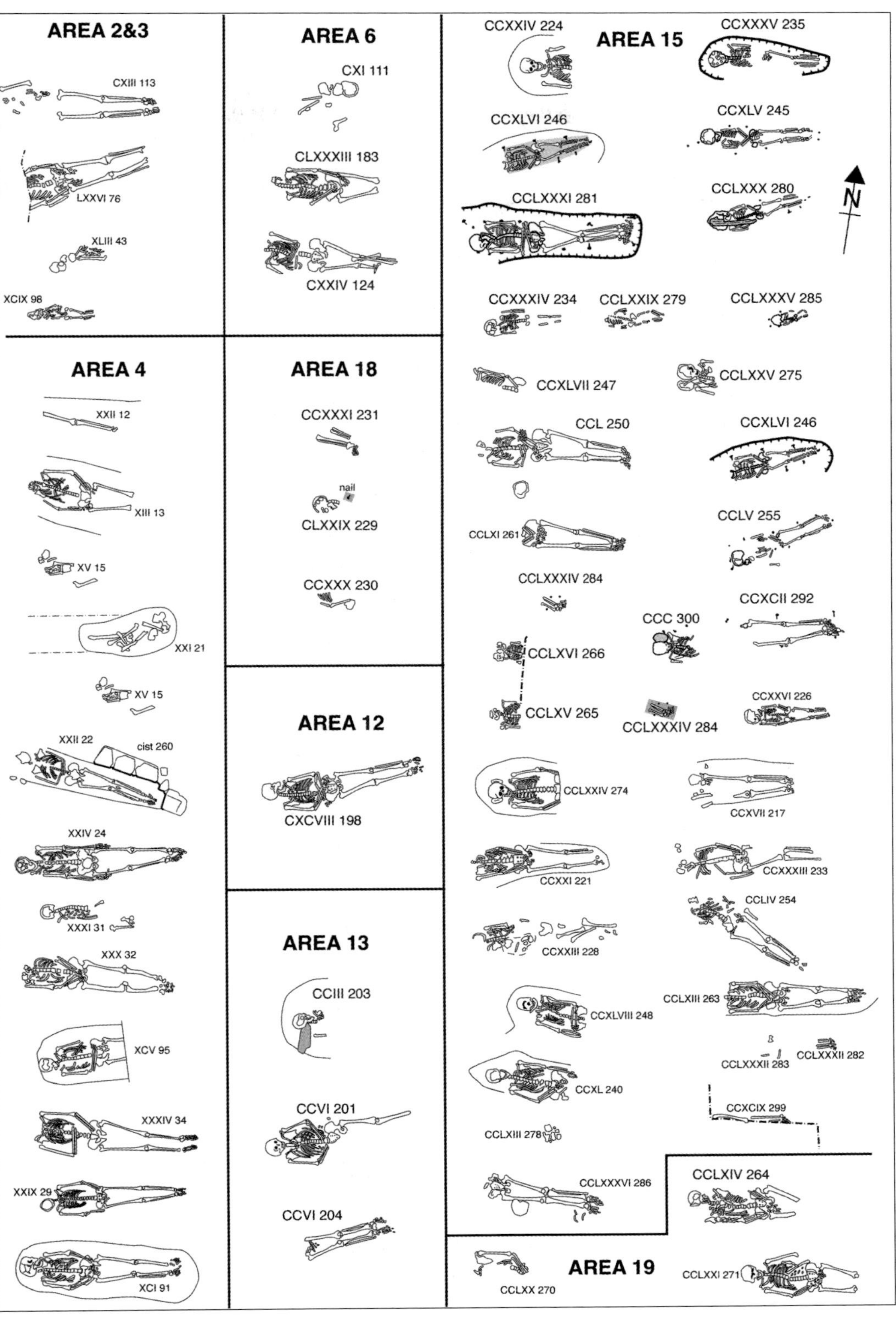

1.41 Burials with iron nails from the Capel Street excavations

1.42 Bronze disc (21E0604:783:1) with woven fabric attached to it in the grave of Burial CXLVI (146), Capel Street

attested. The skeletal analysis also points to a vibrant working population within this bustling quarter of medieval Dublin, demonstrated in various ways including specific wear patterns on teeth that hint at their use as tools or a 'third hand' in leather, wool and textile processing, and also evidence of 'Weaver's Bottom', a type of bursitis, caused by long periods of sitting on hard surfaces.

The dissolution of the abbey

After the dissolution of the monastery, the majestic abbey buildings were eventually dismantled and much of the stone was reused in new building projects. From the seventeenth century onwards the former abbey was gradually absorbed into the new urban development around the Capel Street block and one of Ireland's greatest monasteries disappeared beneath the city streets. In the modern period, late seventeenth- to nineteenth-century houses that replaced the abbey were, in turn, demolished and replaced by a concrete building, including the former Begley's Fruit Market, which sealed the earlier foundations beneath its concrete floor. Impressive cellars from 'Dutch Billy' houses built in *c.*1700 were uncovered on both archaeological excavations on Arran Street East and within the Capel Street site.

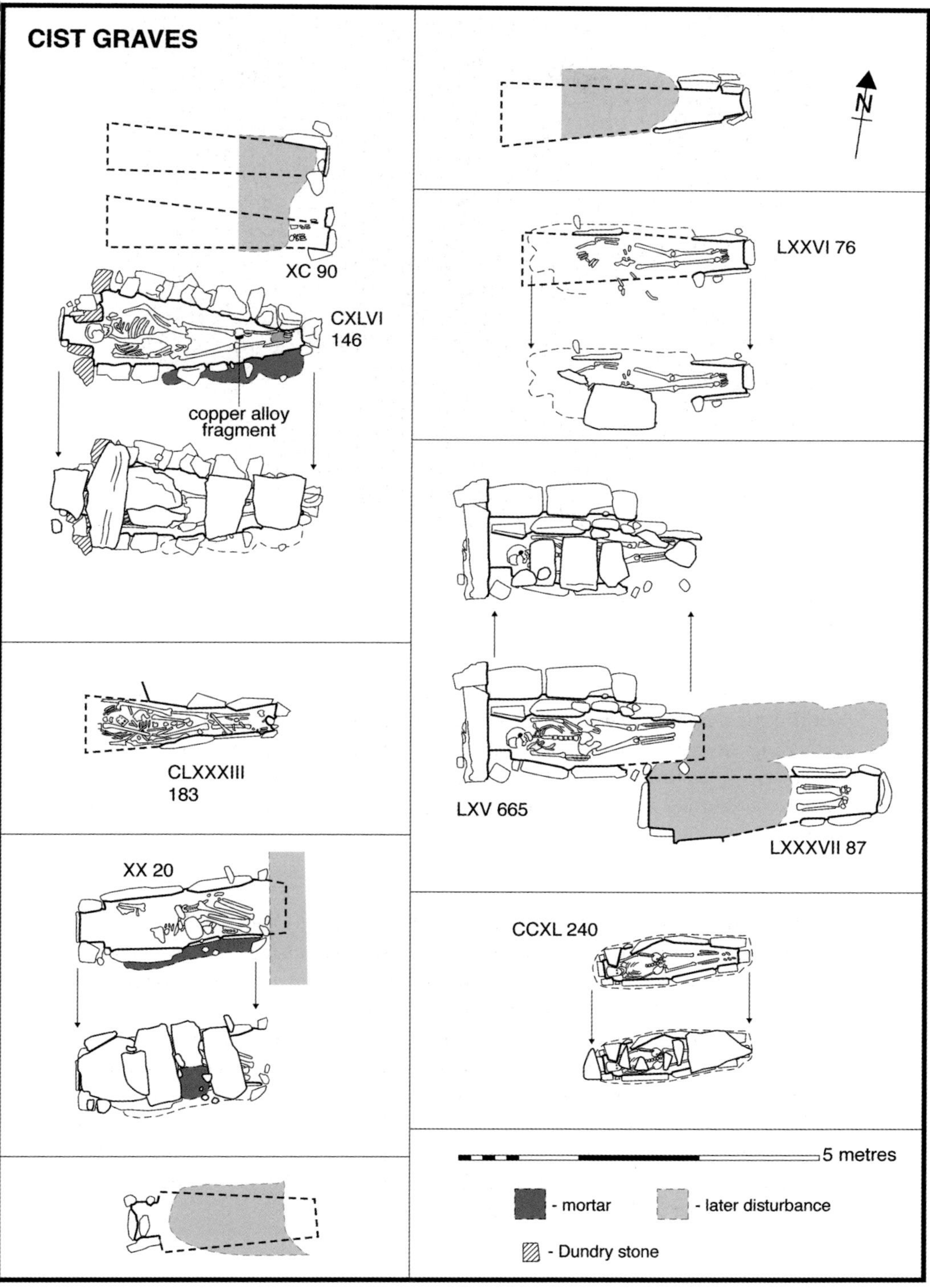

1.43 Burials in stone-lined graves from the Arran Street East excavations

PROVISIONAL RESULTS OF THE C14 DATING PROGRAMME AT ST MARY'S[41]

The programme of C14 dating at St Mary's abbey was undertaken during two phases of test excavation (2017–19) and on two phases of subsequent archaeological excavation (2021–4). Two samples were submitted to the Beta Analytic Lab in Miami from the test excavation at Capel Street (17E0196). A further sample from the Arran Street East test excavation (19E0064) was also processed in the same batch by Beta Analytic (Beta) in 2018. A further date from the Capel Street test excavation (17E0196) was sent to the Chrono Centre in Queen's University Belfast (UBA) and was processed in 2019. The first batch of dates from the Arran Street East excavations (21E0604) was processed by the Chrono Centre in Belfast in 2022. The second and final set of dates from the Arran Street East excavations (21E0604) was processed in January 2025. The final dates from the Capel Street site (21E0802) were processed in February 2025. The results from all of these completed dating programmes are presented below in Table 2 and 3 and in Appendix I where the full calibrated dates are given.

The radiocarbon dates were calibrated in order to convert them from their raw radiocarbon age as illustrated in Table 2 to calendar dates expressed at either one standard deviation (1 sigma) or two standard deviations (2 sigma) from a mean date expressed relative to AD.[42] The results of the calibration of the dates are set out in Appendix I. The 2 sigma calibrated dates have a 95.4% chance of being accurate. The 2 sigma calibrated dates are accepted as the best way of reading the data rather than the 1 sigma calibrated date ranges (which are only likely to be 68.2% accurate).

Evidence for pre-Savignac Hiberno-Norse burial and other early dates

We can definitively say that we have found evidence for pre-Savigniac burial based on three early C14 dates from the excavations at Capel Street (21E0802). The sampling sought to date stratigraphically early and typologically interesting burials on the excavations (UBA-5549; UBA-55149 and UBA-55150). Three of these burials from the Capel Street excavation (Burial

41 The C14 dates presented herein include four dates which were procured as part of the pre-development test excavation undertaken by Courtney Deery Heritage Consultancy (CDHC) (Siobhán Deery) and Linzi Simpson (Excavation Licence ref: 17E0196 and 19E0064); permission to reproduce those dates is gratefully acknowledged. The author (Edmond O'Donovan) directed the subsequent excavations (21E0604 and 21E0802) on behalf of CDHC and the full combined results are presented in this paper.
42 RADIOCARBON CALIBRATION PROGRAM* CALIB REV8.2 Copyright 1986–2020, Minze Stuiver and P.J. Reimer; to be used in conjunction with Minze Stuiver and P.J. Reimer, *Radiocarbon*, 35 (1993), 215–30. Calibration data set: intcal20.14c # Reimer et al. 2020 % area enclosed Cal AD age ranges relative area under probability distribution.

Table 2. The uncalibrated radiocarbon dates from St Mary's abbey, Dublin (after Beta Analytic and the Chrono Centre)

Lab ref. No.	Excavation No. Feature No. Sample ID	Material Type	C14 Age BP	±	F14C	±	Mg Graphite
Beta-525335	17E0196_C8 _SK1	Bone (Non-heated)	820	30			
Beta-525336	17E0196_C27 _SK4	Bone (Non-heated)	940	30			
Beta-525337	19E0064_C8 _SK1	Bone (Non-heated)	560	30			
UBA-37928	17E0196:TP5.1	Human tibia-mid shaft (posterior)	587	36	0.9296	0.0042	
UBA-47871	21E0604:F266 – S#423	Ash fragment retrieved from within mortar in a *c.* 12th century pillar	925	23	0.8912	0.0026	0.960
UBA-47872	21E0604:F54 – S#424	Mortar/charcoal, this sample is from a medieval wall and may be difficult to date due to high mortar and low charcoal content	1072	14	0.8751	0.0015	0.979
UBA-54818	21E0604F1025 – S#460	Fraxinus excelsior (ash)	543	23	0.9346	0.0027	0.985
UBA-54819	21E0604F1047 – S#466	Quercus sp (oak), early charcoal pit	1068	24	0.8755	0.0026	0.991
UBA-54820	21E0604F386:2 – Burial 49	Bone, human sacral fragment	838	26	0.9010	0.0029	0.979
UBA-54821	21E0604F390:6 – Burial 53	Bone, human right fibula fragment	567	26	0.9318	0.0030	0.998
UBA-54822	21E0604F774:12 – Burial 146	Bone, human right tibia fragment	970	26	0.8863	0.0028	0.991
UBA-54823	21E0604F965:1 – Burial 213	Bone, human complete prox pedal phalanx	819	25	0.9030	0.0028	0.996
UBA-55146	21E0802F257:1 – Burial 34	Bone, human left femur fragment	868	20	0.8976	0.0023	0.989
UBA-55147	21E0802F339:1 – Burial 71	Bone, human left rib shaft fragment	891	26	0.8950	0.0029	0.989
UBA-55148	21E0802F1008: 1 – Burial 274	Bone, human cervical neural arch fragment	1028	23	0.8799	0.0025	0.982
UBA-55149	F21E08021017: 1 – Burial 281	Bone, human mid-thoracic vert fragment	1051	21	0.8773	0.0023	0.994
UBA-55150	21E0802F1047 – Burial 290	Bone, human left scapula fragment	1033	22	0.8794	0.0024	0.983

Table 3. Calibrated C14 dates from St Mary's abbey (Cal AD) after OxCcal[43]

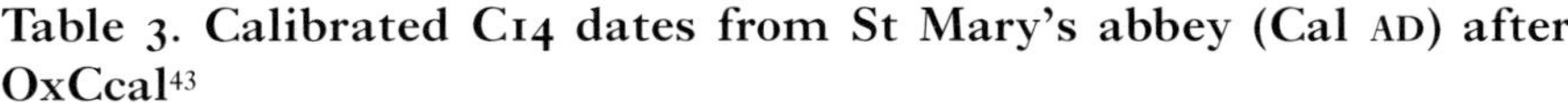

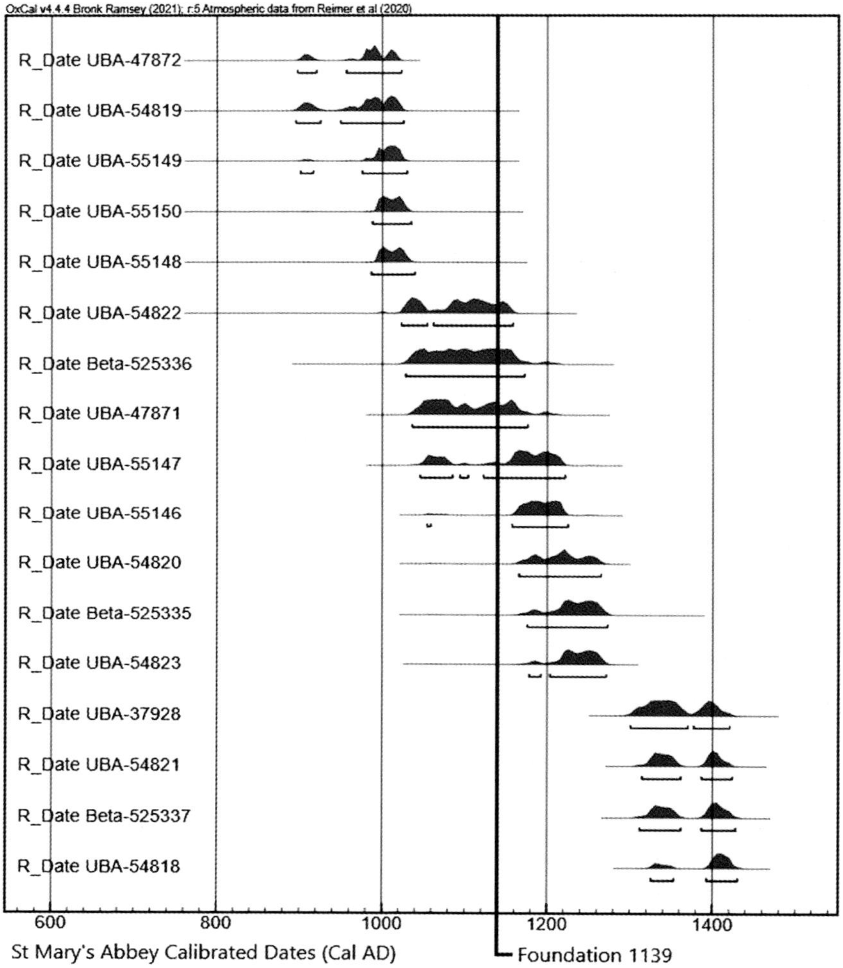

CCLXXIV (274); CCLXXXI (281) and CCXC (290) date from at least the early tenth century and are no later than the early eleventh century. These dates have a narrow standard deviation and prove that the burials were interred at least 100 years before the arrival of the Savignac monks in 1139. All of the other dates from burials at the site (testing and excavation) could be Savigniac

43 The OxCal program is intended to provide radiocarbon calibration analysis of archaeological and environmental chronological information. The current version is 4.4 and works with IntCal20. It is available for online use or downloading at https://c14.arch.ox.ac.uk/oxcal.html (accessed 24/02/2025).

or later Cistercian burials, but the three early dates (UBA-5549; UBA-55149 and UBA-55150) all have a 95.4% chance of dating to between AD Cal 990–1034, AD Cal 902–1028 and AD Cal 979–1038. Statistically there is a *c.*1:20 chance of one of the dates being wrong; however, the identification of three overlapping dates reduces that possibility to negligible levels. A fourth early date was procured from a burial found in Test Trench 5 from Linzi Simpson's test excavation of the Capel Street site which dated AD 1025–1160 (Beta-525336). On Arran Street we have a burial (UBA-54822) that ranges AD 1023–1157, and whilst both dates (Beta-525336 and UBA-54822) could be pre-Savigniac, they also potentially post-date 1139 and statistically are as likely to fall later in that range rather than being selectively early given the wider standard deviation of the calibrated range.

Burials CCLXXIV (274) and CCXC (290) from the Capel Street archaeological excavation were interred with unusual pillow stones and 'ear-muff' stones placed around the head, distinguishing that burial rite from the more typical medieval burials recorded on site, consisting of simple extended inhumations oriented east–west which were occasionally in stone cists. These burials (CCLXXIV (274) and CCXC (290)) were also excavated from amongst the earliest stratigraphic burial levels on the Capel Street site. The 'ear-muff' burials have been uncovered and have strong parallels with the placement of 'ear-muff' stones or even other skulls derived from separate burials around the head on sites excavated in Dublin city, such as at the church of St Michael le Pole,[44] but also in the wider vicinity of Dublin city on Early Christian sites such as Cabinteely,[45] and at Mount Gamble in Swords.[46] Burial CCLXXXI (281) appears to be a plank-lined burial where the timber plank-lining was held in place by iron clinker nails. It can be speculated that this burial (CCLXXXI (281)), dating from the tenth/eleventh century, was lined with fragments of clinkers taken from a dismantled clinker-built boat or ship still partially nailed together as suggested by the type and position of the nails in the grave. These three burials display a burial rite different from that observed within Early Christian Ireland which may reflect a subtly different burial rite relating to evolving Hiberno-Norse burial traditions as they adopted Christianity in the tenth and eleventh century.

The earliest date from the Arran Street East site was derived from oak charcoal from a charcoal production pit that was cut by a later 'Cistercian'

44 Edmond O'Donovan, 'The Irish, the Vikings and the English: new archaeological evidence from excavations at Golden Lane, Dublin' in Duffy (ed.), *MD VIII*, pp 46–8. 45 Malachy Conway, *Director's find findings from excavations at Cabinteely*, Margaret Gowen & Co. (Dublin, 1999), pp 22–7. 46 Edmond O'Donovan, 'Archaeological excavations on Mount Gamble Hill: evidence for a new early medieval church in Swords?' in Duffy (ed.), *MD XV*, pp 13–38; and idem, 'Excavations on Mount Gamble Hill, Swords, Co. Dublin' in Chris Corlett and Michael Potterton (eds), *Death and burial in early medieval Ireland in the light of recent archaeological excavations* (Dublin, 2010), p. 231.

twelfth-/thirteenth-century earthen field-boundary/drainage ditch. The date (UBA-54819) has a 95.4% chance (2 sigma) of being between Cal AD 896–1024. The base of the pit was heat-scorched indicating burning *in situ*. It was an earth-cut feature full of almost exclusively oak charcoal and backfilled clay (F1047). No carbonized seeds were recovered from the feature.[47] The C14 date of the pit suggests it pre-dates the foundation of the Savigniac monastery. The production of charcoal has a wide variety of potential uses including smithing. The location of the feature beyond the Oxamantown Hiberno-Norse settlement presumed to be along Church Street may have been deliberate to confine the practice of intense burning away from thatched buildings. The pit may also be associated with wider Hiberno-Norse settlement located at the site prior to the establishment of the monastery.

The date ranges of the high medieval burials (c.1139–1539)

The skeletal material selected for C14 dating was found to date from the high medieval period and overlaps with the known use of the site as either a Savigniac or Cistercian abbey (AD 1139–1539); this is unsurprising. There are two early dates from burials (Beta-525336 and UBA-54822) that range AD 1025–1160 and AD 1023–1157; these dates overlap with the known foundation of the abbey in 1139. Statistically we cannot deliberately choose from within the date range, i.e., earlier or later, but historically we can infer that the burials are likely to be among the first graves of monks or patrons of the monastery, after its foundation and before the year 1160. Burial CXLVI (146) from the Arran Street East site was a high-status stone-lined grave with Dundry stone placed around the head; the date from this skeleton (UBA-54822) indicated that the individual died before AD1157. This is the earliest dated occurrence of Dundry as a building stone in Ireland. The association and placement of Dundry at the head of the skeleton (Burial CXLVI (146)) is unique within all of the 500 burials uncovered at the site, which suggests that the individual, an adult male *c.*35–45 years old, was a senior monastic cleric or perhaps even a mason involved in the original construction of the site after 1139. Both dates are as likely to be roughly contemporary or date from shortly after the foundation of the Savigniac abbey in 1139, up to 1157 and 1160. They could statistically also pre-date the foundation of the abbey by *c.*100 years. The reminder of the dated burials are from between the late twelfth and thirteenth century (Beta-525335, UBA-54820 and UBA-54823), thirteenth to fourteenth century (UBA-37928) and fourteenth to fifteenth century (Beta-525337 and UBA-54821).

47 The contents of a sample from the feature (charcoal) were examined microscopically by Dr Ellen O'Carroll.

The date of the walls of the church and lime-kiln

Two samples of charcoal were retrieved from the lime mortar bonding the medieval church walls excavated on the Arran Street East site.[48] These samples were processed and prepared for C14 dating.[49] The two C14 dates are present in Table 2 as radiocarbon dates and as calibrated dates in Appendix I. The early date (UBA-47872) is problematic as it should be later (stratigraphically) than the date obtained from the earlier pillar foundation (UBA-47871). The later date is from a church foundation pillar (UBA-47871 21E0604:266 #423) derived from a large ash charcoal fragment. The date should be earlier than the later wall (UBA-47872 21E0604:54 #424); however, the earlier date (UBA-47872) was derived from tiny charcoal fragments that were unidentifiable to species; no other charcoal identifiable to species was recovered from the wall mortar.

The results confirm that there is an early foundation (UBA-47871) that has a 95.4% chance (2 sigma) of being between Cal AD 1036–1199 and it is highly likely to be between AD 1036–1175. The date was derived from a large lump from a small ash roundwood and fits with the known history of the site. The second date has a 95.4% chance (2 sigma) of being between Cal AD 898–1021. This date was derived from tiny flecks of charcoal within the mortar in the wall which could not be identified by our charcoal specialist. Whilst the science of obtaining a date (UBA-47872) from the charcoal fleck is impressive, the wall was excavated and recorded as stratigraphically later than the other foundation (UBA-47871). This wall (Cistercian?) should be later than the pre-Cistercian wall referenced above. The 'Old Wood Effect' is a possible explanation: any charcoal or wood sample that is carbon dated will have an apparent age, which may result in errors of up to hundreds of years unless short-lived tree species or twigs are selected for radiocarbon dating.[50] It may also be that sample charcoal is derived from other ruinous buildings close to the site of the monastery that were dismantled and burnt as part of a later lime-production process for building and rebuilding the monastery. The C14 dating of reused timber establishes its original felling date, not the date of its subsequent reuse as fuel or otherwise.

48 The presence of charcoal was identified by Dr Jason Bolton who attended on both the Arran Street East and Capel Street archaeological excavations and examined the composition of the lime mortar from both a descriptive and comparative perspective. 49 The charcoal samples from the medieval lime mortar were analysed by Dr Ellen O'Carroll. The brief included trying to identify species of tree from which the charcoal was derived and also to try and identify branch or twig wood or charcoal from tree species that are not long-lived. It is always preferable (if possible) to choose species other than oak to avoid exposure to the 'Old Wood Effect', where dates from charcoal from trees such as oak date the heartwood of the tree, which can be anywhere between 100 and 200 years older than the outer sapwood which was growing at the time of the felling of the timber; large hardwood timber is also often valued as a resource and reused in secondary contexts, and hance the C14 dating of oak can be problematic. 50 See 'Understanding the old wood effect': https://www.radiocarbon.com/old-wood-effect.htm [accessed 12/02/2025].

The first phase of the lime-kiln dates from the early fourteenth to early fifteenth century; the latest phase of the lime-kiln was when it was finally used to produce medieval floor-tiles dating from the late fifteenth and early sixteenth century.

PRELIMINARY FINDINGS AND PHASES FROM THE EXCAVATION

The phases outlined below are not necessarily individual events but reflect the evolving character of the monastery from its foundation and after its demise. People and organizations do not live in phases but observing changes and attempting to associate them with significant historical events and key datable archaeological findings allows us to frame a discussion on the growth, development and eventual destruction of St Mary's abbey. The excavated remains suggest a continued occupation of the site, certainly from AD 1139 to 1539.

Phase I: pre-Savigniac burial, c.*AD 1000*

An early radiocarbon date has been recorded from the site dating from between the late ninth and eleventh century (AD 896–1024; UBA-54819). Additionally, a number of stick pins dating from the twelfth century or perhaps earlier were recovered from grave fills associated with burials, including a kite-shaped (21E0802:217:1) and a disc spatulate-headed stick pin (21E0802:849:1), both from the Capel Street excavation. The kite-shaped pin is of Celia O'Rahilly's Class 13D and is of the lozenge spatulate-headed type.[51] Ó Floinn refers to them as kite-headed stick pins rather than lozenge spatulate-headed as they are related to kite brooches. They are comparatively rare in Ireland, Scotland and Yorkshire and most of the dated examples come from eleventh-/twelfth-century contexts, though some in York were found (redeposited) in fourteenth-century levels. A very elaborate example was found in the grave of Archbishop Wulfstan of York (d. 1023) used as a dress pin. The disc spatulate-headed stick pin would be of similar date (eleventh–twelfth century). The burial and layers associated with the stick pins at Capel Street have been independently dated and samples of human bone from burials were submitted to the Chrono Centre in Belfast. The results (Table 3) confirm definitively that early burials date from before the establishment of the Savigniac monastery and that there is solid archaeological evidence for earlier burial at the site pre-dating the arrival of the Continental orders by over one hundred years or more. The dating programme is conclusive. The three burials were located in Cutting 15 on the Capel Street site, suggesting that the early

51 Raghnall Ó Floinn pers. comm. and also see Celie O'Rahilly, 'A classification of bronze stick-pins from the Dublin Excavations 1962–72' in Conleth Manning (ed.), *Dublin and beyond the Pale: studies in honour of Patrick Healy* (Dublin, 1998), pp 23–33.

burials are located under or around this specific location. This equates with the area under the Presbyterian meeting-house located at the end of Meeting House Lane in the centre of the modern urban block surrounded by Capel Street, Little Mary Street, Arran Street East and Mary's abbey. It is suggested that the early burials are associated with an earlier church on which the later Savigniac foundation is established. The conversion to Christianity of the Hiberno-Norse of Dublin is attested in the lives of kings of Dublin such as Sigtrygg (Silkbeard) Olafsson who is likely to have walked amongst the graves of his contemporaries at the site.

Phase II: an early pre-Anglo-Norman monastic church, mid-twelfth century

An early pre-Anglo-Norman monastic (Savigniac) church of mid-twelfth-century date, earth-cut land division for drainage (mid-twelfth/thirteenth century), and a burial ground, have been identified that are twelfth-century or slightly later. Burial CXLVI (146) from the Arran Street East site is significant as it dates to before 1157. The burial was stone-lined with Dundry stone placed at the head of the grave (fig. 1.36). This individual may be a significant cleric, a senior clerical mason or early patron of the Savigniac monastery. A bronze (copper alloy) oval disc (21E0604:783:1) was found between at the left knee of the burial (CXLVI (146)). The disc was thin and slightly curved; one side of the disc has traces of woven brown wool above linen, the other side has traces of plain-woven linen adhering to it (fig. 1.42). The disc is broken at one end. It is not clear if it has any decoration as both surfaces are obscured by textile. It appears to be enfolded with linen, as there is evidence of this cloth on both sides of the disc. The linen is probably made from flax and shows a plain or tabby weave with a simple over-under pattern of warp and weft strands. The wool appears undyed and is also plain-woven. The preservation of textile in burials of this period is rare.[52]

The presence of Dundry stone around Burial CXLVI (146) demonstrates that Dundry was used at St Mary's abbey before 1157 and was most likely one of the stone types used decoratively in the Savigniac house. Preliminary analysis of the decorated stone from the site has identified a fragmentary stone taken from the demolished remains of the earliest Savigniac and Cistercian buildings.

The excavations revealed good evidence for an early to mid-twelfth-century church which is likely to be the Savigniac or at least the earliest stage of Cistercian foundation. The western end of the church was revealed suggesting a nave with side-aisles. Earth-cut ditches suggest that the land around the monastery was laid out in fields, and associated burial continued in an open graveyard to the north of the abbey church.

52 Dr Liezl van Pletzen-Vos has prepared the metal finds report and this information is derived from that.

Phase III (a): the enlarged abbey church, mid-twelfth and/or early thirteenth century
The abbey church was significantly enlarged in the mid-twelfth and/or early thirteenth century. It was built with a wider nave and wider aisles and was constructed above, partially removing, the earlier abbey church. The Phase II and III church shared a southern wall, and elements of the earlier building may have survived above ground level, particularly on its southern side where it adjoined the cloister. Dating the later church building archaeologically is problematic and there may have been several episodes of rebuilding and repair.

Phase III (b): thirteenth/fourteenth century
As the power and influence of the religious house grew as a Cistercian monastery, the church buildings were reconstructed and enlarged to reflect the growing power and status of the foundation. The discovery of the lime-kilns is surrogate evidence for church building and renovation. Burnt or orange heat effected staining is present on carved Dundry from the site. This is likely to be a result of the great fire at the monastery in 1304. St Mary's abbey was recognized as the pre-eminent Cistercian house in Ireland in 1313, and the abbot of such a monastery required an edifice befitting such a foundation. Hence additions and modifications to the monastic buildings were required to reflect that in the physical manifestation of the abbey. The narthex church or porch structure recorded at the western end of the church maybe broadly contemporary with the later enlarged church, or it may have been built subsequently. This new west façade (portico or narthex) with high-status burial and child burial is a striking discovery. Significant high-status medieval burials were interred in stone-lined graves in the structure, suggesting that it acted as a quasi-mausoleum for high patrons of the monastery who were granted the familial privilege of burial and prayer at the abbey in return for their benefaction. The dating of the narthex structure is problematic. The masonry remains had been robbed out deliberately after the dissolution of the monastery. Only fragmentary sub-floor remains survived which were significantly rebuilt over the centuries. Associating walls with building levels and burials was difficult due to the constant reworking of the soils and structures, particularly since the late seventeenth century.

Phase IV: later fifteenth-/sixteenth-century floor-tile kiln
A significant archaeological discovery on site was an intact tile-kiln that contained the wasters from its last firing. A large collection of late-medieval decorated floor-tiles was retrieved from the kiln and those finds, in addition to the other floor-tiles from the site, are the subject of research by Joanna Wren. This research is ongoing, although it points to the re-edification of the prestigious abbey with new and unique decorative mosaic tiled floors. Many of the relief tile types from the kiln on Arran Street East were found in the 1880s when the Boland family rebuilt the Presbyterian meeting-house and converted

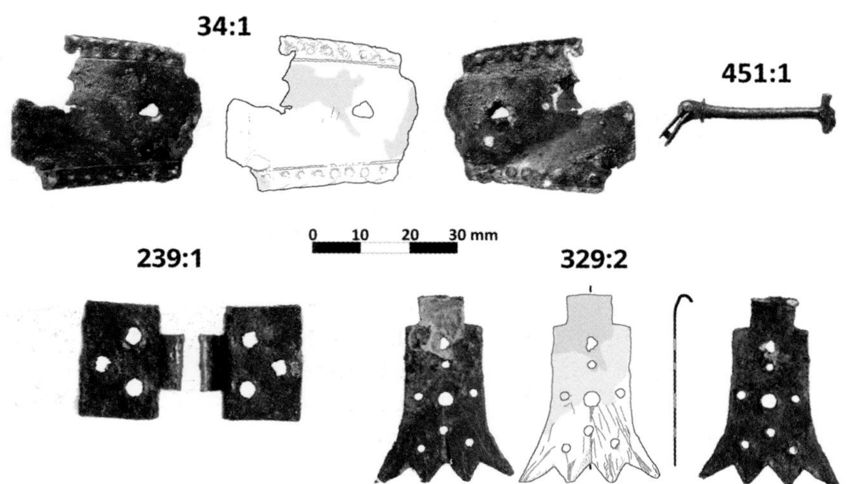

1.44 Medieval book-mounts and clasps from the Capel Street excavations

it into a bakery. This is the presumed approximate location of the chancel and choir in the abbey church where many of the floor-tiles from the kiln once decorated.

Burial XIX (19) from the Arran Street East excavations recovered two copper alloy artefacts (fig. 1.44). The first (21E0604:239:1) is a double-sided hinge plate which corresponds to Howsam Type A8.1. It is a rectangular plate, folded widthways, stepped in at the fold to form a projecting terminal loop, with three perforations through front and back. It was designed to fit onto the end of a leather strap and functioned as part of a book fastener. A book clasp (21E0604:239:2) was also found in the grave fill; it is a decorative front plate clasp with eight attachment holes and a shaped end. The sub-rectangular front plate has bevelled edges with one flared and scalloped (fishtail) end, and a central flat rectangular backward curved hook at the other end. The front plate has incised decoration. This includes four lengthwise feather-like grooves at the fishtail end. There is a central groove running from the central inverted V through the first central perforation, terminating in the largest central hole. Book clasps were riveted in position on the cover to keep the book closed, with a sprung backplate on the reverse and a hook at the other end. Both artefacts (21E0604:239:1–2) were part of the one book fastener. The book clasp (21E0604:239:2) corresponds to Howsam Type A.3 (hooked book fastener). These types of clasps are difficult to date, with examples generally dated to the fourteenth to fifteenth centuries. Similar items were found in Winchester.[53]

53 Martin Biddle and D.A. Hinton, 'Winchester book-clasps and page holder' in Martin Biddle (ed.), *Object and economy in medieval Winchester: artefacts from medieval Winchester*, ii (Oxford, 1990), pp 755–9.

1.45 Cellared remains of Dutch Billy houses dating to the early 1700s, excavated along on the western side of Meeting House Lane on the Capel Street site, looking northwest

Burial clearly continued into the later medieval period, and the association of that with the remnants of a medieval book is fascinating. The St Mary's abbey manuscript (TCD MS 11500) now in Trinity College Dublin is one of a relatively small number of surviving books from the abbey scriptorium and library.[54]

Phase VI: dissolution and later post-medieval burial, quarrying, AD 1540–1600

A significant quantity of the archaeological deposits on site were derived from the activity (spoil heaps) associated with the destruction of the monastic buildings. The archaeological excavation ironically recorded how the monastery was pulled apart.

Phase VII: domestic house building, AD 1600–1800

Localized dilapidation into a back street referred to as Boot Lane in the eighteenth century was revealed by the excavations. Arran Street East evolved

54 Bernard Meehan, 'A fourteenth-century historical compilation from St Mary's Cistercian abbey, Dublin' in Duffy (ed.), *MD XV*, pp 264–76.

from the medieval period when it was the principal thoroughfare leading to the formal abbey entrance. The street continued as a significant location in the late 1600s (Plate 27), before declining into a back street in the late seventeenth century with the development of Capel Street which superseded it as the preeminent local thoroughfare.

ACKNOWLEDGMENTS

A very large group of people dug on the archaeological excavations over a number of years. These include Aaron Kelly, Sean Finlay Scott, Aidan Holmes, Caitlin Gaffney, Daniel Cummins, Eamon Forkan, Edrik Navarro, Elaine Traynor, Fionn Begley, Ingela Wass, James O'Sullivan, Jeff O'Neill, Jenny Ahlqvist, Joe O'Keeffe, Jonathan King, Joseph Gaffney, Laoise O'Donovan, Laura Miucci, Madison Blankenship, Megan Willingham, Michaela O'Donnell, Milla O'Riordan-Little, Niall Garahy, Niamh Barry, Olivia Brown, Paz Alvarez, Ricardo Gayan, Sadhbh Duffy and Thady O'Donovan. The site supervisors were Rory Blount, Jose Silas and Fergal Flannery. Fergal was intrinsic to the post-ex and also took all of the aerial drone photos. The author took all of the still hand-held photos on the Arran Street East excavation, Fergal Flannery taking the majority of the still hand-held photos on the Capel Street site. The site surveying and illustration was all the work of Conor McHale. Yolande O Brien and Liezl van Pletzen-Vos managed the site finds register, prepared finds for specialists and Liezl has prepared many of the small finds reports. Helen Kehoe was the site administrator. All credit goes to them; errors and omissions are my own.

Particular thanks are extended to Courtney Deery Heritage Consultancy (Lisa Courtny and Siobhán Deery) who were the best of project managers and to Linzi Simpson and Paul Duffy who were collegiate frequent visitors at all stages of the digs. The developers, Denis Boland, Alan O'Brien, Bill Wolsey, and James Sinton, were supportive and engaged in the project from beginning to end. Dr Ruth Johnson in Dublin City Council was always on hand with advise and direction as the scale of the discoveries required design changes to the buildings and to the extent and location of subsequent archaeological investigations.

We befriended many archaeologists and historians in Dublin during the excavations such as Matthew and Geraldine Stout. Raghnall Ó Floinn, who has sadly since passed away, was a welcome visitor and expert finds advisor: I think of him happily rummaging through the artefacts and answering queries with his usual good humour. To him and all of you (who are mentioned and referenced in the footnotes) who have helped out, I extend a sincere thanks for what was a privilege of a site with which to be associated.

APPENDIX I
THE FULL CALIBRATED RESULTS OF THE C14 DATING OF ST MARY'S ABBEY

Beta-525335	Radiocarbon age BP 820 ± 30 of a human burial Sk#1		
68.2% (1 sigma)	Cal AD	1206–1259	65.1%
		1193–1197	3.1%
95.4% (2 sigma)	Cal AD	1165–1265	95.4%
Beta-525336	Radiocarbon Age BP 940 ± 30 of a human burial Sk#4		
68.2% (1 sigma)	Cal AD	1081–1151	55.7%
		1035–1051	12.5%
95.4% (2 sigma)	Cal AD	1025–1160	95.4%
Beta-525337	Radiocarbon Age BP 560 ± 30 of a human burial SK#1		
68.2% (1 sigma)	Cal AD	1392–1416	34.3%
		1322–1347	33.9%
95.4% (2 sigma)		1307–1362	49.9%
		1385–1429	45.5%
UBA-37928	Radiocarbon Age BP 587 +/- 36 of a human burial TP#5.1		
68.3% (1 sigma)	Cal AD	1312–1358	72.5%
		1387–1406	27.5%
95.4% (2 sigma)	Cal AD	1298–1373	68.7%
		1377–1416	31.3%
UBA-47871	Radiocarbon Age BP 925 +/- 23 of an abbey wall (F266)		
68.3% (1 sigma)	Cal AD	1046–1084	51.2%
		1094–1103	9.5%
		1124–1142	20.2%
		1146–1162	19%
95.4% (2 sigma)	Cal AD	1036–1175	99.2%
		1195–1199	0.8%
UBA-47872	Radiocarbon Age BP 1072 +/- 14 of an abbey wall (F54)		
68.3% (1 sigma)	Cal AD	905–909	7.8%
		977–995	61.4%
		1005–1017	30.8%
95.4% (2 sigma)	Cal AD	898–919	18.8%
		957–967	4%
		974–997	48.8%
		1001–1021	28.3%
UBA-54818	Radiocarbon Age BP 543 +/- 23 Phase I lime-kiln (F1025)		
68.3% (1 sigma)	Cal AD	1397–1423	100%
95.4% (2 sigma)	Cal AD	1325–1353	22.4%
		1394–1428	77.6%

UBA-54819	Radiocarbon Age BP 1068 +/- 24 of a charcoal pit (F1047)		
68.3% (1 sigma)	Cal AD	903–913	13.3%
		976–997	44.1%
		1002–1021	42.6%
95.4% (2 sigma)	Cal AD	896–923	20.3%
		951–1024	79.7%
UBA-54820	Radiocarbon Age BP 838 +/- 26 of a human burial SK#49		
68.3% (1 sigma)	Cal AD	1178–1192	22%
		1202–1230	53.8%
		1243–1258	24.2%
95.4% (2 sigma)	Cal AD	1167–1263	100%
UBA-54821	Radiocarbon Age BP 567 +/- 26 of a human burial SK#53		
68.3% (1 sigma)	Cal AD	1326–1352	62.7%
		1394–1408	37.3%
95.4% (2 sigma)	Cal AD	1310–1313	0.5%
		1317–1361	56.8%
		1388–1423	42.7%
UBA-54822	Radiocarbon Age BP 970 +/- 26 of a human burial SK#146		
68.3% (1 sigma)	Cal AD	1029–1048	29%
		1082–1097	20%
		1100–1127	38.1%
		1139–1150	12.9%
95.4% (2 sigma)	Cal AD	1023–1053	26.7%
		1061–1067	1.4%
		1075–1157	71.9%
UBA-54823	Radiocarbon Age BP 819 +/- 25 of a human burial SK#213		
68.3% (1 sigma)	Cal AD	1219–1234	38.9%
		1237–1261	61.1%
95.4% (2 sigma)	Cal AD	1178–1192	5.9%
		1202–1271	94.1%
UBA-55146	Radiocarbon Age BP 868 +/- 20; 21E0802; F257:1 – burial 34		
68.3% (1 sigma)	Cal AD	1175–1196	53.6%
		1198–1217	46.4%
95.4% (2 sigma)	Cal AD	1054–1058	0.6%
		1157–1223	99.4%
UBA-55147	Radiocarbon Age BP 891 +/- 26; 21E0802; F339:1 – burial 71		
68.3% (1 sigma)	Cal AD	1053–1061	8.9%
		1156–1215	91.1%
95.4% (2 sigma)	Cal AD	1046–1084	23.9%
		1094–1103	1.9%
		1124–1142	4.2%
		1145–1220	70%

UBA-55148	Radiocarbon Age BP 1028 +/- 23; 21E0802; F1008:1 – burial 274		
68.3 (1 sigma)	Cal AD	995–1006	49.9%
		1013–1025	50.1%
95.4 (2 sigma)	Cal AD	979–983	0.4%
		989–1038	99.6%
UBA-55149	Radiocarbon Age BP 1051 +/- 21; F21E0802; F1017:1 – burial 281		
68.3 (1 sigma)	Cal AD	992–997	15.6%
		1001–1021	84.4%
95.4 (2 sigma)	Cal AD	902–913	3.9%
		976–1028	96.1%
UBA-55150	Radiocarbon Age BP 1033 +/- 22; 21E0802; F1047 – burial 290		
68.3% (1 sigma)	Cal AD	995–1007	51.4%
		1012–1023	48.6%
95.4% (2 sigma)	Cal AD	990–1034	100%

Reference for calibration datasets:

P.J. Reimer, W.E.N. Austin, Edouard Bard, *et al.*, 'The IntCal20 Northern Hemisphere Radiocarbon Age Calibration Curve (0–55 cal kBP)', *Radiocarbon* 62.4 (2020), 725–57: doi:10.1017/RDC.2020.41

Comments:

* This standard deviation (error) includes a lab error multiplier.
** 1 sigma = square root of (sample std. dev.^2 + curve std. dev.^2)
** 2 sigma = 2 x square root of (sample std. dev.^2 + curve std. dev.^2)
where ^2 = quantity squared.
[ ] = calibrated range impinges on end of calibration data set
0* represents a "negative" age BP
1955* or 1960* denote influence of nuclear testing C-14

Note: Cal ages and ranges are rounded to the nearest year which may be too precise in many instances. Users are advised to round results to the nearest 10 yr for samples with standard deviation in the radiocarbon age greater than 50 yr.

Excavations at Riverhouse, Chancery Street, Dublin 7: a riverside dumping ground in medieval Oxmantown

MUIREANN NÍ CHEALLACHÁIN

INTRODUCTION

This paper describes the results of an archaeological excavation in 2019 at Riverhouse, Chancery Street, Dublin 7, located at the site of a hotel development (ITM 715013/734381; fig. 2.1). A 'top down' construction strategy was approved for the development which involved the construction of a transfer slab supported by piles at 8m above the modern ground level. This allowed construction to proceed from the slab upwards while at the same time facilitating the archaeological excavation of the basement from ground level.

The site at Riverhouse is located within the first recorded settlement north of the Liffey; the medieval suburb of Oxmanstown, which centred on a main route leading from the north of the country into the city (Oxmantown Street, now Church Street) that led to the only bridge across the Liffey to the main medieval settlement. Many of the thirteenth-century land grants demonstrate that from the late twelfth century Oxmanstown was composed of a mixed population of Ostmen (Hiberno-Norse), Irishmen and Anglo-Normans.[1] The traditional view of the Oxmantown suburb is that it was established when the Anglo-Normans took Dublin in 1170 and cast out the Hiberno-Norse people to the northern side of the Liffey; however evidence of earlier Hiberno Norse settlement is being revealed through recent archaeological investigations (fig. 2.2).[2] The Riverhouse site is located directly to the north of the foreshore of the confluence of the Liffey and one of its main tributaries, the Bradogue, an area which was known as 'the Pill' during the medieval and post-medieval periods. Speed's map of Dublin (1610) depicts the Pill as a series of mudflats interspersed with narrow water channels and nearby excavations have shown that up to the mid-eleventh century this general area would have been marshy marginal ground of open fields,[3] which would have been subject to salt-water inundation from high-season tides and floodwaters as far north as Pill Lane,[4] abutting the southern end of the Riverhouse site (modern Chancery Street).

1 Emer Purcell, 'Land use in medieval Oxmantown' in Duffy (ed.), *MD IV*, pp 9–112. 2 On the historicity of the supposed expulsion of the Ostmen, see Emer Purcell, 'The expulsion of the Ostmen, 1169–71: the documentary evidence', *Peritia*, 17–18 (2003–4), 276–94; on the excavations, see Linzi Simpson, 'Fifty years a-digging: a synthesis of medieval archaeological investigations in Dublin City and suburbs' in Duffy (ed.), *MD XI*, pp 161–9, and papers by O'Donovan, Moore, and Duffy in this volume. 3 Sinéad Phelan, 'The bank, the ditch and the water: Hiberno-Norse discoveries at Church Street and Hammond Lane' in Duffy (ed.), *MD X*, pp 165–97. 4 Clarke, *Dublin, Pt 1* (IHTA).

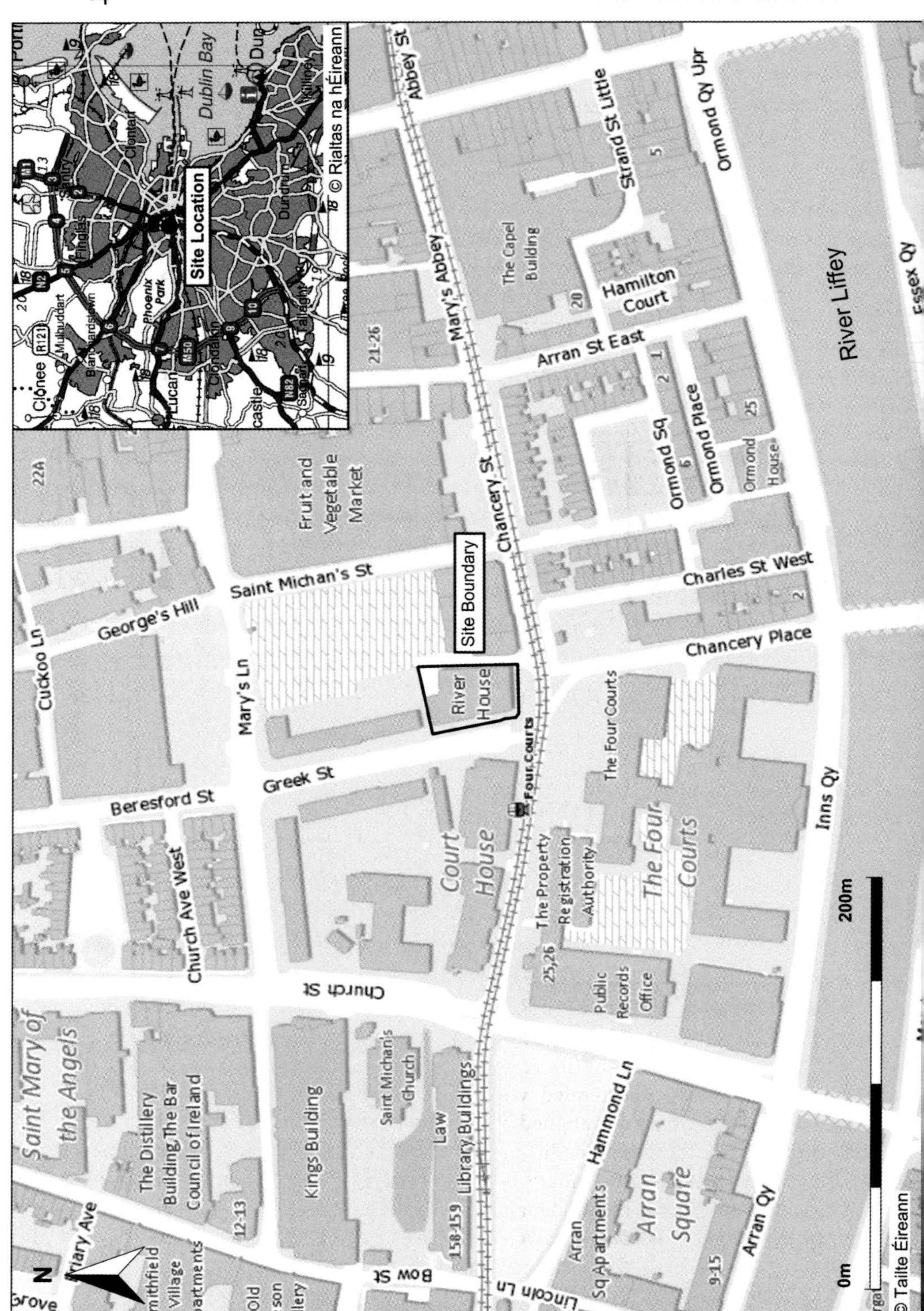

2.1 Site location

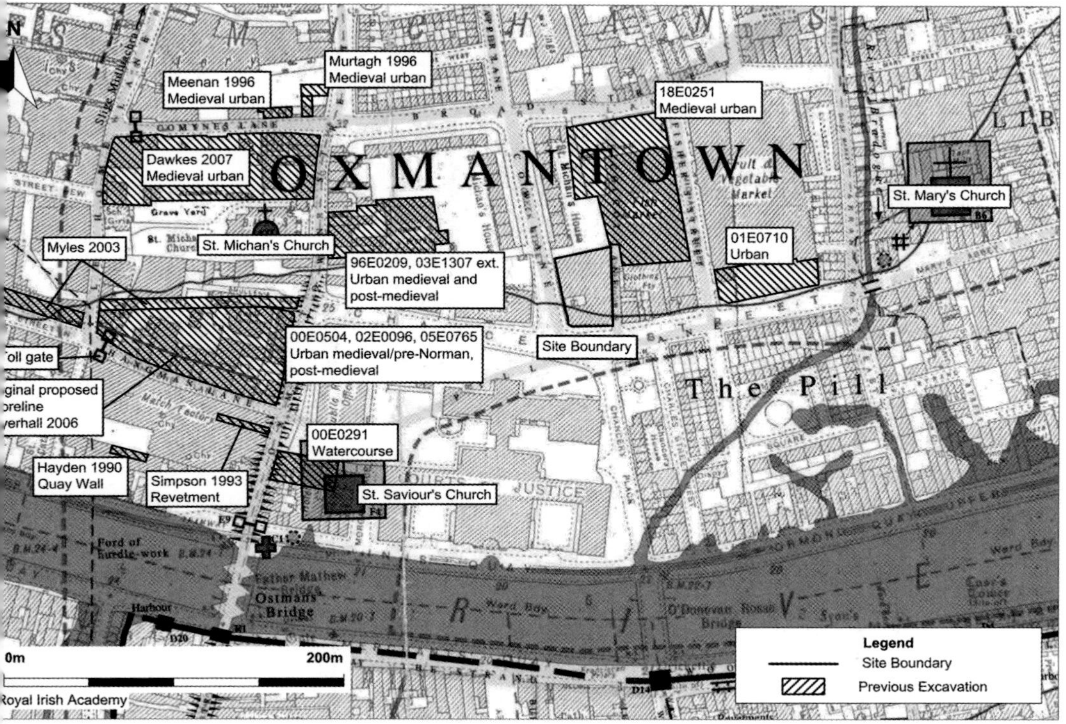

2.2 Extract from Clarke, *Dublin, Pt 1* (IHTA), map 4, showing surrounding archaeological sites

Throughout its lifetime the site at Riverhouse was located in proximity to the precincts of St Michan's church (est. eleventh century or earlier) to the west, St Mary's Cistercian abbey (est. twelfth century) to the east and finally St Saviour's Dominican priory (est. thirteenth century) to the south.

RESULTS

Phase 1 activity: tenth to mid-eleventh century

The earliest recorded activity at Riverhouse consists of a 13m-long section of a linear ditch (fig. 2.3) that returned a two-sigma calibrated radiocarbon date of AD 897–1037 from a basal fill. A heavily truncated terminus was recorded at the east and the ditch extended westward outside the limit of excavation. The tenth-century ditch was aligned west–east running parallel with the river foreshore which suggests it did not function as a drainage ditch but rather perhaps as a property boundary or as a physical barrier to prevent livestock from wandering on to the tidal marshy foreshore to the south. No artefacts and a limited amount of domestic refuse was identified in the basal fills which

2.3 Mid-excavation of the tenth-century ditch, facing east

perhaps suggests it was constantly being cleared out. Six wood taxa were identified in the basal fill, with hazel and blackthorn occurring most frequently, followed by ash, oak, alder, and yew.[5]

Phase 2 activity: mid eleventh to fourteenth century

The second phase of activity at Riverhouse focused on the period from the mid-eleventh to the fourteenth century; it comprised the reclamation of lands along the foreshore at the south, the quarrying of limestone and the dumping of domestic and small-scale industrial refuse, including medieval pottery, antler, animal bone and charcoal into the redundant ditch and in waste-pits of varying size. Two layers indicative of land reclamation were recorded in the south-eastern corner of the site where a medieval watercourse may have been located. This area of the site was investigated by sondage as the layers in question were located below the formation level of the development (fig. 2.4). As such, these layers were only identified in section and are now preserved *in-situ*. Animal bone and marine molluscs (mussels and limpets) were recovered from both reclamation layers which have been interpreted as being associated with the reclamation of the marshy foreshore. The lower of the reclamation deposits returned a two-sigma calibrated radiocarbon date of AD 1031–1202.

5 Lorna O'Donnell, 'Charcoal and wood specialist report, Riverhouse, Chancery Street, Co. Dublin', unpublished report for IAC Archaeology, 2020.

2.4 Sondage showing reclamation layers, facing east

The earlier of two large pits, recorded in the southeast corner of the site at the edge of the reclaimed shoreline, contained frequent calp inclusions and the base was cut into the calp limestone bedrock. The frequent calp inclusions along with the large size of the pit suggests it may have been associated with local limestone quarrying along the marshy foreshore of the River Bradogue. The majority of the Riverhouse waste-pits were irregular in shape and located at the south of the site, adjacent to the historic river foreshore, to the west of the large pits cutting the reclamation layers (fig. 2.5). Several larger and deeper square pits were located towards the middle of the site and only two pits were recorded to the north of the backfilled early medieval ditch. Several shallow deposits of refuse material along with a possible small midden and a small cobbled surface were also recorded amid the waste-pits. Six of the waste-pits from across the site were radiocarbon dated and the 2–sigma calibrated results consistently ranged from between AD 1023–1224, which suggests that many of the waste-pits were open at the same time. No particular contextual variation was apparent within the features, however the pits at the centre of the site did contain more antler-waste than the southern or northern pits.

Pottery 545 sherds of medieval pottery were recovered from the waste-pits and deposits at Riverhouse and date to between the eleventh and the fourteenth century which corresponds to the period immediately before and after the Anglo-Norman conquest (fig. 2.6). The majority (*c*.174 vessels)

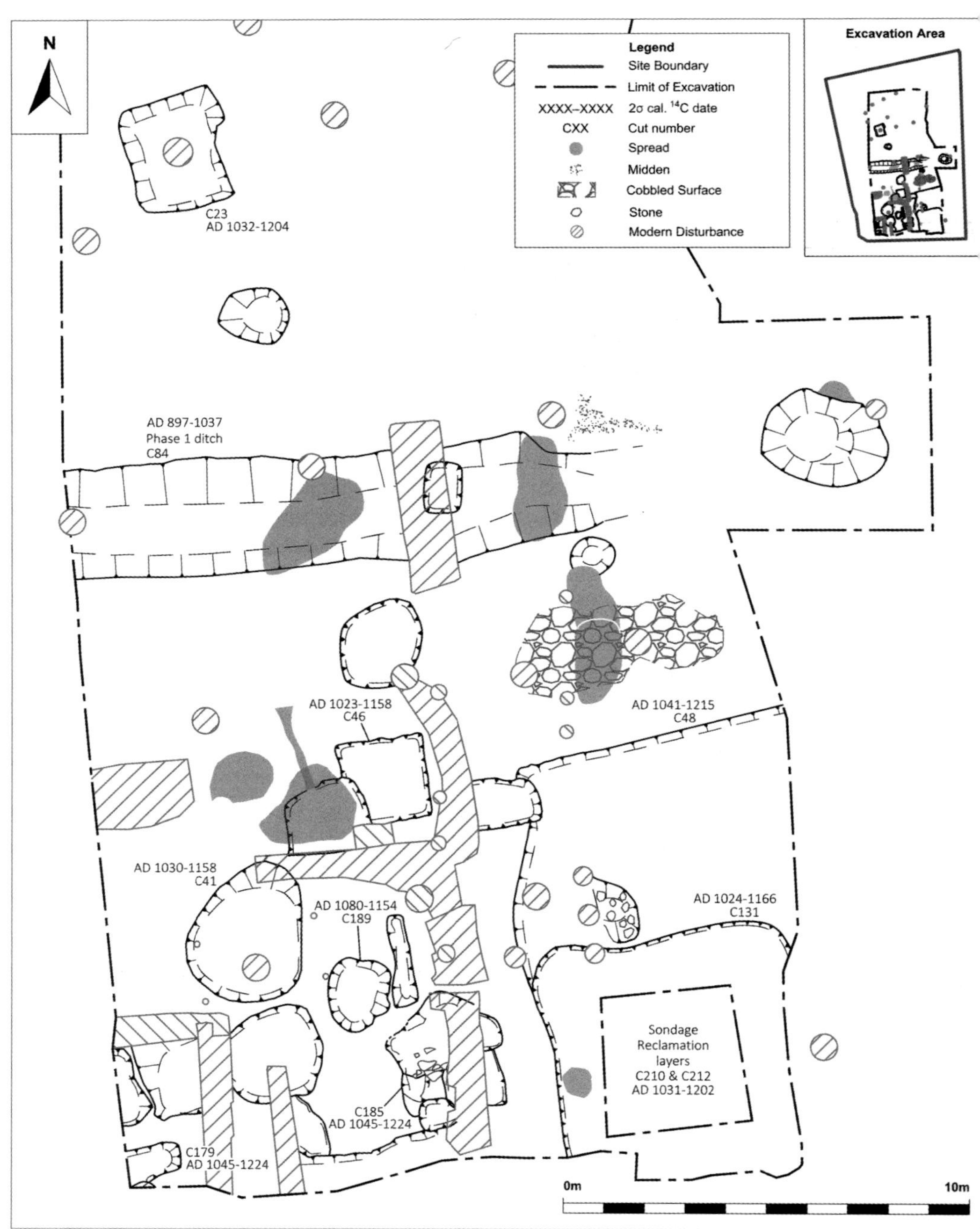

2.5 Plan of Phase 1, early medieval, and Phase 2, medieval features

2.6 Selection of Irish medieval pottery from Riverhouse

consist of locally-made pottery ranging in date between the late twelfth and the fourteenth century. The local wares are dominated by the Dublin wares; particularly Dublin-type ware while Leinster cooking-ware only represents 9% of the locally-produced pottery, and the Dublin-type cooking ware produced in the city accounts for only 5% of the assemblage. Over three-quarters of the English medieval pottery assemblage is made up of early hand-built wares dating between the eleventh and the thirteenth century which include Southeast Wiltshire ware, Minety-type ware, and Ham Green wares. The wheel-thrown English pottery represents a quarter of the English medieval assemblage and is dominated by Bristol-Redcliffe ware which dates between the early thirteenth and the fourteenth century. The English medieval pottery assemblage may represent 66 vessels while the French medieval pottery assemblage, including miscellaneous French wares and Saintonge, may represent 22 vessels. The assemblage consists of cooking pots, jugs/pitchers, tripod pitchers, storage jars, pipkins and dishes which can be associated with domestic or commercial use for food storage, preparation, and consumption as well as health and hygiene, rather than any particular industrial function.[6]

6 Siobhán Scully, 'Medieval pottery specialist report, Riverhouse, Chancery Street, Co. Dublin', unpublished report for IAC Archaeology, 2020.

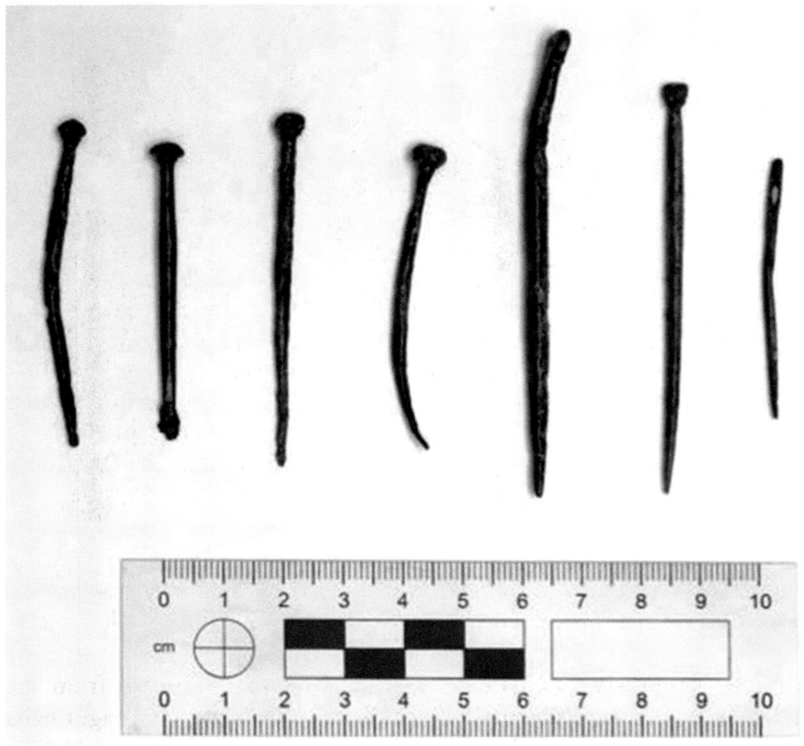

2.7 Stick pins and gilded needle from Riverhouse

Pins The only artefacts of personal adornment recovered at Riverhouse comprised six copper alloy stick pins, four of which were recovered from the eleventh–fourteenth-century waste-pits (fig. 2.7). A very rare form of disc-shaped, spatulate-headed stick pin dated to the eleventh century was recovered from one of the large medieval pits. It is flat on either face of the head and has dot-in-ring decoration on each side of the head. A spatulate-headed stick pin with a squared spatulate head with two opposing faces dating between the late twelfth and mid-thirteenth centuries was recovered from the overlying demolition fill. A club-headed pin from Dublin (Class 9) dated between the last quarter of the eleventh and the end of the thirteenth century was recovered from one of the waste-pits while a second was recovered from the overlying demolition fill. A copper alloy needle with what appear to be the remains of gilding was retrieved from a fill of a large medieval pit at the south of the site.[7]

7 Siobhán Scully, 'Metal artefacts specialist report, Riverhouse, Chancery Street, Co. Dublin', unpublished report for IAC Archaeology, 2020.

2.8 Selection of antler waste from Riverhouse

Iron objects Twenty-two items of structural iron were recorded from the excavations at Riverhouse. The majority of these (17) are hand-wrought nails but there is also one clench bolt, two bolts, one staple and one strap in the structural iron assemblage. Two hollow bone cylinders and three possible bone pin fragments were recovered from the eleventh–fourteenth-century waste-pits. Similar hollow bone cylinders have been produced from many excavations in Ireland, but their purpose is unknown. They were at one time suggested to be gaming pieces but their lack of resemblance to other well-recognized gaming pieces and the use-wear and polish generally exhibited on their surfaces would suggest that they were used in conjunction with rope, wool, or some other textile, which would have produced these polished surfaces. This type of artefact is described as one of the most enigmatic finds from medieval excavations in Ireland.[8]

Antler-waste A total of 112 artefacts of cut antler-waste from manufacturing were recovered from the excavations at Riverhouse, which had a total weight of 2858.5g (fig. 2.8). The presence of the cut antler-waste suggests that there was a craft industry producing objects made of antler either on the site or nearby. The majority of the antler-waste came from a central waste-pit and adjacent deposit along with a smaller waste-pit located directly to the south. The antler,

8 Siobhán Scully, 'Iron artefacts specialist report, Riverhouse, Chancery Street, Co. Dublin', unpublished report for IAC Archaeology, 2020.

for the most part, probably represents shed antler that was gathered in the wild at particular times of the year and the three antler burrs with natural ruptures present in the assemblage would be indicative of this. There is, however, one pedicle and burr present which would indicate that antler was also removed from the skulls of slaughtered animals.[9] The antler-waste from Riverhouse can be divided into primary waste, which represents the initial cutting up of the antler into smaller pieces but constitutes waste pieces that did not receive any further modification, and secondary waste where the primary material has been reworked in some way but has been discarded rather than being further worked to form completed objects. The presence of all parts of the antler in the assemblage indicates that the antlers were sawn up on site. Use of saws in cutting the antler at Riverhouse was obvious from the cut surfaces and from four antler tines which display saw marks. There was no evidence of smoothing or polishing. Tines could be used for a wide range of objects, including components in bone combs and various small items such as gaming pieces. There are 81 tines in the Riverhouse assemblage and 12 of these are the tips of the tine. The tips of tine are often sawn off the tine and discarded as they are not needed in the production of an item and too small to be used for anything else. They too strongly indicate the manufacture of antler objects on the site. Three tines have a hole drilled in the base and four other tines have a slight hollow in the base which may represent unfinished perforations.

Horn-waste There is proportionally much less horn-waste in the Riverhouse assemblage. Cattle, sheep, and goat horn-cores, some of which were sawn or otherwise bore cut-marks, provide evidence of small-scale horn-working at the site. Horn is very prone to decay and disintegration when in the ground even when it is buried in conditions usually favourable to organic materials. Horn-working was probably a very localized industry reliant on locally bred animals for a supply of horn. It is likely that there were close links between skinners and tanners who worked animal hides, and horners who could utilize the discarded horn from hide-working. Horn was probably most commonly used to produce lantern lenses and windows and items such as combs, and boxes are also known.

Food-waste A variety of food-waste was recovered from the eleventh–fourteenth-century waste-pits and the backfilled ditch, and this gives us an insight into the diet of the inhabitants of this area of Oxmantown. In common with other collections in Dublin, livestock animals and fish constitute the most abundant classes in the identified assemblage from Riverhouse, with considerably fewer wild mammals and birds. Comparing percentages from the

9 Siobhán Scully, 'Antler-waste specialist report, Riverhouse, Chancery Street, Co. Dublin', unpublished report for IAC Archaeology, 2020.

main food-forming livestock animals indicates that cattle were most frequent and ageing evidence from the limb bones and the mandibles fragment indicates that cattle continued to be slaughtered at an advanced age, which suggests that these animals were valued as much for their secondary products as their meat. The remains include some primary meat bones as well as metapodia and skull fragments, indicating that live cattle were slaughtered and butchered on or near the site. Two newborn-calf bones, a radius and a second phalanx, along with an adult cow skull-fragment were found in a deposit and the presence of calf bones is of particular interest as it suggests that a certain number of cows were kept in the town during the medieval period as providers of milk.

Second in importance to cattle came sheep/goat and ageing evidence indicates that wool and woolfells were also important trade commodities. Remains of pigs, as at many other sites in Dublin, were relatively scarce when compared with those from cattle and sheep/goat. In common with cattle, the range of skeletal elements for sheep/goat and pig indicates the presence of non-meat-bearing elements and meat-bearing bones, indicating that these livestock animals were also transported live from the rural hinterland and slaughtered locally. It is clear that little was wasted when a carcass was butchered and once all the meat had been removed, the bones themselves were cracked open to extract marrow. Other species identified are horse and dog, mostly found in a large refuse-pit. A withers height of 142cm was estimated from a single complete horse tibia, representing a pony-size individual. There are four dog-bones from a single adult sheepdog-size individual. Three horse-bones (a metacarpus and two tibia) recorded in the ditch are from a single adult individual that would have stood at 123cm at the shoulder, considerably larger than the pony-size individual found in the pit. A cat tibia was found in a central pit and an adult rabbit metapodial bone was found in a nearby pit. The diet was supplemented to some extent by domestic laying-fowl, but there are also elements of domestic goose and perhaps duck.

Evidence that the nearby marine resources were also exploited was evident from the recovery of deep-water fish species such as cod, ling, hake and pollock. The species present reflect fishing offshore from boats using baited lines for the catch of the medium to very large gadids (i.e., fish belonging to the cod family) as well as other species such as herring and gurnard. Skeletal elements from the head and vertebral column were recovered implying that the fish were brought to the site whole, probably gutted. All the fish remains derived from pit fills, ditch fills and midden deposits, implying they are a product of domestic rubbish-disposal; some of the bones were calcined which further suggests burning and disposal of food-waste. Marine mollusca were retrieved from all areas of the site and identified species include oyster, mussel, and cockle.[10]

10 Margaret McCarthy, 'Faunal remains specialist report, Riverhouse, Chancery Street, Co. Dublin', unpublished report for IAC Archaeology, 2020.

The site provided evidence for cereal and legume presence in the local landscape. It would appear that cereals were cultivated elsewhere and imported close to the site; no evidence for habitation or cereal-drying was present during excavation. Very small-scale processing and discard of refuse associated with cereals is visible in the form of low numbers of chaff and arable weeds. The cereals were preserved by charring, while all others were preserved due to waterlogging, but dried out at some stage. Free-threshing wheat was found in sixteen of the samples and much of the flour produced during the medieval period was produced from wheat. Barley, both naked and hulled varieties, was identified at Riverhouse, and it was used as animal fodder and to produce malt, although the use of oat malt superseded barley malt. Oats were noted in fifteen of the samples, although in very low numbers. This is unusual, given the findings of Lyons, which suggest barley and oat dominate Viking and Hiberno-Norse settlements.[11] Oats were often grown alongside barley; they were processed and ground together to make porridge, bread, biscuits, and cakes. Rye was noted in very small quantities in six of the fills while charred legumes, one field pea and over twenty vetch seeds were also present. Legumes were often found in the early-medieval period, and they increased in importance as the Middle Ages proceeded. They were used for both food and fodder and were consumed in breads and pottages.[12]

Twelve wood taxa were identified in the medieval waste-pits, spreads, and backfilled ditch (alder, birch, hazel, beech, ash, holly, pomaceous fruitwood, pine, blackthorn/cherry, oak, willow, yew, and elm). Charcoal could have been deposited into these features in a number of ways. Primary dumps from hearths or multiple hearths could have been thrown into open features, as a means of organization and cleaning living and working quarters. Charcoal could have been swept into features and layers and could also have blown across the site, a residual process. No particular contextual variation was apparent from the site and the variety of wood taxa within the fills is high, on average five taxa. This suggests that the fills could represent repeated dumping of hearths.[13]

Phase 3 activity: fifteenth to seventeenth century

A small number of post-medieval waste-pits, deposits and a stone-lined well were recorded across the site with inclusions of red brick and/or post-medieval ceramics within their fills (fig. 2.9). Similar to the medieval waste-pits, the densest cluster of pits was identified at the south of the site while the well was recorded at the east of the site and may be a precursor to a Phase 4

11 Susan Lyons, 'Food plants, fruits and foreign foodstuffs: the archaeological evidence from urban medieval Ireland', *PRIA*, 115C (2015), 111–66. 12 Nikolah Gilligan, 'Plant macro specialist report, Riverhouse, Chancery Street, Co. Dublin', unpublished report for IAC Archaeology, 2020. 13 O'Donnell, 'Charcoal and wood'.

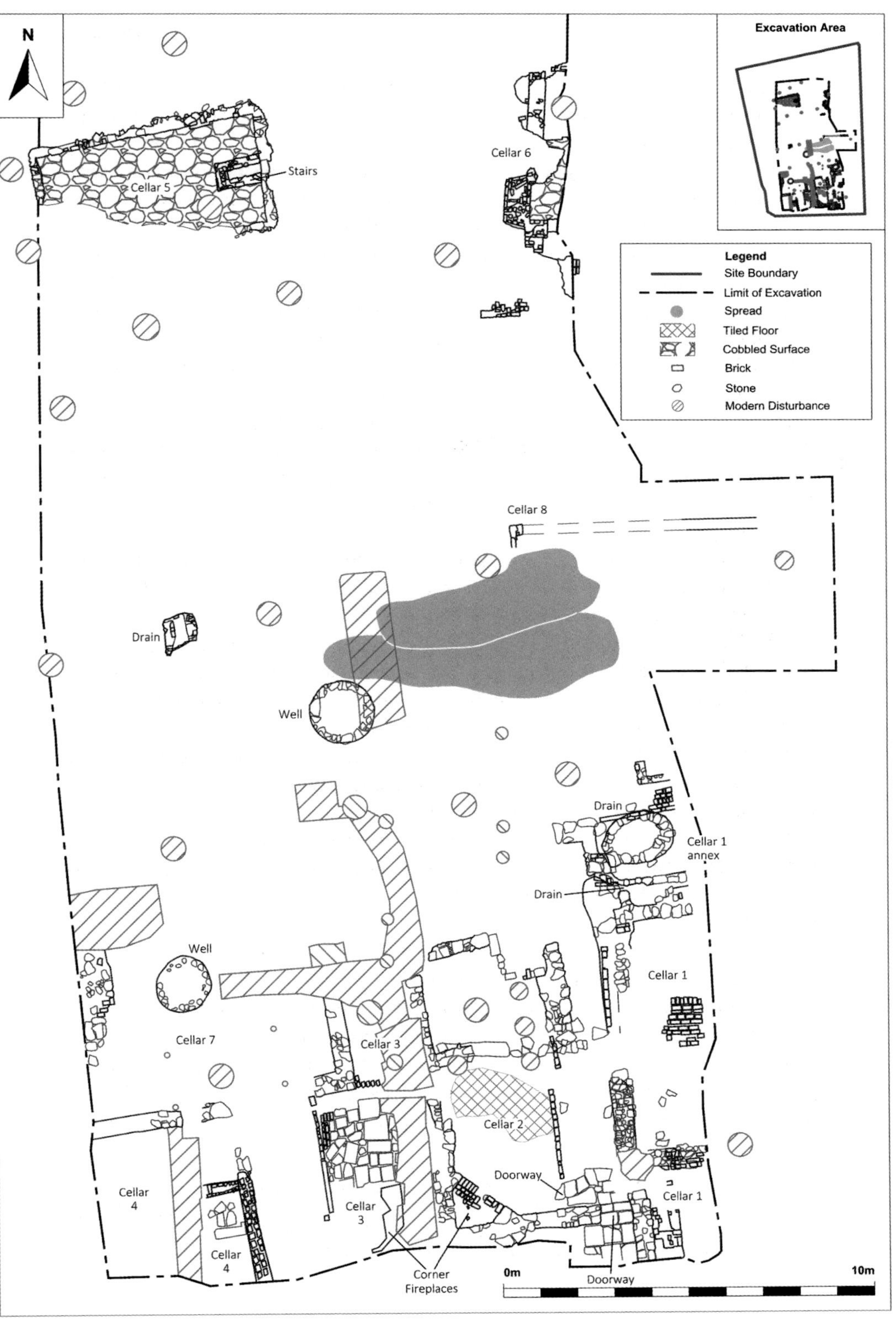

2.9 Plan of Phase 3, post-medieval features

well recorded abutting it to the north. The ceramic assemblage recovered from the pits and deposits demonstrates that they date to between the fifteenth and seventeenth century which suggests that the site at Riverhouse continued to function as a communal dumping area up until the time the area of Oxmantown witnessed a period of rapid growth and development towards the end of the seventeenth century when redevelopment of medieval streets, large-scale reclamation, quay- and bridge-building transformed the suburbs.[14] A shallow spread of material sealed the deep medieval deposits at the southeast of the site and may have been deliberately spread out in that location to solidify the ground surface. Refuse from the Phase 3 pits and deposits included sherds of jugs, jars, and bowls of Transition-type ware along with Beauvais monochrome glazed ware, Raeren and Saintonge green- and brown-glazed ware dating from the fifteenth–sixteenth centuries.

The approximate area of Riverhouse was first noted as developed on Speed's 1610 map of Dublin while the earliest detailed representation of Dutch Billy houses fronting onto Pill Lane, Cow Lane and to a lesser extent Bull Lane is shown on John Rocque's 1756 map. A reference table which accompanies the map identifies all the buildings as dwelling houses, with a stable or outhouse at the rear. These eighteenth-century buildings were of various plot widths and those fronting onto Pill Lane had gardens extending back with returns attached to several of the rears. Today the streets that surround the Riverhouse site have been significantly widened, meaning that the residential houses that once fronted onto Chancery Street and Greek Street are now located under the current streetscape. The heavily disturbed houses at Riverhouse therefore probably represent the returns attached to the rear of the main houses and only survived at basement level.

The excavated evidence seems to tie in with the documentary evidence, as a terrace of four houses was identified during the excavation fronting onto Chancery Street at the south with a further four more fragmentary structural remains recorded, possibly fronting onto Greek Street to the west and Bull Lane to the east towards the north of the site. Each house and yard area appeared to go through varying degrees and phases of alteration and development after construction. The southern terrace of houses was cut into the medieval and no boundary garden walls or fences survived on the site probably due to later nineteenth-century activity.

DISCUSSION

The ditch recorded at Riverhouse with a two-sigma calibrated radiocarbon date of AD 897–1037, adds to a growing database of evidence demonstrating

14 Abi Cryerhall, 'Excavations at Hammond Lane, Dublin: from hurdle-ford to iron foundry'

that the northern suburb of Oxmantown was inhabited by a Hiberno Norse population prior to the arrival of the Anglo-Normans in 1170. The suburb of Oxmantown was served by St Michan's church (*c.*164m to the west of the site), which dubious tradition asserts to have been founded in the late eleventh century,[15] though Purcell suggests that an earlier church may have existed on the site,[16] and excavations to the north of St Michan's have shown that a large ditch interpreted as a possible earlier enclosing ditch of the church contained Hiberno-Norse burials dating to AD 950–1050 along its base.[17] A large excavation by Dawkes immediately south of May Lane may have identified the continuation of this ditch to the west along with activity that probably pre-dated the late tenth century.[18] The earliest activity comprised small pits, ditches and gullies dug into natural clays and sands; however, no scientific dating has been presented.[19] Further evidence of possible contemporary activity has been identified at excavations at 161–168 Church Street/3–15 Hammond Lane *c.*173m to the southeast which was excavated in three phases by Cryerhall (03E0721), Phelan (05E0765) and Moriarty (09E0517). A wattle-lined sunken structure of unknown function, along with several west–east rows of stakes dating to the tenth century, were recorded in the second phase of excavation in the northeast corner of the overall site of Hammond Lane.[20] A large wattle-lined pit or ditch was excavated in the third phase of excavation at the southeast corner of the overall site of Hammond Land which was truncated by eleventh/twelfth-century activity.[21]

The tenth-century ditch at Riverhouse may form part of extensive tenth/eleventh-century flood-relief efforts recorded at a variety of locations along the former Liffey shoreline of Oxmantown. The Riverhouse site is located directly to the north of the foreshore of the confluence of the Liffey and one of its main tributaries, the Bradogue; an area which was known as the Pill during the medieval and post-medieval periods. Speed's map of Dublin (1610) depicts the Pill as a series of mudflats interspersed with narrow water-channels. Nearby excavations have shown that up to the mid-eleventh century this general area was marshy marginal ground of open fields,[22] that would have been subject to salt-water inundation from high-season tides and floodwaters as far north as Pill Lane abutting the southern extent of the Riverhouse site

in Duffy (ed.), *MD VII*, pp 9–50. **15** See Wadden in this volume. **16** Purcell, 'Land use in Oxmantown', pp 9–112. **17** Roseanne Meenan, 'The excavation of pre-Anglo-Norman burials and ditch near St Michan's church' in Duffy (ed.), *MD V*, pp 91–110. **18** Giles Dawkes, 'Interim results of excavation at 152–3 Church Street, Dublin: St Michans early enclosure and late medieval timber-framed buildings' in Duffy (ed.), *MD X*, pp 189–219. **19** As noted in Simpson, 'Fifty years a-digging', pp 161–9. **20** Phelan, 'Hiberno-Norse discoveries at Church Street and Hammond Lane'. **21** Colm Moriarty, 'Phase IIB archaeological excavation at 3–5 Hammond LNE/161–169 Church Street, Dublin 7', Licence 09E0517, unpublished final excavation report (2010). **22** Phelan, 'Hiberno-Norse discoveries at Church Street and Hammond Lane'.

(modern Chancery Street).[23] The earliest activity recorded during Phase 1 excavation at Hammond Lane consists of pre-eleventh-/twelfth-century earthen bank and ditches running west–east interpreted as water-management efforts at the west of the overall site.[24] Several short (11–12m-long) flood-relief ditches of an average width of 1m and depth of 0.8m were recorded running parallel to the shoreline. No finds or ceramics were recovered from the ditches, and they were filled with layers of sand or coarse gravel. The ditch at Riverhouse was slightly larger measuring 13m+ in length, 2.8m wide and 0.92m deep; however, the similar orientation and morphology of the basal fills suggests they may have formed a similar flood-relief function.

The Phase 2 reclamation deposits recorded at Riverhouse add to growing excavated evidence of land-reclamation and land-organization in the later eleventh/twelfth century. It is possible that the Phase 1 ditch became redundant due to these later land-reclamation efforts. The lower of the reclamation deposits returned a two-sigma calibrated radiocarbon date of AD 1031–1202. This date aligns with nearby excavated evidence that shows that control of the river was of primary importance and land-reclamation on the north side of the river had already begun before the arrival of the Anglo-Normans in 1170.[25] Nearby excavation at 161–168 Church Street/3–15 Hammond Lane *c.*173m to the southeast has also shown that land-reclamation began along the riverfront in the late eleventh to twelfth century. Four reclamation boxes constructed of stake and wattle fences were filled with gravel and organic-rich material to build up the level of the foreshore to that of the dryland.[26] A series of wooden front-braced revetments, the earliest dated by dendrochronology to *c.*1305, were recorded at Arran Quay *c.*227m southeast of the site. Organic refuse, river silt, stones, sand, and gravel were dumped behind it to build up the ground level.[27] No such reclamation boxes or wooden revetments were identified at Riverhouse, although the reclamation deposits at Riverhouse were only investigated by sondage as the layers in question were located below the formation level of the development. As such, these layers were only identified in section. It is therefore possible that similar instances of land-reclamation engineering may be preserved *in-situ* at Riverhouse.

The location of the deep reclamation deposits recorded at Riverhouse may suggest that the course of the River Bradogue lies further northwest than originally believed. Speed's map of Dublin shows the River Bradogue running north–south parallel to and to the west of St Mary's abbey before it turns southwest towards the Liffey. On Clarke's well-known map of *Medieval Dublin* c.*840*–c.*1540*,[28] the River Bradogue appears to run directly to the east of the

23 Clarke, *Dublin, Pt 1* (IHTA). 24 Cryerhall, 'Excavations at Hammond Lane'. 25 Simpson, 'Fifty years a-digging'. 26 Cryerhall, 'Excavations at Hammond Lane'. 27 Alan Hayden, 'Excavations of the medieval river frontage at Arran Quay, Dublin' in Duffy (ed.), *MD V*, pp 149–242. 28 Clarke, *Dublin, pt 1*, map 4.

2.10 Working shot of waste pit excavation in southeast corner, facing north

current day line of Arran Street East. De Gomme's map of 1673, however, shows a 'Bradogue Lane' (now Halston Street) lying to the west of Boot Lane (now Arran Street East) and a Wide Street Commission plan by Thomas Serard from 1795 shows a narrow channel named the 'River Bradogue' at the rear of the properties on Boot Lane (Arran Street East) and in alignment with Halston Street to the north (WSC 220/1). A designated watercourse DU018-020566 was identified during pre-development testing under licence 94E0160 running north–south along Halston Street which in tandem with the cartographic evidence suggests that the River Bradogue possibly ran along Halston Street as it is known today to the west of Arran Street East rather than to the east.[29] The original name (Bradogue Lane) and the unusual curving nature of the current Halston Street further adds to this theory. Excavation evidence from test-trenching in 2001 at the carpark to the rear of the Fruit and

29 Margaret Gowen, 'Archaeological assessment of a development site at Halston Street, Ball's Lane, Dublin 7' (Licence 94E0160), unpublished report: Margaret Gowen & Co. Ltd.

Vegetable Market on Chancery Street (previously Pill Lane) also suggested the course of the River Bradogue may have been further west than indicated on the *Medieval Dublin* c.*840*–c.*1540* map. The 2001 testing showed that substantial silty clay deposits containing medieval artefacts were preserved at depths exceeding 2.5m below present ground level which may represent reclamation of a waterway; potentially the River Bradogue.[30] The location of the River Bradogue on the 1795 Wide Streets Commission plan suggests that it runs beneath the current Fruit and Vegetable Market building and probably turned west at the location of the 2001 testing. This would indicate that the deep silty clay deposits identified in the southeast corner of the Riverhouse site, *c.*90m west of the 2001 test excavation, may represent the northern reclaimed shoreline of the River Bradogue as it ran southwest towards the Liffey.

The site at Riverhouse appears to have remained as marginal ground after the land directly to the south was reclaimed as it was used extensively for dumping in the twelfth–fourteenth centuries, marked by the lack of domestic structures and the large number of intercutting rubbish pits (fig. 2.10). Further evidence for damp conditions and hedgerow growth was provided by the large numbers of waterlogged ruderal and hedgerow taxa found in the plant macro assemblage including hazelnuts and blackberries. A similar interpretation was put forward for multiple rubbish pits recorded at Hammond Lane although in that instance there is documentary evidence of the area being used for dumping in the fifteenth century.[31]

While no structural evidence was recorded at Riverhouse, the eleventh–fourteenth-century waste-pits are likely associated with nearby Hiberno-Norse habitation, small-scale industrial activity and shops. Land-reclamation directly south of the Riverhouse site would have allowed expansion into land that was originally part of the river and subject to flooding and would also facilitate the construction of Pill Lane. Pill Lane was a narrow but important artery on the route from the bridge across the Liffey to St Mary's abbey and as such probably existed from the late eleventh century onwards.[32] Purcell suggests that the development of the Dominican priory of St Saviour's on the northern riverbank in AD 1224 may have encouraged further secular settlement in the area and aided the development of Pill Lane.[33] Pill Lane is first referred to as a lane called 'Le Phill' in AD 1539 and later called the 'Lane of St Mary's Abbey' in AD 1581.[34]

The domestic and small-scale industrial waste dumped in the pits adds to our understanding of the everyday diet and possible occupations of inhabitants

30 Emmet Stafford, 'Archaeological testing of The Daisy Market, Dublin 7' (Licence 01E0711), unpublished report for IAC Archaeology (2001). 31 Cryerhall, 'Excavations at Hammond Lane'. 32 J.W. de Courcy, *The Liffey in Dublin* (Dublin, 1996). 33 Purcell, 'Land use in Oxmantown'. 34 Clarke, *Dublin, pt 1*, p. 15.

around Pill Lane, Colcot Lane and Cow Lane in the eleventh–fourteenth centuries. The charcoal analysis also provides information about the fuel-gathering strategies on the site at the time. Charcoal results from this site indicate that different types of woodlands were being harvested for firewood. These include woods probably with oak/ash/elm as their canopy layer and smaller trees forming the shrub layer including hazel/holly/pomaceous fruitwood/blackthorn/cherry. Other types of environment are also represented including riparian or wet woods (including alder, birch, and willow), while the softwoods yew and pine were also noted, along with beech.

There is growing evidence therefore that a mixed Hiberno-Norse community, probably associated with St Michan's church, was living and farming, and managing the high-season tides and floodwaters, within the suburb of Oxmantown and the archaeological features recorded at the Riverhouse site relate to these activities. The footprint of the building has been archaeologically resolved to natural subsoil, apart from the south-eastern area of the basement where the deep reclamation layers which were identified extending beneath the formation level were preserved *in situ*. All other archaeological features, structures and deposits within the footprint have been preserved by record.

ACKNOWLEDGMENTS

I would like to thank the excavation crew that worked tirelessly and cheerfully under the dark unusual conditions brought on by the top-down construction technique undertaken by the developer. I would also like to thank my project manager Paul Duffy for all his help and advice and all the specialists and the post-ex and graphics departments in IAC Archaeology for helping in the successful submission of the final report.

Beyond Clontarf: links between Dublin and the earldom of Orkney

CAITLIN ELLIS

This essay concerns direct links between Dublin and the earldom of Orkney. It focuses on the eleventh and twelfth centuries because this is the period when contemporary evidence for the earldom emerges. These sources are from Britain and Ireland, but the more extended accounts of the earldom in thirteenth- and fourteenth-century Norse sagas will also be taken into consideration, despite the time that elapsed between the events described and the writing of the texts. Four major instances of military and political contact are explored, though other categories of contact and material evidence will also be briefly considered. The earldom of Orkney comprised the Northern Isles of Orkney and Shetland and, at least at times, Caithness in the northernmost tip of the Scottish mainland. Both the earldom and the Hiberno-Scandinavian town of Dublin were part of what has been variously termed the Viking world or the Viking diaspora.[1] Dublin was an important centre of the interlinked trade around the Irish Sea. The concept of the medieval Irish Sea region was extended to include the Scottish Isles (both the Western Isles and the Northern Isles) by Colmán Etchingham, forming what he dubbed the 'Insular Viking zone', as these isles were part of the same 'political nexus' as Ireland and Wales.[2] This essay aims to shed some light on connectivity and regionalism within the Insular Viking Zone.

One problem for this investigation is the imprecise terminology of 'Isles' in the contemporary or near contemporary sources. In Irish, *Innsi Gall*, 'Islands of the Foreigners' (suggesting vikings or Scandinavians), is usually taken to refer to the Western Isles but could have included the Northern Isles.[3] The term *Eyjar*, 'Islands' in Old Norse, is even more ambiguous. There are more specific terms: *Suðreyjar*, 'Southern Islands' (which gives rise to the name Sodor), denoting the Hebrides and Man; *Norðreyjar*, 'Northern Islands', denoting Shetland and Orkney. *Eyjar* alone is usually associated with the Northern Isles specifically.[4]

The spheres of influence of Dublin and the earldom most clearly overlap in Man and the Hebrides. Rulers of Dublin often had influence in Man and the

1 For the 'Viking diaspora' see Lesley Abrams, 'Diaspora and identity in the Viking Age', *Early Medieval Europe*, 20:1 (2012), 17–38; Judith Jesch, *Viking diaspora* (London, 2015). 2 Colmán Etchingham, 'North Wales, Ireland and the Isles: the Insular Viking one', *Peritia*, 15 (2001), 145–87; England was excluded from Etchingham's conception of this zone. 3 Alex Woolf, *From Pictland to Alba: 789 to 1070*, The New Edinburgh History of Scotland 2 (Edinburgh, 2007), p. 298. 4 Jesch, *Viking diaspora*, p. 177.

Isles, as particularly demonstrated in the involvement of Irish dynasties, notably the Uí Briain, in the islands following on from their takeover of Dublin.[5] The relationship between the earldom of Orkney and the Hebrides is less clear. There are references in Norse sagas, particularly in *Orkneyinga saga* ('The saga of the Orkney islanders'), to Orcadian attempts to gather tax in Man and the Hebrides, which should not be given too much credence given the thirteenth-century context of these sources.[6] Control of the Hebrides is claimed for a couple of notable Orcadian earls,[7] but this likely reflects a back projection of later Norwegian dominion over the Isles.[8] There is, though, a contemporary reference of interest, in a stanza of a skaldic poem by the Icelandic poet Arnórr *jarlaskáld* ('poet of earls'), which was composed in honour of Earl Thorfinn Sigurdsson:

Hringstríði varð hlýða
herr frá Þursaskerjum
— rétt segik þjóð, hvé þótti
Þórfinnr — til Dyflinnar

'People had to heed the ring-harmer [generous ruler] from Þursasker to Dublin; I tell men truly how Þorfinnr was regarded'.[9]

Since Dublin is perhaps being claimed as the southern edge of Thorfinn's zone of influence, presumably Þursasker ('Giant skerries') represents its northern edge, suggesting an identification with rocks off Shetland, such as Muckle Flugga or the Outer Skerries.[10] Naturally, praise poetry is prone to exaggerated flattery of the patron and so this wide sway may be more aspirational than realistic. Rather than overlordship, it could refer to the earl having faced opponents over this broad area (and not necessarily at the same time).[11]

* * *

5 See Seán Duffy, 'Irishmen and Islesmen in the kingdoms of Dublin and Man, 1052–1171', *Ériu*, 43 (1992), 93–133, at 101–6; Anthony Candon, 'Muirchertach Ua Briain, Politics and Naval Activity in the Irish Sea, 1075–1119' in Gearóid Mac Niocaill and Patrick F. Wallace (eds), *Keimelia: Studies in medieval archaeology and history in memory of Tom Delaney* (Galway, 1988), pp 397–416, at pp 401–5. 6 William P.L. Thomson, *The new history of Orkney* (Edinburgh, 2008), p. 61. 7 For instance, *Njáls saga* claims that Earl Sigurd Hlöðvisson collected tribute from the Hebrides: ch. 85, 89, *Brennu-Njáls saga*, ed. Einar Ól. Sveinsson (Reykjavík, 1954), pp 205, 224. 8 See for example Richard Oram, 'Ouncelands, quarterlands and pennylands in the Western Isles, Man and Galloway: tribute payments and military levies in the Norse west' in Steinar Imsen (ed.), *Taxes, tributes and tributary lands in the making of the Scandinavian kingdoms in the Middle Ages* (Trondheim, 2011), pp 57–75, at p. 68. 9 Arnórr *jarlaskáld*, *Þorfinnsdrápa*, stanza 23 (in Diana Whaley in Kari Ellen Gade (eds), *Poetry from the Kings' Sagas 2: from* c.*1035 to* c.*1300*, Skaldic Poetry of the Scandinavian Middle Ages 2, 2 parts (Turnhout, 2009), pt 1, p. 257). 10 Barbara E. Crawford, *The northern earldoms: Orkney and Caithness from AD 870 to 1470*, 2nd edn (Edinburgh, 2023), p. 162. 11 It might even refer to the expedition of 1058,

The first, and most famous, recorded instance of interaction between Orkney and Dublin is the battle of Clontarf in 1014. When Sitric *silkiskegg* ('silkbeard'), Hiberno-Scandinavian king of Dublin, rebelled with Leinster against Brian Bóraime, king of Munster and claimant to kingship of Ireland, he was joined by forces from elsewhere in the Insular Viking Zone. These included the earl of Orkney, Sigurd Hlödvisson. The notice of the earl's death in the Annals of Ulster, listed among other 'Foreigners', is the first contemporary reference to the earldom of Orkney.[12] The length of the full annalistic item about the battle of Clontarf indicates the importance that was attached to this event.[13]

But why did Orkney get involved in this Irish battle? The Irish sources provide no explanation.[14] The twelfth-century pseudo-historical work of Munster propaganda *Cogadh Gáedhel re Gallaibh* relates that the Foreigners of Dublin and Laigin [Leinster] 'invited to them also Siucrad, son of Lotar, earl of the Orc islands, and of other islands also (*Ro tuchured cucu, dana, Siucraid Mac Lotair, iarla insi Orc ocus na ninsi archena*)'.[15] It gives no insight into why Sigurd would accept the invitation; presumably as far as the *Cogadh* is concerned he is merely conforming to type (that of the barbarous violent Foreigner). Sigurd's mother was said to be Irish in *Orkneyinga saga*, though the details are murky.[16] It is still possible that his mother was genuinely Irish but

which will be discussed presently, assuming that Thorfinn was still alive for this event (*contra* Woolf, see below). **12** ... *cecidit uero a Gallis ... Siuchraidh m. Loduir iarla Innsi Orcc* ('... of the Foreigners there fell ... Siucraid son of Lodur, jarl of Innsi Orc') (AU1014.2). See Woolf, *Pictland to Alba*, p. 300. The next contemporary surviving reference to an earl of Orkney is in the description of the battle of Stamford Bridge in Manuscript D of the Anglo-Saxon Chronicle: ASC D 1066, trans. Dorothy Whitelock in D.C. Douglas and G.W. Greenaway (eds), *English historical documents, 1042–1189*, 2nd edn (London, 1981), p. 146. **13** The various annalistic items are covered in depth by Seán Duffy, *Brian Boru and the battle of Clontarf* (Dublin, 2014), ch. 4. **14** Other Irish annals do not specifically mention the earl. For example, the Annals of Inisfallen simply comments that 'the Foreigners of the western world were slaughtered in the same battle' *ar Gall iarthair domain isin chath chetna* (AI 1014.2). **15** *CGG*, pp 152–3. **16** *Orkneyinga saga*, ed. Finnbogi Guðmundsson, Íslenzk Fornrit 34 (Reykjavík 1965), pp 24–5 (§11). His mother is identified as Eðna (Eithne or Ethne in Gaelic) daughter of Kjarvalr *Írakonungr* ('king of the Irish'). This Eðna of *Orkneyinga saga* is the only one of Kjarvalr's children not to feature in the *Landnámabók* ('The book of settlements') account of his descendants. Kjarvalr has been assumed to be Cerball mac Dúnlainge (842–88), which Downham notes would make this marriage 'chronologically implausible' (Clare Downham, 'The career of Cerball mac Dúnlainge, overking of the Osraige' in her *No horns on their helmets? Essays on the Insular Viking-Age* (Aberdeen, 2013), pp 91–110, at p. 96). Seán Duffy suggested an alternative identification of Kjarvalr *Írakonungr* as the Leinster king Cerball mac Muirecáin of Uí Fáeláin (r. 884/85–909) (Duffy, *Brian Boru*, p. 229), and therefore it is plausible that Sigurd could have been born *c.*950 to a woman whose father died in 909 (see also, Colmán Etchingham, Jón Viðar Sigurðsson, Máire Ní Mhaonaigh & Elizabeth Ashman Rowe, *Norse-Gaelic contacts in a Viking world* (Turnhout, 2019), p. 200, n. 7). It is also possible that *Kjarvalr* became a generic name in Norse for an Irish king. The genealogies involving him in *Landnámabók* (which do not seem connected to the mentions of Cerball mac Dúnlainge's

that the precise details were invented.[17] However, this aspect is not connected to his involvement in Clontarf in the saga accounts. Admittedly, *Orkneyinga saga* itself is not particularly interested in Clontarf, whereas *Njáls saga* is – both in terms of an Icelandic feud playing out abroad and representing the battle between pagan and Christian. According to *Njáls saga*, Sitric of Dublin visited the earl's court the Christmas before the battle (which occurred at Easter) to try to gain his support. Initially the earl is resistant, but it is agreed 'that earl Sigurd promised to join the expedition, and king Sitric promised to him his own mother and the kingdom (*at Sigurðr jarl hét ferðinni, en Sigtryggr konungr hét honum móður sinni ok konungdómi*)'.[18] This episode seems more like a literary motif and perhaps a bit of comedy given that Gormlaith (or Kormlöð in Norse) is also offered to Bróðir or Brodir of Man in the same fashion. In reality there were likely to have been more pragmatic, mercenary reasons. One scholar has also suggested that Gormlaith would not be such a prize because we can estimate she was at least in her 50s in 1014.[19] In *Njáls saga*, the attack on Brian is her idea, including encouraging her son to gather more forces; this connects to the trope of the 'whetting' or goading woman that is common in the Norse sagas.[20]

Scholars have also sought to contextualize Orkney's involvement in Clontarf by way of the wider political and military situation at the time. Clare Downham suggests that Sigurd may have hired some of the viking fleets that were present in the British-Irish Isles due to the contemporary renewal of raids associated with the Danish king Sven Forkbeard's eventual conquest of England to assist in the conflict with Brian.[21] Distrusting the later saga

family in the Fragmentary Annals of Ireland) appear to date to the twelfth century (see Sverrir Jakobsson, 'The Old Norse high medieval tradition about the Scandinavian kings of Dublin and York (*c.*860–960)' in Matthew Firth (ed.), *The reception of pre-Conquest history beyond English borders* (York, forthcoming). Therefore, it is possible that *Orkneyinga saga* was influenced by this. **17** Duffy, *Brian Boru*, pp 229–30. **18** *Njáls saga*, ch. 155 (ed. Einar Ól. Sveinsson, p. 444; my translation). **19** Having suggested that Gormlaith was born *c.* 955 and was therefore around 58 years old at the time of Clontarf, Muireann Ní Bhrolcháin asserts that Gormlaith was 'hardly the catch she had been some 25 years earlier' on the occasion of her first marriage ('Who was Gormlaith's mother? A detective story' in Joe Fenwick (ed.), *Lost and found II – rediscovering Ireland's past* (Bray, 2009), pp 83–94, at pp 86–7, quote at p. 87). Máire Ní Mhaonaigh similarly calculates that Gormlaith's first marriage would have taken place in the 970s when she was 'still very young' but does not speculate about when she was born ('Tales of three Gormlaiths in Medieval Irish Literature', *Ériu*, 52 (2002), 1–24, at 18). **20** Ní Mhaonaigh argues that Gormlaith's depiction contrasts to that of the 'saintly king' Brian ('Tales of three Gormlaiths', 23). This trope of women inciting violence is evident elsewhere in *Njáls saga*, in the figure of Hildigunnr particularly, and there are also other powerful and potentially dangerous widows as well as Gormlaith in the text: Ní Mhaonaigh, 'Tales of three Gormlaiths', 23; Heather O'Donoghue, 'Women in *Njáls saga*' in John Hines and Desmond Slay (eds), *Introductory essays on* Egils saga *and* Njáls saga (London, 1992), pp 83–92 at pp 84–8, 90 (where Kormlöð is included in the list of goading women, as 'the vengeful instigator of the battle of Clontarf'). **21** Clare Downham, 'England and the Irish Sea zone in the eleventh century',

evidence, Alex Woolf made the intriguing suggestion that it was not Harald *hárfagri* ('fairhair', 'finehair') of Norway in the late ninth century but Harald Bluetooth of Denmark in the late tenth century who had a hand in the early earldom, making it 'a creation of the Danish empire'.[22] Harald Bluetooth's success in establishing control over Denmark was followed by the further expansion of his son Sven Forkbeard and his grandson Cnut. Patrick Wadden offered two hypotheses for Sigurd's involvement in Clontarf: the first accords the earl greater agency in that he 'might have been the instigator of the battle himself' in an expansionist effort 'to bring the Hiberno-Scandinavian kingdoms of the Irish Sea world under his sway'; the second builds on Woolf's arguments about the creation of the earldom, in that Sigurd 'might have been acting on behalf of his putative overlord, the Danish king'.[23] Some scholars have noted that 'there is no supporting evidence' for Woolf's claim.[24] If the Danish king had had the power to direct Sigurd's martial endeavours, as Wadden speculates, one suspects that he would have summoned the earldom's resources to aid his own efforts in England, as Harald *harðráði* ('harsh-ruler', 'resolute', commonly anglicized as Hardrada)), king of Norway, would do in 1066. Indeed, Clontarf occurred at Easter 1014, which was a critical, uncertain time in the Danish conquest of England, as Sven had died in February shortly after being declared king and the former king, Æthelred II, had returned from exile in spring, forcing Cnut to leave Gainsborough and put to sea after Easter.[25] Sven and Cnut were surely too occupied with securing England at this stage to think about Ireland; there was no reason to expect that Æthelred would have received support from any Irish kings.

Therefore, the first of Wadden's suggestions for Sigurd's involvement in Clontarf, that he sought to expand his own sphere of influence, is more likely than the purported Danish connection. The intensification of Scandinavian military activity in England may have meant that smaller bands of mercenaries were on hand to participate in other conflicts. However, it seems that the earldom's participation and its support for Dublin fits better within the geopolitical context of the Isles and Irish Sea region.

* * *

The second major known instance of direct political contact between Dublin and Orkney occurred a few decades later, in 1058. The events of that year

Anglo-Norman Studies, 26 (2003), pp 55–73, at p. 62. **22** Woolf, *Pictland to Alba*, p. 308. **23** Patrick Wadden, 'Brian Boraime, the Insular Viking world and the battle of Clontarf' in Seán Duffy (ed.), *Medieval Dublin XVI: proceedings of Clontarf 1014–2014: national conference marking the millennium of the battle of Clontarf* (Dublin, 2017), pp 144–69 at p. 168. **24** Etchingham et al. (eds), *Norse-Gaelic contacts*, p. 4, n. 121: they also note that the theory would render the chronology of the Icelandic work *Landnámabók* 'completely unreliable'. **25** Anglo-Saxon Chronicle 1014 (manuscripts C, D and E), trans. Dorothy

brought together not only Dublin and the earldom of Orkney, but also Gwynedd in north Wales, England, the Western Isles, and the kingdom of Norway. Neither Dublin nor Orkney spearheaded this cooperation, however. It was a response to Edward the Confessor, king of England (d. 1066), exiling Ælfgar, earl of Mercia (son of Leofric and the subsequently famous Lady Godiva or Godgifu). On his first outlawry in 1055 Ælfgar had been reinstated, after sacking Hereford and then coming to terms with Edward. He had been aided by his son-in-law Gruffudd ap Llywelyn, king of Gwynedd, and by ships from Ireland, probably from Dublin but perhaps from another Hiberno-Scandinavian town.[26] It is therefore the addition to this coalition of elements outwith the Irish Sea, that is the Scottish Isles and Norway, which is striking in 1058.[27] The former are only included in the one Irish account of the event, the Annals of Tigernach, which refers to the fleet 'with the Foreigners of the Orkneys and the Hebrides and Dublin (*co nGallaib Indsi Orcc ⁊ Indsi Gall ⁊ Atha Cliath*)'.[28] Perhaps it was only the Irish source (as opposed to the English and Welsh ones) that cared to – or was able to – differentiate between the different groups of 'Foreigners', or those other sources included the Isles under the banner of the Norwegian fleet.

According to the annalistic item, the fleet was led by 'the son of the king of Norway (*macríg Lochland*)', referring to Magnus Haraldsson, whose father Harald *harðráði*'s attempted invasion of England would fail in 1066.[29] Magnus's presence in the British-Irish Isles in 1058 may have been aimed at securing Norwegian domination over Orkney. *Orkneyinga saga* relates that Thorfinn, earl of Orkney died in the later days of King Harald, which Alex Woolf stretches to 1058, suggesting that Norway's royal line seized the opportunity of Thorfinn's death to assert their authority.[30] This may have been resolved amicably given the kinship ties between Magnus and the earls, leaving

Whitelock, in *English historical documents* c.*500–1042* (London, 1979), pp 246–7. **26** Anglo-Saxon Chronicle 1055 (manuscripts C and D), trans. Whitelock in *English historical gocuments 1042–1189*, p. 133. See Etchingham, 'Insular Viking zone', 154–5. **27** The involvement of Orkney is more noteworthy than that of the Hebrides, given that rulers of Dublin often also had influence over the Hebrides (as mentioned above) and that those islands are mentioned more frequently in the Irish annals. For more on the Norwegian and Scottish elements to the expedition of 1058, see Caitlin Ellis, 'Go west: contextualizing Scandinavian royal naval expeditions into the Insular world, 1013–1103', *Historical Research*, 95:270 (November 2022), 481–505. **28** AT 1058. 4 **29** AT 1058.4. A leader is not supplied in the Anglo-Saxon Chronicle (MS D) or the twelfth-century chronicle of John of Worcester, who instead casts Ælfgar as the main actor, as he regains his earldom with Welsh and Norwegian support: *The Chronicle of John of Worcester. Volume II: The Annals from 450 to 1066*, ed. R.R. Darlington and P. McGurk (Oxford, 1995), p. 584. In contrast, Welsh sources name him as Magnus son of Harald: *Annales Cambriae*, ed. John Williams ab Ithel, Rolls Series 20 (London, 1860), p. 25; *Brut y Tywysogyon, or The Chronicle of the Princes: Red Book of Hergest Version*, ed. and trans. Thomas Jones (Cardiff, 1955), pp 26–7; *Brut y Tywysogyon or The Chronicle of the Princes Peniarth MS. 20 Version*, trans. Thomas Jones (Cardiff, 1952), p. 14. **30** Woolf, *Pictland to Alba*, pp 267–8.

the Norwegian fleet eager for action, with plundering England as part of Ælfgar and Gruffudd's enterprise proving tempting.[31] This scenario would also help explain the presence of the Orcadians on the expedition, as accompanying Magnus through the Irish Sea. But how would Magnus have learnt of these events? Perhaps word reached him via Dublin or the Hebrides, whose men are also recorded as part of the campaign in the item in the Annals of Tigernach. Nevertheless, the earldom's involvement was still largely driven by Norway, given its later participation in Harald *harðráði*'s expedition to England.

Frustratingly for the modern historian, the chronicler who provided the account of 1058 in Manuscript D of the Anglo-Saxon Chronicle found it 'tedious to relate fully how things went (*langsum to atellanne eall hu hit gefaren wæs*)'.[32] Norwegian participation is nonetheless noteworthy enough to feature quite prominently in every account of the events of 1058, while other parties were often omitted.[33] Where the Norwegian naval expedition does not feature is in fact in later Norse sagas; this is presumably because of its lack of impact in Norway itself and to what would prove to be Magnus's brief reign and short-lived line of descendants.[34] Despite being lost to later Norse tradition, it was the involvement of Norwegian royalty that, in contrast to 1055, apparently brought Orkney into the pre-existing nexus of connections across the Irish Sea between (northern) Wales, England and the Hiberno-Scandinavian towns.

* * *

Tied together as mercenaries in the mid-eleventh century, at the start of the twelfth century Dublin and Orkney were linked by their overlords. Muirchertach Ua Briain, king of Munster and most powerful Irish king of the time, controlled Dublin. He had been appointed its governor in 1075 by his father Tairdelbach; this was the occasion of Muirchertach's first mention in

31 Woolf, *Pictland to Alba*, p. 268. 32 Anglo-Saxon Chronicle 1058 (manuscripts D), ed. G.P. Cubbin, *The Anglo-Saxon Chronicle MS D*, The Anglo-Saxon Chronicle: a Collaborative Edition, 6 (Cambridge, 1996), p. 76; trans. Whitelock, in *English historical documents, 1042–1189*, p. 138. 33 As noted above, the Scottish Isles are mentioned only by the Annals of Tigernach. The same annals do not mention the English and Welsh dimension in 1058, which makes it perhaps unsurprising that the Irish aid for Ælfgar and Gruffudd ap Llywelyn in 1055 is not recorded at all in the Irish annals. The Welsh sources omit Ælfgar from both attacks on England, the first being attributed to Gruffudd and the second to Magnus with Gruffudd's help: *Annales Cambriae*, ed. Williams ab Ithel, p. 25; *Brut y Tywysogyon (RB)*, ed. and trans. Jones, pp 24–7; *Brut y Tywysogyon (Pen. 20)*, trans. Jones, pp 14–15. Rebecca Thomas suggests that this was 'a deliberate choice' for the presentation of Gruffudd: 'The view from Wales: Anglo-Welsh relations in the time of England's conquests' in Laura Ashe and Emily J. Ward (eds), *Conquests in eleventh-century England: 1016, 1066* (Woodbridge, 2020), pp 287–306, at p. 295. 34 See Woolf, *Pictland to Alba*, p. 267; Caitlin Ellis, 'Remembering the Vikings: ancestry, cultural memory, and geographical variation', *History Compass*, 19:4 (2021), 1–15, at 4, 9.

the Irish annals.[35] Magnus *berfœttr* ('barelegs'), king of Norway, launched two expeditions to the British-Irish Isles, in 1098 and 1102–3.[36] During the former he removed the earls of Orkney from power and installed his own son Sigurd as ruler. There is no evidence that Muirchertach and Magnus encountered each other in 1098.[37] They certainly did on Magnus's second expedition, however. In 1102 most of the Irish annals describe an agreement with Muirchertach and Magnus as 'a year's peace (*síth m-blaidhna*)'.[38] It is likely that such a treaty would have been accompanied by the exchange of gifts.[39]

This third instance of a known Dublin–Orkney political connection is perhaps the least direct of the four discussed here since it is filtered via their overlords. It seems likely that Magnus gathered extra troops and ships from the earldom as he travelled to Dublin, so that at least some individuals from the earldom may have been in Dublin with him.[40]

The Annals of Inisfallen record the outcome of diplomatic relations between the two kings: 'In this year Muirchertach Ua Briain made a marriage-alliance with the French and with the Norsemen (*In quo anno doróne Muircheartach h-Ua Briain clemnas re Francaib & Lochlannchaib*)'.[41] Magnus's son Sigurd was betrothed to the daughter of Muirchertach. It might have had

35 Candon, 'Muirchertach', pp 397, 399. 36 For further treatment of these expeditions see Rosemary Power, 'Magnus Barelegs' expeditions to the West', *Scottish Historical Review*, 65 (1986), 107–32; Ellis, 'Go west'. 37 Candon, 'Muirchertach', p. 406. 38 Daniel Brown, 'Pacific kingship and legitimate diplomacy in Ireland and the Norse world: Muirchertach Ua Briain's treaty with Magnús Berfœttr (1102)', *Cambrian Medieval Celtic Studies*, 80 (2020), 9–43, at 16. The exception is the Annals of Inisfallen, which usually favours Munster in its accounts, in that it only refers to the marriage alliance (to be discussed presently) omitting the treaty or peace with Norway, which leads Brown to suggest that it may have been deemed 'potentially damaging from a Dál Cais perspective' (Brown, 'Pacific kingship', 21). 39 Brown, 'Pacific kingship', 22. 40 In *Heimskringla* (*Magnúss saga berfœtts*, ch. 23), on his second expedition to the British-Irish Isles Magnus Barelegs stops in Orkney and takes Earl Erlend's two sons away with him as he sails to the Hebrides and onwards to Ireland (though Magnus Erlendsson, who would later be proclaimed a saint, is said to have swum ashore on the coast of Scotland): *Snorri Sturluson Heimskringla. Volume III: Magnús Óláfsson to Magnús Erlingsson*, trans. Alison Finlay and Anthony Faulkes (London, 2015), pp 141–2. In the *Fargskinna* account (ch. 84), only one son of Erlend (Erling) is mentioned as being taken from Orkney by Magnus Barelegs but it does add that some other men were taken too, though without going into detail: Alison Finlay, *Fagrskinna, a catalogue of the kings of Norway. A translation with introduction and notes* (Leiden, 2004), p. 250. *Morkinskinna* claims that Magnus Barelegs left 'his officers and administrators (*gísla sína ok gæzlumenn*)' in Dublin (*Morkinskinna: the earliest Icelandic chronicle of the Norwegian kings (1030–1157)*, trans. Theodore M. Andersson and Kari Ellen Gade (Ithaca, 2000), p. 310; *Morkinskinna II*, ed. Ármann Jakobsson and Þorður Ingi Guðjónsson, Íslenzk Fornrit XXIV (Reykjavík, 2011), ch. 63, p. 66), though they might be assumed to have been Norwegian or other long-standing followers. 41 AI 1102.6. A fuller account is found in the seventeenth-century Annals of Four Masters. For the Norman angle, see Candon, 'Muirchertach', pp 411–13; Caitlin Ellis, 'Ireland and the Anglo-Normans within the Irish Sea world: rebels, mercenaries, allies 1066–1169' in Daniel Armstrong, Áron Kecskés, Charles C. Rozier & Leonie V. Hicks (eds), *Borders and the Norman world*

greater impact, though, if it were not for Magnus's premature death in Ireland, resulting in Sigurd's return to Norway to secure his patrimony. The precise circumstances of Magnus's killing in 1103 are unclear: 'Magnus, king of the Foreigners, was slain when taken unawares by the Ulaid (*Magnus, ri Gall, do marbad do Ultaib tria baegul*)'.[42] Duffy and Etchingham have interpreted it as a souring of relations between Magnus and Muirchertach with the implication that the latter essentially had the former assassinated by his Ulaid allies.[43] Power suggests that the Ulaid may simply have not known who Magnus was when they attacked him.[44] The interests which brought the two rulers together as allies might likewise have led to competition and even fatal rivalry. The speculation will likely never be settled, but whether due to misadventure or mistrust Magnus's death meant that his longer-term ambitions in the British-Irish Isles were not realized. Nevertheless, their existence is still important, however short-lived. Had Sigurd remained as ruler of Orkney and married the daughter of the overlord of Dublin, closer relations between the two regions would surely have developed.

* * *

The fourth and final documented instance where Dublin and Orkney were brought into direct contact is during the Anglo-Norman or English invasion of Ireland (1169–72). The Hiberno-Scandinavian king of Dublin, Ascall Mac Torcaill, had opposed Diarmait Mac Murchada, the king of Leinster whose banishment and subsequent turning for aid to Anglo-Normans lords initiated the invasion. One of the major sources for the invasion, the *Expugnatio Hibernica* by Gerald of Wales, relates that when Raymond de Gros and Miles de Cogan attacked the city of Dublin many inhabitants were killed. Some escaped, including their king: 'But the greater part of them, led by Askulv [i.e., Ascall] went on board ship, taking their most precious belongings, and sailed off to the northern isles (*Pars tamen eorum potior, Hasculpho duce, scaphas cum his que preciosora possederant intrantes, boreales ad insulas se navigio transtulerunt*)'.[45] The *boreales insulas* could refer to the Northern Isles and therefore to the earldom.[46] Man and the Hebrides are of course also north of Dublin and north of Gerald's own area of operation. Ian Beuermann suggests

(Woodbridge, 2023), pp 17–42, at pp 27–34. **42** AI 1103.5. The item in the Annals of Ulster is essentially the same but without the 'unawares' part (AU 1103.6). **43** Duffy, 'Irishmen and Islesmen', 113; Etchingham, 'Insular Viking zone', 150. In contrast Candon ('Muirchertach', p. 407) felt that Magnus's raid on Ulster was coordinated with Muirchertach's unsuccessful offensive against Domnall Mac Lochlainn. **44** Power, 'Magnus Barelegs' expeditions', 128. **45** Gerald of Wales, *Expugnatio Hibernica*, ch. 17 (*Expugnatio Hibernica: The Conquest of Ireland by Giraldus Cambrensis*, ed. and trans. A.B. Scott and F.X. Martin (Dublin, 1978), pp 68–9). **46** Clare Downham writes that 'Ascall had escaped … probably to the Orkneys': 'Living on the edge: Scandinavian Dublin in the twelfth century' in her *No horns on their helmets? Essays on the Insular Viking-Age*

that for Gerald 'the Hebrides were sufficiently far north to merit this description'.[47] In his *Topographia Hibernie*, Gerald uses this expression in quite a general way, referring to all islands north of Man, even including Iceland.[48] It therefore seems likely that the usage in the *Expugnatio* encompasses but is not limited to the Northern Isles. Man and the Hebrides would historically have been a more common place of refuge for rulers of Dublin.[49] Yet perhaps the scale of the invasion of Dublin encouraged a more distant refuge. Ascall presumably hoped to be received well there, which might imply previous connections and diplomatic relations.

In 1171, Ascall tried to retake the city of Dublin with aid from the Scottish Isles, perhaps including Orkney. Gerald relates that 'Askulv the former chief of the men of Dublin ... put in to the banks of the Liffey with Norwegians and men from the isles in sixty boats (*Hasculphus olim Dublinensium princeps ... cum Norwagiensibus et insulanis in sexaginta navibus... Avenliphense litus obtinuit*).'[50] It does seem likely that wherever Ascall sought refuge would also be the place whence he hoped to gain mercenaries and reinforcements to support his bid to regain power in Dublin. It is possible that 'Norwegian' is being used more generically as 'Norse' here; indeed, in his *Topographia*, Gerald refers to 'The northern islands almost all of which are held by Norwegians (*De insulis borealibus quarum fere omnium dominium Norwagenses habent*)'.[51] This suggests an awareness of the cultural milieu of the Isles, and perhaps particularly of Orkney and Shetland. The other major source for the invasion is what has been dubbed *La geste des Engleis en Yrlande* ('The Deeds of the Normans in Ireland', still commonly referred to as *The Song of Dermot and the Earl*, the title given to it by Goddard Orpen in his 1892 edition). It too refers to the presence of forces from beyond Ireland: 'They came from the Islands and from the Isle of Man (*De Eir vindrent e de Man*)'.[52] The French word *Eir*

(Aberdeen, 2013), pp 157–78, at p. 157. **47** Ian Beuermann, 'Sveinn Asleifarson and the Irish Sea: *Mestan Ójafnaðarmann í Vestrlöndum*' in Alex Woolf (ed.), *Scandinavian Scotland – twenty years after. The proceedings of a day conference held on 19 February 2007* (St Andrews, 2009), pp 131–68, at p. 148. **48** John J. O'Meara, 'Giraldus Cambrensis in *Topographia Hibernie*. Text of the First Recension', *PRIA*, 52C (1948–50), 113–78, at 117, 175; for Iceland being the largest of the islands of the north see 120 and 141. **49** For example, Echmarcach Rognvaldsson /mac Ragnaill fled to Man on his expulsion from Dublin in 1052.The Annals of Inisfallen relate that Gofraid mac Arailt meic Ragnaill, king of Dublin, was 'over sea' *dar muir* (AI1075.2), which Benjamin T. Hudson assumes is a reference to 'the Kingdom of the Isles': *Viking pirates and Christian princes: dynasty, religion, and empire in the North Atlantic* (Oxford, 2005), p. 167. **50** Gerald of Wales, *Expugnatio Hibernica*, ch. 21 (ed. and trans. Scott and Martin, pp 76–7). Overall see Duffy, 'Irishmen and Islesmen'. **51** Gerald of Wales, *Topographia Hibernica*, ed. O'Meara, p. 117, trans. John J. O'Meara, *Gerald of Wales, The history and topography of Ireland* (London, 1982), p. 24. Gerald also writes that the Ostmen came 'from Norway and the northern islands (*de Norwagie et insularum borealium*)', ed. p. 175, trans. p. 122. **52** *The Deeds of the Normans in Ireland: La Geste des Engleis en Yrlande. A new edition of the chronicle formerly known as The Song of Dermot and the Earl*, ed. and trans. Evelyn Mullally (Dublin, 2002), p. 111, l. 2260.

'Islands' appears to be a new coinage and borrowed from Old Norse *Eyjar*.[53] As with the Norse term, there is some ambiguity about which archipelagos are intended; the opposition of this to Man might suggest somewhere further away, namely the Northern Isles, or it might be the more usual pairing of Man and the Hebrides.[54] There has also been some support for identification with Orkney, though.[55] As noted above, the Norse *Eyjar* more often denotes the Northern Isles. Lindy Brady notes that in these lines about Ascall's attempt on Dublin the 'poem makes clear that there is still an Irish Sea "Viking" network in the insular region, operating late in the twelfth century'.[56] For *The Song*'s purposes, it was perhaps not the specific origins of the combatants that mattered, but conveying a sense of the assembled coalition faced by the side it favours.

According to Gerald, the forces of 'Norwegians and men from the isles' were 'led by John, surnamed "the Wode", which means "the mad" or "the impetuous"' (*duce Iohanne agnomine 'þe Wode', quod Latine sonar 'insano' vel 'vehementi'*).[57] John the Wode dies in the fighting while Ascall is captured and afterward executed. John's presence in the battle is corroborated in *The Song*, where he is listed after those from the islands and Man:

E de Norwiche I vint Johan:
Un vassal, Johan le Devé,
Ad Mac Turcul od sei mené
Nevu ert cil [al] riche reis
De Norwiche, solum les Yrreis

'and from Norway there came John: /
Mac Turcail brought with him /
a vassal called John the Wode. /
He was the nephew of the mighty king /
of Norway, according to the Irish'[58]

53 Mullally, *Deeds of the Normans*, p. 160, n. on l. 2261. 54 Evelyn Mullally, the text's recent editor, supports the latter: *Deeds of the Normans*, p. 160, n. on l. 2261. 55 Goddard Orpen stated that *Eir* referred to 'the Islands, here meaning Orkney' in his edition's Index Locorum (*The Song of Dermot and the Earl: An Old French poem from the Carew Manuscript No. 596 in the Archiepiscopal Library at Lambeth Palace* (Oxford 1892), p. 330) but in his Notes to l. 2263 opted for a more general identification as 'the islands off the north and west coasts of Scotland' (p. 290). Martin in the notes to *Expugnatio* refers to the *The Song* as providing the information that 'they came from the Orkneys and the Isle of Man' (p. 305 n. 106). 56 Lindy Brady, 'Heroic biography and the Viking age around the Irish sea', *PRIA*, 122C (2022), 123–41, at 138. Brady does not identify the islands (though cites Mullaly's Hebridean identification) or John the Wode. 57 Gerald of Wales, *Expugnatio Hibernica*, ch. 21 (ed. and trans. Scott and Martin, pp 76–7). 58 *The Deeds of the Normans in Ireland* (ed. and trans. Mullally, p. 111, ll. 2261–6).

It seems unlikely that a nephew of the king of Norway would be the vassal of the king of Dublin. Noting that the then Norwegian king Magnus Erlingsson was fifteen years old, Evelyn Mullally suggests that *nevu* might denote a kinsman rather a nephew specifically.[59] It is possible that John the Wode was a potential vassal of Ascall, in the sense that he had been promised land in return for his military aid.[60] Given the audience of the poem, as well as its sources of information, the description of John's affiliation could reflect how he was perceived by Diarmait Mac Murchada's Irish and Anglo-Norman circles.[61] Apart from the brief reference to 'Norwegians' in Gerald's account, which was cited above, there is no other evidence of direct involvement from Norway itself. This was the period of the Norwegian civil wars (1130–1240); although in the early 1170s there was a lull in opposition to the rule of Magnus Erlingsson, one wonders if Norwegians with royal blood would have concerned themselves with events in Ireland given the changeable situation in Norway, unless they purposely fled the unrest.[62] Items for 1171 in the Irish annals refer to an Eoan who aids Ascall and is killed in the process; he is surely the same figure as John the Wode in Gerald and *The Song*. Eoan is an acceptable Irish rendering of John or Johannes.[63] In the Annals of Tigernach he is simply 'Eoan the Norseman (*Eoan Lochlandach*)', but in the Annals of Ulster he is 'Eoan (the Mad) from the Orkney islands (*Eoan (Mear) a h-Innsibh Orc*)'.[64] This certainly suggests an Orcadian involvement in the failed effort to reclaim Dublin.

John of the colourful epithet has been identified as the similarly vivid character Svein Asleifsson (Sveinn Ásleifarson), who is otherwise known almost exclusively from *Orkneyinga saga*, due to similarities in the way their deaths are presented in the saga and in accounts of the invasion.[65] The internal chronology of the saga would provide a date of Svein's raid on Dublin between

59 Mullally, *Deeds of the Normans*, p. 160, n. on ll. 2263–6. 60 Patrick Wadden, pers. comm. 61 See Beuermann, 'Sveinn Asleifarson', p. 147. 62 In the 1150s there was an alliance between Earl Erling *skakke*, the *de facto* ruler of Norway and the earlier Earl Rögnvald Kali Kolsson (d. 1158), so it is not inconceivable that Erling might have sent some men to Orkney to help his allies in later years. However, such an event does not feature in *Orkneyinga saga*, which has a strong interest in Norwegian affairs. The later submission of Earl Harald *ungi* ('the young', d. 1198) to King Magnus Erlingsson is recorded in *Orkneyinga saga* (ed. Finnbogi Guðmundsson, p. 290 (§109)). This occurs in the chapter following the death of Svein Asleifsson (§108), who will be discussed presently. 63 Old Irish generally does not have initial /j/. The examples in annalistic items of ecclesiastical figures with the name Mael Ioin/Eoin (AU 918.1; AU 931.3) support the identification of Eoan with Johannes, following the element *Máel* 'servant/devotee of'. 64 AT 1171.7; AU 1171.2 (my trans.). The Orkney identification made by AU is also found in the later AFM 1171.17 and ALC 1171.2, though not the 'mad' cognomen; likewise, the fifteenth-century Mac Carthaigh's Book 1171.1, as discussed by Beuermann, 'Sveinn Asleifarson', pp 147, 163–4. 65 Thomson, *New history*, p. 119. There is mention of Sveinn and a son in *Íslendinga saga* where they are connected to real historical personages (James H. Barrett, 'Svein Asleifarson and 12th-century Orcadian society' in Olwyn Owen (ed.), *The world of the Orkneyinga Saga: the broad-cloth Viking trip* (Kirkwall, 2005), pp 213–23, at p. 215).

1165 and 1180 though it is specifically stated to have occurred in autumn, whereas in Gerald of Wales's account the battle is around Pentecost (16 May) 1171.[66] Attempts have been made to reconcile the chronology.[67] Born in Caithness, Svein is a warrior with an uneasy relationship with the earls, prone to feud but influential enough to be dubbed 'the great earlmaker' in modern scholarship.[68] The exploits of Svein amount to a quarter of *Orkneyinga saga* as a whole, while the first version of the saga concluded with his death.[69] Judith Jesch detects 'clear evidence of local, oral traditions based on an eyewitness account' in 'the "Sveinian" strand' of the saga.[70] On the other hand, Thomson comments that 'absence of confirmation for his adventures casts doubts on the whole corpus of stories' about Svein Asleifsson.[71] For the present discussion, it is most relevant that *Sveinn* and *Eoan* or *John/Johannes* are not the same name.[72] By way of comparison, renderings of *Sveinn* (Forkbeard), father of Cnut all retain the initial 's'.[73] There is, moreover, a recognized form of *John/Johannes* in Norse, *Jón*. While it is conceivable that Svein Asleifsson went by an alternative or suppletive name in the Irish Sea region, there are also likely to have been warriors and leaders from the earldom who do not feature in *Orkneyinga saga*. It is also possible that Svein participated in an expedition to Dublin led by someone else.

While the specific involvement of Svein Asleifsson is uncertain, this does not rule out the possibility of an Orcadian presence at the siege of Dublin. References in the accounts of Gerald and *The Song* both to 'Islands' and to 'Norway' may have referred to, or at least included, the earldom. The relevant item in the Annals of Ulster confirms the presence of a specific Orcadian. Given the magnitude of the engagement, it seems likely that the ruler of Dublin would have sought aid from far and wide, as was certainly the case with the battle of Clontarf over 150 years earlier.

* * *

Thus far, only political or military interactions have been explored, but other types of links between Dublin and the earldom must also be considered. There

66 Barrett, 'Svein Asleifarson', p. 219. **67** Beuermann, 'Sveinn Asleifarson', pp 141–8; to explain *The Song*'s reference to Norwegian kinship, he also highlights that not much is known of Sveinn's mother's background, implying that she might have been Norwegian (pp 141, 160). **68** Judith Jesch, 'Presenting traditions in *Orkneyinga saga*', *Leeds Studies in English*, 27 (1996), 69–86, at 71. **69** Ian Beuermann, '*Jarla Sögur Orkneyja*: status and power of the earls of Orkney according to their sagas' in Gro Steinsland, Jón Viðar Sigurðsson, Jan Erik Rekdal and Ian Beuermann (eds), *Ideology and power in the Viking and Middle Ages: Scandinavia, Iceland, Ireland, Orkney and the Faroes* (Leiden, 2011), pp 109–62, at p. 148, stating Sveinn's death as being in 1171. **70** Jesch, 'Presenting traditions', 83, see also 81. **71** Thomson, *New history*, p. 119. **72** Beuermann, 'Sveinn Asleifarson', p. 140. **73** AU1035.1: *Sain*; AT 1035.1 *Sdaín*; CS 1035.1: *Stain*. Admittedly this is a small sample, as he features in the Irish annals only in the obit for his son.

are no obvious ecclesiastical links. The patron saint of the earldom was the martyred earl Magnus Erlendsson (d. *c.*1117), but there is no church of St Magnus in Dublin.[74] Indeed, there is no evidence of churches or devotion to Magnus in the Hebrides or the western seaboard of Scotland.[75] This lack of the usual intermediary perhaps decreased the likelihood of it reaching Dublin and Ireland. The cult of Magnus did achieve some popularity in the North Atlantic, particularly in Iceland, but this was not until the thirteenth and fourteenth centuries.[76] This was of course after Dublin was taken over by the Anglo-Normans.

The picture provided by archaeological evidence is mixed. Architecturally, there are distinct differences between house types in Dublin and the Northern Isles.[77] However, true comparison cannot be made due to the lack of rural buildings associated with the Norse presence in Ireland. In terms of the earldom's material culture, David Griffiths highlights an Irish Sea element, which might have impacted Orcadian identity.[78] He highlights contacts 'with Dublin and the Irish Sea' being among those 'most persistently visible amongst the finds' from the settlements in the Bay of Skaill area.[79] A notable example is a copper-alloy crutch-headed ringed pin that has parallels in Dublin to pins which date to the eleventh or early twelfth century.[80] Aside from another instance from Jarlshof, Shetland, this type is very rare in Scotland, although a similar type, crutch-headed stick pins, are extant from Jarlshof and from the Udal, North Uist. Dublin is the most likely origin of the crutch-headed ringed pin, since the majority of ringed pins have been found there, along with signs of their production.[81] Steven Ashby argues that the types of combs found at the Bay of Skaill reflect 'contact with Ireland, the Irish Sea or the Western Isles' in the tenth and eleventh centuries, but no specific mention is made of Dublin.[82] Irish Sea connections are also suggested by items in the

74 For the cult as a whole, see Haki Antonsson, *St Magnús of Orkney: aspects of his cult from a European perspective* (Leiden, 2007). **75** See Rosemary Power, 'Scotland in the Norse sagas' in G.G. Simpson (ed.), *Scotland and Scandinavia, 800–1800* (Edinburgh, 1990), pp 13–24, at p. 20; Caitlin Ellis, 'The development of the cult of Magnús: the interplay between saints, bishops and earls of Orkney' in Ragnhild M. Bø and Jón Viðar Sigurðsson (eds), *The cult of saints in Nidaros archbishopric: manuscripts, miracles, objects* (Turnhout, 2022), pp 111–41, at pp 127–8. **76** Margaret Cormack, *The saints in Iceland: their veneration from the conversion to 1400* (Brussels, 1994), pp 119–21; Ellis, 'Development of the cult', p. 128. **77** For the most recent treatment of Hiberno-Scandinavian house types, see Rebecca Boyd, *Exploring Ireland's Viking-Age towns: houses and homes* (Abingdon, 2023). **78** David Griffiths, 'Status and identity in Norse settlements: a case study from Orkney' in James H. Barrett and Sarah Jane Gibbon (eds), *Maritime societies of the Viking and medieval world* (Leeds, 2015), pp 219–36, at p. 232. **79** Griffiths, 'Status', p. 232. **80** Thomas Fanning, *Viking Age ringed pins from Dublin* (Dublin, 1994), pp 41–6. **81** Griffiths, 'Status', p. 226. See also David Griffiths, 'Copper-alloy finds' in David Griffiths, Jane Harrison and Michael Athanson, *Beside the ocean. Coastal landscapes at the Bay of Skaill, Marwick, and Birsay Bay, Orkney: archaeological research, 2003–18* (Oxford, 2019), pp 238–42, at p. 239. **82** Steven P. Ashby, 'Combs' in Griffiths et al. (eds), *Beside the ocean*,

Skaill hoard from Sandwick, Orkney, which is thought to have been deposited about 960–80, particularly by the elaborate brooches, though the decoration suggests they may have been made on Man specifically.[83] A large number of motif-pieces have been found in Dublin, but these are scarce in the area of the earldom, perhaps due to its more rural environment compared with the urban concentration of motif-pieces; comparisons between motif-pieces from the Northern Isles and the Dublin examples have occasionally been suggested.[84] The ring-chain motif on a bone strap-end from Sandwick, Mainland has parallels in Dublin and beyond.[85]

Plain silver arm-rings, known as 'ring-money', were produced in Scandinavian-influenced Scotland *c.*950–1065 and were most likely associated with the earldom of Orkney.[86] There are very few examples of Scotto-Scandinavian ring-money in Ireland, where it has only been found in four hoards and as a handful of stray finds.[87] None of these are near Dublin.[88] Some coins minted in Dublin have been found in southern Scotland and the southern Hebrides.[89] As Aaron Critch notes, this distribution is 'away from the areas of strongest Orcadian influence' but instead closer to the Irish Sea region, so either Dublin coinage was not reaching further north due to a lack of economic traffic or it was melted down on arrival.[90] The latter was generally the case in England, but crucially that kingdom had a regulated currency, which excluded foreign coinages, unlike the earldom. Either way, it is a noticeable lack.

On the subject of the economy, it is difficult to specifically prove direct trade between Dublin and the earldom of Orkney, though it is likely to have

pp 243–51, at p. 251. **83** James Graham-Campbell, *Viking art* (London, 2013), pp 105–6. **84** Uaininn O'Meadhra, 'Viking-Age sketches and motif-pieces from the northern earldoms' in Colleen E. Batey, Judith Jesch, and Christopher D. Morris (eds), *The Viking Age in Caithness, Orkney and the North Atlantic: select papers from the proceedings of the Eleventh Viking Congress, Thurso and Kirkwall, 22 August–1 September 1989* (Edinburgh, 1993), pp 423–440, at respectively pp 435 and 438. **85** Caroline Paterson, 'A Viking-Age bone strap-end from near St Peter's Kirk' in Griffiths et al. (eds), *Beside the ocean*, pp 305–6. **86** Barbara E. Crawford, *Scandinavian Scotland* (Leicester, 1987), pp 133–4; Aaron Critch, '"How are princely gifts repaid by your powerful friends?": ring-money and the appropriation of tradition in Insular Viking politics, AD 900–1065' (PhD, University of Cambridge, 2015), pp 10–11, 191, 238. **87** Maeve Sikora, 'A hoard of Viking-Age silver ring money from Lugrabrack, Horn Head, Co. Donegal', *JRSAI*, 142–3 (2012–13), 191–6, at 193. **88** There are finds from Woodstown and from Knockmaon, Co. Waterford (Critch, 'Princely gifts', 9, fig. 1.3) and hence therefore near other Hiberno-Scandinavian centres. **89** There are two single finds from Whithorn, one coin in a southern Hebridean hoard, sixteen coins in a Perthshire hoard and ten from a lost hoard from Fife: Gareth Williams, 'Monetary economy in Viking-Age Scotland in the light of single finds', *Nordisk Numismatisk Årsskrift* (2002), 163–72, at 165; D.M. Metcalf, 'The monetary significance of Scottish Viking-age coin hoards, with a short commentary' in James Graham-Campbell (ed.), *The Viking-Age gold and silver of Scotland (AD 850–1100)* (Edinburgh, 1995), pp 16–25, at pp 23–4. **90** Critch, 'Princely gifts', pp 158–9.

occurred. The Northern Isles have been seen as a stopping off point between mainland Scandinavia and the Irish Sea region, where ships could resupply.[91] Norwegian-produced steatite vessels seem to have been traded across the North Atlantic and to have stimulated intensified production from Shetland's steatite outcrops; the increase in Orkney of the use of Shetlandic steatite vessels has been associated with the Norse presence there.[92] There are some finds of steatite objects in Dublin which could be from Norway or Shetland.[93] However, these are low in number compared to other settlements.[94] Unlike steatite, many of the traded goods are likely to have been perishable and therefore have not left much trace in the archaeological record. The earldom was able to exploit its marine resources and become involved in the stockfish trade. It thus took part in the general trend of the eleventh-century rise of cod fishing as part of North Atlantic trade in dried cod as suggested by stable isotope analysis from many sites, as well as anecdotal documentary evidence.[95] In Orkney and Caithness there is evidence of 'highly intensive and extensive fishing for cod and saithe' from the eleventh to thirteenth or fourteenth centuries.[96] Additionally, Orkney produced a grain surplus in the Viking Age and medieval period.[97] Some of this may have ended up in Ireland. It does seem, though, that Dublin was increasingly economically orientated towards southern Britain and the continent, at least by the twelfth century. Of the merchants recorded as a member of Dublin's guild merchant in the period from *c.*1190 to 1265 only one or two can be identified as being from the earldom.[98] There are a handful from the Isle of Man,[99] and more from western

91 Olwyn Owen, 'The Scar boat burial and the missing decades of the Early Viking Age in Orkney and Shetland' in Jonathan Adams and Katherine Holman (eds), *Scandinavia and Europe 800–1350: contacts, conflict, and coexistence* (Turnhout, 2004), pp 3–34, at p. 26, referring to the eighth and ninth centuries. **92** Amanda Forster, 'Steatite, resource control and the Orkney earldom' in Owen (ed.), *The world of the Orkneyinga Saga*, pp 55–74, at pp 55–9. **93** Patrick F. Wallace, 'The archaeology of Viking Dublin' in Howard Clarke and Anngret Simms (eds), *The comparative history of urban origins in Non-Roman Europe: Ireland, Wales, Denmark, Germany, Poland and Russia from the 9th to the 13th century* (Oxford, 1985), pp 103–46, at p. 135. **94** Forster, 'Steatite', p. 61 see also p. 68 for the distribution map, where Ireland is not included even in the 'low numbers of Shetland vessels'. **95** Griffiths, 'Status', p. 227; James H. Barrett, 'Economic intensification in Viking Age and medieval Orkney, Scotland: excavations at Quoygrew' in Andras Mortensen and Símun V. Arge (eds), *Viking and Norse in the North Atlantic: select papers from the proceedings of the Fourteenth Viking Congress, Tórshavn, 19–30 July 2001* (Tórshavn, 2005), pp 264–83. Fish-processing middens have been found at Freswick, Robert's Haven, St Boniface and Quoygrew. **96** Jennifer F. Harland and James H. Barrett, 'The maritime economy: fish bone' in James H. Barrett (ed.), *Being an islander: production and identity at Quoygrew, Orkney, AD 900–1600* (Cambridge, 2012), pp 115–38, at p. 137. **97** See James H. Barrett, 'Introduction: the study of island societies' in idem (ed.), *Being an islander*, pp 1–10, at p. 5. **98** *DGMR*: Johannes de Boue, which the editors identify as being Bow in Devon or Orkney, pp 46, 136; Johannes de Hoirk, which they identify as Dunnet Head, Caithness, pp 39, 141. **99** *DGMR*: Isle of Man, pp 31, 40, 84, 93, 103. **100** *DGMR*:

Scotland, particularly Galloway, Renfrewshire and Argyll.[100] Many are from eastern and central Scotland.[101] Presumably merchants from the earldom could obtain goods from Dublin via such mainland Scottish merchants without personally having to make the longer journey to Ireland.

* * *

In conclusion, the surviving written record testifies to a few specific instances of direct political links between the earldom of Orkney and the town of Dublin. These amount to big events across the British-Irish Isles, notably the battle of Clontarf and the invasion of Ireland, which had reverberations across Europe. Temporary cooperation occurred in 1058 and in the early twelfth century under Muirchertach Ua Briain and Magnus Barelegs. This also underlines the importance of Norwegian involvement in bringing together areas of Scandinavian settlement or influence in Britain and Ireland. Three case studies also involved Man and the Hebrides as political and military players, while in the remaining case study Magnus Barelegs raided those islands on his way from the earldom to Ireland. The archaeological evidence suggests some commonalities and connections, but not to a noticeably high degree; again, Man and the Hebrides may have been intermediaries for material culture as well as being the meeting place of these two important spheres of influence. There was, of course, regionalism within the Insular Viking Zone, and not all the interconnections were of equal frequency and strength. While direct links have been difficult to pinpoint, Orkney and Dublin were clearly part of the same world.

Argyll, pp 79, 85; Carrick, Scotland (Karrec, Karrek), pp 83, 84; Cathcart (near Glasgow), p. 44; Dumfries, pp 13, 16, 18, 22, 31, 53, 55, 106; Galloway, pp 4, 7, 47, 69, 94, 104, 105; Galston, Ayrshire, p. 42; Greenock, Renfrewshire, pp 12, 14, 69, 72, 77, 78, 81, 83, 85, 99, 103, 107; Kirkcudbright, pp 21, 40, 45, 53; Kirkton, Dumfries, p. 9; Knockdolian, Ayrshire, p. 56; Ochiltree, Ayrshire, p. 73; Port Lamont, Renfrewshire, p. 93; Renfrew, pp 15, 23, 25, 94, 105; Rutherglen, near Glasgow, pp 53, 92, 93, 106; Saddell, Argyll, p. 74; Salen, Argyll, p. 13. **101** *DGMR*: Berwick, pp 29, 70, 79, 86, 91, 105, 107; Burnmouth, Berwickshire (Burmeide,)p. 12; Carnbo, pp 58, 80, 83, 102; Edinburgh, p. 7; Holyrood, Midlothian, pp 17, 25, 31, 51, 100; Hume, Scotland, p. 45; the Isle of May, p. 8; Jackton, Lanarkshire, pp 30, 62; The Lothians, pp 76, 82; Melrose, p. 86; Musselburgh, Midlothian, pp 42, 55; Riddell Selkirks, p. 107; Stirling, pp 1, 6. 7, 9, 15, 16, 24, 28, 102; Temple, Midlothian, p. 104. This includes a couple quite far north (and therefore closer to Caithness and the earldom), near the southern coast of the Moray Firth: Coleburn (near Elgin), pp 20 44, 95; Rafford (near Forres), p. 85. There are also a number of merchants that are not localized beyond 'Scottish' or 'Scotland' in general (e.g., *Scoche*, *(le) Scot*, *Albanach*): Scotland, pp 11, 16, 18, 29, 36, 44, 59, 65, 78, 80, 82, 88, 92, 93, 96, 99, 100, 101, 103, 104, 106, 108, 109. The present author could not confidently localize four places: Ardnurcher, pp 23, 21, 56, 61 (identification 135), Crosshill, p. 29 and Crosslee, p. 75 (both identified, p. 139), and Loch Loch, pp 55, 71 (identified, p. 146). Likewise, the editors identify (at p. 148) Newark (pp 41, 105) as 'Fife, Renfrews./Selkirks'.

The leather finds from excavations at Chancery Lane and Ship Street Great, Dublin

JOHN NICHOLL

INTRODUCTION

The excavations at Chancery Lane/Ship Street Great which began in 2018 (conducted by Archaeological Projects Ltd), recovered a total of 263 identifiable leather artefacts, as well as approximately 1,600 pieces of leatherworking scrap. The identifiable finds included 6 knife sheaths, 34 lengths of belts or straps, 26 complete or almost complete medieval shoes and boots, 22 medieval shoe upper fragments, including 14 with vamp-stripes, 18 top-bands, 110 individual soles or sole parts, 2 off-cuts with clear bite marks from human teeth and 13 finds of incomplete bags or pouches. The large quantity of scrap consists mainly of off-cuts of worn shoes as well as unusable pieces of hide trimmings. The bulk of the finds can be dated from the eleventh to the fourteenth century with thirty examples of late seventeenth-century footwear parts and two shoes of late nineteenth- to early twentieth-century date.

OFF-CUTS AND WASTE

The manufacturing process of leather generated a variety of waste pieces of differing size and shape, which can be classified as primary, secondary and tertiary waste. Primary waste was generated in the preparation of hides for leatherworking and can be recognized as flesh-shavings, fur-trimmings or off-cuts of rough leather trimmings from the edge of a hide. Secondary waste was produced when individual parts were being cut to shape and such waste is frequently recognized as regular, geometrically-shaped off-cuts of various sizes. A particularly significant off-cut piece, a triangular shape with one concave side, is usually the product of soles being cut from a hide. Such intersectional off-cuts are a good indicator of footwear manufacture or repair. Tertiary waste is composed of narrow strips of leather, which were trimmed from artifacts in the final stages of assembly (Mould 2003, 3245–7).

Glossary of footwear terms (see Goubitz 2001, Swann 1982)

Backpart: the part of the upper which wraps around the heel of the foot.
Flesh side: inner surface of leather or hide.
Forepart: front part of shoe or sole.
Grain: outer surface of leather with hair follicles.

Heel seat: part of shoe on which the heel of the foot rests.
Insole: the inside sole of shoe on which the foot rests.
Latchet: top edge of the quarters extended into straps for tying shoe with laces or buckles.
Outsole: sole in contact with the ground.
Quarters: parts of shoe which wrap around the heel, joining the vamp at the side seam and each other at the back seam.
Rand: narrow strip of leather between the upper and sole.
Sole Seam: also referred to as 'lasting margin', the seam joining the upper and sole of a turnshoe.
Tongue: extension of the vamp above the instep.
Top-band: an extra band of leather stitched to the top-edge of shoe to raise the height of the quarters.
Upper: consists of the vamp and quarters.
Vamp: front part of the upper covering the toes and instep.
Waist: narrow part of shoe under the arch of the foot.

MEDIEVAL FOOTWEAR

There are a total of twenty-six complete or almost complete examples of footwear, where elements of both upper and sole are present. There are a further twenty-five upper fragments, which are sufficiently intact as to allow classification by style or type. All fifty-one examples can be divided into two basic footwear types, consisting of wrap-around upper ankle boots and wrap-around upper ankle shoes. In both cases, the pattern for the upper is cut from a single piece of leather, which wraps around the foot with a seam on the medial (inner) side. Any gaps in the pattern are filled with completion pieces or inserts. The two types can be differentiated by the height of the quarters. In the case of the shoe, the top-edge of the quarters is generally at, or below, the ankle while the top-edge of the boot is above the ankle. A further distinction can be made by the pattern of sole employed.

All of the boots and shoes in the assemblage were made with separate soles and uppers. There are no examples of one-piece shoes in which the sole and upper were cut from the one piece of leather. Various sub-types can be identified by the manner in which the shoe or boot was secured to the foot through the use of front-lacing, side-lacing or wrap-around thonging. A distinct sub-group is not secured to the foot with either lacing or thonging and can be classified as a slip-on style.

Front-laced ankle boot with V-extension to the sole

There is only a single example of this type of boot, 1945:2 (fig. 4.1), which was recovered from a late tenth- to eleventh-century context. It was worn on the

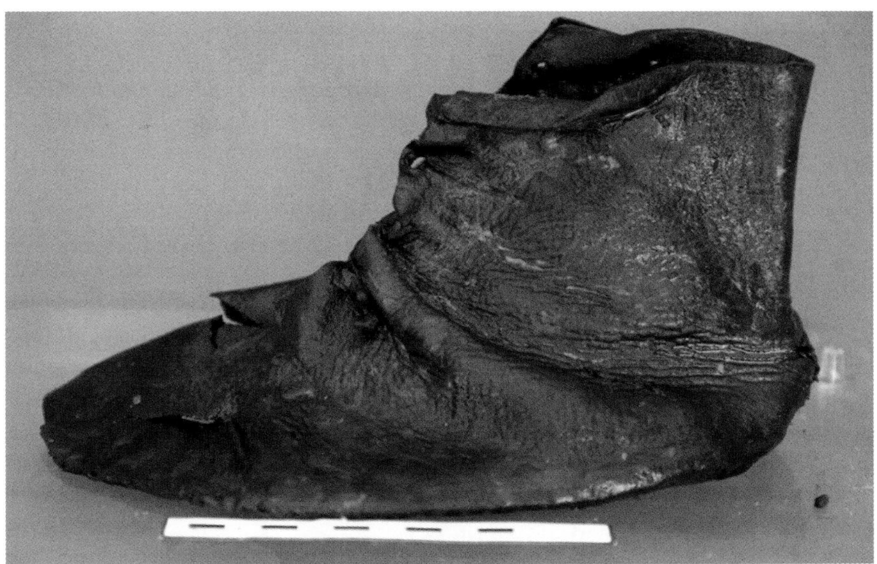

4.1 10th-century front laced boot (Photo: J. Nicholl)

left foot and has a high medial side seam. The quarters would have reached to mid-calf height on the wearer's leg. The boot is open at the instep and the lateral quarters extend slightly over the instep. The boot was secured with a lacing-thong, which passed through four pairs of lace-holes in the leading edges of each quarter. A fragment of this leather lacing-thong is still in situ. The effect of pulling the lace tight has caused the leather to gather in a series of folds above the instep, a feature noted on similarly high boots of tenth-century origin from Drumclay crannog, Co. Fermanagh (Nicholl 2016).

The forepart of the vamp has broken into three pieces, but it is possible to reconstruct it accurately and to match the two faces of the side seam. Only a fragment of the sole remains, but a V-shaped slot at the back of the heel identifies it as once having fitted a sole with a distinctive V-extension. This heel extension is a very significant feature. It is generally associated with footwear of Scandinavian origin or influence from the late ninth to late eleventh century (Hald 1972). The boot is similar to examples of the Class 1b wrap-around ankle boots with V-extensions to the sole recovered from Fishamble Street 2 in the Dublin excavations (O'Rourke 1988, 56–7; Wallace 2016, 276–8). However, it differs in the fastening method, as the Fishamble Street examples do not use front-lacing but were secured with a length of thong, which tied around the foot. The Fishamble Street Class 1b boots are dated from the mid- to late tenth century (ibid., 61).

There have been numerous examples of shoes and boots with V-shaped heel extensions recovered from Viking-Age sites such as York in England (Mould

2003) and Haithabu (Hedeby) in Schleswig (Groenman-van Waateringe 1984). The cutting patterns for the Haithabu Type 6 and 7 ankle boots are almost exactly similar to this boot, the only difference being in the method of closing the ankle boots. The Haithabu examples were secured with a length of thong, wrapped around the ankle and anchored by a pair of keeper-slots on either side of the instep (ibid. 29, taf. 3, 11 and 12).

None of the York ankle boots of comparable date and with V-extensions to the soles were front-laced, the preference here being for toggle and loop fastening. A number of ankle boots recovered from tenth-century levels in the excavations at Drumclay crannog had V-extensions to the soles. However, the uppers were of a completely different design, with a separate vamp and backpart and were closed with toggles and loops (Nicholl forthcoming). In Waterford, two fragmentary examples of soles with V-extensions at the heel were found in a mid-twelfth-century context and were considered to be a very late example of this style of footwear (O'Rourke 1997a, 718).

Apart from the sole, there are no exact parallels for 1945:2 in the literature, except for a single shoe, described by O'Rourke as 'miscellaneous footwear' and recovered from an eleventh-century context in Fishamble Street site 2 (O'Rourke 1988, 131, fig. 30). It is an ankle boot, for the right foot, with four pairs of lacing-holes on the leading edges of the quarters. On the medial side, two of the lacing-holes are located below the side seam and two are located above it, matching the layout of the lacing-holes on 1945:2.

Ankle-boot with keeper-slots and drawstring fastening around ankle

There are six examples of this style of wrap-around upper, which use a length of thong, threaded through keeper-slots to secure the boot to the foot. The slots can be cut as single pairs on either side of the instep, or as a line of multiple slots. In general, the keeper-slots are cut with vertical incisions. However, in the case of 1788:4, the slots are cut obliquely, to give a distinctive trapezoid shape to the keeper, which was fashionable in the mid- to late twelfth century (Volken 2014, 114, fig. 193). A second fragmentary upper from the same context, 1788:3, has the more common vertical slot pairing, which gives a rectangular shape to the keeper and was in use from the mid-twelfth century onwards (ibid., 140–3, fig. 187).

1237:152 is an almost complete, child's size, ankle-boot with a composite sole and a pair of anchor slots on either side of the instep. It is unclear whether the sole was originally a composite type or whether this is the result of repair. This type of sole tends to be a feature of late twelfth- to fifteenth-century footwear (Goubitz 2001, 85). The seat section is missing, and the remaining forepart was seamed at the waist/tread area. There is some wear damage to the toe area of the sole and the upper toe area is scuffed and worn. Ankle-boots, using this style of fastening, have been recovered from mid-twelfth to mid-thirteenth-century contexts at Patrick Street (O'Rourke 1997b, 167–8, fig. 77) and High Street in Dublin. The High Street example is particularly interesting as it is coin-dated to the mid-twelfth century (O'Rourke 1988, 123, fig. 49).

A variation of the basic paired anchor slots arrangement, using threaded thong keepers, began to appear in the late twelfth to early thirteenth century (Volken 2013, 141–3; Goubitz 2001, 57–9). It employed two or three vertical lines of keeper-slots on either side of the ankle, which allowed the lacing thong to be wrapped securely and evenly around the foot several times. A short length of thong was threaded through the keeper-slots and the lace proper was then treaded through the loops formed by the vertical thong. 1237:160 is an almost complete boot upper, which uses this arrangement. A second example from the same context 1237:161 is a boot upper completion piece with two vertical lines of keeper-slots with the lengths of thong *in situ*. Ankle boots with similar lacing arrangements have been recovered from twelfth-century contexts at High Street in Dublin (O'Rourke 1988, 123, fig. 51). The Chancery Lane/Ship Street examples are also similar to the Class VI ankle boots recovered from mid- to late twelfth-century contexts in Waterford (O'Rourke 1997a, 705–07, figs 18.1–2) and to the Type B ankle boots excavated from mid- to late twelfth-century contexts in Aberdeen in Scotland (Thomas 2021, 132). Ten boots of this style were recovered from early twelfth- to thirteenth-century contexts in excavations at 16–22 Coppergate in York (Mould 2003, 3319–21, fig. 1654).

Ankle boot with front toggle fastening

There are two incomplete examples of this style of closure. They were recovered from late thirteenth- to early fourteenth-century levels. 309:17 (fig. 4.2) consists of a torn section of the lateral quarter of an ankle boot. The top edge extends into a single, broad, integral latchet with three long slits at its terminal for toggle closing. A length of very narrow edge-binding remains. This was sewn around the outer edge of the latchet and continued along the top-edge. 320:1 is also the lateral quarters of a front toggle fastened boot; however, in this case, the latchet only has two toggle slits, both of which appear to have been torn in use. There is also a short length of edge-binding, which is confined to the top-edge and does not continue round the entire latchet as with 309:17.

Latchet terminals with single or multiple toggle anchor slits are a common feature of thirteenth- and early fourteenth-century footwear. Latchet fastening boots and shoes with two toggle anchor slits were recovered in excavations at Tobin Street (Gleeson 2003, 362–3) and Christchurch in Cork (O'Rourke 1997c, 319) and dated to the late thirteenth to early fourteenth century, as were examples from York (Mould 2003, 3322–4). At King John's Castle in Limerick, similar finds from the castle ditch were given a mid-thirteenth- to early fourteenth-century date (Hodkinson 2016, 422–3). Examples from Waterford, classified as Class VII, included a shoe recovered from a stone-lined pit, with a

4.2 Child's ankle shoe (Photo: J. Nicholl)

pair of toggle slits on the latchet, and was dated to the early to mid-thirteenth century (O'Rourke 1997a, 707–10, fig. 18.2.1). 309:17 is exceptional in having three anchor slits with only a single example from London, dated to the mid-thirteenth century, having a similar arrangement (Grew and deNeergaard 1988, 58, fig. 91).

Ankle boot with side-lace fastening

A third method of ankle-boot fastening utilized a side-lacing arrangement. A vertical line of four or six paired lacing-holes was located on either side of the foot opening, on the medial side of the shoe. A reinforcing facing piece was sewn on the inner flesh face using tunnel stitching. This fastening method was popular from the late twelfth to the fifteenth century (Goubitz 2001, 175–8, fig. 4; Volken 2014, 147–9, fig. 201).

Four almost complete uppers and six completion pieces with side-lacing holes were recovered, as well as three lace-hole facing-pieces. The impressions of a missing facing with a line of tunnel stitching can be seen on each upper and completion piece. 1955:30, an incomplete upper, still retains both sides of the closing seam. The opening had been cut into the quarters on the medial side from the top-edge to within 20mm of the sole seam. Four pairs of holes were made on either side of this opening. The impression of the facing is clearly visible on the inner flesh face. 1320:394 and 1955:492 are incomplete facing-pieces. The outer edges of both have clear impressions of the whip stitching with which they were sewn in place. Side-laced ankle boots are common finds and have been recorded in Dublin from thirteenth-century levels at Site D in Patrick Street (O'Rourke 1997b, 166–7, fig. 77) and from thirteenth-century levels at Thomas Street (Nicholl 2018b). In Aberdeen, examples were recovered from mid-twelfth to mid-thirteenth-century levels (Thomas 2021, 133) and from early thirteenth-century levels in London (Grew and deNeergaard 1988, 56–7, figs 89, 90).

Ankle shoe with side-lace fastening

1237:162 is the only example of this style of shoe and it was recovered from a thirteenth-century context. It is an incomplete single piece upper, which wraps around the foot and is closed on the medial side. The lower section of the wing and sole seam has been torn away and only the upper three lacing-holes remain. The impression of a facing-piece with tunnel stitching is visible on the inner flesh face. The opposing wing has also been torn away. A continuous line of edge/flesh whip-stitch impressions indicate where an edging band was sewn along the top-edge. The thirteenth-century dating is consistent with the fashion for side-laced ankle boots as outlined above.

Ankle shoe with drawstring fastening in keeper-slots

There are nine examples of wrap-around shoes or shoe uppers using this method of fastening but differing in the number of keeper-slots. It is a method of fastening shoes, which was popular from the mid-tenth to the late twelfth century (Volken 2014, 131–4). Three of the finds use widely spaced pairs of keeper-slots while all of the others have a single, continuous line of keeper-slots around the foot.

1857:1 is an almost complete example of an ankle shoe with a continuous line of keeper-slots around the ankle, commencing at the medial side seam and ending at the opposite point on the lateral quarter. It was recovered from a tenth-century context. It consists of a one-piece wrap-around upper for the right foot. The upper has a line of keeper-slots running around the ankle, just below the top-edge with fragments of the lacing thong still *in situ*. The area at the heel was reinforced internally with a half-moon-shaped heel-stiffener and a length of rand. The shoe appears to have been repaired in antiquity. A broad top-band has been added to raise the height of the quarters and two triangular-shaped inserts to close the instep opening and form a tongue. These inserts are not joined and the gap between them continues as a short slit in the instep, to facilitate putting on the shoe. The effect has been to convert the original ankle-shoe into an ankle-boot. The sole is broad and heavily worn with traces of tunnel stitching showing where a repair clump had been added. The sole is not waisted and is essentially straight from toe to heel, both of which are slightly oval in shape. Broad soles of this basic shape are recorded from tenth-century levels in York (Mould 2003). A line of fine tunnel stitch holes, similar to those used for vamp-stripes also runs obliquely across the toe area and may have helped to fix the clump in place. Alternatively, a toe-cap similar to 653:20 may

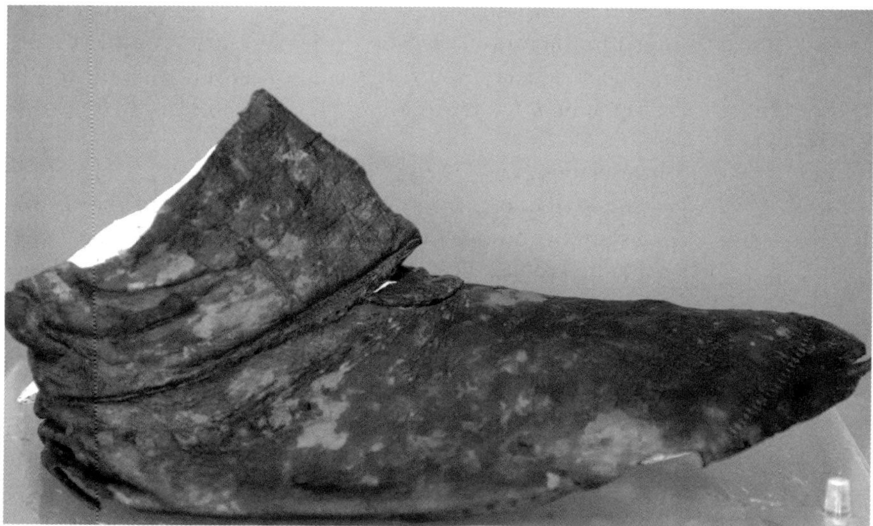

4.3 Ankle shoe with drawstring fastening in keeper-slots and impression of toe cap (Photo: J. Nicholl)

have been added. Two further fragmentary uppers, also from tenth-century contexts, were fastened with a single thong through a continuous line of keeper-slots.

1810:50 (fig. 4.3), from a late eleventh- to early twelfth-century context, also has a line of stitching across the toes and the imprint of a toecap can be seen on the outer grain surface. In this case, the shoe was secured to the foot by drawstring threaded through widely spaced and rectangular keeper-slot pairs. The sole, while still broad and straight, is slightly waisted and has a rounded seat and blunt pointed toe, which suggests an evolution of the earlier unwaisted sole. Toecaps were a feature of a number of Class 1 shoes recovered from Site B, Level 2 and Site D, Level 1 in excavations at Patrick Street in Dublin and dated to the early thirteenth century and late twelfth century respectively (O'Rourke 1997b, 165–7, fig. 76).

1742:4, from a twelfth-/thirteenth-century context, is another example of an upper using a continuous line of thong keepers to fasten the shoe with most of the thong still *in situ*. It differs slightly from the Patrick Street Class 1 in the shape of the instep as it lacks the extended tips on either side of the foot-opening slit. However, the lacing thong continues across this slit as in the Class 1. The vamp has also been decorated with two vamp-stripes, which suggest a mid- to late twelfth-century date for this upper. An upper of similar pattern, decorated with a row of punched circle-and-dot motifs instead of a vamp-stripe, was recovered from a mid- to late twelfth-century context at excavations in Dean Street, Dublin (Nicholl 2018a). The combination of continuous anchor keeper-slots and a vamp-stripe is a feature of the Class III ankle shoes from Waterford, dated to the mid-twelfth century (O'Rourke 1997a, 704–10, fig. 18.3). Shoes of this style were also recovered from mid- to late twelfth-century levels at King John's Castle in Limerick (Hodkinson 2016, 421–3, fig. 190a).

1237:168 is an interesting example of a fashionable shoe, which has been decorated with a vamp-stripe and a short, pointed, out-turned toe. It was fastened with a drawstring running through a row of keeper-slots on either quarter but not continuing around the ankle. Shoes with short, out-turned toes and vamp-stripes were recovered from early to mid-twelfth-century contexts in London (Pritchard 1991, 230–34). The combination of all three features in 1237:168 suggests a mid- to late twelfth-century date for this upper, after which these design features, particularly the vamp-stripe, fell out of fashion.

1829:2 is a low-cut ankle shoe with a deep, concave instep. Two carefully made incisions follow the curve of this opening across the instep and appear to be an extra decorative feature, which would have allowed a coloured sock to be seen. A decorative vamp-stripe runs from the edge of the outer incision at the instep to the toe. It was fastened to the foot with a drawstring through paired, trapezoid-shaped keeper-slots on the quarters, a twelfth-century fashion (Volken 2014, 114, fig. 193). The upper style is similar to the Class I shoes from Waterford, which are dated to the late twelfth century (O'Rourke 1997a, 709, fig. 183).

Slip-on style ankle shoe

There are three examples of slip-on style shoes with wrap-around uppers and medial side seams in the assemblage. The most intact is 669:3, which is virtually complete and is from a twelfth-century context. The upper is probably goatskin and the vamp was decorated with a pair of vamp-stripes from instep to toe. To complete the upper, an extra piece was added to the quarters on the medial side and a heel-stiffener was added internally to strengthen the rear of the shoe. The sole is broad across the tread and straight from waist to seat. The curving out-turned toe is quite distinctive. The shoe is a good example of the fashion for a short, out-curving toe-extension as seen also on 1237:168, which first appeared in the eleventh to twelfth century (Swann 2001, 52–3). The combination of vamp-stripes and out-turned-toe suggest a mid- to late twelfth-century date for this shoe.

1237:17 (fig. 4.4) is an almost complete upper for the left foot. It is seamed on the medial side. The instep pattern has been shaped with a deep V, which forms two peaks on either side of the opening. At the rear of the ankle, a rectangular tab projects upwards to facilitate pulling the shoe on to the foot. At some point in its use, the shoe had become too tight and a roughly-cut slit was made at the instep to make it less tight a fit. The top-edge had been decorated

4.4 Slip-on indoor shoe with low-cut sides (Photo: J. Nicholl)

4.5 Slip-on shoe (Photo: J. Nicholl)

with whip stitching all along its length. Shoes from early twelfth-century contexts in London, with a single peak at the instep, slightly raised at the ankle and no lacing thong, have been interpreted as indoor shoes (Grew and deNeergaard 1988, 12–13, fig. 11). Shoes of similar style were also recovered from early to mid-thirteenth-century contexts and seem to suggest the continued use of indoor shoes (ibid., 15–16, figs 18, 19). Shoes of this design were also recovered in twelfth- to thirteenth-century contexts at Swinegate in York (Mould 2003, 3300–01, fig. 1633). The double peak at the instep of 1237:17 and the raised tab at the rear of the ankle are unusual and perhaps represent a development of the single peak and raised backpart design of the York and London shoes. The absence of any fastening method may also suggest its use as an indoor shoe.

1952:8 (fig. 4.5) is an almost complete slip-on shoe worn on the left foot. It was recovered from a late thirteenth- to early fourteenth-century context. The one-piece, wrap-around upper is seamed on the medial side. The upper design is very similar to the York examples mentioned above. The vamp rises to a pointed tongue at the instep with a matching raised point at the heel. The upper is made of goat leather and is quite thin. There is some wear damage to the forepart and a hole has worn through in the area of the big toe. The composite-type sole is also of very thin leather, only 1.5mm thick, with a seam at the waist. A section of the forepart has broken away. The light materials used in making the shoe suggest it was intended as an indoor shoe; however, the wear damage indicates it may have been worn outdoors as well. Goubitz assigned this type of shoe to his Group 1B with examples ranging from the ninth to the fifteenth century. He speculated as to the evolution of the design from earlier Coptic-style shoes, especially in Ireland and to their occurrence in clerical graves on the continent, funerary shoes not being required to be very robust, as they were not intended for use in the normal way (Goubitz 2001, 219–23, figs. 1–7). Figures on the late fifteenth-century Creagh tomb in Ennis friary, Co. Clare are depicted wearing shoes of this style (Hunt 1974, pls 238, 242), which suggests the continuation of the style in Ireland as well.

Vamp-stripes (fig. 4.6)

There was a total of fourteen examples of shoe vamps still bearing the traces of decoration with embroidered vamp-stripes. Three of the group had been decorated with a pair of parallel lines of embroidery while the other eleven examples had only a single stripe. In all cases, the decorative stripes ran from toe to instep. This form of decoration, using coloured silk or woollen thread, is thought to have derived from the vamp seam closures of early medieval shoes. The thread was sewn through the grain surface of the leather using a plait-stitch through tunnel stitch holes, which leaves two parallel lines of fine stitch holes (Pritchard 1988, 75–9). Such stitch holes are visible on the vamps of the Chancery Lane/Ship Street examples. Of the ten complete vamps and vamp fragments recovered from the Deer Park Farms excavations, all were decorated with a single vamp-stripe from toe to instep, which suggests its popularity during the seventh and eighth centuries (Neill 2011, 370–72). In Denmark, examples are known from excavations in the cathedral city of Lund, which have been dated to the period 1020–50 (Hald 1972, 143–8). Finds of footwear with embroidered stripes on wrap-around uppers from London (Grew and de Neergaard 1988, 13) and on Class I, Class II and Class III shoes from Waterford (O'Rourke 1997a, 704–8) indicate a twelfth- to mid-thirteenth-century date range for the popularity of this decoration in urban settings. At York, twenty-five examples of embroidered vamp-stripes were found on shoes recovered from eleventh- to early thirteenth-century levels after which they

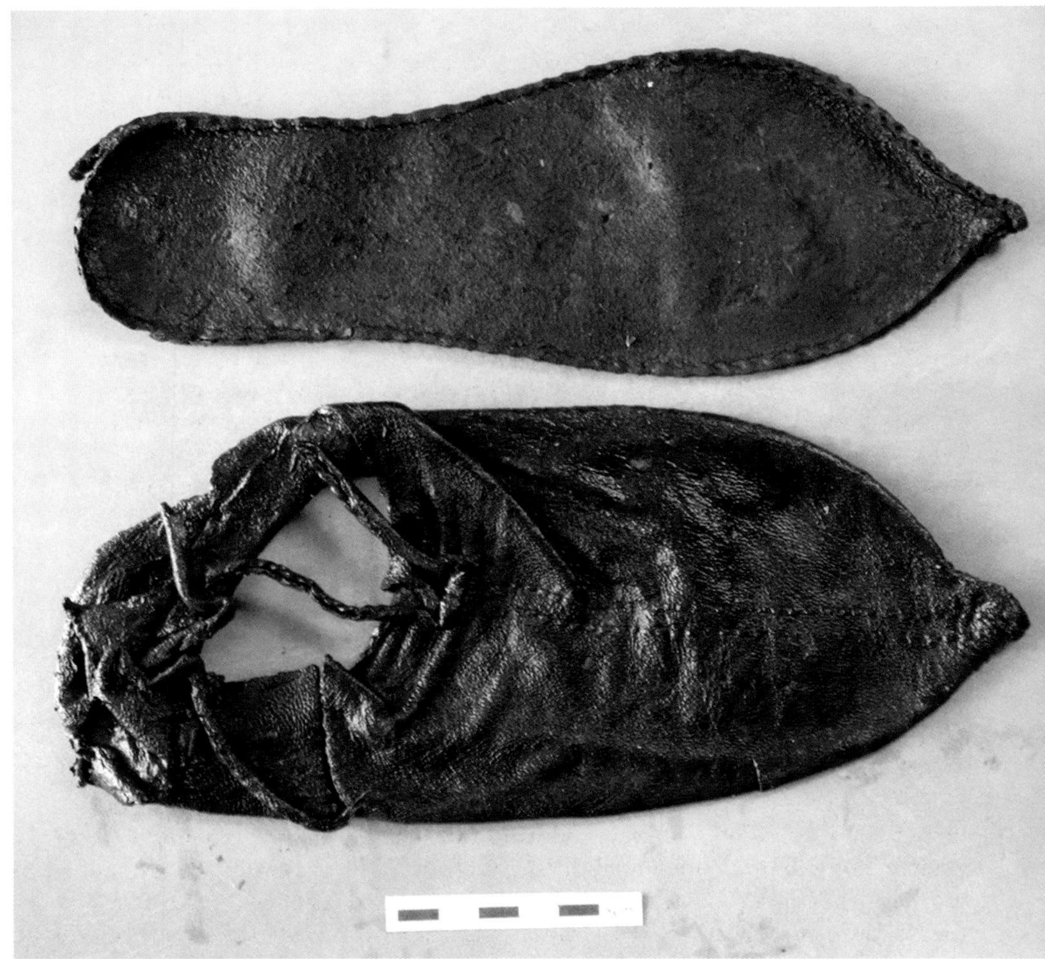

4.6 Shoe with double vamp-stripe and projecting toe (Photo: J. Nicholl)

appear to have fallen out of fashion (Mould et al., 2003, 3341–2). A single example of a late twelfth to early thirteenth-century shoe was recovered in excavations in Dundalk, Co. Louth. It was made with a one-piece wrap-around upper with a single seam on the medial side of the foot. This style of shoe had a blunt or oval pointed-toe with a distinct waist and seat. The vamp shows faint traces of stitching from a decorative embroidered stripe (Nicholl 2019). The Chancery Lane vamp-stripes are in keeping with the general fashions of twelfth- to thirteenth-century footwear and display a good variety of the footwear styles of the period.

Top-bands

There was a total of 18 top bands recovered in the excavation. All of the top-bands are from late tenth- to early twelfth-century contexts with the exception of two examples of thirteenth-century date. Top-bands were generally made from lengths of folded leather, which were closed with a binding stitch before being sewn to the top-edge of a shoe or boot. Occasionally, a single, unfolded strip was used. Top-bands functioned as a way of raising the height of the quarters to give more protection to the foot. Three of the examples are made of wide folded strips and are similar to the top-band on 1797:1, an eleventh-century shoe. A similar style of wide top band was recovered from a late twelfth-century context in Dublin (O'Rourke 2000, 148–9) and from a mid-twelfth-century context in Waterford (O'Rourke 1997a, 722–7). A narrower example, 1237:35a, from a late twelfth-/thirteenth-century context had been decorated with two parallel rows of incisions, which may have been embroidered. Two examples of this style of decorated top-band were recovered from a late twelfth- to early thirteenth-century context in Waterford (ibid.). A number of shoes with decorated top-bands were recovered from late eleventh- to thirteenth-century levels in York (Mould 2003, 3315–17).

Soles (fig. 4.7)

There was a total of 110 soles and sole fragments recovered, which included 18 intact soles, 32 incomplete soles, 11 composite sole parts, 5 clump repair pieces, 4 tread off-cuts, 10 seat off-cuts and 30 sole fragments. Prior to the twelfth century, shoe soles tended to be almost straight and tapered from the widest area at the tread to the seat. This resulted in a very broad waist of almost 90mm in width. However, during the twelfth century, shoemakers began to cut soles, which followed the shape of the foot more closely (Goubitz 2001, 82–5). Waists became narrower and more defined and this trend can be seen in the swayed soles of the Chancery Lane/Ship Street assemblage, of which there are 50 examples.

A swayed sole curves to follow the shape of the foot. This curve, at the lateral edge of the tread can be quite extreme, producing a wide tread area and giving a very asymmetrical shape to the sole. Soles with a narrower tread have a more symmetrical shape. The soles can be differentiated as broad-, medium- and narrow-waisted and loosely dated as follows: broad (40–50mm), twelfth to mid-thirteenth century; medium (35–40mm), early to mid-thirteenth century; narrow (30–35mm), mid-thirteenth to fourteenth century. This grouping and date range is similar to sole assemblages recovered from Waterford (O'Rourke 1997a), Dublin (O'Rourke 1997b), King John's Castle in Limerick (Hodkinson 2016) and to the very large assemblage of soles recovered from High Street in Dublin (Waterer 1969). Generally there can be an overlap in the use of broad- and medium-waisted soles or in the use of medium- and narrow-waisted ones. Interestingly, all three styles can be seen in the soles from C1237 and C1240,

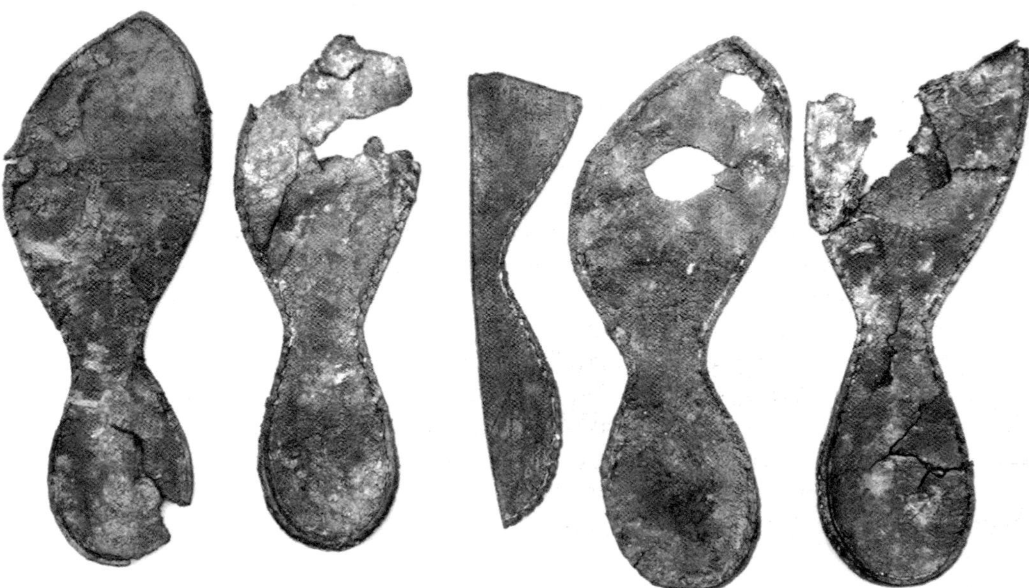

4.7 Swayed soles (Photo: J. Nicholl)

with the broader examples in C1237 and the narrower-waisted soles in C1240 and medium-width examples in both contexts.

There are thirty-two examples of incomplete swayed soles, which were categorized on the basis of two of the areas of the tread, waist or seat remaining intact or almost intact. In all cases, either the tread or seat areas have been completely worn away and the remnant was considered as beyond repair. They show the same style and date range as the intact examples and can be grouped on the basis of waist-width. Two of the intact soles are for children's shoes. Both are slightly swayed at the tread but are almost straight from waist to seat. 651:18 has never been used and may have been intended as a repair sole. The remaining sixteen intact soles are in adult sizes and, while complete, they show varying degrees of wear damage in the toe and seat areas, where the original thickness of the leather has been worn down.

Composite swayed soles

Composite soles were made from a heel and forepart, which were seamed across the waist and there are eleven composite sole parts in the assemblage. An edge/flesh butt seam was used to join the two parts. It is impossible to tell whether the use of a composite sole resulted from a repair or the shoe had been assembled with a two-part sole to begin with. Worn or damaged soles could be repaired by the removal of either the seat or tread and its replacement with a new piece of leather. Composite soles are a feature of late thirteenth- to fourteenth-century footwear (Grew and deNeergaard 1988, 49; Goubitz 2001, 85).

1592:8, is an example of a shoe with its composite sole *in situ*. The seat and tread were joined with a seam across the waist. It is possible the shoe was originally made in this way. However, given the damaged nature of the sole forepart and upper it is more likely a repaired shoe, which was beyond any further use. A second example, 1320:397, is the waist section of a composite sole with a length of rand *in situ*, which is holding the two parts together at the waist seam. 1955:32 is a good example of an unused seat repair section. 1955:33 consists of a damaged seat section, which had been cut across the waist and removed for replacement. In the case of 1955:17, the lateral edge of a left shoe sole was removed and replaced with a narrow, crescent-shaped insert. The leatherwork retrieved from C1955 would appear to have come from a workshop specializing in repair. The remaining forty-four sole fragments consist of torn and damaged pieces of tread, waist and seat areas, which were of no further use and beyond repair.

Clump repair

Another, simpler form of repair work involved the use of clump soles. These were roughly-shaped pieces of leather, which were sewn over the damaged area of the sole, usually at the tread or heel. The repair pieces were attached to the shoe using tunnel stitching to protect the seams from damage (Grew and deNeergaard 1988, 89–90; Goubitz 2001, 85). There were only five examples of clump repair soles recovered in the excavation. 653:5 is typical of this type of repair piece. It is roughly shaped to cover the tread area of a sole with a line of tunnel stitches running around the edge of the clump sole. A second example, 1793:2, was shaped to cover the tread area of a swayed sole and attached with tunnel stitching around its edges.

Pouches and bags

There was a total of fifteen finds, which could be classified as having originally functioned as bags or pouches, based on their size, shape and seams. There were no intact bags or pouches. 1864:18, from a tenth-century context, consists of the remnants of the front and rear panels of a large D-shaped pouch, measuring approximately 200mm x 240mm. A short length of the side panel also remains. The three parts were sewn inside out with a closed seam and then turned to have the seam on the inside. 1320:2 is an off-cut section of a roughly-made bag, probably of D-shape. The front and back panels were sewn with a length of thong, which was knotted at one end and then passed from side to side through opposing awl holes. Other fragments appear to have been deliberately cut up for salvage before being discarded. Each consists of a large remnant of what must have been a larger artefact. 1237:367 is a roughly square fragment, 160mm x 140mm, torn on three sides but with a decorative edge binding *in situ*. This edging is sewn in place with three parallel lines of stitching. Another rectangular fragment, 1237:170, measuring 150mm x 70mm, has lost its edge binding but the lines of parallel awl holes clearly show where it had been located. 1240:58, measuring 360 mm x 130mm, retains traces of seams on two edges and has been cut for salvage on the other two sides.

Harness and belts

There were forty sections of belts and straps of various lengths and widths recovered in the excavation. Four were found in C1237 and a further twenty-four in C1240 along with a large quantity of off-cut shoe parts and other leatherworking waste. The remaining twelve straps were isolated finds. The location of C1240, as a concentrated deposit of leatherworking waste within C1237, and the clustering of twenty-four strap and belt lengths in a single context, suggests the debris from a workshop with an emphasis on the making and repair of harness and belts rather than simply shoe repair. Eleven of the straps recovered from Chancery Lane/Ship Street have had buckles removed for reuse before the damaged piece was discarded.

Harness (fig. 4.8)

There is a variety of different strap types ranging from a single thickness belt to a heavy reinforced strap. Some of the strap lengths were folded around a reinforcing strip of thick leather and seamed along one edge with grain/flesh stitches, which passed through the full thickness of the layers. Other examples were wrapped around a reinforcing core and closed with a central, edge/grain butt seam on the inner side. A number of straps of this style were recovered from medieval levels in York (Mould et al. 2003, 3396–9). In the case of 1240:38, a short section was removed on the inside of the strap to create a single layer to facilitate the fixing of a buckle. This single layer was folded back over the buckle pin and bar and fixed with six rivets. A folded, back-seamed strap of this style was recovered from an early thirteenth-century context in London, still attached to an iron stirrup (ibid.). Unusually, one edge of 1240:38 has been cut to resemble the zigzag pattern of saw teeth. The cuts are very precisely made and avoid damaging the centre seam and may have been intended as a decorative element of the finished strap. Alternatively, as this would have weakened the finished strap, it may actually represent some whittling by the leatherworker in an idle moment.

Other pieces show clear impressions of decorative metal studs and may represent the remnants of decorated horse-harness. An almost intact example of a decorated palfrey or chest-strap from a horse's harness was recovered from a medieval well during excavations at Caherduggan Castle, Co. Cork. The

4.8 Harness straps (Photo: J. Nicholl)

palfrey was fitted with an elaborate copper alloy buckle at both terminals and studded with over forty shield and hanger decorative pieces (Nicholl 2012).

Belts: dress accessories

There were twelve other fragments of leather belts, which are probably best considered as dress accessories rather than harness. The relative fragility of these examples compared to the heavier reinforced straps suggest their use as items of dress. Single layer pieces have lines of awl holes along each edge and rivet holes at intervals along the centre line. Belts and girdles decorated with coloured thread, strap-ends, buckles, metal studs and fittings were common articles of dress in the medieval period (Pritchard 1991). The excavations at Dublin Castle in 1985–7 uncovered a total of thirty-four similar examples from the moat fill and were dated to the thirteenth/fourteenth century (Lynch and Manning 2001; O'Rourke 1988). A number of belts of this style was also recovered from excavations at Christ Church in Cork (O'Rourke 1997c, 329–31) and Waterford (O'Rourke 1997a, 724–5, fig. 18.8). Another example, dated to the early thirteenth century, was recovered at Patrick Street in Dublin (O'Rourke 1997a, 170–73, fig. 80). A belt fragment from the excavations in Winetavern Street in Dublin still retained a line of decorative studs set between a line of stitch holes along each edge and is a good example of what the Chancery Lane examples may originally have looked like (O'Rourke 2000, 148–9, fig. 74).

Decorated leather

Apart from the knife sheaths (below), there were only three other small pieces of decorated leather. Two are probable remnants of belts and show a simple form of impressed linear decoration, which runs parallel to the edges on the grain side. 1864:22 of tenth-century date, is a short, rectangular piece cut from a belt. The impressed decoration runs along both edges and represents the only attempt at embellishment. The second example, 1952:3, is of late thirteenth-/early fourteenth-century date and appears to be the terminal of a narrow belt. It is also decorated with impressed lines and one terminal has been shaped to a point to facilitate the use of a buckle. The third piece, 1556:11a, of thirteenth-century date, has been cut from a larger object than a belt. A single impressed line runs along its length, close to one edge. However, there is no indication as to what its original function might have been.

Teeth marks (fig. 4.9)

The semi-circular impressions of human teeth or bite marks can be seen on two irregularly-shaped off-cut pieces. The two pieces were found among a large quantity of leatherworking debris. 1237:4 has been bitten on twice and the impressions are quite distinct. The teeth appear to be flat and blunted through wear. 1240:23A also has two closely spaced bite marks but the impressions are less distinct and some teeth appear to be missing. Such teeth or bite marks on leather were first recognized and identified on pieces of secondary waste leather from York. In all, there were five examples found there from various locations at tenth-century levels. Some of the fragments had single bite marks while others had several (Carlisle 1998, 7). It would appear to have been a fairly widespread practice with other finds being recorded elsewhere in England, Scotland, and Germany. The reason for the bite marks is unclear with various suggestions ranging from an element of the manufacturing process to a person in severe pain biting on the leather (Mould 2003, 3264–5). A single example was recorded in the excavations at the Corke Tower in Dublin Castle where a triangular off-cut piece with one set of teeth impressions was found in a Viking-Age cesspit (O'Rourke unpublished excavation report). The 2014 excavations at Drumclay crannog, Co. Fermanagh, recovered four examples of triangular off-cuts with bite marks. They were found in association with footwear, of a style which suggests a tenth- to eleventh-century date. Three of the off-cuts were found amongst other leatherworking waste while the fourth is located on a vamp completion piece of a shoe. In this case it seems possible the shoemaker was biting on the vamp to hold the shoe while working on it (Nicholl 2016).

4.9 Scrap pieces with impressions of human teeth marks (Photo: J. Nicholl)

Knife sheaths (fig. 4.10)

There were six knife sheaths (five decorated and one undecorated) recovered in the excavation. Three of the finds are of the Dublin B2 winged type (Cameron 2007, 27–31) although they differ significantly in the detail of their decoration and their state of preservation. 1233:29 is an incomplete top section of a B2 type winged sheath. The closing seam at the back is offset to the left side of the centre line. A pair of suspension holes is located to the outside of the seam. Both the front and back faces are decorated with blank panels within a narrow frame, infilled with oblique hatching.

A second example is almost complete although a section of the blade area is missing. The handle section is almost intact although the right side of the flap appears to have been cut in antiquity. It is fully decorated on the front and back surfaces with impressed linear and interlace motifs. Two suspension holes are punched through the flap on the upper right corner of the front. They cut through elements of the design in this area and indicate they were made after the decoration was completed. The front is decorated with a panel of four-strand plait which wraps slightly around to the back. The pattern is completed with a panel on either edge, infilled with transverse lines. The seam on the reverse of the handle is offset to the left of the centre line. However, a triangular-shaped insert was required to close and complete the seam. This insert is also decorated. The left edge of the insert is sewn with an edge/flesh butt seam, which indicates it was attached before the sheath was sewn shut. The right edge of the triangle forms part of the main seam and is a closely stitched butt seam with edge/grain stitches at 5mm intervals. The triangular insert or completion piece is an interesting detail. Of the one hundred and thirty B2 type sheaths examined by Cameron, only seven had a triangular insert used to complete the seam at the rear of the handle. Of these, six were recovered at Wood Quay and the seventh was of 'unknown context'. All sixty-eight sheaths from Wood Quay are dated 1180–1250 (ibid., 84–112). An eighth

4.10 Decorated knife sheaths (Photo: J. Nicholl)

example of this use of a triangular insert was recovered in an excavation at Vicar Street/Thomas Street in Dublin. Only the complete handle survives. The triangular insert is slightly longer and narrower than 1955:454; however, the decorative motif of four-strand interlace with panels of transverse lines is almost identical (Nicholl 2018b). It is tempting to speculate that both sheaths were made and decorated by the same sheath-maker.

1237:138 is the smallest of the B2 type. It is almost complete, although it too appears to have been deliberately cut in antiquity and a small section is missing from the right front of the handle and right tip of the blade at the rear. A small triangular completion piece is also missing but the combination of edge/flesh butt seam and grain/flesh closed seam on either side of the gap confirm it had once been in place. The handle decoration consists of a single wrap-around panel containing two knotted interlace motifs. The pattern is further embellished with tiny, punched circle-and-dot motifs where the interlace strands overlap. The panel sides are defined with rows of vertical and transverse lines. The decoration on the lower, blade section shows some similarities with 1955:454. In both cases the blade and point are defined with impressed lines and infilled with a single knotted interlace motif. A similar interlace motif can be seen on DLS 194 (Cameron 2007, 109). Knife sheaths of this type have been recovered from early to mid-thirteenth-century contexts in London (Cowgill et al. 1987, 115–19), from early thirteenth-century contexts in Dublin (O'Rourke 2000, 148–52) and Christ Church in Cork (O'Rourke 1997c, 174–5) and from late twelfth- to thirteenth-century contexts in Waterford (O'Rourke, 1997a).

1955:49 is a short segment of the blade area of a sheath, making it impossible to assign to a given type. It is narrow and tapering towards the tip of the blade. A central seam is located at the rear, which is undecorated. The front is decorated with a narrow panel containing an impressed crouching-animal motif. The body of the animal is infilled with a pattern of small dots. This style of decoration was widely used in the late twelfth and the thirteenth century.

1952:160 is an almost complete example of the Dublin B3-type sheath with an offset back-seam to the left of the centre line. The tip and lower section of the blade are broken away. Both the handle and blade areas were decorated but only faint traces of stamped lozenge and impressed plaited motifs remain. Similar sheaths are dated to the late twelfth and thirteenth century in Dublin (Cameron 2007, 114–18).

The final example is best described as a possible knife sheath. It is very roughly made, incomplete and undecorated. It is seamed to the side and retains the shape of the object it was moulded around, possibly a knife blade. Both ends are torn.

Slingshots

1710:7 and 1952:19 are two small elliptical-shaped panels. The central section of each panel has been slashed with four long slits, which may have been intended to increase the flexibility of the piece in order for it to function as a slingshot. In each case, the narrow terminals have been cut away, removing any evidence for a sling-cord and making it impossible to confirm this interpretation. A similarly shaped piece with ten horizontal slits was recovered from an early thirteenth-century context in Waterford, but its function was unknown (O'Rourke 1997c, 730, fig. 18.9.13). A very similarly shaped and sized piece was recovered from a later fourteenth- to fifteenth-century layer at Arran Quay in Dublin. It has four slits along its length and a single perforation at one end and was interpreted as a slingshot (O'Rourke 2004, 217, fig. 24.5). Eight examples were recovered from excavations at 16–22 Coppergate in York, from contexts of tenth- to late thirteenth-century date. In each case, the elliptical-shaped panels had a number of long slits through the wider central section (Mould 2003, 3408–10, fig. 1731).

Off-cuts and trimmings (fig. 4.11)

A large quantity of off-cuts and trimmings was recovered from across the site in general with particular concentrations of material from contexts 1320, 1237 and 1240. As well as the obvious off-cuts and strips, the debris from 1237 and

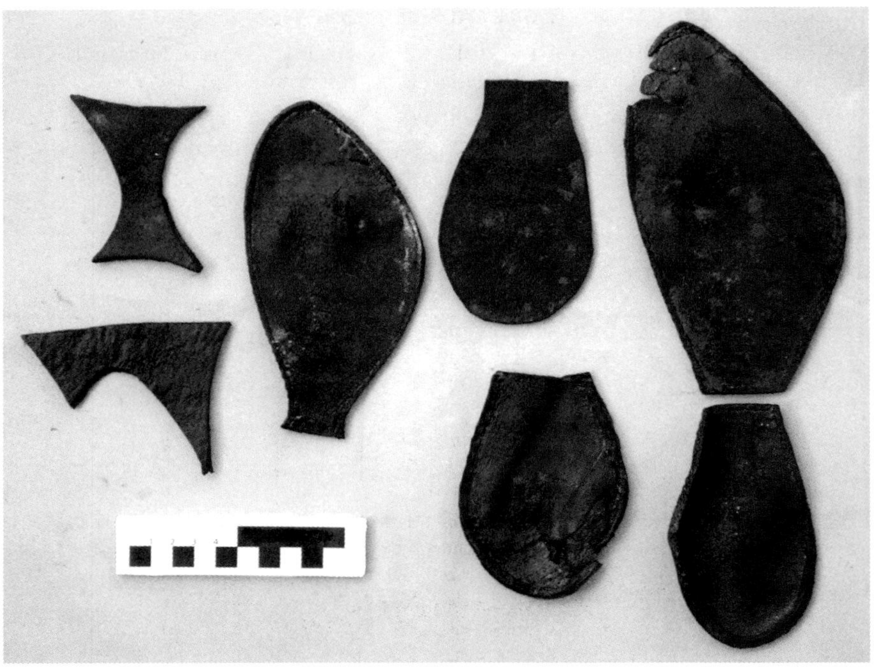

4.11 Cobbling scrap with intersectional pieces and composite soles (Photo: J. Nicholl)

1320 also included numerous worn soles and upper fragments, typical of the refuse from a cobbler's workshop. In the medieval period, the work of the cobbler involved salvaging reusable leather from worn and damaged footwear for use in repair work. Generally, this work involved separating the upper and sole of worn shoes. The cobbler would cut along the sole seam of the upper, which resulted in narrow waste strips. The strips, perforated with the original awl holes, were discarded, leaving the intact upper, which could be used for a smaller shoe or boot. If the upper itself was badly worn, it too would be cut into smaller pieces for reuse. Intact pieces of soles could be reshaped as clump repair patches, with the patch being sewn over a damaged sole area using tunnel stitching. Alternatively, a damaged section of sole could be removed and replaced with an off-cut from a second sole. There are also a number of pre-shaped sole sections such as 1955:32, the seat area of a sole, which was cut from new leather but never used as a repair piece.

As well as the obvious off-cut pieces of worn shoes and boots, there is a large amount of unusable strips and panels of leather, which were trimmed from around the edges of a hide. In the case of wrinkled strips, the perforations and wrinkled appearance are the result of the skin being stretched on a frame while being treated. 1237:365 was discarded due to its blemished surface and the presence of a skin-tag. Large quantities of leatherworking waste similar to the material from Chancery Lane/Ship Street were recovered from the deep deposits of discarded leather of twelfth- and thirteenth-century date at High Street in Dublin. The High Street material was interpreted as the accumulated debris from a community of leatherworkers, working in the area over a long period of time (Waterer 1969).

BIBLIOGRAPHY

Cameron, E. 2007 *Scabbards and sheaths from Viking and medieval Dublin*. Medieval Dublin Excavations 1962–81. Ser. B, vol. 8. Dublin. National Museum of Ireland.

Carlisle, I. 1998 *'Man bites leather' shock in York*. Archaeological Leather Group, Newsletter 7.

Cowgill, J. et al. 1987 (repr. 2000). *Knives and scabbards*. London. Boydell Press.

Gleeson, C. 2003 'Leather artefacts'. In M. Hurley and R.M. Cleary et al. (eds), *Excavations in Cork city 1984–2000*. Cork. Cork City Council.

Goubitz, O. et al., 2001 *Stepping through time: archaeological footwear from prehistoric times until 1800*. Zwolle. Foundation for Promoting Archaeology.

Grew, F. and de Neergaard, M. 1988 *Shoes and pattens*. London. Boydell Press.

Groenman-van Waateringe, W. 1984 *Die lederfunde von Haithabu*, Neumunster.

Hald, M. 1972 *Primitive shoes*, National Museum of Denmark, Copenhagen.

Hodkinson, B.J. 2016 'Leather objects'. In K. Wiggins (ed.), *A place of great consequence: archaeological excavations at King John's Castle, Limerick, 1990–8*. Dublin. Wordwell.

Hunt, J. 1974 *Irish medieval figure sculpture 1200–1600*, Irish University Press. Dublin.

Lynch, A. and Manning, C. 2001 'Excavations at Dublin Castle 1985–7'. In Duffy (ed.), *MD II*, Four Courts Press, Dublin.

Mould, Q. 2003 'Everyday life'. In Q. Mould, I. Carlisle and E. Cameron, *Leather and leatherworking in Anglo-Scandinavian and medieval York*: The Archaeology of York, 17, The Small Finds. York. Council for British Archaeology.

Neill, M. 2014 'The leather objects'. In C. Lynn et al. (eds), *Deer Park Farms*, The Stationery Office, London.

Nicholl, J. 2019 'The leather finds from Church Street, Clanbrassil Street and Bridge Street, Dundalk'. Unpublished excavation report for Archaeology Plan Ltd.

Nicholl, J. 2012 'The leather finds from Caherduggan Castle, Doneraile, Co. Cork'. Unpublished excavation report for Rubicon Archaeology.

Nicholl, J. 2016 'The leather finds from Drumclay Crannog, Co. Fermanagh'. Unpublished excavation report for Northern Ireland Dept. of Communities.

Nicholl, J. 2018a 'The leather finds from Dean Street, The Coombe, Dublin'. Unpublished leather finds report: for ACAS.

Nicholl, J. 2018b 'The leather finds, Thomas Street/Vicar Street, Dublin'. Report for ABH Ltd.

O'Rourke 1988 'The leather finds from Dublin', MA thesis (UCD).

O'Rourke, D. 1997a. In M.F. Hurley et al. (eds), *Late Viking Age and medieval Waterford*, Waterford. Waterford Corporation.

O'Rourke, D. 1997b 'The leather finds'. In C. Walsh (ed.), *Archaeological excavations at Patrick, Nicholas and Winetavern Streets, Dublin*, Dingle. Brandon Press.

O'Rourke, D. 1997c 'The leather'. In R.M. Cleary et al. (eds), *Skiddy's Castle and Christ Church Cork, Excavations 1974–77*. Cork. Cork Corporation.

O'Rourke, D. 2000 'The leather finds'. In A. Halpin (ed.), *The port of medieval Dublin: archaeological excavations at the Civic Offices, Winetavern Street, Dublin, 1993*. Dublin. Four Courts Press.

Pritchard, F. 1988 'Embroidery' in F. Grew and M. deNeergaard (eds), *Shoes and pattens*. Museum of London.

Pritchard, F. 1991 'The small finds'. In A. Vince (ed.), *Aspects of Saxo-Norman London:2 finds and environmental evidence*, London and Middlesex Archaeological Society, Special Paper 2.

Swann, J. 2001 *History of footwear in Norway, Sweden and Finland*. Kungl. Vitterhets Historie och Antikvitets Akademien, Stockholm.

Thomas, C. 2021 'Leatherwork'. In M. Roy et al. (eds), *Pits and boots: excavation of medieval and post-medieval backlands under Bon Accord Centre, Aberdeen*. Archaeopress, Oxford.

Volken, M. 2013 *Archaeological footwear: development of shoe patterns and styles from prehistory till the 1600s*. Lausanne.

Wallace, P. 2016 *Viking Dublin: the Wood Quay excavations*. Kildare. Irish Academic Press.

Waterer, J.W. 1969 'Leather from the High Street excavation, Dublin'. Unpublished interim report for the NMI.

Richard Stanihurst's account of the founding of Ostmantown in 1095: historical fact or fiction?

PATRICK WADDEN

INTRODUCTION

It was widely reported in the summer of 2023 that a team of archaeologists led by Edmond O'Donovan had uncovered a number of human burials while digging on the site of a planned new hotel on Capel Street in Dublin. Media coverage noted that the site was associated with St Mary's abbey, established on the north bank of the Liffey in the twelfth century, initially as a Savigniac and subsequently as a Cistercian monastery. What really caught the eye was that initial findings suggested that some of the burials predated the foundation of St Mary's by potentially as much as a century.[1] Breakingnews.ie quoted O'Donovan as saying

> We have one [burial] that's carbon dated to the 11th century and we have a second burial that was found with a diagnostic stick pin from the 11th century. And that suggests that there was an earlier Christian and potentially monastic foundation here which predates the Savigniac and Cistercian abbey.[2]

As the *Irish Times* pointed out, the find 'indicates the existence of a Christian church predating the foundation of St Mary's abbey, previously thought to be the earliest post-Viking settlement in this part of the city'.[3] The 'part of the city' referred to was Oxmantown, formerly Ostmantown, the medieval suburb of Dublin located on the north bank of the Liffey.[4] There is a long-standing tradition that Ostmantown was established in the aftermath of the English invasion and conquest of Dublin in the late twelfth century, when the Hiberno-Scandinavian inhabitants of Dublin were supposedly expelled from the city proper, which was then located on the south side of the river.[5] In addition to

1 The foundation date most commonly cited is 1139, but there are reasons to doubt the veracity of this. On the shrouded history of the origins of St Mary's, see Aubrey Gwynn, 'The origins of St Mary's abbey, Dublin', *JRSAI*, 79:1 (1949), 110–25. 2 David Young, 'Skeletal remains dating back 1,000 years found on site of planned Dublin hotel', *breakingnews.ie*, 7 July 2023 (accessed online on 10 July 2023 at https://www.breakingnews.ie/ireland/skeletal-remains-dating-back-1000-years-found-on-site-of-planned-dublin-hotel-1498998.html). 3 Olivia Kelly, 'Thousand-year-old skeletons discovered off Capel Street in Dublin city', *Irish Times*, 7 July 2023 (accessed online on 10 July 2023 at https://www.irishtimes.com/ireland/dublin/2023/07/07/thousand-year-old-skeletons-discovered-in-dublin-city-centre-site/). 4 Since we are concerned with the medieval history of the area, I will refer to it consistently hereafter as Ostmantown. 5 For a discussion and

raising the possibility that St Mary's was founded in 1139 on what was already an ecclesiastical site of some kind, the discovery of these skeletons therefore also raises questions about the origins and early history of Ostmantown.

An alternative account of the origins of Ostmantown was reported by Richard Stanihurst (or Stanyhurst) in the late sixteenth century. Stanihurst's account contradicts the traditional narrative by asserting that Ostmantown was established nearly a century *before* the English invasion, in the wake of a distinct and specific Scandinavian invasion of Ireland in 1095. His version of events has not garnered much notice or support, but perhaps warrants further examination in light of the recent archaeological discoveries noted above. The goal of the present article is to identify the sources on which Stanihurst drew, and to examine how he combined them to construct his version of events. Ultimately, it will argue that while Stanihurst's narrative likely owes something to a potentially contemporary, eleventh- or twelfth-century source written in Dublin, it is best understood as a creative blending of sources reflective of his own concerns and preoccupations.

RICHARD STANIHURST AND THE ORIGINS OF OSTMANTOWN

Richard Stanihurst (d. 1618), 'Ireland's greatest humanist', was born in Dublin in 1547 and remained a proud Dubliner throughout his life.[6] His family was part of the social fabric of the city, intimately involved in its economic, cultural, and political life. He attended school in Kilkenny before departing for Oxford, where he graduated in 1568, subsequently studying at Furnivall's Inn and Lincoln's Inn, London. At Oxford he met Edmund Campion, who became his mentor. When Stanihurst returned to Dublin in 1570, Campion accompanied him, and lived for a while in the Stanihurst family home during his six-month stay in Ireland.[7] Beginning in 1577,

critique of this idea, see Emer Purcell, 'The expulsion of the Ostmen, 1169–71: the documentary evidence', *Peritia*, 17–18 (2003–4), 276–94. Seán Duffy has argued on the basis of the surviving charter granting civic liberties to Dublin's residents, that Ostmantown existed prior to Henry II's visit to Ireland in the winter of 1171–2: 'Town and crown: the kings of England and their city of Dublin' in Michael Prestwich, Richard Britnell and Robin Frame (eds), *Thirteenth-Century England X: Proceedings of the Durham Conference 2003* (Woodbridge, 2005), pp 95–117, at pp 95–7. 6 On Stanihurst's life, see Colm Lennon, *Richard Stanihurst the Dubliner, 1547–1618: a biography, with a Stanihurst text, on Ireland's past* (Dublin, 1981); Ian Campbell, 'Irish political thought and intellectual history, 1550–1730' in Jane Ohlmeyer (ed.), *The Cambridge history of Ireland. Vol. II, 1550–1730* (Cambridge, 2018), p. 512. For Stanihurst's self-identification as a Dubliner, see the title page of *De rebus in Hibernia gestis,* ed. and trans. John Barry and Hiram Morgan, *Great deeds in Ireland: Richard Stanihurst's* De Rebus in Hibernia Gestis (Cork, 2013), pp 72–7. For his pride in the city, see his description of it in the same work (*De rebus*, 1.21, ed. and trans. Barry and Morgan, 96–9). See also Lennon, *Richard Stanihurst*, p. 24. 7 On Campion, see Anthony M. McCormack and Terry Clavin, 'Campion, Edmund' in *DIB*

Stanihurst was employed in the London household of the eleventh earl of Kildare as tutor to his eldest son. Political and confessional pressures, compounded by some personal trauma – the deaths of his mentor, wife, and pupil in the space of just two years – precipitated Stanihurst's departure to the Dutch city of Leiden in 1581; he spent the rest of his life on the Continent, writing, studying, and eventually joining the Society of Jesus and entering the priesthood.[8]

Stanihurst identified with those he sometimes called in Latin *Anglo-Hiberni*, and who would later become known as the 'Old English'.[9] These descendants of the Anglo-Norman invaders who came to Ireland in the late twelfth century were overwhelmingly Catholic; as a result, their position in Ireland was coming under increasing pressure in Stanihurst's time from more recent, English-born arrivals, who asserted that 'only those who had proven their loyalty to the crown by becoming Protestant could promote the reform of Ireland'.[10] Confronted by questions regarding their civility, honour, and loyalty, the Old English responded in part through writing history.[11] Stanihurst was at the forefront of this historiographical campaign; his most famous historical work, *De rebus in Hibernia gestis*, published in Leiden in 1584, was a polemical account intended to demonstrate the coarseness of the Gaelic Irish and the role of the Old English community in resisting the Gaels' efforts to expel them and preserving the civility they had introduced to the island. This history, Stanihurst believed, demonstrated that the Old English, rather than the Protestant New English, remained best placed to govern Ireland into the future.[12]

De rebus was not Stanihurst's first historiographical endeavour, however. He had played a crucial role refining and preparing for publication Campion's *Two bokes of the histories of Ireland*, written hastily prior to Campion's departure from Ireland in 1571 from notes compiled while he had lived with the Stanihursts. Thereafter, with Campion's encouragement, Stanihurst contributed two essays to Raphael Holinshed's *Chronicles of England, Scotland, and Ireland,* which was published in 1577. The first of these is called 'A treatise containing a playne and perfect description of Ireland, with an Introduction, to the better

(https://doi.org/10.3318/dib.001436.v1, accessed 21 August 2024). **8** Lennon, *Richard Stanihurst*; for briefer discussions, see Colm Lennon, 'Stanihurst, Richard', *DIB* (https://doi.org/10.3318/dib.008249.v1, accessed 19 August 2024); Margaret Lantry, 'Richard Stanihurst (1547–1618)' (2014) (https://www.ucc.ie/en/cnls/resources/findinglist/richardstanihurst/, accessed 19 August 2024). **9** See, e.g., Stanihurst, *De rebus in Hibernia gestis*, 1.30, ed. Barry and Morgan, pp 108–9. For discussion, see Colm Lennon, 'Richard Stanihurst (1547–1618) and Old English identity', *IHS*, 21 (1978–9), 121–43. **10** Nicholas Canny, 'Afterword: interpreting the history of early modern Ireland: from the sixteenth century to the present' in Ohlmeyer (ed.), *Cambridge history of Ireland II*, p. 639. **11** Lennon, *Richard Stanihurst*, pp 107–8; Brendan Kane, 'A world of honour: aristocratic *mentalité*' in Ohlmeyer (ed.), *Cambridge history of Ireland II*, p. 487. **12** Canny, 'Afterword', pp 638–40.

understanding of the hystories, appertaining to that Island' (hereafter, the 'Treatise'), and the second is an essay on the history of Ireland during the latter part of the reign of Henry VIII.[13] The Treatise includes an abundance of historical information embedded within what is primarily topographical description. In its list of 'The names of the streetes, bridges, lanes and other notorious places in Dublyne', appears the following account:

> Ostmantowne, so called of certayne Easterlings[14] or Normans, properly the Danes that were called Ostmanni. They planted thēselues harde by the waterside néerè Dublyne, & discōfited at Clontarfe in a skyrmishe diuers of the Irishe. … There arriued a fresh supply of Easterlings at Dublyne in the yeare 1095. & setled themselues on the other side of the ciuitie, which of them to this day is called. Ostmantowne, that is, the towne of the Ostmannes, wherof there aryseth great likelyhoode to haue béene a separate towne from the Citie, being parted from Dublyne by the Liffye, as Southwarcke is seuered frō London by Thamesse.[15]

Stanihurst labels all the Scandinavians who came to Ireland 'Ostmen', a term he describes as a synonym of 'Danes' and 'Normans' (i.e., Northmen). In noting the violent nature of the original Scandinavian invasion and settlement of Ireland, he identifies the battle of Clontarf as reflecting the animosity between the (Gaelic) Irish and the new arrivals, though Stanihurst's belief that the Scandinavians 'discomfited' the Irish in the battle is an interesting inversion of the more common view that it was a victory for Brian Bóraime.[16] There is no suggestion that the arrival of another wave of Ostmen in 1095 resulted in comparable conflict; rather, Stanihurst states simply that the new

13 Richard Stanihurst, 'A treatise containing a playne and perfect description of Ireland, with an Introduction, to the better understanding of the hystories, appertaining to that Island', and 'The thirde booke of the Historie of Ireland, comprising the raigne of Henry the eyght' in Raphaell Holinshed, *The first volume of the chronicles of England, Scotlande, and Irelande* (London, 1577), iii.1r–28v, 76–115 (leaves are numbered in the portion of the volume containing the Treatise, while pages are numbered elsewhere). 14 The term E(a)sterlings originated in England in the thirteenth century to refer to people from the east, most commonly traders from the Baltic coasts and the Hanseatic League (*Oxford English dictionary*, s.v. 'Easterling (*n.*)', December 2024, https://doi.org/10.1093/OED/4147694790). The term is more famous with some due to its use by Tolkien for one of the races of men in *The Lord of the Rings*. Stanihurst, and following him Meredith Hanmer (see below), use this term, one probably more familiar to their contemporaries, as a synonym for the Ostmen. But both authors clearly identify their Easterlings/Ostmen as Scandinavians, Stanihurst in the section quoted here and Hanmer elsewhere. 15 Stanhurst, 'A treatise', 11v. 16 The idea that the Dubliners 'won' the battle of Clontarf is not without support in either medieval sources or modern scholarship. See, e.g., Benjamin Hudson, *Viking pirates and Christian princes: dynasty, religion, and empire in the North Atlantic* (Oxford, 2005), pp 103–4. For a more recent discussion of the different sources in which the battle is recorded and their varying assessments of the outcome, see Seán Duffy, *Brian Boru and the battle of*

migrants established themselves opposite Dublin on the north side of the Liffey, creating a settlement that was subsequently incorporated into the city.

This story does not appear in Stanihurst's later, more famous work. There, the foundation of Ostmantown is discussed in passing during his account of the invasion of Dublin in 1171 by its Hiberno-Scandinavian former king, Askulf, after it had been conquered by the Anglo-Normans. In describing Askulf's background, Stanihurst wrote:

> Men of his race were called Ostmen by our people. Their breed stems from Danish stock. Historians report that they invaded Ireland quite frequently. Their most recent arrival – for it is not relevant at this point to write about any other – is dated to the year 1050 after the birth of our saviour and preserver, at which time they came to the island with an armed and marshalled war band. They provoked the Irish to war, routed their battle array, and finally after slaughtering a huge number of the inhabitants, settled in that region of Dublin, the nearest suburb on the north side of the river. Even now that suburb is called Oxmanstown, i.e. town of the Ostmen.[17]

This account differs from the earlier one in a number of significant ways. In claiming that the last of the frequent invasions by Ostmen occurred in 1050, it effectively contradicts the reference in the Treatise to an influx of Scandinavian settlers in 1095.[18] It also specifies that the 1050 enterprise was a military expedition from the outset, and depicts the establishment of Ostmantown as the result of the defeat and slaughter of the Gaelic Irish. It is difficult to know why Stanihurst changed his mind regarding these events, whether he had uncovered new sources, or lost faith in (or access to) ones on which he had previously relied. For current purposes, this question will be set aside and the present study will focus on the narrative in the Treatise.

Clontarf (Dublin, 2013), pp 167–238. 17 Stanihurst *De rebus*, iii, pp 214–15: *Huius gentilitatis homines nostri Oostma(n)nos nuncuparunt: quorum genus est ex Danorum stirpe generatum. Sæpius illos in Hiberniam inuasisse, historici referunt. Citerior eorum aduentus, nam de alio nihil ad hunc locum attinet scribere, numeratur anno, post nostrum sotera, & seruatorem natum, 1050. quo tempore, instructa armataque manu, ad insulam venire, Hibernos bello lacessere, eorum aciem profligare, postremò magna multitudine incolarum occisa, eam Dublinij plagam, finitima suburbanitate, incolere, quæ aquilonem versus trans flumen consistit, eaque etiam nunc Oostmantown, id est, Oostmannorum opidum nominatur.* 18 James Ussher likewise claimed, in a letter to William Camden in 1606, that the Ostmen had settled 'Oastmantown' in about 1050, referring to the authority of 'our annals'; in all likelihood, his source was actually Stanihurst, since Ussher cites both the Treatise and *De rebus* in the same letter. James Ussher, 'Letter to William Camden' in *The whole works of James Ussher, with a life of the author and an account of his writings*, ed. Charles Richard Elrington, 17 vols (Dublin, 1847), xv, p. 11. On Stanihurst and Ussher, see further below pp 157–8.

Stanihurst's account linking the origins of Ostmantown to a specific migration and settlement of Scandinavians in 1095 was repeated and elaborated upon by Meredith Hanmer (1543–1604). His *Chronicle of Ireland* was published posthumously by James Ware in 1633, alongside Campion's *Histories of Ireland* and Edmund Spenser's *View of the present state of Ireland*.[19] Hanmer had a colourful career in Britain before being sent to Ireland to serve the interests of the Established Church. He held numerous benefices in Ireland, among them a prebend of Christ Church, Dublin, to which the parish church of St Michan's in Ostmantown was annexed; when he died in 1604, Hanmer was buried in St Michan's.[20] Hanmer was a historian of considerable ability.[21] A highly regarded preacher with links to the earl of Ormond, he was hardly a disinterested party in this era of highly fraught historiographical debate. But he was less given to open polemic than many of his contemporaries, and his work has a good reputation among modern scholars of his period; in the view of Deana Rankin, for example, Hanmer's is 'the most resolutely historical of Ware's three texts'.[22] Hanmer was also deeply and genuinely interested in the history of Ireland; his surviving papers show that he often had a particular concern with collecting and retelling the histories of places with which he had a personal association.[23] It is therefore of interest that in the midst of a generally well-informed account of the history of Ireland in the eleventh and twelfth centuries, the following appears:

> Stanihurst findeth that *Anno* 1095. there came certaine Esterlings to the North side of Dublin adjoyning to the Liffie, and seated themselves there, so that of them to this day, the place is called Ostomontowne, and corruptly, Oxmonton, and the Parish, Saint Michans, of one *Michanus* a Dane and a Bishop which founded the Church, unto whom *Murchard*, or *Moragh* King of Leynster, gave that parcell of land to that use.

19 Meredith Hanmer, *Chronicle of Ireland*, in James Ware (ed.), *The historie of Ireland, collected by three learned authors, viz. Meredith Hanmer Doctor in Divinitie: Edmund Campion, sometime fellow of St Iohns Colledge in Oxford: and Edmund Spenser Esq.* (Dublin, 1633), ii, pp 1–206. The published version of his *Chronicle* draws extensively on surviving historical notes compiled by Hanmer. But its final form may owe a considerable debt to later editors, specifically the Ulster King of Arms, Daniel Molineux (1568–1632). See Angela Andreani, *Meredith Hanmer and the Elizabethan church: a clergyman's career in 16th century England and Ireland* (New York, 2020), pp 187–8. **20** Andreani, *Meredith Hanmer*, p. 160. **21** On Hanmer's career, including his historical writings, see Andreani, *Meredith Hanmer*, especially pp 159–98; Alan Ford, 'Hanmer, Meredith (1543–1604), Church of England and Church of Ireland clergyman and historian', *ODNB* (https://doi-org.ezp-prod1.hul.harvard.edu/10.1093/ref:odnb/12204, accessed 2 August 2019); Judy Barry. 'Hanmer, Meredith', *DIB* (https:// doi.org/10.3318/dib.003783.v1, accessed 2 August 2019). **22** Deana Rankin, *Between Spenser and Swift: English writing in seventeenth-century Ireland* (Cambridge, 2005), p. 89. **23** Andreani, *Meredith Hanmer*, pp 160, 167–8, 203–14.

Hanmer continues:

> The faire greene or Commune, now called Ostmontowne-greene, was all wood, and hee that diggeth at this day to any depth, shall finde the ground full of rootes. From thence, *Anno* 1098, King *William Rufus*, by license of *Murchard*, had that frame which made up the roofe of Westminster Hall, where no English Spider webbeth or breedeth to this day.[24]

Hanmer has followed Stanihurst's account from the Treatise. But where his source made the events of 1095 look peaceful through a subtle and implicit contrast with the previous Scandinavian incursion that led to the battle of Clontarf, Hanmer makes the whole thing seem positively amicable; certainly, his claim that St Michan's was founded on land granted by a Gaelic Irish king, Murchard, implies a peaceful process of settlement.[25] That Murchard was in a position to authorize the harvesting and exportation of wood from Ostmantown for the construction of Westminster Hall is likewise suggestive of relations having been more cordial that one might have expected between the new arrivals and the locals.[26]

Hanmer's account includes some clear historical inaccuracies that may cast a doubt on the whole. For instance, although his wording is slightly ambiguous, it seems likely that Hanmer understood that the foundation of St Michan's occurred at the time of the invasion and settlement of Ostmantown. The Murchard who donated the land for the foundation should in that case be understood to be the same individual who permitted the taking of wood from Ostmantown for the roofing of Westminster Hall. Hanmer calls him king of Leinster and there was a Murchad from Leinster who ruled Dublin for nearly two decades prior to his death in 1070, Murchad son of Diarmait mac Maíl na mBó.[27] He is sometimes said to have governed Dublin under the authority of his father, the king of Leinster, and he likely did so at first. But Murchad's obit in the Annals of Ulster and the Annals of Tigernach call him king of Leinster and of the Foreigners (i.e., the Hiberno-Scandinavians of Dublin), so he had apparently succeeded his father before his death.[28] Whatever about the possibility that this Murchad had a role in the foundation of St Michan's, the date of which is uncertain, he was dead more than a quarter of a century before

24 Hanmer, *Chronicle of Ireland*, ii, p. 97. For the Ostmen/Esterlings as Scandinavians, see ibid., ii, pp 83, 55. **25** On St Michan's, and the saint to which it is dedicated, see Emer Purcell, 'Michan: saint, cult and church' in Bradley et al. (eds), *Dublin in the medieval world*, pp 119–40. **26** On land use in Ostmantown in the later medieval period, including the Green, see Emer Purccell, 'Land use in medieval Oxmantown' in Duffy (ed.), *MD IV* (Dublin, 1999), pp 193–228. **27** For discussion, see Seán Duffy, 'Irishmen and Islesmen in the kingdoms of Dublin and Man, 1052–1171', *Ériu*, 43 (1992), 93–133, at 99–101. **28** *AU*, *AT*, 1070.

the construction of Westminster Hall (1097x1099). The ruler of Dublin in the late 1090s was Muirchertach Ua Briain, who governed the city under his father's authority between 1075 and 1086, and subsequently in his own right as claimant to the kingship of Ireland in 1089–91 and for two decades beginning in 1094.[29] It is possible that Hanmer conflated the two Irish kings and telescoped their involvement in Dublin affairs into a single event. But the balance of probability is that he had Muirchertach Ua Briain in mind as both the donor of the land for St Michan's and the king responsible for permitting the sale of wood from Ostmantown in the late 1090s.

While its historical accuracy on certain points is doubtful, on the other hand, some of the uncorroborated details in Hanmer's account have gained a degree of acceptance among modern scholars. The archaeologist and architectural historian Richard Gem, for instance, suggested that Hanmer's report that wood from Dublin was used for the construction of the roof of Westminster Hall may have had a basis in reality. As he pointed out, it would have been 'a pointless detail for Hanmer to have invented and he probably saw a relevant document, perhaps in his office as prebendary of St Michan's'.[30] These details, both the historically problematic ones and those uncorroborated but plausible, are not in Stanihurst's account, of course. But it bears keeping in mind that Hanmer may well have had access to material now lost, as Gem supposes, and that Stanihurst's version of events made sense in light of whatever additional information Hanmer had.

What we have in Stanihurst's Treatise is thus an account of the arrival in Dublin, in 1095, of a fresh wave of Scandinavian migrants known as Ostmen, who established a new settlement on the north bank of the Liffey that was subsequently named for them. If it could be shown that Stanihurst based his narrative on reliable sources written contemporary with the events described, then this neglected account could perhaps provide a key to understanding the historical context for interment of human remains in Ostmantown during the eleventh century. It is to his sources that we therefore turn.

29 On his career, see Seán Duffy, '"The western world's tower of honour and dignity": the career of Muirchertach Ua Briain in context' in Damian Bracken and Dagmar Ó Riain-Raedel (eds), *Ireland and Europe in the twelfth century* (Dublin, 2006), pp 56–73. **30** Richard Gem, 'St Flannán's oratory at Killaloe: a Romanesque building of *c.*1100 and the patronage of king Muirchertach Ua Briain' in Bracken and Ó Riain-Raedel (eds), *Ireland and Europe*, pp 86–7. That Hanmer might have had access to now lost material was also suggested by H.J. Lawlor: 'Notes on the church of St Michan's, Dublin', *JRSAI*, 56 (1927), 11–21, at 14. For an alternative view, see Howard B. Clarke, 'Christian cult centres in Hiberno-Norse Dublin and its hinterland' in Ailbhe MacShamhráin (ed.), *The Island of St Patrick: church and ruling dynasties in Fingal and Meath, 400–1148* (Dublin, 2004), pp 147–8. Geoffrey Keating, writing about thirty years after Hanmer's death, claimed that William Rufus requested wood from Ireland to roof Westminster Hall in 1098, and that this was granted by Tairdelbach úa Briain: Geoffrey Keating, *Foras Feasa ar Éirinn. The history of Ireland*, ed. David Comyn and Patrick Dinneen, 4 vols, Irish Texts Society 4, 8, 9 (London,

STANIHURST'S SOURCES I: GERALD OF WALES

The somewhat obvious starting point is the *Topographia Hibernie* by Gerald of Wales.[31] Gerald was both the chronicler of and a participant in the English invasion and conquest of Ireland in the late twelfth century.[32] His *Topographia*, the first of his two intimately connected books on Ireland, was a key source for information pertaining to Irish history prior to the coming of the English among sixteenth- and seventeenth-century historians, and as a result was hugely influential in shaping early modern views of Gaelic Ireland.[33] Gerald's narrative is structured around a series of invasions, the final of which was the English invasion of his own time. Gerald borrowed this framework from the Gaelic Irish historiographical tradition, specifically *Lebor Gabála Érenn* ('Book of the Taking of Ireland'), thus usurping local tradition to justify the English conquest.[34] Whereas *Lebor Gabála Érenn* recounts a series of prehistoric

1902–14), iii, pp 294–5. The specific locality where the wood was sought is not mentioned. In any case, Keating was mistaken to some degree, since Tairdelbach died in 1086. Nonetheless, his account suggests that there existed another historical tradition linking the wood of Westminster Hall to Ireland, beyond that recounted by Hanmer. I am grateful to Dr Caitlin Ellis for bringing Keating's reference to my attention. 31 Giraldus Cambrensis, *Topographia Hiberniae* [first recension], ed. John J. O'Meara, 'Giraldus Cambrensis in *Topographia Hibernie*: text of the first recension', *PRIA*, 52C (1948–50), 116–77; trans. John J. O'Meara, *Gerald of Wales, The history and topography of Ireland* (London, 1982). Unless otherwise stated, all references are to the first recension by chapter number, using the numbers in O'Meara's translation, followed by the page number for O'Meara's edition and his translation, in that order. James Dimock edited the expanded fifth recension for the Rolls Series (Giraldus Cambrensis, *Topographia Hiberniae* [fifth recension], ed. James F. Dimock, *Giraldi Cambrensis Opera*, v (London 1867), pp 3–204). This edition will be cited only in instances when the quoted text was an addition to the first recension and therefore not included in O'Meara's edition. In those instances, the translations are my own unless otherwise stated. 32 On Gerald's reporting on Ireland, see F.X. Martin, 'Gerald of Wales, Norman reporter on Ireland', *Studies: an Irish Quarterly Review*, 58:231 (1969), 272–86. For recent studies of his multi-faceted career, see Georgia Henley and A. Joseph McMullen (eds.), *Gerald of Wales: new perspectives on a medieval writer and critic* (Cardiff, 2018). 33 Stanihurst admitted his debt to Gerald for information pertaining to the English invasion of the twelfth century: *De rebus*, ed. and trans. Barry and Morgan, pp 144–5. For discussion, see Barry and Morgan, *Great deeds in Ireland*, pp 13–24; Lennon, *Richard Stanihurst*, p. 108. For more general discussions of Gerald's influence on Tudor chroniclers, see John Brannigan, '"A particular vice of that people": Giraldus Cambrensis and the discourse of English colonialism', *Irish Studies Review*, 6 (1998) 121–30; Hiram Morgan, 'Giraldus Cambrensis and the Tudor conquest of Ireland' in idem (ed.), *Political ideology in Ireland, 1541–1641* (Dublin 1999), pp 22–44. On the relationship between the *Topographia* and Gerald's other Irish work, *Expugnatio Hibernica*, see Patrick Wadden, 'Gerald of Wales, the *Topographia Hiberniae*, and the history of the Vikings in Ireland', *Viator*, 51:1 (2020 [2021]), 273–310, at 295–6; and idem, 'History and identity in late medieval Ireland: *Lebor gabála Érenn*, the Irish, and the English of Ireland' in Antoni Furió (ed.), *Imagined identities and imagined communities in the late Middle Ages* (forthcoming). 34 Wadden, 'Gerald of Wales', pp 281–2, 296; Jeanne-Marie Boivin, *L'Irlande au Moyen Âge. Giraud de Barri et la* Topographia Hibernica *(1188)* (Paris, 1993), pp 97–106.

invasions of Ireland culminating in the arrival of the Gaels, Gerald extended the list to include two further Scandinavian invasions and that of the English. Drawing on another Gaelic Irish historical tradition, that represented by the surviving copies of *Cogadh Gáedhel re Gallaibh* ('The War of the Gaels with the Foreigners'), he described a Norwegian conquest of Ireland led by Turgesius.[35] According to Gerald, Turgesius conquered Ireland and ruled for thirty years, during which time his followers built strongholds throughout the island. Turgesius was eventually killed in an ambush by his Irish enemies, after which the Norwegians were either executed or expelled from Ireland, and their castles destroyed.[36]

'Not very long' after the death of Turgesius, according to Gerald, there was a second Scandinavian invasion, which he labelled 'the coming of the Ostmen'.[37] Gerald explains that this group was descended from the earlier Norwegian invaders, and that their name meant 'eastern men' in their own language.[38] Gerald relates that the Ostmen initially came in peace, as merchants and with the permission of Irish kings who wished to benefit from their commercial activity. They were led by three brothers, Amelavus, Sitaricus, and Yvorus, who were responsible for the foundation of Dublin, Waterford, and Limerick, respectively. After initially settling peacefully, the Ostmen later turned against their Irish neighbours and asserted their independence. The idea that any of the Scandinavian settlers who came to Ireland did so in peace and with the support of the Irish kings is foreign to the Gaelic historical tradition, and I have suggested elsewhere that Gerald's account of these events was potentially based on historical traditions current among the Dubliners themselves in the twelfth century.[39] It is clear from Gerald's account that he considered the Dubliners of his own time to be the descendants of this second wave of Scandinavian settlement. For one thing, Turgesius's Norwegians had all been expelled or killed. For another, Gerald asserts that the Dubliners were 'now called Ostmen'.[40]

Stanihurst's accounts of the origins of both Dublin and Ostmantown in the Treatise were clearly influenced by certain specific elements of Gerald's narrative. These include the assertion that the Scandinavians who came to Ireland in 1095 belonged to a second wave of immigration, the implicit suggestion that the Ostman settlement was carried out peacefully, and potentially his use of the term *Ostmanni*. Stanihurst also repeated the claim that Dublin, Waterford, and Limerick had been established by the three

35 Wadden, 'Gerald of Wales', pp 285–6. 36 *Topographia Hiberniae*, §§ 111–16, pp 173–5, pp 118–22. 37 *Topographia Hiberniae*, §117: *De Ostmannorum aduentu*, ed. Dimmock, pp 186–7, trans O'Meara, p. 122. 38 *Topographia Hiberniae*, §117, ed. O'Meara, p. 175 n. 552: *Dicti sunt autem Oustmanni lingua ipsorum, corrupto quodam Saxonico, quasi orientales homines*. This comment appears in only one manuscript copy of the first recension, but was fully integrated into later recensions, for which see *Topographia Hibernica*, ed. Dimock, p. 187. 39 Wadden, 'Gerald of Wales', pp 293–4. 40 *Topographia Hiberniae*, §117, pp 175, 122:

brothers named by Gerald as leaders of the Ostman settlement, though he dated the event to the second century.[41] This anachronism seems to have been intended to justify the claim that the Alexandrian geographer Ptolemy had recorded the existence of Dublin in his *Geography*, naming it *Eblana*, which Stanihurst interpreted as a corruption of *Auellana*, which he asserted was derived from the city's supposed founder, Gerald's Amelavus.[42] Hanmer criticized Stanihurst for this dating and, quoting Gerald for support, posited a more plausible, ninth-century date for the coming of the Ostmen.[43] By the time he came to write the *De rebus*, Stanihurst had himself come to realize the error of his former argument, and partly corrected his error by redating the coming of the Ostmen to after 880.[44] Nonetheless, he reasserted his claim that the ancient name of Dublin was derived from its Ostman founder.[45] The name recorded by Ptolemy in the second century, Eblana, which Stanihurst takes to refer to Dublin, is thus presented by him in *De rebus* as derived from the name of a man who arrived in Ireland 700 years later!

Gerald was therefore demonstrably a key influence on Stanihurst's account of the origins of Ostmantown. And for a scholar who was willing to posit that Dublin's original name was derived from a founding figure named by Gerald, it was surely no great stretch to see in the same author's record of the coming of the Ostmen the origins of Ostmantown. On the other hand, since Gerald has nothing to say regarding the date of these events other than that they occurred after the death of Turgesius and before the English invasion, it is also clear that the *Topographia* was not the source for Stanihurst's dating of the foundation of Ostmantown in 1095.

STANIHURST'S SOURCES II: THE 1095 ANNAL

As it happens, it is possible to identify with some certainty Stanihurst's source for the date of the Ostman invasion. A number of related, late-medieval Irish chronicles record the occupation of Ireland's coastal cities in 1095 by a group of Scandinavians identified as Norwegians, Ostmen, or Normans. Three of these texts date in their surviving form to the sixteenth century. The earliest of these three is extant in London, British Library, Cotton MS Vespasian D X, f. 139r–140v, one of several short historical texts in the hand of Philip

nunc Ostmannica gens uocatur. 41 Stanihurst, 'Treatise', 9v. 42 Stanihurst, 'Treatise', 9v. 43 Hanmer, *Chronicle of Ireland*, ii, pp 85–6. Hanmer wisely notes that 'there is no certaintie' about how soon after the death of Turgesius these events occurred. In his letter to William Camden cited above (pp 147–8), James Ussher also criticized Stanihurst's dating of the foundation of the cities of Dublin, Limerick, and Waterford by the Ostmen to the second century in the Treatise, and noted with approval that Stanihurst corrected his error in *De rebus.* 44 Stanihurst *De rebus*, i, p. 23, Appendix; ed. and trans. Barry and Morgan, pp 100–1, 420–1. 45 Stanihurst *De rebus*, i, p. 23, ed. and trans. Barry and Morgan, pp 100–1.

Flattisbury in this section of what is a composite manuscript.[46] Flattisbury was a scribe and scholar active in the first quarter of the sixteenth century, who was closely associated with the earls of Kildare, for whom he penned the famous Red Book – a collection of documents relating to their landed possessions – in 1503.[47] Among Flattisbury's other surviving work is a transcription he made in 1517 of a set of annals of Ireland covering the period 1162–1370 originally compiled in the fourteenth century by John de Pembridge.[48] The text in the Vespasian manuscript is distinct from these annals; it is a short Dublin chronicle covering the period from 948 to 1165.[49] The first entry records the supposed foundation of St Mary's abbey in 948; that for 1095 reports the following:

> *Dungus qui et Donatus episcopus Dublinensem in Christo quievit.*
> *Eodem hoc tempore, Norwagenses sive Ostmanni qui ciuitates Hibernie et maritima occuparant. Normanni vocati sunt.*[50]
>
> Dungus, also known as Donatus, bishop of Dublin, rested in Christ.
> At the same time, the Norwegians or Ostmen, who had occupied the cities and coasts of Ireland, were called Normans.

Another scribe who copied Pembridge's annals was James Grace, who potentially belonged to both the priory of St John in Kilkenny and a notable family in the area.[51] Grace's annals, which he compiled between 1537 and 1539, are distinguished from those of Pembridge by the fact that they have been extended at both the beginning and the end. The opening section of the annals is what concerns us; after a summary of the various invasions and conquests of Ireland reported by Gerald of Wales,[52] it transitions into an annalistic format with an undated reference to the foundation of St Mary's abbey. Shortly thereafter, under the year 1095, the following annal appears:

46 Viewed 4 July 2023 at https://www.bl.uk/manuscripts/Viewer.aspx?ref=cotton_ms_vespasian_d_x_f138r. For the scribe, see K.W. Nicholls, 'Flattisbury, Philip (fl. 1503–1526)', *ODNB*, viewed online on 4 July 2023: https://doi-org.ezp-prod1.hul.harvard.edu/10.1093/ref:odnb/9676. **47** *Red Book of the earls of Kildare*, ed. Gearóid Mac Niocaill (Dublin, 1964). **48** *Chronica Hiberniae auctore Phillippo Flatisbury de Johnstowne iuxtas Naas AD 1517* can be found in Dublin, Trinity College MS 584. Pembridge's annals have been published three times, first by Camden in his *Britannia* (London, 1607), pp 794–836, then by Gilbert (ed.), *CStM*, ii, pp 303–98, and most recently by Williams (ed.), *Pembridge*. **49** This is not the 'Dublin chronicle' edited by Alan J. Fletcher, which covers the sixteenth century: 'The earliest extant recension of the Dublin chronicle: an edition, with commentary' in Bradley et al. (eds), *Dublin in the medieval world*, pp 390–409. **50** London, British Library, Cotton MS Vespasian D X, f. 139v, ll. 3–5. Translation by the current author. I am currently preparing an edition of this brief text for publication. **51** James Grace, *Annales Hiberniae*, ed. Richard Butler (Dublin, 1842). For a discussion of the author, see Butler's introduction, pp v–vii. **52** On these summaries of the invasions of Ireland, which ultimately draw on Gaelic historical traditions encapsulated in *Lebor Gabála Érenn*,

> *Moritur Donatus. Norwegii sive Ostmanni, qui et Normanni vocati sunt, civitates Hiberniae et loca maritima occuparant.*
>
> Donatus dies. The Norwegians or Ostmen, who were also called Normans, had occupied the cities and sea coasts of Ireland.[53]

What appears to be a superior version of the text ascribed to Grace – at least as Grace's text is represented by the edition published in 1842 – has been preserved in London, British Library, Cotton MS Domitian A XVIII. The relevant portion of this composite manuscript comprises what the catalogue calls 'transcriptions of chronicles and other historical material, much of it in the hand of Laurence Nowell (d. *c.*1570), made in England in the 3rd quarter of the 16th century'.[54] Nowell's text, like Grace's, opens with a summary of the invasions of Ireland based on the works of Gerald of Wales, before the annalistic section proper begins with a record of the foundation of St Mary's abbey, the difference being that Nowell's text dates this event to 948, while Grace's omits the supposed foundation date.[55] The entry for the year 1095 also differs slightly from Grace's text in wording and provides additional information about the election of Samuel as successor to Donatus:

> *Donatus moritur. Norwegii siue Ostmanni qui et Normanni uocati sunt urbes Hyberniae et loca maritima occuparant. Samuel fit episcopus Dublinensem.*[56]
>
> Donatus dies. The Norwegians or Ostmen, who are also called Normans, had occupied the cities and coastal areas of Ireland. Samuel was made bishop of Dublin.

In addition to these three sixteenth-century texts, there is one older chronicle that preserves a record of the events of 1095, namely the so-called Annals of St Mary's, Dublin. These survive only in a fifteenth-century manuscript, Dublin, Trinity College MS 175A (formerly E.3.11).[57] They cover

see Wadden, 'History and identity in late medieval Ireland'. 53 Grace, *Annales Hiberniae*, ed. and trans. Butler, pp 8–9 (I have altered Butler's translation slightly). 54 http://www.bl.uk/manuscripts/Viewer.aspx?ref=cotton_ms_domitian_a_xviii_fs001r (accessed 4 July 2023:). For the scribe, see Retha M. Warnicke, 'Nowell, Laurence (1530–*c.*1570)', *ODNB* (revised ed. 2008; originally published 2004) (https://doi-org.ezp-prod1.hul.harvard.edu/10.1093/ref:odnb/69731, accessed 28 August 2024). Nowell visited Ireland in 1560. 55 London, British Library MS Domitian A XVIII, f. 57v–58r, 59r, l. 1. 56 London, British Library MS Domitian A XVIII, f. 59r, ll. 12–14. Translation by the current author. 57 'The annals of St Mary's Dublin', *CStM*, ii, pp 241–86. For discussion of this chronicle, see Andrew Breeze, 'Annals of St Mary's, Dublin' in Graeme Dunphy and Cristian Bratu (eds), *Encyclopedia of the medieval chronicle* (Leiden, 2010; consulted online on 8 June 2020 at http://dx.doi.org.ezp-prod1.hul.harvard.edu/10.1163/2213-2139_emc_SIM_00186); Donnchadh Ó Corráin, *Clavis litterarum Hibernensium: medieval Irish books and texts (c.400–c.1600)*, 3 vols (Turnhout, 2017), §718 (ii, pp 971–2); Aubrey Gwynn, 'Some unpublished texts from the Black Book of Christ Church, Dublin', *AH*, 16

the period from Christ's birth to the early fifteenth century, though the initial compilation seems to have occurred in the thirteenth and there are considerable gaps in coverage. Their record of events in the late eleventh century is largely derived from Henry of Huntingdon's mid-twelfth-century *Historia Anglorum* and other sources.[58] But in 1095 they report the following, which is not from the *Historia Anglorum* or any other known source:

> *Dungus, qui et Donatus, Episcopus Dublinie, in Christo quievit. Notandum vero quod Norwagenses seu Ostmanni, qui tunc civitates Hibernie et maritima occupabant, Normanni, in Christo, sunt vocati.*[59]
>
> Dungus, also known as Donatus, bishop of Dublin, rested in Christ. Let it be noted, truly, that the Norwegians or Ostmen, who were then occupying the cities and coasts of Ireland, are called Normans in Christ.

James Ware (d. 1666) made a series of extracts from what seems to have been a superior text of the annals of St Mary's in the seventeenth century.[60] These extracts do not include the record of the 'foundation' of St Mary's in 948, but Ware was familiar with such a tradition and noted it twice elsewhere in his published work, in one instance associating the foundation with Danes, and in the other with 'Danes or Ostmen'.[61] Aubrey Gwynn believed Ware must have learned of this from his text of the annals of St Mary's.[62] The 948 date for the establishment of St Mary's provided by these chronicles is interesting in light of the evidence emerging from archaeological excavation of the monastic site in summer 2023, though Gwynn gave no credence to this early date in his study of the monastery's origins.[63]

These four fifteenth- and sixteenth-century chronicles are clearly related, and presumably all ultimately derived their information about the events of

(1946), 316–19; Bernadette Williams, 'The Dominican annals of Dublin' in Duffy (ed.), *MD II* (Dublin, 2001), p. 153; Ellen O'Flaherty, 'Manuscript sources for the history of medieval Dublin in Trinity College Library, Dublin' in Duffy (ed.), *MD XII* (Dublin, 2012), pp 301–3. **58** Gwynn, 'Some unpublished texts', 316–17; Williams, 'The Dominican annals', p. 152; Gearóid Mac Niocaill, *The medieval Irish annals*, Medieval Irish History Series 3 ([Dublin], 1975), pp 37–9; A.B. Scott, 'Latin learning and literature in Ireland, 1169–1500' in Dáibhí Ó Cróinín (ed.), *A new history of Ireland I: prehistoric and early Ireland* (Oxford, 2005), p. 991; Alan J. Fletcher, 'The annals and chronicles of medieval Dublin: an overview' in Duffy (ed.), *MD VIII* (Dublin, 2008), pp 196–7, 201, 204. **59** *CStM*, ii, p. 251; Gwynn, 'Some unpublished texts', 334. **60** Printed in *CStM*, ii, pp 278–92. **61** James Ware, *Archiepiscoporum Casseliensium et Tuamensium vitae* (Dublin, 1626), pp 60–61 (the relevant section is part of an appendix called *Coenobia Cisterciensia Hiberniae*, which was reprinted in *CStM*, ii, pp 218–27, with the relevant section at pp 218–19); James Ware, *De Hibernia & antiquitatibus ejus disquisitiones* (London, 1654), p. 141 (a version of this from the 1658 edition, in which the pagination is slightly different, is also reprinted in *CStM*, ii, pp 229–37, with the relevant entry at pp 229–30). **62** Gwynn, 'Origins', 111. **63** In Gwynn's opinion ('Origins', 111), the 948 date 'may be set aside as fictitious'.

1095 from a common source. The existence and identity of this source text was suggested by Aubrey Gwynn nearly eighty years ago in his study of the annals of St Mary's. The 1095 annal is one of a cluster of entries spanning the period from the late eleventh to the early twelfth century in that highly derivative text that are not taken from other identifiable sources. As a group, these distinct entries are characterized by an interest in the history of Christ Church, Dublin. For instance, they include the obituaries of the first three bishops of Dublin (Dúnán, alias Donatus, who died in 1074; Gilla Pátraic, or Patricius, who died in 1084; and Donngus, who also went by Donatus in Latin, who died in 1095), as well as notices of the consecration of the second and third of these by Archbishop Lanfranc of Canterbury.[64] Some of the information reported in these entries can be verified from other sources, but part of it – such as the statement that Dúnán was buried beside the altar in Christ Church and the precise date of Gilla Pátraic's death – is unique to this source, and there is good reason, therefore, to accept Gwynn's proposal that a reliable contemporary record lies behind them: 'some early record of Christ Church, Dublin, which is no longer extant'.[65] Christ Church was built in the 1030s at the behest of the king of Dublin, Sitriuc mac Amlaíb, alias Sigtrygg 'Silkbeard' Olafsson.[66] A chronicle written there could therefore be taken as representing a Dublin perspective on events. A more thorough study of the relationship between the annals of St Mary's and the sixteenth-century chronicles discussed above in which the events of 1095 are recorded – especially Philip of Flattisbury's Dublin chronicle – may help us identify more of the contents of a Dublin chronicle apparently written in Christ Church prior to the English invasion.

Stanihurst's source is unlikely to have been the original twelfth-century text whose existence was proposed by Gwynn. Rather, he seems almost certainly to have possessed a copy of Flattisbury's 'Dublin chronicle'. Shortly after 1609, while living on the Continent, Stanihurst received a letter from his nephew, James Ussher, who would go on to become one of the most celebrated biblical scholars and historians of his age.[67] Ussher requested that his uncle send him various books that Stanihurst owned or could access, for his own study of patristic authors and for the 'gathering together [of] the scattered antiquities of our nation', which Ussher described as 'a kind of recreation'.[68] Alongside

64 Gwynn edited these entries in 'Some unpublished texts', 333–4. **65** Gwynn, 'Some unpublished texts', 314; Fletcher, 'Annals and chronicles', p. 201, is more circumspect, but does not cast serious doubt on the veracity of the record. **66** For a discussion of the foundation, see Dagmar Ó Riain-Raedel, 'New light on the beginnings of Christ Church cathedral, Dublin' in Duffy (ed.), *MD XVII* (Dublin, 2019), pp 63–80; Stuart Kinsella, 'From Hiberno-Norse to Anglo-Norman, *c.*1030–1300' in Kenneth Milne (ed.), *Christ Church cathedral: a history* (Dublin, 2000), pp 25–52. **67** On Stanihurst's relationship with Ussher, see Lennon, *Richard Stanihurst,* pp 62–3. **68** Ussher, 'Letter to Richard Stanihurst at the English College at Louvain' in *The whole works*, ed. Elrington, xv, pp 3–4.

Pembridge's annals and various other works, Ussher specifically requested 'Philip of Flatesbury's Chronicle, for I could never get sight of it'. The fact that he also specifically requested Pembridge's annals suggests it was not Flattisbury's copy of that text Ussher had in mind, and it seems likely he actually sought the shorter Dublin chronicle in which the 1095 annal is found. Stanihurst may have acquired this text while he was employed by the eleventh earl of Kildare; he certainly gained access to other Kildare documents during this period, which shaped his account of the reign of Henry VIII in Ireland in his contribution to Holinshed's *Chronicles*.[69] Alternatively, Stanihurst may have had access to Flattisbury's text at an earlier date. As noted above, Edmund Campion wrote his *Histories of Ireland* while in hiding in Dublin in the spring of 1571, basing his work largely on notes he had written while staying at Stanihurst's home over the previous six months.[70] Campion states that he had access to three versions of the copy made by Philip Flattisbury in 1517 for the earl of Kildare of the text we now know as the 'Annals of Ireland' by John de Pembridge, and, moreover, that one of these three was sent to him by 'M. Stanyhurst', potentially either Richard or his father.[71] Campion also recorded both the foundation of St Mary's in 948, the rebranding of the Ostmen as Normans in 1095 – though not the Ostman invasion specifically – and again identified his source as Philip Flattisbury.[72] Since these events are not reported in Pembridge's annals but are to be found in Flattisbury's Dublin chronicle, it seems highly likely that Campion had access to this text also, and that he encountered it, too, at the home of the Stanihursts in 1570–1.

Stanihurst interpreted Flattisbury's version of the 1095 annal as reporting an invasion of Ireland's coasts by Ostmen – also known as Norwegians, also known as Normans. But it is far from certain that that is what either Flattisbury or the author of the proposed twelfth-century source intended. If we take the four extant versions of the annal as a group, there are three aspects of the language that are unclear. First, the Latin verb *occupare* could mean either 'to inhabit' in a peaceful sense or to seize forcibly.[73] Additionally, while

69 Lennon, *Richard Stanihurst*, pp 35–6, 110. 70 Lennon, *Richard Stanihurst*, pp 26–33. 71 Campion, *Historie of Ireland*, p. 68. It seems likely that only one of the three was Flattisbury's transcription. 72 Campion, *Historie of Ireland*, pp 53, 58: 'in the yeare of CHRIST 1095. Perceiving great envy to lurke in the distinction of Easterlings and Irishe utterly west, and because they magnified themselves in the late conquest of their Countreymen, who from Normandy flourished now in the realm of England, they would in any wise be called and counted Normans'. Campion was the source for Holinshed's comments to the same effect: *Historie of Irelande*, p. 20. Campion's suggestion that the rebranding of the Ostmen was a response to the Norman invasion of England anticipated Aubrey Gwynn's interpretation by four centuries: 'Some unpublished texts', 334. For a more recent discussion of this episode, some of which I no longer agree with, see Patrick Wadden, 'Ostmen, Normans, or Norwegians? Names and identities in the Irish Sea world *c.*1100', *Haskins Society Journal*, 32 (2020 [2021]), 73–91. 73 *Dictionary of medieval Latin*

the annals of St Mary's employ the imperfect tense of the verb, the other three extant versions use the pluperfect. Finally, whereas the versions recorded in Grace's annals and in Nowell's text report the occupation of Ireland's coastal areas by the Ostmen or Norwegians in the main clause, using a subordinate clause to note that they were also known as Normans, Flattisbury's copy and that in the annals of St Mary's reverse this structure, emphasizing a change in the name of those who occupied Ireland's cities. All of this is to say that the common source behind the four extant versions of the 1095 annal may have been intended to report the invasion of Ireland by a group known as Ostmen or Norwegians, and who were also known as Normans, or it may have been intended to report the adoption of a new name by those Ostmen/Norwegians, who had been occupying Ireland's cities and coasts for some time already.

Flattisbury's version of the 1095 annal does not read particularly like it was intended to report an Ostman invasion. Nevertheless, Stanihurst seems to have found in this reference to the occupation of Ireland's cities corroborative evidence and a date for the coming of the Ostmen as reported by Gerald of Wales.

CONCLUSION

What has been determined so far is that the story of the Ostman invasion of 1095 in Stanihurst's Treatise – whence it was derived by Meredith Hanmer – is ultimately based on the author's reading of Gerald's account of the 'coming of the Ostmen' and the 1095 annal. The first of these is not an accurate account of the history of the Scandinavian invasions and settlements of Ireland. It potentially had its roots in local historical traditions in Dublin at the time of Gerald's visit to the city in the late twelfth century, but was likely adopted and adapted by Gerald himself to fit the broader historiographical purposes of his Irish works.[74] The second source potentially originated in a contemporary record of events in late eleventh-century Dublin, though Stanihurst likely accessed it through a sixteenth-century copy. Neither of these sources actually mentions the foundation of any settlement on the north bank of the Liffey. It was Stanihurst who, eager to illuminate the origins and the place names of his beloved city, brought these two sources together to explain the establishment of Ostmantown.

This is not to exclude the possibility that the 1090s witnessed events of significance to the establishment of Ostmantown, or that the suburb was initially inhabited by migrants who arrived from Scandinavia at a relatively late

from British sources online (Turnhout, 2015), *s.v. occupare* (http://clt.brepolis.net.ezp-prod1.hul.harvard.edu/dmlbs/pages/QuickSearch.aspx, accessed 7 July 2020). 74 Wadden, 'Gerald of Wales'.

date, but clear historical evidence is entirely lacking. The first appearance in the written record of a bridge over the Liffey in 1112 would make sense if the settlement had come into existence in the immediately preceding decades, for example.[75] Moreover, the earliest references to the existence of Ostmantown, dating to 1192 and 1200, name the settlement as *Houstmanebi*.[76] Alexander Bugge took this to represent *Austmannabýr*, with its distinctive Old Norse ending, and saw it as evidence that Old Norse was still spoken in Dublin at this date.[77] An alternative interpretation might possibly be that Ostmantown was more linguistically Norse than the rest of the city because its inhabitants were more recent arrivals from Scandinavia. Before any firm conclusions can be drawn regarding the origins of Ostmantown and the possibility that it was established in the 1090s, further study of various sources, including Philip Flattisbury's Dublin chronicle, is necessary.

Stanihurst's eagerness to link the foundation of Ostmantown with Gerald's account of the 'coming of the Ostmen' and the 'invasion' reported in the 1095 annal was more likely influenced by his personal concerns, preoccupations, and prejudices than by awareness of such matters, however. In his *Topographia*, Gerald posited that Irish history was framed by a series of foreign invasions, the last of which, that of the English in the twelfth century, was justified on the basis of its civilizing mission. One of the signs of the backwardness of the Gaelic Irish, according to Gerald, was their failure to live in towns and cities and their lack of interest in the commercial enterprises of urban settlements.[78] Yet it was not the English whom Gerald credited with introducing these features to Ireland, it was the Ostmen.[79] While they had not conquered the entire island, as Gerald expected the English would, the Ostmen had at least established commercial hubs along the coast. The Ostmen thus appear in the *Topographia* in the guise of civilizers whose coming anticipated that of the English.

Such an image may have been attractive to Stanihurst. As noted above, Stanihurst was concerned to distinguish between the barbarism of the Gaelic Irish and the civility of the Old English. The distinction was founded on a number of bases, including the fact that the Gaels still lacked any interest in urban settlement or in the pursuit of commercial enterprise. According to

75 *AFM*, *s.a.* 1112: *Crech la Domhnall Ua Lochlainn tar Fine Gall, .i. co Droichet Dubhghaill, co t-tucc bóromha mhór 7 braitt iomdha* ('A predatory excursion was made by Domhnall, grandson of Lochlann, across Fine-Gall, i.e. as far as Droichet-Dubhghaill; and he carried off a great spoil of cattle and many prisoners'). For an important discussion of the bridge and the surrounding topography in relation to St Michan's, see Purcell, 'Michan', 131–40. On the other hand, Seán Duffy, *Brian Boru*, p. 210 argued it was the bridge on the Tolka at Ballybough. 76 Gilbert (ed.), *HMDI*, pp 52, 57. 77 Alexander Bugge, 'Nordisk sprog og nordisk nationalitet i Irland', *Aarbøger for nordisk old-kyndighed og historie*, 2 række, 15 (1900), pp 279–332, at p. 333. 78 Gerald, *Topographia*, §§ 93, 117; 163, 175; 101–2, 122. 79 Gerald, *Topographia*, § 117, 175, 122.

Stanihurst, while the Gaelic Irish of his own time did not live in thickets and bogs as some outsiders claimed, they continued to be a rural people whose leaders inhabited castles in close proximity to their herds.[80] The Old English, in contrast, resided in towns and cities, 'in accordance to the customs and institutions of Englishmen', and engaged in trade and commerce to the betterment of the community.[81] Stanihurst does not repeat Gerald's claim that the Ostmen were primarily merchants who came to Ireland to establish commercial enterprises, yet he undoubtedly knew about it. The idea that the cities and towns Stanihurst and his fellow *Anglo-Hiberni* inhabited were established by other commercially minded foreigners was potentially attractive, therefore, in part because it removed from those settlements any potential stain of association with the Gaelic Irish.

80 Stanihurst, *De rebus in Hibernia gestis*, 1.32–3, ed. and trans. Barry and Morgan, pp 112–13. 81 Stanihurst, *De rebus in Hibernia gestis*, 1.21, 23–4, 30, ed. and trans. Barry and Morgan, pp 96–9, 100–3, 108–11.

'What shall we hang — the holly, or each other?': Henry II's Christmas Court (Dublin, 1171)[1]

DENIS CASEY

Anthony Harvey's 1968 film *The lion in winter* (based upon James Goldman's play of the same name) dramatizes Henry II of England's supposed 1183 Christmas court at Chinon, where his sons Richard, John and Geoffrey each plot to succeed him, his imprisoned wife, Eleanor of Aquitaine, gives him a tombstone as a Christmas gift – to which he exclaims 'Eleanor, you spoil me!' – and his nemesis, the teenage King Philip II of France, schemes to set them all against each other. Henry, played by the regal Peter O'Toole, is determined to have John on the throne, Eleanor in the dungeon, and Philip's sister in his bed. Queen Eleanor, interpreted magnificently by Katharine Hepburn, schemes to have Richard succeed to the throne, organizes a jail break, and goads Henry that she may have slept with both his father and his close friend, St Thomas Beckett.

Such an average Christmas court that you cannot but help wonder why Goldman picked 1183 and not any other, for example that held in Dublin in 1171. All the ingredients are there for a historical drama that would make *Game of thrones* look like an episode of *Fair city*. The blood of the martyred Thomas Beckett has barely stopped flowing and Henry has hightailed it to Ireland to escape papal wrath, and bolted the door shut behind him. There he will play at being a true son of the church, hold reforming synods and hopefully stall the papal legates whose impending arrival could easily spark yet another civil war in his English and French domains.[2] He is surrounded by the new masters of much of eastern Ireland, men like Strongbow who backed the wrong horse in the last civil war and who have little reason to love him. And then there are the fawning Irish kings, whose loyalty will melt away before that winter's snow, and who are already looking to make alliances with the newcomers in the hope of settling old local scores.[3] In a display of magnificence, Henry holds a Christmas court in Dublin and the Irish kings who flock to it find themselves obliged to eat crane (a bird that apparently did

1 Quotation from *The lion in winter*, dir. Anthony Harvey (1968). 2 Henry's involvement with the Irish church has recently been discussed in Donnchadh Ó Corráin, *The Irish church, its reform and the English invasion*, Trinity Medieval Ireland Series 2 (Dublin, 2017), pp 97–116. 3 That Henry was willing to engage in a winter expedition to Ireland suggests a sense of urgency, especially considering the weather-related disasters of his previous campaign in Wales, in the summer of 1165: Paul Latimer, 'Henry II's campaign against the Welsh in 1165', *Welsh History Review/Cylchgrawn Hanes Cymru*, 14 (1988–9), 523–52.

not normally deck the Christmas table), and do so in a wicker palace seemingly constructed to provide rods for their backs. Storms rage in the Irish Sea cutting Henry off from news from Britain, forcing the arch-schemer to create a new royal household to act as a counterbalance to those among his subjects who had been more rewarded by Strongbow than by him.[4] All the while, Ruaidrí Ua Conchobair is watching from the other side of the Shannon; the once and would-be high-king, who preferred to nail traitors' hands – rather than Christmas wreaths – to the door.[5]

Historians have long recognized that Henry's arrival was a game-changer in Irish history, and Beckett's blood, the wooden hall and taboo roast bird have all become staples of this Christmas story – but who is telling it? For Henry's Christmas court we are reliant upon three writers: Roger of Howden, Gervase of Canterbury and Gerald of Wales. Each 'English', possessing a particular perspective (or axe to grind), none of them present,[6] and all writing over a decade or more later.[7] In the short essay that follows, a brief overview of these three sources will be followed by a discussion of the venue, the attendees and what was on the menu on a Christmas day when both birds and kingdoms went under the carving knife.

4 It was a balancing act, as he was still in need of Strongbow: F.X. Martin, 'Allies and an overlord, 1169–72', *NHI*, ii, pp 67–97 at pp 96–7. See also, Orpen, *Normans*, pp 103–4. Nonetheless, Strongbow appears to have been restored to royal favour, as implied by his loyalty to Henry upon the outbreak of the rebellion of Henry the Young King in 1173: Marie Therese Flanagan, 'Henry II, the council of Oxford and Angevin overlordship in Leinster, 1177–85', *PRIA*, 124C (2024), 119–62 at 120. 5 Ruaidrí nailed the hand of Domnall (mac Andaig) Ua Ruairc – who betrayed Ruaidrí's ally, Tigernán Ua Ruairc of Bréifne, to Hugh de Lacy – to the exterior of Tuam castle: *AT*, *sub anno* 1173, p. 288. It has recently been suggested that Domnall was a member of the Uí Ragallaig and not Uí Ruairc: Seán Ó Hoireabhárd, 'The assassination of Tigernán Ua Ruairc, the last king of Meath', *Peritia*, 29 (2018), 111–41. 6 However, John Gillingham has made a case for Roger of Howden being present in Ireland, working on the theory that there is a personal element to Roger's historical writings, such that coverage and level of detail may be taken as an indicator of his presence at a given location/event. See, John Gillingham, 'The travels of Roger of Howden and his views of the Irish, Scots and Welsh' in John Gillingham (ed.), *The English in the twelfth century: imperialism, national identity and political values* (Woodbridge, 2000), pp 69–91 at pp 85–6. (This essay was originally published as 'The travels of Roger of Howden and his views of the Irish, Scots and Welsh', *Anglo-Norman Studies*, 20 (1998), 151–69, and I am grateful to Seán Duffy for drawing my attention to it.) However, as Flanagan has suggested, there may be other reasons for Roger's uneven coverage of events. He may have been silent at times not because he was absent, but because it was a means of emphasizing royal initiative, for example, in order to present the king in a positive and proactive light, he chose not to recount Strongbow's success in Ireland and its role as a spur to Henry's involvement there: Flanagan, 'Henry II, the council of Oxford and Angevin overlordship', 124–5 n. 21. Additionally, given Roger's ability to incorporate documentary sources into his writing, it does not automatically follow that he had to be in Ireland to have generated his account of Henry's expedition. 7 Surprisingly, the poem known as *The Song of Dermot and the Earl* (sometimes known as the *Deeds of the Normans in Ireland*) has no mention of the Christmas feast, even though it records Henry's sojourn in Dublin in some detail: *Deeds of the Normans*, pp 121–3, ll. 2649–734.

THE SOURCES

Roger of Howden

Our first informant is Roger of Howden/Hoveden, a parson from east Yorkshire who was a clerk of Henry II's court between 1174, if not earlier, and that king's death in 1189. Like many modern historians, Roger had multiple overlapping works on the go, and he mentions the feast in two chronicles, his *Gesta regis Henrici secundi* (which he finished around 1192) and the *Chronica* (upon which he was already working by that time).[8]

Roger has gained a reputation as a dull man, with the inability to tell an interesting story even after witnessing it. His nineteenth-century editor, Bishop William Stubbs, wrote that Roger was representative of historians of the time, who 'however striking the scene which he witnessed, and however interesting the personal character of its actors, treats us to a passionless, colourless narrative'.[9] Frank Barlow savaged Roger in a manner modern historians normally reserve for reviewing their contemporaries' monographs, saying (to extract the juiciest bits):

> it is, indeed, difficult to be an enthusiastic admirer of Roger's work. Roger was a trimmer, and his bias accurately represents the forces exerted on him. [...] he had neither the personality nor the literary skill to give his work a value much greater than that of inflated annals [...] he is not even impeccable as a recorder.[10]

He finally damns him with faint praise, saying:

> But if Roger disappoints, it is surely because the standard of judgement is set too high. If we regard him as a retired administrator of the second class, then his historical work appears characteristic and praiseworthy.[11]

Slightly later, to Sir Richard Southern (wearing an explicitly royalist hat), Roger was the 'best historian of the English Crown in the twelfth century', who 'recorded what he knew with immense elaboration'.[12] Nevertheless, he was a 'dour Yorkshire parson [...] without a spark of warmth for either of the masters whom he had served [Henry II and Richard I]', incapable of emotion 'in circumstances that called out for pity and regret' (i.e., those kings' deaths) and his writings were characterized by the 'strain of malice highly destructive

8 David Corner, 'Roger of Howden [Hoveden]', *ODNB*, available at: https://doi.org/10.1093/ref:odnb/13880, accessed 23 July 2024. 9 William Stubbs (ed.), *Chronica magistri Rogeri de Houedene*, RS 51, 4 vols (London, 1868–71), i, p. lxix. 10 Frank Barlow, 'Roger of Howden', *English Historical Review*, 65:256 (1950), 352–60 at 360. 11 Ibid., 360. 12 R.W. Southern, *Medieval humanism and other studies* (Oxford, 1970; reprint Oxford, 1984), p. 150.

of the royal charisma', which Southern believed was common among twelfth-century English chroniclers.[13] Recently, Michael Staunton has viewed Roger as a 'civil service historian' in profession and outlook, in that he was both a royal functionary and a supporter of the government who possessed a long-term view, as opposed to being a partisan of particular kings.[14] His works stand out for the innovative and in-depth use of documentary material available to him,[15] and whatever about their 'standard', he was well placed to observe royal matters, for although it has been assumed that he entered into royal service a few years after the Dublin Christmas celebration,[16] Marie Therese Flanagan has suggested that:

> his description of the palace built by the Irish kings for Henry must ultimately derive from a firsthand account of the event; it may have been drawn from some form of dispatch, such as Robert of Torigny tells us Henry II sent from Ireland to the young King Henry, his son, in Normandy, and if so, it would reflect Henry's interpretation of the event.[17]

Specifically, Roger writes in the *Gesta* (the earlier of the two works):

> *Circa festum Sancti Martini venit rex usque Divelinam, et ibi construi fecit juxta ecclesiam Sancti Andreae apostoli extra civitatem Duvelinae, ad opus suum palatium regium, quod reges et ditiores terrae mirifice construxerunt ad opus ejus per praeceptum ipsius de virgis, ad morem patriae illius; in quo ipse regale festum in Natale Domini tenuit cum regibus et ditioribus Hyberniae.*
>
> About the feast of St Martin [11 November 1171] the king came to Dublin, and there he built near the church of St Andrew the Apostle outside the city of Dublin, a royal palace for his own use, which the kings and the rich of that land had constructed marvellously for his use, by his command, from brushwood according to the custom of that country; in which he himself held a royal feast at Christmas with the kings and rich men of Ireland.[18]

13 Ibid., p. 150. 14 Michael Staunton, *The historians of Angevin England* (Oxford, 2017), pp 51–2. 15 Ibid., pp 56–60. This is not to say Staunton views him as a particularly exciting writer, and he argues persuasively against John Gillingham's attempts to rescue Roger's literary reputation: ibid., pp 64–5. 16 Roger is first identifiable as a royal servant in 1174 (Corner, 'Roger of Howden [Hoveden]', *ODNB*), although it could be argued that his royal service began at the same point as the *Gesta* (Christmas 1169): Gillingham, 'The travels of Roger of Howden', p. 71. 17 Flanagan, *Irish society*, p. 206. If Henry was indeed cut off from Britain due to inclement winter weather, such a dispatch was presumably not sent until early 1172. 18 William Stubbs (ed.), *Gesta regis Henrici secundi Benedicti abbatis: the chronicle of the reigns of Henry II and Richard I, A.D. 1169–1192*, RS 49, 2 vols (London, 1867), i, pp 28–9. My translation and my additions in square parenthesis.

Writing in his *Chronica*, almost twenty years after the events (but largely based upon his own earlier *Gesta*), he claimed:

> *His itaque apud Waterford factis, rex Angliae perrexit inde usque Diveline, et ibi moram fecit a festo Sancti Martini usque ad caput jejunii; ibique fecit sibi construi juxta ecclesiam Sancti Andreae apostoli, extra civitatem Diveliniae, palatium regium, miro artificio de virgis levigatis ad modum patriae illius constructum. In quo ipse cum regibus et principibus Hyberniae solemne festum tenuit die Natalis Domini.*
>
> After these things had been done at Waterford, the king of England went to Dublin, and stayed there from the feast of St Martin [11 November 1171] until the beginning of the fast [Lent]; and there he built for himself, near the church of St Andrew the Apostle, outside the city of Dublin, a royal palace, built with a marvellous artifice of hewn brushwood in the manner of that country. In which he, with the kings and princes of Ireland, held a solemn feast on the day of the Lord's Christmas.[19]

The differences between the two accounts are subtle and given their shared authorship it is difficult to know whether they represent deliberate factual revisions, changes in emphasis, or simply an author searching for synonyms and slight modifications in an attempt to avoid repetition. Two clear changes are, first, the removal of the Irish as the builders,[20] and second, a modification in the description of the attendees, from *regibus et ditioribus* ('kings and rich men') to *regibus et principibus* ('kings and princes'). This gains significance when Roger's accounts are compared with that of Gerald of Wales (below), as together his *Gesta* and Gerald's *Expugnatio* may indicate that Henry II was deliberately engaged in a policy of wooing middle-ranking Irish leaders.

Gervase of Canterbury

Our second source is Gervase of Canterbury (*c.*1145–*c.*1210), a Benedictine monk who spent his entire adult life in the cathedral priory of Christ Church, Canterbury, where he was professed and ordained by Archbishop Thomas Becket in the 1160s.[21] Gervase was a devotee of Becket (although certainly not of his successors) and to him we owe the idea that Henry was motivated to go to Ireland – in addition to a request from the Irish to rein in Strongbow – by papal wrath for the murder of Archbishop Becket during divine services, an assassination that would probably not be imitated for another eight hundred

19 Stubbs, *Chronica magistri Rogeri de Houedene*, ii, p. 32. My translation and my additions in square parenthesis. **20** Flanagan, *Irish Society*, p. 203. **21** G.H. Martin, 'Canterbury, Gervase of', *ODNB*, available at: https://doi.org/10.1093/ref:odnb/10570, accessed 23 July 2024.

years until Archbishop Óscar Romero was gunned down while saying Mass in El Salvador (1980).[22]

Gervase was the author of several historical works, the most relevant of which for this discussion was his lengthy *Chronica*, begun about 1188 and not finished until at least 1199 (covering from the accession of Henry I (1100) to the death of Richard I (1199)).[23] Among the sources he relied upon were Roger of Howden, but it seems he also had a unique informant in Hervey de Montmorency (Strongbow's uncle), who had become a monk of Canterbury sometime between 1179 and 1185.[24] In general, his *Chronica* is a defence of Canterbury's rights, and fits into an established tradition of Canterbury writings on its struggles to maintain its liberties.[25] Unlike the methodologically unreflective Roger of Howden, Gervase was one of the 'most theoretically aware historians of the period',[26] even if – in the judgment of one prominent late nineteenth-/early twentieth-century historian – he was 'not one of the great historians of his age'.[27]

Gervase has gained a reputation as something of a copyist, but this is not a simple matter of reproducing existing texts, for while in many respects Gervase was a compiler of earlier works (as he stated himself), nonetheless the act of compiling a text from earlier sources can be viewed, in the words of Henry Bainton, as a 'conscious creative choice' that is 'legitimate and creative rather than derivative and unimaginative'.[28] Additionally, as Bainton has noted, some of the copied texts had not yet reached a canonical form:

> it is clear that the texts that would respectively become Howden's *Gesta* and his *Chronica* circulated in abbreviated forms before they were 'completed' by any modern sense of that word. Gervase of Canterbury used Howden's *Gesta* in 1188 (or thereabouts) as the basis of his own annals for the years 1171–79, but the *Gesta* as we have it today was not finished until 1191–92.[29]

In the *Chronica*, Gervase gives a list of Irish kings and ecclesiastics who submitted to Henry, adding:

22 William Stubbs (ed.), *The historical works of Gervase of Canterbury*, RS 73, 2 vols (London, 1879–80), i, pp 234–5. On Henry's motives, see also Gervase's *Gesta regum*: ibid., ii, pp 79–80. The Irish invitation is peculiar to Gervase: Flanagan, *Irish society*, p. 169. Although a devotee of the martyred Becket, he does not appear to have been involved in the archbishop's struggles or in the promotion of his cult: Staunton, *Historians of Angevin England*, p. 110. **23** Stubbs, *Historical works of Gervase of Canterbury*, i, pp 84–594. **24** Flanagan, *Irish society*, pp 169–70. **25** Staunton, *Historians of Angevin England*, p. 113. **26** Henry Bainton, *History and the written word: documents, literacy, and language in the age of the Angevins*, The Middle Ages Series [no number], (Philadelphia, 2020), p. 46. **27** Reginald Lane Poole, 'Gervase of Canterbury' in Leslie Stephen (ed.), *Dictionary of national biography*, 63 vols (New York and London, 1885–1900), xxi, pp 239–40 at p. 240. **28** Bainton, *History and the written word*, p. 36. **29** Ibid., p. 72.

> *Hii omnes juraverunt fidelitatem regi Henrico, cum primo fuit in Hibernia post martyrium sancti martyris Thomae. Construxerunt autem regi virgeum apud Duvelinam palatium magnum, in quo rex festivitatem Natalis Domini more regio celebraret.*
>
> All these swore allegiance to King Henry when he was first in Ireland after the martyrdom of the holy martyr Thomas. And they built a great palace of brushwood at Dublin, in which the king would celebrate the festival of the Lord's birth in the manner of the kingdom.[30]

In contrast to Roger's account, Henry is not ascribed any agency in building the palace and there is no mention of the guests. It is disappointing that Gervase – whose detailed account of the rebuilding of the choir of Canterbury after the fire of 1174 is one of the most cited accounts of medieval construction works – should have nothing more to say of Henry's Christmas palace, and this might suggest that really he had nothing more to go on than the account of Roger of Howden.[31]

Gerald of Wales

Unlike Roger of Howden, nobody could accuse our third source, Gerald of Wales, of being uninteresting. In many respects Gerald was the best-informed of the three, but unreliable in his own way, as he was a man who (in the magnificent words of F.M. Powicke) 'lived every day an existence of dramatic egotism'.[32] He has traditionally been viewed as the invasion's apologist-in-chief, becoming the *bête noire* of Irish writers of the early modern period, like Geoffrey Keating, Philip O'Sullivan Beare, and John Lynch.[33]

Although Gerald was living and studying in Paris during the initial years of the invasion, there is little doubt that his account of it is of the utmost importance, not least because he had access to some of its principal figures. Unlike the previous two informants, Gerald also had first-hand knowledge of

30 Stubbs, *Historical works of Gervase of Canterbury*, i, p. 236 (my translation). On the submissions, see below. 31 On the rebuilding, see Carol Davidson Cragoe, 'Reading and rereading Gervase of Canterbury', *Journal of the British Archaeological Association*, 154:1 (2001), 40–53. 32 Quoted in Robert Bartlett, 'Gerald of Wales [Giraldus Cambrensis, Gerald de Barry]', *ODNB*, available at: https://doi.org/10.1093/ref:odnb/10769, accessed 23 July 2024. 33 Aidan Breen, 'Gerald of Wales (Giraldus Cambrensis)', *DIB*, available at: https://doi.org/10.3318/dib.003490.v1, accessed 23 July 2024. Brendan Kane points out that he continued to be read in the late medieval/early modern period, but he did not leave a substantial imprint upon policy tracts and treatises, and 'we might wonder if the role played by his writings was more one of *ex post facto* historiographical framing and justification for, rather than generative spur of, sixteenth-century colonial expansion': Brendan Kane, 'Did the Tudors read Giraldus? Gerald of Wales and early modern polemical historiography' in Georgia Henley and A. Joseph McMullen (eds), *Gerald of Wales: new perspectives on a medieval writer and critic* (Cardiff, 2018), pp 259–81 at p. 275.

Ireland, visiting it four times,[34] including spending nearly a year there during the expedition of Henry II's son, the Lord John (1185), shortly after entering into royal service.[35] In his *Expugnatio Hibernica* (the first recension of which dates to 1189), he acts as the 'chronicler … apologist and mouthpiece' for the marcher lords (namely his Geraldine kinsmen), expressing resentment toward royal interference that he feels held them back from winning greater lands and renown.[36] Similarly, over the course of his own frustrated ecclesiastical career, he displayed increasing resentment toward the Angevin kings for their failure to support his ambitions.[37]

According to Gerald's account of late 1171:

> *Imminente vero Dominici natalis solemnitate, Dubliniam terre illius principes ad curiam videndam accessere quam plurimi. Ubi et lautam Anglicane mense copiam, venustissimum quoque vernarum obsequium plurimum admirantes, carne gruina, quam hactenus abhorruerant, regia voluntate passim per aulam vesci ceperunt.*
>
> As the solemn festival of Our Lord's birth drew near, the princes of that land came to Dublin in great numbers to view the king's court. There they greatly admired the sumptuous and plentiful fare of the English table and the most elegant service by the royal domestics. Throughout the great hall, in obedience to the king's wishes they began to eat the flesh of the crane, which they had hitherto loathed.[38]

The clearest differences between Gerald's account on the one hand, and those of Roger and Gervaise on the other, lie in his silence on the construction of the hall and his inclusion of crane as a food.[39] Significant too is the status of the attendees, which Roger had also commented upon (discussed further below), and while Gervase could be read as implying that Henry spent an 'Irish-style' Christmas, there is no room for such an interpretation in Gerald's account.

34 Robert Bartlett, *Gerald of Wales, 1146–1223*, Oxford historical monographs [no number], (Oxford, 1982), p. 20. 35 Ibid., p. 58, n. 1. 36 Ibid., p. 21. In the colourful words of F.X. Martin, the *Expugnatio* 'may be seized upon, arraigned for trial, condemned and gibbeted in public, but it cannot be disregarded': F.X. Martin, 'Gerald of Wales, Norman reporter on Ireland', *Studies: An Irish Quarterly Review*, 58:231 (1969), 279–92 at 279. 37 On Henry II impeding the Geraldines, see Colin Veach, 'The Geraldines and the conquest of Ireland' in Peter Crooks and Seán Duffy (eds), *The Geraldines and medieval Ireland: the making of a myth*, Trinity Medieval Ireland Series 1 (Dublin, 2017), pp 69–92 at pp 83–4. 38 Giraldus, *Expug. Hib.*, pp 96–7 (book 1, chapter 33). 39 Caoimhe Whelan points out to me that the crane is not mentioned in the later medieval translation of *Expugnatio Hibernica* into Hiberno Middle English. On the translation process, see Caoimhe Whelan, 'Translating the *Expugnatio Hibernica*: a vernacular English history in late medieval Ireland' in Carrie Griffin and Emer Purcell (eds), *Text, transmission, and transformation in the European Middle Ages, 1000–1500*, Cursor Mundi 34 (Turnhout, 2018), pp 165–92.

DISCUSSION

The Dublin celebration of 1171 was not an isolated event, but rather Christmas courts were an essential aspect of the political culture of the Angevin world; occasions for the practice of religion and piety, but also for dispensing of justice, the manufacture and demonstration of socio-political consensus, entertainment, and intrigue.[40] Such was their importance that chroniclers note the location of almost every Christmas court Henry II held during his 34-year reign.[41] The 1171 Christmas celebrations took on added significance, not simply because they were being held in (and introducing a fundamental aspect of royal practice to) a new part of the Angevin domain, but because of the grave consequences of the Christmas court twelve months previous.[42] At Bur-le-Roi (near Bayeaux) – perhaps on Christmas day itself – Henry supposedly uttered the fateful words 'What miserable drones and traitors have I nurtured and promoted in my household who let their lord be treated with such shameful contempt by a low-born clerk!'[43] The result was the infamous 'murder in the cathedral'; the martyrdom of St Thomas Beckett. Now, in Dublin, the celebration of that same ecclesiastical feast was carried out with due solemnity according to Roger (in his *Chronica*) and with 'elegant service' (according to Gerald). There is a sense that everyone was on their best behaviour (notwithstanding the convention of using 'solemn' in association with Christmas), and that Henry may have been making a show of piety, just as he had at St David's before sailing to Ireland and again on his return.[44]

The palace: location, builders and function

Only Roger of Howden offers a location for the 'royal palace' (as Flanagan notes, *palatium* has a more imperial flavour than *domus*, and better expresses the sense of wealth and power Henry wished to project);[45] it was built near St Andrew's church, outside the enclosed area of the city. As Seán Duffy has observed, Roger is surprisingly specific on this point, given that he was generally not well-informed regarding Ireland.[46] We can only speculate at the exact location and choice of site, but Duffy makes a strong case for it being at the Thingmoot, which he shows was not an assembly mound, but a parcel of

40 On Henry's court, see Nicholas Vincent, 'The court of Henry II' in Christopher Harper-Bill and Nicholas Vincent (eds), *Henry II: new interpretations* (Woodbridge, 2007), pp 278–334. **41** Flanagan, *Irish society*, pp 201–2. **42** This is not to say that the Irish did not observe Christmas as a religious festival, engage in feasting, or use it as a time for political activities. For Irish celebrations of Christmas, see Niamh Wycherley, '(Not) dreaming of a white Christmas in "pre-Norman" Ireland' in Salvador Ryan (ed.), *Christmas and the Irish* (Dublin, 2023), pp 14–17. **43** Quoted in Frank Barlow, 'Beckett, Thomas [St Thomas of Canterbury, Thomas of London]', *ODNB*, available at: https://doi.org/10.1093/ref:odnb/27201, accessed 23 July 2024. **44** Giraldus, *Expug. Hib.*, pp 92–3 (book 1, chapter 30) and pp 104–7 (book 1, chapter 38). On his return, he made a show of his piety by approaching St David's on foot and with a pilgrim staff. **45** Flanagan, *Irish society*, p. 206. **46** Seán Duffy, 'Ireland's Hastings: the Anglo-Norman conquest of Dublin' in Christopher Harper-Bill (ed.), *Anglo-Norman studies xx: proceedings of the Battle conference* (Woodbridge, 1998),

land located east of St Andrew's (itself just east of the junction of modern Dame St and Palace St) and west of Hoggen Green (now College Green, with the *hauger* or mound of its name probably located at the meeting of Suffolk St and Church Lane).[47] Why build it here? Was the fortified area within the enclosure of Dublin too small for Henry's needs? Were there security concerns? Conversely, did Henry seek to flaunt his lack of need for security by building on a greenfield site and not within an existing fortification? Afterall, he had not experienced any armed resistance since landing in Ireland.[48] A location east of the city would have given some protection from attacks that were most likely to come from the west or northwest, and allowed for swift escape to royal ships that were presumably moored at the deep water near the Steine.[49] Duffy proposes that reusing the Dubliners' own assembly area could be read as an act that 'definitively established himself as the city's new master'.[50] There is certainly a sense of ownership on the part of Henry, as he may have subsequently granted the site to Aldhelm 'the rich' of Bristol.[51]

Noticeably, Roger (in the *Gesta*) claims the palace was built both at Henry's command and for Henry, but by the Irish and *ad morem patriae illius/ad modum patriae illius* ('in the manner of that country').[52] The desire for/construction of an Irish-style building could be viewed as a deliberate cultural performance; the Irish may have sought to showcase their craftsmanship or Henry was attempting to demonstrate (rare) cultural sensitivity.[53] However, Gervase

pp 69–85 at p. 82. See Flanagan (above) on Roger possibly having a source emanating directly from Henry. **47** Duffy, 'Ireland's Hastings', pp 82–4; idem, 'A reconsideration of the site of Dublin's Viking Thing-mót' in Tom Condit and Christiaan Corlett (eds), *Above and beyond: essays in memory of Leo Swan* (Dublin, 2005), pp 351–60. **48** Seán Duffy, *Ireland in the Middle Ages* (Dublin, 1997), p. 71. F.X. Martin notes that the siege towers Henry brought would probably have been redundant in an Irish context, and that he was engaged in a show of military power rather than intending to campaign: Martin, 'Allies and an overlord', pp 87–8. The lateness of the expedition suggests he was not intending to campaign: Orpen, *Normans*, p. 95. **49** I owe this latter suggestion to Linzi Simpson. **50** Duffy, 'Ireland's Hastings', p. 85. Henry possessed an eye for strategic sites, and from his first arrival in Ireland indicated where he thought castles should be built, which were subsequently erected by King John, see for example, Giraldus, *Expug. Hib.*, pp 351–2, n. 471 (Tibberaghny) and *Deeds of the Normans*, p. 121, ll. 2663–70 (Lismore). **51** Orpen, *Normans*, pp 100–1, n. 44; Seán Duffy, 'Town and crown: the kings of England and their city of Dublin' in Michael Prestwich, Richard Britnell, and Robin Frame (eds), *Thirteenth Century England X. Proceedings of the Durham Conference 2003* (Woodbridge, 2005), pp 95–117, at p. 102. Similarly, the establishment of the exchequer nearby (during the late twelfth century) gave royal government 'a more stable, if more intimidating, presence' in that area: H.B. Clarke, *Dublin, part 1, to 1610*, Irish Historic Towns Atlas 11 (Dublin, 2002), p. 7. **52** I understand the general tenor of the sources to suggest that the builders were those who might now be termed 'Gaelic Irish' and not necessarily 'Hiberno-Scandinavian' (which is not to rule out their potential contribution to the construction work). The lines of demarcation might be somewhat blurred given that the typical (and near ubiquitous) Dublin Type-1 building may have its origins in Irish, rather than Scandinavian, architecture. For Type-1 buildings, see: Patrick F. Wallace, *The Viking Age buildings of Dublin*, Medieval Dublin excavations 1962–81 Series A volume 1, 2 vols (Dublin 1992), i, 9–14 and ii, figures 32, 46–8 and 183. **53** For the opinion that Henry was appreciating Irish craftsmanship and

almost inverts Roger's *Gesta*; to him it was seemingly built on the initiative of the Irish and there is no mention of Henry's order. Significantly, Gervase implies that the palace builders were those who had already submitted to Henry, something not found in Roger's works. He lists almost all the bishops of Ireland and the kings of Cork, Limerick, Ossory and Mide (all by title only).[54] It seems likely that Gervase was compressing his narrative at this point, and the many ecclesiastics who submitted to him probably did so at the Council of Cashel, which subsequently took place in 1172, and so the list cannot be relied upon as an indication of who built the palace.[55]

Overall, there is a hint of admiration in the writings of Roger (and to a lesser extent Gervase) for the craftsmanship, but none in Gerald's *Expugnatio*, where the only admiration is that of the Irish for what occurred within the hall. The building's magnificence, Nicholas Vincent has suggested, puts it on par with the admired great assembly tent that Henry sent to Emperor Frederick Barbarossa.[56] Its form can only be speculated; Roger's *Gesta* and Gervase's *Chronica* (which probably drew upon Roger) suggest a wattle building, possibly an enlarged Dublin Type-1 building. Such a building would typically have had a floor space of approximately 40m^2, but Henry's hall presumably covered a greater area, in order to accommodate the guests and servants.[57] It is possible that many of Dublin's buildings – vacant owing to the fleeing or killing of their occupants during the recent sieges – furnished building materials for the palace.[58]

As Flanagan notes, there are Irish historical and literary descriptions of underlings erecting houses for their superiors and arguments for viewing the construction of Henry's hall as part of the act of submission,[59] but linking these depictions to the 1171 hall is difficult, and Patrick Sims-Williams' minimalist conclusion has much to commend it: 'the action of the Irish kings and nobles in building the house for Henry II should not necessarily be construed as more than a (possibly reluctant) gesture of hospitality'.[60] As he also notes, 'there is no suggestion that it was intended to be the setting in

living freely among the Irish, see Orpen, *Normans*, p. 98. Gervaise might almost be understood to suggest that Henry adopted Irish practices in the celebration of Christmas, but it seems unlikely that Henry would have 'gone native' (indeed Gerald suggests he did quite the opposite) and the *more regio* ('in the manner of the kingdom') may have been a result of his condensing of Roger's accounts, where it is the hall that was built *ad morem patriae illius/ad modum patriae illius* (according to the *Gesta* and *Chronica* respectively). **54** Stubbs, *Historical works of Gervase of Canterbury*, i, pp 235–6. **55** Orpen makes this point regarding Roger of Howden's *Gesta* and *Chronica* (Orpen, *Normans*, pp 95–6, n. 21), and it seems equally applicable to Gervase. **56** Vincent, 'The court of Henry II', p. 327. However, if admiration it was, it was for something they had not seen. **57** Some idea of the potential occupancy of Irish buildings might be seen in the *Annals of Ulster*'s account of the killing of 38 people assembled in one house for a feast in 1119 (*AU* 1119.3) and the *Annals of Inisfallen*'s description of the burning of over 80 people in a single house, a century earlier (*AI* 1029.2). **58** It would have required several kilometres of wattle (I owe this observation to Stephen Harrison) and recycling material would have made sense. **59** Flanagan, *Irish Society*, pp 203–6. **60** Patrick Sims-Williams, 'The submission of Irish kings in fact and fiction' in idem, *Irish influence on medieval Welsh literature* (Oxford, 2011), pp 208–29 at p. 220.

which Henry received the submission of the Irish kings', with Roger's *Gesta* portraying the submission of the Irish occurring at Waterford the previous October.[61] If it was intended for taking the submission of the Irish kings, it is difficult to see the value of building it at the site of the Thingmoot, a Dublin institution that would probably have held little significance for them. For the family of Mac Murchada it would have been a particularly galling choice, given that the Dubliners had supposedly murdered Diarmait Mac Murchada's father and buried him with a dog (for added insult) within the confines of their own assembly structure (presumably nearby).[62] Instead, as Sims-Williams suggests, the building was 'apparently so that he could spend Christmas and the winter months in his accustomed royal fashion, lording it over his new subjects while placating their residual resentment with food and gifts'.[63] The one source that might suggest that Henry II used his Dublin palace as a venue for taking submissions – the fifteenth-century *Mac Carthaigh's Book* – is problematic, and justifiable doubt has been cast upon it.[64]

The attendees

It is evident that all the commentators viewed Henry's Dublin court as more than a Dublin or even Angevin affair. As already noted, between Roger's *Gesta* and his *Chronica* the attendees changed from *regibus et ditioribus Hyberniae* ('kings and rich men of Ireland') to *regibus et principibus Hyberniae* ('kings and princes of Ireland'), while Gervase makes no mention of attendees. Gerald claimed that *terre illius principes* ('princes of that land') visited the king's court, which ought to be read in light of his understanding of the hierarchical structure of contemporary Irish kingship. He assigned the royal title to significant overkings like the high-king Ruaidrí Ua Conchobair, Domnall Mór Ua Briain of Thomond and Diarmait Mac Carthaig of Desmond,[65] but considered men farther down the political pecking-order, such as Domnall Mac Gilla Pátraic of Osraige (Ossory) and Máel Sechnaill Mac Fáeláin of the Déisi (Decies), to be princes *quanquam non tam principalibus, magnis et autenticis tamen in gente sua* ('although they were not of such cardinal importance, were nevertheless influential and had real authority among their

This is a revision of his earlier article, 'The submission of Irish kings in fact and fiction: Henry II, Bendigeidfran, and the dating of *The Four Branches of the Mabinogi*', *CMCS*, 22 (1991), 31–61. **61** Sims-Williams, 'The submission of Irish kings', p. 215. **62** Giraldus, *Expug. Hib.*, pp 66–7 (book 1, chapter 17). The claim is repeated, doubtless under Gerald's influence, in *AMisc*, *sub anno* 1169.4 (pp 52–5). **63** Sims-Williams, 'The submission of Irish kings', pp 214–15. Similarly, Martin suggests 'Henry had learned in Wales the importance for Celtic peoples of the open door and prodigal entertainment': Martin, 'Allies and an overlord', p. 90. **64** Sims-Williams, 'The submission of Irish kings', pp 216–17; *AMisc*, *sub anno* 1172.5 (pp 56–7). For recent discussions on the 'entered into his house' submission formula, see Denis Casey, 'A man of no mean standing: the career and legacy of Donnchad mac Briain (d. 1064)', *Peritia*, 31 (2020), 29–57 at 43, n. 70 and Caitlin Ellis, '"Brian's sword" and the "Standard of the king of the Saxons" in the Irish annals: the Godwinsons, Hastings and Leinster–Munster relations', *Ériu*, 73 (2023), 43–62 at 51–6. **65** They are called kings in

people'), and they were worthy to receive royal gifts.[66] They, in turn, stood above other men of consequence, like Diarmait Mac Murchada's son, Domnall, who *quanquam non legitimo in sua tamen gente pervalido* ('although illegitimate, [was] a man of great influence among his people').[67] In some respects, this hierarchical perception is reflected in the poem known as the *Song of Dermot and the Earl* (otherwise, *Deeds of the Normans in Ireland*), which says the Irish recognized Domnall as a king, and 'in Ireland kings were as numerous as earls were elsewhere' but the kings of Meath, Leinster, Desmond, Munster, Connacht and Ulster were the 'chief kings' among them.[68]

It appears that Henry was engaged in something of a 'charm offensive'. Displaying royal power and munificence to the 'middling sort' – and allowing them access to his person – had the potential to undermine the networks of both the great kings like Ua Conchobair and those among the invaders who were not entirely within royal favour, like Strongbow. There is much to Orpen's cynical assessment of Henry's strategy that 'it was Henry's cue throughout this expedition to appear as the friend of the natives, Welsh and Irish, and the stern repressor of the Anglo-Norman march-lords; his real object being to secure the control of the Crown over both'.[69] Although it is an *argumentum ex silentio*, none of the three sources make mention of the presence of Henry's barons and neither is there mention of the clergy, even though among Henry's first acts in Ireland were a visit to Lismore (where the papal legate was located) and Cashel (the seat of an archbishopric and site of his intended church council),[70] while both Archbishop Lorcán Ua Tuathail (Laurence O'Toole) of Dublin and Bishop Áed Ua Cáellaide of Clogher-Louth witnessed Henry's (undated) confirmation of an earlier grant/charter to All Hallows by Diarmait Mac Murchada.[71] As for the poor, who were often the recipients of royal charity at Christmas, they too are unmentioned, and as Otway-Ruthven noted, 'Dublin must of course have been largely denuded of citizens at this time' owing to how many were killed in the recent sieges or had fled.[72]

The Christmas fare

Gerald claims the guests ate *carne gruina, quam hactenus abhorruerant* ('flesh of the crane, which they had hitherto loathed'), but not that it was forbidden them. Notions of crane as a taboo food for the Irish are probably little more than instances of taking Gerald's statement and working backwards to its illogical conclusion, and it would be more profitable to consider his account in light of evidence for crane consumption in Ireland, hunting crane as an elite

Giraldus, *Expug. Hib.*, pp 92–3 (book 1, chapter 31). **66** Ibid., pp 94–5 (book 1, chapter 32). **67** Ibid., pp 32–3 (book 1, chapter 3). **68** *Deeds of the Normans*, p. 109, ll. 2185–96. **69** Orpen, *Normans*, p. 93. **70** F.X. Martin, 'Allies and an overlord', p. 89. **71** Orpen, *Normans*, p. 101, n. 45. On the possible existence of a (now lost) charter, see Marie Therese Flanagan, *Irish royal charters: texts and contexts* (Oxford, 2005), pp 64–6 and 385–6 (§4). **72** A.J. Otway-Ruthven, *A history of medieval Ireland* (London and New York, 1968), p. 50,

activity, the food situation in Ireland in Christmas 1171, and Gerald's cultural views on matters of diet and consumption.

The common crane (*Grus grus*) was once (but is no longer) a widespread resident of Ireland, and although it is frequently difficult to distinguish it in the written sources from the outwardly similar heron, it appears that cranes were occasionally domesticated and kept as a pets.[73] This does not preclude it from being a source of food, for although adult crane is tough and sinewy, its young are more tender (although apparently both are awkward to prepare).[74] Crane bones have been found at the high-status early medieval sites of Ballinderry and Lagore, where it was likely consumed as food.[75] Given the small number of bones found among the large bone assemblages at these sites, it appears that crane was neither a forbidden nor a common food, or that its consumption was an emergency measure; it was simply optional and a rarity. This stands in contrast to England where crane was hunted continuously for food from the Mesolithic period until its local extinction in the late Middle Ages.[76] Gerald previously discussed the crane in his *Topographia Hibernie* (the first recension dates to 1187, slightly pre-dating the *Expugnatio* (*c.*1189),[77] where it is portrayed as a symbol of watchfulness and no mention is made of eating it (although Gerald claims of its own digestive system that it possesses 'such a warm and fiery liver that, if it should eat iron, it will not let it through undigested').[78]

Despite its less-than-optimal flavour, consuming crane was a display of high status in England and Wales, where hunting it was reserved for elites.[79] The preferred method of hunting was falconry, and the size of the prey required the largest and most expensive of raptors and skilful handling; a successful hunt required one to be an elite performer in an elite sport. Given

n. 38. See also, Orpen, *Normans*, p. 99. 73 Fergus Kelly, *Early Irish farming: a study based mainly on the law-texts of the 7th and 8th centuries AD*, Early Irish Law Series 4 (rev. ed. Dublin, 2000), pp 125–8. Herons were considered a nuisance owing to their impact on fish stocks: Fergus Kelly, *A guide to early Irish law*, Early Irish Law Series 3 (Dublin, 1988), p. 106. 74 Umberto Albarella and Richard Thomas, 'They dined on crane: bird consumption, wild fowling and status in medieval England', *Acta zoologica cracoviensia*, 45 (2002), 23–38 at 23. 75 Kelly, *Early Irish farming*, p. 127, n. 171. See H. O'Neill Hencken and A.W. Stelfox, 'Ballinderry crannog no. 2', *PRIA* 47C (1941–2), 1–76 at 21, 67 and 73 and Hugh Hencken, Liam Price and Laura E. Start, 'Lagore crannog: an Irish royal residence of the 7th to 10th centuries A.D.', *PRIA*, 53C (1950–1), 1–247 at 229–30. For references to the consumption of crane from late imperial Rome to late medieval/early modern Europe, see László Bartosiewicz, 'Crane: food, pet and symbol' in Gisela Grupe and Joris Peters (eds), *Feathers, grit and symbolism: birds and humans in the ancient old and new worlds*, Documenta Archaeobiologiae 3 (Rahden, 2005), pp 259–69 at pp 263–6. 76 Lee Raye, 'The ugly, greedy crane of medieval Wales', *Peritia*, 29 (2018), 143–58 at 144. 77 Five recensions of his *Topographia* were made during his lifetime, all probably by him: Caoimhe Whelan, 'The transmission of the *Expugnatio Hibernica* in fifteenth-century Ireland' in Henley and McMullen (eds), *Gerald of Wales: new perspectives*, pp 243–58 at p. 254, n. 1. 78 John J. O'Meara (trans.), *The history and topography of Ireland*, Dolmen Texts 4 (rev. ed. Mountrath, 1982), pp 40–1 (book 1, chapter 10). This is a 'characteristic' of the ostrich, borrowed from Pliny: Raye, 'The ugly, greedy crane', 149–50. 79 Raye, 'The ugly,

that, in England, hunting with birds was forbidden to ordinary people, there may be an implied slur in Gerald's account (i.e., the Irish do not hunt crane as they are not noble). Henry II was obsessed with falconry (many of the rents from Ireland subsequently payable to him included hawks)[80] and according to Gerald, while the king was waiting to sail from Wales to Ireland, he put in an order for Welsh falcons after seeing their ability to beat off the Norwegian goshawks he had brought with him.[81] It is possible that the crane served at Christmas were hunted by Henry himself and, if read together, the accounts of the Welsh raptors and Christmas fare may have a subtext (admittedly at a stretch) that the Welsh 'hawks' of the Angevin aviary would bring down the largest of Ireland's native 'birds'.

Did Henry know that crane was not normally eaten in Ireland and thus deliberately introduced it at his table in an act of dominance, played out against a time of food shortage? (If so, it would jar against his supposed cultural sensitivity in the palace's construction materials/methods.) The evidence for shortages that Christmas is considerable: the *Annals of Inisfallen*,[82] the *Song of Dermot*,[83] and Welsh chronicles all indicate that it was a harsh winter. According to the Peniarth 20 version of *Brut y Tywysogion*: 'mortality befell those who had gone with the king to Ireland because of the novelty of the unaccustomed foods, and also because the ships had not been able to sail with merchandise in winter, on account of the fury of the Irish Sea',[84] while Ralph de Diceto reports outbreaks of dysentery in the king's army.[85]

Finally, somewhat overlooked, but perhaps more significant was the manner in which the bird was served. The Irish, Gerald informs us, admired not only the quantity and quality of the food, but also the 'most elegant service by the royal domestics'. Gerald had little time for Irish cuisine and eating habits, reporting sailors' tales of semi-naked Connachtmen rowing the Atlantic surf who had never seen bread or cheese and lived only on meat, fish and milk, and famously summed up the Irish saying 'they are a wild and inhospitable people. They live on beasts only, and live like beasts. They have not progressed at all

greedy crane', 146–8. 80 Nicholas Vincent, 'Angevin Ireland' in Brendan Smith (ed.), *The Cambridge history of Ireland I, 600–1550* (Cambridge, 2018), pp 185–221 at p. 204. 81 Giraldus, *Expug. Hib.*, pp 90–1 (book 1, chapter 29). 82 *AI*, *sub anno* 1172.2 (pp 304–5). Given this is the second entry for 1172 (and the first merely contains chronological information), it is likely that it refers to the winter of 1171–2. 83 The *Deeds of the Normans in Ireland* says that supplies were expensive throughout Leinster, and none came from elsewhere: *Deeds of the Normans*, p. 122, ll. 2689–924. The shortages in Leinster may have been aggravated by Ruaidri Ua Conchobair's burning of their crops earlier in the year: *AFM*, *sub anno* 1171 (ii, pp 1184–5) and *AT*, *sub anno* 1171 (p. 282). 84 Quoted in Duffy, *Ireland in the Middle Ages*, p. 86. Thomas Jones (ed. and trans), *Brut y Tywysogyon, or, the chronicle of the princes: Peniarth MS 20 version*, History and law series 11 (Cardiff, 1952), *sub anno* 1172 (p. 63). 85 William Stubbs (ed.), *Radulfi de Diceto decani Lundoniensis opera historica (The historical works of Master Ralph de Diceto, Dean of London)*, RS 68, 2 vols (London, 1876), i, p. 350.

from the primitive habits of pastoral living'.[86] For Gerald, the Christmas feast was an episode in the display of polite manners, cultural superiority, and set a lesson in civility.[87]

CONCLUSION

Henry II's Christmas court of 1171 was a minor event, which can be viewed through a variety of lenses. For students of the municipal history of Dublin, it holds interest in the possible continuity of assembly site and that it may have been the occasion at which were issued the first English royal charters in Dublin, including that which granted it to the city of Bristol. For those who study the Angevin court, it takes its place among the many royal, ducal and other assemblies of Henry II. For many, its significance probably rests in its ostentatious show of English royal presence in Ireland and the duplicitousness of Henry II in his dealings with the Irish. Whatever its significance, if we were to rely on the Irish annals we would probably have no inkling that it occurred.[88] Instead, we are fortunate to have the testimonies of Gerald of Wales, Roger of Howden and Gervaise of Canterbury – an egotist, a dullard and a second-rater – which, for medievalists, is as good as you will get.[89]

86 O'Meara, *History and topography of Ireland*, p. 101 (Book 3, chapter 93) (quotation); the sailors' story is at p. 111 (Book 3, chapter 103). **87** A 'civilising mission' and sense of cultural superiority on the part of the invaders was not a universally held view among them: Colin Veach, 'Henry II and the ideological foundations of Angevin rule in Ireland', *IHS*, 42:161 (2018), 1–25. A negative view of Henry II's expedition can be found in the work of William of Canterbury: Marcus Bull, 'Criticism of Henry II's expedition to Ireland in William of Canterbury's miracles of St Thomas Becket', *Journal of Medieval History*, 33:2 (2007), 107–29. **88** Alone among the Irish annals the *Annals of Inisfallen* (in a curt entry) note that Henry wintered at Dublin, but make no mention of his departure: *AI* 1171.5. Of the annals that mention his journey to Dublin (but not wintering): the *Annals of Ulster* compress his entire expedition into one short entry, and another simply noting his departure (*AU* 1171, 1172); the *Annals of Loch Cé* report his arrival and departure in similar terms (*ALC* 1171, 1172); the *Annals of Tigernach* portray his expedition (likewise over two entries) as obtaining more substantial results (*AT* 1171, 1172). Of the annals that make no mention of Henry at Dublin: the *Annals of the Four Masters* note he arrived in Waterford and reports nothing further of his actions or departure (*AFM* 1171) and the *Annals of Clonmacnoise* record that Henry arrived in Ireland in person to complete the conquest in 1173: Nollaig Ó Muraíle (ed.), *Annals of Cluain Mhic Nóis (to AD 1408) also known as Mag Eochagáin's Book ('Leabhar Conaill Mhig Eochagáin') translated by Conall Mag Eochagáin, AD 1627 together with a remnant of 'Annals of Leacán', AD 1443–68 translated by Dubhaltach Mac Fhir Bhisigh, AD 1666* (Dublin, 2022), *sub anno* 1167.5, p. 309. On the entries in *Mac Carthaigh's Book* (*AMisc*), see n. 64 above. **89** I would like to thank the following: Ben Snook for assistance with Latin translation and discussing the site of Henry's winter palace with me, Linzi Simpson for her thoughts on its location, Stephen Harrison on the logistics of its construction, Caoimhe Whelan on Gerald of Wales, Seán Duffy for various suggestions and references, and the participants of the 25th Medieval Dublin Symposium (5 October 2024) for comments and good-natured engagement.

Revealing the medieval riverfront: excavations at 42–51 Strand Street Great/31–34 Abbey Street Upper, Dublin

CAITRÍONA MOORE

INTRODUCTION

From late May to early November 2019, excavations at 42–51 Great Strand Street/31–34 Abbey Street Upper, Dublin, revealed significant evidence for the medieval Liffey riverfront comprising multiple phases of wooden revetments, associated stone and timber structures and the remains of a substantial portion of the medieval precinct wall of St Mary's abbey (DU018-020048). The excavation site covered some 0.35 ha., its northern limit taking in the plots of 31–34 Abbey Street Upper, while its southern boundary encompassed 42–51 Great Strand Street. The site also included a significant section of Byrne's Lane which runs east–west across its centre (fig. 7.1). The excavation was directed by the author for Archaeology and Built Heritage Ltd under licence 19E0110 from the National Monuments Service. It was completed in advance of the development of two hotels by the Marlet Property Group who funded the excavation and post-excavation programme.

ARCHAEOLOGICAL AND HISTORICAL BACKGROUND

The site lies within the environs of the medieval St Mary's abbey, the topographic and archaeological evidence for which has been presented in much detail in a previous volume,[1] and does not need detailed repetition here; suffice to state that the results of this excavation have allowed for some revision of the exact location of the abbey precinct, as it extended along this section of Great Strand Street. Of greater significance perhaps when beginning the project was the 2002 excavation at 52–56 Great Strand Street on which a substantial early thirteenth-century timber revetment (DU018-115-) was uncovered.[2] That excavation greatly expanded the knowledge of the northside waterfront throughout the medieval period. This section of shoreline was part of the liberty of St Mary's, under the jurisdiction of the Cistercian monastery located some 320m to the west, and it is likely the revetment was constructed for the monastery, their main harbour being upstream at the mouth of the Bradogue.

1 Geraldine Stout, 'The topography of St Mary's Cistercian abbey and precinct, Dublin' in Duffy (ed.), MD XII, pp 138–60. 2 Claire Walsh, 'Archaeological excavation of the Anglo-Norman waterfront at Strand Street Great, Dublin' in Duffy (ed.), MD VI, pp 160–87.

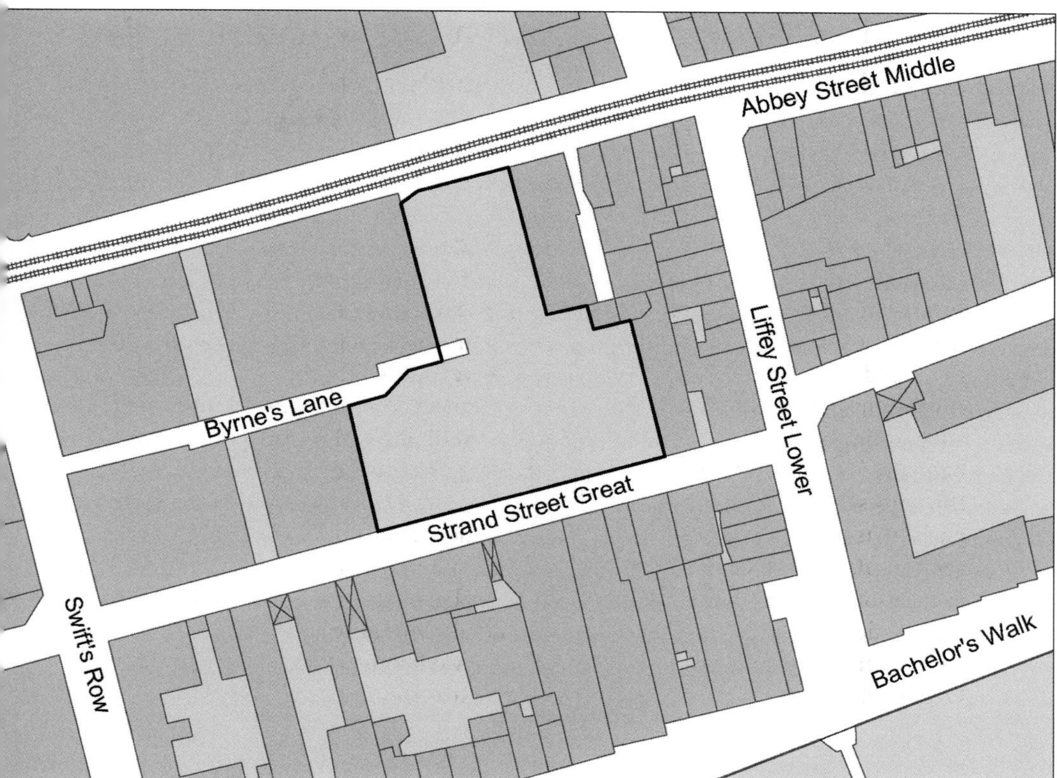

7.1 Site location

The revetment almost certainly relates to an inlet, depicted by Speed on his 1610 map as enclosed by the outer precinct wall of the abbey, which accommodated the watercourse through its thickness just to the north of its confluence with the Liffey (fig. 7.2).

The earliest archaeological investigations on the excavation site were completed in 2008 when a series of test-trenches was opened to assess the potential impact of a proposed development.[3] This trenching sought to identify the extension of the known thirteenth-century revetment but, while the structure was not uncovered along its expected trajectory, oak planking was detected in the northern part of the site. Occurring in tandem with the 2019 excavation was that of the site of 35–36 Abbey Street Upper, on which was found the well-preserved remains of a thirteenth-century vertical mill,[4] clearly related to the revetments and indeed the abbey itself.

3 James Hession, 'Archaeological assessment and impact statement. 31–34 Abbey Street/ 42–51 Great Strand Street. Bounded by Byrnes Lane, Dublin 1', unpublished report, 2008.
4 Ian Russell, 'Archaeological excavation of a proposed development at 35–36 Abbey Street Upper, Dublin 1 (18E0293)', unpublished report, 2023.

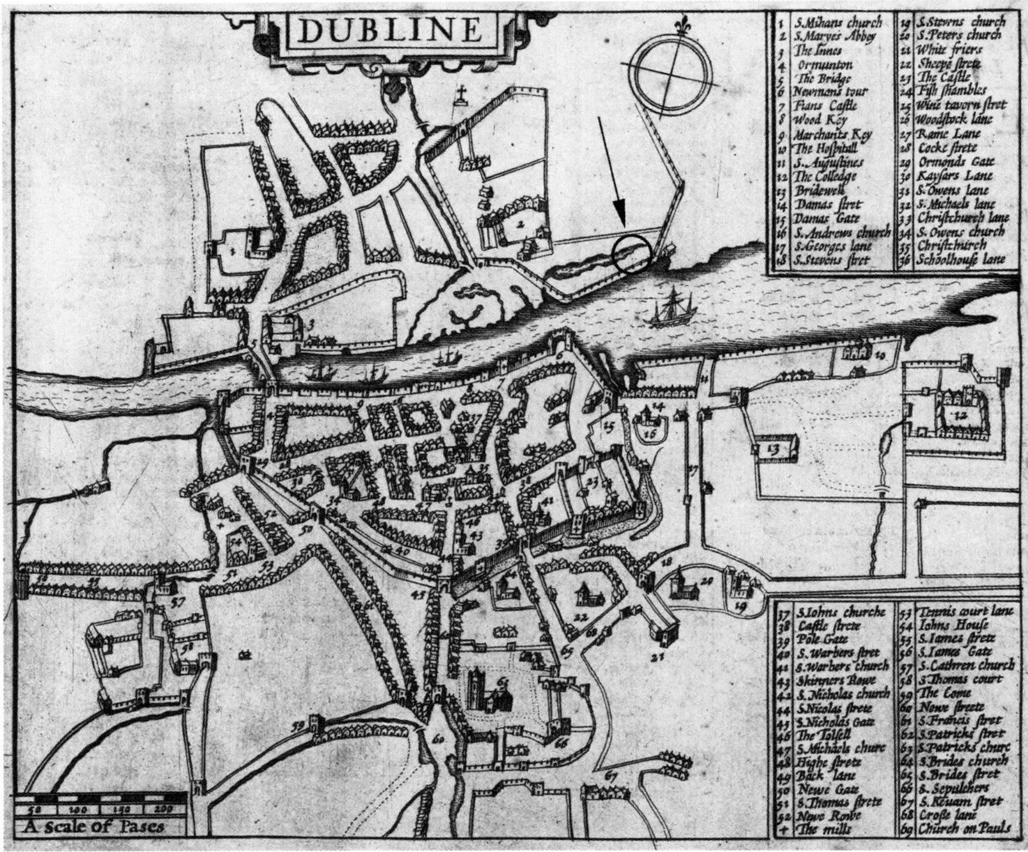

7.2 Speed's map of Dublin, 1610, site location circled

EXCAVATION RESULTS

Revetment C093/DU018-115-

Revetment C093, the continuation of DU018-115-, was found at the southwest edge of the site, adjacent to Byrne's Lane (fig. 7.3). It was disturbed along the site boundary, as evidenced by the recovery of *ex situ* timbers within the backfill of the pile trench for the adjacent modern building. A well-preserved portion, 5000mm long, with a maximum surviving height of 700mm, was found beneath a modern concrete tank. The revetment was orientated ENE–WSW and comprised transverse subsidiary baseplates set 770–1040mm apart and pegged in position on the riverine silts. Half-laps in the upper surface of these held two longitudinal primary baseplates, the ends of which were joined with a splayed scarf joint. As was seen on the adjacent site, the scarfs indicated

7.3 Revetment C093/DU018-115- as it entered the site adjacent to Byrne's Lane

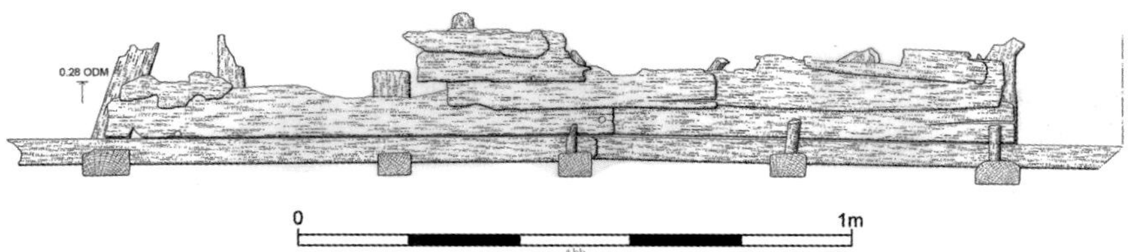

7.4 Southeast east-facing elevation of C093/DU018-115- (Johnny Ryan)

construction from east to west.[5] All of the basal timbers were additionally secured in place with small posts and stakes set alongside their edges, preventing lateral movement. Sturdy vertical posts set into mortises in the baseplates supported up to four longitudinal planks set horizontally on their edges, facing south towards the modern river (fig. 7.4). Just one raking brace survived, set into a chase mortice on a subsidiary baseplate. This would have supported the planking from the rear and was reinforced with an east–west orientated timber (a reused subsidiary baseplate), set 260mm above the level of the baseplates on a layer of grey clay and gravels. These were undifferentiated

5 Walsh, 'Waterfront at Strand Street Great', p. 174.

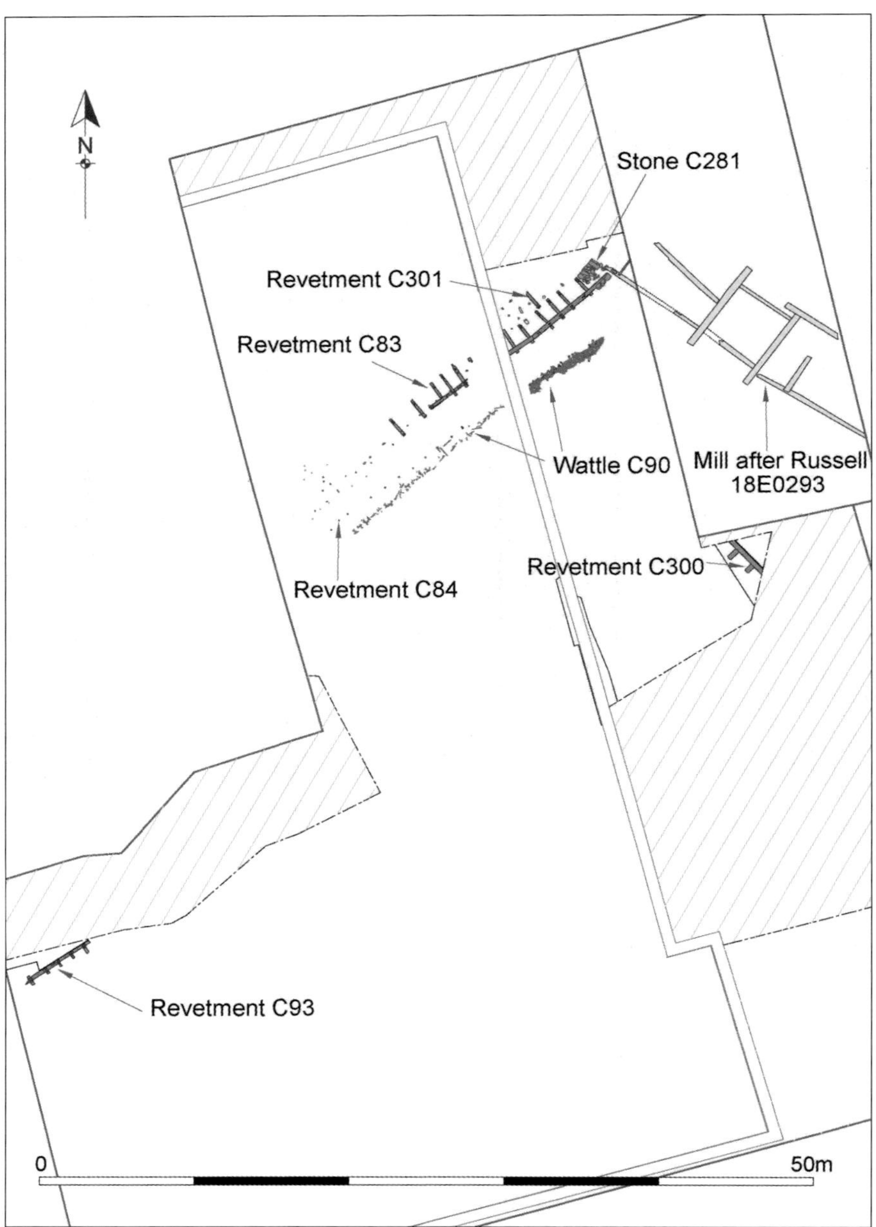

7.5 Excavated medieval revetments

from the natural riverine deposits across the site but were clearly introduced during the construction of the revetment. The angle of the brace suggested an original revetment height of *c.*2000mm. Redundant carpentry joints in posts,

7.6 Looking WSW at the poorly preserved remains of revetments C083 (R) and C84 (L) as they crossed the central part of the site

and dowel holes in planks, indicated the reuse of several elements; all of the timbers were oak. Again in keeping with the evidence on the adjacent site, no nails were used in the timber construction.

C093 was sealed by multiple bands of silty grey alluvial clays and grey/orange gravels. At its ENE end the planking of C093 was missing and the primary baseplate terminated with a splayed scarf, beyond which no further timbers were encountered. At this point, however, was C400, a stone surface comprising a single course of well laid limestone flags set at the same level as the timber baseplates. This was orientated NE–SW signifying a change in direction of the features in this area. Only a short portion 760mm long of C400 was excavated, as it extended beneath a rubble embankment alongside Byrne's Lane which could not be removed for health and safety reasons, and beneath which any surviving archaeological features are now preserved. Approximately 1300mm east of the ENE end of C093 was C155, the remains of two truncated baseplates joined with a face-pegged scarf. C155 was not in line with trajectories of either C093 or C400, and appeared to be *ex situ* but may have originally have been part of C093 or another dismantled revetment (see below).

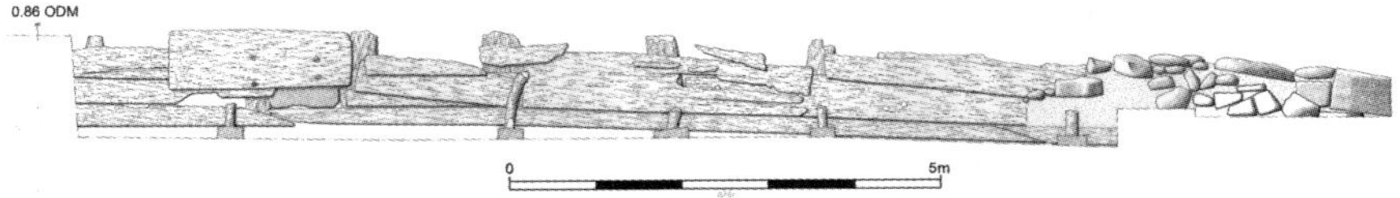

7.7 Southeast-facing elevation of C083 in the ENE part of the site, its ENE end enclosed by stone structure C281

7.8 Looking northwest at revetment C083 with inset of carpentry detail; to the rear of C083 are the remains of several stone and timber structures including the single subsidiary baseplate C301

Revetment C083

Some 20m further north were found the remains of two parallel timber revetments, C083 and C084, along with a wattle fence C090 (fig. 7.5). All were orientated ENE–WSW and were constructed on riverine silts and covered with exceptionally compact gravel deposits. The WSW ends of both C083 and C084 were disturbed by the pile trench of the adjacent modern building, but *ex*

7.9 The end of the baseplate of revetment C083 where it abutted a timber from the mill headrace

situ timbers within the construction backfill again suggested that one or both of these structures extended through that site. Archaeological testing of that site did not identify either revetment,[6] but it is possible that they only crossed

6 Claire Walsh, Archaeological assessment of a site at 21–29 Abbey St., Dublin 1, unpublished

7.10 Stone plinth C281 as it covered the ENE end of revetment C083

its southwesternmost corner (see below), and in any case may not have survived well. Across the centre of the excavation site these structures formed three parallel lines; however, as they moved ENE, the timber revetment C084 and the wattle fence C090 merged.

C083 was the northernmost of the two timber revetments and extended across the site for a length of 24.6m. Its preservation varied considerably, its ENE end surviving only as a line of upright oak posts spaced an average of 800mm apart, paired with occasional brushwood stakes (fig. 7.6). Moving WSW, however, the structure became gradually more substantial and was clearly built to the same design as C093 with the planking facing southwards. Across the centre of the site, C083 consisted of six subsidiary baseplates, set 700–800mm apart and pegged in position. Chase mortices at their northwest ends were occasionally cross-dowelled, but all were empty. At the opposite southeast end of each was a small mortice into which was set a peg holding the timber in position on the river silts. Adjacent to these, cut into the upper surface, were half-laps into which was set a longitudinal primary baseplate.

At its ENE end, revetment C083 was very well-preserved, buried by successive layers of alluvial clays and gravels, and had a surviving height of

report, [online, available from: https://heritagemaps.ie/documents/Therefore_Archaeology Reports/00E0240.pdf [Accessed 27 February 2025].

750mm (fig. 7.7). It followed the same structure of evenly spaced subsidiary baseplates with half-lap joints into which two primary baseplates were secured. The primary baseplates were joined with a face-pegged scarf (fig. 7.8). Sturdy vertical posts set in stopped mortices on the baseplates supported *c.*11 horizontal planks set longitudinally on edge, and stacked 4–5 planks high. Several planks had unused or truncated fixings indicative of reuse, and at least three (possibly four) were ship timbers. In one location a large flat stone, rectangular in shape and set horizontally on its edge, had been used to plug a gap in the planking but, as seen in C093, no nails were used in the construction. Despite the good preservation in this area, none of the raking braces survived, but chase mortices in the subsidiary baseplates, some of which held smaller packing posts, indicated their position.

C083 terminated within the ENE corner of the site where it abutted C305/C312, part of the headrace of the mill on the adjacent site (fig. 7.9). The baseplate of C083 was cut with a blunt end, clearly respecting the edge of the headrace timber. Both features were covered by C311, an irregular deposit of limestone blocks over which was C281, a solid square construction (L1500; W1700; D310mm) of 2–3 courses of regular limestone blocks consolidated with packing clay (fig. 7.10). Both C281 and the blunt end of the baseplate suggest a formal gap in the revetment, related to the adjacent mill. Revetment C083 did continue beyond the headrace on the other site where it had suffered some disturbance by post-medieval activity.

Revetment C084

Across the central part of the site, 1600–2000mm south of and parallel to C083, were the remains of a second timber revetment, C084. This survived largely as a line of 17 posts and stakes spaced 690–1100mm apart (see figs 7.5 and 7.6). At its ENE end lay the heavily degraded remains of two subsidiary baseplates and two very fragmentary planks. The better preserved of the baseplates had a half-lap cut into its upper surface. This would originally have held the longitudinal primary baseplate and its position suggests that this revetment faced the opposite direction to C083 (and C093), i.e., its planking faced northwards. C084 did not extend into the ENE corner of the site but rather merged with a post-and-wattle fence, C090. The point where they met was truncated but while C090 continued into the ENE area, C084 appeared to terminate.

Wattle fence C090

Across much of the central part of the site C090 was located 400–500mm south of C084 and consisted merely of occasional fragmentary and degraded horizontal rods. Moving ENE, the space between the two features gradually reduced and the evidence for C090 became more substantial. The exact point where they merged was truncated by a test-trench and modern pile-wall;

7.11 Looking north at post-and-wattle fence C090

however, in the ENE part of the site, parallel to the well-preserved section of C083, C090 was also in very good condition having been covered with the same successive layers of alluvial clay. In this area it presented as a substantial post-and-wattle fence with a maximum surviving height of 1450mm. The posts were worked to long shallow points and although very unevenly spaced, were frequently set in pairs with the majority set securely into the underlying silts. They sloped downwards from top to bottom at *c*.80°. The posts within C090 were characterized by a slight bend or kink along their length. This is a known feature of coppiced hazel, caused by the topping process resulting in a forked stem or kink in the stem which occurs after a year's growth.[7] The tips of several posts were exposed at a significantly higher level within the weave suggesting several episodes of construction (fig. 7.11).

This was further indicated by the weave that occurred in three distinct bands. The lowest band (H160mm) comprised scant rods (diam. 15–25mm) woven around the lower parts of the posts. Above this was a more substantial band (W250mm) of loosely woven rods (av. diam. 22mm). The uppermost portion comprised a band (W300mm) of heavy rods woven around the posts, these elements being poorly preserved, brittle and fragmentary. Although

7 Oliver Rackham, *Ancient woodland: its history, vegetation and uses in England* (London, 1979).

sturdy and substantial, C090 was generally roughly built. Its ENE end was truncated by a post-medieval pit and the boundary with the adjacent site; however, it did align with a more complex structure on the adjacent site, which was related to the mill.[8] In the ENE corner of the site where it merged with C084, C090 was located 2300mm south of revetment C083, and between them lay fairly undifferentiated layers of grey alluvial clays interspersed with river gravels.

Wooden and stone structures north of C083

The small area available for excavation immediately north of C083 contained the remains of several wooden and stone structures, all orientated ENE–WSW parallel with the more substantial revetment (see fig. 7.8). These are summarized below, but their fragmentary nature somewhat limits their interpretation.

Located 950mm north of the primary baseplates of revetment C083 was a single subsidiary baseplate, C301. This was laid on the same orientation as those in C083 and was truncated by a test-trench at its NNW end. Its opposite end was held in position with two brushwood pegs, one of which was set through a mortice, adjacent to which in the upper surface of the timber was a half-lap. Seven brushwood stakes (C319) extended out from each side of the timber forming a line 4000mm long, parallel with revetment C083. If this was all that remained of a timber revetment of the same form as C083, the position of the half-lap, which would have held the primary baseplate, suggests that like C083 the planking faced south.

In this same small area, just north of C301 and some 1500mm north of revetment C083, was C285, a line of split-timber posts again orientated ENE/WSW. Roughly woven around the lower portion of the posts was wattle C299. The rods were very thin (av. diam. 4mm), and dispersed, with no formal weave evident. The combination of timber posts and such thin wattle is unusual, and it is possible that this structure originally included more substantial components at a higher level. C285 extended ENE–WSW for a distance of 6.94m, parallel to C083, C301/C319 and C090 further south. Its ENE end extended below the portion of the mill headrace which occurred on the site, and it also probably continued across the adjacent site where a similar structure was uncovered below the continuation of revetment C083. The WSW end of C285 ran beneath C298, a dispersed line (approx. 7m long) of rough limestone blocks orientated ENE/WSW. These were directly north of post-and-wattle structure C285. The stones in C298 were irregularly set and the feature was truncated by the archaeological test-trench which also truncated C301. The most structured portion of C298 was at the ENE end

8 Russell, '35–36 Abbey Street Upper'.

where several split-timber posts, at least one of which was set in a square cut, were inserted among six large blocks. The WSW end of this structure extended beyond the limit of excavation and potentially also into the adjacent site.

Revetment C300

At the return of the boundary wall between 34 and 35 Abbey St Upper was revetment C300 (see fig. 7.5). The excavation of C300 was hampered by the rising water table and depth of excavation meaning that only a short section (L1700; H700mm) was exposed. The revetment was orientated NW–SE and was of the same design as C083 and C093, comprising transverse subsidiary baseplates pegged in position with half-lap joints in their upper surface to hold a longitudinal primary baseplate. Chase mortices at the southwest end of the subsidiary baseplates indicated the position of the raking braces. These were absent as were two upright posts which would have sat within mortices in the upper surface of the primary baseplate. Three horizontal planks set edge to edge formed the plank shuttering. It is remarkable that the planking was still *in situ* given that all of the supporting elements were missing. The northwest end of C300 was truncated by the return of the boundary wall; however, attempts to trace it beyond this proved fruitless. Its southeast end was truncated by a post-medieval robber-trench related to the wall C177 (see below). Beyond this lay a steep bank which could not be removed and it is possible that C300 extended further southeast towards the river. C300 was roughly parallel with the tailrace of the mill and the two were likely associated.

The abbey precinct, C177

C177 comprised the remains of a substantial stone wall believed to be part of the outer precinct of St Mary's abbey (DU018-2048). Its survival on the site was first indicated through the discovery of C162, a wide (W2400mm) band of irregularly dispersed limestone blocks (av. L300; W200; thk. 50mm), and smaller debris which ran ENE–WSW across the central portion of the site, south of the revetments which had the same orientation. C162 lay immediately north of the *in situ* remains of the wall and is interpreted as displaced material from the same.

Across the site the wall had a surviving length of 44.6m and varied in width from 2200mm to 2300mm and in height from 10mm to 800mm (0.27m to -0.59m OD). It is best described as drystone foundation courses formed with large dressed façade blocks containing internal basal blocks and slabs, over which was laid an internal rubble core. The façade blocks were mostly rectangular (max. L600; W450; thk. 150mm), and laid with their long axes set into the wall centre. Up to four courses of blocks survived containing the internal rubble core of irregularly-sized pieces of angular limestone.

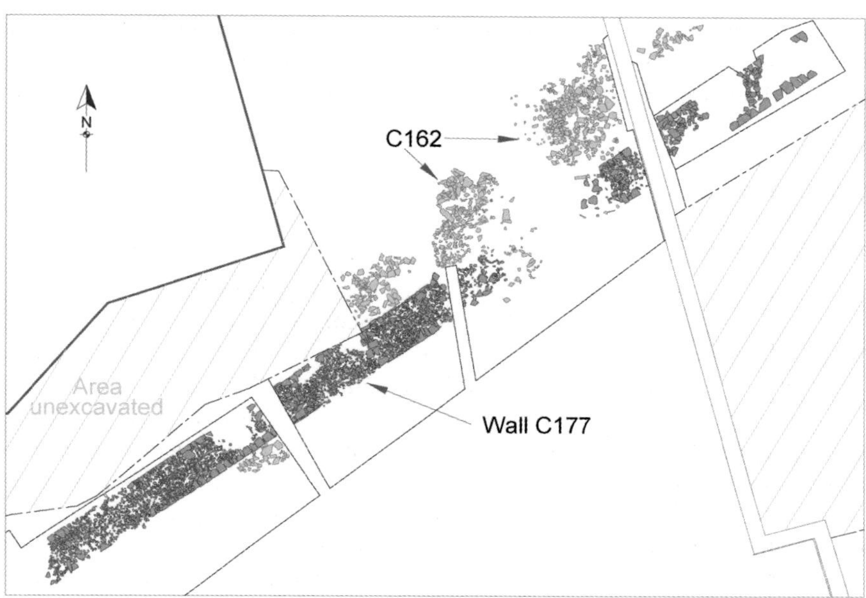

7.12 Wall C177 and stone spread C162

The survival of C177 varied considerably across the site (figs 7.12 and 7.13). Its WSW extent lay approximately 2500mm south of revetment C093/DU018-115-, and, like the revetment, was extensively disturbed along the boundary with the adjacent site. This end comprised only a linear deposit of the rubble core, almost all the larger elements having been removed. Further disturbance was evident across the centre of the site, where in addition to truncation by a post-medieval well, the wall was almost entirely absent but was flanked to its north by the rubble spread C162. At its ENE end, C177 was heavily disturbed by post-medieval robber-trenches. Possible mortar was encountered within the rubble core in this area, but this is the only location where such material was found. Hand excavation of C177 recovered a stratified sherd of thirteenth-century Dublin-type pottery and samples of wood and animal-bone.

C177 was built on compacted river silts and across the centre of the site was covered by C164, a 600mm deep natural deposit of orange/brown sandy silt with gravel, and C181, a thin deposit of soft black silt. The disturbance at its ENE end saw it additionally covered with tumbled deposits of stone. At this end, along its northern face, was C151, a deep (D450–480mm) deposit of organic material containing frequent brushwood, plant remains, fragments of leather and medieval ceramics. Analysis of the plant remains by Dr Penny Johnston identified seeds from mostly wild plants including sedges, rushes, daisies, buttercups and grasses, along with moss and leaf fragments. These

7.13 Looking west along the remains of wall C177 during excavation with stone spread C162 visible on the right

probably originated from damp meadows, including the types of plants that naturally colonized the flood plain of the river.[9] This supports the interpretation of C151 as primarily natural, with the seeds originating from

9 Penny Johnston, 'Organic plant remains from Abbey St, Dublin (19E0110)', unpublished

plants that grew by the river's edge and were carried by water and washed up against the wall to form the deposit. Adjacent to C151 and above the wall was a rough linear feature, possibly a small channel containing laminated bands of compressed organic material, frequent wood fibres, grasses and seeds (C179). Fragments of brushwood, some upright, suggested the presence of wattle within this feature; however, the evidence was poor and it may simply have been a natural accumulation related to C151.

CHRONOLOGY

Dendrochronological dating was completed on timbers from revetments C083, C300 and C301. The selection of timbers sought to avoid, insofar as was evident, any reused elements. Radiocarbon dating was completed for wattle structures C090, C299 and on material associated with the precinct wall C177 and the overlying C179. In general the results indicate that the structures likely date to the thirteenth century.

Dendrochronology (David Brown)

Dendrochronological dating on suitable timbers from C083, C300 and C301 was undertaken in the Palaeoecology Centre, Queen's University, Belfast. As revetment C093 was clearly a continuation of DU018-115- it was not dated, and no timbers suitable for dendrochronology were recovered from revetment C084.[10]

Only one timber from C083 retained complete sapwood and returned a felling-date of late AD 1206 or early AD 1207 (Q12702). Two of the other three samples (Q12699 and Q12700) had estimated felling-date-ranges late in the twelfth century; these could easily, and are more likely to, date from the early thirteenth century. Only one sample (Q12701) was earlier and this timber was heavily squared indicating that a large number of the rings could be and probably are missing from the sample. It is probable that the timbers from context C083 date to AD 1206 or early AD 1207.

All the samples from context C300 had partial sapwood present and all the estimated felling-date-ranges can fit into the first decade of the thirteenth century. The dendrochronological average estimated felling-date for this structure would be AD 1206 ± 9 years.

The single timber from C301 (Q12704) has an estimated felling-date-range after AD 1235. It is noted that this sample had a squared edge. The felling-date

report, 2021. **10** What follows is a summary of the dendrochronological report completed by Mr David Brown, for the medieval structures on the site (David Brown, 'Dendrochronology Laboratory Report 9/2020. Dendrochronological report on the wood samples from 31–34 Abbey Street Upper, Dublin 1', unpublished report, 2020).

for the tree from which this sample was taken could be much later in the thirteenth century or even into the fourteenth century. Table 1 below summarizes the results of the dendrochronological dating.

Table 7.1 Dendrochronological dating results

Lab Code	Context No./ Timber No.	Rings (sapwood)	Start date	End date	Felling-date or Best Estimated felling-date-range
Q12699	C083/T7	110 (0)	AD 1032	AD 1141	After AD 1173
Q12700	C083/T29	132 (0)	AD 1027	AD 1158	After AD 1190
Q12701	C083/T33	136 (0)	AD 996	AD 1101	After AD 1133
Q12702	C083/T19	183 (29C)	AD 1024	AD 1206	AD 1206/AD1207
Q12703	C300/T5	274 (4)	AD 896	AD 1169	AD 1197 ± 9 Years
Q12704	C301/T1	137 (0)	AD 1067	AD 1203	After AD 1235
Q12705	C300/T2	331 (6)	AD 850	AD 1180	AD 1206 ± 9 Years
Q12706	C300/T4	115 (16)	AD 1088	AD 1194	AD 1210 ± 9 Years
Q12707	C300/T6	159 (11)	AD 1031	AD 1189	AD 1210 ± 9 Years

All nine samples were used to construct the Abbey Street Upper site master chronology. This site chronology is 357 years in length and dates from AD 850 to AD 1206. The site chronology gives extremely significant and consistent correlation values with all the site and regional master chronologies in Ireland. Table 2 below gives the correlation values with a series of most used site and regional chronologies from Ireland.

Table 7.2 Cross-correlation values for the samples from 31–34 Abbey Street Upper

Site Master chronology	Start and end date	Abbey Street Upper correlation value
Dublin Index Master chronology	AD 855 to AD 1306	12.05***
New Ross Chronology	AD 907 to AD 1278	10.31***
Waterford City Chronology	AD 839 to AD 1216	10.12***
Drogheda City Chronology	AD 921 to AD 1194	10.11***
Cork City Chronology	AD 957 to AD 1219	6.57***

The dendrochronological dating results indicate that the revetments on the site were broadly contemporary with DU018-115- timbers from which returned felling-dates of AD 1203/1204, AD 1214±9 years or later, and after AD 1180.[11]

Radiocarbon dating

Radiocarbon dating of a piece of blackthorn from wattle fence C090 returned a result of cal. AD 1052–1254 (866±25 BP; UBA-45080). A piece of holly from C299, the thin wattle rods woven around posts C285, was dated to cal. AD 1047–1260 (874±31 BP; UBA-45081).

A twig of holly found between the horizontal plane of two large flat stones within the precinct wall C177 returned a date of cal. AD 1048–1221 (885±24 BP; UBA-46009). A piece of elm brushwood from the rough linear feature above the wall was dated to cal. AD 1034–1198 (930±26 BP; UBA-46008). The results of the radiocarbon dating are summarized in Table 3 below.

Table 7.3 Summary of radiocarbon dating results

Lab Code	Context No.	Material	14C years BP	Calibrated 14C date 2 sigma
UBA-45080	C090	Blackthorn	866±25	AD 1052–1254
UBA-45081	C299	Holly	874±31	AD 1047–1260
UBA-46009	C177	Holly	885±24	AD 1048–1221
UBA-46008	C179	Elm	930±26	AD 1034–1198

DISCUSSION

All of the medieval features excavated on the site relate to the river and to the inlet depicted by Speed in the early seventeenth century, as enclosed by the abbey precinct. The mill at 35–36 Abbey St Upper is also central to their interpretation. While the discovery of revetment DU018-115- was expected, what was also expected was that it would continue across the site on a straight ENE–WSW trajectory. Careful exploratory work along its anticipated line failed to identify any traces. Had it continued along this line, at least some elements such as posts would have been expected to survive, similar to the remnants of C083 and C084 to the north. The timber structure of C093/DU018-115- clearly terminated close to where it entered the site. C400, the NE–SW orientated stone surface at its ENE end was laid at the same level

11 David Brown, 'Appendix 1. Dendrochronological analysis on wood samples from Strand Street Great, Dublin' in Walsh, 'Waterfront at Strand Street Great, Dublin', 182–4.

as the baseplates and is evidently broadly contemporary. It could represent part of a different but associated structure such as a jetty, or be a continuation, repair or replacement of the revetment with stone. The change in orientation here is notable as it occurs at the point where the line of Byrne's Lane shifts very slightly. This is depicted on Rocque's *Exact survey of the city and suburbs of Dublin* (1756), as a stagger in the footprint of the buildings. The reason for this small bend is unclear and it is possible that the lane was laid out to partially follow an early and/or established boundary, albeit one which perhaps no longer functioned as such. The exact nature of the remaining archaeological features below Byrne's Lane is unknown but the change in orientation is clear. Coupled with the position of the contemporary C083 some 20m further north, it is suggested that the thirteenth century structures in this location turned north–east and ran beneath the lane for a short distance, before remerging and turning once more to follow an ENE–WSW trajectory.

The timber structure of C093/DU018-115- may originally have been continuous, and considering the evidence further to the north, this seems most likely. Found in isolation, DU018-115- was originally interpreted as a front-braced revetment, due in part to the uniformity of the alluvial deposits on each side of the structure. The planking was not nailed and so it was suggested that the deposits on the riverward or south-facing side must have been introduced to support the planks, with the whole structure held up by the raking braces on the opposite side.[12] If C083 was indeed the continuation of C093/DU018-115-, the evidence across the centre of the site is that it was flanked by a parallel revetment C084 (which, further to the ENE, became the post-and-wattle fence C090). C084 faced the opposite direction to C083, its planking facing northwards. If we accept C093/DU018-115- and C083 as a single structure with south-facing planking, it can now be interpreted as back-braced and mirrored by C084, an identical but front-braced revetment. This layout would have created a 1600–2000mm-wide channel, infilling of which would have held the planks of both in place and created a strong revetment along the medieval shoreline (fig. 7.14). The post-and-wattle fence C090 was, across the centre of the site at least, a separate structure to C084 but, towards its ENE end, C084 terminated and C090 became the southernmost of the two parallel revetments. No evidence for C084 was found parallel to C093 (or DU018-115- when it was excavated); however, the *ex situ* baseplates (C155) found close to C093 could have been the remains of C084, removed here by the building of the precinct wall, the scant remains of which in this area were lower than the baseplates of the revetment. Alternatively C155 could have been part of C093/DU018-155- removed when the stone surface C400 was laid.

The end of C084 was encased in C281, a substantial stone plinth that abutted the headrace of the mill. The revetment was, however, seen to continue

12 Walsh, 'Waterfront at Strand Street Great', 164–5.

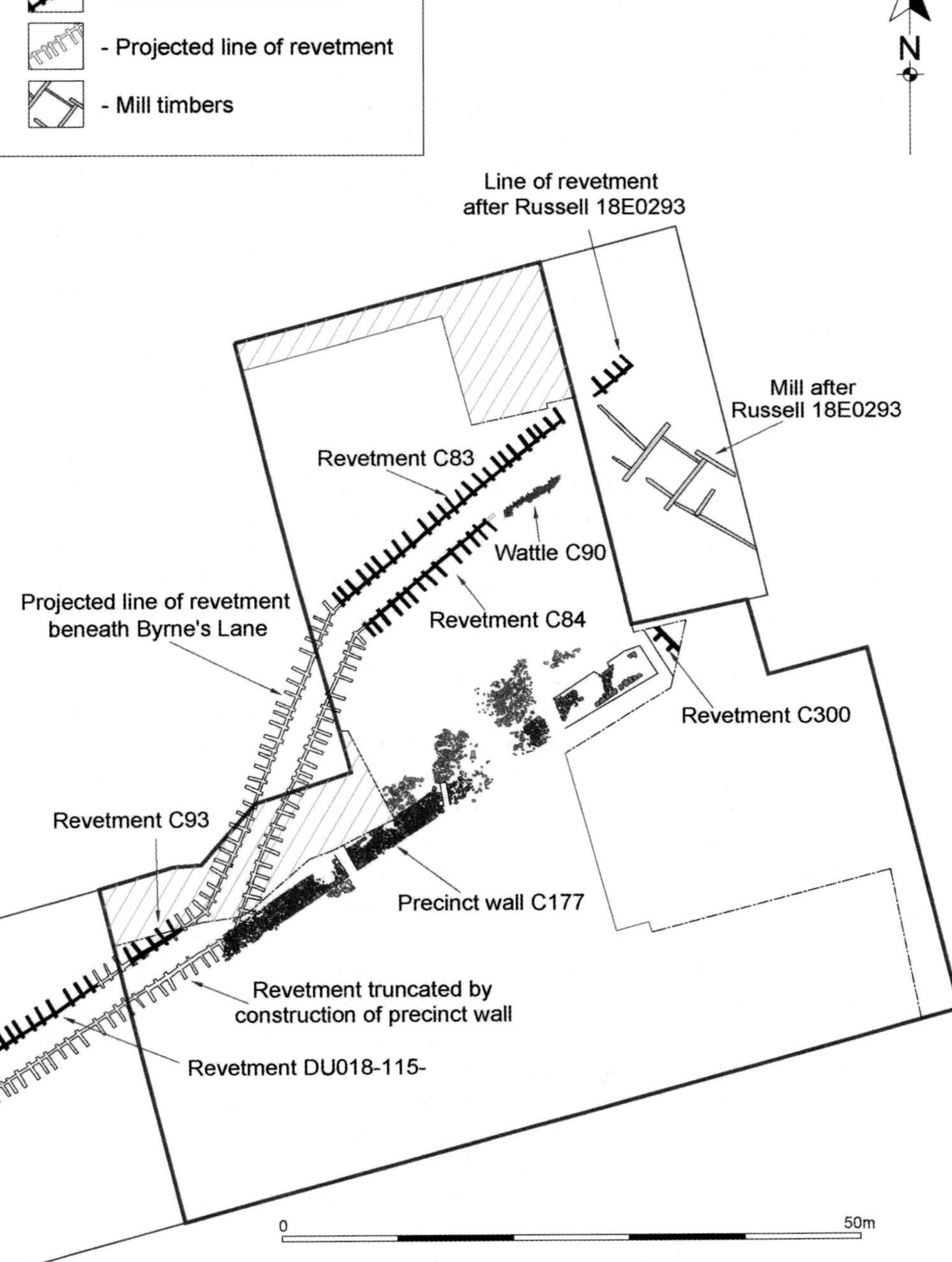

7.14 Plan of excavated medieval features and proposed original trajectory of revetments

beyond the headrace on the adjacent site and so there appears to have been a formal gap in the structure. A key structural component of the mill was dendrochronologically dated to AD 1233/4 (Q12800), the latest exact felling-date returned for the assemblage.[13] This falls almost thirty years after the likely construction date of C083 and DU018-115-, and so it seems that a gap within an existing revetment was opened and consolidated with stone to facilitate the mill headrace. The blunt cut end of the C083 baseplate in this area also lends credence to this idea. It should, however, be noted that both the dating of the mill and analysis of the timber assemblage by this author,[14] identified significant reuse and the strong likelihood of an earlier phase of mill(s) on that site, which could relate directly to the revetments. Critical to both the revetments and the mill is the position of the inlet depicted on Speed. Accepting that the revetments were built along the medieval shoreline, it is almost certain that the inlet lay to their north and very likely fed the mill, possibly canalized to a degree and managed with sluices to control the flow. The proximity of the mill is also related to the multiple parallel stone and timber structures north of C083 in the ENE corner of the site. Although disturbed and fragmentary, all proceeded on the same ENE–WSW trajectory as the revetments, and appear to represent multiple attempts to create barriers in this area, which could be very close to the confluence of the inlet and mill. The estimated felling-date of after AD 1235 for the single baseplate C301, suggests that it might have been part of a revetment contemporary with the final phase of the mill. In contrast, the probable continuation of C285/299 across the adjacent site where it was stratigraphically lower than the continuation of C083, means that it was an earlier structure. The isolated revetment C300 was built very close and almost parallel to the mill tailrace. Like the revetments further north, it appears to predate the mill or final phase thereof, but nonetheless could have been related to it. It may have been part of an overflow channel, an earlier race or have served to protect the mill from the tidal ebb and flow of the river.

The precinct wall of St Mary's abbey is shown by Speed as a substantial construction with crenelations. It formed a polygonal boundary around the abbey and enclosed the inlet which ran NE–SW, approximately parallel to the Liffey which lay to the south. Documentary evidence for the precinct wall includes three phases of building, the first beginning after 1216 and constructed by 1247.[15] The second comprised the fortification of the south quays in 1317, and so assumed to be the point at which the inlet became enclosed.[16] The third phase dates to 1455 and involved the building of a tower by the boundary wall at the pier of St Mary's, which was located at the

13 Brown, 'Wood samples from 35–36 Abbey Street Upper'. 14 Caitríona Moore, '18E0293: worked wood and timber report', unpublished report, 2023. 15 Stout, 'Topography of St Mary's abbey', p. 150. 16 Ibid.

southwestern corner of the precinct.[17] A twig of holly found between the horizontal plane of two large flat stones within wall C177 returned a radiocarbon date of cal. AD 1048–1221 (885±24 BP; UBA-46009). The dated piece was well-stratified and, even allowing for the riverine location, is unlikely to have washed in between two large, heavy blocks. If this date is accepted as indicative of the construction date for the wall, the actual date must surely fall towards the later end of the range. This would mean that the wall excavated on the site was built in the early thirteenth century, potentially contemporary with or not long after the construction of the revetments. An early thirteenth-century date for this wall would also suggest that the southern quays were established and fortified before 1317.

It is somewhat difficult to marry the potentially early date for the wall with the evidence of the mill. As it neared the mill, the wall was very heavily disturbed and there was no evidence of it on the adjacent site. The mill was a substantial structure certainly in use *c.* AD 1233/4 and potentially also for the preceding decades. If it was contemporary with C177, a formal opening for the mill outfall would have been required. There is no indication of such on Speed which shows the wall as a continuous quay along the river, before returning to the northeast. Just beyond this turn, Speed does indicate an isolated building on a small inlet, usually interpreted as a boathouse or warehouse,[18] but this seems too far east to be the mill which in any case was certainly not extant in the seventeenth century. Although well stratified between two slabs, it is possible that the dated holly twig was intrusive and that the wall is later than the mill, constructed after the mill had fallen out of use.

The piece of elm brushwood from the rough linear feature above the ENE end of C177 was dated cal. AD 1034–1198 (930±26 BP; UBA-46008). This channel was poorly defined, its edges formed with laminated bands of compressed organic material. Considered during the excavation to be the remnants of a possible fence, the returned date makes this unlikely as, regardless of when the wall was constructed, its foundation courses cannot have been exposed and remained so from the twelfth century.

Prior to this excavation the survival of the precinct wall had only been hinted at in scattered locations, with possible sections identified along Arran Street East,[19] Mary's Abbey Street,[20] and Liffey Street.[21] Another significant section has, however, since come to light at Mary's Abbey Street and Strand Street Little. Archaeological monitoring at this location in 2003 and 2004 uncovered the baseplates of a NW–SE orientated revetment, a timber from which returned an estimated felling-date of AD 1201 ± 9 years or later.

17 Ibid. **18** Ibid., p. 146; Walsh, 'Waterfront at Strand Street Great', p. 160. **19** Emmet Stafford, '2001:632–Dublin: Daisy Market, Arran Street East, Dublin' [online, available from: https://excavations.ie/report/2001/Dublin/0006300/. [Accessed 20 February 2024]. **20** DU18-344. **21** NMI 1971:1063.

7.15 Timber revetment and wall at Mary's Abbey Street/Strand Street Little (Credit: Helen Kehoe)

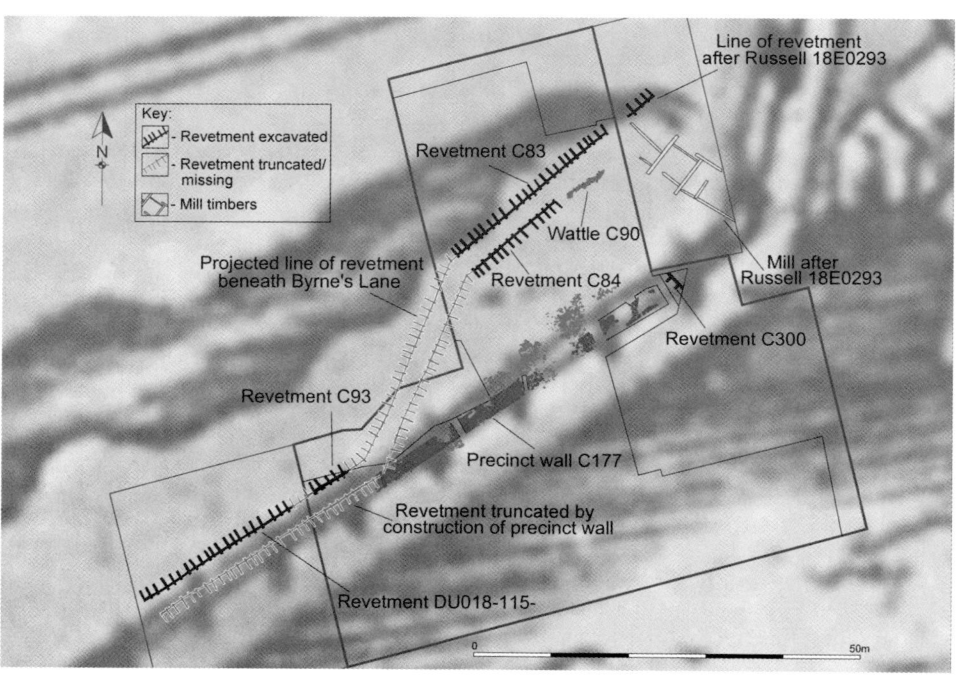

7.16 Excavation results overlaid on Speed

7.17 Proposed layout of the abbey precinct to incorporate wall C177 and that at Strand Street Little

Immediately adjacent to the baseplates of the revetment was a substantial stone wall 9.5m in length and 2300mm wide, identical to the remains of C177 (fig. 7.15).[22] The positioning of these two structures matches that of C093 and C177, and there is no doubt that this too was a section of the precinct as it ran NW–SE across the area of Strand Street Little, bounding the southwestern part of the abbey.

C177 is the longest section of the precinct wall that has been found to date. An overlay of the excavation results onto Speed aligns the tip of the inlet with the mill headrace, while the outfall occurs at the point where the wall returns to

22 Helen Kehoe, 'Archaeological monitoring report for the site area bounded by: Mary's abbey and Strand Street Little, Dublin 1. Licence No. 03E0002', unpublished report, 2005 [online, available from: https://heritagemaps.ie/documents/Therefore_ArchaeologyReports/03E0002.pdf [Accessed 20 February 2024].

the northeast (fig. 7.16). If both C177 and the wall found on Strand Street Little ran along the straight trajectories shown by Speed they would intersect in the middle of the river. Thus a working hypothesis is that the wall turned slightly along Great Strand Street (fig. 7.17).

CONCLUSION

The timber revetments found at the site were part of a substantial thirteenth-century structure along the medieval Liffey shoreline, consolidating the land to the north and enclosing the inlet which very likely powered the mill on the adjacent site. The discovery of the precinct wall has demonstrated that the southern quays ran on a sharp ENE–WSW orientation along this stretch of the river. Combined with the evidence from Strand Street Little, it is suggested that the precinct wall turned slightly along the shoreline, a small shift in orientation not captured in its later mapping.

ACKNOWLEDGMENTS

The hard-working excavation crew included Johnny Ryan, James Kyle, Wayne Malone, Maggie Kobik, Rory Blount, Peter Dodd, Ivor Kenny, Louise Callan, Clare Ryan, Martha Revell, Ian Dunne, Georgia Vakasira, Deanna Lee, Killian Foley, Noel Carroll, Servane Buckle, Amy O'Keefe, Jordan Hanson and Isobel Walsh. I am particularly grateful to Johnny Ryan for his illustrations of the timbers and work on the mapping, also to Maggie Kobik for final edits on the same. Thanks are also due to Claire Wash for advice and input and to Ian Russell for discussions regarding both sites and permission to include his dating results. Thanks to Franc Myles for commenting on an early draft of this paper. Marlet Property Group funded the excavation and post-excavation work.

The 'cemetery gate' and outer precinct of St Mary's abbey, Dublin

PAUL DUFFY

INTRODUCTION

Archaeological investigations at a former warehouse site bounded by Little Mary St, Little Green St and Anglesea Row, Dublin 7, were undertaken by IAC Archaeology in several phases from 2019 to 2022 in advance of the site's redevelopment as a Staycity aparthotel.[1] A further programme of archaeological test-trenching was carried out on a site fronting Little Britain St, *c*.40m to the north in December 2022 (fig. 8.1). The excavation areas both lie in a landscape of high archaeological potential on the north bank of the River Liffey within the vicinity of Oxmantown,[2] a Hiberno-Norse suburb of Dublin, likely established in the tenth/eleventh century.[3] Oxmantown faced the walled town established by the Vikings on the south bank of the Liffey in the ninth century. Taken in tandem, the results of both archaeological investigations provide important new information on the topography and layout of St Mary's abbey and allow speculation as to the nature of potential Viking age activity on the north shore of the Liffey.[4]

The largest medieval complex on the north side of the river was St Mary's abbey (DU018–020048), founded in 1139 by Benedictine monks belonging to the congregation of Savigny, which later joined the Cistercian order, St Mary's then became subject to Combermere, Cheshire, before being assigned to Buildwas in Shropshire in 1156.[5] The chapter house, which is the only upstanding element of the abbey, is located 80m south–southeast of the excavation area, while the conventual buildings and church are suspected to lie

1 The differing stages of excavation were directed by Paul Duffy and David McIlreavy under licence 19E0156 issued by the National Monuments Service (NMS) of the Department of Housing, Local Government and Heritage (DHLGH) in consultation with the National Museum of Ireland (NMI) and the Archaeology Section of Dublin City Council. The work was undertaken on behalf of LMS Investments DAC in response to planning conditions attached to the proposed development (Planning Ref.: ABP 3629/17). 2 On the term Ostman, meaning 'east man', see *Oxford English dictionary*, s.v. 'Ostman (*n.*)', July 2023, https://doi.org/10.1093/OED/9631995359; see also, Wadden in this volume, p. 146. 3 Clarke, *Dublin, Pt I* (IHTA), p. 6. 4 This area of Dublin is undergoing extensive redevelopment and numerous ongoing excavations will enhance our understanding of many aspects of the abbey. For example, a pre-twelfth-century date from a burial close to the chapter house may suggest a pre-existing foundation (see O'Donovan, this volume, pp 68–72). 5 Bill Doran and Linda Doran, 'St Mary's Cistercian abbey, Dublin: a ghost in the alleyways,' in Bradley et al. (eds), *Dublin in the medieval world*, pp 188–201 at pp 188–9.

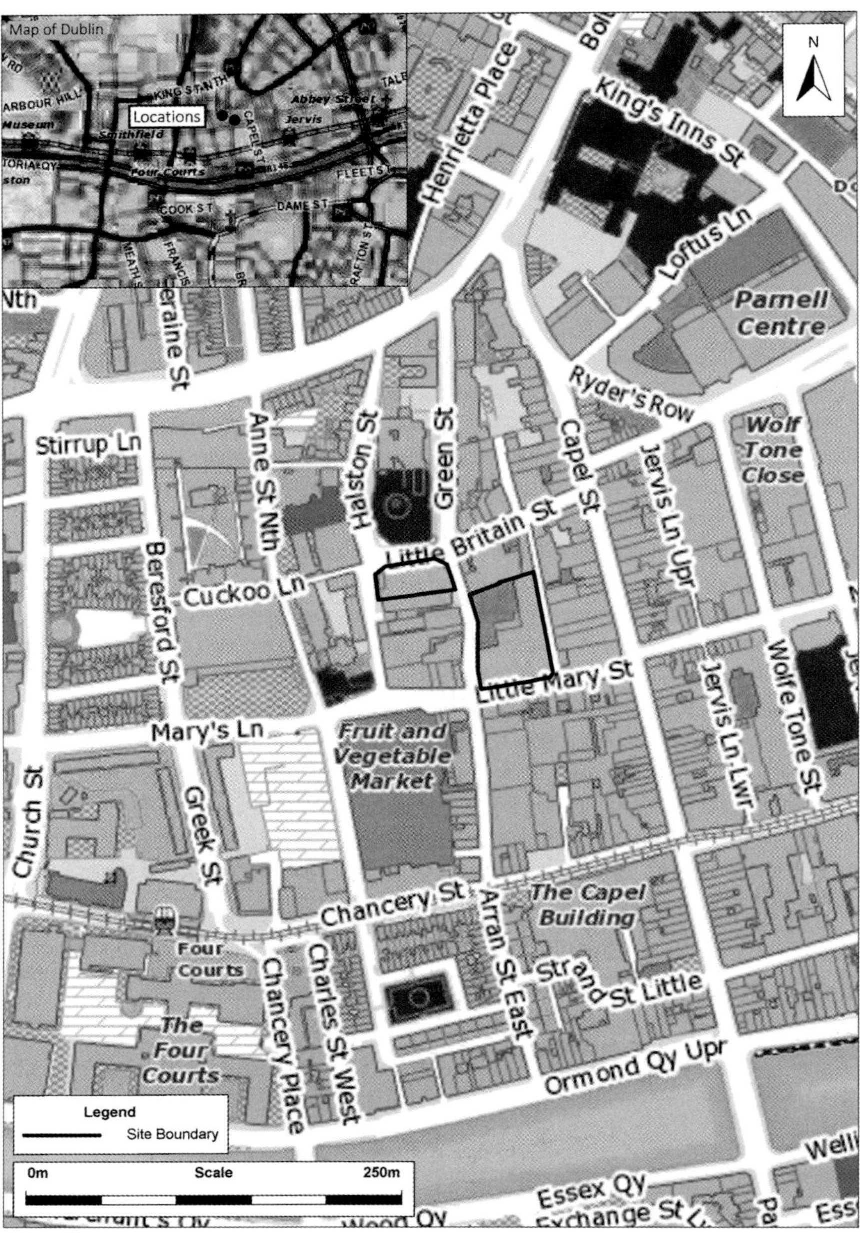

8.1 Site locations

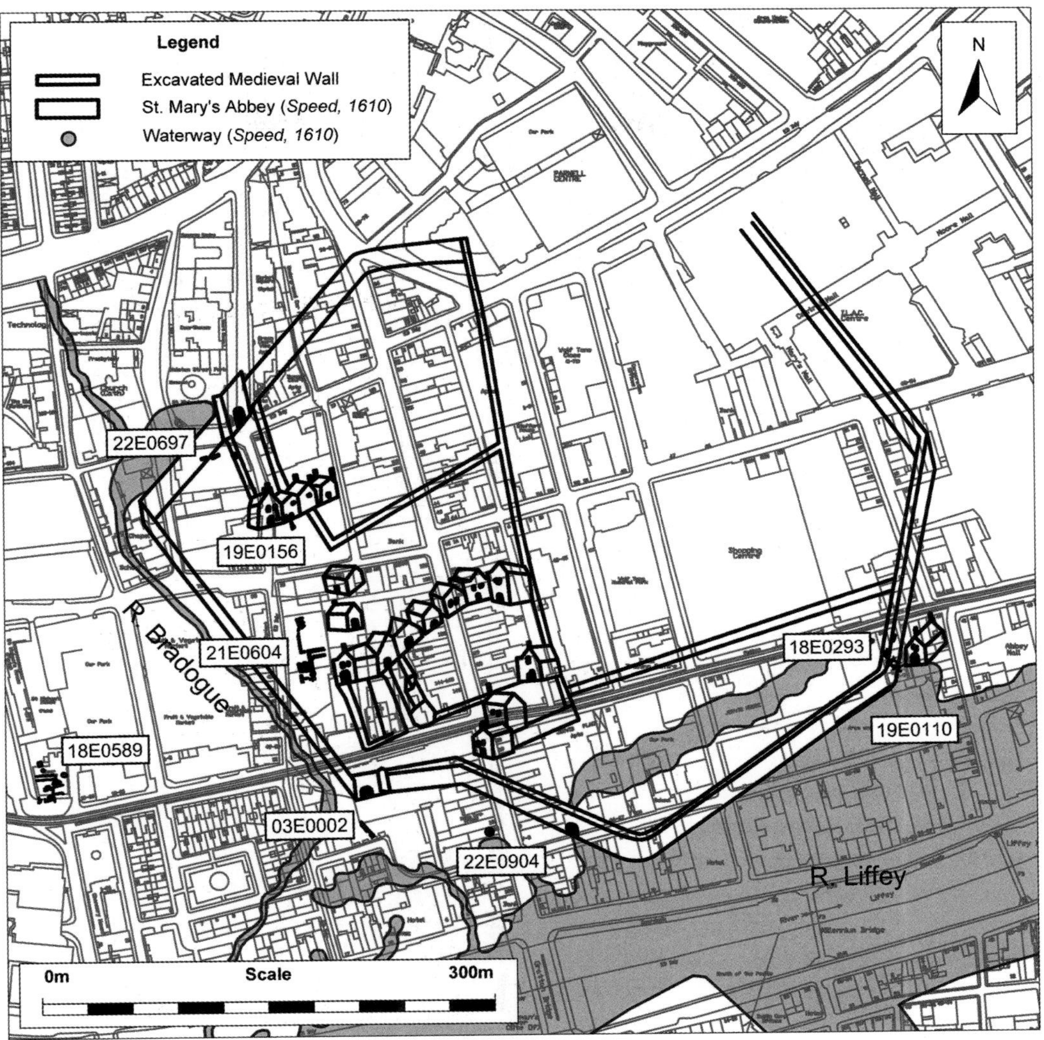

8.2 Overlay showing John Speed's 1610 depiction of St Mary's abbey with reference to recent excavations in Dublin

50m to the south.[6] At its largest extent, St Mary's was the richest monastery in Ireland with combined holdings of 30,000 acres.[7] Using John Speed's map of 1610, calibrated with archaeological findings in the wider area, the scale of the monastic precinct can be set in the modern streetscape (fig. 8.2).

6 See Geraldine Stout, 'The topography of St Mary's abbey and precinct, Dublin' in Duffy (ed.), *MD XII* (Dublin, 2012), pp 138–60, at p. 153. Recent excavations in this area have confirmed the location of the abbey church: O'Donovan, this volume. 7 Colmcille

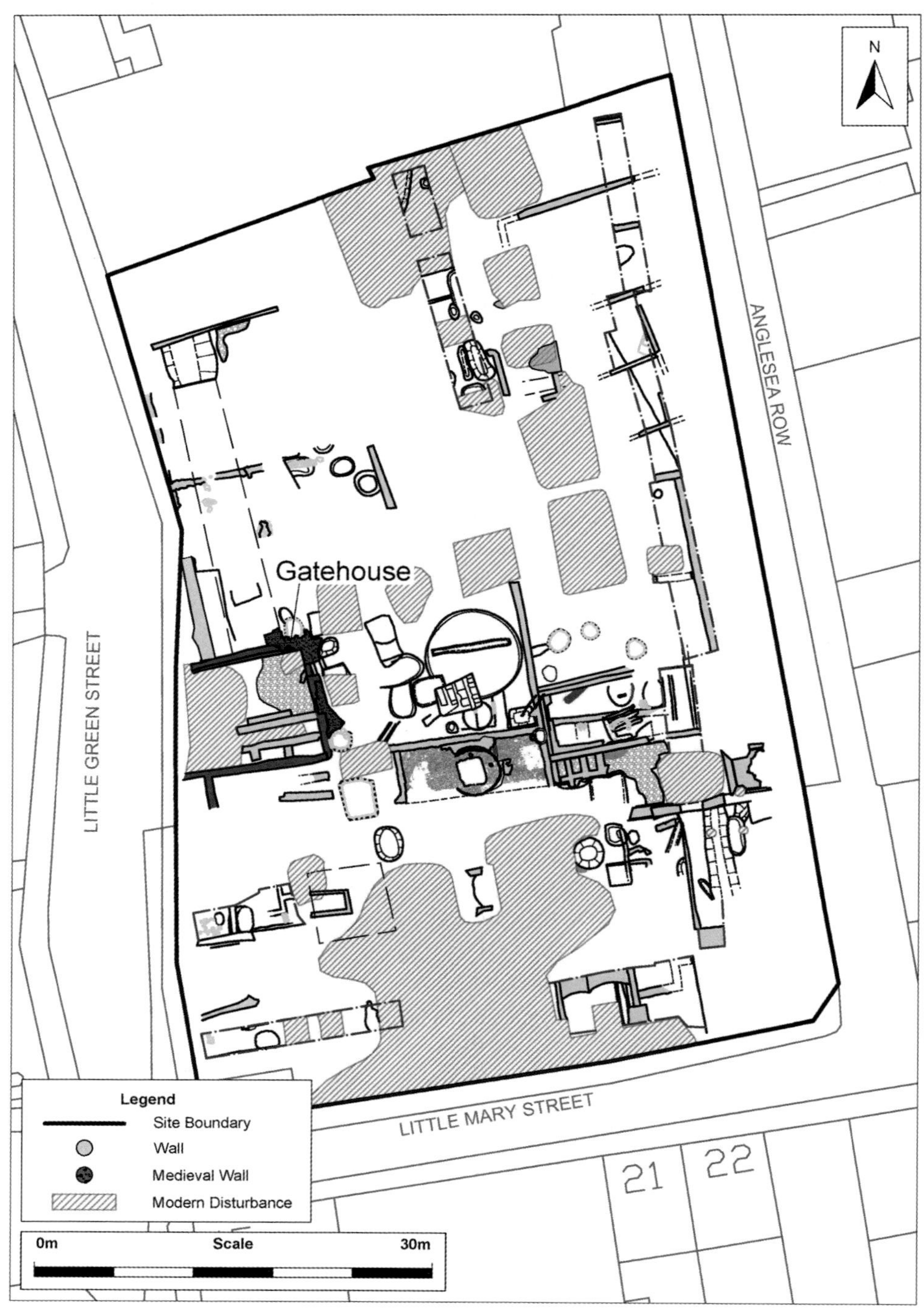

8.3 Overall excavation plan (gatehouse in middle left of image)

THE 'CEMETERY GATE' (19E0156)

A large, open-plan excavation was carried out across this site following the demolition of a two-storey concrete-built warehouse in advance of redevelopment (fig. 8.3). Despite extensive disturbance from large concrete foundations and infilling in the 1970s, several areas of stratified archaeology and fragmentary structures were identified. The bulk of the archaeology encountered, however, related to the residential and subsequent industrial development of the site from the later seventeenth century onwards. The final design of the Staycity development was modified in light of the archaeological findings, allowing a substantial element of this archaeology to be preserved in situ, particularly where located outside the footprint of the basement and below the construction levels of the ground-floor structure.

Phase 1 (early twelfth to late thirteenth century)

The earliest phase of activity comprised features which may correspond to agricultural activity associated with the abbey in the twelfth and thirteenth centuries. These included a truncated earthen bank (C305) identified along the eastern limit of excavation, with a relict plough-soil extending from its north face; this banked material may represent a 'headland'. A large north–south-running ditch (C389) extending over a projected length of *c*.35m was partially excavated adjacent and parallel to Little Green St along the site's western boundary; this feature was *c*.7m in maximum width, with a maximum depth of 0.5m. The ditch profile suggests a steeper western face and a gentler, eastern stepped profile suggesting a property boundary enclosing the area to the east (including the development site); however, potential remains for this feature to represent a hollow-way or longstanding medieval routeway. The two ditch fills contained within the feature may support the latter interpretation: the basal fill comprised a largely sterile silty clay, consistent with natural infilling; the upper fill contained abundant water-rolled cobbles and may have been a deliberate backfilling episode to form a road surface. A charred grain of bread wheat was retrieved from the basal fill of this ditch; this returned an AMS 2 sigma date of AD 1299–1398, and suggests that the feature was backfilled in the fourteenth century.[8] Immediately east of the ditch, a truncated but well-preserved metalled surface was recorded, extending eastwards, likely relating to a well-constructed pathway flanking the ditch (fig. 8.4). A continuation of this path may be traced in the patch of cobbles and cut features identified in the southwest corner of the site (C117, C118). A range of charred cereal grains from these levels reveals that typical medieval crops including wheat, emmer wheat, bread wheat, barley and oat were processed at this site.

Ó Conbhuidhe, 'The lands of St Mary's abbey', *PRIA* (1962), 21–84. 8 Vilnius lab number: FTMC-KG89-1.

8.4 Metalled path leading to the gatehouse, facing east

Phase 2 (fourteenth to mid-sixteenth century)

The heavily modified remains of the northern and eastern walls of a medieval building constructed of rubble-coursed local limestone and a cream-coloured lime mortar were identified midway along the western boundary of the site (figs 8.5 and 8.6). This structure appears to have been built on top of the infilled ditch C389. The east–west-running wall survives to a length of 9m and the north–south one runs to 7.6m; wall thickness is up to 1.2m wide and it survives to a maximum height of six courses. Diagonal corner buttress foundations and a short section of a well-executed sloping batter on the eastern wall survive, while foundations of a square buttress were evident at the northern wall. Ten fragments of architectural stone were recovered from the vicinity of the structure: nine of these are of imported oolitic limestone, which has been shown, through thin section analysis, to have come from quarries at Dundry near Bristol.[9] The fragments include several chamfered quoin stones, a moulded springer with rebate, a painted respond and a hood moulding. A trefoil/triple roll colonette of what appears to be local Waulsortian limestone was also retrieved.

9 Paul Duffy and Sara Pavia, 'Quarrying the past: petrographic analysis of Dublin's medieval building stone' (unpubl. Royal Irish Academy research report, 2021).

8.5 Gatehouse under excavation, facing southwest

A fragment of charcoal from a pomaceous tree retrieved from the fill (C142) within the foundation cut for the square buttress returned an AMS 2 sigma date of AD 1316–1427,[10] indicating a construction date in the fourteenth century. However, when the architectural fragments are considered, a date in the earlier part of that century is likely.

This building was substantially reconstructed in the seventeenth century, with its walls modified to carry a redbrick vault, the floor level lowered to accommodate a cellar, and a redbrick fireplace inserted into the cellar's northeast corner.

Discussion

Some comparisons can be made with the surviving medieval features of the structure. For example, the sloping batter can be seen nearby on the remains of the early thirteenth-century chapter house at Christ Church cathedral; Linzi Simpson discovered a similar batter executed in Dundry at St Patrick's cathedral.[11] This type of ornament implies a building of some significance. Diagonal corner buttresses are also a feature of medieval buildings, but very

10 Vilnius lab number FTMC-TT26-1. 11 Linzi Simpson, 'St Patrick's cathedral, Dublin: the recent discovery of the thirteenth-century south nave wall' in Duffy (ed.), *MD XIV* (Dublin, 2014), pp 110–17.

8.6 Rectified orthophoto of the gatehouse

rare in an Irish context, being more common in France in the thirteenth century and in England in the fifteenth, as at the gatehouse of Malvern priory. This may be significant as St Mary's abbey acquired the Irish lands of Little

Malvern in the fifteenth century.[12] One example of a corner buttress has recently been highlighted at the remains of a residential tower at Beaubec, Co. Meath (ME020–031) and may be the only other example surviving in the country; tentatively dated to the first quarter of the thirteenth century, it forms part of the Cistercian grange farm of Beaubec.[13]

This identification of a diagonal buttress at Beaubec is particularly pertinent to the Little Mary St find given the location of the newly identified structure relative to the core of the (Cistercian) abbey and to Little Green St. Speed's map (1610) shows a row of structures in the general vicinity (see fig. 8.2). When the orientation of Speed's map is corrected and the outer northern gatehouse positioned at the top of Little Green St (50m to the north), these structures appear to straddle the main approach to the former abbey from the north. Bernard de Gomme's map of 1673 clearly shows a gatehouse straddling the roadway at this point. The rebuilding of the gatehouse very soon after and the noted installation of a redbrick vault and cellar would have necessitated the blocking-up of the gate passage from Little Green St; this in turn would have required a realignment of the street to bypass the building – precisely what can be seen in the streetscape today, where Little Green St kinks dramatically to the west at this point (fig. 8.2).

Examination of the lease records for the area has identified a small plot held by Lord Drogheda, comprising an 'old house' together with a small adjoining, street-front plot to the south.[14] This house was just one of two structures known to have been then standing on the east side of Little Green St. The old house was listed as in the possession of Captain John Jeacock of Kinsale, whose will is dated 1686. The Jeacock house is described in a deed of 1711 as 'commonly called by the name of St Mary's Chappell'. The presence of a chapel is corroborated by an extensive grant of diverse holdings by the newly crowned James I to Sir William Taaffe of Ardee in 1604, which mentions 'a messuage and garden extending to the outer gate of the abbey of the Blessed Virgin Mary near Dublin, lately in the tenure of Francis Agard, with a chapel adjoining and a green called the Abbey Green; parcel of the estate of the said abbey'.[15]

Historic reference to this building as a chapel poses no impediment to its identification as a gatehouse. In discussing the monastic gatehouse of St Benet's Holm, Julian Luxford states:

> A curial function is often envisaged (if less often documented) for the chambers over grand gates … Upper chambers might also house

12 *CStM*, i, p. 26. 13 Geraldine Stout and Matthew Stout, 'Excavation in the time of coronavirus', *Archaeology Ireland*, 34:4 (2020), 14–18; eidem, *Beaubec, Co. Meath: excavation of French Cistercian grange in the Boyne Valley* (Julianstown, 2023). 14 Peter Keenahan, 'Little Mary St report on the lease records' (unpubl. report undertaken on behalf of IAC Archaeology, 2022). 15 Ibid.

> chapels: this was true of Norwich's Ethelbert gate, other Benedictine examples at Durham and Peterborough, and at least two Cistercian ones, at Beaulieu and Whalley.[16]

Morant, meanwhile, lists gatehouses with chapels at the abbeys of Mailing, Kirkstall, Faversham, Durham and Barking and, most importantly given the Irish Cistercian context, at Tintern abbey in Wales.[17]

The alignment of our excavated medieval building, relative to new information emerging from excavations south of Little Mary St,[18] would appear to corroborate the interpretation of this structure as a gatehouse giving access to the abbey's inner precinct and graveyard (see fig. 8.2) and it is potentially the building referenced in 1543 as the 'gate of the cemetery … north of the abbey church'.[19] This is an important breakthrough for the understanding of the spatial extent of the precinct and the features depicted on Speed's map given that the most detailed study of the layout of the abbey published to date had placed this thoroughfare at Capel St, not Little Green St.[20]

Conclusions

The excavated site, from at least the early twelfth century, was probably in agricultural use and associated with the foundation of St Mary's abbey. The construction of a precinct wall around the broader area in the thirteenth century seemingly did not greatly alter land-use and boundary ditches and possible evidence for ploughing and cultivation were identified. A boundary ditch running along the site's western side followed what appears to have been the original line of the road that would become Little Green St. This boundary ditch appears to have been partially infilled and used as a hollow-way in later years, perhaps reflecting a westward move of the abbey boundary, presumably as far as the recorded limit of the Bradogue River (the minor tributary that rises in Cabra and joins the Liffey at Ormond Quay).

In the main, however, medieval activity is not well represented before the fourteenth century when a substantial mortared stone building was constructed over the line of the boundary ditch/hollow-way. On the balance of the evidence, this building formed the gatehouse opening into the inner precinct of the abbey that contained the conventual buildings and the graveyard. This building likely had a first-floor chapel, as with many monastic gatehouses in England, including Tintern abbey near Chepstow, mother-house to the Cistercian Tintern abbey in Wexford.

16 Julian Luxford, 'Architecture and environment: St Benet's Holm and the fashioning of the English monastic gatehouse', *Architectural History*, 57 (2014), 31–72, at 55. **17** R.W. Morant, *The medieval abbeys of England and Wales: a resource guide* (Bloomington, 2004). **18** Excavation licence number 21E0604. **19** Stout, 'Topography of St Mary's abbey', 151. **20** See Stout, 'Topography of St Mary's abbey'.

8.7 Conjectural reconstruction drawing of the 'cemetery gate' *c.*1450 by artist Matthew Ryan (http://matthewryanhistoricalillustrator.com/)

The remains of the gatehouse have been preserved beneath a glass floor within the development and are available for public viewing. Several interpretation panels detailing the archaeological findings are mounted in the Staycity foyer and incorporate a fine conjectural reconstruction of the 'cemetery gate' (fig. 8.7).[21]

THE OUTER PRECINCT (22E0697)

Archaeological investigations at a former warehouse fronting Little Britain St and Little Green St, Dublin 7, were undertaken by IAC Archaeology in late 2022. This site is located only 20m to the northwest of the Little Mary St site and presented the opportunity to explore further the suspected layout of St Mary's abbey precinct. Speed's map and other cartographic sources suggest that the outer precinct wall traversed this site and the new understanding gleaned from the excavations at Little Mary St point to the outer gate being

21 http://matthewryanhistoricalillustrator.com/.

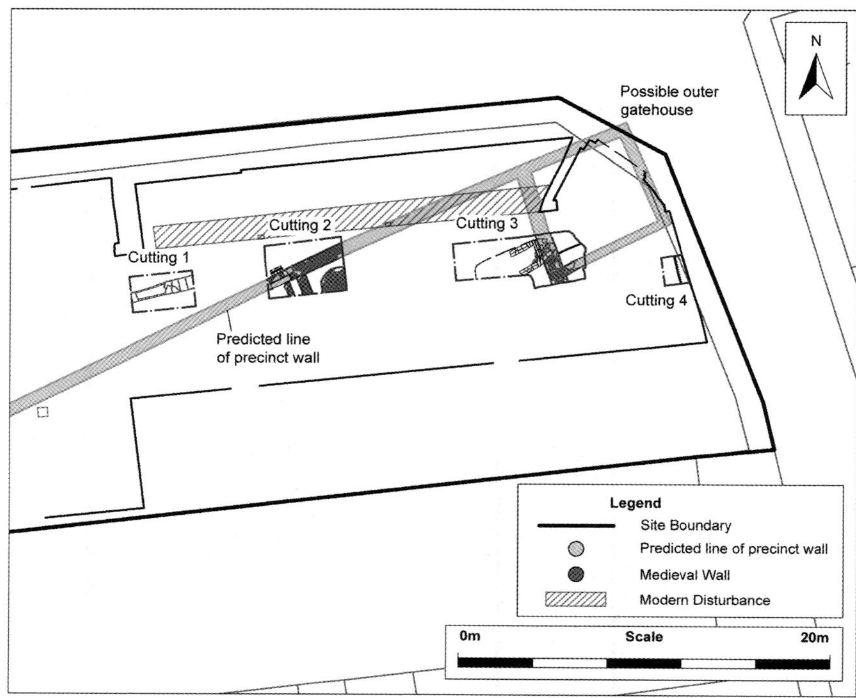

8.8 Little Britain Street site showing test trenches and medieval walls and their conjectural lines

situated at the junction of Little Britain St and Little Green St (see fig. 8.2). Testing revealed up to 2.7m of stratified archaeological deposits and confirmed that the eastern rubble-built limestone wall of the standing warehouse is of post-medieval date, but substantial walls of probable medieval date were identified below the current ground level along with seventeenth- and eighteenth-century structural remains. Significantly, a large wall was identified running northeast–southwest in the centre of the site (C6) and a second wall running north–northwest to south–southeast (C11) was encountered towards the east of the site (fig. 8.8). Both walls were constructed of calp limestone bonded with a cream-coloured lime mortar, though the lower courses of C6 were either denuded of, or devoid of lime mortar.

Testing Results

A large wall (C6) was identified running northeast–southwest through Cutting 2 in the centre of the site (fig. 8.9). The cutting was extended to the north to allow excavation on the northern side of the wall. The wall is constructed of calp limestone, its upper courses bonded with lime mortar, and survives to a height of 1.2m and is a maximum 0.75m wide. At the western side of the

8.9 Precinct wall emerging in Cutting 2, Little Britain St, facing west

cutting, a probable seventeenth-century intervention (C7) is evident where the wall has been broken through, a doorway installed and subsequently infilled with what appear to be late seventeenth-/early eighteenth-century bricks (figs 8.10 and 8.11). A clay layer (C19) with abundant water-rolled cobbles and smaller stones abutted C6 on its northern side at the level of the bottom of this infilled ope – appearing to form a metalled surface. Beneath this clay layer, the natural gravel was identified along with a shallow construction-cut (C20) for the wall C6. A sample of the fill (C2) of this construction-cut was taken. A charred hulled barley grain was retrieved from this fill and returned a radiocarbon date of AD 924–1026.[22] Three stone and brick walls and a sloping mortared surface, all of late seventeenth- or eighteenth-century date, were identified immediately south of and abutting the wall C6 (C8, C9 and C10).

22 2 sigma range FTMC-LL82–2.

8.10 Wall C6 showing location of foundation cut and dated sample

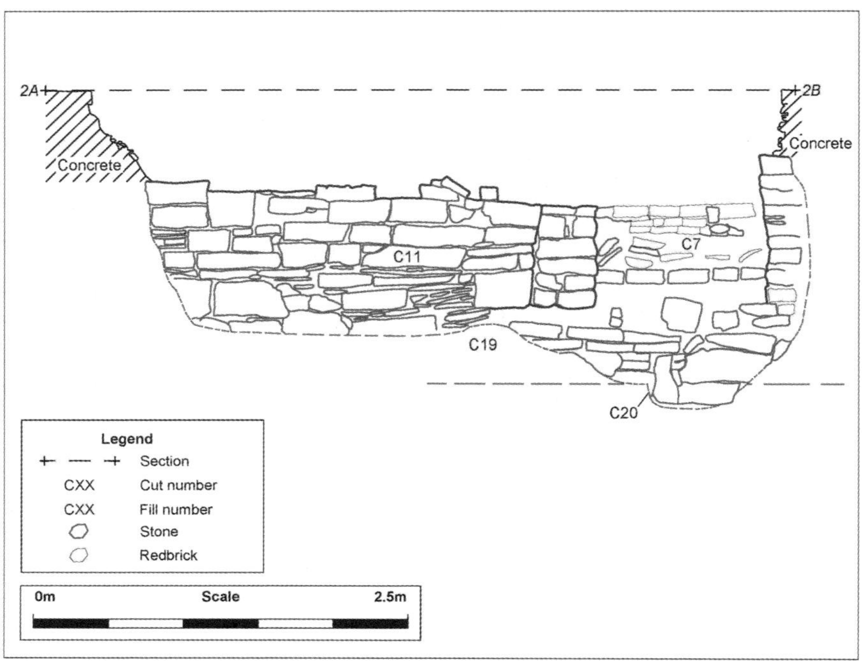

8.11 North facing elevation of wall C11

8.12 Cutting 3 with wall C11 emerging, facing west

A large wall (C11) was identified running north–northwest to south–southeast through the eastern side of Cutting 2 (figs 8.12 and 8.13). A smaller wall (C12) running east–northeast is bonded into (therefore contemporary with) C11. The wall is constructed of calp limestone bonded with a cream-coloured lime mortar, survives to a height of 1.3m and is a maximum 0.83m wide. The internal space defined by walls C11 and C12 contained two layers of

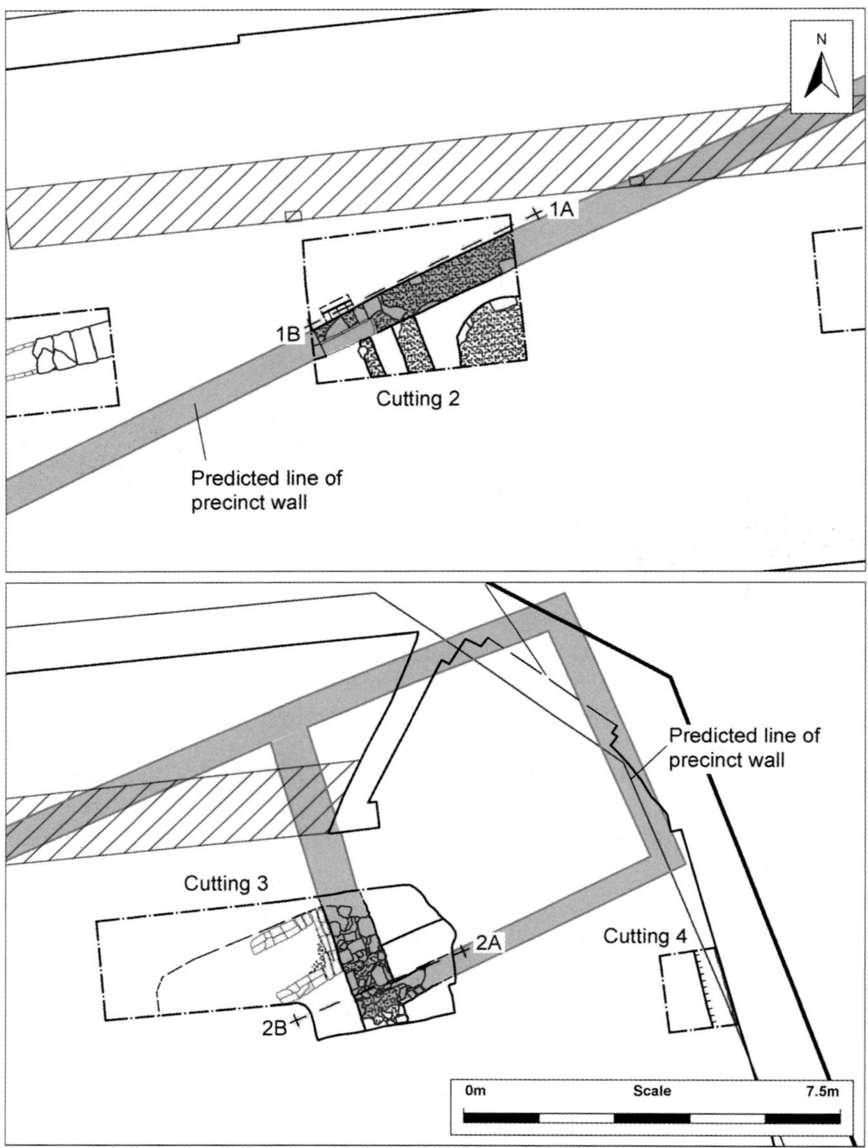

8.13 Plan of cuttings showing medieval walls

silty clay. The upper layer, 41cm in depth C13, was of post-medieval date and contained occasional redbrick fragments, mortar and slate. The lower layer, C14, was a mid-brown compact silty clay with common inclusions of stone. No artefacts were recovered from the excavated portion of C14, though it was cut through where it abutted wall C12 and backfilled with a post-medieval fill with

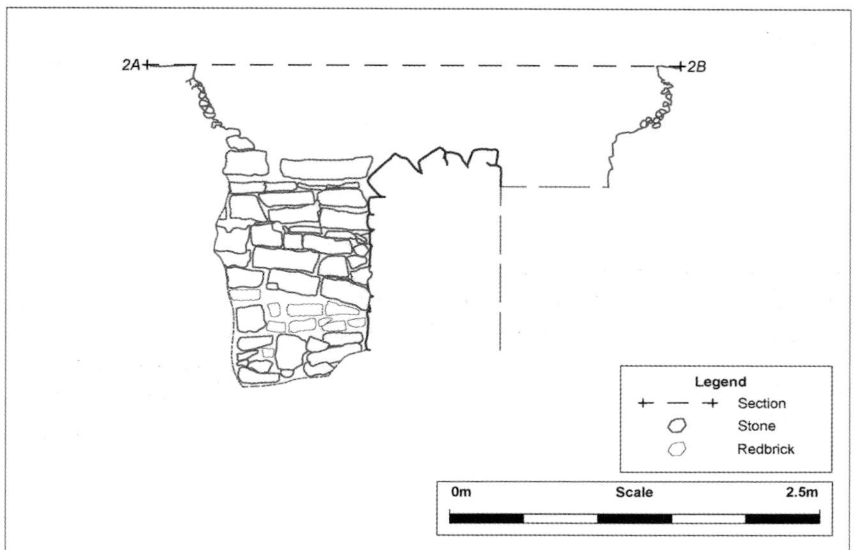

8.14 North-facing elevation of wall C12

frequent inclusions of redbrick and broken slate. The location of this cut corresponded to the location of a redbrick intervention in wall C12 which appears to represent the bricking up of a relieving arch in the structure – though this could not be confirmed with certainty given the restricted size of the cutting (fig. 8.14). Wall C11 is aligned perpendicular to Wall C6, while wall C12 is perpendicular to it, suggesting they form part of the same overall phase of construction.

Discussion

St Mary's abbey had at least two substantial phases of precinct wall-building around the abbey that might relate to the wall C6. The first recorded wall was built around 1216.[23] Sometime between 1213 and 1228, St Mary's abbey sought permission from Henry, archbishop of Dublin, to construct a wall at the site. This was constructed by 1247 when there is reference to lands outside the 'walls'. In 1263 maintenance of these walls was mentioned.[24] A second phase of precinct wall-building began when the south quays were fortified in 1317 due to the Bruce invasion. This second wall would have enclosed the inlet ('the Pil(l)') that runs into the south of the precinct on Speed's map. In 1443 there is a reference in a deed to a stone boundary wall around the abbey which formed the boundary with Oxmantown.[25] In 1539–40 the boundary wall and

23 *CStM*, i, pp 152, 180, xxxvi. 24 *CStM*, i, p. 518. 25 H.B. Clarke, 'Urbs et suburbium: beyond the walls of medieval Dublin' in Conleth Manning (ed.), *Dublin and beyond the Pale:*

outer gates and the monastery wall in the north are mentioned in the extents relating to the Dissolution. The date retrieved from the foundation cut of the gatehouse 40m to the southwest (AD 1316–1427) is suggestive of it belonging to the second phase of building.

The structure formed by walls C11 and C12 is similar in construction, scale and alignment to C6. While the possibility remains that these are post-medieval foundations for structures shown on Rocque's map, the build-up of aceramic clays (C14) against the base of the walls would suggest an earlier date. Should these features be connected it is likely that these walls represent the foundations or lower levels of the western side of the gatehouse through the outer precinct of St Mary's abbey that would have opened onto Little Green St. Further archaeological work is expected on the site and it is hoped that this hypothesis can be clarified in due course.

CLOSING THOUGHTS: OXMANTOWN AS VIKING EMPORIUM?

The early date retrieved from the construction-cut of the precinct wall (C6) at Little Britain St (AD 924–1026) presents some challenges to interpretation. While no artefactual material was recovered to complicate this dating – i.e., no twelfth- or thirteenth-century ceramics were retrieved from the clay layers abutting the lower courses of the wall – a construction date in the tenth–eleventh century would see the precinct predating the historically attested establishment of the abbey by, at the very least, a century. While initially this seems improbable, emerging evidence from excavations across the abbey precinct is beginning to build a picture of a significant earlier, pre-abbey phase of activity. It is worth bearing in mind that the Hiberno-Norse city wall surrounding the historic core of Dublin, traditionally ascribed a date sometime in the years either side of 1100 is a substantial calp and lime-mortar structure between 5m and 7m in height and 1.50m to 3m in width.[26] Dating evidence from several lime kilns in the city, all associated with church sites, provides further confirmation that the Dubliners of the eleventh century were more than capable of building large structures in stone.[27]

With the above in mind, it is relevant that St Mary's abbey is located in the same general location known as Ostmanby/Ostmantown/Oxmantown in the historical record. This name has attracted much attention in recent years with Patrick Wadden posing fresh questions about the antiquity of this northern,

studies in honour of. Patrick Healy (Bray, 1998), p. 49. **26** Linzi Simpson, *Dublin city walls and defences*, an action of the Dublin City Heritage Plan (Dublin, 2006), p. 22; Patrick Wallace, *Viking Dublin: the Wood Quay excavations* (Newbridge, 2016), p. 138. **27** See Paul Duffy, 'Structures of import: St Peter's church, a unique sunken floored structure and Dublin's southern suburb' in Duffy (ed.), *MD XIX* (Dublin, 2022), pp 53–104; idem, 'St Canice's church, Finglas and the Hiberno-Norse churches of Dublin' *Archaeology Ireland*,

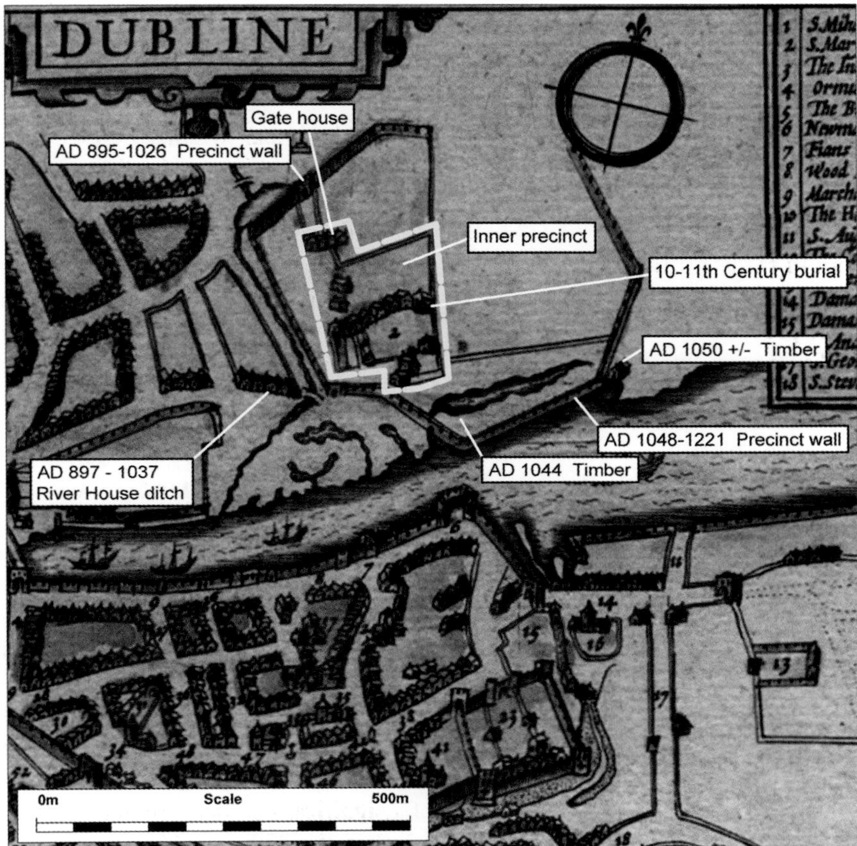

8.15 Emerging dates from excavations within and adjacent to the abbey precinct over Speed's map

transpontine suburb.[28] A pre-Anglo-Norman presence in the area around St Michan's church and Hammond Lane has been archaeologically proven, with many identified features dating to the ninth and tenth centuries,[29] and burials and a large enclosing element around the church site pre-dating the traditional founding date of 1095.[30] In this context, the date retrieved from the base of the wall at Little Britain St, very close to the banks of the Bradogue, accords well with dates retrieved by Muireann Ní Cheallacháin from the confluence of the Bradogue and the Liffey 260m to the southwest.[31] Even more pertinent to the early date at Little Britain St are the very recent findings from within the

145 (2023). **28** Wadden, this volume, pp 143–61. **29** Ní Cheallacháin in this volume (pp 83–101) presents a comprehensive review of this archaeological information. **30** Roseanne Meenan, 'The excavation of pre-Anglo-Norman burials and ditch near St Michan's church' in Duffy (ed.), *MD V* (Dublin, 2004), pp 91–110. **31** Ibid.

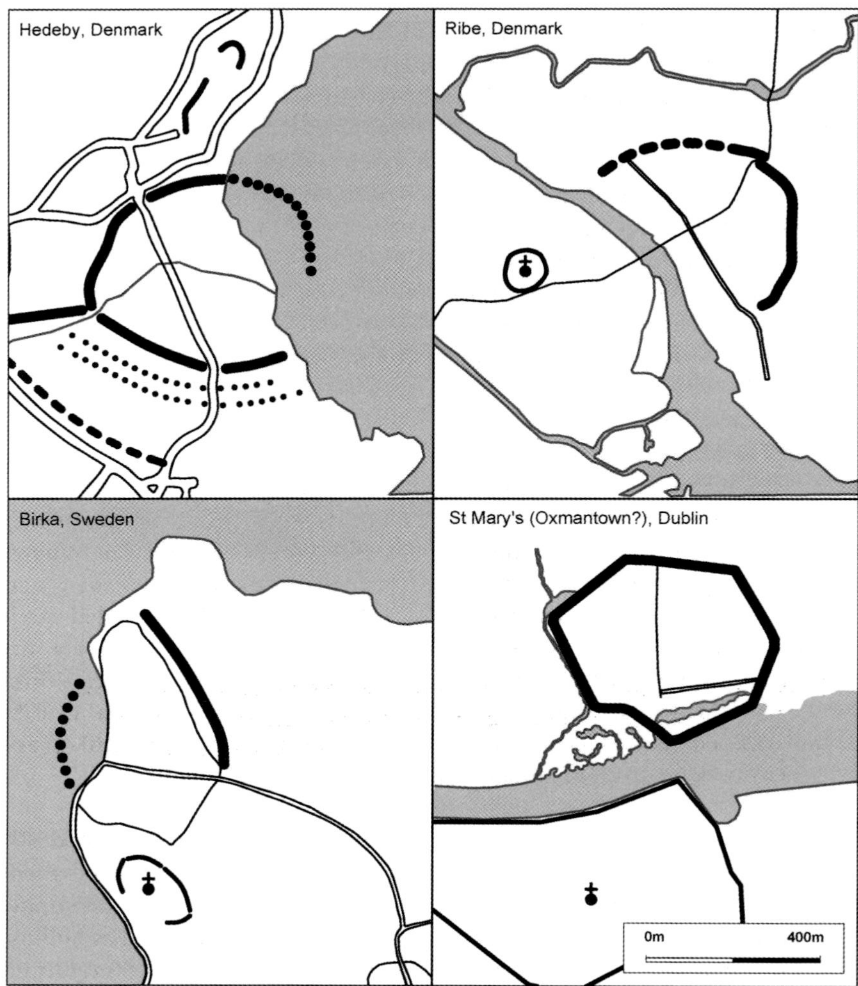

8.16 St Mary's enclosure as depicted by Speed compared to the principal 'Viking emporia'

abbey precinct (fig. 8.15). Eleventh-century burials have been identified within the core of the abbey complex that clearly pre-date the traditional foundation date of 1139.[32] The length of precinct wall excavated along Strand St Great by Caitríona Moore contained within its fabric a wood fragment that returned a date of AD 1048–1221,[33] while further dating of overlying features seemed to

32 O'Donovan, this volume; the earliest date prior to this is from a burial found in Test Trench 5 from Linzi Simpson's test excavation at Begley's Fruit Market, 14–20 Little Mary Street, 28–32 Arran Street East, Dublin (19E0064) which dated between AD 1025–1160 (Beta-525336) (pers. comm.). **33** Caitríona Moore, this volume.

suggest a date earlier in this range rather than later. The adjacent mill building excavated by Ian Russell contained a re-used timber that was dendrochronologically dated to *c.*AD 1050[34] while a revetment timber of very similar date (*c.*AD 1044) has recently been retrieved from estuarine levels at Strand St Little.[35]

While each of these early dates, taken in isolation, could be explained as intrusive or residual, viewing them collectively provides scope for speculation. Supposing for the remainder of this paper that the early date from the foundation cut of the wall at Little Britain St can be taken at face value and is supported by the dating retrieved from the precinct wall at Strand St Great, let us consider that the line of the outer precinct enclosure at St Mary's abbey is a Hiberno-Norse construction. What might such an early precinct relate to, or enclose?

One approach to this question is to take some basic characteristics from the precinct/enclosure and search for parallels to sites with a similar range of characteristics in the wider world to which Dublin was connected by trade routes in the tenth and eleventh centuries. The defining characteristics of such an enclosure at Oxmantown could be described as follows: a large, notably hexagonal/angular enclosure of *c.*500m across fronting a significant watercourse in an urban area connected to wider Scandinavian-founded trade routes. When this description is applied to the wider tenth-/eleventh-century world of the Dubliners, three parallels immediately suggest themselves – these are the settlement and trading centres described as Viking 'emporia' at Ribe (Denmark), Hedeby (Germany) and Birka (Sweden; see fig. 8.16). Corsi describes the Viking Age emporia as follows:

> The emporia consisted of permanent settlements that were modestly sized but swelled seasonally into large markets. The types of goods traded at the emporia fell into two categories or levels: prestige and utilitarian. Prestige goods included things such as coins used as bullion, precious metals, decorated metalwork, arms, basins and cauldrons, textiles, ceramic tableware, glass vessels, windowpanes, beads, precious stones, hunting dogs, hides, spices, wine, dyes, honey, and slaves. The more utilitarian goods were lava quernstones, honestones, soapstone vessels, linen smoothers, foodstuffs, salt, metal and bone tools, and pottery.[36]

34 David Brown, 'Dendrochronological report on wood samples from 35–36 Abbey Street Upper, Dublin 1', QUB Dendrochronology Laboratory Report 8/2022, unpublished report prepared for ACSU, 2022. 35 Paul Duffy, Joe Moran and Femke Vleeshouwer, *Preliminary excavation report, 162–164 Capel St and 33–36 Strand St Little, Dublin 1, Licence: 22E0904* (unpubl. 2024). 36 Maria Corsi, *Urbanization in Viking Age and medieval Denmark: from landing place to town* (Amsterdam, 2020), p. 51.

While the artefactual evidence for such a concentration of trading on the north bank of the Liffey is thus far absent, the market function associated with Oxmantown is strongly attested in the medieval period, enduring to this day. Caitlin Ellis has explored the significance of the term *austmann* in sources from across the Scandinavian realms and has suggested that, in some contexts, this was a designation that could be applied to foreign merchants.[37] Dating of the ramparts at Ribe points to a construction in the period 889–974 and a use-life of at least 50 years.[38]

A similar date range has been obtained for Hedeby,[39] and both dates overlap with the date obtained from the wall at Little Britain St. In all of the three Scandinavian examples presented above, the primary focus of the emporium was trade-related with a separate but adjacent centre comprising a fortress or stronghold containing also the primary church site (fig. 16). This compares very favourably with the situation at Dublin where the primary *dún* or fortress along with associated royal palace and church site were likely to be located on the ridge overlooking the Liffey and Poddle on the south bank of the Liffey opposite to St Mary's abbey.

With regard to the lack of archaeological evidence for early habitation within the precinct of St Mary's abbey, it might possibly be the result, not only of limited programmes of excavation and historic deep cellaring, but also of the attested layout of the emporia sites. At early Ribe there was an 'apparently typical streetscape in the middle of the so-called market area' and excavations have revealed 'substantial parts of two housing plots facing each other on either side of the main street leading through the settlement'.[40] This longitudinal trend in settlement is evident not only at Ribe but also at Hedeby (fig. 8.16).[41] Perhaps such a trend is fossilized in the strong, east–west line of modern Abbey St that is visible throughout the historic mapping (see fig. 8.2).

This interpretation is not without problems, particularly as no archaeological evidence for urbanization or trade-related infrastructure has yet been found from within the precinct, whereas house plots and a church site

37 Caitlin Ellis, 'Degrees of separation: Icelandic perceptions of other Scandinavian settlements in the Faroes, Orkney, Ireland and the Hebrides', *Viking and medieval Scandinavia*, 16 (2020), 1–26, at 10. Though Ellis does not apply this to Dublin, stating instead that 'in an Irish context the use of *austmenn* denoting Hiberno-Scandinavians was perhaps in opposition to *vestmenn* ('west men'), denoting Gaelic Irish'. **38** Sarah Croix, Olav Elias Gundersen, Søren M. Kristiansen, Jesper Olsen, Søren M. Sindbæk, Morten Søvsø, 'Dating earthwork fortifications: integrating five dating methods in Viking-age Ribe, Denmark', *Journal of Archaeological Science: Reports*, 26 (2019). **39** Ibid. **40** Søren Sindbaek, 'Northern emporium: the archaeology of urban networks in Viking-Age Ribe' in Rubina Raja and Søren M. Sindbaek (eds), *Urban network evolutions: towards a high-definition archaeology* (Aarhus, 2018), p. 162. **41** Volker Hilber, 'The access to raw materials and its impact on Hedeby's development in the Viking period' in Petra Eisenach, Thomas Stöllner and Arne Windler (eds), *The RITaK conferences 2013–2014. Raw materials, innovation, technology of ancient cultures RITaK 1. Der Anschnitt Bd. 34* (Bochum/Rhaden, V.

clustered between St Michan's and the Liffey shore would seem to suggest a focus of activity along Church St, some 300m to the west. However, in recent years, previously unsuspected eleventh-century suburbs have been identified at Aungier St and Dean St illustrating the potential for new discoveries to reshape previous understanding of the urban landscape. One association of the emporium function that may prove pertinent to understanding the Oxmantown precinct may prove to be that of slave-trading. A significant volume of this trade is suggested at Dublin in the historical sources with, it has been suggested, a peak period in the late eleventh century when some believe that Dublin became an international slaving hub.[42] The infrastructure, marketplace and holding areas to facilitate such a trade are poorly understood. Perhaps a large tenth-/eleventh-century precinct on the north bank, with market associations, serviced by a small inlet not dissimilar to that leading to the Dubh Linn on the southern bank, might, in future, be found to hold some solutions to these problems. Given the rate of redevelopment of the area formerly comprising the precinct of St Mary's abbey, along with associated archaeological investigations, evidence to progress our understanding of the situation may be forthcoming, perhaps even by the time this paper makes it to print!

2017), pp 253–70. **42** Poul Holm, 'The slave trade of Dublin, ninth to twelfth centuries', *Peritia,* 5 (1986), 317–45; David Wyatt, *Slaves and warriors in medieval Britain and Ireland, 800–1200* (Leiden, 2009).

The occupational profile of pre-modern towns: the case of Dublin, *c.*1190–1640*

BRUCE M.S. CAMPBELL

'Cities', wrote Jan de Vries in 1984, 'are places that have populations, population densities, percentages of the workforce in non-agricultural occupations and a measure of diversity in the occupational structure, all of which are *sufficiently large* … to separate urban from non-urban places'.[1] Richard Holt and Gervase Rosser concur: to them, 'a relatively dense and permanent concentration of residents engaged in a multiplicity of activities, a substantial proportion of which are non-agrarian' constitutes 'an acceptable working definition' of a town.[2] In the case of England, they stress that 'it was the heterogeneity of its composition, rather than the sheer weight of human numbers, that produced the distinctively urban character of the medieval town'. Further, 'many town dwellers were non-natives, who lacked the shared experience of a common upbringing in a local environment'. In short, what differentiated towns from non-agricultural nucleated settlements devoted primarily to fishing, mining, defence, or religion was their economic and occupational diversity. Hence the debate as to whether Early Christian Ireland's nucleated monastic settlements constituted fully fledged towns.[3] For instance, was tenth-century Armagh already as urban as its late eighteenth-century successor clearly was, as revealed by the household survey of this small archiepiscopal city and county town conducted in 1770 by Revd Dr William Lodge?[4] By then, on the evidence of L.A. Clarkson's pioneering analysis of this census-type source, 44 per cent of the city's 471 male heads of households were occupied in crafts, construction and labouring and 54 per cent were engaged in commerce and a variety of service occupations.[5]

* I am grateful to Seán Duffy for the invitation to present an abridged version of this paper at the 2022 symposium of the Friends of Medieval Dublin at Trinity College Dublin. The final version has benefited from helpful comments by Niall Brady, David Dickson, Maryanne Kowaleski and Steve Rigby. 1 Jan de Vries, *European urbanization, 1500–1800* (London, 1984), p. 22. 2 Richard Holt and Gervase Rosser, 'Introduction' in eidem (eds), *The English medieval town: a reader in English urban history, 1200–1540* (London, 1990), pp 3–4. 3 Charles Doherty, 'The monastic town in early medieval Ireland' in Howard Clarke and Anngret Simms (eds), *The comparative history of urban origins in non-Roman Europe: Ireland, Wales, Denmark, Germany, Poland, and Russia from the ninth to the thirteenth century* (Oxford, 1985), pp 45–75; M.A. Valante, 'Reassessing the Irish "monastic town"', *IHS*, 31 (1998), 1–18; John Soderberg, 'Anthropological "civitas" and the possibility of monastic towns', *JRSAI*, 144:5 (2014–15), 45–59. 4 Catherine McCullough and W.H.Crawford, *Armagh: Irish Historic Towns Atlas 18* (Dublin, 2007); L.A. Clarkson, 'An anatomy of an Irish town: the economy of Armagh, 1770', *Irish Economic and Social History*, 5:1 (1978), 27–45. 5 Clarkson, 'Anatomy of an Irish town'; idem, 'Household and family structure in

Urban occupations obviously reveal much about the economic functions and specialisms of individual towns. More generally, they matter because, in aggregate, towns spearheaded the growth of the value-adding activities of manufacturing, commerce and services, upon which the transition to higher levels of per capita economic output and rising living standards ultimately depended. Thus, any increase in the urban share of the population drove a concomitant expansion in the relative importance of secondary and tertiary occupations. Hence the importance attached to urbanization as a proxy for economic progress.[6] Charting GDP per head is one way of measuring the latter, reconstructing changes in occupational structure another, with the latter a fundamental component of GDP estimates.[7] Extending analyses of occupational structure back before the advent of systematic census information in the nineteenth century is consequently a research priority. In the case of England, male occupational trends have been reconstructed in outline from 1379 and then in impressive detail from 1700.[8] Sebastiaan Keibek's sophisticated reconstruction of the male occupational structure of England and Wales in 1710 reveals the clear contrast which, by then, existed between the occupations of the quarter to a third of the national workforce who lived in towns of at least 2,000 inhabitants and those of their non-urban counterparts. Strikingly, 96 per cent of urban workers were employed in the secondary and tertiary sectors and a mere 4 per cent in the primary sector, in contrast to rural workers where these proportions were reversed, with 63 per cent employed in primary occupations and 37 per cent in secondary and tertiary occupations.[9] Were information available for the female workforce, this contrast between urban and rural occupation structures would undoubtedly be even greater, for women typically outnumbered men in the service sector and men were more actively involved than women in primary production.[10]

Armagh City 1770', *Local Population Studies*, 2 (1978), 14–31. For a comparable analysis of Carrick-on-Suir, Co. Tipperary, in 1799, based on a similar household survey, see idem, 'The demography of Carrick-on-Suir, 1799', *PRIA*, 87C (1987), 13–36; idem, 'The Carrick-on-Suir woollen industry in the eighteenth century', *Irish Economic and Social History*, 16:1 (1989), 23–41. 6 Bruce M.S. Campbell, 'National incomes and economic growth in pre-industrial Europe: insights from recent research', *Quaestiones Medii Aevi Novae*, 18 (2013), 167–96. 7 Stephen Broadberry, Bruce M.S. Campbell, Alexander Klein, Mark Overton and Bas van Leeuwen, *British economic growth, 1270–1870* (Cambridge, 2015), pp 194–7, 345–64. 8 The Cambridge Group for the History of Population and Social Structure, 'The occupational structure of Britain 1379–1911', https://www.campop.geog.cam.ac.uk/research/occupations/overview/ accessed 9/10/22; Leigh Shaw-Taylor and E.A. Wrigley, 'Occupational structure and population change' in Roderick Floud (ed.), *The Cambridge economic history of modern Britain, I, Industrialization, 1700–1860* (2014), pp 53–88. Also, Broadberry et al., *British economic growth*, pp 343–64. 9 Sebastiaan Antonius Johannes Keibek, 'The male occupational structure of England and Wales, 1600–1850' (PhD, University of Cambridge, 2016), p. 201. 10 For the bias of female employment towards the service sector and the bias of service-sector employment towards women, see Broadberry et al., *British economic growth*, pp 346–64. Preliminary

Keibek's estimates clearly vindicate de Vries's emphasis upon the distinctive occupational characteristics of towns.[11]

Whether towns were already occupationally thus differentiated some four to five centuries earlier nevertheless remains to be demonstrated. Certainly, the Campop occupational project, from which Keibek's estimates have emanated, lacks any explicit aspiration to extend analysis back before the poll taxes of the late fourteenth century into the preceding urbanizing era of the twelfth- and thirteenth-century commercial revolution.[12] Yet these earlier centuries are not without relevant data, as analyses of the male occupational structures of such leading pre-Black Death English provincial cities as York, Norwich, Winchester and Canterbury demonstrate.[13] In the case of Norwich the information comes from the names and occupations of 1,160 men enrolled in the city's deeds between 1286 and 1305 as buyers or sellers of property.[14] Occupationally, this was a broad cross-section of Norwich's economically active population but upwardly biased towards those with the means to engage in the city's property market. The equivalent information for 426 property owners at Winchester retrieved prosopographically from an array of sources between 1300 and 1339 is similarly biased but nonetheless reveals the potential of this unavoidably laborious approach.[15] More readily amenable to analysis, although far from unproblematic, is the occupational information contained in the freemen's registers that survive for numbers of towns.[16] Of these, none have received as much attention or generated as much discussion as those for

findings from the project 'Forms of labour: gender, freedom and experience of work in the preindustrial economy', funded by the European Research Council and directed by Jane Whittle (University of Exeter) and co-investigator Mark Hailwood (University of Bristol), confirm that by the sixteenth century an array of service occupations dominated female employment in large English towns and gave more employment to females than males. Additionally, primary activities were of small importance in towns, crafts and construction provided more employment to males than females, and males and females were equally, if differently, involved in commerce. I am grateful to Professor Whittle for sharing these unpublished results with me. 11 De Vries, *European urbanization*, p. 22. 12 Cambridge Group, 'Occupational structure of Britain'; Bruce M.S. Campbell, *The great transition: climate, disease and society in the late-medieval world* (Cambridge, 2016), pp 121–5. 13 Edward Miller and John Hatcher, *Medieval England: towns, commerce and crafts 1086–1348* (London, 1995), pp 324–30; Richard Britnell, 'The economy of British towns 600–1300' in D.M. Palliser (ed.), *The Cambridge urban history, I, 600–1540* (Cambridge, 2000), pp 121–3. 14 Elizabeth Rutledge, 'Economic life' in Carole Rawcliffe and Richard Wilson (eds), *Medieval Norwich* (London, 2004), pp 157–88, at pp 168–72. 15 Derek Keene, *Survey of medieval Winchester, I, Part I*, Winchester Studies, 2 (Oxford, 1985), pp 252–64. For a prosopographical reconstruction of the occupational structure of late fourteenth-century Exeter, see Maryanne Kowaleski, *Local markets and regional trade in medieval Exeter* (Cambridge, 1995), pp 120–75, 334–52, and Tables 4 and 5. 16 D.M. Woodward, 'Freemen's rolls', *Local Historian*, 9:2 (1970), 89–95; John F. Pound, 'The validity of the freemen's lists: some Norwich evidence', *Economic History Review*, 34:1 (1981), 48–59; Heather Swanson, 'The illusion of economic structure: craft guilds in late medieval English towns', *Past and Present*, 121 (1988), 29–48.

York.[17] Between 1272 and 1349 the York registers furnish the occupations of 2,389 freemen. This can be compared with the 245 freemen with known occupations recorded for the substantially smaller city of Canterbury between 1297 and 1346 and 216 freemen with occupations contained in the Exeter registers between 1300 and 1349.[18] Rates of admission, and consequently the amount and range of the available occupational information, varied between towns according to the gravitational draw of their respective economies, level at which entry fines were set, and whether constraints were placed upon the admission of certain occupational groups.[19]

Among the earliest extant freemen's registers for any 'English' town are those for Henry III's Irish capital of Dublin. These span the 1230s and 1240s and preserve the names of 391 new freemen, with occupational information given for 158 of them.[20] This information is mostly in the form of the attribution made by the clerk who enrolled the admission, as in the case of Henry Oeyn *factor armorum*, but also includes men with occupational surnames, as, for instance, Alan *Clericus* and Walter *Tannator*, all of whom were admitted in the early 1230s.[21] These occupations, along with those of men admitted at the same time to the lesser privilege of the guild merchant, are conveniently indexed in Philomena Connolly's edition of the *Dublin guild merchant roll* and, apart from a few revisions and additions, these are the occupations analysed here.[22]

Since Dublin and the new English Lordship of which it was the capital were actively recruiting immigrants, few preconditions appear to have been placed in the path of those who wished to settle in the city and become freemen beyond payment of an unspecified entry fine. The value of the latter reflected the fact that those enfranchised as freemen were entitled to vote in municipal elections and run for office but were also obliged to bear the costs and responsibilities of doing so. It was therefore set higher than the lesser fine of

17 P.M. Tillott (ed.), *A history of the county of York: the city of York* (London, 1961), Appendix, 'The later Middle Ages: admissions to freedom', pp 114–16, *British History Online* (http://www.british-history.ac.uk/vch/yorks/city-of-york/pp114-116 [accessed 1 April 2022]); R.B. Dobson, 'Admissions to the freedom of the city of York in the later Middle Ages', *Economic History Review*, 26:1 (1973), 1–22; Swanson, 'The illusion of economic structure'. Also, John Patten, 'Urban occupations in pre-industrial England', *Transactions of the Institute of British Geographers*, n.s., 2:2 (1977), 298–9. 18 A.F. Butcher, 'Canterbury's earliest rolls of freemen admissions, 1297–1363: a reconsideration' in Felix Hull (ed.), *A Kentish miscellany*, Kent Archaeological Society (Chichester 1979), pp 1–26; Margery M. Rowe and Andrew M. Jackson (eds), *Exeter freemen, 1266–1967*, Devon and Cornwall Record Society (Exeter, 1973), pp 6–29. 19 Mary Bateson (ed.), *Records of the borough of Leicester: being a series of extracts from the archives of the corporation of Leicester, 1103–1327* (London, 1899), pp xxvii–xxxv; Eleanora Carus-Wilson, 'The woollen industry' in M.M. Postan and Edward Miller (eds), *The Cambridge economic history of Europe, II, Trade and industry in the Middle Ages* (Cambridge, 2nd edn 1987), p. 641; Miller and Hatcher, *Towns, commerce and crafts*, pp 104–6. 20 *DGMR*, pp 113–20. 21 *DGMR*, p. 114. 22 *DGMR*, pp 157–9.

9 shillings charged for admission to the guild merchant which merely guaranteed the right to trade freely and conduct business within the municipality's jurisdiction (a requirement that was periodically enforced by the civic authorities).[23] Traders and craftsmen, of course, needed the latter privilege; labourers, servants, carters and mariners did not. As a result, during these two decades, admissions to the freedom were outnumbered by those to the more affordable guild merchant by a ratio of over four to one.

Occupations are given for 480 of the 1,689 guildsmen admitted at this time, which, in combination with the freemen, raises the total number of men with recorded occupations to 638, equivalent to 29 per cent of the total admitted. Per year this is barely half the amount of occupational information available for Norwich over fifty years later but is on a par with that available for York. The Dublin guildsmen information has the further merit that it spans a substantially longer period than the corresponding record of freemen's admissions, beginning in the final decade of the twelfth century and continuing to 1265 and over these 75 years recording the occupations of 1,544 of the 8,477 men thus admitted.[24] Initially, this information is given for only one in seven of new guildsmen but from the 1220s this proportion rises to a little over one in five. In fact, given the amount of immigration and in-migration taking place, the guild merchant's clerks were more interested in recording the geographical origins than the occupations of these new guildsmen. Those with both types of information comprise a precious 14 per cent of the total (Table 9.11). Why occupations are recorded for some men and not others is unclear but there is nothing to suggest that those with this information are unrepresentative of the whole.[25] Indeed, analysis of the available information yields results which are as credible as they are consistent over time (Tables 9.2 and 9.12).

As well as greatly amplifying the volume of available occupational information, the Dublin guildsmen's admissions extend coverage to include those further down the socio-economic pyramid for whom becoming a guildsman was the cheaper and less onerous option and usually sufficient to their purpose. As Table 9.1 shows, including the guildsmen significantly improves the visibility of those occupied in direct production, provisioning, and certain branches of commerce. Rarely did butchers and fishermen, many of them based outside the city, become freemen, and millers, bakers, brewers and maltsters are all much better represented among the guildsmen than the freemen. Similarly, the middling and petty traders – mercers, drapers, mongers, chapmen and hucksters – were less likely to become freemen than the great merchants, spicers and vintners, not least because they were less

23 Bruce M.S. Campbell, 'Dublin 1190–1290: provincial capital or capital city?' in Seán Duffy (ed.), *Medieval Dublin XIX* (Dublin, 2023), pp 230–1. **24** Geoffrey Martin, 'Introduction' in *DGMR*, pp x–xi. **25** Below, pp 236–42.

likely to have been permanent residents of the city, as was almost certainly required of those who became freemen.[26] Wealth was also clearly a factor. Within the textile trades it was those who specialized in the capital-intensive occupations of fulling, finishing, and dyeing who show up most strongly in the freemen's register, in contrast to those engaged in the less remunerative occupations of wool preparation and weaving, who are better recorded in the guild merchant roll. In fact, without the guildsmen's register, the textile and clothing trades would be significantly under-represented, in direct contrast to those occupied in leather-working – hatters, glovers, shoemakers, cobblers, harness-makers and saddlers – and especially the skinners, tanners and curriers who show up particularly strongly in the freemen's register.

Table 9.1. Numbers of Dublin guildsmen admissions (1230–49 and 1190–1265) per freeman (1230–49) for specific occupational groups

Occupational category	Guildsmen 1230–49 per freeman 1230–49	Occupation	Guildsmen 1190–1265 per freeman 1230–49
		Fishermen & butchers	86.00
Provisioning	8.30	Mercers, drapers & mongers	27.00
Primary	6.00	Millers, bakers, brewers, maltsters	18.88
Misc. crafts	3.00	Petty traders	14.00
Construction	2.45	Clerks & scribes	12.43
Commerce	2.45	Clothing	10.33
AVERAGE	2.39	AVERAGE	9.54
Textiles & clothing	2.15	Wool preparation & weaving	9.50
Metal-working	2.06	Leather-working	8.36
Services	2.03	Personal, professional & public services	7.60
Tanning & leather	1.09	Dyeing, finishing, fulling	6.33
		Great merchants	4.54
		Cooks	4.33
		Painters	4.17
		Hides, skins & tanning	3.86

Source: *DGMR*.

26 At York the franchise was restricted to 'those who lived as well as traded within the walls of the city': Dobson, 'Admissions to the freedom of the city of York', p. 11.

De facto, the higher entry fine paid by those who became freemen served as a means test and numbers of these occupational differences between the ratio of guildsmen to freemen are consequently to be explained by the relative incomes of the groups concerned, with those on the lowest incomes mostly confined to the ranks of the guildsmen. There was also the issue of which status best served the business interests of the parties concerned. Seemingly, there was little incentive for almost all butchers and fishermen and the majority of middling and petty traders to become freemen when admission to the guild merchant was sufficient to their needs. Problematically, it was also the case that not all guildsmen were permanent residents of the city and therefore eligible to become freemen.[27]

Undoubtedly, some of those who became guildsmen were established Dubliners. Others, as their recorded places of origin sometimes reveal, were betterment migrants who had been drawn to the expanding city by the economic opportunities that it offered and arrived with the intention of making Dublin their home. In contrast, some had every intention of leaving once the business which had brought them temporarily to Dublin had been concluded. In other towns these men, whose permanent places of residence were elsewhere, were described as *forinseci*.[28] They were part of the constant turnover of personnel that was characteristic of busy commercial entrepôts like Dublin. While in the city, they joined the guild merchant for the trading privileges which membership granted and the cultural and social perks that it offered.[29] Finally, there were those, like most of the butchers and fishermen and many of the millers engaged in provisioning the city, plus the many mercers and chapmen who serviced its trade and retailed its wares, who maintained a regular presence in the city and were active in Dublin's marts and markets but who for the most part operated from permanent bases elsewhere within its hinterland.[30] The city could not have functioned without them even though, strictly, they were non-residents. Residence, in fact, was a relative thing.

To differentiate on a systematic basis between those who were resident and those who were not with little more to go on than the place-of-origin information provided for one in seven of those guildsmen with recorded occupations is a vain proposition. Nor, even if it could be done, would it necessarily make a significant difference to the overall picture obtained from the available information. Table 9.2 summarizes the city's occupational profile of the 158 freemen recorded 1230–49 and the corresponding profiles for the 1,544 guildsmen recorded 1190–1265 and subset of 480 guildsmen recorded

27 Cf Leicester: Bateson (ed.), *Records of Leicester*, p. xxxviii. 28 James Masschaele, 'Urban trade in medieval England: the evidence of foreign gild membership lists' in P.R. Coss and S.D. Lloyd (eds), *Thirteenth Century England*, 5 (Woodbridge, 1995), pp 116, 125. 29 Campbell, 'Dublin 1190–1290'. 30 Below, pp 236–8.

Table 9.2. The occupational profiles of Dublin guildsmen 1190–1265 and 1230–49 and freemen 1230–49 (see Appendix 1 for the occupational classification)

Occupation group	Guildsmen 1190–1265	Guildsmen 1230–49	Freemen 1230–49	Guildsmen & freemen 1230–49
A) Primary/Secondary/Tertiary occupations [%]:				
Primary	3.6	6.3	1.9	5.2
Secondary	63.0	61.9	65.8	62.9
Tertiary	33.4	31.9	32.3	32.0
TOTAL NUMBER	1,544	480	158	638
B) All occupations [%]:				
Primary	1.4	1.7	0.6	1.4
Provisioning*	15.5	19.4	6.3	16.1
Cloth	7.6	10.0	9.5	9.9
Clothing	8.0	7.3	7.6	7.4
Tanning	5.3	5.2	13.3	7.2
Leather-working	7.6	5.4	8.9	6.3
Metal-working	10.9	9.2	11.4	9.7
Miscellaneous crafts	4.5	3.8	3.2	3.6
Construction	5.7	6.3	7.0	6.4
Commerce	13.3	12.7	12.0	12.5
Services	19.1	18.5	20.3	19.0
High titles	1.0	0.6	0.0	0.5
TOTAL NUMBER	1,544	480	158	638
C) Secondary occupations [%]:				
Food processing	21.2	23.9	7.7	19.7
Cloth	12.0	16.2	14.4	15.7
Clothing	12.7	11.8	11.5	11.7
Tanning	8.4	8.4	20.2	11.5
Leather-working	12.1	8.8	13.5	10.0
Metal-working	17.3	14.8	17.3	15.5
Misc crafts	7.2	6.1	4.8	5.7
Construction	9.0	10.1	10.6	10.2
TOTAL NUMBER	973	297	104	401

* Gardening, fishing and food processing.
Source: DGMR.

1230–49. At the most basic level, of primary, secondary and tertiary occupations (Table 9.2A), the results obtained for freemen and guildsmen, both separately and in combination, are virtually identical. Further, the similarities remain strong when the results are broken down in greater detail into twelve basic occupational groupings (Table 9.2B), with the most conspicuous differences being the greater prominence of provisioning occupations among guildsmen and superior importance of tanning and leather-working among freemen. Correlations of guildsmen to freemen range from +0.66 (1230–49 to 1230–49) to +0.76 (1190–1265 to 1230–49), which confirms that each reveals a broadly similar picture, with that conveyed by the guildsmen based upon a substantially larger number of observations which extend further down the socio-economic hierarchy.

Only when comparison is confined to secondary occupations alone do the differences between the occupational profiles of the guildsmen and freemen outweigh the similarities, owing, as observed, to the substantially greater involvement of guildsmen in the out-of-town activity of provisioning and of freemen in the urban and urban-fringe activities of tanning and leather-working. Probably the most reliable occupational profile, which makes the most of the fuller and more representative information available for the guildsmen (towards whom it is weighted) and the surer residential credentials of the freemen, is therefore that revealed for the combined total of 638 guildsmen and freemen recorded 1230–49. Its relatively muted emphasis upon provisioning, tanning and leather-working reflects its weighting towards the guildsmen by a factor of three to one.[31] Henceforth, it is this comprehensive but warts-and-all occupational profile for the 1230s and 1240s which is mostly used for comparison with the profiles of other pre-1350 cities and Dublin at later periods in time.

Faced with a plethora of different occupational descriptions, classification is, of course, fundamental to this whole exercise. In their analyses of urban occupations historians have employed a variety of often bespoke schemes designed to suit the purpose of a particular analysis or tailored to accommodate the idiosyncrasies of a specific dataset.[32] For late fourteenth-century Exeter, for example, Maryanne Kowaleski applied a 'types of raw materials/types of product' scheme.[33] This differs from that applied by J.F. Pound to sixteenth-century Norwich, which is derived from a scheme developed for other sixteenth-century towns by W.G. Hoskins as a pragmatic response to the information contained in Tudor tax returns.[34] This is the scheme applied by Colm Lennon to the occupations listed in the Dublin City Franchise Roll of 1468–1512.[35] Different again is that applied by Clarkson to the census-like household surveys of Armagh in 1770 and Carrick-on-Suir in 1799, which had

31 Hence its stronger correlation of +0.98 with the equivalent profile for guildsmen alone than that of +0.79 for freemen. 32 Patten, 'Urban occupations in pre-industrial England', 305–10. 33 Kowaleski, *Local markets and regional trade*, pp 120–75, 344–5, 350–52. 34 J.F. Pound, 'The social and trade structure of Norwich, 1525–1575', *Past and Present,* 34 (1966), 67–9; W.G. Hoskins, 'English provincial towns in the early sixteenth century', *Transactions Royal Historical Society*, 5th Ser., 6 (1956), 1–16. 35 Colm Lennon, 'Introduction' in *DCFR*, p. xxi.

its origins in one elaborated by W.A. Armstrong and intended, on the one hand, to make sense of the detailed information contained in nineteenth-century census returns and, on the other, to facilitate systematic comparison.[36] It was with the clear ambition to make valid occupational comparisons between communities, across space, and over time that in 2006 E.A. Wrigley elaborated a new detailed classification scheme intended to differentiate between primary-, secondary- and tertiary-sector (PST) occupations.[37] This has since been widely adopted by a growing number of studies of occupational structure.[38] It is a simplified version of that scheme, adapted to suit the period-specific and often ambiguous nomenclature employed by medieval clerks, that has been adopted here (Table 9.2), as set out in Appendix 1. The most obvious departure from Wrigley's strict PST scheme is the creation of a separate category for the core pre-modern urban activity of provisioning, which includes both the primary occupations of gardening and fishing and the secondary food-processing occupations of butchering, dairying, milling, baking, malting and brewing. When necessary, however, as in Tables 9.2A and 9.2C, these individual provisioning occupations are reallocated to their respective primary and secondary sectors.

THE OCCUPATIONAL PROFILE OF THIRTEENTH-CENTURY DUBLIN IN COMPARATIVE PERSPECTIVE

The reconstruction of Dublin's occupational profile 1230–49 is currently the earliest available for any leading provincial city under English rule and the only such reconstruction available for any medieval Irish town.[39] Obviously, it would be revealing to be able to make comparison between Dublin and such high-ranking Irish towns as Drogheda and Waterford, but without extant freemen's registers or their equivalent that is scarcely feasible.[40] Instead, it is possible to make comparison with five early fourteenth-century English cities of broadly

36 Clarkson, 'Anatomy of an Irish town', pp 33–45; Clarkson, 'Carrick-on-Suir woollen industry', p. 32; W.A. Armstrong, 'The use of information about occupation' in E.A. Wrigley (ed.), *Nineteenth-century society: essays in the use of quantitative methods for the study of social data* (Cambridge, 1972), pp 228–30. 37 E.A. Wrigley, 'Categorizing occupations: the primary, secondary, tertiary (PST) system', unpublished paper, Department of Geography, University of Cambridge (2006). 38 For example, Shaw-Taylor and Wrigley, 'Occupational structure and population change'; Broadberry et al., *British economic growth*, pp 345–60; Keibek, 'Male occupational structure of England and Wales'; Osamu Saito and Leigh Shaw-Taylor (eds), *Occupational structure, industrialization and economic growth in a comparative perspective* (Cambridge, forthcoming). 39 D.M. Palliser, Peter Clark, and Martin Daunton (eds), *The Cambridge urban history of Britain*, 3 vols (Cambridge, 2000–1) does not include Ireland. 40 On extant Irish freemen's records, see Mary Clark, 'Sources for Irish freemen' in M.D. Evans and Eileen Ó Dúill (eds), *Aspects of genealogy: proceedings of the first Irish genealogical congress* (Naas, 1993), pp 44–53; Lennon, 'Introduction', p. xiii.

comparable rank and size, namely York, Norwich, Canterbury, Winchester and Exeter.[41] This places the results for Dublin in comparative context and marks a first step in the reconstruction of an overall profile of urban occupational structures across the English realm before the Black Death.

York, like Dublin, had Viking origins, was located at the head of navigation on a tidal river, and was the ecclesiastical, political and cultural capital of the north of England, a region which for the previous two hundred years, following William I's brutal wasting of the North, had been experiencing active post-conquest resettlement.[42] By 1300, when Dublin had a population of maybe 11,000, York, England's second city, was probably twice as large.[43] Norwich was of lesser rank than York but nonetheless ranked among the top five English cities. As such it was more closely comparable to Dublin in size (Table 9.3). It was an episcopal city, the county town of the most populous county in England, an important centre of manufacturing, and was connected to the busy outport of Great Yarmouth via the navigable River Yare. Winchester, the former Anglo-Saxon royal capital of England, was probably slightly smaller than Dublin. It was strategically located between London and the sheltered deep-water port of Southampton on England's south coast favoured by growing numbers of continental merchants.[44] It was a major episcopal centre, contained wealthy religious houses, and hosted the annual international St Giles Fair, although by the end of the thirteenth century the fair was waning in prosperity.[45] Exeter was the smallest and lowest ranking of these cities, and less than half the size of Dublin (Table 9.3). Nevertheless, it was the largest and most important city in the southwest of England, was an episcopal capital and county town, like Dublin had a strongly pastoral hinterland, and conducted an extensive maritime trade, with numbers of Exeter men becoming guildsmen of Dublin.[46]

The published occupational information available for each of these cities has been reclassified according to the modified PST scheme set out in Appendix 1. In every case, as set out in Table 9.3, males with primary occupations (agriculture, horticulture, fishing, forestry, quarrying and mineral extraction) accounted for no more than an eighth of the total and usually closer

41 For the results of applying alternative classification schemes, see Miller and Hatcher, *Towns, commerce and crafts*, pp 324–30; Britnell, 'Economy of British towns', pp 121–3. 42 Sarah Rees Jones, *York: the making of a city, 1068–1350* (Oxford, 2013). 43 Bruce M.S. Campbell, 'Benchmarking medieval economic development: England, Wales, Scotland, and Ireland, *c.*1290', *Economic History Review*, 61:4 (2008), 908, 911. 44 Campbell, 'Benchmarking', 908, 911; Bruce M.S. Campbell, James A. Galloway, Derek J. Keene, Margaret Murphy, *A medieval capital and its grain supply: agrarian production and its distribution in the London region, c.1300*, Historical Geography Research Series, 30 (n.p., 1993), pp 9–11. 45 J.Z. Titow, 'The decline of the fair of St Giles, Winchester, in the thirteenth and fourteenth centuries', *Nottingham Medieval Studies*, 31:1 (1987), 58–75. 46 Kowaleski, *Local markets and regional trade*, pp 81–175; Campbell, 'Dublin 1190–1290', Table 7.4, p. 251.

Table 9.3. The percentages of males with primary, secondary and tertiary occupations: York, Norwich, Dublin, Canterbury, Winchester and Exeter pre-1350, Exeter 1377, and England and Wales 1710

City	Years	Approx. population in 1290	No. men with occupations	% total occupations: Primary	Secondary	Tertiary	Other
York[b]	1272–1349	22,700	2,389	3.6	67.3	29.1	0.0
Norwich[c]	1286–1305	12,000	1,160	12.7	52.8	34.5	0.0
Dublin[a]	1230–1249	11,000	638	5.2	62.9	32.0	0.0
Canterbury[b]	1297–1346	8,800	245	0.8	72.2	25.0	2.0
Winchester[c]	1300–1339	6,800	426	4.9	51.2	43.9	0.0
Exeter[b]	1300–1349	3,700	216	0.0	76.4	23.6	0.0
Exeter[b]	1377	[d]2,500	396	2.0	74.7	23.2	0.0
Mean of 6 pre-1350 cities:			782	4.2	64.9	30.7	0.3
England & Wales 1710:				4.0	68.0	28.0	0.0

[a] guildsmen and freemen [b] freemen [c] property owners. [d] 1377

Sources: Campbell, 'Benchmarking', 908; Clarke, *Dublin, Pt I* (IHTA), p. 12; Tillott (ed.), *York*, pp 114–16; Rutledge, 'Economic life'; *DGMR*; Butcher, 'Canterbury's earliest rolls of freemen'; Keene, *Winchester*; Rowe & Jackson (eds), *Exeter freemen*; Keibek, 'Male occupational structure of England and Wales', p. 201. The figures for Exeter in 1377 have been recalculated from Kowaleski, *Local markets and regional trade*, pp. 128–9 (for its population see, p. 374).

Note: all occupations have been classified according to the detailed scheme set out in Appendix 1.

to a twentieth. Males with secondary occupations (manufacturing and construction) accounted for at least half and often closer to two-thirds of the total. The remaining quarter to a third were occupied in the tertiary sector (commerce and services).[47] The figures for Dublin sit well within these ranges, as might be expected of a city of its size, diversity and developed economic and administrative functions. Nor is it a surprise that already by this early date the occupational profile of each of these six cities anticipated that of England and Wales as a whole some four hundred years later (Table 9.3). In fact, of these six cities, it is Dublin whose PST occupational profile most closely matches that

47 For the results of applying alternative classification schemes to York, Norwich and Winchester, see Miller and Hatcher, *Towns, commerce and crafts*, pp 324–30; Britnell, 'Economy of British towns', pp 121–3.

of England and Wales in 1710 (correlation = +0.9996). By implication, 'English' urban occupational structures were deep rooted, early established and, in their essentials, long enduring.

More detailed breakdowns of the data allow these inter-urban comparisons to be pushed closer. Grouping occupations into the six categories, (i) primary (farming, horticulture, forestry, hunting, fishing, quarrying and mineral extraction), (ii) the provisioning of food and drink, (iii) crafts and construction, (iv) commerce, (v) services and (vi) other (unknown and high titles), yields the results summarized in Table 9.4. Again, the occupational profiles of all six cities emerge as closely correlated, with the weakest matches being those between Norwich and Exeter (+0.82) and Canterbury and Winchester (+0.85) and the strongest those between Dublin and York and Dublin and Canterbury (both + 0.99), for all three of which the available occupational information comes from freemen's registers or, in the case of Dublin, from its guildsmen's equivalent. The match between Dublin and Exeter in 1377 is also an impressive +0.98 and, in fact, the pre-1350 profiles of York, Norwich, Dublin, Canterbury and Winchester all correlate better with the 1377 profile for Exeter than that for 1300–49, which is based upon information for little more than a quarter of freemen which, in its details, looks less than randomly representative of those admitted. Nonetheless, this does not detract from the strength of these similarities which sprang from the need of all six of these cities to feed, clothe, house and service their substantial populations. Each also discharged core religious, governmental and administrative functions and all were actively engaged in local, regional, national and international orbits of commerce conducted by river, sea and land. They also belonged to a functioning urban hierarchy which extended across the Irish Sea to incorporate the port towns of Ireland's east and south coasts.[48]

In none of these cities were primary occupations of any importance, and hence between an eighth and a quarter of those men with recorded occupations were engaged in victualling them with essential foodstuffs, both unprocessed and processed, in the form of grain, flour, bread, malt, ale, fruit and vegetables, fish and meat (Table 9.4). Their activities ensured that close ties existed between these towns and their immediate provisioning hinterlands upon whose productivity and prosperity they depended.[49] With these needs satisfied, collectively it was crafts and construction that accounted for by far the largest share of occupations, ranging from around 40 per cent in Norwich to over 55 per cent in York and Canterbury and an improbable 72 per cent in Exeter (but a more credible 57 per cent in 1377). This created a constant

48 Campbell, 'Dublin 1190–1290'. **49** For case studies of urban provisioning, see Campbell et al., *Medieval capital*; Margaret Murphy and Michael Potterton, *The Dublin region in the Middle Ages: settlement, land-use and economy* (Dublin, 2010).

Table 9.4. The occupational profiles of York, Norwich, Dublin, Canterbury, Winchester and Exeter pre-1350, and Exeter 1377

City	Years	No. men with occupations	% of total occupations: Primary	Provisioning	Crafts & construction	Commerce	Services	Other
York[b]	1272–1349	2,389	0.0	15.5	55.4	15.7	13.4	0.0
Norwich[c]	1286–1305	1,160	0.2	25.4	39.9	19.1	15.3	0.0
Dublin[a]	1230–1249	638	1.4	16.1	50.5	12.5	19.0	0.5
Canterbury[b]	1297–1346	245	0.4	16.3	56.3	6.1	18.8	2.0
Winchester[c]	1300–1339	426	0.5	12.9	43.9	27.0	15.7	0.0
Exeter[b]	1300–1349	216	0.0	5.1	71.8	12.5	11.1	0.0
Exeter[b]	1377	[d]396	2.0	17.7	57.1	11.4	11.9	0.0

[a] guildsmen and freemen [b] freemen [c] property owners [d] 1377
Sources: see Table 9.3. For classification scheme see Appendix 9.1.

demand for raw materials and fuel. If manufacturing lay at the core of their urban economies, commerce was the mainstay of them all, albeit rarely the main source of livelihood of more than a fifth of those with recorded occupations. This is hardly because commercial occupations are significantly under-recorded, for merchants, mercers, and chapmen are among the most visible occupational groups within the available sources. Rather, it was because for many men commerce was conducted as an adjunct to some other provisioning or craft activity. Only in Winchester, helped no doubt by the annual St Giles Fair and the city's location between Southampton and London, was commerce the primary occupation of as much as a quarter of those recorded. Finally, everywhere service-sector occupations account for a more modest share of recorded occupations than, in reality, must have been the case. Present in all these cities were religious and governing elites with their bureaucracies and households, professional providers of legal, financial, clerical, medical and essential services, and numbers of public, domestic and personal servants, both male and female. All were centres of hospitality and entertainment, and generated a constant flow of traffic, freight, and travellers. Yet nowhere did services account for more than a fifth of those with recorded occupations and in York and Exeter the proportion was around an eighth. It therefore seems certain that services are the least reliably recorded component of these cities' respective occupational profiles.

Table 9.5. Secondary occupations at York, Norwich, Dublin, Canterbury, Winchester and Exeter pre-1350, and Exeter 1377

City	Years	No. men with secondary occupations	% of total secondary occupations:					
			Food processing	Cloth & clothing	Tanning & leather	Metals	Misc.	Construction
York[b]	1272–1349	1,608	*17.7*	*15.7*	*40.5*	*15.9*	*4.4*	*5.8*
Norwich[c]	1286–1305	613	*24.5*	*15.7*	*41.3*	*10.8*	*1.6*	*6.2*
Dublin[a]	1230–1249	401	*19.7*	*27.4*	*21.5*	*15.5*	*5.7*	*10.2*
Canterbury[b]	1297–1346	177	*22.0*	*20.9*	*23.2*	*14.7*	*9.0*	*10.2*
Winchester[c]	1300–1339	218	*16.5*	*38.5*	*26.1*	*7.3*	*1.8*	*9.6*
Exeter[b]	1300–1349	165	*6.7*	*21.2*	*47.3*	*6.7*	*12.1*	*6.1*
Exeter[b]	1377	[d]296	*23.6*	*18.9*	*25.0*	*12.5*	*6.4*	*13.5*

[a] guildsmen and freemen [b] freemen [c] property owners [d] 1377
Sources: see Table 9.3. For classification scheme see Appendix 9.1.

Differences between these cities are most apparent in the composition of their secondary sectors. Food processing, cloth-making and clothing manufacture, tanning and leather-working, smithing and a variety of other forms of metal-working, assorted other crafts, and construction, were activities common to all of them, but the relative importance and corresponding level of development of each, as set out in Table 9.5, varied a good deal.[50] Occupationally, York and Norwich had the most similar mix of manufactures (correlation = +0.96). In both cities the tanning of hides and working of leather eclipsed all other craft activities and accounted for over 40 per cent of recorded secondary employment. It is at these scales of occupational development that it is possible to talk about an industry having outgrown the subsistence needs of its immediate host city and region and become a genuine economic specialization.[51] At Exeter 1300–49, where the minority of freemen with recorded occupations look less than randomly representative, skinners, tanners, cordwainers, and glovers made up almost half of the recorded total, but this proportion reduces to a quarter in 1377 when the evidence is more representative (Table 9.5). Significantly, in all three of these cities tanning and

50 Much the same array of occupations features in the late twelfth-century guild roll of Leicester: Bateson (ed.), *Records of Leicester*, pp xxix–xxx. **51** Nigel Goose, 'English pre-industrial urban economies', *Urban History*, 9 (1982), 25–7.

leather-working led food processing and cloth and clothing by a considerable margin. Craft specialization on this scale was absent from Dublin and Winchester, whose secondary sectors were broadly similar (correlation = +0.93). In both cities cloth and clothing were the biggest employers but less overwhelmingly so than were the tanning and leather industries of York, Norwich and, maybe, Exeter. Unsurprisingly, the lowest correlations are between the least and most specialized of these cities, namely Winchester and York (+0.53) and Winchester and Norwich (+0.57), although it is Exeter 1300–49 which, for the reasons already given, looks the odd man out, in contrast to Exeter in 1377 which gives consistently stronger correlations (that with Dublin rising from +0.47 to +0.79). Canterbury also lacked any single dominant secondary occupation, and, after Winchester, it was Canterbury that Dublin most closely resembled (correlation = +0.90). These cities were notable for the diversity of their secondary sectors but lacked the comparative advantages and access to substantial markets that might have boosted a greater concentration upon any single branch of manufacturing activity. Thus, important as Dublin's tanning and leather crafts were, they contributed barely half of the share of secondary urban employment achieved by the same industries in York and Norwich, both of which served larger, wealthier and more populous hinterlands.

In the 1230s and 1240s Dublin's occupational profile reflected the subsistence and material needs of the city and its relatively limited and underdeveloped hinterland. These were those of a regional capital of unusual political importance but modest size, for, in the second quarter of the thirteenth century, it must still have had far fewer than 10,000 inhabitants.[52] Over a third of all those with recorded occupations were engaged in providing for the essential subsistence needs of food, clothing, and housing, while a further third made their livings processing animal fibres and skins into cloth and leather and fashioning leather, metal, wood, clay and bone into the material goods of everyday life. As yet, the local luxury demand from religious, landed and urban elites fell a long way short of that available to the craftworkers of York, let alone those of London.[53] Only by expanding the market that Dublin's craftworkers served both within and beyond the city could they have achieved a greater division of labour and sustained higher levels of specialization.[54] That, in turn, was contingent upon Dublin extending

52 This is on the assumption that it was some way short of the 11,000 given for *c.*1300 by Clarke, *Dublin Pt I* (IHTA), p. 12. The same figure had been proposed by Josiah Cox Russell, *Medieval regions and their cities* (Newton Abbot, 1972), pp 136–7. Estimates as high as 20,000 and 25,000 have also been suggested (Murphy and Potterton, *Dublin region*, p. 30), which would put Dublin on a par with York, which seems unlikely. 53 Christopher Dyer, 'The consumer and the market in the later Middle Ages', *Economic History Review*, 42:3 (1989), 306–20. 54 George J. Stigler, 'The division of labor is limited by the extent of the market', *Journal of Political Economy*, 59:3 (1951), 185–93.

its administrative, commercial and social reach within Ireland and promoting the security and prosperity of the region of which it was the capital. In the 1230s and 1240s there was a real prospect that these developments were in train and that Dublin's similarities to comparable leading English cities would be consolidated.[55] Half a century later, when the occupational profiles of other cities come into view, the opportunity for Dublin to extend its influence beyond a limited radius within eastern Ireland had passed.[56]

DUBLIN'S OCCUPATIONS 1190–1265: A CLOSER LOOK

Between 1230 and 1249 the Dublin guild merchant roll and freemen's register record 111 unique occupations, a number which increases to 150 over the entire 75 years, 1190–1265. Some occupations are mentioned just once, such as William of Leicester, *Ductor Aque*, Robert the Boothwright (son of William the Fletcher), and the bookmonger, John of Coventry, admitted respectively in 1238–9, 1245–6, and 1259–60, along with the cup-maker (*cipharius*), Gregory of Bristol, admitted as a freeman in 1247–8.[57] Other occupations are recorded time and time again, as in the case of the bakers, butchers and fishermen who victualled the city, the dyers, tailors, tanners, and smiths active in its textile, leather and metal trades, the mercers and chapmen who handled much of its middling and petty commerce, and the clerks whose literacy skills underpinned a growing dependence upon written records. The sheer number and range of these occupations, from right across the employment spectrum, identifies Dublin as a city of some rank and scale, since, the greater the market that was served, the greater the division of labour that was sustainable.[58] This chimes with Derek Keene's observation that the 'numbers of medieval urban occupations seem broadly to reflect population and commercial development'.[59] Thus, at the end of the thirteenth century, tax rolls list over 300 occupations for Paris, at that time the largest European city north of the Alps, and 175 for London, the second largest.[60] On this crude measure, Dublin was clearly lower in rank and smaller in scale than London but maybe a cut above the shire town and former royal capital of Winchester, for which about 70 occupations are recorded.[61]

55 Campbell, 'Dublin 1190–1290', pp 258–61, 269. 56 Bruce M.S. Campbell, 'From boom to bust: the Lordship of Ireland and the European "commercial revolution"' in Peter Crooks and Seán Duffy (eds), *Invasion 1169* (Dublin, forthcoming). 57 *DGMR*, pp 75, 84, 101, 119. 58 Stigler, 'Division of labor'. 59 Derek Keene, 'Continuity and development in urban trades: problems of concepts and the evidence' in Penelope J. Corfield and Derek Keene (eds), *Work in towns, 850–1850* (Leicester, 1990), p. 7. Also, R.H. Britnell, 'Specialization of work in England, 1100–1300', *Economic History Review*, 54:1 (2001), 2. 60 Keene, 'Continuity and development', p. 7. 61 Keene, 'Continuity and development', p. 7.

Primary production and provisioning

As already observed, those occupied in primary-sector activities were conspicuous by their effective absence from Dublin (Table 9.2).[62] Fishermen alone were an exception (Table 9.6), since Dublin had its own fleet which fished the waters from Holmpatrick in the north to Dalkey in the south and, in a devout age, fish were a staple foodstuff.[63] It is for the latter reason that fishing (sometimes synonymous with fish-mongering) is here classified under provisioning (Appendix 1). Otherwise, these primary activities, so characteristic of the surrounding countryside, had no place in the city.[64] Instead, around a sixth of the male workforce was employed in some branch of the provisioning trades without whose efforts the city's essential victualling needs could not have been met.

As in all late medieval cities, grain, ground and baked into bread or malted and brewed into ale, was Dublin's single most important staple foodstuff and in the thirteenth century those who dealt in these products and processes dominated the provisioning trade, with millers, bakers, maltsters and brewers accounting for almost two-thirds of the men with occupations recorded in this sector (Table 9.6).[65] No doubt the brewers were the least numerous of this occupational group because so much of the brewing was still undertaken domestically by women.[66] Women, too, would have been the chief producers and suppliers of dairy produce – milk, butter, cheese and eggs – which explains why this small but vital component of the city's provisioning trade is wholly missing from the occupational record.[67] In contrast, the supply of fruit and vegetables is represented by the admission of three gardeners.[68] More numerous were the millers, who, in lieu of middlemen cornmongers (of whom there is no mention), played a leading role in provisioning Dublin's bakers with flour from their mills outside Dublin (Table 9.6).[69] Commonest of all, however,

62 Exceptions include a churl, a villein, two *famuli* (farm servants), a mower, a stocker, a possible goatherd, a franklin, and two grangers. The admission of seven foresters probably reflects the city's dependence upon timber, wood and firewood. For the sources of Dublin's fuel supply, see Murphy and Potterton, *Dublin region*, pp 367–8; Peadar Slattery, 'Woodland management, timber and wood production, and trade in Anglo-Norman Ireland, *c.*1170 to *c.*1350', *JRSAI*, 139 (2009), p. 72. **63** Murphy and Potterton, *Dublin region*, p. 399. **64** The presence of two falconers, two hawkers and a fewterer (who kept and handled hounds) among the pre-1265 guildsmen is a reminder of the proximity of the countryside and suggests that some at least of Dublin's urban elite indulged in the pleasures of the chase: *DGMR*, pp 14, 32, 54, 67, 103. **65** Murphy and Potterton, *Dublin region*, pp 409–32. For a reconstruction of the grain requirements and supply hinterland of London, a city with at least six times the provisioning requirements of Dublin, see Campbell et al., *Medieval capital.* **66** Murphy and Potterton, *Dublin region*, pp 430–1; Peadar Slattery, *Social life in pre-Reformation Dublin, 1450–1540* (Dublin, 2019), pp 136–76; Judith M. Bennett, *Ale, beer, and brewsters in England: women's work in a changing world, 1300–1600* (Oxford, 1996). **67** Murphy and Potterton, *Dublin region*, p. 443. **68** *DGMR*, pp 23, 73, 88. **69** Murphy and Potterton, *Dublin region*, pp 416–26. Cornmongers operated as middlemen: for their role in the provisioning of London, see Campbell et al., *Medieval*

were the bakers themselves, who produced the daily bread upon which all Dubliners relied and, in the process, generated a constant demand for fuel to fire their ovens.[70] The three charcoal burners admitted to the guild before 1221 testify to the existence of this important trade.[71] Those bakers recorded as coming from places too distant from Dublin to have been able to supply it with fresh bread, including all those from outside Ireland, were probably immigrants relocating their activities to the city. Before 1265, Dublin's recruitment of so many men with this occupation implies that this was a city with an expanding population needing to be fed.

Table 9.6. Numbers of Dublin guildsmen and freemen occupied in supplying provisions, *c.*1190–1265 and 1230–49

	Guildsmen *c.*1190–1265 No.	Freemen 1234–49 No.	Guildsmen & freemen 1230–49 No.
Fish	31	1	21
Meat	55	0	21
Dairy	0	0	0
Fruit & vegetables	4	1	4
Grains & flour	40	2	14
Bread	94	4	32
Malt	3	1	2
Ale	14	1	10
Wine	12	2	6
TOTAL	253	12	110

Source: *DGMR*.

Dublin also consumed live animals in great quantity, slaughtered to provide meat, tallow (for manufacture into candles and soap), and the raw hides upon which Dublin's substantial tanning industry depended. Butchers were therefore vital to the city's economy and were the last link in a supply chain which drew animals in from relatively remote rearing regions which bred the animals ultimately destined for the Dublin market. The butchers needed pastures near the city on which to fatten up and finish off animals driven in from further away, and stalls and shops within the city where the fresh meat was sold; here, too, they sold the hides that were so vital to the city's prominent tanning industry.[72] In the thirteenth century, as at Exeter in the following

capital, pp 3, 46–53. **70** Murphy and Potterton, *Dublin region*, pp 431–2. **71** *DGMR*, pp 27, 33, 39. A coaler and four colliers may also have dealt in either charcoal or coal: *DGMR*, pp 2, 9, 24, 37, 58. **72** L.F. Salzman, *English industries of the Middle Ages* (Oxford, 1923),

century, many Dublin butchers were based outside the city rather than within it, with a County Dublin address favoured by numbers of those who became guildsmen (Table 9.7).[73] Admission to the guild entitled them to trade within the city's precincts and, thus licensed, none is recorded as having aspired to become a freeman (Table 9.6). This anticipated the situation at Exeter in 1300–49 where a single butcher became a freeman compared with 34 skinners and thirteen tanners, with the clear implication that the butchers operated from outside the city and the skinners and tanners from within it.[74]

Those supplying sea and fresh-water fish to the city similarly mostly operated from outside its bounds and were thus, with a single exception, ineligible to become freemen.[75] In contrast, 31 fishermen and dealers in fish became guildsmen (Table 9.4). Dublin, although a port, lacked a deep anchorage (hence the two steersmen or pilots who became guildsmen and a third who became a freeman) but was accessible to fishing vessels with their shallow draughts and it was on its extensive wharves that fishermen from across the river at Oxmantown and from the east-coast ports of Howth, Drogheda and Ardglass, landed their catches.[76] Those who came from such land-locked locations as Rathcoole, Kildare and Castledermot are more likely to have been dealers in, than catchers of, fish.[77]

The bulk of those occupied in these staple provisioning trades plainly operated from outside the city and consequently were content with the commercial privileges conferred by admission as a guildsman. This explains the exceptionally high ratio of guildsmen to freemen among those occupied in these provisioning occupations (Table 9.1). Of men with a provisioning occupation and a recorded place of origin, 30 per cent came from outside Ireland and are likely to have been recent immigrants to the city and its hinterland (Table 9.7). It was, however, from within Ireland that the great majority of men with these occupations originated, of whom 85 per cent hailed from the four immediately neighbouring counties of Dublin, Louth, Meath and Kildare (Table 9.7). It was this limited region, extending no more than 90 kilometres from Dublin, which formed the core hinterland from which the city drew the bulk of its staple foodstuffs, with the extramural suburb of Kilmainham and the towns of Drogheda, Kells, Naas, Kildare and Castledermot all actively involved in servicing that trade.[78] Each formed a hub in the urban hierarchy headed by Dublin.

pp 245–6. 73 Maryanne Kowaleski, 'Town and country in late medieval England: the hide and leather trade' in Corfield and Keene (eds), *Work in towns*, pp 57–73; Campbell, 'Dublin 1190–1290', p. 234. Butchers with an origin in Ireland came from the extramural suburbs of Patrick Street, Oxmantown and Kilmainham (two), from Palmerstown, Saggart, Santry and Swords (two), Co. Dublin, from Castledermot (two), Kildare and Naas in Co. Kildare, from Drogheda in Co. Louth and from Trim in Co. Meath. 74 Rowe and Jackson, *Exeter freemen*, pp 6–29. 75 *DGMR*, p. 115. 76 *DGMR*, pp 48, 55, 74, 80, 87, 90, 118. 77 Murphy and Potterton, *Dublin region*, pp 395–6; *DGMR*, pp 79, 81, 88, 91. 78 Murphy and Potterton, *Dublin region*.

Table 9.7. The recorded origins of Dublin guildsmen and freemen occupied in the provisioning trades, *c.*1190–1265

Origin	Fish	Meat	Grain	Bread	Ale	TOTAL	%
Co. Dublin	3	10	4	5	3	25	*27.2*
Louth, Meath, Kildare	5	6	5	11		27	*29.3*
Rest of Ireland	1	2	1	5		9	*9.8*
Wales		1		2		3	*3.3*
England	1	7	3	13	1	25	*27.2*
Scotland				1		1	*1.1*
Europe			1	1		2	*2.2*
TOTAL	10	26	14	38	4	92	*100.0*

Source: *DGMR.*

Crafts and construction

The admission of many alien merchants from across northern Europe to the Dublin guild merchant testifies to the active involvement of the city in international commerce.[79] Apart from imported spices, wine, luxury fabrics and furs, the bulk of what medieval Dubliners ate, drank and wore was nevertheless produced locally and it was to the home market that the city's economy was overwhelmingly geared.[80] In fact, the scale of its own consumption-needs helps explain why, in the late thirteenth century, customs receipts at Dublin from the export of surplus hides, wool fells and wool were so much smaller than those collected at Ireland's smaller south-coast ports of Cork, Waterford and New Ross.[81] Locally produced wool and hides went into locally made cloth and leather and gave employment to many in Dublin and its immediate environs. Tailors, shoemakers and glovers always ranked among the most frequently recorded occupations. Similarly, potters, wood-workers, soap-makers, and building workers relied upon local sources of supply, respectively, for their clay, wood, tallow, stone, lime and timber. Keeping the city's many

79 Campbell, 'Dublin 1190–1290', pp 245–6. **80** Imports were typically high in value, low in bulk, and lacked local substitutes, thus the *DGMR* records the admission of fourteen spicers, six vintners and a single mustarder as guildsmen *c.*1190–1265 and three spicers and one vintner as freemen 1234–49. On wine imports, see Wendy Childs and Timothy O'Neill, 'Overseas trade' in Art Cosgrove (ed.), *A new history of Ireland, II, Medieval Ireland, 1169–1534* (Oxford, 1987), pp 507–8; Timothy O'Neill, *Merchants and mariners in medieval Ireland* (Dublin, 1987), pp 44–7, 84–5, 90. For imported pottery, see Clare McCutcheon and Rosanne Meenan, 'Pots on the hearth: domestic pottery in historic Ireland', *PRIA*, 111C, *Special issue: Domestic life in Ireland* (Dublin, 2011), pp 96–9. **81** During the boom years 1275–89 customs receipts at Dublin were 60 per cent those at Cork, 40 per cent those at Waterford, and 33 per cent those at New Ross: calculated from T.E. McNeill, *Anglo-Norman Ulster: the history and archaeology of an Irish barony, 1177–1400* (Edinburgh, 1980), pp 132–5.

ovens, forges and kilns fired with a sustainable supply of firewood and charcoal was therefore a perennial challenge. It was one faced by all pre-modern towns of any size.[82] In return, Dublin's immediate hinterland provided the city's craftsmen with their second most important market after that of the city itself. Together, demand from the city and its region for a wide range of staple wares ensured that industries of one sort or another lay at the heart of Dublin's urban economy and accounted for the single largest share of all recorded male occupations (Table 9.2).

Clothing Dublin's population was a major source of employment. In the thirteenth century a total of 134 guildsmen and freemen were recorded as engaged in one of the branches of cloth manufacture (Table 9.7) and a further 136 were involved in clothing manufacture, as tailors, parmenters (makers of facings and trimmings) and wimplers. The fabric-specific occupations of wool-beater, comber, blanket-weaver, burel-weaver (a densely woven and virtually waterproof cloth), fuller, napper and shearer confirm that the bulk of the cloth being made and then fashioned into garments was woollen. Linen cloth made from local flax was also used, as witnessed by the admission of a single linen draper and the four wimplers, but self-evidently on a far smaller scale.[83]

Table 9.8. Numbers of Dublin guildsmen and freemen occupied in cloth manufacture, *c.*1190–1265 and 1234–49

Textile process	Guildsmen 1190–1265 No.	Freemen 1234–49 No.
Wool preparation	9	2
Spinning	0	0
Weaving	32	1
Fulling & finishing	19	1
Dyeing	57	11
TOTAL	117	15

Source: *DGMR*.

The preparation and then spinning of wool and flax created considerable employment for spinners, none of whom appear in the admissions of guildsmen and freemen since they were mostly women.[84] Their conspicuous

82 Murphy and Potterton, *Dublin region*, pp 367–8; James A. Galloway, 'The economic hinterland of Drogheda in the later Middle Ages' in Vicky McAlister and Terry Barry (eds), *Space and settlement in medieval Ireland* (Dublin, 2015), pp 179–80; James A. Galloway, Derek Keene, and Margaret Murphy, 'Fuelling the city: production and distribution of firewood and fuel in London's region, 1290–1400', *Economic History Review*, 49:3 (1996), 447–72. 83 *DGMR*, pp 68, 79, 85, 86, 97. 84 Clarkson, 'Carrick-on-Suir woollen industry', p. 33, estimates that at Carrick-on-Suir in 1799 it required three female spinners

omission is a reminder that Dublin's considerable female workforce is hidden in plain sight. Weavers, who were mostly male, are more visible, although those that are recorded can only be a fraction of the total, for, instead of greatly outnumbering the dyers, it was the dyers who outnumbered them by two to one (Table 9.8).[85] It was the dyers, along with the fullers, who finished the cloth and, in the virtual absence of drapers, were the most directly involved in organizing its production and marketing the end product. Dyeing required capital and expertise and it was consequently the dyers who had the potential to dominate production and make the greatest profits.[86] This gave them both the incentive and the means to seek admission to the guild or become freemen. Almost two-thirds of all textile producers known to have become guildsmen were involved in the finishing trades and they accounted for four out of five of those who became freemen (Table 9.8). Many were clearly doing so as Dublin residents but not all of them, for Kilmainham (Co. Dublin) contributed a weaver, three shearers and a fuller and other dyers and fullers came from such places within the city's wider hinterland as Ardee, Drogheda and Dundalk (Co. Louth), Athboy and Kells (Co. Meath), Athy and Naas (Co. Kildare), and Arklow (Co. Wicklow) and, by implication, were active in the city as *forinseci*.

This all suggests that Dublin served as the commercial and organizing centre of an industry which gave employment to many within an extensive surrounding area and in the thirteenth century accounted for a greater share of manufacturing employment within the city than at any subsequent time (Table 9.12). Its command of this domestic demand sustained the industry but ultimately restricted the scale of its development, since, to have expanded further, cloth would need to have become a significant item of export and in this it was handicapped by its distance from overseas markets and the coarse and inferior quality of Irish wools.[87] Insofar as yarn (both woollen and linen) and locally made coarse friezes, checkers, mantles, burels and blankets were exportable, it was probably only to the markets with which Dublin traded on the opposite shore of the Irish Sea.[88]

and carders to keep each male weaver of woollen rateens supplied with yarn; also, that overall rateen manufacture provided more employment for females than males. **85** At Carrick-on-Suir in 1799 weavers outnumbered dyers by twenty to one: Clarkson, 'Carrick-on-Suir woollen industry', p. 33. **86** E.M. Carus-Wilson, *Medieval merchant venturers* (London, 1954), pp 226–38. **87** John H.A. Munro, *Wool, cloth, and gold: the struggle for bullion in Anglo-Burgundian trade, 1340–1478* (Toronto, 1972), p. 2. **88** For minor exports of 'Irish cloth' from Boston in Lincolnshire in 1303, see Stephen H. Rigby and Robert C. Nash, *The overseas trade of Boston, 1279–1548* (Vienna and Cologne, 2023), p. 43 (I am grateful to Professor Stephen Rigby for this reference). For later textile exports from Dublin to Chester, see Kevin Patrick Wilson (ed.), *Chester customs accounts, 1301–1566*, Record Society of Lancashire and Cheshire, 111 (Chester, 1969); Jennifer Kermode, 'The trade of late medieval Chester, 1500–1550' in Richard Britnell and John Hatcher (eds), *Progress and problems in medieval England: essays in honour of Edward Miller* (Cambridge, 1996), p. 293; Slattery, *Social life*, pp 112, 217–20.

Tanning and leather-working came a close second to textiles and clothing in the amount of male employment that they provided, although they provided fewer opportunities for women (Table 9.2).[89] They, too, formed part of a wider enterprise suffused throughout the wider city region, as is reflected in the fact that fifteen of the 26 tanners with known Irish origins came from the three immediately neighbouring counties of Kildare (six), Louth (five) and Meath (four), with others coming from as far away as Ferns (Co. Wexford), Kilkenny (Co. Kilkenny), Leighlin (Co. Carlow), and Mullingar (Co. Westmeath).[90] The implication is that these out-of-town tanners were becoming guildsmen in order to sell their products to the city's leather-workers and to the shippers and merchants involved in the substantial export trade in hides and skins. They were matched in numbers by immigrant skinners and tanners who had come and settled in Dublin from places with equally well-established leather industries: in descending rank order of importance, from London, York, Bristol, Lincoln, Shrewsbury, Nottingham, Worcester, and Pontefract in Yorkshire.[91]

Tanning was a polluting activity that required oak bark and water in quantity and produced quantities of wet and odorous industrial waste. Typically, as at London, Winchester, Canterbury, Leicester and Exeter, it was therefore relegated to locations on the urban fringe.[92] In Dublin the extramural location of Patrick Street, a low-lying suburban area close to the River Poddle became and long remained a focus for this activity.[93] Notwithstanding the noxiousness of their craft, Dublin-based tanners seem to have belonged to the upper echelon of the city's industrial labour force as evidenced by the fact that in no other craft activity, not even dyeing, was the ratio of guildsmen to freemen as low (Table 9.1).[94] Like their country counterparts, they prospered supplying hides, untanned and tanned, to the export trade and locally-produced leather to a host of other Dublin-based craftworkers among whom the material was in constant demand. Collectively, the skinners and tanners were matched in number by the cappers, hatters, glovers, shoemakers, cobblers, girdlers and scabbard-makers.[95] When combined with the tailors,

89 For accounts of the tanning of hides, the tawing of skins and the working of leather, see John Cherry, 'Leather' in John Blair and Nigel Ramsay (eds), *English medieval industries: craftsmen, techniques, products* (London, 1991), pp 295–318. 90 Kowaleski, 'Town and country in late medieval England', pp 60–1. 91 For the early importance of Norse-speaking traders in supplying skins, pelts and furs to Dublin, see Catherine Swift, 'Norwegian *scing*-traders and other skinners in early Dublin' in Duffy (ed.), *Medieval Dublin XIX*, pp 17–35. 92 For similar patterns within Exeter and its hinterland and related interactions between butchers and tanners, see Kowaleski, 'Town and country in late medieval England', pp 60–2. 93 Murphy and Potterton, *Dublin region*, pp 440–2. 94 17 tanners became freemen 1234–49, plus three skinners and one currier, compared with 11 dyers and 11 tailors: *DGMR*. 95 For archaeological evidence of specialized leather-working dating from the twelfth and thirteenth centuries see: Breandán Ó Ríordáin, 'Excavations at High Street and Winetavern Street, Dublin', *Medieval Archaeology*, 15:1

parmenters and wimplers, this ensured that the clothing trades formed Dublin's single largest male occupational grouping, in 1230–49 accounting for a quarter of all recorded craftworkers and 14 per cent of guildsmen and freemen with known occupations. The admission to the guild of 24 saddlers is also a reminder that, in a horse-drawn age, leather was in strong demand for saddles and harness, which, in turn, created work for lorimers (the makers of bits, spurs, stirrups and other small metal fastenings and objects), spurriers and bucklers.

Leather-working and metal-working were complementary activities, best conducted on the urban fringe where the adverse side effects of smithing and forging – noise, dirt, smoke, and a constant risk of fire – were least objectionable. Dublin's transpontine suburb of Oxmantown was home to five of the smiths who became guildsmen, Kilmainham the base of another three plus three lorimers and a locksmith, and others came from the extramural western suburb of St Thomas and from nearby Clontarf, Howth, and Finglas.[96] Other metal-workers with an Irish origin came from substantially further away, from Loughsewdy (Co. Westmeath), Roscrea (Co. Tipperary), and the cities of Waterford and Cork. Whether they were *forinseci* who came just to trade or in migrants who had come to settle is unclear. As with the many metal-workers who came to Dublin from outside Ireland, they may have been drawn to the growing city by the economic opportunities that it offered.[97]

The concentration within the city of households with substantial disposable incomes helps explain why, in response to this luxury demand, three goldsmiths became freemen and a further 24 (plus one gilder, one gold-beater and four jewellers) became guildsmen. They represent the high end of metal-working. Other non-ferrous metal-workers are exemplified by a cup-maker, ewerer,[98] coppersmith, lead-beater and four smelters.[99] Several steel-workers are recorded, notably five furbishers (who finished sword blades and similar weapons), two cutlers (one of them, Walter le Cutiler de Taxstede in 1238–9, from the cutlery-making centre of Thaxted in Essex), two armourers and a sieve-maker.[100] Most numerous, however, were the ironworkers: 70 smiths, 19 marshals or farriers, 23 lorimers, and 12 locksmiths. Products of their work retrieved from excavations include 'barrel-padlocks and their keys, belt-buckles, tanged knives, socketed arrow-heads, horseshoes, fish-hooks and a

(1971), p. 75. **96** *DGMR*. **97** Metal-workers are recorded as coming from Ayr in Scotland, St Helens in Cumberland, Gloucester, Bristol, Coventry, Lincoln, Thaxted in Essex, Cowdray in Sussex, and Beauvais and Paris in France: *DGMR*. **98** The ewerer might either manufacture ewers (water-pitchers) or supply guests at table with water for hand-washing: see *Oxford English dictionary*, s.v. 'ewerer (*n.*)', September 2024, https://doi.org/10.1093/OED/4930175184. **99** *DGMR*, pp 47, 69, 74, 91, 92, 96, 99, 109, 119. **100** *DGMR*, p. 73 (this is the earliest explicit reference to the Thaxted industry); Kenneth Charles Newton, *Thaxted in the fourteenth century: an account of the manor and borough, with translated texts*, Essex County Record Office Publications 33 (Chelmsford, 1960), p. 21; https://en.wikipedia.org/wiki/Thaxted [accessed 8 September 2022].

variety of iron nails, some of which are of the kind used in boat- and shipbuilding'.[101] By shoeing horses, making the metal components of their harness, fitting the wheels of carts and wagons with iron tyres and making other moving metal parts, they performed an indispensable role in maintaining Dublin as the hub of the local transport network and helped keep moving the considerable traffic that thronged its streets. They worked with local and imported raw materials and their forges were voracious consumers of fuel.[102] Although less numerous than the cloth and clothing manufacturers and tanners and leather-workers (Table 9.2), the metal-workers were equally essential and long remained at the core of Dublin's manufacturing economy.

An assortment of other crafts utilizing a variety of raw materials accounted for a further 8 per cent of recorded manufacturing employment. In the thirteenth century, joiners and turners who fashioned furniture, tools, eating and drinking vessels, and other items from wood were prominent among these craftsmen, alongside coopers who bound staves with metal hoops to create the barrels in universal use for storing and transporting an array of commodities.[103] Two fletchers made the arrows, needed in quantity for hunting and war, by attaching metal arrowheads to slender wooden shafts fitted with feather fletchings to make them airborne.[104] More numerous were the potters, although how many of the 23 who are recorded were 'founders of copper-alloy pots and other domestic utensils' and how many were makers of earthenware pottery is entirely unclear.[105] Given that copper and brass were scarce and clay abundant and that Dublin-ware earthenware pottery of a range of qualities dominates the assemblages of local pottery recovered from excavations in Dublin city and many of the rural sites around it, the suspicion has to be that the latter predominated.[106] Whichever material the potters worked in, like the tanners and smiths, they were drawn to the outskirts of Dublin – numbers of them congregating outside the city's west gate – due to the smoke and smell emitted by their forges and kilns and the need for a constant supply of wood and charcoal to fire them.[107] Here, and at other industrialized extramural locations, as Elizabeth Rutledge observes of medieval Norwich, emissions from kilns, the noisome smells associated with tanning, fulling and dyeing, and the discordant sounds of metal-working, must have been an intrinsic part of the urban landscape.[108]

101 Ó Ríordáin, 'Excavations at High Street and Winetavern Street, Dublin', p. 76. **102** Murphy and Potterton, *Dublin region*, pp 444–6, 449. **103** Aidan O'Sullivan, 'Woodland management and the supply of timber and underwood to Anglo-Norman Dublin' in Frans Verhaeghe (ed.), *Environment and subsistence in medieval Europe: papers of the 'Medieval Europe Brugge 1997' conference*, 9 (Brussels, 1997), pp 137–8. **104** *DGMR*, pp 57, 72. **105** Claude Blair and John Blair, 'Copper alloys' in Blair and Ramsay (eds), *English medieval industries*, p. 93. **106** Murphy and Potterton, *Dublin region*, pp 451–6. **107** Murphy and Potterton, *Dublin region*, p. 451. **108** Rutledge, 'Economic life', p. 160.

Six guildsmen specialized in making rope from hemp, which was needed in quantity for ships' rigging, fishermen's nets and much else.[109] Soap, whose ingredients were alkaline lye (derived from the wood ashes produced in abundance by the city's many domestic fires), lime, mutton fat and flour, was manufactured by four guildsmen.[110] Curiously, though, chandlers make no appearance in the guildsmen's and freemen's lists until the sixteenth century.[111] Finally, bone, ivory and antlers were turned into combs and the dice used by many Dubliners to while away their idle hours and gamble away their scanty earnings.[112] This list of niche craft activities would undoubtedly be longer were occupational information comprehensively available for all guildsmen and freemen. Their diversity is, however, plain to see as is the recruitment from outside Ireland of so many of the skilled craftsmen who worked in them, the latter outnumbering those coming from within Ireland by almost three to one.[113] The attraction of the city to non-Irish craftsmen testifies to the dynamism of Dublin's urban economy during its first hundred years as the capital of the king of England's Irish Lordship.

Through their efforts, this wide array of craftsmen kept Dublin and its region reasonably self-sufficient in staple manufactured goods. Much of this work was undertaken in small-scale workshops staffed by individual household units, with husbands assisted by their wives and other family members and aided by their servants. Manufacturing was fundamental to Dublin's prosperity and, as the city grew and market demand from all sources expanded, so the extent of craft specialization continued to develop and craftworkers from elsewhere were drawn to the city. Respectively, 58 per cent and 65 per cent of guildsmen and freemen recorded as coming from a non-Irish origin had craft occupations of one sort or another. Of the 34 Dublin guildsmen and freemen known to have come from London, almost three-quarters had craft occupations.[114] That so many skilled workers from such a high-status place were willing to make this move is a clear indication that mid-thirteenth-century Dublin was thriving.

For Dublin to grow physically, housing needed to be built to accommodate an expanding workforce, churches erected for them to worship in, the city's defences extended and strengthened, and investments made in the physical infrastructure that enabled the city to function, including developing its quays and providing an improved supply of fresh water.[115] The prestige early

109 *DGMR*, pp 37, 52, 76, 84, 101, 105. **110** *DGMR*, pp 50, 58, 74, 77. **111** Henry S. Guinness, 'Dublin trade gilds', *JRSAI* 6th ser., 12:2 (1922), 153–4; Mary Clark and Raymond Refaussé, *Directory of historic Dublin guilds* (Dublin, 1993), pp 29–30. **112** *DGMR*, pp 47, 71, 116; Ó Ríordáin, 'Excavations at High Street and Winetavern Street, Dublin', p. 75. **113** *DGMR*. **114** From London came four clothing manufacturers, eight skinners and tanners, five leather-workers, a goldsmith, a potter, a dicer, and five painters. Bristol contributed seven cloth-makers, four clothing manufacturers, two tanners, one marshal, one cup-maker, five miscellaneous craftsmen and three building workers. *DGMR*. **115** Clarke, *Dublin Pt I* (IHTA), pp 6, 19, 22.

thirteenth-century building projects of the royal castle, St Patrick's cathedral and a new nave for Christ Church cathedral created further demand for skilled construction workers assisted by teams of labourers.[116] No matter how great or small the project, the necessary building materials of timber, stone, mortar, and much else had to be obtained from sources outside the city and assembled on site. Since brute strength was an advantage, the bulk of these different tasks were typically undertaken by men, but not invariably so, since it is known from elsewhere that women and children were also sometimes employed on building sites.[117] Building labourers did not become freemen and had neither the means nor the need to become guildsmen, and hence it is mostly only the higher grades of building workers who show up in the record of guildsmen admissions, where they outnumber those who became freemen by eight to one.

Among construction workers, carpenters are the single most numerous occupational group, with 35 guildsmen and just one freeman. They are followed by 31 painters, of whom six became freemen, identifying them as the aristocrats of the construction sector. Both groups far outnumber the six stone masons and eight wallers and gablers, which is a reminder that there was far more building in wood than stone and the available architectural evidence implies that skilled stone masons were in short supply.[118] Of the handful of masons, two are known to have come from Gloucester and a third from Coventry.[119] One lime-burner became a freeman and three sawyers, three thatchers, two plumbers, one tiler and an assortment of others became guildsmen and thereby testify to the existence of these occupations within the city, but clearly those recorded are just a fraction of those who must have practised these essential trades. Collectively, those with occupations in construction accounted for just 6 per cent of guildsmen and 7 per cent of freemen whereas the scale of this sector within the city's economy must have been substantially larger, especially when account is taken of the omitted legion of building labourers. Christopher Dyer reckons that 'for every skilled building craftsman there were two labourers, digging foundations, hauling stone and timber, and mixing and applying daub to wattle walls'.[120] Only a full occupational census could have exposed the latter's real numbers: in 1770

116 Campbell, 'Dublin 1190–1290', p. 260. **117** John L. Langdon, 'Women as workers on royal building sites before the Black Death', unpublished paper presented at the Ninth Anglo-American Seminar on the Medieval Economy, Durham, 2010. I am grateful to Professor Langdon for providing a copy of this paper. **118** Ó Ríordáin, 'Excavations at High Street and Winetavern Street, Dublin', pp 76–7; O'Sullivan, 'Woodland management', pp 135–9; Murphy and Potterton, *Dublin region*, pp 366–72; Rachel Moss, 'Building the Anglo-Norman church' in Peter Crooks and Seán Duffy (eds), *Invasion 1169* (Dublin, forthcoming); for the possibility that some of the many guildsmen described as *taillur*, *talliur*, *tailiator* may have been cutters of stone rather than of cloth see Roger Stalley, 'The medieval sculpture of Christ Church Cathedral, Dublin', *Archaeologia*, 106 (1979), 107–22, n.12. **119** *DGMR*, pp 65, 78, 118. **120** Christopher Dyer, *Making a living in the Middle Ages: the people of Britain, 850–1520* (New Haven and London, 2002), p. 201.

labourers alone comprised 15 per cent of the male workforce at Armagh and in 1799 13 per cent of that in the larger textile-producing town of Carrick-on-Suir (co. Tipperary), which at that time was the size that Dublin may have been *c.*1300.[121] Physically, the thirteenth-century city could not have grown without a concomitant expansion of those employed in the building trades.

Collectively, this large and diverse secondary sector processed a range of organic and inorganic raw materials, manufactured a wide array of both essential and luxury commodities, and in the thirteenth century accounted for half of the guildsmen and 60 per cent of the freemen with recorded occupations. Including the food-processing crafts of butchering, milling, baking and brewing would further increase these proportions to over 60 per cent (Table 9.2). The sector had grown and developed in skill and specialization in response to the needs of the city and its region for housing, clothing and all the other essentials of daily life. Dublin's craft activities were those that lay at the core of every medieval urban economy of any scale.[122] Each developed as far as domestic demand would allow. No single industry was ever dominant because, apart from tanned hides and a modest export trade in yarn and textiles, none ever became geared to producing surpluses for sale to overseas markets. Rather, it was the raw materials surplus to the needs of these crafts – notably wool, wool fells, skins, and hides – that were destined for export.

Of course, most craftsmen, by the nature of their work, engaged in commercial activity – purchasing raw materials, trading component parts, and marketing their wares – which is why so many of them found it expedient to seek admission to the merchant guild or become fully fledged freemen. That those practising these trades are given the single occupational descriptor of craftsmen, even though, inevitably, there must have been a considerable crossover between activities, especially when the economic contributions of other household members are taken into account, is because that was the individual guildsman's or freeman's primary source of livelihood. Using a single occupational descriptor has the merit of keeping analysis simple but at the expense of masking much of this occupational fluidity.[123] Nonetheless, since crossovers between occupations occurred in both directions, and by-employment was more likely to be a household than head-of-household phenomenon, the net effect of taking each occupational description at face value is unlikely to misrepresent too seriously the relative shares of occupations between categories.[124] Exceptions there obviously were, especially

121 Clarkson, 'Anatomy of an Irish town', p. 45; Clarkson, 'Carrick-on-Suir woollen industry', p. 32. **122** Goose, 'English pre-industrial urban economies', pp 24–6; Britnell, 'The economy of British towns 600–1300', pp 121–3. **123** For evidence of urban multi-tasking, see Swanson, 'The illusion of economic structure'; Kowaleski, *Local markets and regional trade*, pp 124–6, S.H. Rigby, *Medieval Grimsby: growth and decline* (Hull, 1993), pp 70–72. **124** Broadberry et al., *British economic growth*, p. 345; Sebastian A.J. Keibek,

among the city's elite whose economic interests could be quite diverse. Thus, English-born and Oxmantown-based William Hogeson, who served as mayor of Dublin in 1514–15, owned agricultural land outside the city and houses within it, operated a lighter and larger vessel to bring goods into and out of Dublin's shallow port, traded as a merchant in iron, salt, coal and wine, and, probably as a goldsmith, was involved in manufacturing and training apprentices.[125]

Non-residency is a further complication, since a minority of these craftworkers may have been based outside the city's precincts but enrolled in the merchant guild so that they could operate without let or hindrance within the city's markets. This need for legal legitimacy would long prevail. Others, although Dublin-based, were reliant upon extramural producers for the yarn and cloth which they finished and processed, and the leather which they worked into hats, gloves, shoes, saddlery and much else. None could have survived without the raw materials supplied from the surrounding countryside or the market which the rural population provided for their products. It was a relationship which was mutually reciprocal.

Commerce

Commerce, of course, pervaded these provisioning and craft activities and bound Dublin into regional, national and international orbits of exchange but, as the primary means of earning a living, it was the occupation of only an eighth of the total recorded male workforce (Table 9.2).[126] These specialist traders and dealers exercised an economic importance and came to perform a civic role out of all proportion to their numbers. Their commercial role was, of course, complemented by those engaged in the various provisioning trades, which, as already noted, engaged significantly more guildsmen than freemen (Table 9.1). Possibly, too, some branch of commerce may have been the default occupation of many of those for whom no occupation was recorded. Certainly, it is difficult to believe that at this time, when the recorded origins of its guildsmen reveal Dublin to have been a magnet for traders from far and wide, so small a share of the city's occupied workforce made its living primarily by commerce (Table 9.2).

In the thirteenth century a commercial occupation plainly took many forms and could be pursued at a range of different levels. Some, the merchants, spicers, and vintners, traded internationally and embraced the risks and reaped the profits of doing so. They were attracted to Dublin because no other Irish

'By-employments in early modern England and their significance for estimating historical male occupational structures', *Cambridge Working Papers in Social and Economic History* 29 (Cambridge, 2017). **125** Randolph Jones, 'William Hogeson, mayor of Dublin, *fl.* 1493–1519' in Duffy (ed.), *Medieval Dublin XIX*, pp 307–19. **126** Campbell, 'Dublin 1190–1290', pp 233–46.

city offered so great a concentration of luxury demand or headed a more extensive distribution network. More numerous were the mercers, drapers, haberdashers and commodity-specific dealers and mongers, whose commercial horizons were narrower and who serviced a distributional network which straddled the Irish Sea. Many within this mercantile group were based in Dublin, others were based elsewhere in the network of towns that made up the urban system headed by Dublin, but all were active participants in Dublin's markets. Finally, there were the itinerant chapmen, hucksters and hawkers who formed the lowest tier of this loose hierarchy of traders and who peddled the wares that had originated with the merchants and mercers, disseminating them to all within the city and its region. Some, like Adam le Custurer (costermonger), were street traders, typically operators of a fruit stall.[127] Others went from periodic market to periodic market and from door to door, no doubt becoming footsore in their endeavours to earn a modest livelihood. Among the freemen, it was the high-end merchants who predominated and outnumbered the mercers and chapmen by two to one (Table 9.9). After all, they made the greatest profits and could best shoulder the costs and responsibilities of becoming a full citizen. In due course, merchants would almost monopolize civic office and dominate government of the city.[128] Among the guildsmen that ratio was reversed and it was the mercers and chapmen who outnumbered the merchants by two to one. Guild membership was sufficient to the needs of these more modest traders, especially those who were impermanently resident in Dublin.

As the numbers summarized in Table 9.9 show, the great merchants were the least likely of these three overlapping groups to have come to Dublin from elsewhere within Ireland. Two thirds of them came from Great Britain and usually from towns of some size and commercial standing, such as Chester (five), Winchester (three), and Bristol, Coventry, Leicester and London (two each).[129] European merchants were also more likely to be encountered among this mercantile group than any of the others, as in the case of Luke the merchant of La Rochelle (France), John of Lucca (Italy), merchant, and James of Lombardy, merchant of Florence (Italy), respectively admitted to the merchant guild in 1253–4, 1262–3 and 1263–4.[130] Their appearance underlines the point that men active within this tier of Dublin's commerce must often have travelled overseas and no doubt were absent from the city a great deal on business. Probably they were no strangers to the great international trade fairs of England, Flanders and especially the county of Champagne in France, which were all then at the zenith of their importance and prosperity.[131] It was

127 *DGMR*, p. 53. **128** Brendan Fitzpatrick, 'The municipal corporation of Dublin 1603–40' (PhD, Trinity College Dublin), 2 vols (1984), i, pp 39–64. I am grateful to David Dickson for alerting me to this important thesis. **129** *DGMR*. **130** *DGMR*, pp 93, 107. **131** Campbell, *Great transition*, pp 82–4, 127–8, 139–40.

through the activities of these men that Dublin had become firmly integrated into the wider pan-European orbit of commerce centred upon France, the Low Countries and northern Italy. They supplied the exotic commodities and luxury goods which the local economy was incapable of producing and in return bought up and exported the primary raw materials – hides, skins, fells and wool – that were surplus to the Dublin region's own needs.

Table 9.9. The commercial occupations of Dublin guildsmen, *c.*1190–1265, and of freemen, 1234–49, and the recorded origins of guildsmen and freemen, *c.*1190–1265

Occupation	Guildsmen *c.*1190–1265		Freemen 1234–49	
	Number	%	Number	%
Merchant etc	60	*30.9*	14	*70.0*
Mercer etc	105	*54.1*	4	*20.0*
Chapman etc	29	*14.9*	2	*10.0*
TOTAL	194	*100*	20	*100*
	All guildsmen and freemen *c.*1190–1265			
	Number	*% from Ireland*	*% from Great Britain*	*% from Europe*
Merchant etc	39	*25.6*	*66.7*	*7.7*
Mercer etc	73	*49.3*	*49.3*	*1.4*
Chapman etc	15	*60.0*	*40.0*	*0.0*
TOTAL	127	*42.9*	*54.0*	*3.2*

Merchants etc = merchants, spicers, vintners and others
Mercers etc = mercers, drapers, haberdashers, glass merchants and others
Chapmen etc = chapmen, pedlars and hawkers

Source: *DGMR*.

There was a good deal of overlap between this elite of Dublin's mercantile class and the mercers, drapers, and assorted dealers (four glass-merchants, three haberdashers, two ironmongers, one bookmonger) who handled the bulk of Dublin's trade with its wider hinterland. Among the guildsmen these middling merchants were by far the most numerous commercial group and their respective descriptions imply that they often specialized in particular commodities and branches of trade (Table 9.9). Almost half of them came to Dublin from places elsewhere in Ireland, particularly from the secondary towns within Dublin's wider hinterland, notably Castledermot, Kildare, and Naas (Co. Kildare), Kells (Co. Meath), Wexford (Co. Wexford), and Downpatrick (Co. Down), where local and regional orbits of trade intersected. Geographically, these places demarcated the region within Ireland of which Dublin was the commercial capital and which extended from Co. Wexford in the south to Co. Down in the north and extended no further inland than Co. Westmeath.[132] A bilateral relationship should be imagined between mercers operating out of these towns and their counterparts based in Dublin. Through their activities as wholesalers and retailers, these men linked Dublin into the wider networks of commerce and exchange upon which the city's continuing prosperity in large measure depended. Their activities complemented those of the dealers in provisions and the craftworkers who marketed their own wares, for commerce was not the exclusive preserve of members of the professional mercantile class. As a reminder that Dublin was now closely bound into the developing commercial spheres of influence of England's chief west-coast ports, strong ties had also developed between Dublin and men of this commercial class on the opposite side of the Irish Sea. From Bristol, for example, had come at least four mercers and two drapers, two more mercers came from Gloucester and three from Chester. Men from Europe were not excluded from this level of commerce but the French mercer, Robert of Champagne, is the sole named example.[133]

Chapmen, pedlars and hawkers are less well recorded (Table 9.9) even though they probably constituted the most numerous mercantile group. They operated on an altogether more modest commercial scale, which is why only two chapmen are recorded as having been admitted as freemen compared with the 29 petty traders who became guildsmen (Table 9.9). Essential as was the function which they performed in the Dublin region's commerce, belonging to the Dublin guild merchant was less essential to them than it was to the mercers and merchants, and foregoing the 9-shilling entry fine was an economy which many must have been happy to make. None of those with a named place-of-origin came from mainland Europe and fewer than half came from outside Ireland, with those that did so tending to come during the prosperous 1230s and 1240s and from places on the facing shore of the Irish Sea: Greenock (Scotland), Swansea (South Wales) and Bristol (England).[134] In keeping with the humbler scale of their activities, more of these petty traders came from within Ireland than either the mercers or merchants and they tended to come from places lower down the urban hierarchy: Carlow (Co. Carlow), Ballymore (Co. Kildare), Dundalk (Co. Louth), and Dunshaughlin and Ratoath (Co. Meath).

Collectively, the places from which Dublin's professional mercantile class originated define the region over which the city held commercial sway. Of the 53 merchants, mercers and chapmen known to have come from Ireland, 85 per cent came from a region which extended from Dublin northwards as far as Co. Antrim, westwards as far as Athlone on the River Shannon, and southwards as far as Wexford. Two-thirds of those who came from within this region hailed

132 Campbell, 'Dublin 1190–1290', pp 237–41, 265–9. **133** *DGMR*, p. 88. **134** *DGMR*, p. 69, 76, 78.

from Dublin's three immediately neighbouring counties of Louth, Meath and Kildare. In fact, Co. Meath alone contributed as many mercantile guildsmen and freemen as the combined total from Cos Waterford, Cork, Kerry, Limerick and Clare, while most of Connacht and Ulster outside of the earldom contributed almost none at all. Commercially, during the years spanned by the guild merchant roll, *c.*1190–1265, Dublin's ties were much closer with the Irish Sea ports of Britain's west coast than those of Ireland's own south coast. From north to south, collectively, Greenock, Ayr, Furness, Chester, Haverfordwest, Swansea, Cardiff, Gloucester, Bristol and Exeter contributed five times as many guildsmen and freemen with commercial occupations as those sent by the Irish ports from Waterford round to Limerick.[135] On this measure, Dublin's ties with the towns of the Severn Valley (Gloucester, Tewkesbury and Shrewsbury) were strong, as were those with the prominent regional English cities of Coventry and Winchester and the commercial and political capital of London. Such ties evidently served Dublin's commercial sector well and anchored the city firmly within England's commercial orbit of influence which, in turn, was part of a wider European orbit centred on Flanders, eastern France and central and northern Italy.

Services

As a major religious centre, the seat of royal and civic governments, and the location of Ireland's most important law courts, Dublin was always a major provider of public and professional services. Of necessity, as recorded occupations confirm, the city was supported by essential transport services both by water and land, and offered hospitality, entertainment and catering services to its permanent and temporary residents and visitors. The city's wealthiest households will have made great use of personal and domestic servants. In late fourteenth-century Exeter, for example, 'at least 40 per cent of … households employed servants and several had between five and seven servants each'.[136] Nevertheless, few of these service workers, and least of all the lowliest, had the need or possessed the means to become guildsmen or freemen, which is why men with service occupations accounted for barely a fifth of the total (Table 9.2). This under-recording of male service workers is reinforced by the almost complete omission of women, upon whose extensive employment the service sector depended.[137]

Since Dublin was characterized by a constant flow of people and goods in and out of the city, transport services by land and water were integral to the smooth running of its economy. Given the poor quality of Ireland's roads, the use of pack animals must have been widespread, as in the case of the three sumpterers, of whom one was from Ardee (Co. Louth) and another from Trim

135 Campbell, 'Dublin 1190–1290', pp 233–46. 136 Kowaleski, *Local markets and regional trade*, p. 168. 137 Above, note 10. Swanson, 'Illusion of economic structure', p. 35.

(Co. Meath).[138] Only a single drover is recorded, even though the importance of cattle and sheep and hides and wool to the region's economy implies there must have been many, although this was an intrinsically rural and semi-agricultural occupation.[139] Wheeled transport was plainly important as witnessed by the four wheelwrights who became guildsmen.[140] Two-wheeled carts would have been ubiquitous and better able to cope with the poor-quality roads than the heavy four-wheeled wagons needed for the biggest and bulkiest loads. Hence the fact that the single recorded waggoner (*quadrigator*) was outnumbered by the twelve carters who became guildsmen, all from the hinterland counties of Dublin, Kildare, Meath and Westmeath.[141] Transport of bulk loads by water was always cheaper and easier and a shipmaster, three steersmen (who helped pilot vessels in and out of port), a boatswain, nine mariners and an oarsman reflect Dublin's location on the tidal Liffey and its role as a seaport.[142] Loading and unloading cargoes gave work to the four porters who became guildsmen and who likely worked alongside many others on Dublin's quays. In all cases, the numbers formally recorded fail to do justice to the numbers actually employed but do at least document the existence of these activities, name a few of those who made their living from them, and record where two of them had come from.[143]

Catering, hospitality and entertainment were further important urban service-sector activities. Of the 32 cooks, 26 were admitted as guildsmen and six as freemen. Some may have been in domestic employment, others, like the bakers, may have been intent upon producing food for sale given that many of the poorest households will have lacked their own cooking facilities. Hospitality was provided by a dozen taverners, one publican and a single innkeeper (although there must have been many more), which bears out Swanson's point that 'hostels were thick on the ground in late medieval towns, although they are not easy to find in the records'.[144] A complementary service for horses was provided by a groom, two ostlers and a stabler. Entertainment went with eating and drinking and is represented by two poets, two rhymers, seven harpists, four pipers, two organists, a lutenist and a singer, but presumably there was much more music-making in thirteenth-century Dublin than they alone can have provided.[145] These specific examples testify to the existence of these occupations but no more than hint at their importance.

Men with clerical skills – three summoners, five scribes and a small army of clerks – constitute the single most numerous service-sector group and their recorded origins reveal them to have been attracted to the growing city from an

138 *DGMR*, pp 88, 92, 104. 139 *DGMR*, p. 35. 140 *DGMR*, pp 30, 47, 73, 82. 141 *DGMR*, p. 29. Dublin St Mary's and Oxmantown (Co. Dublin), Athy (Co. Kildare), Kells and Trim (Co. Meath), Athlone and Mullingar (Co. Westmeath). 142 *DGMR*. 143 Athlone (Co. Westmeath) and Roscrea (Co. Tipperary). 144 Swanson, 'Illusion of economic structure', p. 35; eadem, 'Artisans in the urban economy' in Corfield and Keene (eds), *Work in towns*, pp 50–1. 145 *DGMR*.

exceptionally wide area. They travelled light with quill, ink and parchment and could be confident of finding employment wherever they went. Their literacy and numeracy skills underpinned the city's administrative and legal functions and its growing dependence upon written records as exemplified by creation and preservation of the guild merchant roll itself.[146] Civic occupations are represented by just six burgesses, a reeve and three sergeants. Religious occupations are exemplified by a miscellany of ordained and conventual clergy, whose numbers give little indication of the scale of ecclesiastical employment provided by the city's two cathedrals, a dozen or more monasteries and hospitals, and many churches and chapels.[147] The appearance of thirteen knights, two esquires, two spearmen, three archers, and four artillery men (with a fifth admitted as a freeman) is a reminder that there was also a permanent military presence within the city. Dublin may have contained the greatest concentration of government officials, civil servants, and members of the legal profession within the Lordship of Ireland but the record of guildsmen and freemen admissions fails to do justice to these high-end service functions. This is because few of these elite occupational groups found it strictly necessary to become either guildsmen or freemen. Only their clerks and scriveners did so and consequently show up in some numbers.

Professional services were provided by eleven physicians, a surgeon, and a financier (*finaculator*) and public services by a rat catcher, four barbers, and five water-carriers. Household officials included seven butlers (a further two became freemen), a cellarer and a chamberlain, two bursars, five stewards, and six watchmen. Conceivably, the fewterer and four falconers should also be included with this group of household staff and indicate that the better-off Dubliners were not averse to the pleasures of the hunt. Finally, three-dozen personal servants are recorded, numbers of them associated with named masters including the three who became freemen.[148] This cannot, however, do justice to the numbers of servants employed in the city. Instead, it is a reminder that, whereas the list of unique service occupations is impressively long, the list of those named as thus employed is disappointingly short.

CONTINUITY AND CHANGE IN DUBLIN'S OCCUPATIONAL PROFILE FROM THE 1230S TO THE 1630S

A documentary gap of over two hundred years separates the extant Dublin guildsmen and freemen's rolls of 1230–49 from the next extant run of freemen's registers that span the forty-five years from 1468 to 1512.[149] In the

146 Michael T. Clanchy, *From memory to written record: England, 1066–1307* (London, 1979). **147** Clarke, *Dublin Pt I* (IHTA), pp 17–20. **148** For example, Henry servant of G. of Coventry, Robert of England servant of N…, John servant of the son of William of St Edmunds: *DGMR*, pp 113, 116, 117. **149** Entries in the *DCFR* differ fundamentally and

interim much had changed. The heyday of the English Lordship and Dublin as its capital was long past. Politically and economically, the Lordship of Ireland was neither a land of opportunity nor the recipient of active immigration and the area over which the crown exercised effective control had contracted to the lands of the Pale, comprising the defensible portion of Dublin's immediate hinterland counties of Dublin, Kildare, Meath and Louth, and a scatter of other protected coastal enclaves.[150] Repeated plague outbreaks, adverse weather, harvest failures, endemic warfare, Gaelic advances and commercial recession had all taken their toll and Dublin was much diminished in both size and economic vitality.[151] Maintaining a secure food supply from its shrinking and increasingly beleaguered hinterland had become a growing challenge. This led to intensified scrutiny of the activities of the haggardmen who dealt in grain and maintained stores of it in the city and, at times of extreme scarcity, as in 1462 and again in 1471–2, the banning of grain exports.[152] Want of investment in the city's port infrastructure compounded these problems, for its wharves and approaches were silting and lacked depth at a time when the draught of ocean–going ships was increasing.[153] Bristol merchants had more or less forsaken the city for Waterford and the other ports of Ireland's south coast, their place taken by the merchants of Chester with whom Dublin's merchants now found themselves struggling to compete.[154] In David Dickson's words, Dublin was now a 'stagnant and embattled place', a dismal verdict borne out by a drop of over two-thirds in annual rates of freemen's admission (Table 9.11).[155]

inexplicably from the electronic version available via Dublin City Archives at https://databases.dublincity.ie/freemen/about.php and purportedly transcribed in 1919 by Gertrude Thrift. The latter also span only the years 1468–85. For the earlier history of this roll, see Lennon, 'Introduction', p. xiv. There is a significant falling off in both the quantity and quality of the available occupational information from the mid-1490s, and hence analysis is here confined to the twenty-eight years 1468–95 when occupations are given for at least four out of every five new freemen. **150** Art Cosgrove, 'The emergence of the Pale, 1339–1447' in idem (ed.), *A new history of Ireland, II*, pp 533–56. **151** Gearóid Mac Niocaill, 'Socio-economic problems of the medieval Irish town' in David Harkness and Mary O'Dowd (eds), *The town in Ireland: Historical Studies XIII* (Belfast 1981), pp 16–20; David Dickson, *Dublin: the making of a capital city* (Cambridge, MA, 2014), pp 25–9; Bruce M.S. Campbell and Francis Ludlow, 'Climate, disease and society in late-medieval Ireland', *PRIA,* 120C, special issue, James Kelly and Tomás Ó Carragáin (eds), *Climate and society in Ireland* (Dublin, 2021), pp 221–31. **152** James A. Galloway and Margaret Murphy, 'Food security and insecurity in medieval Irish towns', *Journal of Medieval History,* 49:5 (2023), 626–7. **153** I am grateful to Dr Niall Brady of the Archaeological Diving Company for this information. **154** Childs and O'Neill, 'Overseas trade', pp 495, 514; Wendy Childs, 'Ireland's trade with England in the later Middle Ages', *Irish Economic and Social History,* 9:1 (1982), 26–9; D.M. Woodward, *The trade of Elizabethan Chester* (Hull, 1970); Susan Marie Flavin, 'The development of Anglo-Irish trade in the sixteenth century' (MA, University of Bristol, 2004), 26, 31–2, 34; Dickson, *Dublin*, p. 28; Slattery, *Social life*, pp 102–7; Galloway and Murphy, 'Food security', p, 627–8. **155** Dickson, *Dublin*, pp 40–1.

Table 9.10. Modes of admission to the Dublin city franchise 1468–95, 1575–1602 and 1603–40

Mode of admission	% of total admissions:					
	1468–95		1575–1602		1603–40	
	M	F	M	F	M	F
Special grace	27.5	7.5	3.2	0.5	3.0	0.4
Special grace + entry fine	2.9	0.2	0.8	0.0	12.1	0.0
Entry fine	0.4	0.0	5.7	0.0	1.4	0.0
Inheritance	8.0	2.0	13.2	5.1	14.7	11.1
Marriage	5.4	0.1	2.4	0.0	2.0	0.0
Apprenticeship	37.8	5.9	66.3	2.0	55.5	0.0
Other	2.2	0.0	0.5	0.3	0.0	0.0
SUB-TOTAL	84.3	15.7	92.1	7.9	88.7	11.5
TOTAL	N = 957		N = 1,474		N = 2,804	

Sources: 1468–95: Lennon & Murray (eds), *Dublin city franchise roll*, pp 1–47; 1575–1602: *Dublin City Archives Libraries and Archive: Ancient Freemen of Dublin* (2011), https://databases.dublincity.ie/freemen/about.php; 1603–40: Fitzpatrick, 'Municipal corporation of Dublin', ii, pp 40–97.

Where once a clear distinction had existed between the guild merchant, open to all prepared to pay a relatively modest entry fine and with no requirement of residency, and the freedom, restricted to residents prepared to pay a higher fine and shoulder the responsibility of direct participation in the corporation's affairs, by the 1460s the two groups had become subsumed into a single enfranchised class of citizens. Citizenship was heritable and a fifth of those admitted did so either by inheritance from their fathers or through marriage with an inheriting daughter (Table 9.10).[156] A further third were granted citizenship by 'special grace' of the corporation or at the sponsorship of individual civic officials (the mayor, treasurer, recorder, bailiffs, etc.), sometimes in conjunction with payment of an entry fine.[157] For them the city's franchise had assumed an honorific character. Typically, these were landed proprietors within the surrounding region who thereby gained a say in the city's affairs plus the right to do business there and, in return, may have given the city 'some measure of control' over its food supply.[158] That there were so many of them – over the twenty-eight years from 1468 to 1495, twelve high churchmen, three noblemen, two knights, nine esquires, thirty-seven

156 Unlike some other towns, 'There is no explicit case of widowhood in itself conferring citizenship': Lennon, 'Introduction', p. xviii. **157** Fitzpatrick, 'Municipal corporation of Dublin', i, pp 4, 16–19. **158** Fitzpatrick, 'Municipal corporation of Dublin', i, p. 16. For a similar phenomenon in York during the closing decades of the fifteenth century (where the numbers thus admitted were far smaller), see Dobson, 'Admissions to the freedom of the city of York', p. 12. Mac Niocaill, 'Socio-economic problems', p. 20.

gentlemen and six gentlewomen, seven husbandmen and 123 yeomen – testifies to the close links that existed between the city and its immediate hinterland.[159] On occasion, admission by special grace was also the means utilized by the corporation to recruit individuals with useful skills and assets.[160]

The single-largest group of new freemen, however, comprising 44 per cent of the total, became citizens by dint of having served a seven-year apprenticeship to a master craftsman in one of the growing number of trade guilds, followed by a usually three-year probation as a journeyman, and, finally, payment of the requisite substantial entry fine.[161] Although protracted and costly, and potentially with a high drop-out rate, this was now firmly established as the most common route to becoming a citizen.[162] Its rewards were the right to practise a craft within the city's limits, the skill (provided that they had been well trained by an experienced master) to make a success of it, and a say and a stake in the government of both their respective guild and the municipal corporation. The downside was that, under these rules, those without the need, means, opportunity, or determination to serve a lengthy apprenticeship were less and less likely to feature in the city's freemen's rolls.

In the face of repeated plague outbreaks, in 1439, 1447, 1466, 1468, 1478 and 1488, recruiting replacements to repair the depleted ranks of the freemen presented both an institutional and a demographic challenge, to which wider deployment of admission by special grace provided one solution and the growing popularity of apprenticeships another.[163] By the 1480s almost half of those becoming freemen were doing so via the apprenticeship route, but then, in the troubled 1490s, when dismal weather, poor harvests, high prices and, eventually, famine hit urban populations hard, rates of admission by this and other conventional routes began to fail.[164] In response, the mayor, bailiffs and other civic officials began enlisting new freemen via a process of sponsorship. Their motives were not entirely altruistic, for, as Colm Lennon points out, they seized the opportunity to consolidate their influence by promoting those to whom they were related by blood or kinship.[165] Even so, these self-interested efforts failed to arrest the decline and admissions sank to a historical nadir in

159 The occupational term 'yeoman' is ambiguous in an urban context. In fifteenth-century London the journeymen of trade guilds, who had completed their apprenticeships but not yet become admitted as master craftsmen and full guild members were known as the 'yeomanry or bachelors' of their companies: Caroline M. Barron, 'London 1300–1540' in Palliser (ed.), *Cambridge urban history, I*, p. 429. Whether it had acquired this meaning in Dublin is unknown, although the lack of any additional occupational description beyond 'yeoman' suggests not. **160** Lennon. 'Introduction', pp xix–xx. **161** Slattery, *Social life*, pp 121–2; Fitzpatrick, 'Municipal corporation of Dublin', i, pp 19, 51–2, 71–2. **162** Patrick Wallis, 'Apprenticeship and training in premodern England', *Journal of Economic History*, 68:3 (2008), 832–61. **163** Campbell and Ludlow, 'Climate, disease and society', 220, 226, 230; Mac Niocaill, 'Socio-economic problems', pp 16–17, 20–1. **164** Campbell and Ludlow, 'Climate, disease and society', pp 233–4. **165** Lennon, 'Introduction', p. xx.

Table 9.11. Numbers of admissions, rates of admission and numbers of unique occupations recorded in the Dublin guild merchant and freemen's roll of 1230–49, and the freemen's rolls of 1468–95, 1575–1602 and 1603–40

	Guildsmen & freemen 1230–49	Freemen 1468–95	Freemen 1575–1602	Freemen 1603–40
Total no. admissions	2,080	957	1,474	2,804
Average total admissions per year	104	34	53	76
No. males	2,080	807	1,358	2,486
% males	*100*	*84*	*92*	*89*
% females	*0*	*16*	*8*	*11*
No. males with occupations	637	761	1,240	2,358
% males with occupations	*29*	*94*	*91*	*95*
% males with occupations & origins	*14*	*0*	*0*	*0*
Unique occupations per 10 years	57.0	*21.4*	*26.8*	*29.5*
Unique occupations per 250 occupied males	44.7	19.7	15.1	11.9

Sources: see Table 9.10.

the opening decade of the sixteenth century. For the four consecutive years from 1505 to 1508 there were fewer than twenty male admissions per year, compared with an average of over thirty in the 1480s, with apprenticeships contributing barely a third of them.[166] It did not help that immigration from Britain had long since dried up and that recruitment from within Ireland was restricted by the requirement that new freemen should be 'of free condition and not of the Irish nation'.[167]

This shortfall of eligible men provided openings for women, an occupational group wholly absent from freemen's admissions in 1230–49.[168] In default of sons, daughters could inherit citizenship rights from their fathers. Joan Blake, the daughter of Thomas Blake of Oxmantown, who was admitted to the freedom on 3 May 1493, is a case in point. When she married, her husband, William Hogeson from Wakefield in Yorkshire, then qualified for admission to the franchise.[169] Elected a freeman on 25 October 1493, William

166 *DCFR*, pp 40–43. **167** Lennon 'Introduction', pp xvi, xxvii. In October 1490, after 21 years as a freeman, Alexander FitzJohn, painter, was 'discharged of the liberty of the aforesaid city because he is of the Irish nation and for other crimes and offences': *DCFR*, p. 8. **168** The only two female exceptions in 1230–49 both became guildsmen: Alice of Haverfordwest in 1240–1 and Susanna widow of Henry Clerk of Arklow in 1243–4: *DGMR*, pp 77, 81. **169** Jones, 'William Hogeson, mayor of Dublin', pp 308–11; Lennon,

in due course proceeded to become a bailiff, alderman and, eventually, mayor before he died, probably of plague, in 1519. It was to take advantage of this male right of enfranchisement by marriage that civic officials advanced their female relatives to the freedom, since this was as good as providing them with a dowry and thereby enhanced these women's eligibility as marital partners.[170] From the 1470s to the 1490s daughters accounted for a sixth of those who became freemen by patrimony but in the 1500s that proportion increased to a quarter.[171] Remarkably, by then women made up a quarter of all new freemen. Including those women whose rights had passed to their husbands through marriage raises this proportion to a little over a quarter, a larger share of admissions than had ever been the case before or would be again (Tables 9.10 and 9.11).

Men, of course, continued to dominate civic life and office but for a time the mortality induced suppression of male replacement rates boosted the frequency of female inheritance and thereby elevated Dublin women to a degree of economic and municipal prominence which they would forfeit once male replacement rates recovered and more populous times returned. As Caroline Barron has observed of London at this time, 'women were needed to fill a gap in the workforce and they were willing and able to do this'.[172] Moreover, in Dublin as in London, numbers of women at this time – 56 between 1468 and 1495 and a further thirteen 1496–1512 – became apprentices and on that basis became admitted to the franchise in their own right.[173] Of these 43 apprenticed women, ten are known to have engaged in a range of secondary occupations – butcher, seamstress, leather-worker, smith, armourer – and, as is to have been expected, more than three-times that number served their apprenticeships in the tertiary sector, 28 of them (under the umbrella heading of merchants) within various branches of commerce. It is also worth noting that in five cases it was free women who had provided the apprentice women with their training.[174]

'Introduction', p. xviii. **170** Lennon, 'Introduction', p. xx; Clark, 'Sources for Irish freemen', p. 45. **171** For the significance of such a high rate of female succession, see R.M. Smith, 'Some issues concerning families and their property in rural England, 1250–1800', and Bruce M.S. Campbell, 'Population pressure, inheritance, and the land market in a fourteenth-century peasant community' in R.M. Smith (ed.), *Land, kinship and lifecycle* (Cambridge, 1984), pp 40–54, 97. **172** Barron, 'London 1300–1540', p. 428. Also, eadem, 'The "Golden Age" of women in medieval London', *Reading Medieval Studies,* 15 (1989), 35–58, and, for a review of the controversy this paper generated, Jeremy Goldberg, 'Some reflections on women, work, and the family in the later medieval English town' in Jesús Ángel Solórzano Telechea and Amélia Aguiar Andrade (eds), *Ser mujer en la ciudad medieval europea* (Logroño, 2013), pp 191–214. **173** Lennon, 'Introduction', pp xxiii–xxiv; Slattery, *Social life,* p. 126. On the phenomenon of female apprentices, see Sheilagh Ogilvie, *The European guilds: an economic analysis* (Princeton, 2019), pp 266–71, 299–303. **174** Agnes Wodbone to Margaret Dennyse in 1478; Joan White to Jacoba Mosse in 1480; Rose Downe to Joan Waren in 1484, Genet FitzWyllan to Mauude Parrys in 1500; and Anne Barbi to Elen Roch in 1503: *DCFR*, pp 12, 14, 19, 35, 39.

By the end of the fifteenth century Dublin had plainly contracted to maybe half its peak thirteenth-century population and the number of unique occupations recorded in the freemen's rolls had similarly shrunk substantially in number.[175] Compared with the situation in 1230–49, the number of unique occupations per 10 years and per 250 occupied males were both down by well over half (Table 9.11). In part, this may have been the result of the reduced opportunities for specialization consequent upon shrinking market demand, but it also reflected a change in the nature of the occupational information entered on the franchise roll. It was now the norm (at least until the mid-1490s) for the occupations of all new freemen to be recorded, especially those who had successfully completed their apprenticeships. Other things being equal, therefore, this ought to make the available information more representative. Instead, and increasingly, it was the guild to which a freeman belonged that was recorded, not the specific craft or trade occupation by which they made their living. This was in accordance with the principle of 'everyone to one Mystery' (i.e., one craft per person) established by statute in late fourteenth-century England.[176] The result is a significant loss of detail.

Those occupied in one of the many branches of commerce are a case in point. In 1230–49 the 74 men thus occupied went by the occupational descriptions of merchant (6), spicer (10), vintner (6), mercer (31), linendraper (1), glass merchant (1), ironmonger (1), and chapmen (18). By 1468–95 there were more than three times as many men with commercial occupations but, with the exception of three vintners, all went by the generic description of merchant. This loss of occupational detail followed the foundation in 1438 of what became Dublin's largest, wealthiest and most influential guild, the merchants' guild of the Holy Trinity (not to be confused with the former non-trade-specific guild merchant established in the late twelfth century). It was rechartered in 1451 and granted a virtual monopoly over the city's wholesale and retail trades.[177] Henceforth, all within the city who made their living from commerce, on whatever scale, found themselves obliged to join the Trinity guild, which is why merchants swiftly became the single largest occupational group, far outnumbering all others. They might operate in any branch of commerce, great or small, but, irrespective of their exact specialism, in the freemen's roll they all went under the umbrella title of 'merchant'. The exceptions were the vintners who remained distinct because they belonged to the separate guild of cooks and vintners founded in 1444.[178] Likewise, once the Dublin smiths' guild had been founded in 1474, all those included among its

175 Mac Niocaill, 'Socio-economic problems', pp 18–19. **176** Swanson, 'Illusion of economic structure', p. 33. **177** Guinness, 'Dublin trade gilds', pp 144–5; Clark and Refaussé, *Dublin guilds*, pp 23–5; Slattery, *Social life*, pp 116, 119–20; Fitzpatrick, 'Municipal corporation of Dublin', i, pp 39–44. **178** Guinness, 'Dublin trade gilds', p. 152; Clark and Refaussé, *Dublin guilds*, p. 18.

members – first the ironmongers and girdlers, then later the braziers, embroiderers, founders, glaziers, pattern-makers, pewterers, pin-makers, tinplate-workers and trunk-makers – tended to become subsumed under the occupational descriptor of 'smith'.[179] Thus, 26 smiths were recorded between 1475 and 1512 compared to just three pewterers and a single brazier.[180] The net effect of this suppression of detail is to make Dublin look as though it supported substantially fewer specialist occupations than was actually the case.

Craft guilds began to become a feature of several English towns in the fourteenth century and by 1415 York already boasted fifty-seven.[181] In London the heyday of the city companies was the fifteenth century and by the close of that century it had at least forty.[182] In Dublin the proliferation of craft guilds began somewhat later, in the mid-fifteenth century, and by 1508 there were still only ten, in contrast to the twenty at Hereford by 1503, thirty at Chester in 1499/1500 (whose population was barely half that of Dublin), and the thirty-three at Coventry by 1522.[183] As elsewhere, Dublin's guilds were established by charter and were governed as property-owning corporations by masters and wardens who were elected annually.[184] Each guild looked after the interests of its members, performed civic, religious and ceremonial functions, regulated and protected the trades over which it had jurisdiction, and, through formal apprenticeships, trained the next generation of guildsmen who were eligible to become enfranchised in their own right, once they had completed a period of probation as a journeyman.[185] The tailors' guild, chartered in 1418 and 1419, was the first to break away and become independent of the ancient guild merchant.[186] The Trinity guild of the merchants followed in 1438 and then the guilds of the cooks and vintners in 1444, the barber-surgeons and the weavers in 1446, the shoemakers in 1465, the smiths in 1474, the glovers and skinners in 1476, the bakers in 1478, the carpenters, masons, millers, heliers (roofers) and coopers in 1508, and early incarnations of the tanners and curriers and the goldsmiths at unspecified dates.[187] In addition, ten of Dublin's eleven religious guilds were founded between 1418 and 1476, plus, in 1466 and 1474, the military guilds of St Edmund and St George.[188]

179 Guinness, 'Dublin trade gilds', p. 146; Clark and Refaussé, *Dublin guilds*, p. 27. 180 *DCFR*, pp 9–47. 181 Jennifer Kermode, 'The greater towns 1300–1540' in Palliser (ed.), *Cambridge urban history, I*, p. 450. 182 Caroline M. Barron, 'London 1300–1540' in Palliser (ed.), *Cambridge urban history, I*, pp 428–32. 183 Mac Niocaill, 'Socio-economic problems', p. 18; Guinness, 'Dublin trade gilds'; Clark and Refaussé, *Dublin guilds*, pp 14–31; Lennon, 'Introduction', p. xx; Kermode, 'The greater towns', p. 450; Kermode, 'Trade of late medieval Chester', p. 303. 184 Fitzpatrick, 'Municipal corporation of Dublin', i, pp 66–9; Guinness, 'Dublin trade gilds', p. 145; Clark and Refaussé, *Dublin guilds*, p. 11. 185 For a critical evaluation of the functions and effects of European guilds, see Ogilvie, *European guilds*. 186 Guinness, 'Dublin trade gilds', pp 143, 145–6; Clark and Refaussé, *Dublin guilds*, p. 28. 187 Guinness, 'Dublin trade gilds', pp 146–57; Clark and Refaussé, *Dublin guilds*, pp 14–31; Dickson, *Dublin*, p. 27; Jones, 'William Hogeson, mayor of Dublin', p. 314. 188 Clark and Refaussé, *Dublin guilds*, pp 32–42.

Figure 9.1. The chronology of Dublin freemen's and guildsmen's admissions, 1220s to 1630s (10-year averages)

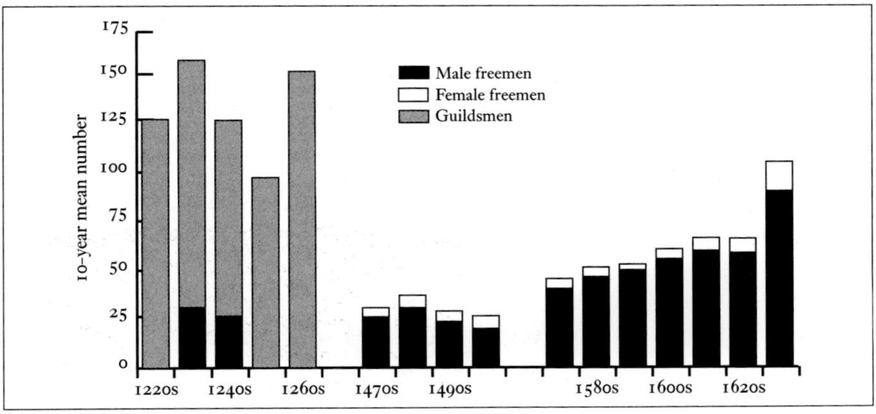

Sources: see Table 9.10.

As will be noted, secondary-sector occupations were disproportionately served by Dublin's new institutional infrastructure of guilds. The Trinity guild of the merchants apart, by the close of the fifteenth century the only tertiary-sector trades with their own guilds were the cooks (and vintners) and the barber-surgeons. This helps to explain why service-sector occupations accounted for a substantially smaller share of the total by 1468–95 than in 1230–49 (Table 9.12). Workers in this sector were often of humble origin and their employment in a range of personal, domestic, hospitality and transport services required no lengthy training or apprenticeship. Moreover, a majority of these essential service-sector workers are likely to have been women and it is women's occupations, even in those cases when a woman had served an apprenticeship, which are most hidden from sight.[189] The service sector's contribution to the city's economy did not erode or disappear but, as the transition to self-governing guilds and formal apprenticeships progressed, the extensive employment that it provided became increasingly hidden from sight.[190] Hereafter, it is through the opaque and restrictive lens created by this new institutional framework that the visible components of Dublin's occupational structure must perforce be viewed.

After a further documentary void of sixty years, the freemen's rolls again become continuous from 1575. From then until the end of Elizabeth I's reign almost 1,500 individuals were admitted as freemen and for 1,240 of them,

189 In England, female employment was biased towards the service-sector and employment in the service-sector was biased towards women: above note 10; Broadberry et al., *British economic growth*, pp 346–64. **190** Kermode, 'The greater towns', p. 451; Swanson, 'Illusion of economic structure', discusses these omissions with reference to the York freemen's rolls.

representing 92 per cent of the males, an occupation is given (Table 9.11).[191] This constitutes the largest and most representative body of occupational information available to date. Steadily improving annual rates of admission (Figure 9.1) imply that the city was slowly recovering both economically and demographically, as the English crown, from its administrative base in Dublin, made determined efforts to reassert its power in Ireland.[192] Maybe, too, the wider Pale was beginning to experience the return to positive demographic replacement rates that is so evident at this time in England.[193] From a low point of 22 per year in 1496–1511, male admissions recovered to 53 per year in 1575–1602 (Table 9.11). At the same time, there was a big percentage drop in those admitted by special grace and sponsorship and a rise from 38 per cent to 66 per cent in those admitted by apprenticeship (Table 9.1), with a fivefold increase in the annual numbers admitted via this route from an average of 8 per year in the 1500s to 40 per year. Clearly, Dublin's guilds were again recruiting strongly, expanding their influence, and, in the process, training a growing number of apprentices.

Over the sixteenth century more guilds had continued to be founded: the saddlers in 1558, the butchers in 1569 (if not before) and the tallow chandlers in 1583.[194] These additional foundations reinforced the existing bias of Dublin's guild structure towards the secondary sector to the neglect of service-sector occupations, whose share of freemen's admissions continued to contract to barely 6 per cent of the recorded total (Table 9.12). What was declining was not the service sector but its visibility. Advance of the guilds also fostered wider adoption of blanket occupational descriptions, so that, paradoxically, between 1468–95 and 1575–1602 the rate per head at which unique occupations are named in the rolls shrank by a quarter (Table 9.11). This was despite the numbers of guilds, apprentices and admissions to the franchise all growing. Meanwhile, female admissions as a proportion of the total halved as women became economically and institutionally more marginalized. Fewer women were admitted by special grace and, although women continued to account for over a quarter of those who became freemen by patrimony (Table 9.10), there was a relative drop in the number of men who became freemen through marriage to an inheriting woman. The days when women had made up a quarter of those admitted to the freedom had long passed.

These trends maintained their momentum right up to the eve of the outbreak of the Great Rebellion in 1641.[195] Annual rates of male admission

191 Transcribed in 1919 by Gertrude Thrift, electronic version available via Dublin City Archives at https://databases.dublincity.ie/freemen/about.php. **192** S.G. Ellis, *Tudor Ireland: crown, community and the conflict of cultures, 1470–1603* (London and New York, 1985), pp 278–313. **193** E.A. Wrigley and R.S. Schofield, *The population history of England, 1541–1871: a reconstruction* (Cambridge, 1989), pp 174–9. **194** Guinness, 'Dublin trade gilds', pp 149–57; Clark and Refaussé, *Dublin guilds*, pp 17, 25–6, 29–30. **195** The information used here is the transcription contained in Fitzpatrick, 'Municipal

rose from 53 per year in 1575–1602 to 64 per year in 1600–29 and then peaked at 105 per year in the boom decade of the 1630s, when they were finally approaching the levels last recorded in the 1230s (Figure 9.1). It was now again the norm for the occupation of each new freeman to be recorded, although the existing trend towards the use of blanket descriptions continued. The upshot is that although from 1603–40 the chief occupations of 2,358 men are known, which is more than ever before, fewer unique occupations are recorded per head than at any previous time (Table 9.11). In fact, the rate per head of the recording of specific occupations in 1603–40 is only a quarter of what it had been in 1230–49, when occupations are given for only 29 per cent of those admitted. The seventeenth-century occupational information may be the more representative of the entire body of freemen but, owing to the advance of the guilds, this is at the price of being significantly less detailed.

After 1603 there was some reduction in the relative importance of admissions via apprenticeship, although the general upward trend was so strong that apprenticeship admissions rose from 36 to 42 per year. Tellingly, fewer than one in twenty of those who became freemen via this route had service occupations, for this type of work mostly lay outside the purview of the guild system. In contrast, the admission of those apprenticed to the influential mercantile Trinity guild went from strength to strength, rising by almost 40 per cent from 13 to 18 per year. Meanwhile, admissions of craft and construction workers rose from 21 to 30 per year. On these numbers the city's economy was plainly thriving, boosted no doubt by contemporary political, military and commercial developments which were reinforcing Dublin's effective status as Ireland's capital.[196] A rise in the numbers paying an entry fine in order to become freemen (Table 9.10) implies that once again the city was becoming a magnet to migrants.

With reference to the classification scheme set out in Appendix 1, Dublin's occupational profile in each of these four benchmark periods – 1230–49, 1468–95, 1575–1602 and 1603–40 – is summarized in Table 9.12. Correlations between these respective profiles are set out in Table 9.13. All four occupational profiles are unmistakably urban, insofar as each displays an overwhelming predominance of a diversity of secondary- and tertiary-sector occupations. Across these 400 years, it is a picture which changes more in detail than in outline. Unsurprisingly, the match is closest between the two consecutive periods with the fullest information and most developed guild structures, namely 1575–1602 and 1603–40. Correlations of a perfect +1.000 and near perfect +0.999 at the macro levels of (A) primary, secondary, and tertiary occupations and (B) the sixfold breakdown of primary, provisioning, crafts and construction, commerce, services and high titles, indicate that the city's basic occupational structure remained essentially the same across these

corporation of Dublin', ii, pp 40–97. **196** Dickson, *Dublin*, pp 52–8.

Table 9.12. The changing occupational profile of Dublin guildsmen and freemen 1230–49 and freemen 1468–95, 1575–1602, and 1603–40 (see Appendix 9.1 for the occupational classification)

Occupation group	Freemen & guildsmen 1230–49	Freemen 1468–95	Freemen 1575–1602	Freemen 1603–1640
A) Primary/Secondary/Tertiary/High titles [%]:				
Primary	*5.2*	*0.0*	*1.0*	*0.5*
Secondary	*62.6*	*30.6*	*62.8*	*64.0*
Tertiary	*31.7*	*44.0*	*32.4*	*31.4*
High titles	*0.5*	*25.4*	*3.8*	*4.2*
TOTAL NUMBER	637	761	1,240	2,358
B) All occupations [%]:				
Primary	*1.4*	*0.0*	*0.1*	*0.0*
Provisioning*	*16.1*	*7.4*	*16.3*	*15.1*
Crafts & construction	*50.5*	*23.3*	*47.4*	*49.3*
Commerce	*12.5*	*32.7*	*26.5*	*25.7*
Services	*19.0*	*11.3*	*5.9*	*5.7*
High titles	*0.5*	*25.4*	*3.8*	*4.2*
TOTAL NUMBER	637	761	1,240	2,358
C) Secondary occupations [%]:				
Food processing	*19.7*	*24.0*	*24.5*	*23.1*
Cloth & clothing	*27.4*	*23.2*	*18.9*	*22.0*
Tanning & leather	*21.5*	*19.7*	*27.7*	*24.3*
Metal-working	*15.5*	*22.7*	*8.7*	*8.7*
Misc crafts	*5.7*	*1.7*	*6.4*	*10.1*
Construction	*10.2*	*8.6*	*13.7*	*11.7*
TOTAL NUMBER	401	233	779	1,508

* Gardening, fishing and food processing.
Sources: see Table 9.10.

75 years, notwithstanding the physical growth which Dublin was experiencing at the time and the considerable political and religious turmoil to which it was being subjected as the English government sought to reassert its power in Ireland.[197] Secondary occupations accounted for an impressive 62.8–64.0 per cent of the recorded total and the relative importance of that sector's six core occupations (Table 9.12C), led by tanning and leather and closely followed by food provisioning and then cloth and clothing, changed scarcely at all (correlation = +0.95).

197 Dickson, *Dublin*, pp 42–8.

Table 9.13. Inter-period correlations in Dublin's occupational structure as specified in Table 9.12 (listed in rank order according to the strength of the mean correlation)

Inter-period occupational correlation	Minimum correlation	Mean correlation	Maximum Correlation
1575–1602 to 1603–1640	0.947	0.986	1.000
1230–1249 to 1603–1640	0.798	0.919	0.995
1230–1249 to 1575–1602	0.716	0.896	0.994
1468–1495 to 1575–1602	0.511	0.556	0.592
1468–1495 to 1603–1640	0.494	0.546	0.583
1230–1249 to 1468–1495	0.232	0.506	0.862

Source: Table 9.12.

Such pronounced occupational continuity had not always prevailed, for correlations of both these periods with the equivalent occupational profile for the end of the fifteenth century are significantly weaker and in all cases below +0.6 (Table 9.13). This is hardly unexpected given the distorting effect in 1468–95 of the unusually large number of freemen with 'high titles' as an occupational group (i.e., men of yeomen's rank and higher), a majority of them admitted by special grace. Omitting those with high titles and repeating the correlations improves the results somewhat but fails to eliminate the difference. Plainly, significant changes in Dublin's occupational structure occurred over the course of the sixteenth century. Chief among these were a relative contraction of the tertiary sector, involving both commerce and services, and a counterbalancing expansion of the secondary sector (Table 9.12). Among secondary occupations, tanning and leather gained relative to cloth and clothing, metal-working contracted and construction expanded. Telling though these developments are, too much should not be made of them, for the sample size in 1468–95 is modest, especially respecting secondary occupations. Overall, these occupational shifts and adjustments are characteristic of a city that was regaining its economic and demographic dynamism. As a result, the need to recruit men from the rural landed classes to help bolster freemen numbers faded. They remained a feature of the citizenry but not on the scale of the late fifteenth century when Dublin's fortunes were at their lowest ebb.

The contrast between the occupational profile of the late fifteenth-century city and that of the 'thrusting Anglo-Norman town of the thirteenth century' is even greater.[198] Correlations between these two benchmark periods are the weakest of all (Table 9.13) and excluding men with high titles from the

198 Dickson, *Dublin*, pp 40–1.

comparison does little to improve them. Between 1230–49 and 1468–95 the share of those with secondary occupations dropped dramatically as mass enrolment into the mercantile Trinity guild prompted a leap in the proportion of those reported as engaging in commerce. At the same time, those with service occupations began to fade from view and large numbers of landed gentlemen replaced the many non-resident guildsmen formerly active in provisioning the thriving city and acting as commercial intermediaries within Dublin's expanding hinterland. Where, in the second quarter of the thirteenth century, it had looked as though Dublin was on course to become the effective political and economic capital of the greater part of the then actively expanding Lordship of Ireland, by the close of the fifteenth century it had settled into its diminished role as a decaying regional capital with a decidedly circumscribed hinterland.[199]

Given the evident dynamism of the early thirteenth-century city when it was benefiting from its role as the seat of English power in Ireland, it is perhaps hardly surprising that Dublin's occupational profile at that time correlates far more closely with those of the late sixteenth- and early seventeenth-century city, when English power in Ireland was again in the ascendant, than that of the late fifteenth century when it was at almost its lowest ebb (Table 9.13).[200] Thus, correlations between the occupational profiles for 1230–49 and 1575–1602 fall within the range +0.72 to +0.99 and those between 1230–49 and 1603–40 into the slightly higher range of +0.80 to +0.995. Paradoxically, the correlations are strongest between the two periods furthest apart in time, with the least and most developed guild and apprenticeship structures, and differing most conspicuously in the quality and quantity of the available occupational evidence (Table 9.11). What underpinned their strong occupational similarities was their common political, economic, and demographic expansionism. The balance struck between primary, secondary and tertiary occupations was virtually identical in both periods (+0.99). In both, also, the spread of craft occupations remained relatively wide, with tanning and leather-working, the cloth and clothing trades and food processing all well represented but none so pre-eminent as to constitute clear market specialization in a single branch of manufacturing. The distinguishing feature of the city's economy in both the early thirteenth and the early seventeenth centuries was the wide spread of activities and diversity of occupations to be found within it.

These marked similarities in occupational structure between two eras separated by almost 400 years are a reminder that by 1603–40 Dublin had finally come full circle and was back more or less where it had been during its confident first century as the king of England's Irish capital. The political and economic promise of the first half of the thirteenth century had, however,

199 Campbell, 'Dublin 1190–1290', pp 256–62, 268–9. **200** Dickson, *Dublin*, pp 40–1.

proved to be a false dawn, and, by the end of the fifteenth century, progress plainly had not only stalled but had gone into reverse.[201] Recovery began in the sixteenth century but it would then take until the opening decades of the seventeenth century for Dublin's economy to be restored to the level of development achieved four centuries earlier. It was upon that firmer foundation that the city's subsequent continuing growth and development would be built until, by 1770 when Revd Dr William Lodge undertook his house-to-house detailed survey of the small county town of Armagh, Dublin had grown to become the political, administrative, legal, financial, educational, commercial and cultural capital of Ireland, the effective head of an all-Ireland urban system, and second only to London in size among British and Irish cities with, presumably, an occupational profile to match.[202]

DUBLIN'S OCCUPATIONAL PROFILE IN CONTEXT

Together, the Dublin guildsmen's and freemen's rolls allow the analysis of urban occupational structures to be extended further back in time than has been possible for any other British or Irish town of broadly comparable urban rank and size. Moreover, later freemen's rolls enable the evolution of Dublin's occupational structure to be traced over the ensuing 400 years. The results that emerge are in line with what is already known about the occupational structures of other large pre-modern towns both collectively and individually and affirm the timelessness, universality and durability of these structures. All large towns had to feed, house, clothe and organize their substantial populations and, to do so, all engaged in commerce at a range of scales and distances to secure the essential provisions, raw materials, and luxury goods upon which their survival and prosperity depended.[203] Of counter-balancing importance was securing markets for the goods produced and the services provided by their secondary and tertiary workers, upon whose sale these towns were equally dependent. Hence the unimportance of employment in primary production, except, as in the case of coastal ports like Dublin, of sea-fishing, and the absolute pre-eminence of a diversity of manufacturing, commercial and service occupations. It was these occupational characteristics which were for long their most diagnostic urban feature, until, with the transition to modern economic growth, occupational diversity and the overwhelming dominance of secondary and tertiary occupations became features of the entire economy.[204] A component of that transition, of course, was an expansion of the

201 Above, pp 261–7; Dickson, *Dublin*, pp 26–9. **202** David Dickson, 'The place of Dublin in the eighteenth-century Irish economy' in T.M. Devine and David Dickson (eds), *Ireland and Scotland, 1600–1850* (Edinburgh, 1983), pp 177–92; Dickson, *Dublin*, pp 152–87. **203** Patten, 'Urban occupations in pre-industrial England'; Goose, 'English pre-industrial urban economies'. **204** Between 1381 and 1851 in England and Wales the urban share of population and employment from a minority to a majority of the total.

England and Ireland were at the beginning of that process in the thirteenth century and by its close Dublin may have supported a population of about 11,000. At that time the city's economy was rooted in that of a hinterland which straddled the Irish Sea. In the twelfth century Gerald of Wales had observed that environmentally Ireland enjoyed a comparative advantage in pastoral production.[205] Grain for bread was crucial but cattle, sheep and swine and horses for transport were fundamental to the city's economy. This explains why butchers, tanners and leather-workers, processors of tallow, horn and bone, spinners and weavers of wool, fullers and dyers of cloth, and manufacturers of clothing, including tailors, shoemakers, glovers and hatters, were all well represented occupational groups within the city. Hides, wool and woolfells surplus to the city's requirements were exported, along with quantities of leather, yarn and coarse woollen cloth produced within the city and its hinterland. In return came grain, salt, wine, spices, ingots of iron and much else. This was a commercial economy geared above all towards maintaining the self-sufficiency of the city and its dependent region. It was underpinned by a sophisticated exchange system which, on the evidence of the recorded places-of-origin of its guildsmen and freemen, extended further by sea than by land.[206] In the 1230s and 1240s, had prevailing political, commercial and economic circumstances remained favourable, it was a commercialized production system with real potential for further sustained expansion.[207] Dublin was as yet too small for the need to feed and fuel the city to have been a constraint, rather, it was insufficient investment in improved urban institutions and infrastructure, the absence within Ireland of an integrated urban hierarchy, and the associated limited scale of aggregate and *per capita* demand for Dublin's goods and services that held its urban growth in check.[208]

Any reconstruction of occupational structure based upon the information contained in freemen's rolls is unavoidably skewed towards the upper echelons of urban society. In Dublin until 1265 – when they cease – the city's guildsmen's rolls allow that reconstruction to extend further down the socio-

primary sector's estimated share of the labour force contracted from 57 to 24 per cent, while those of the secondary and tertiary sectors expanded from 19 to 46 per cent and from 24 to 31 per cent. Meanwhile, the urban share of the population grew from approximately 12 per cent in 1290 to 54 per cent in 1851 and GDP per head increased by 450 per cent: Broadberry et al., *British economic growth*, pp 227, 244, 344; Campbell, 'Benchmarking', 931; Christopher M. Law, 'The growth of urban population in England and Wales, 1801–1911', *Transactions of the Institute of British Geographers*, 41 (1967), p. 130. **205** Gerald of Wales, *The history and topography of Ireland*, trans. and intro. John O'Meara (Dundalk, 1951), pp 34–5, 53–4. **206** Campbell, 'Dublin 1190–1290', pp 233–46. **207** Campbell, 'From boom to bust', forthcoming. **208** Campbell, 'Dublin 1190–1290', pp 263–5, 268–9. On the challenges of feeding and fuelling medieval cities, see Campbell et al., *Medieval*

economic hierarchy than would otherwise be possible. Even so, the occupations of the bulk of those at the bottom of the occupational hierarchy – the domestic and industrial servants, unskilled labourers, messengers, fetchers and carriers, and those engaged in providing transport, hospitality and entertainment – mostly elude investigation and certainly quantification, as do the occupations of most women. The available evidence may be both abundant and richly informative but by its nature can never provide anything more than a partial picture. As Jennifer Kermode has lamented, 'the unskilled sector in the greater towns ... lies beyond our historical reach'.[209] Also missing in Dublin's case are most of the top tier of officials charged with running its ecclesiastical and governmental administrations, for they remained detached from the corporation's affairs and had little need to become either guildsmen or freemen. Only towards the end of the fifteenth century, when the corporation deemed it expedient to enlist some of them as honorary freemen, do they begin to make an appearance.

Paradoxically, the occupational information contained in the guildsmen's and freemen's rolls is most detailed in the thirteenth century before the advent of trade guilds led to the stereotyping of occupational descriptions. From the fifteenth century, as the first guilds were founded and a system of formal apprenticeship became established, the use of blanket occupational descriptions based upon guild membership came to predominate, with a consequent loss of occupational detail. Per head, the amount of detailed occupational information halved between the early thirteenth and the late fifteenth century (Table 9.11). The advance of guilds also explains the progressive marginalization and exclusion of service workers, the heightened representation of 'merchants' (for whom the freedom to operate legally within the city was conditional upon admission to the mercantile Trinity guild), and, within the record of freemen's admissions, the substitution of guild affiliations for actual occupations. The post-1265 occupational information may look more complete, since it is generally given for nine out of ten freemen, but it is less occupationally comprehensive and detailed than the equivalent pre-1265 information. These distortions and omissions endorse the importance of qualifying and contextualizing the occupational evidence provided by freemen's rolls with that available from other historical sources. Where such sources exist – wills, witness statements, property transactions, coroners' reports and much else – the methodologies are now being developed which allow useful occupational information to be extracted, systematized and codified.[210]

capital; Galloway et al., 'Fuelling the city'. **209** Kermode, 'The greater towns', p. 451. **210** Examples include Kowaleski, *Local markets and regional trade*; Keibek, 'Male occupational structure of England and Wales'; Cambridge Group, 'Occupational structure of Britain'; and Whittle and Hailwood's project, 'Forms of labour: gender, freedom and experience of work in the preindustrial economy'.

As demonstrated by the other contributions to this volume, archaeology also has an important contribution to make. Whereas the freemen's rolls offer a wide-angle view of the city's economy as a whole, embracing its extramural franchises and transpontine suburbs and such outlying semi-industrial settlements as Kilmainham, with their butchers and bakers, textile-workers, leather-workers, smiths and metal-workers, carters and ostlers, archaeology provides a sharp-focus view of the activities undertaken at specific sites. It can pin down where particular crafts were located, what techniques, tools and raw materials were used, where the raw materials came from and much else. Thereby it can also greatly amplify the invariably laconic information contained in the documents. For example, where the guildsmen's rolls record just two comb-makers, archaeological excavations at Winetavern Street reveal that the fashioning of combs and similar artifacts from antlers and bones was a well-established craft activity with a substantial legacy of industrial waste.[211] Future insights into Dublin's wool-textile, tanning and leather, metal-working and pottery industries are more likely to come from ongoing urban archaeology than closer examination of the city's remarkable but nonetheless limited range of manuscript records.

The documentary evidence does, however, raise the tricky question of where exactly the line should be drawn between resident and non-resident Dubliners, and the complementary but somewhat contrasting occupations which they pursued. To distinguish between the two is anything but straightforward. It might be thought that, by definition, all freemen should be construed as residents, since there was a clear expectation that they would reside within the city. Nevertheless, the stipulation in a bye-law of 1485 that all mayors of Dublin during their years of office should live within the walls of the city implies that not all mayors had been complying with that expectation.[212] Cities were places with a constant traffic of people and goods and it was not unusual for their permanent residents, especially those engaged in commerce, to be regularly absent on business for periods at a time. Thus, in 1468, the year before he was enfranchised as a Dublin citizen, James Welles made ten voyages across the Irish Sea, mostly between Dublin and Chester, which thereby enforced his absence from Dublin for much of that time.[213] In his stead, no doubt, came traders and shippers from elsewhere who became temporary residents of Dublin for as long as their business required. Between 1180 and 1265 many of those arriving from Britain and beyond found it expedient, while in Dublin, to pay the entry fine of 9 shillings, enrol in the city's guild merchant and be legitimized to go about their business.[214] At one and the same time they were resident and impermanent.

211 *DGMR*, pp 47, 116; Ó Ríordáin, 'Excavations at High Street and Winetavern Street, Dublin', p. 75. **212** Lennon, 'Introduction', pp xv–xvi. **213** Slattery, *Social life*, p. 105. **214** Campbell, 'Dublin 1190–1290', pp 228–34.

There were also those closer to home, notably the many mercers and related traders who acted as commercial intermediaries between Dublin and the towns, markets and fairs of its trans-Irish Sea hinterland, who were familiar participants in its wholesale and retail markets. Collectively, they had a very real presence within the city even though individually they did not necessarily reside there. Dublin's many butchers constitute a similar case. They operated from bases outside the city but maintained an almost permanent commercial presence within its walls, where they marketed their meat and supplied hides to the city's many tanners. The city could not have coped without them. It was also to the city's franchises (its extramural and suburban fringe) that many of its tanners, smiths and potters were drawn due to the noxious and polluting nature of their activities.[215] Functionally, their fortunes were tied to those of the city even if, strictly, they did not necessarily reside within it. The key point to emerge from this is that there was no simple and clear distinction between residents and non-residents, for the personnel of the city and its environs were mutually dependent and the city was the regular resort of both. The turnover of population was also too great given that many residents were in fact recent arrivals. Only at the end of the fifteenth century, when the city was struggling to recruit freemen, is there a line perhaps be drawn between genuine Dubliners and the large number of landed proprietors who, at the instigation of the corporation and often for reasons of family aggrandizement, became enfranchised as citizens.

These issues of definition and demarcation are not exclusive to Dublin but nor are they of such moment as to invalidate the comparisons drawn with York, Norwich, Canterbury, Winchester and Exeter. The same is true of the gap of at least half a century between the evidence for them and that for Dublin. These limitations apart, what emerges strongly from these comparisons, including that with Keibek's urban benchmark estimates for England and Wales in 1710, is just how characteristic Dublin's pre-1250 occupational structure appears to have been of other leading pre-modern towns (Tables 9.3–9.5). Differences there were, of course, but in Dublin's case these were more of detail than of kind. Insofar as its occupational structure differed from York's or Norwich's, it was in the absence from its secondary sector of any single pre-eminent craft activity. In this respect it more closely resembled Canterbury and Winchester, neither of which exhibited the degree of craft specialization evident in York and Norwich. As both were modest county towns and probably had fewer than 10,000 inhabitants, maybe their manufacturing sectors were inhibited from becoming more specialized by the circumscribed extent and limited wealth of the markets, both internal and external, which they served?[216] If so, perhaps the same was true of Dublin. While it remained small in size and served a

215 Clark, 'Sources for Irish freemen', p. 44. **216** Campbell, 'Benchmarking', 908.

territorially restricted, comparatively thinly peopled and economically underdeveloped hinterland, greater occupational specialization would remain elusive.[217] Norwich and especially York, in contrast, were in a different league.

Dublin looked more like these comparator English cities when its economy was buoyant, in the early thirteenth and then again in the late sixteenth and early seventeenth centuries, than towards the end of its prolonged late-medieval decline, at the end of the fifteenth and opening of the sixteenth centuries. At that time it also looked least like its former and later self (Tables 9.12 and 9.13). In both England and Ireland, the great and lasting reductions in population and economic output which followed the demographic disaster of the Black Death, and the concurrent shifts in the orientation and conduct of international trade, presented serious challenges to the economic prosperity of most towns, which now found themselves in greater competition with each other and especially with London.[218] They met these challenges with mixed degrees of success. Resilience, or the want of it, often came down to specific local circumstances, geographical, locational and institutional.[219] In an era when centripetal outweighed centrifugal forces, distance from the emergent commercial and economic nexus of the southern North Sea region – Flanders, Brabant, Holland and London – counted as a disadvantage.[220] Hence the widening divergence within England between the north and the south.[221] Inescapably, it was with the underdeveloped and undynamic north that Dublin's lot was cast, on account of its geographical location and established commercial ties. Local environmental circumstances did not help. At a time when maritime shipping was gaining in relative importance and ocean-going

217 Campbell, 'Benchmarking', 911; Campbell, 'Dublin 1190–1290', pp 264–9. **218** Alan Dyer, *Decline and growth in English towns 1400–1640* (Basingstoke, 1991), pp 25–36; Derek J. Keene, 'Changes in London's economic hinterland as indicated by debt cases in the court of common pleas' in J.A. Galloway (ed.), *Trade, urban hinterlands and market integration, c.1300–1600: a collection of working papers given at a conference organized by the Centre for Metropolitan History and supported by the Economic and Social Research Council, 7 July 1999*, Centre for Metropolitan History, Working Papers 3 (London, 2000), pp 59–81. For a rare discussion of the phenomenon in Ireland, see Howard B. Clarke, 'Decolonization and the dynamics of urban decline in Ireland, 1300–1550' in T.R. Slater (ed.), *Towns in decline, AD 100–1600* (Aldershot, 2000), pp 157–92; Campbell, *Great transition*, pp 355–71. **219** Revealing case studies include R.H. Britnell, *Growth and decline in Colchester, 1300–1525* (Cambridge, 1986), pp 159–264; Rigby, *Medieval Grimsby*, pp 113–46; Jennifer Kermode, *Medieval merchants: York, Beverley and Hull in the later Middle Ages* (Cambridge, 1998); Charles Phythian-Adams, *Desolation of a city: Coventry and the urban crisis of the late Middle Ages* (Cambridge, 2002); Helen Clarke, Sarah Pearson, Mavis Mate and Keith Parfitt, *Sandwich the 'completest medieval town in England': a study of the town and port from its origins to 1600* (Oxford, 2010), pp 119–45; Rigby and Nash, *Overseas trade of Boston*. **220** Campbell, *Great transition*, pp 384–5. **221** Bruce M.S. Campbell, 'North–south dichotomies 1066–1560' in Alan R.H. Baker and Mark Billinge (eds), *Geographies of England: the north–south divide, imagined and material* (Cambridge, 2004), pp 161–74, reprinted in Bruce M.S. Campbell, *Land and people in late medieval England*, Variorum Collected Studies Series (Aldershot, 2009).

ships were getting larger, the shallowness of Dublin's port and anchorage were a further handicap. Without significant investment in the port's infrastructure to redress the problem, big ships were obliged to dock at Dalkey, a distance of 14 kilometres to the south, and, at some risk, trans-ship their cargoes into lighters for the final journey to Dublin.[222] Its rival east-coast port of Drogheda did not labour under these difficulties, which are also likely to have been one of several reasons why Bristol merchants forsook Dublin in favour of Waterford.

Following the innovative first century of English rule, Dublin had settled into a state of institutional inertia.[223] It lagged behind other cities in the foundation of trade and craft guilds, one of whose purposes was to protect and enhance the commercial and manufacturing interests of those they represented. Such protectionism could, of course, backfire but cities with well-developed guilds, such as London, tended to do well.[224] In a world where demographic decline had long been the norm, keeping up numbers was also of obvious importance. Here Dublin was doubly handicapped as the epicentre of most Irish plague outbreaks and by a ban on enfranchising Irishmen.[225] In a divided land, war, too, was never far away. Twice, in October 1478 and April 1480, the business of the corporation was suspended while the mayor, bailiffs and commons went on campaign with the lord deputy against his Irish enemies.[226] Here was the rub, for compounding everything was the dwindling benefit Dublin derived from being the diminished capital of the shrinking and beleaguered rump of England's Irish Lordship. While this remained the case, Dublin's fortunes stagnated, as manifest in the depressed freedom admission rates of the opening decade of the sixteenth century (Figure 9.1). Political factors therefore loomed large in shaping Dublin's own experience of late-medieval urban decline and set it apart from that of most of its English urban contemporaries. The problems the city faced and how it coped invite closer examination and, beginning with its franchise roll, might well repay the kind of prosopographical analysis which has been applied so revealingly to cities such as Exeter and London.[227]

This investigation of Dublin's early occupational structure, viewed in comparison with those of four nearly contemporary English cities plus three later profiles of Dublin across a 400-year period, represents a beginning rather than an end. It demonstrates the potential for extending this type of analysis back to before the Black Death to include the phase of urbanization which accompanied the commercial revolution of the twelfth and thirteenth

222 Information supplied by Dr Niall Brady of the Archaeological Diving Company; Slattery, *Social life*, pp 94–5. **223** Campbell, 'Dublin 1190–1290', pp 257–62, 269. **224** Barron, 'London 1300–1540', pp 412–32. **225** Campbell and Ludlow, 'Climate, disease and society', pp 220, 226. **226** *DCFR*, pp 12, 14. **227** Kowaleski, *Local markets and regional trade*; Maryanne Kowaleski, 'A new digital prosopography: the medieval Londoners database', *Medieval People*, 36:1 (2022), Article 13; https://medievallondoners.ace.fordham.edu.

centuries.[228] It also highlights the benefits of viewing Dublin's economic development within a wider geographical and historical context and illustrates the kinds of insights to be gained from comparisons made with other well-documented English and Irish towns provided they are undertaken systematically and employ a common scheme of occupational classification. The challenge now must be to extend this type of analysis down the urban hierarchy to establish whether the results obtained for this top tier of medieval regional capitals hold true for the greater number of lesser towns with populations of around 5,000 or less, for numbers of which appropriate sources do exist especially if, in Ireland's case, investigation is broadened to include the sixteenth and seventeenth centuries.[229] By any standard, Dublin is uniquely blessed by the remarkable survival of its intermittent series of guild and franchise rolls which span a period of 450 years from *c.*1190 to 1640 and continue thereafter. They are a national treasure. When so much else of relevance to Ireland's urban history perished in the explosion and fire of June 1922 which destroyed the Public Record Office of Ireland, they were secure in the Dublin City Archive. Beginning with Sir John Gilbert, who published selections from these rolls in his *Calendar of ancient records of Dublin*, a succession of dedicated archivists and scholars – Gertrude Thrift, Brendan Fitzpatrick, Philomena Connolly, Mary Clark, Colm Lennon, and James Murray – have transcribed, edited and made available (now, thanks to Dublin City Library and Archive, online) the thousands of individual personal entries which they contain.[230] This paper is a tribute to their painstaking and expert work.

228 Robert S. Lopez, *The commercial revolution of the Middle Ages, 950–1350* (Englewood Cliffs, 1971); Campbell, *Great transition*, pp 85–6, 121–5. **229** For Leicester, see Bateson (ed.), *Records of Leicester*; for Ipswich, Masschaele, 'Urban trade in medieval England'. For occupational differences between the lowest tier of towns and agricultural villages, see John Patten, 'Village and town: an occupational study', *Agricultural History Review*, 20:1 (1972), 1–16. **230** https://databases.dublincity.ie/freemen/about.php. Note that discrepancies exist between the hard copy and online versions of these texts.

APPENDIX 9.1: OCCUPATIONAL CLASSIFICATION SCHEME

Primary-, Secondary-, Tertiary-occupation:				
		Occupational main category:		
			Occupational sub-category:	
				Occupation:
P	1	Primary production:		
P		1	Agriculture	
P			01	Farm worker
P			02	Shepherd
P			03	Warrener
P			04	Husbandman
P			05	Franklin
P			06	Bailiff
P		2	Forestry	
P			01	Forester
P		3	Hunting	
P			01	Huntsman
P	2	Provisioning		
P		1	Primary provisioning	
P			01	Gardener
P			02	Fisherman
P			03	Fisher
S		2	Food processing	
S			01	Butcher
S			02	Poulterer
S			03	Hatcher
S			04	Cheesemonger
S			05	Fruiterer
S			06	Cornmonger
S			07	Oats seller
S			08	Miller
S			09	Baker
S			10	Maltster
S			11	Brewer
S			12	Distiller
S			13	Misc. provisioning

Primary-, Secondary-, Tertiary-occupation: (*continued*)				
		Occupational main category:		
			Occupational sub-category:	
				Occupation:
S	3	Cloth-making		
S		1	Wool preparation	
S			01	Comber
S			02	Wool-beater
S		2	Spinning	
S			01	Spinner
S		3	Weaving	
S			01	Weaver
S			02	Blanker-maker
S			03	Burel-maker
S			04	Cloth-maker
S			05	Challoner
S			06	Quilter
S		4	Fulling & finishing	
S			01	Dubber
S			02	Napper
S			03	Fuller
S			04	Felter/Felt-maker
S			05	Shearman
S			06	Tapener
S		5	Dyeing	
S			01	Dyer
S			02	Silk dyer
S	4	Clothing		
S			01	Clothier
S			02	Tailor
S			03	Parmenter
S			04	Lacemaker
S			05	Embroiderer
S			06	Hosier
S			07	Wimpler
S			08	Capper
S			09	Button-maker
S			10	Misc. clothing
S	5	Hides & skins		
S			01	Skinner
S			02	Tanner
S			03	Tawyer

Primary-, Secondary-, Tertiary-occupation: (*continued*)				
		Occupational main category:		
			Occupational sub-category:	
				Occupation:
S	5	Hides & skins (*continued*)		
S			04	Curer/Currier
S			05	Parchment-maker
S	6	Leather-working		
S		1	Clothing	
S			01	Hatter
S			02	Glover
S			03	Cordwainer
S			04	Shoemaker
S			05	Cobbler
S			06	Girdler
S			07	Bursar or Purse-maker
S			08	Scabbard-maker
S		2	Harness	
S			01	Bridle-maker
S			02	Harness-maker
S			03	Saddler
S		3	Misc. leather	
S			01	Bottle-maker
S			02	Leather dresser
S			03	Leather-worker
S			04	Other
S	7	Metal-working		
S		1	Non-ferrous	
S			01	Goldsmith
S			02	Coppersmith
S			03	Brazier
S			04	Cup-maker
S			05	Bell founder
S			06	Pewterer
S			07	Leadbeater
S		2	Iron & steel	
S			01	Smelter
S			02	Iron-worker
S			03	Smith
S			04	Marshal/(Farrier)
S		3	Metal wares	
S			01	Lorimer

Primary-, Secondary-, Tertiary-occupation: (*continued*)				
		Occupational main category:		
			Occupational sub-category:	
				Occupation:
S		3	Metal wares (*continued*)	
S			02	Spurrier
S			03	Buckler
S			04	Locksmith
S			05	Watchmaker
S			06	Gunsmith
S			07	Cutler
S			08	Sword-maker
S			09	Furbisher
S			10	Armourer
S			11	Axe-burner
S			12	Other
S	4	Miscellaneous crafts		
S		1	Wood	
S			01	Joiner
S			02	Turner
S			03	Cooper
S			04	Fish cooper
S			05	Box-maker
S			06	Wheelwright
S		2	Pottery	
S			01	Potter
S		3	Tallow & wax	
S			01	Soap-maker
S			02	Chandler
S			03	Tallow chandler
S		4	Bone & ivory	
S			01	Dicer
S			02	Comb-maker
S		5	Various	
S			01	Fletcher
S			02	Hatcher
S			03	Bookbinder
S			04	Printer
S			05	Misc. crafts
S	5	Construction		
S		1	Carpentry	
S			01	Carpenter

Primary-, Secondary-, Tertiary-occupation: (*continued*)				
		Occupational main category:		
			Occupational sub-category:	
				Occupation:
S	5	Construction (*continued*)		
S			02	Carpenter/Fuster
S			03	Sawyer
S		2	Bricks & masonry	
S			01	Lime-burner
S			02	Brickmaker
S			03	Bricklayer
S			04	Waller
S			05	Gabler
S			06	Plasterer
S		3	Roofing	
S			01	Roofer
S			02	Thatcher
S			03	Slater
S			04	Helier (tiler/slater)
S		4	Building workers	
S			01	Architect
S			02	Mason
S			03	Labourer
S			04	Painter
S			05	Plumber
S			06	Tunneler
S			07	Aqueductor
S			08	Glazier
S			09	Wright
S			10	Boothwright
S		5	Other	
S			01	Other construction
T	6	Commerce		
T		1	Great merchants	
T			01	Merchant
T			02	Wool merchant
T			03	Spicer
T			04	Mustarder
T			05	Vintner
T		3	Middling traders	
T			01	Dealer

Primary-, Secondary-, Tertiary-occupation: (*continued*)				
		Occupational main category:		
			Occupational sub-category:	
				Occupation:
T		3	Middling traders (*continued*)	
T			02	Saltman
T			03	Apothecary
T			04	Money lender
T			05	Mercer
T			06	Draper
T			07	Linen draper
T			08	Woolen draper
T			09	Haberdasher
T			10	Upholsterer
T			11	Ironmonger
T			12	Oil/unguent seller
T			13	Stationer
T			14	Flaxman
T			15	Woolmonger
T			16	Woad dealer
T			17	Featherman
T		4	Petty traders	
T			01	Chapman
T			02	Huckster
T	7	Services		
T		1	Transport	
T			01	Carter
T			02	Wagoner
T			03	Sumpturer
T			04	Drover
T			05	Boatman
T			06	Gabbardman
T			07	Mariner
T			08	Steersman
T			09	Boatswain
T			10	Coalman
T			11	Porter
T		2	Hospitality & entertainment	
T			01	Publican
T			02	Taverner
T			03	Innkeeper
T			04	Stabler

Primary-, Secondary-, Tertiary-occupation: (*continued*)				
		Occupational main category:		
			Occupational sub-category:	
				Occupation:
T	7	Services (*continued*)		
T		2	Hospitality & entertainment (*continued*)	
T			05	Rhymer
T			06	Musician
T			07	Piper
T			08	Harpist
T			09	Organist
T			10	Trumpeter
T		3	Catering	
T			01	Cook
T			02	Saucemaker
T			03	Puddling seller
T		4	Personal services	
T			01	Servant
T			02	Butler
T			03	Steward
T			04	Cellarer
T			05	Hoarder
T			06	Chamberlain
T			07	Usher
T		5	Professional & public services	
T			01	Illuminator
T			02	Picture-maker
T			03	Scribe
T			04	Scribe/Scrivener
T			05	Clerk
T			06	Summoner
T			07	Attorney
T			08	Justice
T			09	Schoolmaster
T			10	Fencing master
T			11	Physician
T			12	Surgeon
T			13	Barber-surgeon
T			14	Barber
T			15	Watchman
T			16	Trone operator
T			17	Water carrier

Primary-, Secondary-, Tertiary-occupation: (*continued*)				
		Occupational main category:		
			Occupational sub-category:	
				Occupation:
T	7	Services (*continued*)		
T		6	Religious, urban & military services	
T			01	Monk
T			02	Pastor
T			03	Chaplain
T			04	Burgess
T			05	Sergeant
T			06	Officer
T			07	Artillery man
T			08	Gunner
T			09	Spearman
T		7	Misc. services	
T			01	Other
T	8	High titles		
T		1	Churchmen	
T			01	Bishop
T			02	Abbot
T			03	Prior
T			04	Other ecclesiastic
T		2	Titled	
T			01	Earl
T			02	Baron
T			03	Knight
T			04	Esquire
T		3	Untitled	
T			01	Gentleman
T			02	Gentlewoman
T			03	Yeoman
T			04	Husbandman
T	9	No information		

The spectrum of occupations and the influence of guilds and *Gaffeln* in medieval Dublin and Cologne

VALENTIN ROTHAUPT

In 1417 the scribe Sibert von Eilsich drew up a poll-tax list of 1,373 citizens of Cologne, subdivided into twenty-two so-called *Gaffeln* that existed there between 1396 and the late eighteenth century. This list is an extraordinarily revealing source as it contains a survey of the wealthy craftsmen and merchants living and working in Cologne at the time.[1] And in 135 cases, occupations were added to this list, making it an invaluable source of the crafts carried out by these people. In some ways this poll-tax list bears similarities to the Dublin Guild Merchant Roll (*DGMR*), which dates from *c.*1190–1265, and is the earliest such town record roll to have survived in Britain or Ireland and certainly one of the best preserved and most striking documents of its kind, according to Geoffrey Martin, the co-editor of the roll.[2] Many of the names on the *DGMR* are toponymics, allowing historians to reconstruct the origins of many names of merchants trading in Dublin in the late twelfth and thirteenth century.[3] Four of the names mentioned are *Ace de Colonia*,[4] *Werri Colonicensis*,[5] *Bertolf Colonicensis*,[6] and *Gerardus de Koloyne*,[7] all of whom originally came from Cologne. However, the following analysis does not focus on toponymics like these, but on another aspect both lists have in common: the fact that the *DGMR* in many cases contains information on the occupations which these people carried out, just as the poll-tax list does in Cologne.[8]

This essay aims at comparing two things: first the spectrum of occupations, crafts and trades found in both medieval Dublin and Cologne and second the political roles and influence exercised in both cities by the guilds and *Gaffeln*, respectively the crafts and trades assembled in these organizations. Therefore it is necessary to begin by defining guilds as well as German *Zünfte* and *Gaffeln*. Only in this way is it possible to contextualize both sources. Subsequently, the guilds, which existed in Dublin throughout the late medieval and Early Modern period, will be studied and compared to the *Gaffeln* of Cologne,

1 Klaus Militzer, *Die vermögenden Kölner 1417–1418. Namenlisten einer Kopfsteuer von 1417 und einer städtischen Kreditaufnahme von 1418* (Vienna, 1981), pp i, x. 2 *DGMR*, p. x. For more detailed descriptions of the Dublin merchant guild and the guilds of Dublin in total, see Elmar W. Eggerer, 'The merchants guild of Dublin' in Duffy (ed.), *MD VI*, pp 144–59; John J. Webb, *The guilds of Dublin* (Washington etc., 1929, repr. 1970); B.M.S. Campbell, 'Dublin 1190–1290: provincial capital or capital city?' in Duffy (ed.), *MD XIX*, pp 226–69. 3 Patricia Becker, 'An analysis of the Dublin Guild Merchant Roll, *c.*1190–1265' (M.Phil, TCD, 1995), p. 14. 4 *DGMR*, p. 32. 5 *DGMR*, p. 39. 6 Ibid. 7 *DGMR*, p. 50. 8 Becker, 'Analysis', p. 14; and see the important study by Campbell in this volume.

followed by an analysis of the influence of these organizations in the respective cities. Eventually the different occupations mentioned in the Cologne poll-tax list of 1417 will be analysed and compared to the occupations listed in the *DGMR*. Besides the two sources already mentioned, two other were indispensable for this essay: the Cologne *Verbundbrief* of 1396,[9] a kind of late medieval Cologne *basic law* constituting the twenty-two *Gaffeln* and their political role, and the *Directory of historic Dublin guilds* produced by Mary Clark and Raymond Refaussé.[10] For the purpose of this essay, German occupations were translated into or described in English,[11] whereas some terms like *Gaffel* and *Verbundbrief* are not translated and are written in italics. In some cases, the German dictionary of historical occupations by Jakob Ebner was helpful in correctly identifying and translating the occupations mentioned in the different sources.[12]

One question remains to be answered at this point: what makes the city of Cologne so interesting in terms of a comparative study with Dublin? First of all, and not very surprisingly, both Dublin and Cologne were connected by trade, at least to a limited extent, as the examples in the *DGMR* above show. Second, both cities were by the late thirteenth century the largest in their respective countries, with already about 40,000 people living in Cologne throughout the high and late Middle Ages,[13] making it the largest German city at the time, and 10,000–15,000 people living in Dublin in the second half of the thirteenth century.[14] Though Dublin was the biggest city in Ireland, it must be mentioned that it was still outranked by at least five English cities at the time, as Bruce Campbell points out.[15] Third, in both cases, only the survival of sources like the DGMR and the poll-tax list allows us to compare Dublin and Cologne. It must be taken into account that the Cologne sources were written up to 227 years after the first entries in the *DGMR*. However, both primary sources date back to the high and late Middle Ages, periods of time in which the size and likely also the spectrum of occupations in Cologne did not vary significantly, which allows a comparison to thirteenth-century Dublin. Moreover, this study of Dublin and Cologne enables exemplary

9 Manfred Huiskes, 'Kölns Verfassung für 400 Jahre: Der Verbundbrief vom 14. September 1396' in Joachim Deeters and Johannes Helmrath (eds), *Quellen zur Geschichte der Stadt Köln, Band II. Spätes Mittelalter und Frühe Neuzeit (1396–1794)* (Cologne, 1996), pp 1–28. **10** Mary Clark and Raymond Refaussé (eds), *Directory of historic Dublin guilds* (Dublin, 1993). **11** The Langenscheidt German–English dictionary was helpful in finding the best translations in each case: Langenscheidt (ed.), *Online Wörterbuch* (https://de.langenscheidt.com/), accessed 11 March 2023. **12** Jakob Ebner, *Wörterbuch historischer Berufsbezeichnungen* (Berlin and Boston, 2015). **13** Huiskes, 'Verbundbrief', p. ix; Militzer, Klaus, *Ursachen und Folgen der innerstädtischen Auseinandersetzung in Köln in der zweiten Hälfte des 14. Jahrhunderts* (Cologne ,1980), p. 135. **14** Bruce M.S. Campbell, 'Dublin 1190–1290: provincial capital or capital city?' in Duffy (ed.), *MD XIX*, pp 211–54, at p. 212. **15** Ibid.

insights into the society of both Ireland's and Germany's largest cities at the time.

Defining guilds and Gaffeln

To carry out a comparison of the merchants and craftsmen that worked in the guilds of medieval Dublin and Cologne, it is first of all necessary to define guilds and ostensibly similar associations. Philomena Connolly and Geoffrey Martin, the editors, who fully published the *DGMR* for the first time in 1992, define the purpose of a guild:

> They were solidarities, originally rooted in pagan religious practices, which used the rituals of eating and drinking, but particularly of drinking, in common, to establish a surrogate brotherhood between the participants. They were also characterized by oaths, and by payments to a common fund … Once the brotherhood was established it was reaffirmed at every feast, and newcomers could readily be admitted to its number. It could also be directed to an agreed purpose: to confraternity as an end in itself, to pious observances, to maintaining common interests, to negotiating with the king, or even, as kings were all too ready to suspect, to conspiring against him.[16]

In order to maintain these 'common interests', guilds controlled prices, the quality of their products and the admission of new members.[17] Whereas the term *Gilde* also exists in the German language, the similar use of the word *Zunft* is rather common there.[18] Ruth Schmidt-Wiegand pointed out that the German historiography of recent decades tends to use *Gilde* for confraternities of merchants and *Zunft* for such groups of craftsmen.[19] There is another special kind of group in Cologne and other medieval cities in the Rhineland which has to be defined: the so-called *Gaffel*.[20] In Cologne there were originally four *Gaffeln* which were confraternities of merchants similar to guilds, founded throughout the second half of the fourteenth century.[21] In

16 *DGMR*, p. xvii. **17** Becker, 'Analysis', p. 9. **18** As there are numerous Latin synonyms for *Guild* as pointed out by Becker, there are also other terms for this in Germany. In Cologne, for example, guilds were contemporarily called *Ämter* (Engl. 'agencies'); Becker, 'Analysis', p. 9; Huiskes, 'Verbundbrief', p. 2. **19** Ruth Schmidt-Wiegand, 'Die Bezeichnungen Zunft und Gilde in ihrem historischen und wortgeographischen Zusammenhang' in Konstanzer Arbeitskreis für mittelalterliche Geschichte (ed.), *Gilden und Zünfte. Kaufmännische und gewerbliche Genossenschaften im frühen und hohen Mittelalter (Vorträge und Forschungen XXIX)* (Sigmaringen, 1985), pp 31–52, at p. 52. **20** Since there is not an adequate way to translate this term into English, the German term will henceforth be used in this essay. **21** Christian Hillen, Art. 'Die Kölner Gaffeln' in *Portal Rheinische Geschichte* (https://www.rheinische-geschichte.lvr.de/Epochen-und-Themen/Themen/die-koelner-gaffeln/DE-2086/lido/5e98015879dc69.22344533), accessed 11 March 2023.

1396, however, these *Gaffeln* got a new meaning as 'political corporations':[22] each *Gaffel* was permitted to elect a certain number of representatives to the Cologne city council.[23] The approximately fifty existing guilds or *Zünfte* of craftsmen were also united in eighteen *Gaffeln*, which together with those of the merchants added up to twenty-two *Gaffeln*.[24] In 1417, about 30 per cent of the male population of Cologne were members of the *Gaffeln*.[25] Although the words *Gaffel* and *Zunft* are often used synonymously in German, as Christian Hillen points out, the pre-existing guilds or *Zünfte* as separate confraternities were not dissolved in the course of the changes that occurred in 1396.[26] Therefore it must be taken into account that the terms *Gaffel* and guild do not have the same meaning at least after 1396.[27]

It may be asked why such a detailed distinction between these terms is made. This is necessary to understand the context of one of the primary sources to be analysed in this essay, the so-called Cologne *Verbundbrief* of 1396. It was in that year that three of the merchants' *Gaffeln* and some goldsmiths managed to overthrow the existing political predominance of old patrician families in Cologne.[28] They created a council of 49 members instead, which would control the city for the following four hundred years.[29] The *Verbundbrief*, written by city-clerk Gerlach vanme Hauwe,[30] listed the most important rules for the procedure of elections and the duties and responsibilities of the councillors.[31] It is therefore often described as the basic law or constitutional charter of Cologne.[32] However, for the purpose of this essay the *Verbundbrief* is not only interesting for its political history, but also for the fact that it contains a list of all the twenty-two *Gaffeln* of Cologne and of some guilds (respectively, in Cologne, *Ämter*)[33] and trades incorporated in them. The analysis of these guilds and *Gaffeln* will be presented below when they are also compared to the guilds and occupations mentioned in the *DGMR*.

The latter document is interesting with respect to the fact that it gives us a glimpse of the population of Dublin only a few decades after the English invasion and therefore after the old Viking-elites were killed or had to escape.[34] Connolly and Martin date the earliest preserved entries on the parchment-rolls to around 1190, whereas the latest of them are dated around 1265.[35] Something

22 Hillen, 'Kölner Gaffeln'. **23** Huiskes, 'Verbundbrief', p. 2. **24** Ibid. **25** Ibid. **26** Hillen, 'Kölner Gaffeln'. **27** Huiskes, 'Verbundbrief', p. 2. **28** Huiskes, 'Verbundbrief', p. 1; Hillen, 'Kölner Gaffeln'. **29** Historisches Archiv der Stadt Köln (ed.), *Stadtrat, Stadtrecht, Bürgerfreiheit. Ausstellung aus Anlaß des 600. Jahrestages des Verbundbriefes vom 14. September 1396* (Cologne, 1996), p. 7; Huiskes, 'Verbundbrief', p. 2. **30** Gerlach vanme Hauwe wrote 23 copies of the *Verbundbrief*, 22 for each of the *Gaffeln* and one for the Cologne city council. According to Huiskes, ten of these copies survived. In his edition, he published the copy that could be identified as the one written for the city council: Huiskes, 'Verbundbrief', pp 3–4. **31** Huiskes, 'Verbundbrief', pp 1–2. **32** Historisches Archiv der Stadt Köln, 'Stadtrat, Stadtrecht, Bürgerfreiheit', pp 7, 37. **33** Huiskes, 'Verbundbrief', p. 25. **34** *DGMR*, p. xv. **35** *DGMR*, pp xiv, 109.

that both sources have in common is the fact that they include local elites: in the case of Dublin, 'well-heeled members from Ireland itself as well as from the neighbouring kingdoms and territories, and from many places at a greater distance',[36] and, in Cologne, 30 per cent of the male population.[37] Therefore both sources tend not to reflect the trades of lower social classes.

Before both primary sources are analysed and compared, some notes about the names and occupations mentioned there must be added. As to the Cologne *Verbundbrief*, the German name of the *Gaffeln* will be used in italics. These German names, however, are not written in the original medieval way, which can be read on the original copies of the document.[38] Instead, the modern German 'translations' of these names, as adopted by Manfred Huiskes, will be used. This way the common German names of these organizations can be understood and the translation into English can be reconstructed more easily. The guilds and occupations are translated into English. Since there is not always a direct translation of specific occupations, however, some of them have an additional description rather than a single title.

In case of the *DGMR*, the work of Philomena Connolly is essential. In the edition published by Connolly and Geoffrey Martin, she added an 'Index to occupations'[39] in which she translated into English 171 Latin occupations mentioned among the more than 8,400 recorded names. Patricia Becker points out that it is not always possible to determine whether people whose names are connected with an occupation actually still practised it or whether it had already become a part of their surname.[40] But since this essay does not aim at comparing the detailed numbers of people in these occupations but rather the wide spectrum of crafts and trades existing in both cities, Connolly's index can nevertheless be used.

Cologne's Gaffeln

The names of the Cologne *Gaffeln* and in some cases of guilds included in these *Gaffeln* are the following, in the order of the document: the *Wollenamt* (the guild of wool-weavers, including nappers, curriers and weavers of *Tirtei*, the latter of which is blended fabric of linen and wool), *Eisenmarkt*, *Schwarzenhaus* (including merchants of woad and linen-dyers), *Goldschmieden* (goldsmiths, including goldbeaters), *Windeck*, *Buntwörter* (skinners), *Himmelreich*, *Schilderer* (signwriters/painters/shield-makers, including embroiders of coats of arms, saddlers and glaziers), *Aren* (guild of lorimers), *Stonemasons* (including the guilds of carpenters, wood-cutters, joiners, slate-roofers, plasterers for timbered-houses), *Schmiede* (smiths), *Bäcker* (bakers), *Brauer*

36 *DGMR*, p. xix. 37 Huiskes, 'Verbundbrief', p. 2. 38 For the original spelling, see Huiskes, 'Verbundbrief', pp 4–15. 39 *DGMR*, pp 157–9. 40 Becker, 'Analysis', p. 18; this problem also affects the Cologne poll-tax list of 1417: Militzer, 'Namenlisten', p. VI; Becker, 'Analysis', p. 17.

(brewers), *Gürtelmacher* (girdlers, with the guilds of leather-craftsmen, needle-makers, turners, purse-makers and glovers), *Fleischamt* (the guild of butchers), *Fischamt* (the guild of fish-merchants), *Schneider* (tailors), *Schuhmacher* (shoemakers/cordwainers, including the guilds of tanners and of the makers of wooden shoes), *Sarwörter* (armourers, including the guilds of bag-makers, swordsmiths,[41] and barbers), *Kannengießer* (tinsmiths, including the guilds of collar-makers), *Fassbinder* (barrel-makers, including the guilds of wine-taverners and wine-carriers), *Ziechenweber* (sackcloth-makers, including blanket-makers and linen-weavers).[42] As regards these names and the bracketed occupations that are also mentioned in the *Verbundbrief* some aspects are interesting: first, most of the *Gaffeln* are named after occupations but five are not: *Eisenmarkt, Schwarzenhaus*, *Windeck*, *Himmelreich* and *Aren*. Four of them are named after their *Gaffel-houses*; the origin of *Himmelreich* is unclear.[43] Second, the *Gaffeln* listed in this document only consist of craft-guilds. There are no guilds, respectively *Ämter* of merchants, mentioned within any *Gaffel*. It has to be added that the *Gaffeln* just mentioned, except for *Aren,* are the four merchant *Gaffeln*, which in fact were quite influential in overthrowing the patricians.[44]

Dublin's guilds and the city council

In Dublin, the guild of merchants was the oldest of the guilds. As noted above, the first surviving entries in the *DGMR* date back to *c.*1190 at the latest, according to Connolly and Martin.[45] However, it was not the only guild that existed in Dublin, as the *Directory of historic Dublin guilds* by Clark and Refaussé shows: including the guild of apothecaries, which was the last guild established there in 1747, there were in fact at least twenty-five trade and craft guilds in the history of Dublin, a number remarkably close to the twenty-two *Gaffeln* which were formed in Cologne in the aftermath of the events of 1396.[46] The Dublin and Cologne bodies had a common political function. The members of each *Gaffel* in Cologne could elect a certain number of

41 A *Schwertfeger* is a certain kind of swordsmith, who forges and treats swords in the latter stages of manufacture. 42 Huiskes, 'Verbundbrief', pp 16–17, 25–6. 43 Huiskes, 'Verbundbrief', p. 25. 44 Hillen, 'Kölner Gaffeln'. 45 *DGMR*, pp xiv, 109. 46 Clark and Refaussé, *Dublin guilds*, p. 43. The focus on the Dublin guild of merchants in this essay arises from the fact that when the Cologne poll-tax list was written, the Dublin guild of merchants may have been the only one existing there at the time. The guild of tailors tried to trace back its history to the time of King John but was not successful due to a lack of records to prove this: Clark and Refaussé, *Dublin guilds*, 28; Henry F. Berry, 'The merchant tailors' gild: that of St John the Baptist, Dublin, 1418–1841', *JRSAI*, 8:1 (1918), 19–61, at 19. But since the order of precedence between the different Dublin guilds in the Early Modern period was determined by the guild's individual time of foundation, it can be inferred that such records of any guild except for the merchant guild were not known in the Early Modern period. The merchant guild was the first on this list, followed by the guild of tailors and the guild of smiths, created in 1474 (Clark and Refaussé, *Dublin guilds*, pp 43, 27).

representatives to the city council.[47] When a merchant or craftsman joined one of these political unions, it was not possible to change to another *Gaffel* if they changed their occupation and thus also their guild,[48] a regulation intended to safeguard the political function of the *Gaffeln*.[49] It also demonstrates that in Cologne *Gaffeln* and *guilds*, although often used wrongly as synonyms, were practically never the same at least after 1396 when the *Verbundbrief* took effect. In Dublin, the twenty-five guilds mentioned above directly sent a certain number of members to the common council of the Dublin City Assembly.[50]

The mentioned order of precedence of the Dublin guilds, which also includes the number of members each guild sent to the common council of the City Assembly, can help us get an idea of the political and, to some extent, social status which each guild and each occupation had in the late Middle Ages. Arguably, the older a guild was, the earlier the importance of their craft and hence the desire to unite as a guild. By far the most important and influential guild in Dublin, as already outlined, was the merchant guild, which sent thirty-one members to the council.[51] In what follows, the other guilds will be mentioned in the order of precedence and including the number of members they sent to the council, listed in brackets:[52] guild of tailors, established 1418 (four); smiths, established 1474 (four); barber-surgeons, established 1446 (two); bakers, established 1478 (four); butchers, established 1559 (three); carpenters, established 1508 (three); shoemakers, established 1465 (four); saddlers, established 1558 (three); cooks, established 1444 (two); tanners, established 1688 (two); tallow-chandlers, established 1583 (two); glovers/skinners, established 1476 (two); weavers, established 1446 (three); sheerman/dyers (two);[53] goldsmiths, established 1557 (four);[54] coopers, established 1666 (two); feltmakers, established 1667 (two); cutlers, established 1670 (three); bricklayers, established 1670 (two); hosiers, established 1688 (two); curriers, established 1659 (two); brewers, established 1696 (four); joiners, established 1700 (two); and apothecaries, established 1747 (two).

Comparing the precedence of these guilds according to the time of foundation and the number of members in the council, two inconsistencies seem obvious. First, the precedence appears to be wrong. For example, the guild of barber-surgeons, third in rank and officially created in 1446, should rank before the smiths, second in order, which were created almost thirty years

47 Huiskes, 'Verbundbrief', p. 2. 48 Ibid. 49 Ibid. 50 Clark and Refaussé, *Dublin guilds*, p. 43. Also see Henry F. Berry, 'Existing records and properties of the old Dublin city guilds', *JRSAI*, 35:4 (1905), 338–41. 51 Clark and Refaussé, *Dublin guilds*, p. 43. 52 The order of precedence, including the stated number of members which each guild could send to the council, can be found at: Clark and Refaussé, *Dublin guilds*, p. 43; the guilds' foundation-dates are also provided in the same work, at pp 14–31. 53 This guild never had a charter but sent members to the council starting in 1660: Clark and Refaussé, *Dublin guilds*, p. 26. 54 Established before 1557; an earlier medieval charter was burned around this time: Clark and Refaussé, *Dublin guilds*, p. 21.

later. Since most of the guilds claimed an earlier time of foundation but were not able to give proof of it, at least by the end of the Early Modern period, from which the list of Clark and Refaussé dates, one possible explanation might be that earlier records of some of the guilds were in existence when they were introduced to the council but lost by the late eighteenth century when the order of precedence was compiled.[55] The second inconsistency that can be detected is that the official precedence does not reflect the actual political influence each guild had. Take, for example, the guild of brewers which appears in twenty-third place on the list, and yet sent four members to the council, two more than many of the guilds of higher ranking – such as the barber-surgeons who were in third place and yet were only represented on the council by two members.[56] It is worth noting, however, that most of the crafts which were later incorporated in separate guilds already existed within the guild merchant in the thirteenth century, as will be examined below.

Cologne's Gaffeln *and the city council*

The *Verbundbrief* contains a remarkably similar list, primarily not of guilds but of *Gaffeln*, including the number of members each sent to the Cologne city council from 1396 onwards.[57] Therefore it is possible to compare the political relevance of the respective crafts incorporated in the *Gaffeln* to the relevance of equivalent guilds in Dublin.[58] In Cologne, for instance, each of the four merchant *Gaffeln*, Eisenmarkt, Schwarzhaus, Windeck and Himmelreich, sent two members to the council; this adds up to eight members compared to the thirty-one members of the merchant guild who were council members in Dublin.

The other guilds are listed here in order of their position in the Verbundbrief, with the original name and number of members they sent to the council added in brackets: wool-weavers (*Wollenamt*; four);[59] goldsmiths/goldbeaters (*Goldschmiede/Goldschläger*; two); skinners (*Buntwörter*; two); signwriters/painters/shield-makers (*Schilderer*; one); lorimers (*Aren*; two); stonemasons (*Steinmetze*; one); smiths (*Schmiede*; two); bakers (*Bäcker*; one); brewers (*Brauer*; two); girdlers (*Gürtelmacher*; two); butchers (*Fleischamt*; one); fish-merchants (*Fischamt*; two); tailors (*Schneider*; one); shoemakers/

55 A similar theory was suggested by Berry in 1918: Berry, 'Merchant tailors' gild', 19. 56 According to the number of members that each guild sent to the council, the list would have to look different at the end of the Early Modern period: 1. merchants (thirty-one members), 2. tailors, smiths, bakers, shoemakers, goldsmiths, brewers (four members each), 3. butchers, carpenters, saddlers, weavers, cutlers (three members each), 4. barber-surgeons, cooks, tanners, tallow-chandlers, glovers/skinners, sheermen/dyers, coopers, feltmakers, bricklayers, hosiers, curriers, joiners, apothecaries (two members each). 57 See Huiskes, 'Verbundbrief'. 58 The number of councillors whom each *Gaffel* could send to the council is shown in: Historisches Archiv der Stadt Köln, 'Stadtrat, Stadtrecht, Bürgerfreiheit', pp 22–3. 59 The original German names here can best be found in the edition of the *Verbundbrief*: Huiskes, 'Verbundbrief', pp 16–7.

cordwainers (*Schuhmacher*; one); armourers (*Sarwörter/Harnischmacher*; one); tinsmiths (*Kannengießer*; one); barrel-makers (*Fassbinder*; one); sackcloth-makers (*Ziechenweber*; one).[60] Accordingly, the single most powerful *Gaffel* in Cologne were the wool-weavers who sent four members to the council, followed by each of the four merchant *Gaffeln* as well as the goldsmiths/goldbeaters, skinners, lorimers, smiths, brewers, girdlers and fish-merchants, each of which sent two members to the council.

A similarity between Cologne and Dublin lies in the fact that the merchants in total sent the most members to their councils. But since they were split into four *Gaffeln* in Cologne, they did not act as one group, whereas the Dublin merchant guild with its thirty-one members in the council was seemingly far more powerful than its Cologne counterparts. But it has to be added that it was not only the members directly elected by the *Gaffeln* who were sent to the city council: these councillors only made up 36 of the 49 members. Thirteen additional so-called *Gebrechsherren* ('missing men')[61] were chosen by the 36 already elected councillors to join them. They were already experienced councillors and, most importantly in this context, these 13 *Gebrechsherren*, with very few exceptions, were also merchants. Logically therefore there were not only eight, but a total of twenty or twenty-one merchants in the council of Cologne.[62] We can also see that, compared to the remaining guilds and *Gaffeln*, the smiths, goldsmiths and brewers were relatively powerful in both cities as well. The guild of weavers in Dublin, founded in 1446, sent three members to the council, which is one more than thirteen other guilds did, but its position was not as distinguished as the special position which the *Gaffel* of wool-weavers had in Cologne.[63]

Overlap of occupations in Dublin and Cologne

The question of occupations common to both the guilds and *Gaffeln* remains to be answered. Of the 171 occupations Philomena Connolly lists for the *DGMR*, seventy-three can either be directly identified in the *Verbundbrief* or they show striking similarity to the occupations listed there. For example: similar or identical with the occupations already listed above at the

60 Historisches Archiv der Stadt Köln, Stadtrat, Stadtrecht, Bürgerfreiheit, pp 22–3. **61** *gebricht* in this period means something which is missing from the full number (in this case, 49 councillors): Huiskes, 'Verbundbrief', p. 26. **62** Huiskes, 'Verbundbrief', pp 2–3; Hillen, 'Kölner Gaffeln'. **63** Clark and Refaussé, *Dublin guilds*, pp 30, 43. One point should, however, be noted here concerning the *Verbundbrief*. Although it had already taken effect in 1396, it remained in force for 400 years until the end of the eighteenth century (Huiskes, 'Verbundbrief', p. ix). Since the great majority of the Dublin guilds, to our knowledge, were only founded at the end of the Middle Ages or in the Early Modern period, they can only be interpreted as indicators of the upcoming relevance of the respective crafts around 1400. However, since the *Verbundbrief* was still in force centuries later, the comparison drawn in this essay is only valid for the late Early Modern period without the reservations mentioned.

Wollenweber-Gaffel, there is also at least one dyer, fuller, napper, parmenter, roper, teaseler, weaver or woolbeater recorded in the *DGMR*.[64] As for the listed trades in the following brackets, there are also similar findings like the ones concerning the other *Gaffeln*: *Goldschmiede* (goldbeater, goldsmith, smelter); *Buntwörter* (pelterer, skinner); *Schilderer* (gilder, painter, saddler, shield-maker); *Aren* (lorimer); *Steinmetze* (carpenter, joiner, mason, sawyer, stonecutter, thatcher, tiler, waller) *Schmiede* (axe-burner, cutler, locksmith, smith); *Bäcker* (baker, miller);[65] *Brauer* (brewer, malterer); *Gürtelmacher* (cooper, coopersmith, girdler, glover, hatter, leather-carver, leather-dresser, purse-maker, scabbard-maker, turner); *Fleischamt* (butcher); *Fischamt* (fisherman); *Schneider* (tailor); *Schuhmacher* (buckler, cordwainer, tanner); *Sarwörter* (armourer, barber, furnisher); *Zinngießer* (ewerer); *Fassbinder* (cellarer, innkeeper, taverner, vintner) and *Ziechenweber* (blanket-maker).[66]

Thirteen of the occupations mentioned in the *DGMR* are specific merchant-occupations such as linen-drapers.[67] Therefore they are occupations that might well have been represented in the four merchants-*Gaffeln* of Cologne as well. Of the other ninety-eight occupations named on Connolly's index, thirteen were square-bracketed and could not be fully identified by Connolly herself. As to the remaining eighty occupations,[68] they were usually not typical occupations of craftsmen or merchants and therefore not named in the Cologne *Verbundbrief*.[69]

Cologne's 1417 poll-tax list

Luckily other sources have survived that give more details about the occupations of the members of the *Gaffeln* of Cologne and allow us to contrast them with what we know about the people listed in the *DGMR*. When the archbishop of Cologne, Dietrich von Moers, and Duke Adolf von Berg feuded with each other before 1417, they erected bulwarks in Mülheim and Deutz, both of which are part of the city of Cologne today.[70] These bulwarks, however,

64 *DGMR*, pp 157–9. 65 Millers are associated with the *Gaffel* of bakers: Historisches Archiv der Stadt Köln, 'Stadtrat, Stadtrecht, Bürgerfreiheit', p. 22. 66 Ibid. 67 book-monger, chapman, costermonger, draper, fruiterer, haberdasher, ironmonger, linen-draper, mercer, merchant, pitcher, poulterer, vendor: *DGMR*, pp 157–9. 68 archer, bailiff, boatswain, boothwright, bowyer, burel-maker, butler, carrier, carter, chamberlain, chaplain, charcoal-burner, churl, clerk, comb-maker, cook, crocker, crossbowman, ditcher, doubler, falconer, fewterer, fletcher, forester, franklin, gabler, gardener, granger, groom, harper, hatcher, hawker, knight, larderer, latimer, lay-brother, leadbeater, lime-burner, luterer, mariner, marshal, monk, mower, mustarder, parchment-maker, pedlar, physician, plumber, porter, potter, provost, reeve, salt-measurer, saucerer, screen-maker, scrivener, sergeant, servant, sieve-maker, soap-maker, summoner, spicer, spindle-maker, squire, stabler, steersman, steward, stocker, sumpterer, surgeon, templar, tunner, turnspit, usher, waggoner, watchman, water-carrier, wheelwright, whittawyer, wimpler: *DGMR*, pp 157–9. Some of these crafts probably also existed in medieval Cologne but they could not be identified with the ones mentioned in the *Verbundbrief*. 69 It must also be added that ecclesiastical occupations were excluded from the *Gaffeln*. Huiskes, 'Verbundbrief', p. 2. 70 Militzer,

were seen as a threat to the trade of Cologne, which is why Emperor Sigismund ordered that the buildings be destroyed.[71] In order to accomplish this rapidly, the city volunteered to cover the cost of it, although this would have been the responsibility of the two parties to the feud. Financially, this demolition was a great burden for Cologne. Therefore the city introduced a poll-tax in 1417, which had to be paid by everyone in possession of a certain amount of money. Poorer citizens had to swear an oath to the effect that they were not able to pay such a tax.[72]

This *Kopfsteuerliste* or poll-tax list luckily still survives. It lists a total of 1,373 people, among which were forty-five women, subdivided into the twenty-two *Gaffeln*.[73] It is an enormously valuable source in so far as it lists, if not all, the great majority of *wealthy* people and families living in Cologne in 1417. It survived in the historical city archive of Cologne and consists of twenty folios, on which the scribe Sibert von Eilsich wrote the names of these people subdivided into their *Gaffeln*.[74] It is very beneficial for today's historians that Klaus Militzer, archivist in the city archive of Cologne, edited and published this edition. He made it possible not only to print all the names, but, using dozens of further documents, also to identify a great number of the more than one thousand persons mentioned, and in many cases he managed to add further information such as possible membership in the city council, place of residence and occupation.[75] He adjusted people's first names as they would be spelled today but kept the original writing of family names and, if listed, occupations. In cases where some people were known by different names, he added them in the list in brackets.[76] However, in some cases people were not only or not at all listed by their names, but by their occupations, probably simply to distinguish them more easily from others. These entries, for example about a baker, were like this: *Arwijn (von Gusten)*,[77] *pister zom Doym* (i.e., 'Arwijn [von Gusten], baker at the cathedral').[78]

In total there were 135 persons who had their occupation added to their entry, almost exactly ten per cent of all the names. Examining these names, we can find more detailed information about the occupations in the region of Cologne at the time. The occupations listed within the respective *Gaffeln* (in bold) are these:[79]

'Namenlisten', p. I. 71 Ibid. 72 Ibid. 73 See chart 1 in: Militzer, 'Namenlisten', p. iii. 74 Militzer, 'Namenlisten', pp x–xi. 75 Militzer, 'Namenlisten', p. xiv. 76 Militzer, 'Namenlisten', p. xiv. 77 This bracketed part of the name is not written on the list originally but was added by Militzer in his edition. 78 Militzer, 'Namenlisten', p. 160. 79The occupations are found throughout the whole poll-tax list: Militzer, 'Namenlisten', pp 1–259. However, the table of contents before p. 1 includes references to where the name-list of each *Gaffel* begins, and hence each occupation in the following passage can be quickly retraced.

Schwarzhaus: barber-surgeon (*Baitstover,* Badstüber); a dyer specializing in the colour blue (*Blaverwer*, Blaufärber); farmer (*Bouman*, Bauer); someone controlling the sale of dyer's woad (*Weytmesser,* Waidmesser); probably someone who prepared grounds for the cultivation of vines (*Weinröder*, Weinröder);

Windeck: two pharmacists (*Apotheker*, Apotheker); two coopers (*Bodenbender*, Bodenbinder);

Himmelreich: barber-surgeon (*Badstüber*, Bader); crane-master (*Cranenmeyster*, Kranmeister);

Goldsmiths: silver-smelter (*Silberschmelzer*, Silberschmelzer);

Wool-weavers: three persons smoothing and combing cloths (*Slichter*, Tuchschlichter); three cloth-cutters (*Schorre*, Tuchscherer); barber-surgeon (*Baetstover*, Bader); someone refining cloths (*zeuwer*, Tuchbereiter);

Butchers: butcher (*Beynheuwer*, Fleischer);

Tinsmiths: two tinsmiths (*Cannengiesser*, Kannengießer); two horse-collar makers (*Hamecher*, Kumtmacher);

Tailors: two tailors (*Schroder*, Schneider);

Bakers: someone controlling the grain on the market for the city (*Mudder*, Kornmüdder); thirteen bakers (*Pister*, Bäcker); a flatbread-baker (*Fladenbecker*, Fladenbäcker); three millers (*Moelner*, Müller);

Shoemakers: shoemaker for children's shoes (*Kintzschomecher*, Kinderschuhmacher); vinegar-merchant (*Essichmenger*, Essighändler); two shoemakers for wooden shoes (*Houltzschenmecher*, Holzschumacher); glassmaker (*Glaseworter*, Glasmacher); pillowmaker (*Kusmecher*, Kissenmacher);

Skinners: hatmaker (*Hoedemecher*, Hutmacher);

Signwriters/painters/shield-makers: two engravers of coats of arms (*Wapensticker*, Wappensticker); three painters (*Melre*, Maler); two glassmaker (*Glasemecher,* Glasmacher); sexton (*Offerman,* Küster); two saddle makers (*Sadelmecher, Sattler*); crossbow-maker (*Armbostmecher*, Armbrustmacher);

Bag-makers, part of armourers' ***Gaffel***: two tanners (*Conreider,* Lederbereiter); barber-surgeon (*Baitstover,* Bader); fishing rod maker (*Angelmecher,* Angelmacher); two bag makers (*Teschmecher*, Taschenmacher);

Lorimers: salt-worker (*Hallemeister*, Hallenmeister); fishing rod maker (*Angelmecher,* Angelmacher);

Smiths: kettle-smith (*Kesselsleger*, Kesselschläger); someone controlling the grain on the market for the city (*Mudder*, Kornmüdder); two axle-makers (*Assenmecher*, Achsenmacher); two scabbard-makers (*Scheydemecher*, Scheidenmacher); two drill-bit makers (*Bormecher*,

Bohrermacher); kettle-mender (*Kessilboysser,* Kesselschläger); three cutlers (*Metzmecher,* Messerschmied); blacksmith (*Hoifsmit,* Hufschmid); buckle-maker (*Rynkenmecher*, Spangenmacher); two buckle-smiths (*Rynkensmit*, Spangenschmied); scissor-smith (*Scherensmit*, Scherenschmied); two nail-smiths (*Nalesmit,* Nagelschmied); grille-maker (*Roistenmecher*, Rostenmacher); clockmaker (*Uyrclockenmecher*, Uhrenmacher); weaving-comb maker (*Kammenschirper*, Webereikammhersteller); someone crafting stirrups and similar things (*Spormecher*, Sporenmacher);

Girdlers: three turners (*Dreseler*, Drechsler); three tanners (*Conreider,* Lederbereiter); four needle-makers (*Naildemecher*, Nadelmacher); apple-merchant (*Eppilmecher,* Apfelhändler); three coppersmiths (*Kuffersleger*, Kupferschmied); barber-surgeon (*Baitstover,* Bader); purse-maker (*Budelmecher,* Beutelmacher); girdler (*Gurdelmecher,* Gürtelmacher);

Stonemasons: three carpenters (*Zymmerman/zymmerer*, Zimmermann); three stonemasons (*Stynmetzer,* Steinmetz); two chest-makers (*Kistenmecher,* Kistenmacher); candle-maker (*Kertzmecher,* Kerzenmacher);

Barrel-makers: three barrel-makers (*Vasbender,* Faßbender); some craft specializing in chests (*Kistensitzer*);[80] vinegar-merchant (*Essichmenger*, Essighändler), shooter (*Schutze*, Schütze); three wine-carriers (*Wijnschroeder*, Weinschröder).

In very few *Gaffeln* such as the fisherman's *Gaffel*, there are no occupational names within the persons listed there.[81]

It is obvious that many of these occupations, like the barber-surgeons, are mentioned within different *Gaffeln*. Three other findings can be reached. First, this study proves that there were also craftsmen who belonged to a certain *Gaffel,* although their occupation should rather have been covered within another one. Such examples are fairly rare but they did exist, as the case of the apple-merchant shows, who was on the list of the girdlers' *Gaffel*, although it might have been more fitting for him to be part of a merchant *Gaffel*.[82] Second, occupations were most probably added to the list in 1417 in order to distinguish people more easily from one another. When no occupation was added to the person's name, it is quite likely they pursued the occupations which were typical within the respective *Gaffel*. For example when listing the

80 *Kistensitzer*; this occupation could not be identified in detail: Militzer, 'Namenlisten', p. 247. 81 Although there is one person with the family name *Hamecher* and one with the family name *Trumpener*, Militzer suggests that these persons actually did not pursue these occupations but that these titles only were parts of their names: Militzer, 'Namenlisten', pp 178–84. 82 As mentioned above, this seems plausible since craftsmen or merchants could change their occupation and guild, but not their *Gaffel*.

members of the *Gaffel* of brewers, most of them were probably brewers if it does not say otherwise. Thirdly, as, for example, the different crafts in the *Gaffel* of wool-weavers show, there were already relatively specialized occupations at the time.

Accordingly, among the 135 occupations mentioned in the poll-tax list there were 63 different occupations, many of which are listed more than once. Sixteen of these occupations also appear in the *DGMR*, as a comparison with Philomena Connolly's index of occupation shows.[83] Since there are a lot of specialized and therefore rarer occupations listed on the poll-tax list, it is no surprise that most of these occupations mentioned in both sources are rather common such as millers, bakers or painters. However, twenty-five additional occupations mentioned in the poll-tax list do not appear on the *DGMR* but are quite similar to other occupations or they craft certain objects which are possibly traded by certain merchants listed on the *DGMR*.[84] The remaining twenty-two occupations could not be identified within the *DGMR*.[85]

CONCLUSION

In Cologne as well as in Dublin multiple *Gaffeln* and guilds existed, mostly uniting merchants and craftsmen of the same occupation. Since it was possible in Cologne to change one's occupation and guild, but not to change from one *Gaffel* to another, it is unsurprising that there were members of *Gaffeln* that no

83 baker, butcher, carpenter, cooper, coppersmith, cutler (blue-)dyer, girdler, miller, painter, purse maker, saddler, scabbard maker, tanner, tailor, turner. For all the occupations listed in the Guild Merchant Roll, see the 'Index of occupations' in *DGMR*, pp 157–9. The digital version of the *DGMR* also includes a digital index of occupations. By clicking on the respective original Latin occupations on this list, all the individual people named in connection with these occupations are listed on one website, which also links these listings to their original folios. See Dublin City, Dublin Guild Merchant Rolls *c.*1190–1265, Index of Occupations, in *Databases Dublin City* (https://databases.dublincity.ie/dgmr/occupations.php), accessed 17 April 2023. 84 On this list, the Cologne occupations are mentioned followed by partially similar ones from Dublin: flatbread baker, baker; barber-surgeon, barber/physician; bag maker, purse maker; blacksmith, smith; buckle smith, smith; buckle maker, smith; chest maker, joiner/carpenter; scissor smith, smith; cloth cutter, linen-draper; cloth refiner, linen-draper; someone refining cloths, linen-draper; weaving comb maker, comb maker; crossbow maker, armourer; glass maker, glass-merchant; nail smith, smith; salt worker, salt measurer; shoemaker of kid's shoes, shoemaker; shoemaker of wooden shoes, shoemaker; shooter, archer; silver-smelter, smelter; stonemason, stonecutter; vinegar-merchant, merchant; someone preparing grounds for planting vine, vintner; wine carrier, water carrier. 85 axle maker, barrel maker, chest maker, *Kistensitzer* (as noted above, some craft specializing in chests), clockmaker, coats of arms engraver, (horse-)collar maker, someone controlling corn, crane master, drill-bit maker, farmer, fishing rod maker, grille maker, hat maker, kettle mender, kettle smith, needle maker, pharmacist, pillow maker, sexton, stirrups maker, tinsmith, dyer's woad controller.

longer practised the crafts after which the *Gaffeln* were named. Something the Dublin guilds and the Cologne *Gaffeln* had in common was their political function. Each of them could send a certain number of members to the respective city council. In both Dublin and Cologne the *Gaffeln* or guilds of smiths and goldsmiths were relatively powerful compared to others. The politically most influential groups in both cities, however, were the guilds and *Gaffeln* of merchants. In Dublin the merchant guild sent 31 members to the common council, making up almost a third of its members. In Cologne there were 20 or 21 merchants among the 49 members of the city council: each of the four merchant *Gaffeln* sent two members to the council and in addition to these there were 12 or 13 *Gebrechsherren* who almost always consisted of merchants, as demonstrated above. The single most influential *Gaffel* in Cologne was the *Gaffel* of the wool-weavers.

In the second part of this essay, the analysis of the poll-tax list enabled us to go beyond just mentioning occupations within the 1396 *Verbundbrief*, and to have a closer look at 135 individual Cologne citizens named together with their occupation. Among these 135 people there are sixty-three different occupations, sixteen of which also appear on the *DGMR*. Twenty-five others of these occupations do not directly appear in the *DGMR*'s index but they are very similar to other crafts listed there or to objects of trade which are indirectly indicated by specialized trade occupations mentioned in the *DGMR*. The remaining twenty-two occupations included in the poll-tax list could not be identified in the *DGMR*. But since there is a total of 171 occupations mentioned in the *DGMR*, as listed above, there also remains a considerable number of crafts and specialized merchant occupations there which cannot be identified in the two sources for Cologne. This shows that the *DGMR*, although up to 227 years older than the Cologne poll-tax list, and although Dublin was not even half as populous as Cologne at the time, already lists almost two-thirds of the occupations that could be identified in Cologne centuries later. This demonstrates that the *DGMR* is an immensely valuable source for the study of medieval occupations, even more so in comparison to other medieval European sources like the Cologne poll-tax list of 1417.

Purposeful or a parade? Riding the Franchises in Dublin's history

SHEA BRENNAN

Recalling, in 1826, memories of his boyhood in Dublin, the actor and dramatist John O'Keeffe (1747–1833) describes the 'grand triennial sight called the Franchises', a procession in which the trades of Dublin, alongside the mayor and the corporation and citizens, walk and ride in a splendour of pageants, numbering many thousands of people to undertake the perambulation of the city.[1] The trades of the city, distinct and meticulously organized, each represent themselves through grandiose displays, such as the smiths who had a 'grand high phaeton, in which sat the most beautiful young girl that could be found, as Venus', and the vintners who had 'Bacchus, dressed in ivy and vine leaves', perched on a wine casket, followed by a procession of mythical creatures.[2] His memory was of such a spectacle that all of Europe would flock to Dublin to see it (for the full account, see Appendix 7 below).[3]

This picture is a far cry from the earliest accounts of Dublin's ancient tradition of perambulation, known as the Riding of the Franchises, where the good men of Dublin were expected to physically trod the boundaries of the city in a formal legal procedure. The *Calendar of ancient records of Dublin* recounts in detail the Ridings of 1488, 1603 and 1767, showing a civil ritual with both ceremonial and practical purposes.[4] By chronologically surveying these descriptions, alongside unofficial accounts of the Ridings, this essay analyses how the procedure and purpose of the Riding of the Franchises changed throughout its lifetime. It argues that although the Riding of the Franchises started with both explicit ceremonial and practical purposes, over the course of the centuries it ultimately began to lose its practical purpose, culminating in its existence primarily as a civic ceremonial ritual in the nineteenth century.

At its most fundamental level, the Riding of the Franchises is an example of the medieval practice of perambulation. Perambulation acted as an 'ocular demonstration of where the boundaries ran' in any given town or indeed any potentially contested parcel of ground.[5] The purpose of these geographical boundaries, and of their articulation, was to establish the precise area in which the legal rights of jurisdiction, whether that be a city or, for example, a property-owning church, would be enjoyed.[6] The 1192 charter of liberties

1 John O'Keeffe, *Recollections of the life of John O'Keeffe*, vol. 1 (London, 1826), pp 38–42. 2 Ibid. 3 Ibid., p. 43. 4 *CARD*, vols i–xviii. 5 Lennox Barrow, 'Riding the Franchises', *DHR*, 33 (1979–80), 135. 6 Allegra Di Bonaventura, 'Beating the bounds: property and perambulation in Early New England', *Yale Journal of Law & the Humanities*, 19:2 (2007),

granted to Dublin by its then lord, the future King John, first established Dublin's practice of perambulation, granting to the citizens of Dublin the right to have 'their boundaries as they were perambulated' under oath by upright men of the city (see Appendix 1).[7] The charter provides a preliminary outline of Dublin's original city bounds and proceeds to list the franchises, or rights, within such bounds. Although the charter makes no explicit reference to the practice of the Riding, it is an important starting point nonetheless because, as later discussed, the geographical bounds it establishes act as a guide for future Ridings. Its use for early boundary disputes also sets a precedent for the way in which this charter, and subsequent city boundary settings through perambulation, will have practical legal purposes. For example, in 1319, when deciding in which court to settle an inheritance dispute, the 'charter of King John and its ratifications by his successors' was produced to prove that the property lay within Dublin's liberties and so should be tried in the Dublin courts, thus showing the charter's practical uses.[8]

EARLY PERAMBULATIONS: THIRTEENTH TO FIFTEENTH CENTURIES

In the thirteenth and fourteenth centuries, the first and only actual mention of a perambulation occurring comes with a writ of Edward II, issued in 1324, after Dublin's mayor complained about certain religious institutions overstepping their land boundaries.[9] This followed a dispute between the city of Dublin and the abbeys of St Thomas and St Mary over the jurisdiction of their coroners, as a result of which ongoing boundary disputes the king's writ instructed the empanelling of a jury to 'perambulate the city and declare its boundaries'.[10] The *Calendar* prints the outcome of these proceedings in full (see Appendix 1), giving a detailed description of what the 1326 city boundaries would have been, but does not talk to the procedure of the perambulation other than by the jury established for that singular purpose. Once again, however, although the Riding is not explicitly referenced here, this incident is key in establishing perambulation's early role in Dublin as a practical tool for determining the city's geographical boundaries to be used in a legal setting; indeed, the record blatantly declares that the perambulation was ordered by jurors 'with the object of giving a verdict in the most secure form'.

The first explicit mentions of a practice known as the Riding of the Franchises appear to come in the fifteenth century, including a detailed account of the 1488 Riding. As far as I have been able to determine, the first mention comes in a 1455 memorandum:

117–18. 7 *CARD*, i, pp 2; Clarke, *Dublin, Pt 1* (IHTA), p. 31. 8 *CARD*, i, pp 147–8. 9 *CARD*, i, pp 155–8; see here an account of the boundary disputes discussed in the whole paragraph, as well as the account of the 1326 boundaries. The boundaries are very similar to the 1192 charter, although more detailed. 10 *CARD*, i, p. 156.

> Also, hyt was ordeyned yn the sayd semble that the Mayre and the Baylyffes and comynes schold ryd the franches of the sayd cytte, the <...> aftyr feste of Trynyte Sunday, etc., then nexte folowyng, etc.[11]

It is not, however, until the 1488 account that the actual physical procedure for Riding the Franchises begins to materialize. The text of the proceedings was originally transcribed into the White Book of Christ Church,[12] and occurred during the mayoralty of Thomas Meyler in September 1488.[13] The description gives insights into both the potential ceremonial and the more practical aspects of the Riding (see Appendix 3).

Certain aspects of the 1488 account indicate that, to some extent, the Riding of the Franchises was partially done with ceremonial purpose following and a traditional procedure. This is most apparent near the end of the account in a conversation between the riders and an abbot of St Mary's, where, upon being enjoined by the abbot not to do him wrong, the riders respond that they 'wold nothynge do but lyke as ther fore fadres enformed and taght them how they shold ride ther fraunches'.[14] This indicates that there was a set tradition regarding how the franchises should be ridden, and that the procedure was handed down generationally. There were likely practical uses to having a set procedure as well, but if the pure purpose was for practical reasons in setting the necessary bounds, it seems only *where* they rode and not *how* they rode would matter. Another portion of the Riding that seems partially ceremonial is the spear-casting to set a maritime city boundary in the Irish Sea. It is described how at low tide, a young man named William Walsh rode south as far as possible 'and caste a spere in to the see' as far as he could, and so 'extendith the franches of the said cite'.[15] Once again, although there would have been practical reasons for wanting to establish a clear aquatic city boundary, this procedure appears to be more for ceremonial purposes due to its seeming ineffectiveness: William threw the spear at low tide, thereby extending deeper into the water than if he had thrown at full tide but, of course, when the tide returned the spear would simply be washed away. Even if the spear held, a single point would be ineffective for creating a miles-long sea boundary.

On the other hand, the 1488 account implies throughout that the Riding of the Franchises was an overwhelmingly practical ritual. This is mainly seen through the commitment to rigidly following the original city boundaries as documented in the 1192 charter. For example, when the group comes across landmarks that have changed since the twelfth century, they indicate in the account things such as 'as the chartyre makethe mencyonn where the gallowse

11 Ibid., i, p. 285. Similar mentions occur in 1457 (p. 294). 12 Lennox Barrow, 'The franchises of Dublin', *DHR* 36 (1982–3), 68–9. 13 Representative Church Body Library, MS C/6/1.2, fos 65–6; *CARD*, i, pp 492–6; H.J. Lawlor, 'A calendar of the Liber Niger and Liber Albus of Christ Church, Dublin', *PRIA* 27C (1908–9), 1–93, at 33–5; Clarke, *Dublin, Pt 1* (IHTA), pp 31–2. 14 *CARD*, i, p. 495. 15 *CARD*, i, p. 493.

was of old tyme'.[16] The meticulous following of the original text establishes the Riding as a practical procedure, specifically in light of how dedicated the riders are to following its boundaries. Throughout the perambulation, the riding party seemingly crushes and tramples through multiple houses that are on the city lines. For example, at one point the entire throng go 'throw the strete southward till they came to William Englysh is hous, and so throw that house' they went.[17] Considering that William Englyshe is noted to be a bailiff of Dublin at the beginning of the account, it would seem extreme that the party would crush a high-ranking citizen of Dublin's house for a ceremonial procession. Later in the ride, they also made one man climb through the window of a barn with a ladder to put a stone on the floor, thus marking the separation of the city's franchises from those of the liberty of the priory of Holy Trinity at Christ Church.[18] Considering, therefore, the earlier legal uses of the charter's boundaries, as well as the extreme actions of the riders, it would seem that the perambulation fulfilled important practical purposes for the city.

The Riding of the Franchises also appears to be important beyond ceremonial purposes due to the conflict it causes, or brings to a head, between the mayor and the abbot of St Mary's at its end, when the latter returns to scold the party, saying that 'they did hym wrong, for they shold have ridden be west the Abbey, and so forth to the see'.[19] The mayor disagrees, reiterating the correctness of his own path. Although nothing more is written on the conflict, it seems there would be no point in the record relating this dispute if the Riding did not have practical legal implications: it goes without saying that it would be unnecessary for the abbot to feel wronged and threatened, and to confront the mayor in the manner he did, if the issue was simply a matter of a parade taking a wrong turn.

THE MIDDLE YEARS: SIXTEENTH AND SEVENTEENTH CENTURIES

For whatever reason, the record is relatively sparse regarding the Riding of the Franchises for almost the next hundred years until repeated orders for the franchises to be ridden again start appearing. In 1574, a memorandum declared that the 'fraunches and liberties of this citie shalbe rydden about and vywed of the Maior and citizens' the following August, or else there would be a fine to pay.[20] This sentiment is reiterated over the course of the next few years, with the 1588 order even stating:

16 *CARD*, i, pp 194–5. 17 *CARD*, i, p. 493. 18 *CARD*, i, p. 495. 19 *CARD*, i, p. 496. 20 *CARD*, ii, p. 93.

> That forasmoche as the fraunches of this cittie have not of long time ben rydden, to the great danger that the liberties therof for want of ryding and perambulation the same, the citties rights are lycke to be extinguished,[21]

Eventually, the Riding of the Franchises did return, the next confirmed Riding occurring in 1596. This rebirth of the procedure is particularly noteworthy because, during the course of this Riding, a tailor named Rychard Benet made repeated efforts using 'all the meanes he might to hinder the fraunches', leading to his subsequent disenfranchisement and exclusion from the city.[22] That the record notes the city to be in danger for lack of Riding the Franchises, and that a citizen not only tried to hinder the procedure but lost the freedom of the city for doing so, once again points to the earlier franchises as retaining importance beyond the ceremonial.

It seems necessary here to touch also on the question of why the Riding of the Franchises was not performed if it was such an important procedure, such that its absence left even the city's liberties at risk. Lennox Barrow writes that 'the reluctance of mayors to perform the Riding was partly on account of the expense, which was sometimes, but not always it seems, reimbursed by the Assembly'.[23] In light of later discussions pertaining to the expenses of the procession and its surrounding dangers, this certainly seems likely. He also posits that it could have been due to the riding parties' fear of obstruction. As mentioned, there was the 1596 incident, but another situation is recorded from 1692. Here, as the Lord Mayor, Michael Mitchell, and company

> were rideing the franchises of the citty of Dublin, our sword, according to antient custome, was passing in the hand of an officer under one of the arches of the Bow Bridge [at Kilmainham], near to which Bridge, on the north side of it, stood a man whose name is Isaac Davys … who … threatened the officer that if he came through that arch he would beat out his braines, and endeavoured soe to doe by throwing stones at him.[24]

What was happening was an objection to permitting the mayor and commonalty from entering and passing through the grounds of the new hospital at Kilmainham because this stood on the site of the earlier liberty and priory of the knights hospitaller of St John. Chaos ensued and ultimately city troops were called to fetch the mayor and break up the mobs. One of those later charged in connection with the confrontation, a Captain Sankey submitted before the Assembly, stating that he was told by long-time servants

21 *CARD*, ii, p. 188. See other orders in 1577 (p. 118), in 1580 (p. 150), in 1587 (p. 209) and in 1596 (p. 299). 22 *CARD*, ii, p. 299. 23 Barrow, 'Franchises of Dublin', 69. 24 *CARD*, vi, pp 14–21. See here for full 1692 account.

of the hospital that the mayor's 'sword ought not to come within the walls, nor pass through the field of the said Hospitall'.[25] Viewed from this perspective, it is perhaps understandable why the mayor might face opposition in trying to complete the Riding of the Franchises. But the episode again reminds us that the Riding – controversial enough to elicit an armed response from those who do not agree with how it is being executed – remained a serious business.

Stepping back slightly, the most extensive account of the Riding of the Franchises exists from 1603, ridden by the then mayor John Terrell and three hundred companions (see Appendix 4).[26] In many ways this important account is similar to the 1488 description, although it includes some new ceremonial features.[27] For example, throughout the account, there are multiple references to trumpets guiding the party, giving it the aura of a grander procession rather than just a legal riding party. There is also the mention of a 'Swoordberrer', who rode at the front of the group next to the mayor.[28] The sword-bearer would have been carrying one of the mayor's Great Swords of Dublin, a relic of immense symbolic authority.[29] Unlike the 1488 Riding, when the party comes to the barn straddling the city's and priory's franchises, the mayor now simply has the sword-bearer thrust his sword through the window to symbolize the line of the franchise.[30] Here we see the slow process in which certain parts of the Riding are overtaken by symbolism and ceremony, showing a stark contrast from the Riding's original procedural rigorousness. The 1603 account also explicitly describes how, throughout the ride, the party stopped, and citizens met 'the Maior, and welcomed him and his company, and made them drincke'.[31] This fact alone, participants stopping for drinks along the route, indicates that the Riding is becoming closer to a parade rather than a practical legal process for determining a strict demarcation of the city's boundaries.

Another difference from the 1488 account is seen in the treatment of houses. Although quite a few are still trampled, it is also specified that one or more others are spared as 'they would loathly break downe' the house of Sir Thomas Fitz William', instead opting to 'ride a lytetell besydes it'.[32] This is a marked change from the treatment of William Englyshe. This change in the treatment of the houses of Dublin's high-ranking men indicates that, as time moved on, the meticulous application of the procedure of the Riding broke down. This might show that the strict visualization of Dublin's boundaries in the form of a perambulation is no longer necessary as a practical means of determining and reiterating the city's boundaries.

25 *CARD*, vi, p. 20. **26** *CARD*, i, p. 191. See pp 190–8 for the full 1603 account. **27** See Barrow, 'Franchises of Dublin', for a lengthy account of the geographical boundary changes evident in known accounts of the Riding. **28** *CARD*, i, p. 194. **29** Claude Blair and Ida Delamar, 'The Dublin civil swords', *PRIA*, 88C (1988), 96. See here for discussions of swords in the Riding of the Franchises. **30** *CARD*, i, p. 197. **31** *CARD*, i, p. 193. **32** *CARD*, i, p. 192.

Another subtle difference is seen in the section of the Riding where the party casts a spear into the sea to determine Dublin's water boundary. The spear is now cast by one of the water bailiffs.[33] This is interesting since, in subsequent accounts, the mayor himself eventually undertook the job of casting the spear, showing a progression where this portion of the Riding became increasingly ceremonial with the task bestowed upon a titled individual.[34] If it were being used strictly for practical purposes, the party would likely have wanted the strongest or fittest individual to cast the spear, as they could extend the boundary the farthest. Allowing elected public officials to cast the spear turns it into something altogether more ceremonial.

From 1612 to 1710, there was a consistent Riding of the Franchises every three years, as documented in the *Calendar*.[35] This seems a potential consequence of a 1606 order, that explicitly threatens to fine Mayor Bellewes (from 1598), Mayor Handcockes (from 1601), and Mayor Robert Balls (from 1605) ten pounds for failing to ride the franchises during their terms.[36] It also established that the franchises are subsequently to be ridden in the month of September, with 'paine of ten poundes to every one that make defaulte'.[37] It is also notable that, within this time, there are multiple calls for permanent visible barriers to be erected along the boundaries of the franchises. In 1624, and again in 1633, the assembly is petitioned that 'according to auncient custome the fraunches weere to be perambulated, wherein many obstacles may incur, chieflie in obscure and doubtfull [places to which the said] fraunches extend, and therefore praied that certaine permanent markes might be [set up in such places] whereby the true meares may be apparantlie manifest in future time'.[38] This was never done, as seen by the repeated calls for boundary markers, but it is noteworthy in showing how the city had concerns that citizens might not be able to distinguish its exact boundaries.[39] Again, this adds to our understanding of the Riding as not solely a ceremony, but an important practical procedure meant to mark the boundaries of Dublin, given that mayors might be fined for its deferral. However, the need for physical bounds is also possibly indicative of the fact that the Riding is beginning to lose its ability to adequately mark the city bounds. If the Riding itself was sufficient to alert people to the boundaries, there would be no need for physical markers, a possible reason for the changes it undergoes in the generations that followed.

33 *CARD*, i, p. 191. 34 Sir Jonah Barrington, *Personal sketches of his own times*, vol. 1 (London, 1827), pp 260–1. 35 *CARD*, i, pp 264–5. 36 *CARD*, ii, p. 463. See *CARD*, ii, pp 321, 375, 443 for the mayor terms. 37 *CARD*, ii, p. 463. 38 *CARD*, iii, p. 176. 39 *CARD*, iii, p. 276.

CENTURIES OF CHANGE: EIGHTEENTH AND NINETEENTH CENTURIES

Evidence for traditional-style Riding continues to exist throughout much of the eighteenth century. In 1731, for instance, Captain John Vernon gave a speech deriding the lord mayor for encroaching on his property at Clontarf during the Riding, accusing him of destroying old charters and 'riding these pretended Franchises' to claim for the city greater liberties than actually existed.[40] Likewise, in 1753, the city compensated a lessee on St Stephen's Green for the riders trampling his property, and there are records from the period from 1782 to 1800 of the Assembly approving reimbursements for the lord mayor's expenses in undertaking the Riding, and presumably therefore performing a public role akin to that of his predecessors over many generation.[41]

But the eighteenth and nineteenth centuries also brought major changes to how the Riding of the Franchises was executed and by whom, specifically with the entrance into the proceedings of the trade guilds (sometimes known as corporations) and its transition as a result into a grand public parade. In 1743, and reiterated in 1752, there was an order from the city that all guilds must participate fully in the procession, lest they want to be fined anywhere between ten and thirty pounds.[42] This insistence on the guilds taking part is at odds with what we find by 1785 when an order was issued preventing the trades from accompanying the lord mayor in perambulating the city due to the 'general dissipation among the lower class of people' it causes, as well as general injury. This would suggest a shift in attitudes that occurs toward the Riding, some Dubliners seemingly becoming disillusioned by the event as a result of the rowdiness to which it had given rise.[43]

The entrance of the guilds into the Riding of the Franchises, however, seems to coincide with its full-blown transition into a public parade. The last lengthy description of the Riding tells of the 1767 event and is accompanied by a poem, artfully describing the procession of the trades (Appendix 5), in a manner similar to O'Keeffe's noted above (see also Appendix 7).[44] The 1767 account is different from the 1488 and 1603 descriptions, as it offers little picture of what the riders actively did in the course of the ride. It does not tell of either the casting of the spear into the sea or the sword-thrusting into the barn. The poem however does include some similar details such as how the

40 John Vernon, *Dublin August 6, 1731. This day captain john vernon opposed the lord mayor on Riding the Franchises of the city of Dublin, at their attempting to enter on his mannor of Clontarf in the county of Dublin, at large, and made the following speech* (Dublin: Printed by George Faulkner, on Essex Street, 1731). No page numbers, occurs in the fourth paragraph. 41 Barrow, 'Franchises of Dublin', 71. 42 *CARD*, ix, pp 106–7 for the 1743 account. See x, pp 30–2 for 1752. 43 *CARD*, xiii, p. 422. 44 *CARD*, xi, pp 489–95.

riders 'fall to drink' at the end of the procession, aligning with the 1603 accounts, that the Riding itself had a festive environment.[45] In his memory of the Riding, Sir Jonah Barrington (Appendix 8) praises the beauty of the trade procession but also speaks to the eventual decline of the event, the reason for which he cites as an unwillingness to incur the expense. Now, instead, the lord mayor and 'a dozen dirty constables' privately perambulate the city, taking away from its purported purpose which was to be an 'an object of great attraction and pride to the inhabitants' of Dublin.[46] For Barrington, the Riding was a ceremony of civic pride, less focused on perambulation but rather on spurring the city's spirit and industry.[47]

It was therefore in the early part of the nineteenth century that the demise of the Riding of the Franchises took place. Barrow states that there are existing nineteenth-century references to three Ridings, in 1818, 1821 and 1827.[48] Another outsider account exists from 1815 in Watty Cox's *Irish Magazine*, in which the writer expresses shock upon seeing a 'cloud of horsemen, galloping' during the Riding (Appendix 6).[49] Although technically anonymous the piece was probably written by the controversial Cox himself, who makes clear his disdain for the city officials, calling them a 'very criminal masquerade' and mocking that the city officials are 'assuming a military appearance', which is beyond the rank of their positions.[50] Despite the bias of the account, it sheds some light on a few important late aspects of the Riding. For one thing, the description of the party as wearing military costumes reminds us of the Riding's ceremonial nature. Also noteworthy is that as the viewer begins to follow the party, he describes how it would stop and purport to hold a court, where citizens could come forward to settle debts with the city; except, they never stayed in one place long enough to do this, and it was mainly for show.[51] Once again, this shows a lack of practical purpose in the performance of the ceremony of the Riding.

Barrow ultimately contends that the Riding of the Franchises 'died with the reform of the corporation in 1841', bringing to an end the 649-year story (if we trace it back to John's 1192 charter of liberties) of the perambulation of Dublin.[52] Starting as a predominantly practical procedure with some ceremonial aspects, with the entrance of the guilds into the process in the eighteenth century, the Riding of the Franchises ultimately ended largely as a public ceremonial procession. The study of the Riding provides an interesting perspective on how civil rituals change over time, as well as how attitudes towards them shift and vary.

45 *CARD*, xi, p. 495. 46 Barrington, *Personal sketches*, pp 265–6. See 260–6 for whole account. 47 Ibid. 48 Barrow, 'Franchises of Dublin', p. 71. 49 'Account of the late franchise rode by the lord mayor and corporation', *Irish Magazine, and Monthly Asylum for Neglected Biography*, 8 (1815), 410. 50 Ibid. 51 Ibid., 411. 52 Barrow, 'Franchises of Dublin', 71.

APPENDIX 1: JOHN'S CHARTER OF LIBERTIES, 1192

John, lord of Ireland, count of Mortain, to all his vassals and friends, French and English, Irish and Welsh, present and future, sends greetings.

Know that I have given and conceded and by this my charter have confirmed to my citizens of Dublin, both outside the walls and inside the walls, dwelling as far as the boundaries of the town, that they shall have their boundaries as they were perambulated by the oath of upright men of the city itself at the command of King H[enry], my father:

that is to say, from the eastern part of Dublin and the southern part of the pasture that extends as far as the gate of St Kevin's church, and thus along the road as far as Kilmerecaregan, and so by the boundary of the land from Donnybrook to the Dodder, and from the Dodder all the way to the sea, namely, to Clarade near the sea, and from Clarade as far as Renuvielan; and in the western part of Dublin from St Patrick's church through the valley as far as Dolphin's Barn, and thence as far as the boundary of the land of Kilmainham, and beyond the water of Kilmainham near the River Liffey as far as the fords of Kylmehauoc, and across the water of the River Liffey towards the north through Dunocnegauhoc, and then as far as the barns of Holy Trinity, and from those barns as far as the gallows, and so by the boundary between Clonliffe and Crinan as far as the Tolka, and then all the way to the church of St Mary of Ostmanby; and that they shall have all the liberties and free customs set down in writing.

APPENDIX 2: PERAMBULATION OF THE CITY BOUNDS, 1326[53]

Common Pleas at Dublin, before Thomas Fitz John, earl of Kildare, justiciary of Ireland, within the octave of St Hilary, 1326–7.

By writ at Cowyk, 2 August 1324, under the great seal of England, Edward II notifies to his justiciary in Ireland, or his deputy there, that the Mayor and commonalty of Dublin have represented to him that under charters from his progenitors they hold the city of Dublin and its liberties within boundaries specified in those instruments; that members of religious orders and others have acquired, in fee, lands, tenements and rents within the city boundaries since the promulgation of the Statute of Mortmain [1279], and have without royal licence encroached on the citizens, to their great prejudice, detriment and damage.

The King desires to be fully informed as to the grounds for these complaints, commands inquisition to be made on them, and the result to be certified to him with the seals of the justiciary and of the jurors.

Under this writ the Mayor and commonalty of Dublin complain that the prior of the church of the Holy Trinity, Dublin, and the abbot of the house there of St Thomas the Martyr, have acquired and usurped lands and tenements within the city and its boundaries. Jurors are duly impanelled, and, with the object of giving a verdict in the most secure form, they perambulate the city and declare its boundaries to be as follow:

53 *CARD*, i, pp 156–8.

On the eastern side of Dublin and on the south side: the pasture which extends as far as St Kevin's gate and so by the way as far as Kilmerecaregan and by the boundary of the land of Dovenachbrok [Donnybrook] as far as Dodir [Dodder]. And from Dodir as far as the sea at Clarade3 near the sea. And from Clarade [Poolbeg] as far as Rennyvelan. And from the gate of St Kevin's church, by the way towards the north, so far as the stone cross ['Butter cross'] where the old market was formerly, towards the west. Thence by the lane near the church of the Holy Sepulchre, going towards the north so far as an old lane, closed up, near the common of the vicars of St Patrick's church extending as far as the street of that church.

On the western side of Dublin: from St Patrick's church by the middle of the valley so far as the pond of the house of St Thomas the Martyr, leaving the south gate of Weycesthame and the Coulane towards the north on the right hand, and so equally by the centre of that pond. From the pond through the middle of the meadow extending so far as the field called the Irendam towards the north. From the Irendamme so far as the cross at Kylmaynan, going by the boundaries of the land of Kylmaynan. From that cross by the boundaries of the land of Kylmaynan, so far as the ford called Tirelesford, and from that ford between the land of the church of the Holy Trinity at Dublin and the land of Kylmaynan so far as the water of Avenlyf [Liffey]. Thence near that water so far as the ford of Kylmehanoc, and beyond the water of Avenlyf towards the north by Ennocnegannoc, going into the meadow extending towards the west as far as the King's highway which goes towards Cobragh [Cabra] of Dublin. Thence so far as the barns of the Holy Trinity, and from those granaries by the ditch called le Rugh dich so far as the King's highway leading from Fynglas to the city, leaving the ditch on the left hand side. From the King's highway so far as the water of Glascoynok and the hill towards the north where the old gibbet stood. Thence by the middle of the water of Glascoynok so far as the King's highway which leads from the city of Dublin towards Sauntref [Santry] and beyond that way so far as the ditch of the land of Clonlyf [Clonliffe], and by that ditch so far as the Green on the north side of the abbey of the Blessed Virgin Mary at Dublin. Thence between the Green and the ditch so far as the middle of the King's highway from Oustmanton so far as Tulghan by the middle way of the town of Ballyboght so far as the old causeway of the old mill, leaving the abbey and the land of Crinan on the right hand towards the south, and the ditch and that causeway on the left hand towards the north. Thence by the water of Avenlyf so far as St Mary's abbey of Oustmaneby.

The jurors also find that the prior and convent of the church of the Holy Trinity, Dublin, have, during forty years, occupied and usurped upon the Ostmans' Green thirty perches of land on both sides of the old corn mill, worth by the year three halfpence, to the damage of five shillings to the citizens of Dublin.

APPENDIX 3: 'CONCERNING THE METES AND BOUNDS OF THE FRANCHISE OF THE CITY OF DUBLIN', 1488[54]

Memorandum: that Thomas Meylere beynge maire of the citte of Dulyn', Wylliam Englyshe and Robert Boys, bailiffis of the seid citte, withe the aldirmen and comenys, did ryde the fraunches of the forseid citte the fourthe day of September, the yere of the reigne of Kynge Herry the VIIth the iiijth.

In primis: the seid mayre and his bre theme toke ther way, in the name of God, first, owte at the Dammys Gate and so forthe by the Longe Stone of The Stayn' levynge Al Hallous onn ther right hand, and so by Ampanlyffy [River Liffey] is side tylle they came to the Rynges Ende, and from that to Clare Rade, in Englysh the clere rode for shippis, whiche is now called Pole Begge; and fromm that to Remelan', now called the Bar Fote, and so estward vpponn the strone [strand] onn the southe side asfer as a mann moght ride, and caste a spere in to the see; and thenn a yemann named William Walshe rode in to the watyr and keste a spere in to the se at lowe watyr as fere as he moghte, and so ferre extendith the fraunches of the seid cite estward in both sides of the watyr.

And then they rydde backward tylle they came to the Blak Stone be este Myrrionge and fefte Mirryonge onn ther righte hand, and ridde onn a mere westward tylle they came to Our Lady Welle, and so straight onn the seid mere tylle they came by the gate of Smothiscourte, and so about the grene and over the ford of Dannabroke, and lefte the towne and the churche onn ther lyft hand, and so forthe throw the hy wey tylle they came to Kylmagergan' be hy wey is syde, and so forth the streyght wey tille they came to Seynt Kevynesgate, and from that northward vnto the lane that the cros of stone ys in, and be cause the dyche of that lane was faste, they brake a shard and put menn over the dyche, and went throw the lane to the hy wey be este Seynt Pulchris, and so lefte Seynt Pulcrys and alle Seynte Patrikkes Close onn ther lyfte hand tilte they came tylle an old lane runynge faste to the northe side of the chauntor is orchard or hagard place, and throw an orchard that sumtyme belonged to Thomas Suetirby, and so throw the gardynes tylle they came to ann hous be north the hous that John Artoure sumtyme dwelled ynn, and throw that hous in to the street, and so throw the strete southward tylle they came to William Englyshe is hous, and so throw that hous and over the roffe of an other hous, and throw the gardynes tylle they came to The Couimbe, and owte at the Couombe Gate tille they came to the Cowe Lane, and so forthe fromm that to Carnaclonngymothe, that is by Dolfynesberne.

And thenn they turned bakward by the Irnedamm and left it onn ther right hand, as menn rideth to the cros dyche in the lane as ye goeth fromm Dulyn' to Kylmaynan', and so downe tylle they came to the Bowbrige, and throw an arche of the same brige and so throw the watyr of Camoke, but for the moste ayse the[y] rid onn the priour of Crychurches landes tylle they came in to ann acre of Gargetes medues, and left that acre be southe themm.

And thenn they ridde over the watir of Camoke westwarde, for to that place came the watyr of Ampanlyffy in old tyme, and so forth westward levynge the tyllynge land of Kylmaynan' onn ther lyfte hand and parte of the medue onn ther right hand, tylle

54 *CARD*, i, pp pp 492–6; Clarke, *Dublin, Pt 1* (IHTA), pp 31–2.

they kame to the narowest place of the medue, and ther lyethe by the tillyng land a dyche of smale thornes and breres. And then they rid northward in and throw the watyr of Ampanlyffy to the west end of Elynn Hore is medue, for that is caled the ford of Kylmahennoke, for the hylle that is now called the hille of Isoldes Fante of old tyme was called Kylmahenokes Hylle. Ant [sic] at the fote of that hylle be north the west ende of EIynn Horres medue ther is a bushe in the slade by the hye way, and ther they staied and taried and came alle togaddyr and toke ther councelle.

And they said that ther was ann acre benorth Elynn Hoore is medue that shold be comeynn, of the whiche the priour of Kylmaynan' receveth the rente. And so sum of them rid over the northe side of that acre, and sum over the south syde and met to gadyr in the Gibbett Slade, and lefte Knoknecaoke (in the chartre wryttynn and now called Hennok Makenok) onn ther right hand, and so straght to the priour of Crichurche is lessowe [pasture land] be north the gallows and throw the lessow, and lefte the Erbere and parte of the tyllynge land onn ther ryght hand, and so went straght throw the lessow to Sharpis parke and throw aparte of that parke, and so into the hye wey.

And when they came in to the hye wey, they turned northward throw the same wey tylle they came agayns the priour of Crychurch is berne, and so over Russelis parke tylle they came to the bernes end, and thenn the priour made a wey for them in to the berne, and made put vp a laddyr to a wyndow at the west ende of the berne. And John Savage, cittezaynn, and Richard Whyte, one of the mase bererez to the mayre, was send [sic] by the mayre and his bretherne to trye how the francheis went. And they put a mann throw the wyndow onn a laddyr in to the berne flore, and ther lyethe a stone in the myddis of the flore be twix both the franches of the towne and the priors francheis, and so fromm that stone estward over the old kylle, and so estward throw the orchardes of Crychurch vnto the gardynes of the grene, levynge the gardynes onn ther right hand and the tyllynge land onn ther lyfte hand, and so straght to the hy wey that goth vnto Glasnevyng', and so owt of that (as the chartyre makethe mencyonn where the gallowse was of old tyme) be twix the abbote of Seynt Mary Abbay is land onn the este side and the priour of Crichurchis landes onn the west side. And ther the abbott and his covente mett with them and praied them that they wold do them no wronge, and they seid they wold nothynge do but lyke as ther fore fadres enformed and taght them how they shold ride ther fraunches.

And thenn they rode northward vpponn the mere to GIaskoynok, and so forthe over the hie wey that goeth to Drysshok, and lefte the stone welle onn ther lifte hand, and so forthe sowhte ward tylle they came in to the hye wey that goth to Ballyboght, and bi the gate of Blliboght to the watir of Tulkan' by the brige of Balliboght, and over that watir, and so by that watir southestward as fer as they moght ride tille they came to the see, and then they turned abak westward onn the watresside of Ampanlyffy tille they came to Seynt Mary Abbay, and left the abbay onn ther right hand, and be west the abbay onn the watrres side ther lieth a stone, and ther the abbot and his monkes met them agayne. And the abbott said that they did hym wronge, for they shold haue riddynn bewest the abbay and so forthe to the see. And the maire and his bretheme said: "Nay, for by our boke when we did retorne bakward fromm the Tulkan' we shold haue rid to Our Lady Churche of Ostmanneby".

And so they departed, and every mann went home to ther logynge, and thus the maire and his bretherne made an end of ther ridynge of the fraunchese, the day and yere before said, etc.

APPENDIX 4: RECORD OF THE RIDING OF THE FRANCHISES OF THE CITY OF DUBLIN, 1603[55]

The Ryding of the Fraunecheses and Liberties of the Citty of Dublin, according to the auncient custome, and lately perambulated in the yeare of Sir John Terrell's maioralty, viz.: –

First, in the name of God, the Mayor, Sheryfes, Recorder and Aldermen, accompanied with the number of three hundred horse, and above, of the cittizens, tooke their way out at the Dame's Gate, torning presently betwixte the Dame's Mylls and the citty walls, and soe to the ryver syde of Annelyffy, riding directly eastward by the water-side to the Ringe's end, and from thens eastward to Clarade, otherwyse called the Cleare Roade, and now called Poole Begge, and from thens to Ranielean, nowe called the Barr Foote, whear the trompett sounding the company came togeather, and, according [to] the auncient usadge, Richard FitzSimons, one of the Waterbayleyfes, was called uppon and commaunded to ryde as farr into the sea eastward from thens as he could, being then loe water, and thens to cast a speare as far as he could into the sea, which he did, and soe farr extendeth the francheses of the sowth syde of the river and harborowe of Dublin.

Then they bent their course sowthwards, as directly as they could, to the blacke stone, nowe called the Blacke Rocke, opposyte against the place whear the Sheryfes of Dublin doe keape courte uppon the land on the west syde of the Newto[w]n of the Strone [Strand]; wher the trompett sounding, the company againe came togeather and rode westward all the highe waie to the chappell of Merryon; whear the trompett againe sounding, the company came togeather and consulted of their righte passadge ther; and it was agreed that they should ryde uppon a green mear, leaving an acre of land betwixte them and the chapple of Merryon on the sowth syde of the chappell; which acre was then said to be of the land of Raboe.

And so rode westward for a small space to the end of that mear, and then turned northward to the sowth-west corner of the orchard diche of Merryon, through which corner the elder [fathers] of the citty said that of ould tyme they did ryde. And now for that the same was soe strongly fensed with trees and thornes, which, in favor of the gentleman of the house of Merryon [Sir Thomas Fitz William], being the citty tenant, they would loathly breake downe, they rode a lyttell besydes it, upon the left hand throughe the nexte end of a meddowe, and then turnid on their right hand to a diche of blacke sally and hathornes, by which they rode westward, leaving that diche on their right hand till they came to our Lady[s] well, whear they stoode, and the trompett sownded, and from thens downe a short meire north-west to the meddowe, under that; and soe over the meddowe to a faier broad meare norwest of that, and alongest uppon

55 *CARD*, i, pp 190–8.

that meare to the gate of Smothe's Courte, and then tornid to the sowth-easte syde of the green of Smothe's Courte, ryding close by the arrable land alongest that green to the Read Shard; and soe sowthward to the uttermost parte of that green nexte to the land of Raboe; arid then tornid west uppon the myll pound of Donabrooke in the water of Dodder.

And, for that the water was soe deepe ther as it was not passable, they turned for a lyttell space northward, alongest and through the myll pound uppon the land of Donalbrooke; and then tornid sowthward by the myll pound upon the land of Donabrooke, soe farr as it went neer the bridge of Clonskeyghe; and then tornid west uppon the just meare of Donabrooke deviding the lands of Donalbrooke and Mylton [Milltown]; and soe keapte on upon the uttermost meare of Donabrooke, leaving all the land therof within them uppon their righte hand, alongst by the highe waye syde leading to Dublin, till they came to the farthest mear of the land of Donabrooke, in the west syde; and then turnid norward to a meddowe; halfe wherof is of the land of Donabrooke, and past throughe the myddest of that meddowe north-east to the east-south-east corner of a parcell of land called Kilmakeregan nexte adjoyninge to the highe waie leading from Donabrooke to Dublin; and then they turned bake, west-north-west, aboute that land of Kilmakeregan, leaving it upon the right hand betwixte them and the said high way, and rode out into the high way aforesaid at a shard uppon the west corner of the said Kilmakeregan, and rode alongest that high way to St Stephin's green, and tooke the sowth syde of the green <damaged> syde, to St Kevin's Gate, and torned in the lane norward, tyll they came to the east end of the Butter lane, which was broken, and they entred therat; and in that lane lyeth an ould crosse of stone, and it was said that that crosse was called the Butter Crosse, for that in ould tyme the provision of butter that came from the marches and Tooles' country [co. Wicklow] to Dublin was sould ther.

And then they rode to the west end of the lane that leadeth from St Kevin's street by east St Pulcher's [Sepulchre's] and through that lane, leavinge St Pulcher's and St Patrick's close uppon the left hand and west syde of them till they came to an ould lane next on the sowth syde of the poore house lately buylte by Mr Richard Rouncell, Alderman, and on the sowth syde of the Chauntors orchard, that by old records was called Thomas Suetterby his orchard; and ther the Maior and meny of his company lighted, for that the Puddell under that orchard was not passable by horse, and the rest rode about St Kevin's street to the Coumbe, to meet the Maior; and the Maior, Sheryfes, Recordour, Aldermen, with the Swoord-berrer and divers others, through that gardin passed over the Puddell uppon plancks in two severall places, and soe through the gardins, wherin parte of the neighbors ther dwelling mett the Maior, and welcomed him and his company, and made them drincke.

And then they passed through a house nexte on the north syde of a great house named Dowdall's house, and somtyme before that of old tyme wherin one John Arthore dwelt, and soe in to the street, and soe sowthward through the street to the farther syde of the street, and in at a house calid of old tyme William Englysh his house, which is on the sowth syde of the newe house buylte by Sir Thomas le Strandge [Le Strange], knighte, and Margrett le Strandge, alias Bath, his wyfe, and through Englysh his house to the gardin therof, and then turnid uppon their lefte hand sowthward through the gardins of all the houses that way; in one garding wherof it was said and soe fownde ther lay a great stone in ground, shewing the franches in that parte and in the farthest gardin southward to <damaged> betwixt the Cowme to the Freeman's Stone standing in the street; and ther the Maior tooke horse, and rode alongst throughe the Coumbe near the houses, through Washames gate to the myll pound on the sowth syde of the smale gate, at the west end of the Cowmbe leading into St Thomas Courte, over which pound, at theast end of the meddow just against the myddest therof, called the Abbot's meddowe, ther wear planck s putt over by Sir Edward Brabson's people for the Maior and his company to passe, over which the Maior and Swoordberrer, with many others of the company, rode through the meddowe, and in the mydst of that meddowe was a great ould haihorne bonding the franches, which was lately cutt, but, the roote and stocke lefte.

And then they rode through that meddowe to the west end therof and out at a shard that was made for them into the highe way; and then tornid sowthward to the other highe waye leading from Cromlyn to St Patrick's, and so, alongst that highe way westward to Carnoclohoyunaghe, that is by Dolphin's barne, and from thence somewhate more westward to the north syde of that highe way, wher ther was a shard broken uppon the diche, and upon asmale plott of pasture ther caulid Talbot's land.

And they rode through that westward <damaged> the northward to the great leasure [pasture land] called the Iron Damme, leaving it on theire righte hand, ryding compase-wyse to a smale lane then stopped uppe with diches, which nowe wear broken downe uppon the north syde of the said Iron Damme, which lane is above a paier of butts leingth by west another lane or high way, on the north syd of the Iron Damme, leading to Kilmaynehame, and soe throughe that smale lane directly northward to the highe waye leading from Kilmainehame to Dublin, and over that highe waye northward to a blind and a stype [steep] lane betwixte the closes, called by some of the elders ther the Murdring Lane, and downe that lane to the water of Camocke and under the west arch of the bridge called Bowe Bridge, and tornid uppon the left hand under the high grownd of Kilmainehame to a deepe forde ther, wher it was said the Annlyffe came of ould tyme, albeit they mighte ryde farther northward, but for that the water in that place wher they should pass over was not passable with horse, they rode over and through the nexte foord to the bridge, and soe to the great meddowe of Christchurch.

Upon the west end of which meddowe neer to the water of Camocke ther wear pitched severall tents for the Mayor, Sheryfes and the corporacions, and ther the Mayor and his company lighted and dyned, and after dynner tooke boate, himselfe and the Recordour, Sheriffes and Aldermen, the Swoordeberrer, the Clearke reeding the record, and others of the Commens, and past over the water of Cammocke, the horse goeing aboute, and went betwixte the arrable land, called nowe the Leis [pasture land] of Kilmaynehame, and the meddowe under that, and soe directly westward to that parte of the meddowe that lyeth opposite uppon that parte of the hill called Kilmahennockes hill, and nowe the hill of Isold's font, which is a bowshot of the west syde of Isold's font, and west of Ellen Hoare's meddowe, over which font is a great hathome tree, and in that parte of the meddowe of Kilmainehame, the Maior, Swoordberer and others tooke boate and passed upp the water of Aunlyffe, neer Kilmaineham bridg, wher was said was a foorde called Kilmahenockes foord, and then tooke horse and rode eastward over and by north Isold's font, and to the font itselfe, and then rode to the slade by north-west; the west end of Ellen Hore's meddowe, and in and throughe that slade northward, wher was saide of ould tyme was a buyshe of hathorue, and soe to the toppe of the hill, wher they stayed and advysed themselves whear to goe.

And then it was moved that they should ryde on the great meare or way on the north syde of an acre of arrable land on the height of the hill over the north syde of Ellen Hore's meddowe, which acre is parcell of the Newton [New town] of Kilmainehame, and said then, and soe found by auncient record, to be common; throughe which way or broade meare on the north syde of that acre they rode east and then north-east, leaving Knockmakaok, now called Hennocke Magynnocke, of the right hand, and into the gybbett slade [green sward], and soe uppe against the hill in the common pathwaye to the north-west end of the lessoe betwixte the arrable land of Grandge Gorman, called the Prior of Christechurches lessoue, and soe alongest that lessoe, leaving the Earber hill [Arbour hill] on the righte hand to and by northe Sharp's parke, and soe into the Stony bater or highe waye, and from thence to the buysh of the Lyttle Cabraghe, as a memory that the Lyttell Cabraghe and the land thereof is within the franches of Dublin, aboute which land they would have rydden, but that the daie was farr spent.

And then rode backe againe the same way till they came over against Sir Henry Harrington, knighte, his house of Grange Gorman, in tymes past called the Prior of Christe Church his barne, and broke a shard [gap] uppon the west end of a parke called Russell's parke, and through that parke to the west end of a voyde ground whear the ould barne was, in the floer of which barne was a stone shewing the franches, and throughe that grownd to the west end of an other house in ould tyme called the ould Kill, on the west end of which throughe a windowe the Maior caused the Swoordberrer to sett in the Kinges swoord, for that in favour of the said Sir Henrye being a freeman of Dublin they would not have broken a greter passadge, which they mighte; and from thence into the said Sir Henry his hall, in which hall at the sowth end of the chymny ther is a houle or bowell in the stone wall, and ther it was said the swoord should come throughe, and Sir Henry his people made a banquett to the Maior, and, that done, the swoord was putt out at the east wyndowe of the hall, and so throughe the garding directly easteward through the orchards at the north end of the gardings belonging to the houses of Oxmanton Green, and then over two closes or partes into the high waye leading from Dublin to Glasnevin, and then turnid northward to Glascoynoke, which is in the slade, and from thens turnid eastward at the foote of the arrable land to the place called the Ould Galloes, and from thens directly norward uppon a green mear to the north end of the said mear and then turnid eastward directly leadinge betwixte some parkes inclosed of the left hand and the arrable land on the right hand.

And soe to the high way leadinge from Dublin to Dryshoke, and in the said highe way turnid a lytell southward to a parke whear throughe a sharde they passed to a well called the stone well, leavinge it on the left hand, and from thens directly sowth-east to the highe waye, leadinge to Ballyboughte; and soe rode alongest that waye over the hill cauled [forrians?] hill on the north [and partly damaged gully] over the water of Tolchan [Tolka] to and alongest the high waye from Dublin to Clonetarfe, and soe to the furlonge of Clontarfe, and farther mighte yf they would; for the ould records say that their franches stretcheth eastward uppon the north syde of the channell as far as they mighte to the sea, and then from the furlonge to the Iland of Clontarfe, and soe by the river of Anlyffe alongest westward to and without the sowth syde of tlie stone wall of St Marye Abbaye, betwixte it and the river, and soe through the Abbay lane to the street of Oxmanton; and then, for orders sake, they rode in good order over the bridge and about the citty the longest waye till they came to the Maior's dore, where every one, blyssing the Kinge's Majestie, tooke leave of the Maior and parted to their houses.

APPENDIX 5: SURVEY OF THE LIBERTIES AND FRANCHISES OF THE CITY OF DUBLIN, 1767[56]

The whole order and procession of the twenty-five Corporations, with a survey of the Liberties and Franchises of the City of Dublin; as they are to be ridden and perambulated on Tuesday the 4th of August, 1767, by the Lord Mayor, Aldermen, Sheriffs, Commons, and Guilds, with the Masters' and Wardens' names and places of abode; also, the various Colours in each worn Cockade.

Order of procession

I. Merchants, or Holy Trinity Guild, blue and yellow. Richard French, Blind quay, Henry Hart, Eustace street, masters. John Booker, Essex bridge, William Coats, Bagnio slip, wardens.

II. Tailors, or Guild of Saint John Baptist, saxon blue and white. Abraham Loe, Merchants' quay, master. Abraham Creighton, Big Ship street, David Bacon, Trinity lane, worders.

III. Smiths, or Guild of Saint Loy, black and white. William Osbrey, Dame street, master. Richard Nix, Dame street, John Sheen, Dame street, wardens.

IV. Barber-Surgeons, or Guild of Saint Mary Magdalen, purple, cherry and white. Alexander Ross, Blind quay, master. Edmund Chapman, Smithfield, T. Mitchell, wardens.

V. Bakers, or Guild of Saint Anne, orange, cherry and lemon. William Beasley, Marrowbone lane, master. Caleb Smalley, senior, George's lane, warden.

VI. Butchers, or Guild of the Blessed Virgin Mary, red and white. Gust. Wild, Channel row, master. Edward Rice, Fleet street, John Brazell, George Hamilton, New market, wardens.

VII. Carpenters, Millers, Masons, Healers, Turners, and Plumbers, of the Fraternity of the Blessed Virgin Mary and House of Saint Thomas, Dublin, red and white. Richard Cranfield, Hog Hill, master. William Stokes, Clare street, John Morgan, Chequer lane, wardens.

VIII. Shoemakers, or Guild of Saint Michael, Archangel, red, blue, and green. Edward Clark, Capel street, John Sherwood, Cut-purse row, masters. William Sleavin, Crane lane, James McCleary, High street, wardens.

IX. Saddlers, Upholders, Coach and Coach harness makers, or Guild of the Blessed Virgin Mary, crimson, while, and green. William McCready, Bride street, master. Humphrey Curtin, Mary street, John Hale, George's lane, wardens.

56 *CARD*, xi, pp 489–95.

X. Cooks, or Guild of Saint James, Apostle, orange and black. Joseph Watson, Ormond market, master. Paul Presley, Dame street, Terence Sherridan, Sussex street, wardens.

XI. Tanners, blue, white, and yellow. Samuel Henderson, New row, on the Poddle, master. Samuel Nesfield, T. Miller, James's street, W. Vicars, Crooked staff, wardens.

XII. Tallow Chandlers, or Guild of Saint George, blue and sky colour. John Shandly, Pimlico, master. Robert Ferran, Coombe, William Kinsolows, Cole alley, wardens.

XIII. Glovers and Skinners, or Guild of Saint Mary, green and brick colour. T. Tudor, Blind quay, master. J. Brooks, Palmer's row, T. Barrow, Patrick street, wardens.

XIV. Weavers, or Guild of Saints Philip and James, orange and blue. William Worthington, Vicar street, master, J. Wiseheart, Corn market, J. Lynch, wardens.

XV. Sheermen and Dyers, or Guild of Saint Nicholas, blue and white. Benjamin Houghton, Ash street, master. T. Houston, Francis street, Stephen Mara, Coombe, wardens.

XVI. Goldsmiths, or Guild of All Saints, red, yellow, and white. W. Wilme, Hoey's court, master. R. Williams, Castle street, J. Frederick Sherwin and Benjamin Wilson, Skinner row, wardens.

XVII. Coopers, or Guild of Saint Patrick, white and green. J Lane, Anglesea street, master. R. Servant, George's lane, David Hollister, Kennedy's lane, wardens.

XVIII. Feltmakere or Hatters, white hats with sky colour. J. Brady, Meath street, master. Alexander Tate, Temple Bar, N. Tomkins, Church street, wardens.

XIX. Cutlers, Painters, Paper Stainers, Printers, and Stationers, or Guild of Saint Luke, Evangelist, crimson, lemon, and sky blue. John Exshaw, Dame street, master. Sampson Silvester, Castle market, Patrick Wall, Arran quay, wardens.

XX. Bricklayers and Plasterers, or Guild of Saint Bartholomew, blue and orange. Edward Gill, Dorset street, master. Thomas Walsh, Moore lane, John Kennedy, Lazers hill, wardens.

XXI. Hosiers, or Guild of Saint George, white, blue, and. copper colour. Charles Grollier, Castle street, master. J. Carmichael, Castle street, Stephen Malone, Coombe, wardens.

XXII. Curriers, yellow, red, and black. Richard Ginn, Back lane, master. James Hill, Patrick street, Arthur Ord, Nicholas gate, wardens.

XXIII. rewers and Maltsters, or Guild of Saint Andrew, buff colour and blue. Arthur Guinness, James's gate, master. Forbes Jones, Ferry boat slip, Thomas Andrews, New row on the Poddle, wardens.

XXIV. Joiners, Ceilers, and Wainscoters, green, yellow, and white. William Adair, Fleet street, master. William Jones, Charles street, J. Wright, Mary's Abbey, wardens.

XXV. Apothecaries, or Guild of Saint Luke, Evangelist, purple and orange. Edward Caddy, Smock alley, master. J. Pentland, Church Street, J. Crampton, Dame street, wardens.

A survey of the city liberties, 1767

Beginning at the Custom-house, you go down to survey Essex-street, Temple-bar, and to the East End of Lazer's-hill. From thence across the Strand to Ringsend. From thence to the Water-mark, where the Dart is thrown. From thence to the * Black-rock. From thence Westward to a Red-house on the East-side of *Merrion. From thence thro' the Garden on the back of the said House, and across the Fields to Simon's-court. From thence across the Fields into the Road to Bray. From thence Southward along the said Road to two little Cabbins on the South-side thereof. From thence across the Fields into the Road to Clanskeagh opposite a Mill on the River of Donnybrook. From thence along the said Road to the Bridge of Clanskeagh, and under the Eastmost Arch thereof. From thence to the Mill of Clanskeagh, and thro' said Mill. From thence to a Lane called Clanskeagh-lane, and along the said Lane to Milltown-road. From thence Northward to Mr. Roberts's House in said Road. From thence thro' Mr. Roberts's House and Garden across the Fields to Donnybrook Road near a little Cabbin on the Right-hand thereof. From thence Northward along Donnybrook Road to the House with the Sign of the Curran-tree, on the West-side of said Road. From thence by the South-end of the said House, thro' the Garden and across the Fields by the back of Mr. Leeson's, to the Corner-house of Khevan's-port, on the East-side thereof, and thro' the said House. From thence by the West-side of Khevan's-port to Big Butter-lane. From thence thro' Big Butter-lane to Bride-street. From thence along Bride-street to Bull-alley. From thence down Bull-alley to Counsellor Swift's House, and thro' the said House and Garden into Patrick-street. From thence to the House with the Sign of King William and Queen Mary, on the West-side of said Street. From thence along the Coomb, by the Water-course to Crooked-staff. From thence over the Wall the Left-hand of Crooked-staff, between the Willow-trees, and along the Water-course into the Road to Dolphin' s-barn. From thence by the Water-course to the * Malt-house at the West-end of Dolphin's-barn, including the said Malt-house and Garden West-ward of it. From thence Northward across the Fields, and thro' the Garden and Red-house at the North-end of * Cut-throat-lane. From thence to Bow-bridge, and under the middlemost Arch of said Bridge. From thence into the Hospital-fields over the old Deer-park Wall, near the old Slaughter-house. From thence thro' the Hospital-fields and across the Liffey-strand to the round Stone near the * Deer-park-wall. From thence over the Deer-park-wall and thro' the Park to a Corner of the Wall near the Dog-kennel on the North-side thereof. From thence over the Wall Northward by the said wall, to the first half-round or rising on the said wall. From thence Eastward thro' Mr. Brownlow's Fields, and several Gardens to Stony-batter, by Mr. Addison's House, on the South End thereof. From thence thro' the House with the Sign of the Half-moon on the East-side of Stony-batter and Gardens, to Colonel Stanley's, and thro' said House to * Grange-gorman-lane. From thence by the South-end of the House with the Sign of the Half-moon on the East-side of Grange-gorman-lane, and thro' the Gardens into Finglass Road. From thence Northward to the * Broad-stone. From thence thro' the Water-course under the stone and thro' the Gardens into * Drumcondra Road. From thence Southward to a little Cabbin at a Wall in * the Garden, on the East-side of the Road. From thence thro' the Gardens to the Sign of the Coach and Horses in Ballybough-lane. From thence North-ward along Ballybough-lane to Ballybough-bridge. From thence across the River on the West-side of the

Bridge, and along the Strand-side to Clontarif. From thence unto the Shades of Clontarff. From thence to the Mill of Raheny. From thence farther Northward 130 Perches to a * little Brook, which is the End of the Liberties of the City of DUBLIN.

[Note. Where this * is, there a Court is called.]

Anon., Poem (printed by B. Corcoran, Inns Quay, Dublin, 1767)

THOU mighty Sol, who in the East ascend,/ Thy beams display, and all thy glories lend,
Now mount thy chariot, drive each cloud away,/ And bright Aurora usher in this day.
Next Neptune, god and ruler of the main,/ Let not the clouds exhale one drop of rain,
Then will each Hero, at the night's approach,/ Come home with dry cockades without a coach.
And now the glorious Cavalcade's begun,/ Ye Muses open all your Helicon,
Inspire my verse, and assist my song,/ While I relate how each troop moves along.

The **City Praetor** [Lord Mayor], mounted on a steed,/ With ribbons drest, leads on the cavalcade,
Before his Lordship, with a solemn grace,/ They bear the **sword of justice** and the **mace** [sword- and mace-bearers],
His gown of richest scarlet in his hand,/ Majestical he holds the powerful wand,
In awful pomp and state, on either side,/ The City **sheriffs** in like triumph, ride,
Attended by a band, whose gripping paw,/ Poor debtors dread, and keep them still in awe.

Next march the **Guild** [merchants], who plow the frothy main,/ In depth of winter for the hopes of gain,
To distant climates our beef and wool convey,/ And barter wholesome food for silk and tea;
Fearless of rocks, they seek the unknown shore,/ And bring from thence the glit'ring, tempting ore.

The cross-legg'd **Taylors** next in order go,/ Who, by their arts, trim others for this show,
All other arts acknowledge and confess,/ They're grac'd by them in ev'ry gaudy dress,
As well the peasant as the cringing beau,/ Must from the Taylor to fair Silvia go;
No wonder then those Taylors march so gay,/ Since from all others thus they bear the sway.

Next march the **Smiths**, men bravely us'd to fire,/ Without whose aid all arts must soon expire,
Before them, clad in armour in his pride /A brawny Vulcan doth in triumph ride.

Next come the **Barbers**, who can soon repair /Nature's defects, and lend the bald with hair,
Suit all complections, and with little pains,/ Supply the skull with wigs that lacketh brains.

Next comes the well-**bred men** [bakers], who know the way/ To please the ladies in their bread at tea,
And with their white, their wheaten, and their brown,/ Can please the palate of the lord or clown.

Next march the **Butchers**, men inur'd to toil,/ Their brawny limbs, like champions, shine with oil,
Murder and slaughter, knocking in the head,/ Are their delight, the trade to which they're bred.

Next march the **Carpenters**, whose arms can rend,/ The lofty pines, and make proud elms to bend.

Next do the **Shoe-makers** in order go,/ And their dragoons do make a stately show,
Since the wide hoop exposes to the view,/ The well-shaped leg, silk stockings, red-heel'd shoe.

Next march the **Saddlers**, glorious to behold,/ On sprightly beasts, their saddles shine with gold;
A warklike steed most proudly walks before,/ Richly attir'd, led by a Black-a-moor.

Next march the **Cooks**, who study day and night,/ With costly fare to please the appetite;

With these the **Vintners** ride, did they refine,/ As much as they adulterate the wine,
Their every muse would gladly sound,/ And with what pleasure would the glass go round.

Next march the **Tanners**, fam'd in days of yore,/ For tanning hides for shields which heroes bore;
Who has not heard of Ajax's seven-fold shield./ Which neither to the sword nor shield would yield;
And wont you as much admire, as much adore,/ The tanner's hand, as his the buckler bore.

Next march the **Tallow-chandlers**, who expel,/ With cheerful lights, shades from the darkest cell,
Enthusiasts of inward light may boast,/ But these are they, illuminate the most.

Next march the **Glovers**, who, with nicest care,/ Provide white kid for the new-married pair;
Or nicely stitch the lemon-colour'd glove,/ For hand of beau to go and see his love.

The **Weavers** next, in order proudly ride,/ Who with great skill the nimble shuttle guide;
Pity such art should meet such small reward,/ But what art, now-a-days, does meet regard.

Sheermen and **Dyers** next in order come,/ Men who depend entirely on the loom;
The weaver finds employment for them both,/ One gives the colour, 'tother finds the cloath.

Next march the **Goldsmiths** who can form and mould,/ In sundry shapes and forms, the ductile gold;
Men call them traytors, rebels, and what not,/ Nor king, nor queen they spare, all goes to pot;
No pity meets, in the devouring fire,/ Monarchs, and chamber-pots, and rings expire.

Then come the jolly **Coopers**, who confine,/ In casks well bound with hoops, the sparkling wine.

Next march the **Hatters**, once a gainful trade,/ When men wore finest beavers on their heads,
But now, least weight of that the curl should harm,/ Beaux strut along with beaver under arm.

Next **Printers, Stationers, Cutlers, Painters** appear,/ Three men in shields their arms before them bear. And printing-press to show that art so rare.

Next march the **Bricklayers**, by whose hands arise,/ Hibernia's towers, whose top salutes the skies.

The **Stocking-Weavers** next in order come, / Who form the scarlet stocking in the loom,
With clock of gold or silver nicely wrought, / Each step fair Chloe takes, a lover's caught.

Next march the **Curriers**, who both cut and pare, /The hides for saddlers or shoe-maker.

The **Brewers** next well mounted doth appear, / These are the men brew humming ale and beer.

The skilful **Joyners** next in order come, / Whose chairs and tables furnish out the room,
A man in white proceeds the gallant train, /Whose ample shoulders a huge pole sustain.

See, where the proud **Apothecaries** drive, /Who most by fraud and impositions thrive,
Whose monstrous bills immoderate wealth procure, / For drugs that kill as many as they cure,
Well are they plac'd the last of all the rout, For they're the men we best can live without.

In order thus they ride the city round, / View all the limits, and observe each bound,
Then homeward steer their course without delay, /And fall to drink, the business of the day,
Next morning send their horse and coutrements away.

APPENDIX 6: 'ACCOUNT OF THE LATE FRANCHISE RODE BY THE LORD MAYOR AND CORPORATION', 1815[57]

As I was slowly turning the corner house which joins the North-strand, and the new street at the custom-house stores, on Saturday 21st of August, my astonishment cannot be described, when a cloud of horsemen, gallopping with great rapidity, attracted my eyes. Among the foremost I first distinguished John Claudius Beresford, he was dressed in black with a large military hat which also distinguished his companions, the haste they appeared in, the military costume of their heads, and the abrupt manner of our meeting, with the coincidence of the frightful neighbourhood of the riding-house, so appalled me, that I really imagined the days of terror were not passed away, though seventeen years had elapsed...

Immediately I recollected that the day was dedicated to the triennial visitation, which the lord mayor and corporation are bound to make to ascertain or preserve the boundary lines of the city. Still I could not intirely shake away the fright which seised me, nor forbear blaming the very criminal masquerade which the gentlemen appeared in, and the impropriety of a set of corporation folk, assuming a military appearance. What the devil, said I, had the office of pump boarer to the pipe-water board, to do with defence, that requires Mr Coffey to dress like a general officer, his duty and office would be better expressed by an auger, or a pick-axe. Sheriff Harty, the hosier, would be more in character with a legboard to his side instead of a sword. Sim's, the barber, picketting a louse on his comb; Farrel, city auctioneer; with a woman's shift in one hand and hammer in the other; Jack Willis, the breeches maker, instead of the long hat would look more characteristic by peeping through the thigh of Doctor Duigenan's small clothes; Taafe, the cake-man, and clerk to the pipe-water office, shooting gingerbread nuts through the cylinders of the metal main...

While my imagination was thus dressing the rabble, I ventured to follow the procession, to witness the concluding part of the Drama. They stopped at the Rotunda, to hold a court as the custom was in early times. The crier called out in a loud voice, "hear ye, hear ye, all manner of persons who having complaints to make to the Right Hon. John Claudius Beresford our lord mayor, come forth and they shall be heard – God save the king". This was repeated three times. This business was foreseen by many persons in the neighbourhood, particularly the several poor people to whom were due, several small sums by the estate of Mr Beresford, previous to his bankruptcy. The communication of the holding of this court was made by some wag, who contrived to have it circulated that the invitation to be made by the crier, was to settle the small debts due by his lordship. The crowd of poor huxtermen, butchers, bakers and others, exhibiting their several accounts, and their disappointment at the short duration of the court, which sat not longer than while the crier was repeating his lesson, was so great, that were the gentlemen not very quick in retiring from the scene, it would be difficult to restrain the poor sufferers from vengeance on the masqueraders.

From this troublesome quarter they galloped to the old custom-house where another mock court was held, and as the custom they crier called out. "Sir Michael

57 'Account of the late franchise rode by the lord mayor and corporation', *Irish Magazine, and Monthly Asylum for Neglected Biography*, 8 (1815), 410.

Creagh, attend and restore the chain and regalia". This was repeated three times. Sir Michael took no notice of the court. This Sir Michael, was another bankrupt lord mayor, in the days of Charles the II, who ran away with the gold chain and the other part of the the regalia ; and it is the duty of the corporation to call upon Sir Michael every three years to return what he stole. He must be as dead as King Charles, or as poor as John Claudius, or he would not be so long without settling.

The day concluded with a station dinner at the Mansion-house, to which every person in office, of every guild, had access; they all got drunk, as usual, and every man took as much of the wines and broken meat away as his hat, pockets and breeches could contain. Poor Mary Nagginlaw, and other corporation ladies, were entertained at home, as far as the industry or sobriety of their several husbands enabled them to secure the spoil.

APPENDIX 7:

John O'Keeffe, *Recollections of the life of John O'Keeffe*, vol. 1, 1826[58]

In my boyhood and youth I often saw the grand triennial sight called the Franchises. The first view of it made a great impression on my mind: I was seated in the front window of my cousin Kavanagh's house in Thomas-street, and saw the procession pass close under me. It consisted of the riding and walking of the trades of Dublin (there called Corporations). The whole were first assembled and marshalled in the great square of Stephen's Green, and from thence in order commenced their perambulations of the city. Many of the trades were remarkable for the splendour of their pageants, as most persons of rank who had handsome equipages and fine horses and trappings lent them for this day's cavalcade.

The printers had a large splendid open carriage, in which was a printing press, the compositors setting types, and the men working off impressions, which, as fast as they printed, they flung to the populace in the streets: this was a description of the whole procession, masters, wardens, colours, &c., and a *finely-written* explanatory poem.

The smiths had a grand high phaeton, in which sat the most beautiful young girl that could be found, as Venus; at the corners were Cupids and Loves and the Graces, and so forth; and Vulcan in armour rode by her side. The carriage of the weavers was also very handsome: the men wore wigs of wool of different colours. The millers and bakers had men dressed up in wheat sheaves. The masons and carpenters, all the emblems of masonry, with Solomon's Temple, &c. The curriers were represented by men appareled in skins, with large grotesque masks, and great wooden falchions, which they flourished about. The chandlers were remarkably fine for horses, dress, and accoutrements: their insignia was a dove, and their motto "Let your light so shine".

The hosiers had in their carriage the stocking-loom, and a man really weaving stockings, and at the corners of the carriage young women at their wheels, spinning silk, flax, and cotton. The goldsmiths, glass-makers, jewellers, carvers and gilders, had

58 John O'Keeffe, *Recollections of the life of John O'Keeffe,* vol. 1 (London, 1826), pp 38–42.

each their sumptuous pageant expressive of their trade. The linen weavers had in their vehicle a loom, at which they were employed in weaving as they rode along: young women were spinning, and a youth dressed as a collegian, *en badinage*, breaking their threads, &c. The shoemakers displayed a prince and princess – Crispin and Crispiana – dressed in gold and silver robes, and crowns, with two little pages carrying between them a crimson velvet cushion, and on it a gold slipper. The vintners had Bacchus, dressed in ivy and vine leaves, astride upon a tun, with a bowl of wine in his two hands, drinking to the health of the people; and a number of bacchanals, Silenus, fauns, and satyrs, following him.

The upholsterers were headed by a man dressed all in feathers: he was called the Feather-man, and, from his arch gambols and comic attitudes, was the great delight of the crowd. It became a saying to anything of high humour, "Oh, this beats the Feather-man!". The Guild, or corporation of merchants, were all in uniform, and rode remarkably fine horses of their own. Each trade had a band of music, and its own appropriate tune; so that as one party was passing you by, the particular air was heard at a distance, proclaiming the approach of the next.

The cavalcade and procession consisted of many thousand persons, all arranged with strict decorum in their proper places. Each corporation had its masters, wardens, and beadles, dressed and equipped in full paraphernalia. The Lord Mayor, Aldermen, &c. made part of the show. When they reached the end of the North Wall, the Lord Mayor and his attendants got into a barge, and were rowed out into the bay, and at a particular station, he stood up, and with all his force threw a dart from him into the sea, as far as he could: where the dart fell, a buoy was fixed, and as far as that, his warrant, as Lord Mayor of the city, reached, extending to every vessel within that buoy.

In what is called the Earl of Meath's Liberty, the Lord Mayor of Dublin has no jurisdiction, this quarter of the town having a court of its own. This Liberty consists of some of the largest, finest, and richest streets in Dublin; for instance, Meath-street, Francis-street, and the Coombie. In the latter was the Weavers' Hall: over the gate a pedestrian gilt statue, as large as life, of George the Second.

The Lord Mayor walked the boundaries, his sword-bearer before him; but when arrived at the point where the Liberty begins, he was met by a certain chosen number of people, who stopped his progress, and in a kind of seeming scuffle took the sword from the sword-bearer: if not thus prevented, and the Lord Mayor permitted to go on, wherever he went, with his sword of office borne before him, the power of his warrant would reach; but this ceremony is done without the least riot or ill-will, being part of the business previously well prepared.

All this affair took place in one day, the first of August, every third year. To this grand triennial festival people flocked to Dublin from all parts of Ireland, England, Scotland, and even from the Continent: it was always looked to with great joy. The Regatta at Venice was something in this way.

Many years after I wrote a piece, and had it brought out at Crow-street, for the express purpose of introducing the procession, and beautiful pageantry of our Dublin franchises.

APPENDIX 8:

Sir Jonah Barrington, *Personal sketches of his own times*, vol. 1, 1827

One of the customs of Dublin which prevailed in my early days made such a strong impression upon my mind, that it never could be obliterated. The most magnificent and showy procession, I really believe, except those of Rome, then took place in the Irish metropolis every third year, and attracted a number of English quite surprising, if we take into account the difficulty and hazard of a passage at that time from London to Dublin.

The corporation of the latter city were, by the terms of their charter, bound, once in three years, to perambulate the limits of the lord mayor's jurisdiction, to make stands or stations at various points, and to skirt the Earl of Meath's liberties – a part of the city at that era in great prosperity, but forming a local jurisdiction under the earl (in the nature of a manor) totally distinct from that of Dublin.

This procession being in fact partly intended to mark and to designate the extreme boundaries of his lordship's jurisdiction, at those points where they touch the Earl of Meath's liberty, the lord mayor thrust his sword through the wall of a certain house; – and then concluded the ceremony by approaching the sea at low water, and hurling a javelin as far upon the sands as his strength admitted, which was understood to form the boundary between him and Neptune.

The trade of Dublin is comprised of twenty-five corporations, or guilds, each independent of the other, and represented, as in London, by a common council. Every one of these comprised its masters, journeymen, and apprentices; – and each guild had a patron saint, or protector, whose image or emblem was on all great occasions dressed up in appropriate habiliments.

For this procession every member of the twenty-five corporations prepared as for a jubilee. Small funds only were collected, and each individual gladly bore his extra charges – the masters and journeymen being desirous of outvying one another, and conceiving that the gayer they appeared on that great day, the more consideration would they be entitled to throughout the ensuing three years! Of course, therefore, such as could afford it spared no expense: they borrowed the finest horses and trappings which could be procured; the masters rode – the journeymen walked, and were succeeded by the apprentices.

Every corporation had an immense carriage, with a great platform and high canopy – the whole radiant with gilding, ribbons, and draperies, and drawn by six or eight horses equally decked and caparisoned – their colours and flags flying in all directions. On these platforms, which were fitted up as workshops, were the implements of the respective trades; and expert hands were actually at work during the entire perambulation, which generally lasted eight or nine hours! – The procession indeed took two hours to pass. The narrow-weavers wove ribbons which they threw to the spectators: the others tossed into the air small patterns of the fabric they worked upon: the printers were employed in striking off innumerable hand-bills, with songs, and odes to the lord mayor, the lady mayoress, &c.

But the smiths' part of the spectacle was the most gaudy: they had their forge in full work, and were attended by a very high phaeton adorned in every way they could think of – the horses covered with flowers, gilt stars, and coloured streamers. In this phaeton sat the most beautiful woman they could possibly procure, as wife to their patron, Vulcan. It is unnecessary to describe her dress: suffice it to say, it approached that of a Venus as nearly as decency would permit: a blue scarf, covered with silver doves, was used at her discretion, and four or five little Cupids, apparently naked, with goose wings stuck to their shoulders (aiming with bows and arrows at the ladies in the windows) played at her feet. On one side rode, on the largest horse which could be provided, a huge fellow, representing Vulcan, dressed *cap-à-pie* in coal-black armour, and flourishing an immense smith's sledge-hammer as if it had been a light toy! On the other side pranced his rival, Mars, on a tawdry-caparisoned charger, in shining armour (with an immensity of feathers and horse-hair), and brandishing a two-edged glittering sword six or eight feet long – Venus meantime seeming to pay much more attention to her gallant than to her husband. Behind the phaeton rode Argus, with an immense peacock's tail; whilst numerous other gods and goddesses, saints, devils, satyrs, &c. were distributed in the procession, on carriages painted with clouds for the *gods*, and blue flames for the *devil*!

The skinners and tanners seemed to undergo no slight penance – a considerable number of these artisans being dressed up close in sheep and goat skins of different colours. The representatives of the butchers were enveloped in hides, with towering horns, and rode along brandishing knives, marrowbones, and cleavers! – a most formidable-looking corporation! The apothecaries made up and distributed pills and boluses on their platform, which was furnished with numerous metal pestles and mortars, so contrived and tuned as to sound, in the grinding, like bells ringing some popular air. Each corporation had its appropriate band and colours; perfect order was maintained; and so proud was the Dublin mob of what they called their *fringes* [franchises], that on this peculiar occasion they managed to behave with great decorum and propriety.

But the crowd seemed always in the most anxious expectation to see *the tailors*, who were certainly the favourites. The master-tailors usually borrowed the best horses from their *gentlemen* customers; and as they were not accustomed to horseback, the scene was certainly highly ludicrous. A tailor on a spirited horse has ever been esteemed a curiosity; but a troop of a hundred and fifty or two hundred tailors, all decked with ribbons and lace and every species of finery, on horses equally adorned, presented a spectacle outvying description! Their great difficulty in keeping their seats was extremely amusing. But when the beast was *too obstreperous*, a couple of tawdry apprentices led him: this precaution, however, did not prevent occasional misadventures. The journeymen and apprentices walked, except that number of workmen on the platform. St Crispin with his last, St Andrew with his cross, and St Luke with his gridiron, were all included in the show; as were the city officers in their full robes and paraphernalia. The guild of merchants, being under the especial patronage of the *Holy Trinity*, could not, with all their ingenuity, find out any unprofane emblem, except a *shamrock*, of huge dimensions! the three *distinct* leaves whereof are on *one* stalk. This, by the way, offered St Patrick means of explaining the Trinity, and thereby of converting the Irish to Christianity; and hence the shamrock became the national emblem of Ireland. The merchants had also a large ship on wheels, drawn and manned by *real* sailors.

This singular procession I twice witnessed: it has since been abolished, after having worked well, and done no harm, from the days of the very first lord mayor of Dublin. The city authorities, however, began at length to think venison and claret would be better things for the same expense; and so it was decided that the money should remain in the purse of the corporation, and a wretched substitute for the old ceremony was arranged. The lord mayor and sheriffs, with some dozen of dirty constables, now perambulate these bounds in privacy and silence; thus defeating, in my mind, the very *intention* of their charter, and taking away a triennial prospective object of great attraction and pride to the inhabitants of the metropolis of Ireland, for the sole purpose of gratifying the sensual appetites of a city aristocracy, who court satiety and indigestion at the expense of their humbler brethren.

The unnecessary abolition of all ancient ceremonies is impolitic. Such as that of which I speak, tended to keep up an honest feeling of national pride, and to mark epochs in time: gratifying the humbler classes by giving them the prospect, although a distant one, of an attractive object adapted to their taste, their habits, and their station. The *fringes* were a spur to industry, and the poor people took great pride therein.

John Estrete (*fl.* 1474–89): the 'Yorkist' earl of Kildare's 'Lancastrian' lawyer

RANDOLPH JONES

The late fifteenth-century lawyer, John Estrete, is best known for being the king's sergeant-at-law in Ireland and a benefactor of Dublin's Holy Trinity priory at Christ Church cathedral.[1] Once thought to have been born in Ireland, appearing suddenly in the historical record during the second half of Edward IV's reign,[2] new evidence indicates that he probably came from England and was previously in the service of John de Vere, the thirteenth earl of Oxford. This evidence was entered into the Irish exchequer memoranda roll for the year 15 Edward IV (1475–6).

The original roll was destroyed in the Four Courts fire of 1922, but a nineteenth-century calendar of its contents refers to a deed attested at St Michael's Mount in Cornwall on 21 February 1474, by John Fortescue, esquire of the king's body and sheriff of Cornwall. This was enrolled in the Irish exchequer at the request of Estrete, who was then described as being a 'narrator' or pleader.[3] The deed mentions that on 7 December 1473, Edward IV commissioned Fortescue, Sir John Croker and Henry Bodrugan esquire to recover St Michael's Mount, which Oxford and a small band of die-hard Lancastrian supporters had seized at the end of September, though subsequently failing to generate a local uprising against the Yorkist king. Fortescue was empowered 'to promise pardon to any rebels within the Mount who may be willing to submit and take an oath of fealty', with the exception of the earl, his three brothers and William Beaumont, Viscount Beaumont and Lord Bardolf.[4] The deed further states that Estrete was one of those who made their submission, took the required oath of fealty to Edward IV, and was pardoned.[5]

Estrete is described in the deed as the 'serjeant of the said earl', which suggests that he was Oxford's legal advisor. He probably entered the earl's service sometime after 1464, when Oxford was permitted to succeed to his ancestral estates, after his father was executed in 1462 for plotting to kill the

1 A.R. Hart, *A history of the king's serjeants at law in Ireland. Honour rather than advantage?* (Dublin, 2000), pp 24–6, 147, 169. His surname is also rendered as *Esterret, Estrate, Estret, Esterete, Estreyt, Estricte, Estyrrette, Straite, Strayte Streete, Stret,* and *Strete* in the contemporary sources. 2 https://en.wikipedia.org/wiki/John_Estrete. 3 College of Arms, London, MS Ph 15175, pp 243–4 (Irish Exch. Mem. Roll, 14, 15 Edw. IV, mem. 16). 4 *CPR 1467–77*, p. 418. 5 For a contemporary account of the siege, which lasted from 23 December 1473 to 15 February 1474, see Dan Embree and M. Teresa Tavormina (eds), *The contemporary English chronicles of the Wars of the Roses* (Woodbridge, 2019), pp 132–3, 289.

new Yorkist king. Estrete may have been with Oxford when he was defeated at the battle of Barnet in April 1471, fighting for the briefly restored Lancastrian king Henry VI. Estrete may also have fled with Oxford to Scotland and then on to France before St Michael's Mount was seized in September 1473.[6] It is therefore possible Estrete originally came from the east of England, where Oxford's estates were primarily located. This is further supported by Sir John Chalers's inclusion in the grants Estrete later made to the prior and convent of Holy Trinity Dublin, in return for masses to be said and sung for his living benefactors and family members, as well as the souls of those who were deceased.[7] Chalers was a Lancastrian knight whose family's seat was at Whaddon, Cambridgeshire, though he later based himself at Lyford, Berkshire, which he held courtesy of his second wife Maud Cowdray. Chalers was the sheriff of Oxfordshire and Berkshire in 1443–4 and again in 1451–2. He also served as the sheriff of Cambridgeshire and Huntingdonshire in 1445–6 and again in 1446–7. Chalers was elected as a member of parliament for Berkshire in 1447. He also served in the same shire as justice of the peace from 1453 to 1461. Chalers remained loyal to Henry VI throughout the first phase of the Wars of the Roses and was only pardoned by the Yorkist king Edward IV in 1464. Chalers died three years later. He had no apparent connection with Ireland.[8]

Where Estrete obtained his legal training is not known. It is possible that Chalers may have funded this, and hence the remembrance mentioned above. Of the four Inns of Court in London, only Lincoln's Inn has records going back to the fifteenth-century, but Estrete is not mentioned therein. Circumstantial evidence suggests that he may have been trained there for, in the aforementioned masses, Estrete included the soul of William Elliott, who may have been the person specially admitted to Lincoln's Inn in 1461, 'for his faithful service as butler'. Thomas Dowdall, clerk, and keeper of the rolls of the Irish chancery from 1471, whose name is also included in the masses to be said or sung, was admitted to Lincoln's Inn in Trinity term 1459, while William Darcy, one of Estrete's pupils, was admitted there on 10 May 1485.[9]

It is possible that, after obtaining his pardon, Estrete sought a fresh start in Ireland, thanks to the acquaintances he had made at Lincoln's Inn. He may have accompanied Sir Gilbert Debenham, an East Anglian knight, who was sent to Ireland in September 1474 as Edward IV's new chancellor.[10] Estrete

6 James Ross, *The foremost man of the kingdom. John de Vere, thirteenth earl of Oxford (1442–1513)* (Woodbridge, 2011), pp 48–75. **7** *CCD*, nos 349 and 1091. **8** Josiah C. Wedgewood, *History of parliament biographies of the members of the Commons House 1439–1509* (London, 1936), p. 169; Linda Clark (ed.), *The House of Commons 1422–1461* (Cambridge, 2020), 7 vols, iii, pp 795–8. **9** *The records of the Honorable Society of Lincoln's Inn. I. Admissions from A.D. 1420 to A.D. 1799* (London, 1896), pp 14, 15 and 23; *The records of the Honorable Society of Lincoln's Inn: the black books vol. I, From A.D. 1422 to A.D. 1586* (London, 1897), pp 20, 37, 82. **10** Steven G. Ellis, *Reform and revival: English government*

quickly gravitated into the service of the prior and convent of Holy Trinity Dublin and was granted an annual pension of 40*s*. by them, perhaps as a retainer for his legal services.[11] In July 1476, Estrete witnessed Henry Goldynge's homage for the manor of Balscaddan, which the latter held from the prior and convent by military service. Likewise, between December 1478 and December 1479, Estrete performed a similar service for the prior and convent when Edward Balffe did homage for Kinsaley before the high altar in Christ Church. In May 1485, he did so again when Peter Tirrel did homage for his lands in Mabestown.[12] Estrete acted as a witness for the prior when the latter requested the mayor of Dublin, on 10 February 1481, to enrol within the records of the Tholsel a deed he had previously received from William Sutton, late baron of the exchequer, granting Holy Trinity Dublin the ten marks per annum he received from the fee farm of the city.[13] Indeed, by August 1477, Estrete was sufficiently well-established within Dublin's legal community to witness several lands being granted by Robert Noryce of Dublin, esquire, and his wife Joneta Chamber, to the prior and convent of Holy Trinity Dublin, together with Sir Robert Dowdall, chief justice of the common pleas, and Philip Bermingham, chief justice of the king's bench.[14] By the end of Edward IV's reign, Estrete had also established a law school in the city, to instruct the sons of the Pale gentry in 'their tenuors and Natura Brevium'.[15] Steven Ellis has suggested that the 'tenures' were those of Sir Thomas Littleton (d. 1481), justice of the common pleas in England, whose treatise on property law was printed in London within a year of his death. If this was the case, Estrete had a manuscript of the work when he came to Ireland, or obtained a printed copy soon after its publication, thus demonstrating his close contacts with the legal community in England.[16]

Following the duke of Clarence's execution in late February 1478, the king's council in Ireland elected Thomas fitzGerald, earl of Kildare, as justiciar of Ireland until the king appointed a new lieutenant. With Kildare's death on 25 March, the council elected his 22-year-old son and heir, Gerald (Gearóid Mór), into the same office. On 10 March, the king appointed his brother-in-law, John de la Pole, duke of Suffolk, as the new lieutenant and Kildare was instructed to step down as justiciar and refrain from holding a parliament. However, on 6 July 1478, Edward IV changed his mind and appointed his infant son George, duke of Bedford, as lieutenant instead, with Henry, Lord

in Ireland 1470–1534 (Woodbridge, 1986), p. 220. **11** Barra Boydell (ed.), *Music at Christ Church before 1800: documents and selected anthems* (Dublin, 1999), pp 32–3. **12** Hugh J. Lawlor (ed.), 'Calendar of the Liber Niger and Liber Albus of Christ Church, Dublin', *PRIA*, 27C (1908–9), 30–1. **13** *DCFR*, pp 52–4. **14** *CCD*, no. 309. **15** William Lynch, *A view of the legal institutions, honorary hereditary offices, and feudal baronies, established in Ireland during the reign of Henry the Second* (London, 1830), p. 110 (Irish Exch. Mem. Roll 9, 10 Hen. VIII, m. 21.). **16** https://www.dib.ie/biography/darcy-sir-william-a2405; https://doi.org/10.1093/ref:odnb/16787.

Grey, as his deputy.[17] On the very same day, Estrete was granted a pardon by the king, perhaps copper-fastening the one he had received following the surrender of St Michael's Mount in 1474.[18] This suggests that Estrete may have been in England at the time, perhaps as part of an official delegation headed by Robert Preston, Lord Gormanston, who was created Viscount Gormanston on 7 August 1478.[19] Estrete was back in Dublin on 25 August 1478 when he witnessed a deposition concerning a property located in St Werburgh's Street.[20]

When Grey arrived in Ireland in late August/early September, he was opposed by Kildare and his supporters. To cover his disloyalty, Kildare rejected Grey's appointment on a technicality (his letters of appointment having been authenticated with the king's privy seal rather than the great seal of England).[21] James Keating, the Hospitaller prior of St John of Jerusalem, Kilmainham, and constable of Dublin Castle, the seat of English government in Ireland, refused to admit Grey, filling it with armed men and breaking down the bridge into it, while Kildare's father-in-law, Roland Fitz Eustace, Lord Portlester and chancellor of Ireland, refused to hand over the Irish great seal. Kildare had also summoned the Irish parliament to meet again at Connell, Co. Kildare, on 14 September, after meeting previously at Naas on 29 May and Dublin on 6 July. Grey withdrew to Trim, Co. Meath, where he summoned a rival parliament to meet on 6 November, which was adjourned to Drogheda on the 19th of the same month. Estrete, Bishop William Sherwood of Meath, Chief Justice Philip Birmingham, Thomas Dowdall, and the mayor and citizens of Dublin and others accepted Grey's authority. On 18 December Grey appointed Estrete as the king's sergeant-at-law in Ireland, with an annual salary of £10.[22] However, Grey returned to England early in the new year, having failed to make an impression in Ireland. Before departing, he appointed Gormanston as his deputy, who was acting as such by 14 January 1479.[23] He was still acting as Grey's deputy on 15 March 1479, when a bakers' guild was founded in Dublin, dedicated to SS Anne and Clement. Estrete was named in the letters patent as one of the worthies who supported the foundation of the new guild.[24] On 15 May 1480, Estrete was similarly named in a statute passed by the Irish parliament which refounded a fraternity of English merchants based in Dublin, which had been established there twenty years before.[25]

17 *CPR 1476–85*, p. 118. **18** *CPR 1476–85*, p. 121. **19** *CPR 1476–85*, p. 120. **20** *CCD*, no. 314. **21** Grey's retinue was ordered to be mustered at Conway by 19 August, but this seems to have been done on 27 August. See *CPR 1476–85*, p. 121; David B. Quinn, 'Guide to English financial records for Irish history 1461–1558, with illustrative extracts, 1461–1509', *AH*, 10 (1941), 48–9; TNA E 101/55/9, Muster of soldiers going with Henry, Lord Grey, to Ireland, 18 Edw IV. **22** Philomena Connolly (ed.), *Statute rolls of the Irish parliament Richard III–Henry VIII* (Dublin, 2002), p. 322. **23** *CCD*, no. 1014. **24** NLI, MS 680, ff. 166–75; Henry S. Guinness, 'Dublin trade gilds', *JRSAI*, 52 (1922), p. 148. **25** James F. Morrissey (ed.), *Statute rolls of the parliament of Ireland twelfth and thirteenth to*

On 10 February 1479, Kildare, Keating, and his other supporters were granted safe conducts to go to England to help resolve the impasse caused by two rival administrations operating in Ireland.[26] Chief Justice Bermingham also went to England, where he received £10 from the English exchequer during the Easter term of 1479.[27] Thomas Dowdall was also summoned to England to attend the king's council there in August.[28] A compromise was eventually reached: Kildare was appointed the new deputy lieutenant, with Sherwood as chancellor and Portlester as treasurer.

Despite Estrete backing the wrong horse in the struggle for the chief governorship, Kildare accepted his appointment as the king's serjeant-at-law, which was confirmed by the Irish parliament when it met again on 10 December 1479.[29] In the same session, Estrete and other supporters of Grey's administration, including Bishop Sherwood and Chief Justice Birmingham, were pardoned for any treasons and felonies they had committed against Kildare, and any actions or acts of attainder subsequently made against them were to be revoked. The statute was exemplified by Irish letters patent on 5 July 1480 and enrolled in the exchequer's memoranda rolls.[30]

As the king's serjeant-at-law, Estrete represented the crown's interests whenever cases were heard in the Irish courts. Nothing has survived from the records of the king's bench and common pleas in which Estrete is mentioned, but the exchequer memoranda rolls contain several instances of him upholding the crown's feudal dues. For example, in 18 Edward IV [1478–9], Estrete claimed that Sir Thomas Ormond [sic] owed 100*s*. relief for his manor of Carrick, Co. Tipperary on becoming the new tenant-in-chief on the death of his brother John, earl of Ormond.[31] In the following year, Estrete informed the court that Christopher Bernewall of Crickeston had intruded into the manors of Crickstown, Kilmessan, Ringlestown and Belpere, Co. Meath.[32] During the Easter term 20 Edward IV [1480], Estrete also informed the court that James Welles, a London draper and master of the guild of English merchants in Dublin, refused to pay poundage on £80 of imported goods he later put up for sale. Welles claimed exemption from payment of poundage as a citizen of Dublin under a statute recently passed by the Irish parliament. Estrete argued that Welles could not benefit from this exemption, because even though he was admitted to the franchise of Dublin in 1469, he was not continually resident

the twenty-first and twenty-second years of the reign of king Edward the Fourth (Dublin, 1939), pp 768–85 (19 and 20 Edw. IV, ca. 39). **26** *CPR 1476–85*, p. 137. **27** Quinn, 'English financial records', 32. **28** CIRCLE CR 19 Edw IV, nos 14–19. **29** Connolly (ed.), *Statute rolls*, p. 328. **30** James F. Morrissey (ed.), *Statute rolls of the Irish parliament: twelfth and thirteenth to the twenty-first and twenty-second years of the reign of King Edward the Fourth* (Dublin, 1939), pp 768–9; College of Arms, London [hereafter COA] Ph 15175, p. 264 (Irish Exch. Mem. Roll, 20 Edw. IV, mem.15). **31** COA Ph 15175, p. 252 (Irish Exch. Mem. Roll, 18 Edw. IV). Sir Thomas was the younger brother of James (ex. 1461) and John (d. 1478), earls of Ormond, to which title he succeeded. **32** COA Ph 15175, p. 256 (Irish

there. A jury was summoned and found that Welles was indeed not continually resident in the city. For his refusal to pay poundage, his imported goods were forfeited to the king. He also had to pay a fine for contempt.[33] During the Trinity term of 1484, Estrete claimed that letters patent dated 5 May 1462, allowing the mayor and bailiffs of Dublin a £20 reduction on their annual fee farm payment to the king, were 'insufficient', whereupon John Gaydon, one of the two bailiffs concerned, insulted Estrete and, in contempt of the king, threatened him with violence.[34] Also, on 4 January 1485, Estrete and Walter Ever were arbitrators in a dispute between Patrick Burnell, baron of the exchequer, and the prior and convent of Holy Trinity Dublin, concerning 12*s.* rent due from the former to the latter for some houses situated in Fishamble Street.[35]

In addition to holding the office of king's serjeant-at-law, Estrete was appointed deputy to Oliver Fitz Eustace, chief baron of the exchequer, on 12 March 1485, swearing his oath of office on 16 May.[36] These offices gave Estrete a seat on the king's Irish council, which advised Kildare in his role as chief governor. Estrete's previously unknown Lancastrian past throws interesting light on the decisions made by Kildare during periods of crisis following Edward IV's death in April 1483. Like other Lancastrians who survived the dynastic wars in England, Estrete had eventually made his peace with the Yorkist regime, but old loyalties probably surfaced when Edward V was deposed on the grounds of illegitimacy due to the invalidity of Edward IV's marriage to Elizabeth Wydeville. He was replaced by his uncle Richard of Gloucester, who took the throne as Richard III. As Edward V and his younger brother Richard were believed to have been killed by the new king, Edward IV's former supporters now turned to Henry Tudor, in exile in Brittany, the last Lancastrian contender for the English throne. To bolster his dubious claim, Tudor promised to marry Elizabeth, Edward IV's eldest daughter, thereby uniting the houses of York and Lancaster.

Kildare soon clashed with Richard III, over the appointment as chancellor of Robert St Lawrence, Lord Howth, for, on the death of William Sherwood, bishop of Meath, Kildare had granted this office to his brother Thomas for

Exch. Mem. Roll, 19 Edw. IV). 33 RIA MS 24/H/17, p. 77; William Lynch, *The law of election in the ancient cities and towns of Ireland traced from original records* (London, 1831), p.49; COA Ph 15175, p. 263 (Irish Exch. Mem. Roll, 20 Edw. IV, mem. 11). The statutes concerned are 19 and 20 Edw. IV, ca. 24 and 27 and were intended to support a small standing army known as the 'Brotherhood of Arms'. See Morrissey, *Statute rolls 12/13 to 21/22 Edw. IV*, pp 734–7 and 740–47. For Welles's English connections, see ibid., pp 768–85 (19 and 20 Edw. IV, ca. 39); *CPR 1467–77*, pp 72, 309; ibid., 1476–85, p. 282. 34 COA Ph 15175, p. 285; NAI, Dublin, MS RC 8/33, pp 522–3 (Irish Exch. Mem. Roll, 2 Ric. III, mem. 18). For the letters patent concerned, see CIRCLE PR, 2 Edw. IV, no. 4, which confirmed and exemplified an earlier grant made in 1427 for 20 years. The £20 rebate was supposed to be used for repairing, maintaining, and improving the city walls. 35 *CCD*, no. 1055. For the outcome, see ibid., no. 1057. 36 NAI, MS RC 8/33, pp 413–14 (Irish Exch.

life, shortly after the death of Edward IV, using his authority as justiciar of Ireland under the so-called statute of Henry Fitz Empress. When Richard became aware of this in December 1483, he demanded Howth's admission into the disputed office. Kildare ignored him.[37] Richard never forgot this slight to his royal prerogative and began cultivating James fitzGerald, the estranged earl of Desmond, as a replacement for Kildare. In September 1484, Richard wrote to Desmond, lamenting Edward IV's execution of his father Thomas in 1468. Richard also sent him his livery collar, a wardrobe of English clothes, an invitation to come to court soon, and the promise of a suitable bride, perhaps one of his own nieces.[38] Kildare's opportunity to retaliate came in November of the same year, when Oxford escaped from prison in the Calais Pale and joined Tudor, now in France, who was planning to invade England with French help. Although Kildare needed little encouragement, the fact that Oxford was free and actively supporting the Lancastrian cause again, may have prompted Kildare to support the opposition against Richard, prompted by Estrete. There was no immediate sign of opposition, for the Irish council forwarded an estimate of Irish revenues to the king, which it had drawn up in the spring of 1485.[39] However, when the French agreed to support Tudor's intended invasion of England, Kildare increasingly flouted Richard's authority. On 6 June 1485, the Irish parliament confirmed the statute of Henry Fitz Empress and the powers contained therein, as well as confirming Kildare and the other members of the Irish council in their respective offices for life, in defiance of the king's commands.[40] On 7 July, Kildare appointed the Dublin goldsmith Richard Neville as master of the Irish coinage, an appointment that was specifically reserved to the king, with Estrete as the comptroller.[41] Also, despite Richard granting Thomas Butler, earl of Ormond, a licence on 16 February 1485 to be absent from Ireland, Kildare ignored it, refusing to remit the full income of Ormond's Irish lands and his prise of wines imported into Ireland, retaining two-thirds of their respective values for the defence of the land under the statute of absentees.[42]

On 26 July 1485, Estrete granted various properties in Dublin and its suburbs, as well as lands he had recently purchased in Bryanstown

Mem. Roll, 2 Ric. III). 37 H.G. Richardson and G.O. Sayles, *The Irish parliament in the Middle Ages* (Philadelphia, 1952), pp 328–30. 38 James Gairdner (ed.), *Letters and papers illustrative of the reigns of Richard III and Henry VII* (London, 1861), i, pp 67–70, 73–4. 39 Quinn, 'English financial records', 17–27. The document is not dated, but the latest date mentioned within it is 8 March 1485. The document is signed by Estrete and by the other members of the Irish council. 40 Connolly (ed.), *Statute rolls*, pp 61–3. 41 Estrete pleaded a pardon dated 28 April 1485 for his intrusion into the annual profits of the coinage minted in Dublin, both the castle and city. COA MS Ph 15175, p. 288 (Irish Exch. Mem. Roll, 2–3 Richard III, m. 6). 42 TNA, C 49/53/5. In 1485, two-thirds of the receipts and profits of Ormond's manors of Rush, Turvey and Balscaddan; Blackcastle and Donaghmore; and Castlewarden and Oughterard; amounted to £48, £24, and £8 17*s.* 10½*d.* respectively. See Quinn, 'English financial records', 24.

(*Brynestoun*), Ministown (*Mydnyghtestoun)* and Rodanstown (*Balrodan/ Ballirodan*), Co. Meath, in trust to John Waryng, rector of Malahide, and Thomas Laundey, chaplain. From the income generated by these lands, the trustees were to convey four marks annually to the prior and convent of Holy Trinity Dublin, in return for the mass of the Holy Ghost to be celebrated daily by a canon for ever, with the residue of the income generated by these properties conveyed to Estrete for the duration of his life. When he died, this income was to go to Estrete's son and heir George, and his issue lawfully begotten, in tail male, with remainder to the right heirs of Estrete. Failing that, the lands were to be passed to the prior and convent of Holy Trinity Dublin.[43] Estrete may have been ill at the time, for the 'plague', probably the sweating sickness, was ravaging Dublin and elsewhere in Ireland.[44] By 8 October 1485, Estrete may have recovered from this illness, because, in addition to the lands mentioned above, he also granted the same trustees his interest in half of the 'New Rents' situated on Dublin quay, for the term of his life, as well as surrendering the 40*s*. yearly pension he received from the prior and convent of Holy Trinity Dublin, making a total income of £4 4*s*. per annum, in return for a mass of the Holy Ghost to be said daily in St Lawrence O'Toole's chapel. After Estrete's death, the daily masses were to continue, as well as one to be sung every Thursday for himself, his family and other named benefactors, with his obit and dirige observed in Whitsun week.[45] However, there may have been another reason, for, on 7 July 1485, Tudor landed at Milford Haven with his French invasion force. Rallying support as he passed through Wales, he marched into England. On 22 August, he was victorious at Bosworth Field, killing Richard III. Tudor now ascended the throne as Henry VII with his key supporter, the earl of Oxford, as 'the foremost man of the kingdom'. It is possible that Kildare sent Estrete to liaise with Tudor's invasion force, since Estrete later gave thanks for his safe return to Ireland by confirming and enhancing the previous grant he had made to Holy Trinity Dublin.

In early 1486, drawing on his *persona grata* status at the Tudor court, Estrete was sent to England to negotiate for Kildare's continued appointment as chief governor.[46] The outcome was a success, for Kildare was appointed deputy to the new lieutenant of Ireland, Jasper Tudor, duke of Bedford, with the king rewarding Estrete with the royal manors of Ratoath and Chapelizod, together with the collectorship of the customs and cockets in Dublin port on

43 *CCD*, nos 348, 1069–71. Representative Church Body Library, Dublin, *Registrum Novum* II, pp 833–6. My thanks to Dr Stuart Kinsella, archivist at Christ Church cathedral, for supplying me with a copy of this reference. 44 Connolly (ed.), *Statute Rolls*, p. 69; *AFM*, iv, pp 1135–6. 45 *CCD*, no. 349. RCBL, *Reg. Nov. II*, pp 827–9. St Laurence O'Toole's chapel was formerly dedicated to the Holy Ghost. It was located at the east end of the south aisle, where it joined the high choir. See Kenneth Milne (ed.), *Christ Church cathedral, Dublin: a history* (Dublin, 2000), p. 104. 46 Gairdner, *Letters and papers*, i, pp 91–3; ibid., 'Earl of Kildare's petition', *Notes and Queries*, 14 Dec. 1867, p. 481.

7 March.[47] During this visit Estrete also successfully defended Kildare against complaints made against him by Thomas Butler, earl of Ormond, before the lord chancellor and the king's council in England.[48] He also seems to have secured the grant of Carrickfergus Castle in Ulster for his cousin, Robert Strete of London, for on 18 March he and other London merchants entered into bonds with Henry VII totalling £500 which would be voided if the castle was faithfully and securely kept by Robert for the king whenever he obtained possession of it.[49] Estrete had returned to Dublin by 14 August when he informed the barons of the exchequer that, on 20 July 1486, William Chamberleyn and others had entered 'with force and arms' John Waryng's possession near the 'Pollmyll' in Dublin (i.e., the Pool Mill in Ship Street Little), contrary to an Irish statute passed in 11 Henry IV, under which the culprits would suffer imprisonment for a year, pay fines to the king, and compensate the aggrieved parties threefold for their losses.[50] It is probable that Estrete had a personal interest in this case for among the properties he conveyed in trust to Waryng and Laundey on 26 July 1485 were 'a messuage and tanhouse with a bawn and haggard place without the Polegate' as well as 'an orchard called Paradise adjoining'.[51] These properties were returned to Estrete by the same trustees on 31 July 1488.[52]

Shortly after Kildare's appointment, discontent began to grow in Ireland, in which his brother Thomas took a leading part. This was due to a decision made in the English courts that declared Ireland subject to English statutes, thereby jeopardizing the autonomy the country had enjoyed since 1460. In October 1486, the young Edward, earl of Warwick, the son and heir of George, duke of Clarence, and the primary Yorkist claimant to the throne, was abducted from the Tower of London and taken to Ireland where he was accommodated by Thomas. When Henry sent John Yong, Falcon pursuivant, to recover Warwick, Kildare complied but probably as a quid pro quo granted his brother a pardon 'for all manner of treasons'.[53] Estrete seems to have informed Henry VII of the presence of Warwick in Ireland and later assisted Falcon pursuivant when he was sent there, for during the Michaelmas term 1486 Estrete was paid £26 13*s.* 4*d.* by the English exchequer for 'his costs and expenses in parts of Ireland on the king's business'.[54] By 14 February 1487, Falcon was back in England with Warwick, who was put on display in St Paul's cathedral in London on 5 March.[55] Estrete was apparently still in Dublin on 10 February, but he seems to have returned to England soon after, because on 26 March he was appointed master of the Irish coinage by English letters patent with an annual salary of

47 *CPR 1485–94*, pp 64, 78. 48 TNA, C 49/53/5. 49 *CCR 1485–1500*, p. 10; William Campbell (ed.), *Materials for a history of the reign of Henry VII, from original documents preserved in the Public Records Office*, i (London, 1873), pp 389–90. 50 COA Ph 15175, p. 300 (Irish Exch. Mem. Roll 1 Hen. VII, m. 23). 51 *CCD*, no. 349. 52 Ibid., no. 352. 53 BL Add. MS 4793, fo. 149v; COA Ph 15175, p. 303 (Irish Exch. Mem. Roll 2 Hen. VII, m. 15). 54 Quinn, 'English financial records', p. 33. 55 Ibid., p. 51.

£20.[56] Estrete's absence from Ireland, for part of the year 1486–7 at least, is suggested by the crown's interests being represented in the Irish exchequer court by Thomas Cusake, the king's attorney-general.[57]

In the spring of 1487, John de la Pole, earl of Lincoln, Francis, Viscount Lovell, and two thousand German mercenaries, sailed from Flanders and arrived in Ireland on 5 May. They brought with them another boy, 'the son of the duke of Clarence', who had been nurtured by Edward IV's sister, Margaret, the dowager duchess of Burgundy. On Thursday, 24 May, the boy was proclaimed 'Edward VI', and crowned in Christ Church cathedral on the following Sunday. Kildare had been subverted from his allegiance to Henry VII, with the elevation of the lordship of Ireland to kingdom status and his appointment as the new king's lieutenant. The whole cavalcade soon departed for England to make good the boy's claim there, supported by an Irish contingent led by Kildare's brother Thomas. Henry defeated the pretender's forces on 16 June 1487 at the battle of Stoke Field, during which Thomas fitzGerald and many of the Irish contingent were slain.[58]

What Estrete was doing during these trying times is not known. If he managed to return to Ireland before the invasion force from Flanders made landfall there, he failed to influence Kildare's decision to support the pretender king. It is possible that once news reached Kildare of the disaster of Stoke Field, Estrete was commissioned by him to negotiate with Henry VII for a face-saving return to his allegiance. No evidence has been found to date to support this supposition, but there must have been contact between Dublin and London well before Sir Richard Edgcumbe, the king's commissioner, disembarked at Malahide on 5 July 1488, for he brought in his baggage pardons that were pre-sealed and attested by the king at Croydon on 25 May 1488.[59] Estrete was the likely person to conduct these discreet negotiations, thanks to his previous credentials. When Edgcumbe arrived in Ireland, Estrete and John Payne, bishop of Meath, escorted him into Dublin. It is also likely that Estrete played a key role in Edgcumbe's final negotiations with Kildare and the Irish council in the abbey of St Thomas the Martyr later in the same month. It is noteworthy that Estrete's name is absent from those who were required to make their submissions and take oaths of allegiance to Henry VII

56 *CCD*, nos 1077–8; Aquilla Smith, 'Irish silver coins of Henry VIII', *The Numismatic Chronicle, and Journal of the Numismatic Society,* 19 (1879), 180–2; *CPR 1485–94*, pp 158, 169; S.G. Ellis, 'The struggle for control of the Irish mint, 1460–*c.*1506', *PRIA,* 78C (1979), 30. Ellis suggests that this appointment was a retainer, to support Estrete's new status as one of the king's councillors. The same can probably said for his previous appointment as comptroller of the coinage and collector of the customs and cockets in Dublin port. 57 BL Add. MS 4793, fo. 149v; COA Ph 15175, p. 303; TCD MS 1218 fol. 101r (Irish Exch. Mem. Roll, 2 Hen. VII, mems. 9, 17). 58 Randolph Jones, 'The extraordinary reign of "Edward VI" in Ireland, 1487–8', *Ricardian Bulletin* (March 2021), 48–56. 59 *CPR 1485–94*, p. 227.

before receiving their pardons, which suggests he had been absent from Ireland during the coronation of 'Edward VI' and that his allegiance to the Tudor regime was never compromised.[60]

On 26 July 1488, shortly after the negotiations with Edgcumbe were concluded, the lands in Bryanstown, Ministown and Rodanstown, which Estrete had granted earlier to Waryng and Laundey in trust, together with a messuage in Fishamble Street, Dublin, were transferred to a new foundation, the members of which were Estrete himself, Gerald fitzGerald, earl of Kildare, Roland Fitz Eustace, Lord Portlester, Walter de la Hyde, lord of Moyclare, John Waryng, archdeacon of Dublin, and Thomas Laundey, chaplain. The foundation then granted these lands to the prior and convent of Holy Trinity Dublin, for the Holy Ghost mass to be said daily by one of its canons in the Holy Ghost chapel and for the entire convent and choir to sing a mass of the Holy Ghost every Thursday for Estrete and his benefactors, as well as keeping Estrete's obit during Whitsun week. It is noteworthy that the list of Estrete's benefactors to be prayed for now included the Tudor monarch, Henry VII (see Appendix 2), perhaps as a tacit acknowledgment that Kildare had now returned to that king's allegiance.[61]

On 31 July, Edgcumbe boarded his ship for England. Estrete followed soon afterwards, appointing deputies to his collectorship of the customs and cockets in Dublin port on 8 August.[62] He seems to have been part of a delegation subsequently sent by Kildare and the lords of Ireland to the king, which was led by John Payne, bishop of Meath.[63] In September, Henry VII ordered the English exchequer to pay Estrete £10 as a reward for his 'good and acceptable service', with a further ten marks (£6 13*s*. 8*d*.) in December, for his 'long abiding and attending upon' the king. Both payments were made into his own hands. He was also now described as an 'esquire' rather than as a 'gentleman'.[64] John Edmund de Courcy, bishop of Clogher, John Payne, bishop of Meath, Walter Ivers, chancellor of the exchequer, and Thomas Dartas, also received payments from the English exchequer in the same term.[65]

Estrete, together with three London merchants and an esquire of the king's body, were mentioned in recognisances totalling £120, which were enrolled in the close rolls of the English chancery on 4 February 1489. These recognisances would be voided if a 30–ton ship laden with 20 tuns of Rochelle

60 Anon., 'The voyage of Sir Richard Edgecumbe, sent by King Henry VII into Ireland in 1488 to take new oaths of allegiance from the nobility and others, who had declared for (the then Pretender) Lambert Simnell', Walter Harris (ed.), *Hibernica: or, Some antient pieces relating to Ireland, Part 1* (Dublin, 1770), pp 59–77. **61** *CCD*, nos 350, 351, 1090. 1091. William de la Hyde was probably included in the grant because he was the lord of the lands in Bryanstown, Ministown and Rodanstown held from him by Estrete. **62** *CCD*, no. 1096. Estrete's deputies were Philip Bermyngeham, esquire, Thomas Dovedall, gentleman, and Richard Nangle, clerk. **63** Aubrey Gwynn, *The medieval province of Armagh, 1470–1545* (Dundalk, 1946), pp 29–31. **64** Quinn, 'English financial records', 33, 34, 52. **65** Ibid., p. 33.

wine which had been despoiled by two Breton pirates, or the value of the same, was returned to its owners by Estrete or his attorney before the coming Easter [19 April]. In return, the owners' prosecution of a suit of assault against the king was to be quashed. It seems that after the ship was despoiled, the ship had come into the possession of William Tywe, mayor of Dublin, and Patrick Mole and Thomas Byrmyngeham, bailiffs of the same, hence the prosecution brought by the original owners.[66] This matter occurred during a particularly sensitive time for Henry VII because he had recently agreed an extension of a truce with France until January 1490, but the French were threatening to take over the duchy of Brittany, the independence of which Henry was keen to preserve, while avoiding war with France until a time of his own choosing. At the time the recognisances were made, Henry's ambassadors led by Sir Richard Edgcumbe, were busy negotiating a treaty with Duchess Anne's advisors in Brittany to supply 6,000 men to defend her lands in case of further French aggression. The Treaty of Redon was signed on 14 February, which Henry ratified on 1 April 1489.[67]

It seems that Estrete was successful in this undertaking, for, during the Michaelmas term of 1489, the English exchequer paid Estrete a further £10 into his own hands, which had been authorized by the king the previous Easter.[68] He was described in the king's privy seal letters as one of his councillors.[69] In the same term, a further ten marks was paid to him, this time via intermediaries.[70] Estrete may have died before 12 November 1489, when the king granted the royal manors of Ratoath and Chapelizod to Estrete's son and heir George, in consideration for his father's services.[71] Estrete's obit was not recorded in Holy Trinity's martyrology, but he is said to have been buried in Christ Church cathedral, the location of his grave now unknown.[72] No trace of a will has been found. However, Estrete was not replaced as the king's sergeant-at-law, until 8 November 1496, when one of his Dublin law-school pupils, Thomas Kent, took his place.[73] It appears that the office had been in abeyance since Estrete's death because the serjeant-at-law's fee is not listed in the estimate of receipts and payments for 1496 drawn up by William Hattecliffe, the under-treasurer of Ireland, at the end of 1495.[74] Indeed, Kent

66 *CCR 1485–1500*, p. 109. Tywe, Mole and Bermingham held their respective offices for the mayoral year commencing Michaelmas 1488. Estrete's own recognisance was for £40, the other parties £20 each. 67 James Gairdner, *Henry the seventh* (London, 1892), pp 62–9; Terry Breverton, *Henry VII: the maligned Tudor king* (Stroud, 2019), pp 192–5. 68 Quinn, 'English financial records', 34, 53. 69 Ellis mentions that Estrete was 'later sworn to the king's council in England'. Steven G. Ellis, *Defending English ground. war and peace in Meath and Northumberland, 1460–1542* (Oxford, 2015), p. 89. idem, *Reform and revival*, p. 35, n. 101. 70 Ibid., p. 34. 71 *CPR 1485–94*, p. 314. 72 Raymond Refaussé and Colm Lennon (eds), *The registers of Christ Church cathedral, Dublin* (Dublin, 1998), pp 84, 122. 73 Ellis, *Reform and revival*, p. 224; Lynch, *Legal institutions*, p. 110. 74 Agnes Conway, *Henry VII's relations with Scotland and Ireland, 1485–1498* (Cambridge, 1932), pp 186–90.

was only appointed as the new serjeant-at-law after Kildare had been reappointed as the new deputy lieutenant of Ireland on 6 August 1496.[75]

Estrete's previously unsuspected Lancastrian past helps explain the timing of his grant of an annual income to Holy Trinity Dublin, from various lands and properties he had recently purchased, in return for prayers to be said for himself, his family, and his benefactors. This was made in July 1485, just before Henry Tudor mounted his invasion of England, and confirmed in October of the same year, after Tudor had defeated his rival Richard III and assumed the throne as Henry VII. This premise is reinforced by some of those lands and properties later being transferred to a foundation, which then granted them to Holy Trinity priory immediately after Kildare and the Irish lords were brought back to Henry VII's allegiance in July 1488, after flirting with a Yorkist pretender in the previous year. Estrete's previous association with John de Vere, earl of Oxford, made him the ideal person through whom Kildare could touch base in 1485 with the enemies of Richard III, a monarch with whom he had been at odds, following his controversial accession to the throne two years previously. Estrete no doubt encouraged Kildare to support Tudor's cause in 1485, though he was probably pushing at an open door. After Henry's accession, he continued to promote Kildare's interests at the English court, but was increasingly retained by the king himself, resulting in being absent from Ireland during the 'Edward VI' or Lambert Simnel episode in 1487. Nevertheless, his continuing attachment to Kildare's interests resulted in him playing a crucial role in the subsequent negotiations in England, and later in Ireland, which led to the earl's rehabilitation during Sir Richard Edgcumbe's mission.

If Estrete died in England in late 1489, his calming influence at the Tudor court was quickly missed, resulting in a gradual deterioration in Kildare's relations with Henry VII. Kildare was replaced as deputy lieutenant in 1492, arrested and sent as a prisoner to England in 1495, and attainted by the Irish parliament. Kildare did not regain Henry's trust until the following year, when his attainder was reversed by the English parliament and he was reappointed deputy lieutenant, this time to the king's second son, Henry, duke of York, the future Henry VIII. Then a widower, Kildare was also given Elizabeth St John, a cousin of Henry VII's, as his new wife. From then on, Kildare remained loyal to the Tudor regime until his death in 1513.

75 Ellis, *Reform and revival*, pp 217–18.

APPENDIX 1: ESTRETE'S PARDON ENROLLED IN THE EXCHEQUER MEMORANDA ROLL FOR 14, 15 EDWARD IV

John Strete Narrator obtains enrolment of Deed whereby John Fortescu *unus armigeror p[ro] corpe sup[re]mi D[omi]ni n[ost]ri nunc R[e]g[em] Ang[lie]* and Sheriff of Cornwall & John Croker Knight who by Patent at Westminster 7 December 13th year were appointed *ad quar[um]cumq[ue] p[er]sones orta d[i]c[tu]m D[omi]n[u]m Regem supremu[m] D[omi]n[u]m n[ostru]m infra montein S[an]c[t]i Mich[ael]is ut rebelles & inobediencie* would submit & take the Oath of Fealty to receive same & pardon them under the Great Seal. We do now receive the submission & Oath of John Strete Serjeant of said late Earl & said John have pardoned &c. Dated at *Monte S[an]c[t]i Mich[ael]is in Com[itatus] Cornub[ia]* 21 Feb[ruary] 13th year.[76]

APPENDIX 2: PRAYERS TO BE SAID FOR THE FOLLOWING BENEFACTORS AND RELATIVES OF JOHN ESTRETE

(names in italics deceased at the time grants were made).

10 October 1485	**28 June 1488**
	Henry VII
Gerald, earl of Kildare	Gerald, earl of Kildare
Roland fitz Eustace	Roland fitz Eustace, Lord Portlester
	Robert Estrete, his cousin
Thomas Douedall	Thomas Dovedall
Richard Stanyhurst	
John Flemyng	Master John Flemyng
Jeneta Estrete, mother	*Johan, his mother*
George Estrete	George Estrete, his son
	Kateryne, his daughter
William Casshell	*William Casshell*
Margaret Blake	Margaret Blake
John Estrete, senior	*John, his father*
	Roger, his uncle
John Estrete, junior	*John, his son*
Christopher, brother [of John Estrete, junior]	*Cristofere, his son*
Patrick, brother [of John Estrete, junior]	*Patrick, his son*
	Jonet, his daughter
Sir John Chaler	*Sir John Chalers, knight*
William Eliott	*William Elliott*

76 COA Ph 15175, pp 243–4.

APPENDIX 3: ESTRETE'S FAMILY MEMBERS AND BENEFACTORS

The following notes exclude Henry VII, Gerald fitzGerald, earl of Kildare (d. 1513) and Roland Fitz Eustace, lord Portlester (d. 1496), whose lives are amply covered in the *Oxford dictionary of national biography* and the *Dictionary of Irish biography*. Sir John Chalers (d. 1467) is likewise the subject of a substantial biography in the UK's *History of Parliament* series.

Estrete's parents *John* and Jeneta/*Johan*

Nothing is known about Estrete's parents other than the fact that his father died before 1485 and his mother before 1488.

Estrete's children, George, *John, Christopher, Patrick*, Kateryne and *Jonet*

Three of Estrete's sons, John, Christopher and Patrick had died before 1485, probably as minors. A daughter Jonet, who seems to have been born after 1485, was dead by 1488. Only two of Estrete's children, George and Kateryne survived after 1488. The former seems to have survived his father, being granted his interest in the royal manors of Ratoath and Chapelizod in November 1489, but he and his sister seem to have died soon afterwards. The mother of Estrete's children is not known, but she may have been Margaret Blake.

Margaret Blake

On 28 August 1485, Estrete left the remaining term of his 50-year lease on a tenement in Dublin's High Street, recently acquired from the prior and convent of Holy Trinity, to Margaret.[77] Estrete's relationship to her is not stated, but she may have been his wife and the mother of some or all of his children. She may have been related to Thomas Blake of Oxmantown.[78]

Robert Estrete, cousin and *Roger, uncle*

Robert was probably the son of Estrete's uncle Roger. Described as a gentleman, Robert appears to have resided in London, where he was involved in shipping and trade. On 16 May 1484, he was appointed with others to investigate the complaint of several Spanish merchants, who lost their cargo of wine and woad when the ship conveying it was seized by Thomas Prestland of Calais and 'one called Brooke of Dover'. He was also ordered to arrest the culprits and make restitution for the stolen cargo to the owners.[79] Around August of the same year, Richard III granted Robert an annuity of £20 sterling from the revenues of Calais until he was granted an office or offices to the same yearly value or more.[80] It is possible that Richard III later granted him the constableship of Carrickfergus Castle because Robert and two other London merchants were required to make bonds with Henry VII on 18 March 1486 totalling £500, which would be voided if Robert became Henry VII's faithful subject henceforth

77 *CCD*, no. 1047. 78 See Randolph Jones, 'William Hogeson, mayor of Dublin, fl. 1493–1519' in Duffy (ed.), *MD XIX*, pp 307–19, at p. 309. 79 *CPR 1476–85*, p. 446. 80 Rosemary Horrox and P.W. Hammond, *British Library Harleian Manuscript 433* (Gloucester, 1979), i, p. 211.

and kept Carrickfergus Castle for him once he had obtained possession and custody of it, 'by any means whatsoever'.[81] It is perhaps noteworthy that these bonds were entered into when John Estrete was in London, negotiating with Henry VII on behalf of the earl of Kildare. A ship belonging to a Robert Streete was one of the four vessels that made up the fleet of Sir Richard Edgcumbe, which sailed from Cornwall for Ireland on 23 June 1488.[82]

William Elliott

Probably the William Elyot who was admitted and sworn in as the butler of Lincoln's Inn in 1450–1. He was especially admitted as a member of the society in February 1461 for his faithful service as butler 'for a long time'.[83] He may have been the William Elyot, yeoman, who is mentioned as an attorney and witness to several property transactions connected to Estrete in February 1487 and August 1488, for lands in Crumlin, Co. Dublin and Ministown, near Colp, Co. Meath, but according to the list of benefactors drawn up by Estrete on 10 August 1485, Elliott was dead by then.[84] Likewise, he cannot be the William Elyot, former servant of John Bedyll, through whose hands money was paid to Estrete during the Michaelmas term of 1489 by the English exchequer.[85]

Thomas Dovedall

The son of Sir Robert Dowdall, chief justice of the common pleas in Ireland.[86] He was admitted into Lincoln's Inn during Trinity term 1459,[87] and appointed the king's serjeant-at-law in Ireland on 4 March 1462 by English letters patent. He was also granted the king's lordship of Coly (Cooley, Co. Louth) for life on 28 July of the following year.[88] On 28 April 1469, he was admitted to the franchise of Dublin 'by special grace',[89] and appointed clerk and keeper of the rolls in the Irish chancery on 10 September 1471, with an annual salary of £20 drawn from the revenues of the king's manor of Esker.[90] In August 1479 he was summoned to attend the king's council in England, appointing Thomas Archbold as his deputy during his brief absence.[91] On 30 July 1488 Dovedall was pardoned for supporting the pretender king crowned in Dublin the year before.[92] As a consequence of Kildare's replacement as deputy lieutenant by Walter Fitzsimon, archbishop of Dublin, Dovedall was replaced as clerk and keeper of the rolls by Thomas Butler on 10 July 1492, who took up office on 26 September.[93] Likewise, following Kildare's arrest by Sir Edward Poynings, and despatch to England as a prisoner, Dovedall was required to make a recognisance in the Irish chancery on 20 May 1495 for 500 marks, presumably to ensure his continuing loyalty to Henry VII. However, Dovedall was dead by 30 March 1496, when his executors were released from this bond.[94]

81 *CCR 1485–1500*, p. 19; Campbell (ed.), *Reign of Henry VII*, i (London, 1873), pp 389–90). 82 Edgcumbe, *Voyage*, p. 59. 83 *Lincoln's Inn: black books* (London, 1897), i, pp 20, 37. 84 *CCD*, nos 1077–9, 1080, 1092–4. 85 Quinn, 'English financial records', p. 34. 86 COA Ph 15175, p. 284. 87 *Lincoln's Inn: admissions*, p. 14. 88 *CPR 1461–67*, pp 184, 284. 89 *DCFR*, p. 2. 90 CIRCLE PR 11 Edw. IV no. 12. 91 CIRCLE CR 19 Edw. IV, nos 15–18. 92 Edgcumbe, *Voyage*, p. 74. 93 *CPR 1485–94*, p. 386. 94 Conway, *Henry VII's relations with Scotland and Ireland*, pp 156, 158, quoting BL MS Royal 18 C XIV, fos. 13v and 121. A possible fine of 800 marks was imposed on Dovedall in the Easter term of

Master John Flemyng

In 1463, Flemyng was practising as a notary public in Dublin.[95] Circa 1466, he was appointed as clerk to the treasurer of Ireland.[96] He apparently came from Naas, Co. Kildare, where he inherited several properties, the title deeds of which were later enrolled in the exchequer's memoranda roll for 10 Edward IV [1470–1].[97] He was the temporary beneficiary of several escheated lands that were taken into the king's hands for various reasons, being granted custody of them by the court of exchequer.[98] He held the office of chief remembrancer of the same exchequer for a brief period during the tenure as deputy lieutenant of John Tiptoft, earl of Worcester [1467–70], perhaps deputizing for the normal incumbent, but he subsequently reverted to his previous office after Worcester's final departure from Ireland.[99] On 28 April 1469, he was admitted as a citizen of Dublin, 'by special grace'.[100] Flemyng was also appointed one of the keepers of the king's palace in Dublin Castle from 10 December 1471.[101] On 24 March 1478, Roland Fitz Eustace, treasurer of Ireland and John Flemyng clerk, were pardoned all treasons and felonies.[102] In 1483, he was appointed the second remembrancer in the exchequer.[103] He was still alive in July 1488, when Estrete made his grant, but it is not known when he died. Theresa O'Byrne has identified Flemyng as the rubricator of Nicholas Bellewe's English translation of the *Mirror of St Edmund,* which was probably produced sometime in the 1460s.[104]

William Casshell

In 1480 Casshell was a clerk in the Irish exchequer, and two years later, together with James Dillon, clerk, he represented the earl of Kildare in a plea of debt of £40 against Bartholomew Silke, citizen and merchant of Dublin.[105] Between 1485 and 1487 he witnessed several property transactions in which Estrete had an interest.[106] On 7 March 1486, Casshell was granted the office of controller of the customs and cockets, in the ports of Dublin, Drogheda, and Dundalk, with an annual fee of £10, when he

1495, but this seems to have been reduced to 500 marks. **95** Henry F. Berry, 'Some ancient deeds of the parish of St Werburgh, Dublin, 1243–1676', *JRSAI* 6th ser., 5 (1915), 43. **96** NAI Ferguson Coll, iii, 224; COA Ph 15175, p. 210; NAI RC 8/41, pp 33–4 (Irish Exch. Mem. roll, 6 Edw. IV, m. 6). **97** COA Ph 15175, p. 231. **98** E.g., Molynboddyn, in the lordship of Garristown in 1466 (CIRCLE PR 6 Edw. IV, no. 7); Walshestown, in the parish of Lusk, jointly with Philip Bermingham in the same year (ibid., no. 12); manor of Kilmoon, Co. Meath, parcel of the temporalities of the archbishopric of Armagh, jointly with Henry White, in 1470 (COA Ph 15175, p. 228; BL Add MS 4793, fo. 157); lands and profits of Stephen Fitz William, jointly with James Prendergast alias Collyn, and John Ward, in 1471 (CIRCLE PR 11 Edw. IV, no. 9); manor of Clondalkin, parcel of the temporalities of the archbishopric of Dublin, jointly with John Ward, in 1472 (CIRCLE PR 12 Edw. IV, no. 10; BL Add. MS 4793, fo. 157v). **99** NAI, Ferguson Coll. iii, 227; COA Ph 15175, p. 219 (Irish Exch. Mem. Roll, 7, 8, 9 Edw. IV, m. 6). Philomena Connolly (ed.), *Irish exchequer payments, 1270–1446* (Dublin, 1998), p. 626. **100** *DCFR*, p. 2. **101** COA Ph 15175, p. 235 (Irish Exch. Mem. Roll, 23 Edw. IV, m. 11). **102** NAI, Ferguson Coll. iii, 221v (Irish Exch, Mem, Roll, 18 Edw. IV, m. 10). **103** Ibid., fo. 230; COA Ph 15175, p. 280; (Irish Exch. Mem. Roll, 23 Edw. IV, m. 11); NAI RC 8/33, fo. 543 (ibid., 2 Ric. III, m. 27. **104** Theresa O'Byrne, 'Dublin's Hoccleve: James Yonge, scribe, author, and bureaucrat, and the literary world of late medieval Dublin' (PhD, University of Notre Dame, 2012), pp 393–7. **105** *CCD*, no. 1027; COA Ph 15175, p. 275. **106** *CCD*, 1027, 1060, 1064, 1078, 1080.

was in England with Estrete.[107] Casshell was murdered on 7 May 1489 by Stephen Dowdall of le Newton of Termonfeckin, Co. Uriel (Louth), gentleman, for which he received a pardon on 10 June 1490.[108] On 14 May 1489 Casshell's executors conveyed a meadow and a parcel of land in Dundalk worth 20*s*. per annum to Holy Trinity Dublin, for which nine lessons were to be read. A mass was also to be sung for him annually on the Friday in the week of Pentecost.[109]

Richard Stanihurst

One of the two bailiffs of Dublin in 1475–6, he was admitted as a juré of the city on 22 October 1484, and elected mayor for the year 1489–90.[110] With other prominent citizens of Dublin, he swore an oath of allegiance to Henry VII on 27 July 1488 before Sir Richard Edgcumbe in the city's 'gyldehall'.[111] He died in 1501.[112] He is the only person mentioned in Estrete's first list of benefactors who is not included in the second, suggesting perhaps that the two men had fallen out in the interim.

107 *CPR 1485–94*, p. 64. **108** Charles McNeill and A.J. Otway-Ruthven (eds), *Dowdall deeds* (Dublin, 1960), no. 503. **109** *CCD*, 354–5, 379; Refaussé and Lennon (eds), *Christ Church registers*, pp, 56, 84. **110** *DCFR*, pp 10, 19, 25. **111** BL MS Titus B XI, fo. 338v. **112** J.G Smyly (ed.), 'Old deeds in the library of Trinity College – V', *Hermathena*, 71 (May 1948), 48–50.

The records of Dublin's late medieval guild of carpenters

SARAH HENDRIKS

INTRODUCTION

The Dublin guild of carpenters is one of the medieval Dublin guilds whose early records have survived. A minute-book of 1513–64 preserves a range of business at a time of religious, political, and cultural change. It therefore provides a unique insight into how these events shaped the lives of guild members. It also enables an analysis of how guild business evolved during the first half of the sixteenth century, and an opportunity to examine the changing priorities in the management and arrangement of the guild's operations. Furthermore, given the sparse examples of medieval timber architecture in Dublin, the minute-book provides a view into the working life of the guild that physically shaped the now-lost Tudor city.

THE GUILD SYSTEM

While the guild system reached Ireland at a later date than many other countries across Europe, the Lord John's 1192 charter to Dublin licensing guilds established a system that continued to predominate for some six and a half centuries until 1841.[1] Dublin maintained the oldest and most expansive guild system on the island, though it was by no means the only medieval city to have such a system.[2] The Dublin guilds were numbered in the order in which they were incorporated by charter, and pre-eminent amongst them was the merchant guild.[3] Merchant guilds had an important role to play in the development of European cities and trade, and Dublin was no exception. It is thought that their structure provided a blueprint for the creation and

1 Mary Clark and Raymond Refaussé (eds), *Directory of historic Dublin guilds* (Dublin, 1993; rev. edn, 2024), p. 7; Fergus A. D'Arcy, 'The trade unions of Dublin and the attempted revival of the guilds: an episode in mid-nineteenth century Irish labour history', *JRSAI*, 101:2 (1971), 113–27. 2 Other Irish cities with medieval merchant guilds include Carlow (1296); Cork (1342); Drogheda (1229); Dundalk (1379); Inistioge (1209); Kilkenny (*temp.* Henry III); Limerick (1292); New Ross (*temp.* Edward III); Rosbercon (Kilkenny) (1300); Thomastown (*temp.* Henry III); Waterford (1205); Wexford (1317): cf. Tom Hoffman, *Guilds and related organizations in Great Britain and Ireland: a bibliography. Part II: The English provincial guilds, the Irish guilds, the Scottish guilds, the Welsh guilds*, 2011. 3 *GDMR*; Patricia Becker, 'An analysis of the Dublin Guild Merchant Roll *c.*1190–1265' (M.Phil., TCD, 1996).

establishment of craft guilds.[4] Initially, practitioners of various trades were included in the membership of the merchant guild, but over time they separated to form their own distinct franchises.[5] The impetus for this divergence was practical as well as philosophical: craft guilds were able to regulate the activities of their profession, not just the materials that passed through their hands.[6]

By 1747, Dublin had twenty-five trade and craft guilds, though political, religious, and commercial changes led to a steady decline in guild activity and finally, the abolition of guilds in 1846.[7] While various records and transcripts from across the seven centuries of guild activity in Dublin survive, no guild retains an unbroken series of records throughout its existence. This unfortunate situation cannot be blamed solely on the destruction of the Public Record Office of Ireland (PROI), although at the time of the 1922 blaze, select records of seven guilds were housed in its treasury.[8] Being independent organizations, guild records had been subject to the local conditions of their administration and, upon their winding up, any surviving records became the property of the guild trustees.[9] It was certainly with this in mind that Henry F. Berry published his guide to existing Dublin guild records with the hope 'that its being made public may lead to the discovery of records or effects of some of the remaining city companies'.[10] His plea appeared to have had an effect for the majority of guild material donations to the PROI were made after 1905.[11] The most recent survey of existing Dublin guild records was conducted in 1992. This work confirmed the survival of three records of the carpenters' guild, including a sixteenth-century minute-book, a charter of James II, and a 1656 roll of members.[12]

4 John J. Webb, *The guilds of Dublin* (Dublin, 1929), p. 2. 5 Charles Gross, *The gild merchant: a contribution to British municipal history* (Oxford, 1890), p. 107. 6 Webb, *Guilds of Dublin*, p. 11. 7 Clark and Refaussé (eds), *Dublin guilds*, pp 10, 13; D'Arcy, 'Attempted revival of the guilds'. 8 Guilds represented in the PROI in 1922 included the brewers' and malsters' guild, carpenters' guild, feltmakers' guild, merchant taylors' and guild of merchants, shoemakers' guild, and the guild of smiths: see, Herbert Wood, *A guide to the records deposited in the Public Record Office of Ireland* (London, 1919), pp 280–3. For an account of Dublin guild records lost and surviving, see Clark and Refaussé (eds), *Dublin guilds*. 9 Clark and Refaussé (eds), *Dublin guilds*, p. 13. 10 Henry F. Berry, 'Existing records and properties of the old Dublin city gilds', *JRSAI*, 35:4 (1905), 338–41. 11 These included a donation of three volumes from Henry S. Guinness relating to the carpenters' guild: the Minute-book or Entry Book of Proceedings (1792–1835), the Book of Petitions and Stamped Admissions (1772–1835), and the Book of Stamped Admissions (1835–37): Wood, *Guide to records deposited in PROI*, p. 281; Henry S. Guinness, 'Dublin trade gilds', *JRSAI* 12.2 (1922), 143–63. 12 Clark and Refaussé (eds), *Dublin guilds*; building on Berry, 'Records and properties of the old Dublin city gilds'; Guinness, 'Dublin trade gilds'.

THE CARPENTERS' GUILD

The Dublin carpenters' guild was founded by royal charter in 1508, as the Fraternity of the Blessed Virgin Mary of the House of St Thomas the Martyr, near Dublin. Its earliest surviving record, a 206-page minute-book of 1513–64, contains a variety of records including membership lists, notes of ingress, accounts, election of guild officials, day-to-day business, judgments on guild member infractions, and copies of statutes.[13] The volume is not bound in chronological order and some pages are incomplete or missing, though a continuous run of yearly accounts is preserved for the years 1533–9. Their contents cover the range of guild business, from recording quarterage payments to expenditure on wax and wax makers, and payments to a clerk for his yearly services. More than 50% of the extant pages record membership lists, grouped by occupation and rank and recorded at quarterly meetings.[14] These reflect the varied representation between the guilds and indicate that membership was not restricted to carpenters but, despite being colloquially known as the carpenters' guild, it included a variety of trades associated with the building industries. A later copy of its original charter indicated that the fraternity was to include 'the arts of carpenters, millers, masons, and heliers [slaters/tilers]'.[15] This listing of associated trades was not prescriptive, but rather indicative, with representation of the various named trades fluctuating over the years. In 1562 the fraternity referred to themselves as the guild of carpenters, joiners, masons, heliers, millers, and coopers.[16] By 1564, it was officially known as the 'corporacion of the carpendars, masons, juyneres, and heliers' and was seventh in the Dublin City Assembly.[17] This breadth of membership remained largely unchanged until after the Restoration when the coopers (1666), cutlers, painters, paper-stainers and stationers (1670), and joiners, ceylers and winscotters (1700) formed their own separate fraternities.[18]

The brethren (also referred to as the brotherhood, or fraternity) met quarterly at Lamas, Hallowtyde, Candlemas and May. In addition to these quarterly meetings, and in accordance with its charter, the guild also met on the day after the feast of the Assumption of the Blessed Virgin on 16 August. At this meeting, which marked the change in the guild's administrative year, elections took place for the master and two wardens, business was discussed,

13 Dublin City Library and Archives, MS 209. For an overview of the manuscript, see Henry F. Berry, 'The Dublin gild of carpenters, millers, masons, and heliers, in the sixteenth century', *JRSAI*, 35:4 (1905), 321–7. A transcription of early membership lists in the volume may be found in Sarah Hendriks, 'Early membership lists of the Dublin guild of carpenters, 1514–20', *AH*, 53, Special Issue: The Fire of 1922 (2023), 133–64. 14 For membership lists recorded in the earliest years, cf. Hendriks, 'Early membership lists'. 15 Berry, 'The Dublin Gild of carpenters, millers, masons, and heliers, in the sixteenth century', p. 324. 16 Modern spellings have been used for transcriptions. 17 *CARD*, ii, p. 36. 18 Clark and Refaussé (eds), *Dublin guilds*.

and annual accounts were submitted. As was typical, the guild celebrated with religious services and a feast.[19] In accordance with their charter, the guild met within the parish of St Catherine, and had an ongoing relationship with the lady chapel of St Thomas's abbey until the dissolution of the monastery in 1539. In 1565, the year after the minute-book ends, the guild is recorded as meeting at a room in Tailors' Hall, then located in Winetavern Street. No doubt this move was a contributing factor to the survival of the minute-book, for it marks the end of the period recorded, and the location of the records for the years that followed was unknown by 1905.[20]

MEMBERSHIP

Membership of the guild was restricted to those qualified to practise their nominated trades within the limits of Dublin and, notably, to those of English descent.[21] Women were allowed to join, although only one, Margaret Herford, has been identified in a 1536 list. In addition to full members, journeymen, those who had completed their apprenticeships but were employed as workmen rather than masters of their crafts, were also listed. In accordance with English practice, journeymen were required to serve for seven years before gaining full admission.[22] The distribution across the trades for journeymen mirrored those of the full master craftsmen, with carpenters again making up most of the membership. The membership lists divide the names of members by both occupation and rank, with carpenters listed before heliers and masons, and full members before journeymen.

The prohibition of Irishmen in the guilds has long been expounded, although charters from various guilds such as the goldsmiths refer to the inclusion of those of 'English name and blode', rather than any explicit exclusion of the Irish.[23] It is not clear from the extant records of either the carpenters' guild, or any other, that Irishmen were specifically targeted for exclusion. There is, however, a concern for the retention of business and industry control within local markets and a repeated concern for the activity of 'foreigners'. Webb, in his seminal work of the guilds of Dublin, shows how the craft guilds emerged from the merchants guild, the first, largest, and most influential guild in Dublin.[24] His analysis shows that a core driving principle of the guild structure was power – its establishment and retention. Such an aim, whether cognizant or not, can hardly have been without some political overtone in a city and region still undergoing tensions between local and

19 Peadar Slattery, *Social life in pre-Reformation Dublin, 1450–1540* (Dublin, 2019), p. 120. **20** Berry, 'Records and properties of the old Dublin city gilds'. **21** Berry, 'Dublin gild of carpenters', 324. **22** Ibid. **23** Webb, *Guilds of Dublin*, p. 70. **24** John J. Webb, 'The guilds of Dublin', *The Irish Monthly*, 45:530 (1917), 507–14.

foreign communities. The establishment of the Merchant Taylors Guild ensured that Dublin's citizens retained control over the goods and services being sold within the city, and that foreign traders (from both other countries and elsewhere across Ireland) were limited in their ability to capitalize on the market, as well as being required to pay additional tolls and customs.[25] As the craft guilds were derived from this system, they too retained these structures of power and authority and, no doubt, similar concerns for market share. Thus, the exclusion of 'non-English' was, in all likelihood, an exclusion of those from beyond the Pale. Within the guild, there were fines for employing 'foreigners', but it is clear that the issue was a business one, rather than a cultural one, and arose from a concern that such practices deprived guild members of potential income. A familiarity with local customs and environment, coupled with the practical need for builders, appears to have overridden any potential cultural discomfort that inclusion of Irishmen in the guild may have inspired. A similar triumph of necessity occurred in the early seventeenth century, when Irish carpenters were employed in building projects following the Ulster Plantation, suggesting local knowledge and need for craftsmen outweighed any political or cultural sensitivities.[26]

An analysis of the names listed in the volume further supports either a loose interpretation, or lack of observance, of this 'English' clause. The use of occupation as a nominal signifier was already well-established by this time, with occupations used as surnames in the *Dublin guild merchant roll* (*DGMR*).[27] Unlike surnames on the *DGMR*, few in these lists are linked to place-names.[28] Furthermore, the guild lists reflect an overwhelming preference for the use of surnames, rather than geographical, or occupation-based derivatives. The exceptions are few, with only John White of Oxmantown having a place association. Occupation-based names appear, but are readily exchanged with surnames, with those like Donyll Carpynder (for Myller) and Gowery Mason (for Bartholomew) occurring interchangeably across multiple years. This use of established names obfuscates any obvious assignation of 'foreign-ness' to the brethren in the way names such as, say, Daniel de Bruges might.[29] Given Dublin's centrality to the Pale, the association of seemingly Irish names with the native Irish was not a given, and many families of Irish origin had, by this period, adopted anglicized versions of Gaelic names.[30] On this basis, qualifying as English did not mean being born in England, but having an established

25 Webb, *Guilds of Dublin*, pp 12–13. **26** Rolf Loeber, *Irish houses and castles, 1400–1740* (Dublin, 2019), pp 135–6. **27** For analyses of naming conventions in the *DGMR*, see: Becker, 'Analysis of the Dublin Guild Merchant Roll'; Catherine Swift, 'Norwegian *Scing*-traders and other skinners in early Dublin' in Duffy (ed.), *MD XIX*, pp 17–35; B.M.S. Campbell, 'Dublin 1190–1290: provincial capital or capital city?' in ibid., pp 226–79. **28** Becker, 'Analysis of the Dublin Guild Merchant Roll', p. 14. **29** Becker, 'Analysis of the Dublin Guild Merchant Roll', p. 40. **30** Sparky Booker, *Cultural exchange and identity in late medieval Ireland: the English and Irish of the Four Obedient Shires*, Cambridge Studies in

connection to the Pale. Long-standing associations are seen in the listing of both 'O'Tole' senior and junior in the membership lists and reflect a tradition in the building trades, like other occupations, of professions being passed down along family lines.[31] Anglicized versions of Gaelic names occur with great frequency throughout the membership lists. The two aforementioned O'Toles were listed in the original charter as founding members of the guild, and they appear repeatedly in the list of wardens and masters. Traces of Gaelic origins appear elsewhere, in the surnames 'o mory', 'o dukgyn', and 'dowgan', and the forenames such as 'Donyll', 'Germot', and 'Tade'.[32] It is notable that anglicized forenames were most likely to be coupled with occupation-based surnames.

OCCUPATIONS

As stated, various trades appear in the membership lists but, in practice, the guild was heavily dominated by carpenters, a reflection of the primary building trade of the period. Carpenters are consistently listed first throughout the volume. In the earlier years, masons are the only other named group, though on occasion heliers are also included in a joint list.[33] By the mid-century, masons are replaced by heliers as the next most prominent group after carpenters, and by the 1560s only one or two masons are regularly listed. Despite this, carpenters and heliers dominated the leadership roles of the guild throughout the recorded years.[34] Berry, in his 1905 article, prepared a list of masters and wardens of the guild for the years covered in the volume. This shows that until 1556 only carpenters held the role of master and carpenters and heliers alone were elected wardens.[35] In 1558–60, William Dowgan was elected master, the first mason in the guild's recorded history to hold a position in the leadership. Although each of the four trades were part of the one fraternity, there were clear regulations that prohibited the practice of multiple trades. In 1557, guild business records that Dermot Rowertie, a journeyman carpenter, should not undertake any mason's work in Dublin. By this period, few masons were listed in the guild membership. This may be accounted for by the variant trading rules relating to masons, who were allowed to travel and work across the country and therefore not restricted to a single guild.[36]

Medieval Life and Thought (Cambridge, 2020), p. 52. **31** Rachel Moss (ed.), *Art and architecture of Ireland: medieval* c.*400*–c.*1600* (Dublin, 2014), i, p. 496. **32** Booker, *Cultural exchange and identity*, p. 53. **33** Hendriks, 'Early membership lists'. **34** Berry, 'Dublin Gild of carpenters', 326. **35** The trades of Pers Gerrott and John Jordane, wardens in 1538–9 are not given: Berry, 'Dublin Gild of carpenters', 337. **36** Berry, 'Dublin Gild of carpenters', 328.

ADMINISTRATION

The administrative structure of craft guilds was relatively uniform, and the records of this volume suggest the carpenters were not unusual in this respect. As noted above, they were governed by a master and supported by two wardens, all of whom were elected from within the full membership of the fraternity.[37] In addition to these roles, the guild also occasionally employed a clerk and beadle to assist in the administrative management. It is clear from various markings on the manuscript that it was the principal written record of the guild's activities for the years covered and functioned as a working document. The lists not only record the names of the members, but additional markings alongside names in the quarter list appear to track attendance, and the issuing and payment of fines. Monies owing are sometimes crossed out by a later hand. The early dates recorded in the manuscript focus on membership lists, with additional business rarely occurring and, when it does, being noted in the spaces around the lists. As the years progress, the system of record-keeping appears to become more systematized, with business recorded on separate pages to memberships and accounts.

On two occasions is guild business duplicated. The events recorded are not particularly unique, but in the pages for 1559/60, two matters are noted, one regarding an account to be taken from James Kenwyke and another recording the admission of a joiner. These two matters of business are recorded again on a later page in a different hand and with slightly different syntax. On this page, the two items appear as the fourth and fifth pieces of business after three general notices recording that Rowertie the journeyman carpenter shall not undertake any mason's work in Dublin, the beginning of a notice that John White is submitting himself to the guild, and a list of members elected to represent their trades to the City Assembly. These three items cannot be found elsewhere in the volume, though there are numerous pages missing from this section of the manuscript and it is possible they once appeared on those pages. There is little in the content itself to support the need for such business to be transcribed, but the neater arrangement of entries on this page, along with the absence of any membership lists, is indicative of the more formalized approach to managing guild business that emerges by the mid-century. Further evidence for the formalization and working nature of the volume, and the role of clerks in its preparation, are the presence of marks in place of signatures and traces of a wax seal. These declarations, all dating from the 1560s, confirm payments to be made by individual guild members. Each is given its own page and includes a signatory mark from the named members.

37 For a list of these extracted from the manuscript, see Berry, 'Dublin Gild of carpenters', 337.

The manuscript therefore presents an evolution in the operation and business concerns of the guild from the first decades of the sixteenth century through to the mid-1560s. Although membership lists appear throughout the volume, greater space is given over to other types of guild business as the years advance and it is clear from the changing priorities and recorded business that the guild was highly self-regulated. Finances become a stronger focus of the guild's record-keeping, with an unbroken list of annual accounts from 1533 to 1539. The membership lists and record of masters and wardens suggest a relatively stagnant membership pool, but the recorded business provides a window into the conduct of members and operations of the guild. For example Kenwyke, the same mentioned above whose records were duplicated, appears throughout the records and his career within the guild can be reconstructed. He first appears on the membership lists as a carpenter in 1545. In 1548 he serves as warden. It is unclear how long he held this position as the lists for these years are incomplete, but in 1556 he was elected master. In 1559/60 he is mentioned in guild business as being required to give his 'accompte' to guild members John Rede, William Dowgan, Edmond Alen, Patrycke Crosbye, John Branaghe, and Richarde Bleke. Those appointed to take his account were also among the leadership group of the guild. John Rede was the longest-standing member, having served four years as master at various points from as early as 1535. One of these years was directly preceding that of Kenwyke. William Dowgan, mason, joined the guild after Kenwyke in *c.*1549, but appears to have risen up the ranks relatively quickly. He became master in 1558, the first non-carpenter to do so, and was master at the time of Kenwyke's account. Edmond Alen was another carpenter and member of the guild who served as warden under John Rede in the years prior to Kenwyke's mastership. So too did Patrycke Crosbye, though his wardenship took place in 1547–8, also under John Rede. Only the last two members of the group appear not to have held named leadership positions, though it is possible they did so in the years for which records are missing. Kenwyke's account was apparently of some significance, although there is no record of when, where, or how this took place, but another undated record notes the fine he incurred as a result and a further signed declaration of when such payments were to be made is also recorded. Kenwyke did not return to any leadership role within the guild after this, though he was still listed as a member in 1560. Examples such as this, along with the recurrence of names in the membership lists, suggest an organization built on tradition and living knowledge.

Given the increased number of new names in the leadership from the 1550s onwards, and the election of the first mason as warden, one can surmise a slight shift in the balance of power between the carpenters and the masons and from what remains of the business during the 1550s and 1560s, it is apparent that the guild experienced internal tensions between the trades, especially in the years immediately prior to the end of the volume and the guild's relocation. From the opening list recorded in the manuscript, carpenters held the role of master, reflecting their predominance within the guild. In 1558, this tradition was broken with, and for what was possibly the first time in the guild's history, a mason being sworn in as master. By 1564, a carpenter was once again in control of the guild. It is at this point that the volume ends.

RELIGION

1564/5 marked another change in the life of the guild – its relocation to a new guildhall. Initially, the guild had met at St Thomas's abbey, situated outside the walls of the Dublin to the west.[38] This close association with a religious order was an integral part of guild life in Dublin.[39] The religious houses provided a 'home' for the guilds and, in return, the guilds supported the maintenance and operations of their associated church. The carpenters, named 'the Fraternity of the Blessed Virgin Mary of the House of St Thomas the martyr, near Dublin', were designated to meet within the parish of St Catherine.[40] In 1523 the guild elected James Hayn, a carpenter, as master, with John O'Tole, helier, and Nicholas Gowne, carpenter, as wardens in the lady chapel of the abbey.[41] Fines for wax, recorded for non-attendance, were used to make tapers or candles to light the lady chapel. In 1536, payments were made for a choir to sing at Assumption Day, presumably within the same lady chapel of the abbey.

Henry VIII's dissolution of the monasteries did not spare those in Ireland and St Thomas's was dissolved on 25 July 1539, possession passing to William Brabazon that same year.[42] There is no mention of this development in the manuscript and, in practice, the guild continued to associate with its patron saint the Blessed Virgin, though presumably it formed a new association with a chapel elsewhere within St Catherine's parish. Foley has suggested that the church of St Thomas's abbey was demolished soon after its dissolution, an act that would certainly have ensured the relocation of the guild.[43] The condition of the pages dating from *c.*1540–64 in the surviving minutes also supports such a move and suggests that, wherever it was, the guild remained there until 1564/5. These pages are of a different quality and appear to have been kept as

38 Aubrey Gwynn and Neville Hadcock (eds), *Medieval religious houses: Ireland* (London, 1970), p. 172. 39 Myles V. Ronan, 'Religious customs of Dublin medieval gilds', *Irish Ecclesiastical Record,* 5:26 (1925), 225–47; Webb, *Guilds of Dublin*, p. 71. 40 Berry, 'Dublin gild of carpenters', 324. 41 Webb, *Guilds of Dublin*, p. 61; *Reg. St Thomas*, p. xi. 42 Gwynn and Hadcock, *Medieval religious houses*, p. 172; Áine Foley, *The abbey of St Thomas the Martyr, Dublin: Mainistir Thomáis Mairtírteach, Baile Átha Cliath*, Archaeology Section of the Planning and Property Development Department in conjunction with the South Central Office, Dublin City Council (Dublin, 2017), p. 74. 43 Foley, *Abbey of St Thomas*, p. 76.

a discrete packet prior to being bound with the earlier accounts. As late as 1559, the guild paid for a priest to say mass after Lady Day, but the location is unspecified. A medieval Carpenters' Hall is said to have occupied a space on St Audeon's Lane at some point prior to 1565, although there is no reference to any such location in the surviving minutes.[44] In December 1564/5, the guild was granted the lease of an upper room of 'the Taylors haule, in the Wintavern Strett'.[45] This lease was granted by the city, but the building itself was first recorded in 1539 as the property of the tailors' guild, ranked second in the order of precedence.[46] The date of this lease coincides with the end of the extant minute-book, indicating a new phase in the guild's history for which we have no surviving record.

THE DUBLIN CONTEXT

By the sixteenth century, Dublin supported thirteen craft guilds. Only Limerick and Waterford had a similarly diverse range of active guilds by that date (although Waterford did not have a carpenters' guild).[47] Of course, such as system was not a phenomenon unique to Ireland in this period and one might assume a parallel operation to the guilds of London.[48] But although, as stated above, the Dublin guild of carpenters encompassed various building trades (albeit that carpenters were predominant), this was in contrast to the carpenters' guild of London which, during the same period, maintained a more focussed brotherhood.[49] A comparison with the London carpenters' guild, which received its first charter in 1477, shows strong parallels otherwise. The primary observable difference is in the breadth of membership. In the years prior to its incorporation, the London guild grouped carpenters and masons together in a 'brotherhood of fellow-craftsmen'.[50] However, as their status evolved into a full company, their remit narrowed to focus on a single trade, a division that would not begin to take shape in Dublin until the eighteenth century. By contrast, the London guild included a more geographically diverse membership, with names reflecting an attribution of homeland as had appeared on the earlier *DGMR*.[51] This difference is perhaps explained not only by the relative size of the two cities, but the nuanced cultural and environmental differences of the capital and the colony.

44 Clark and Refaussé (eds), *Dublin guilds*, p. 19. **45** *CARD*, ii, p. 36. **46** F.E. Dixon, 'The Dublin tailors and their hall', *DHR*, 22:1 (1968), 147–59, at 151. **47** Hoffman, *Guilds and related organizations*; Kieran Hoare, 'Guilds in Irish towns, 1450–1534', *History Studies (Limerick)*, 7 (2006), 53–65. **48** Michael Potterton, 'Introduction' in idem and Thomas Herron (eds), *Dublin and the Pale in the Renaissance* c.*1540–1660* (Dublin, 2011), pp 19–50, at p. 41; John Bradley, 'The purpose of the Pale: a view from Kilkenny' in ibid., pp 51–67. **49** Worshipful Company of Carpenters, *Records of the Worshipful Company of Carpenters.* (Oxford, 1913), ii, p. x. **50** Ibid. **51** Edward Basil Jupp, *An historical account of the*

The changes reflected in the minutes are also indicative of wider social and architectural changes. Houses and buildings constructed of timber were the norm in medieval Dublin, but the sixteenth century saw a shift towards construction in stone.[52] This shift occurred for a number of reasons including safety (timber was far more susceptible to fire), resource availability (ancient timbers were becoming more scarce), and in Dublin, environmental (timber was more prone to rot in the damp climate). In the Pale, there were also cultural drivers at play. Stone was a demonstration of cultural and political power, holding an aesthetic dominance over the vernacular landscape.[53] Carpenters and joiners were, of course, still required for framing, and timber-caged homes retained a presence in Dublin.[54] But the shift towards a more permanent and less-permeable building material no doubt changed the power balance of the trades within the guild and the relative power of the carpenters. Nevertheless, the integration of the building trades seems to have been a feature of the Dublin architectural environment and one that seemingly lasted into the eighteenth century where, as Casey notes, workmen families would be responsible for every aspect of a build, not just one component.[55] In this way, local culture, environment, and practice had a role to play in the structure, organization, and operation of the Dublin guild.

CONCLUSION

Given the challenges of time and circumstance, the survival of the Dublin guild of carpenters' minute-book for the sixteenth century is somewhat remarkable. Containing records from 1513 to 1564, its workaday nature provides an insight into the activities and membership of this historic guild and the changes wrought on the guild by cultural and political events. Its pages enable insights into the realities of guild life in the Pale, from the inclusion of those of Irish heritage, to the effect (or lack thereof), of the Dissolution of the monasteries. Furthermore, the efforts given to formalizing and recording the guild's operations over the recorded decades are evidence not only of a maturing administrative approach, but also of an organization in development.

Worshipful Company of Carpenters of the City of London (London, 1848). **52** Rachel Moss, 'The building trade in medieval Ireland, *c.*1190–*c.*1600', *JRSAI*, 149 (2019), 124–45, at 134–5. **53** Bradley, 'Purpose of the Pale', p. 63. **54** P., 'Ancient houses of Dublin', *Dublin Penny Journal*, 1:34 (1833), 268–70. **55** Christine Casey, *River, rivalry and revolt: history and the built fabric of Dublin City*, Sir John T. Gilbert Commemorative Lecture, 2008, City Public Libraries (Dublin, 2009), p. 17.